AF322914

BIRDS OF IDAHO

BIRDS OF IDAHO

By

THOMAS D. BURLEIGH

Illustrated With Photographs

The CAXTON PRINTERS, Ltd.
Caldwell, Idaho

1972

International Standard Book Number 0-87004-208-4
Library of Congress Catalog Card No. 79-137769
Lithographed and bound in the United States of America

DEDICATION

TO MY WIFE, DOROTHY BARRETT BURLEIGH, IN GRATEFUL
ACKNOWLEDGMENT OF HER CHEERFUL ACCEPTANCE OF THE
INCONVENIENCES, AND NOT INFREQUENT FRUSTRATIONS,
THAT LIVING WITH A FIELD ORNITHOLOGIST ENTAIL. A BOOK
SUCH AS THIS BEARS TESTIMONY TO THE UNFAILING SUPPORT
AFFORDED DURING THE YEARS WE LIVED AT MOSCOW

CONTENTS

CONTENTS

Page

ILLUSTRATIONS

Page

COLOR PLATES

facing page

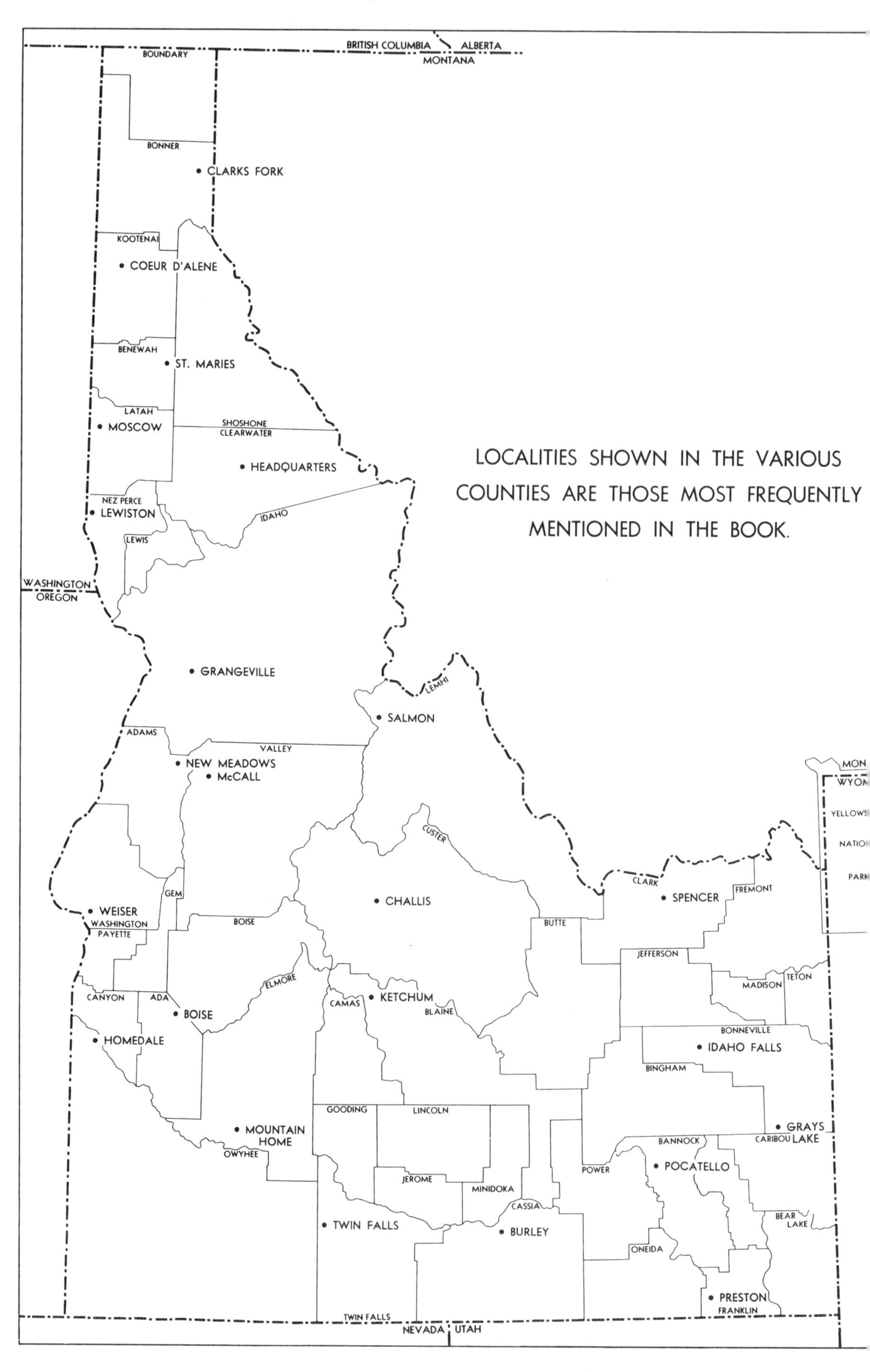

BRITISH COLUMBIA
ALBERTA
MONTANA
BOUNDARY
BONNER
• CLARKS FORK
KOOTENAI
• COEUR D'ALENE
BENEWAH
• ST. MARIES
LATAH
• MOSCOW
SHOSHONE
CLEARWATER
• HEADQUARTERS
NEZ PERCE
• LEWISTON
IDAHO
LEWIS
WASHINGTON
OREGON
LOCALITIES SHOWN IN THE VARIOUS
COUNTIES ARE THOSE MOST FREQUENTLY
MENTIONED IN THE BOOK.
• GRANGEVILLE
LEMHI
• SALMON
ADAMS
VALLEY
• NEW MEADOWS
• McCALL
CUSTER
MON
WYOM
YELLOWS
NATIO
PARK
CLARK
FREMONT
GEM
• WEISER
WASHINGTON
PAYETTE
BOISE
• CHALLIS
• SPENCER
BUTTE
JEFFERSON
MADISON
TETON
ELMORE
CANYON
ADA
• BOISE
CAMAS
• KETCHUM
BLAINE
BONNEVILLE
• IDAHO FALLS
• HOMEDALE
BINGHAM
GOODING
LINCOLN
• MOUNTAIN
HOME
OWYHEE
• GRAYS
BANNOCK
CARIBOU LAKE
POWER
• POCATELLO
JEROME
MINIDOKA
CASSIA
BEAR
LAKE
• TWIN FALLS
• BURLEY
ONEIDA
• PRESTON
FRANKLIN
TWIN FALLS
NEVADA
UTAH

PREFACE

Despite the fact that as far back as 1804, the avifauna of Idaho was reported on by Lewis and Clark during their famous expedition to the Pacific coast, this state has, until recent years, remained one of the few in the country concerning which relatively little was known about the distribution and abundance of its birdlife. In fact, for an interval of over one hundred years, there were but three contributions to our knowledge of the birds of Idaho, that of Charles E. Bendire, in 1871, at Fort Lapwai in what is now Nez Perce County; C. Hart Merriam's biological reconnaissance of the south-central part of the state in 1890, and J. C. Merrill's observations on the birds of Fort Sherman (the present site of Coeur d'Alene) from November, 1894, until December, 1896.

Since 1900 articles of varying length have appeared in such current periodicals as the *Auk* and the *Condor*, the two most important being those of Henry J. Rust, "An Annotated List of the Birds of Kootenai County, Idaho, 1911-1947," and R. L. Hand, "Birds of the St. Joseph National Forest, Idaho, 1921-1941." Others who have contributed information of value include, in chronological order, L. E. Wyman (Boise River Valley, 1909-11), Stanley G. Jewett (The Sawtooth Mountains in the vicinity of Ketchum, 1910), William B. Davis (Rupert, 1919-21, and Owyhee county, 1934), Pierce Brodkorb (Southern Idaho, 1932-34), William H. Marshall (Boise National Forest, 1938-40), M. Dale Arvey (short notes covering much of the state, 1941-50), Robert T. Orr (Northeastern Idaho, 1941, 1948), Fred G. Evenden, Jr. (Mountain Home 1944-47), David W. Johnston (Latah County, 1947), Seymour H. Levy (Northern and Southern Idaho, 1949-50), Paul E. Steel (Grays Lake, 1949-51), and Lewis W. Oring (Northern Idaho, 1959, Southeastern Idaho, 1961).

It was on October 28, 1947, that I arrived in Idaho, my major assignment with the Fish and Wildlife Service to be a detailed study of the birdlife of the State. My residence was established at Moscow, the county seat of Latah County, and for the following eleven years, until September 12, 1958, much of my time was devoted to carrying on field work involving the distribution, relative abundance, and life histories of Idaho's avifauna. A long-accepted policy with regard to distributional lists is the requirement that if a species is to be placed on an accredited list, at least one specimen must have been collected and identified by a competent ornithologist. Accordingly, field activities on my part have involved, where possible, the collection of one or more specimens of all species encountered. Published records too frequently consist of sight observations, and where these consist of species heretofore unrecorded in the state, they are considered hypothetical, regardless of how carefully they have been identified. One exception to this rule concerns the Blue Grosbeak, a photograph taken of both the male and female in the area of Glenns Ferry where they were nesting, leaving no question as to their identity. In the annotated list that follows, such hypothetical species are separated from those accredited to Idaho by having their names enclosed in brackets.

For the sake of uniformity, data with reference to both distribution and migration go from north to south in the state.

Statements relative to ranges, and both common and scientific names, have largely been taken from the fifth edition of the American Ornithologists' Union *Check-List of North American Birds* published in 1957. Any changes in ranges, and the inclusion of recently described races not found in the 1957 Check-list, are the result of information secured from such publications as the *Auk* or *Condor,* or from personal investigations.

ACKNOWLEDGMENTS

Birds of Idaho has been published in co-operation with the U.S. Department of the Interior, Fish and Wildlife Service, Washington, D.C., which graciously relinquished a proprietary interest in the manuscript to permit its publication.

I wish to acknowledge my indebtedness to George D. Frazier for his successful efforts in finding a publisher for this book on the birds of Idaho. Without his continued interest and a generous allotment of his time to the book, the manuscript might still be gathering dust in the files of the Fish and Wildlife Service.

My thanks are also due to David B. Marshall, of the Fish and Wildlife Service, for his cooperation in making available many of the photographs depicting the characteristic birds of the state.

W. C. Royall rendered valuable assistance in assuming responsibility for typing the original manuscript, and his efforts in this respect are much appreciated.

Order GAVIIFORMES: Loons

Family GAVIIDAE: Loons

Gavia immer (Brunnich): Common Loon

General Distribution: Breeds from the Aleutian Islands east across the continent to Newfoundland and as far south in the United States as northern Pennsylvania and northern New York. Winters south to northern Mexico, the Gulf coast and the Florida Keys.

Status in Idaho: A fairly common transient throughout the state, wintering in small numbers as far north as Lake Coeur d'Alene. It is reported as breeding at Lake Coeur d'Alene (Merrill, 1897), at Tamarack, Adams County (Wyman, in litt.), in Minidoka County (Dille, in litt.), and at St. Anthony (Preble, in litt.); but there is no record of a nest having actually been found. Specimens have been taken at Lake Coeur d'Alene (Rust, 1915) and at St. Anthony (Preble, in litt.).

It was first recorded in the state by Merrill (1897) who found it resident on Lake Coeur d'Alene and common except during the winter months. Rust (1915) reported it a rare resident on Fernan Lake in Kootenai County, noting it there from March, 1910, to December, 1914. At Priest Lake, it has been observed from September 30 to October 8, 1897 (Young, in litt.), and April 15 and 16, 1915 (Cottingham, in litt.), and at St. Maries from March 20 to April 30, 1921, to 1941 (Hand, 1941).

Farther south in the state it has been reported at Lewiston October 8, 1955, and October 29, 1957 (Burleigh); Fish Lake, Idaho County, July 31 to late September, 1923, October 3, 1925, September 19-21, 1926, October 17-20, 1928, October 10-11, 1929 (Hand, 1932); Payette Lake, Valley County, July 18-29, 1913 (Wyman, in litt.), and October 11, November 15, and December 18, 1915 (Cottingham, in litt.); Deer Flat, Canyon County, August, 1911 (Dille, in litt.), and April 15, 1915 (Cooper, in litt.); Sawtooth Lake, Sawtooth Mountains, October 2, 1890 (Merriam, 1891); Grays Lake, a rare transient with extreme dates of occurrence, April 29, 1950, and May 14, 1951 (Steel, 1956); Hazelton, Jerome County, July 12, 1949 (Levy, 1950).

Habits: Since it is only on the larger bodies of water that the loon can be found, it is of rather local occurrence in the state. The larger lakes and rivers not only afford comparative safety and food, but where flight is necessary, a sufficient expanse of water to get into the air. Its large heavy body and small wings make it extremely difficult for it to leave the water; and if forced to alight on the ground, it is practically helpless.

Gavia stellata (Pontoppidan): Red-throated Loon

General Distribution: Breeds from northern Alaska east across the continent to Newfoundland and as far south as southern Mackenzie and northern Manitoba. Winters from the Aleutian Islands to Sonora and from the Great Lakes and Maine to the Gulf coast and southern Florida.

Status in Idaho: A rather scarce spring and fall transient. It was first recorded in the state by Rust (1913) who reported a specimen from Coeur d'Alene on October 6, 1912. Davis (1935) noted it in Minidoka County on April 20 and May 7, 1919, April 14, 1920, and May 19 and 21, 1921. There are no other records.

Habits: Unlike the Common Loon, the Red-throated Loon shows a decided preference for salt water and both in migration and during the winter months is largely a bird of the open ocean. As with the preceding species, it will appear in Idaho only on the larger bodies of water and at all times is wary and difficult to approach. Nesting as it does on the tundra pools that are formed by the melting snow, it has developed an ability to leave the water that in this respect is quite at variance with the apparent awkwardness of its near relative.

Order PODICIPEDIFORMES: Grebes

Family PODICIPEDIDAE: Grebes

Podiceps grisegena holböllii (Reinhardt): RED-NECKED GREBE

General Distribution. Breeds in Manchuria and Siberia, and from northern Alaska east to northern Ontario and south to South Dakota and southern Minnesota. Winters south to central California, Georgia, and central Florida.

Status in Idaho. A scarce transient and a rare summer resident.

Merrill (1897) considered this species not uncommon at Coeur d'Alene and reported a nest there that, on June 3, 1895, held four eggs.

Levy (1959) recorded it on three occasions in the northern part of the state. An immature female was taken on Lake Coeur d'Alene on October 11, 1950, and single birds were seen on Priest Lake on September 23, 1951, and on Lake Pend Oreille on October 25, 1961. It has yet to be recorded from southern Idaho.

Habits. This large grebe suggests a small loon both in flight and in the water, and is almost as wary and difficult to approach. Although normally a solitary bird, it may occur in small flocks in migration and will be seen then on the larger bodies of water. If its safety is threatened, it escapes by diving rather than flying; and once under the water, it may not be seen again.

Podiceps auritus cornutus Gmelin: HORNED GREBE

General Distribution. Breeds from central Alaska east to northern Manitoba, south to northern Nebraska and northeastern Iowa. Winters north to southern Alaska, the Great Lakes, and Nova Scotia, and south to southern Florida and the Gulf coast.

Status in Idaho. An uncommon spring and fall transient. It has been noted during the summer months in the southern part of the state, but there are no definite breeding records. It possibly winters sparingly where conditions are suitable.

At Lewiston, in the northern part of the state, I found the Horned Grebe an uncommon transient, one or two birds being noted at infrequent intervals on the reservoir east of Lewiston Orchards. My extreme dates of occurrence in the spring are April 26 (1957) and June 8 (1953) and in the fall November 13 (1956) and December 19 (1956). Two specimens were taken here, males, on November 13, 1956, and April 26, 1957. The latter was in full breeding plumage. Levy (1959) reports a male taken on Lake Coeur d'Alene on October 16, 1951.

Cottingham (in litt.) noted it on Payette Lake on May 10 and August 3, 1915.

Merriam (1891) considered it common on Sawtooth Lake in the Sawtooth Mountains in late September and early October, 1890. He stated that at least one hundred were observed there on October 1.

At Grays Lake in Bonneville and Caribou counties, Steel (1956) noted this species but once, two birds being seen May 30, 1950. His observations covered the intervals from May 16 to October 1, 1949, April 1 to September 13, 1950, and April 5 to September 14, 1951.

Davis (1935) considered it a summer resident at Rupert in Minidoka County but cites no actual breeding records. His extreme dates of occurrence (1919-21) are April 11 and October 27.

Habits. In breeding plumage, the Horned Grebe can be readily distinguished from the Eared Grebe, but after the postnuptial moult, these two species resemble each other so closely that satisfactory identification is often difficult. For this reason, it is possible that it is more common in migration than present records indicate. Nesting as it does in fresh-water marshes, its migrations take it through the interior of the country; but once it reaches its winter quarters, it is found largely on salt water. It is not especially shy; but if alarmed, it escapes pursuit by diving. Under such circumstances, it is adept at disappearing under water for long intervals.

Podiceps caspicus californicus Heermann: EARED GREBE

General Distribution. Breeds from British Columbia east through Alberta, Saskatchewan, and Manitoba, south to northern Baja California, New Mexico, and southern Texas. Winters largely in the southern part of its breeding range and south to Colombia.

Status in Idaho. A fairly common transient both in the spring and in the fall, and a locally common summer resident in the southern part of the state where there is suitable habitat.

Danby (in litt.) reports the Eared Grebe common at Rathdrum, Kootenai County, during the spring of 1902, being first seen on April 11 and frequently noted after April 20. At Coeur d'Alene, Rust (1913) took an immature female on October 9, 1912. Hand (1941) considered this species an uncommon spring transient at St. Maries, appearing there in May (1921-41). One bird was noted on July 11, 1936. He also saw a single bird in September on Steamboat Lake, near Monumental Buttes.

In Latah County there are no large bodies of water, so I noted the Eared Grebe at rather infrequent intervals on the few small ponds near Moscow. Two birds were seen there May 18, 1950, ten on May 8, 1951, and four on May 2, 1952. A single bird was found on the Palouse River at Potlatch on August 22, 1954.

At Lewiston in Nez Perce County, I found it a regular and fairly common transient both in the spring and in the fall, single birds or small flocks being frequently noted on all bodies of water large enough to afford them sufficient protection. My earliest record for the spring migration is that of one bird seen on the reservoir east of Lewiston Orchards, April 26 (1957), my latest three birds seen on the reservoir June 19 (1957). The full migration begins rather early, the first birds appearing each year by the middle of August and being of regular occurrence thereafter. My extreme dates of occurrence then are August 8 (1953), a fairly compact flock of eleven birds on the reservoir, and November 13 (1956), four birds on the reservoir. Over a five-year interval, nine specimens were taken at Lewiston. These were males collected October 12, 1953 and October 21 and November 13, 1956; and females October 21, 1953, August 24, 1954, May 23, 1955, May 28 and October 12, 1957, and September 8, 1958.

In Idaho County, Hand (1932) reported this species as a fairly common fall transient. He gives as extreme dates of occurrence August 22 (1928) and November 3 (1926), the average date of arrival and departure being September 14 and October 16.

Farther south in the state it has been recorded at Payette Lake on May 25, 1915 (Cottingham, in litt.), Sawtooth City (Alturas Lake) on October 3, 1895 (Howell, M.S.), Paris September 1, 1929 (Hayward, in litt.), Hazelton, Jerome County (Wilson Lake) July 12, 1949 (Levy, 1950), Rupert August 1, 1920 (Davis, 1935), Minidoka September 16 to 29, 1916 (Cantwell, in litt.), Council November 24, 1957 (Newhouse, 1960), Deer Flat May 24 and August 21, 1911 (Dille, in litt.), and April 15, 1915 (Cooper, in litt.), Riddle, Owyhee County May 28 to June 3, 1934 (Davis, 1934).

Although it undoubtedly breeds elsewhere in the state where there is suitable habitat, the Eared Grebe is now known to nest only on Grays Lake, in Bonneville and Caribou counties. Here I found it common and well distributed on June 10, 1949, and collected a nestling male that had left the egg within the past twenty-four hours. Steel (1956) considers it an abundant summer resident there and gives as arrival dates April 21, 1950, and April 17, 1951.

Jewett (in litt.) reported it common on Blackfoot Reservoir in Caribou County, May 9-16, 1943, and May 30-31, 1945, but lack of suitable marsh areas eliminated the possibility of its nesting there.

Habits. Unlike the other grebes, this species is extremely sociable and breeds in colonies that are so compact that a group of twenty-five nests will occupy a space not over twenty feet in diameter. It is likewise far less shy than its near relatives; when the nests are approached, the incubating birds will swim away to the nearest open water rather than escape by diving. The nests are seldom concealed in any marsh vegetation and are masses of moist cattail stalks, reeds, marsh grass, and not infrequently mud. The eggs, usually four or five in number, lie in a slight hollow in the top.

Aechmophorus occidentalis (Lawrence): WESTERN GREBE

General Distribution. Breeds from British Columbia east through Alberta and Saskatchewan to Manitoba, south to central California, northern Utah, northern North Dakota, and southwestern Minnesota. Winters mainly on the coast south to Baja California and locally inland to western Nevada.

Status in Idaho. An uncommon transient throughout the state, it breeds locally in small numbers where there is suitable habitat. The Western Grebe was first recorded in the state by Merrill (1897) who reported a specimen taken at Fort Sherman (Coeur d'Alene). It has been reported in migration at Coeur d'Alene by Rust (1915) who considered it uncommon during the fall and winter, being most frequently seen from September to December. Young (in litt.) noted an occasional bird at Priest Lake September 30 to October 8, 1897.

At Potlatch, in Latah County, I saw two birds October 15, 1956, and at Lewiston, four birds on the Clearwater River October 8, 1955, and two on the reservoir November 1, 1956.

Farther south in the state Hand (1932) reported three birds in Idaho County on Fish Lake October 17 and 18, 1928, and a single bird October 26, 1928; American Falls, June 19 and 20, 1953 (Willis, in litt.), Bayview, November 13, 1943 (Longley, in litt.); St. Charles, April 29, 1929 (Hayward, in litt.); Neeley, February 15, 1915 (Teeters, in litt.); Rupert, October 10, 1909 (Kenagy, in litt.); and extreme dates of occurrence May 19 and September 30 (1919-21) (Davis, 1935); Minidoka, September 16 to September 29, 1916 (Cantwell, in litt.); Grays Lake, a rare summer visitant (Steel, 1956); Blackfoot Reservoir, May 9-16, 1943 (Jewett, in litt.); Montpelier, Bear Lake, Swan Lake, May 24 to June 22, 1945 (Jewett, in litt.); Deer Flat, October 29 to November 1, 1914, and September 30 to October 30, 1915 (Cantwell, in litt.), and May 15 to May 30, 1932, and July 16, 1932 (Towle, in litt.).

It was first recorded as breeding in the state by Moody (1903) who found a nest that year near Sandpoint on Lake Pend Oreille that held three eggs. Yocom (1946) noted one breeding pair at the upper end of Lake Coeur d'Alene in Kootenai County, July 1-10, 1943. Levy (1950) states that in 1949 he found it a common breeding bird on Wilson Lake near Hazelton, Jerome County. He also reports a pair with young on the Snake River at Burley, July 8, 1949. Davis (1935) reported it as breeding at Rupert (1919-21) with fresh eggs on June 7. Steel (1956) states that it breeds on Blackfoot Reservoir in Caribou County.

Habits. As with the other grebes, this species occurs on fresh-water marshes during the summer months; and where conditions are favorable, hundreds of pairs can be found nesting in close proximity. The nests are built on the surface of the water rather than in it, and are normally substantial beds of dry fragments of reeds and rushes. The nest found by Moody on Lake Pend Oreille was in a rather unusual situation, being on the top of an old muskrat house. It is a common habit for the other grebes to cover their eggs with moist decaying marsh vegetation when leaving for any length of time, but the Western Grebe seldom, if ever, resorts to this habit.

Bureau of Sport Fisheries and Wildlife

Photo by Eugene Kridler

A WESTERN GREBE ON HER NEST

During the winter months, these grebes assemble in large numbers on the coasts of Washington, Oregon, and California and are then essentially birds of the open ocean.

Podilymbus podiceps podiceps (Linnaeus): PIED-BILLED GREBE

General Distribution. Breeds from British Columbia east across the continent to Nova Scotia and south to Mexico, the Gulf coast and southern Florida. Winters within much of its breeding range and south to western Panama and Cuba.

Status in Idaho. An uncommon transient and a locally common summer resident. Winters rarely.

At Coeur d'Alene, Merrill (1897) noted it during the spring and summer months, while Rust (1915) reported it there only during the fall and winter, with the largest numbers noted in November (1914). Kittredge (in litt.) saw a single bird at Priest River August 24, 1913. Hand (1941) considered it a common summer resident at St. Maries, occurring from April to November and being observed at infrequent intervals during mild winters.

I personally found this little grebe a rather scarce transient in the northern part of the state. Single birds were seen at Moscow on April 27, 1955, and at Lewiston on October 10, 1955, December 30, 1956, and March 9, 1958.

Farther south in the state it has been reported from Fish Lake in Idaho County on September 25 and October 2, 1929 (Hand, 1932); Ben Ross Reservoir in Adams County, April 20, 1958 (Newhouse, 1960); Gary Lake in Blaine County, June 4, 1949, and Wilson Lake, Jerome County, July 18, 1949 (Levy, 1950); Rupert, May 15, 1918 (Davis, 1935); Minidoka, September 16-29, 1916 (Cantwell, in litt.).

At Grays Lake, Steel (1956) found this species an uncommon summer resident. He gives as arrival dates April 21, 1950, and April 15, 1961. Brodkorb (in litt.) collected a young bird of the year, a male, at Bear River Outlet July 15, 1934.

Habits. Because of its wide distribution, the Pied-billed Grebe is a relatively well-known bird. It is far less sociable than the other grebes, and this trait and its small size make the smaller bodies of water acceptable as nesting sites. It is not uncommon to find single pairs nesting in reeds and cattails fringing ponds, although in large marshes, optimum conditions for rearing their young will attract numerous pairs. The nest is always built in water, normally where the depth averages two or three feet, and is a substantial floating mass of moist decaying fragments of reeds, cattails and other marsh vegetation. Both birds incubate but are so shy that only rarely is it possible to see one on a nest. At the slightest alarm, the eggs are hurriedly covered with a layer of material taken from the nest and remain so concealed for long intervals.

Unlike the other grebes, this is essentially a bird of fresh-water ponds and streams, salt water being consistently shunned both in migration and during the winter months.

ORDER PELECANIFORMES

Pelicans: *Family Pelecanidae*

Pelecanus erythrorhynchos Gmelin: WHITE PELICAN

General Distribution. Breeds from British Columbia east through Mackenzie, Alberta, Saskatchewan, and Manitoba to Ontario, south to central California, southern Montana, South Dakota and southeastern Texas. Winters from California south to Guatemala and from the Gulf coast south into Mexico.

Status in Idaho. A common transient and summer resident in the southern part of the state, breeding in a few spots where conditions are suitable. Apparently largely of accidental occurrence north of the open arid desert country.

The White Pelican was first recorded for the state by Merriam (1891) who reported it seen on the Bear River by Townsend in 1834 and on Henrys Lake by the Hayden Survey in 1872. Many years later, it was again seen on Henrys Lake by Rust (1917), three birds during the summer of 1916.

It has also been reported in migration at Deer Flat from October 29 to November 1, 1914, October 1, 1915, and September 4 to September 15, 1916 (Cantwell, in litt.), and March 25 and May 20, 1918 (Cooper, in litt.); Neeley, October 3, 1914, April 1 to April 15, and September 1, 1916, April 20, 1917, and May 1 to May 15, 1918 (Teeters, in litt.); Weiser, March 9, 1926 (a dozen seen on a sandbar in the Snake River) (Hurley, 1926); Wilson Lake Reservoir, August 7, 1949 (Levy, 1950); Grays Lake, a rare summer visitant, 1949-51 (Steel, 1956); Adams County, June 5, 1958 (eleven seen in Indian Valley) (Newhouse, 1960).

Cooper (in litt.) reports that this species nested at Deer Flat in 1914, but gives no further information as to the number of nests actually found.

Teeters (in litt.) states that it breeds in Minidoka County and that it was first seen in 1915 on April 30 and in 1919 on March 16. Cantwell (in litt.) reports one hundred seen "during the nesting season" of 1916. Davis (1935) further verifies the breeding of the White Pelican in Minidoka County, giving June 7 as the date when fresh eggs were found near Rupert and May 19 and October 30 (1919-21) as extreme dates of occurrence.

William D. Rush, Game Agent, Fish and Wildlife Service, reports (in litt.) that this species nested for the first time in 1961 on Blackfoot Reservoir, eighteen miles north of Soda Springs. A total of 206 nests held eggs on May 13. This breeding colony was on Gull Island, near the west side of the reservoir. All were found deserted on June 7, apparently due to molestation by local fishermen.

Habits. In spite of their similarity in appearance and close relationship, the White Pelican differs markedly from the Brown Pelican in its actions.

A WHITE PELICAN REGALLY SURVEYS HIS SURROUNDINGS

It secures its food, largely small fish, from near the surface of the water as it swims slowly along, rather than by plunging spectacularly from the air into deep water. For this reason, small fish form the bulk of its food. Both species nest on islands that afford them protection from such nocturnal predators as the fox and the coyote; but whereas the Brown Pelican normally builds a substantial nest of whatever material is available, the White Pelican usually lays its eggs in a slight hollow in the ground that may or may not have a lining of plant stems and rootlets.

After the breeding season is over, the White Pelican leaves the fresh-water lakes and during the winter months appears on both the Atlantic and Pacific coasts, showing no aversion whatsoever to salt water.

Ward (1924) reports the recovery of two birds banded on Yellowstone Lake in July, 1922, one on Mud Lake, forty miles northwest of Idaho Falls October 1, the other on Swan Lake October 23.

Cormorants: *Family Phalacrocoracidae*

Phalacrocorax auritus auritus (Lesson): DOUBLE-CRESTED CORMORANT

General Distribution. Breeds from central Alberta east across the continent to Newfoundland, south to southern Idaho, New Mexico, southern Minnesota, Ontario, and Massachusetts. Winters in New Mexico and southern Texas, in the Mississippi Valley from Tennessee to the Gulf coast, and on the Atlantic coast from New York to Florida.

Status in Idaho. A common transient and summer visitant in the southern part of the state, at present known to breed there in three widely separated spots. A rare fall transient north of the Salmon River in Idaho County.

The Double-crested Cormorant has the distinction of being included in the first list of birds for the state. Lewis, in his account of the famous Lewis and Clark expedition, mentions the birds, a total of twenty-four species seen in Idaho, and states (*Original Journals*, Lewis and Clark, ed. Thwaites, IV: 141-42) that this species was seen September 26 to October 8, 1805, on the Clearwater River (Jollie, 1953). There are but two other records for the northern part of the state. Merrill (1897) states that while at Fort Sherman on Lake Coeur d'Alene from November, 1894, until December, 1896, several Cormorants were seen September 19. Ranson (in litt.) reports a single bird at Chatcolet on October 2, 1925.

In southern Idaho, it has been noted in migration at Lewis Ferry on October 11, 1890 (Merriam, 1891); Montpelier, April 12, 1912 (Jewett, in litt.); Neeley, May 1, 1915, and from March 1 to April 1, 1918 (Teeters, in litt.); Minidoka County, March 22 to April 3, 1915, and September 16 to September 29, 1916 (Cantwell, in litt.); May 6 and September 1 to November 4, 1919, August 1 to September 5, 1920, and May 19, 1921 (Davis, 1935); Wilson Lake Reservoir, August 10, 1949 (Levy, 1950); Grays Lake, a rare summer visitant, 1949-51 (Steel, 1956).

Bureau of Sport Fisheries and Wildlife

Photo by David B. Marshall

CORMORANTS ON THEIR NESTING ISLAND ON LAKE WALCOTT ON A WINDY DAY

Behle (1941) states that this species nests at Bear Lake in extreme southeastern Idaho, but gives no details as to the number of breeding pairs noted. Jewett (in litt.) reports a small breeding colony on Goose Island in Blackfoot Reservoir, where on May 15, 1943, thirty nests were found. Some held four fresh eggs, while in others there were two to four young "of different sizes."

In 1958 I was shown a small breeding colony of approximately thirty pairs on an island in Lake Walcott, in the Minidoka National Wildlife Refuge, eight miles northeast of Rupert. That day, July 22, the young were well grown and out of the nest, but only a few were fully enough developed to leave the island.

A small series of eleven specimens was examined critically to determine what geographic races occur in Idaho. These were six specimens collected by Pierce Brodkorb—a male at Montpelier, Bear Lake County, May 17, 1930, and four males and a female at Mud Lake, Bear Lake County, May 30, 1930; and five specimens that I personally took on Lake Walcott—two adult females and an immature female on July 22, 1958, and a male and a female on June 17, 1960. These were found to be intermediate in their characters between *auritus* and *albociliatus*, but closer to *auritus*, a conclusion reached by Behle (1941) where the Cormorants of the Great Salt Lake, Utah, are concerned.

Habits. The Double-crested Cormorant is at all times a wary bird, rarely permitting an approach within gunshot range even on its nesting grounds. Its food being almost entirely fish, it is in ill repute with fishermen; and the persecution it receives justifies its attitude toward mankind.

It breeds on both salt and fresh water, and this same impartiality is shown during the winter months when it can be found on the coast and on inland lakes and rivers.

The nests that I examined on Lake Walcott were quite characteristic of this species, being flat but substantial structures of small sticks, twigs, weed stems, grasses and other such material available in the vicinity. Normally three or four chalky white eggs are laid and but a single brood is reared each year.

ORDER CICONIIFORMES

Herons, Egrets, and Bitterns: *Family Ardeidae*

Ardea herodias Linnaeus: GREAT BLUE HERON

General Distribution. Breeds from southeastern Alaska east through Alberta, Saskatchewan, and Manitoba to central Ontario and southern Quebec, south to southern Mexico and the West Indies. Winters from British Columbia and the northern United States south to Colombia and Venezuela.

Status in Idaho. In the northern part of the state, the Great Blue Heron is a regular but uncommon fall transient, an occasional bird wintering where there is sufficient open water to afford a food supply. Farther south it occurs commonly during the summer months, nesting in large colonies in widely separated spots. It also winters in small numbers.

Rust (1915) reported it as rare during the fall and winter in Kootenai County. He collected a specimen on the St. Joe River, February 14, 1913. At St. Maries in Benewah County, Hand (1941) considered it common from July to October (1921-41), an occasional bird being seen in the winter. In Latah County, I found it a scarce fall transient, extreme dates of occurrence at Potlatch being July 19 (1950) and September 28 (1948), and at Moscow July 29 (1950) and September 30 (1948). At Potlatch, single birds were seen on the Palouse River January 13, 1955, and January 28, 1956.

At Lewiston in Nez Perce County, I saw single birds on the Snake River at infrequent intervals during the summer and fall months, my extreme dates of occurrence being July 31 (1952) and October 21 (1950). It was noted here twice during the winter on February 8 and December 28, 1951.

In the central part of the state, it has been reported in migration at Payette Lake August 2, 1915 (Cottingham, in litt.); Fish Lake, in Idaho County, August 19, 1924, September 26-27, 1927, and August 23-24, 1928 (Hand, 1932); New Meadows, September 17, 1955 (Burleigh); Council, several seen, March and April, 1958 (Newhouse, 1960).

In southern Idaho, it has been noted by Merriam (1891) as common on the Snake River in July and August, 1890, and it has also been seen on Birch Creek in August, on the Salmon River near Challis, September 20, and on the Snake River in October. It was also recorded at Dubois August 22 and 23, 1909 (Bailey, in litt.); by Jewett (in litt.) at Nampa, May 15, 1910; on the Snake River at Glenns Ferry July 1 to 7, 1910; at Ketchum on the Big Wood River July 9 to 15; 1910; at Inkom on the Port Neuf River, June 26, 1911; at Shelley on the Snake and Blackfoot rivers, July 26 to August 7, 1911; at Neeley, March 1, 1914, April 1, 1915, April 1 through

A GREAT BLUE HERON STANDS GUARD OVER ITS YOUNG

November 1, 1916, February 10, 1917 (Teeters, in litt.); Meridian, April 17, 1903, May 7, 1904, January 2 and July 23 to November 2, 1913, April 25 to May 1 and September 4, 1914 (Stalker, in litt.); Deer Flat, June 24 to July 10, 1912 (Dille, in litt.); October 29 to November 1 and December 13, 1914, September 30 to October 30, 1915, and September 4 to September 29, 1916 (Cantwell, in litt.); Fremont County, immature male taken on Little Dry Creek near Spencer, July 14, 1916, and five noted on the Snake River, August 18, 1916 (Rust, 1917); Jerome and Twin Falls counties, a common summer resident in 1949 and well distributed (Levy, 1950).

Hurley (1926) first reported the Great Blue Heron as breeding in the state when, on March 9, 1926, he found a colony of approximately one hundred pairs nesting on an island in the Snake River near Payette. He noted that on this date there was an incubating bird on every nest. However, Davis (1935) had previously (1919-21) found this species nesting in Minidoka County, where he states that the earliest nests held eggs on June 1 and young on June 30.

Hayward (1934) reports a colony of several hundred pairs at Bear Lake in 1928. The birds were present there from early April to early November. When examined in early May, the nests all held eggs. Jewett (in litt.) found large breeding colonies at Blackfoot Reservoir in Caribou County May 9-16, 1943, and May 24-June 22, 1945.

Habits. Although a solitary bird much of the year, the Great Blue Heron gathers in colonies of varying sizes to nest; and during this part of the year, it seems to enjoy the proximity of its kind. Although nests are occasionally built on the ground, a tree is preferred if one is available. On Goose Island, in Blackfoot Reservoir, the nests examined by Jewett were in willows from ten to sixteen feet up, while in the rookery at Bear Lake, they were built in cottonwoods "well above ground." The nests are large, flat structures of sticks and twigs, finer twigs in most instances forming the lining. Four eggs are normally laid, occasionally five, and rarely six.

Ardea herodias treganzai Court

On the basis of ten specimens taken at Montpelier, Bear Lake County, by Paul E. Trapier, May 21 to June 9, 1930, *treganzai* is the breeding race in Idaho. The identification was made by Dr. Harry C. Oberholser. There is apparently a northward movement of this species after the breeding season, the males that I took at Potlatch January 5, 1949, and at New Meadows, Adams County, September 17, 1958, being referable to this race.

Ardea herodias fannini Chapman

A male that I took at Potlatch on September 19, 1958, represents the dark race that breeds on the Pacific coast from Alaska to Washington. It is here recorded for the state for the first time.

Ardea herodias herodias Linnaeus

I took a female at Potlatch on July 4, 1958, that is referable to the nominate race. There are no other records for Idaho.

Casmerodius albus egretta (Gmelin): Common Egret

General Distribution. Breeds from Oregon, central Oklahoma, southern Minnesota, northern Ohio and New Jersey south through Mexico, Central America, the West Indies, and South America to the Straits of Magellan. Winters north to southern Oregon, central Nevada, New Mexico, southern Louisiana and coastal North Carolina.

Status in Idaho. Of accidental occurrence in the southern part of the state. There are two records for the occurrence of the Common Egret in Idaho. A specimen, now in the United States National Museum, was collected in June, 1962, on the Deer Flat National Wildlife Refuge, west of Nampa, by Gene H. Crawford; and a wounded bird, its left wing crippled, was picked up in a meadow near Parma by Mike Phariss in early September, 1968.

Habits. It is well known that the Common Egret wanders north after the breeding season, and during the summer months it is found as far north as the Canadian Provinces. Consequently, it was to be expected that it would eventually be recorded in Idaho. In recent years, it has increased noticeably in numbers and has been extending its breeding range northward, so it is not improbable that it may in time be of regular occurrence in the state.

Leucophoyx thula brewsteri (Thayer and Bangs): Snowy Egret

General Distribution. Breeds from northern California, northern Nevada, southern Idaho, northern Utah and Colorado, south to southern Arizona, southern New Mexico and western Texas. Winters from the southern part of its breeding range south into Mexico.

Status in Idaho. A fairly common summer resident in the southern part of the state. The Snowy Egret has been reported from Henrys Lake, June, 1909 (Wetmore, in litt.); Jefferson County, several at Mud Lake during the summer of 1925 (Luther Goldman, in litt.) and "five or six" at Roberts, July 31, 1933 (Murie, 1934); Rupert, September 16, 1919 (Davis, 1935); Jerome County and Twin Falls County, a common "late" summer visitant in 1949 (Levy, 1950); Grays Lake, one recorded in August, 1949 (Steel, 1956); Parma, June 2, 1951 (Burleigh); Burley, June 18, 1949, and April 24, 1954 (Burleigh).

It was first recorded as breeding in the state by G. Tonkin (in litt.), who states that six nests with young were found on the Snake River, at American Falls, July 20, 1922. Hayward (1934) reports a large rookery at Bear Lake in 1928 in which there were two hundred nests. When examined on June 4, a few held small young; but in the rest, there were well-incubated eggs. Davis (1935) found a small colony in June, 1934, nesting on an island in the Snake River near Burley. At Blackfoot Reservoir, two nests, each holding three eggs, were found by Jewett (in litt.) on Goose Island May 15, 1943.

On July 21, 1958, I was shown a small colony of approximately twenty pairs of Snowy Egrets that were nesting on a small island in Lake Walcott on the Minidoka National Wildlife Refuge. On this date, the young were fully grown but still unable to fly well enough to reach the mainland.

Specimens identified as *brewsteri* have been taken at Henrys Lake in June, 1909 (Wetmore), at Rupert, September 16, 1919 (Davis); in Bear Lake County, July 20, 1934 (Brodkorb); at Burley July 8, 1949 (Levy), and at Lake Walcott, July 21, 1958 (Burleigh). It can be distinguished from the nominate race by its larger measurements.

Bureau of Sport Fisheries and WildlifePhoto by R. C. Twist

SNOWY EGRETS "AT HOME"

Habits. Although it is known that, in common with other herons, the Snowy Egret wanders north of its breeding range during the summer months, it apparently does not do so in any appreciable numbers. At least this must be the case with this western subspecies, for it has yet to be recorded anywhere in northern Idaho.

The usual nesting site is the top of a bush, rarely over six feet from the ground, and the nest is usually a flat but fairly substantial structure of sticks and twigs. The rookery at Bear Lake was described by Hayward as occupying ten acres in the most inaccessible part of the swamp, the nests being one to two feet above the water and well built of dry tules. The majority held four eggs, in some instances three or five.

The nests I saw on Lake Walcott were characteristically built of sticks and twigs and averaged five feet above the ground. Jewett states that the two nests he saw on Goose Island, in Blackfoot Reservoir, were in a large colony of Great Blue Herons, Night Herons, and Cormorants.

Nycticorax nycticorax hoactli (Gmelin): BLACK-CROWNED NIGHT HERON

General Distribution. Breeds from Oregon east across the continent through Manitoba and Ontario to southern Quebec, south through Mexico and the West Indies to northern Chile and Argentina. Winters north to Oregon, Utah, New Mexico, the Gulf Coast, and Massachusetts.

Status in Idaho. A fairly common summer resident in the southern part of the state, an occasional individual wandering as far north as Nez Perce County during the summer months.

In southern Idaho, it has been recorded from Payette, April 18-27, 1910 (Jewett, in litt.), and June 2-8, 1913 (Wyman, in litt.); Sweet, "abundant" on Squaw Creek, August 19 and 20, 1913 (Wyman, in litt.); Midvale, "several" seen June 24-29, 1913 (Wyman, in litt.); Deer Flat, one hundred noted September 30 to October 30, 1915 (Cantwell, in litt.); Rupert, extreme dates of occurrence May 2 and September 4 (1919-21) (Davis, 1935); American Falls, June 12, 1935 (Mrs. J. S. Collier, in litt.); Homedale, Owyhee County, June 23, 1949 (Burleigh); Jerome, Cassia, and Twin Falls counties, uncommon summer resident in 1949; "many" at Greene's Trout Farm (near Twin Falls) August 7, 1949 (Levy, 1950); Grays Lake, a rare summer visitant; several seen in August, 1949 (Steel, 1956); Montpelier, Bear Lake County, April 27, 1954 (Burleigh).

It was first reported as breeding in the state by F. M. Dille (in litt.) who examined twelve nests at Dear Flat in 1912. Davis (1935) stated that it bred near Rupert, in Minidoka County, in 1919, 1920, and 1921, fresh eggs being found as early as May 30. A large rookery comprising "from 300 to 400 nests" was found by Hayward (1934) in Bear Lake in 1928. He stated that the birds were present there from April to late November. Jewett (in litt.) found twenty pairs nesting on Goose Island, in Blackfoot Reservoir, May 15, 1943. Two years later, May 30-31, 1945, he noted many pairs nesting at the reservoir in association with other herons.

There are very few records for the occurrence of this species in the northern part of the state. I saw single birds in adult plumage on the Snake River at Lewiston, August 21 and 27, 1950, and at the reservoir east of Lewiston Orchards July 5, 1953; and I collected one bird in immature plumage at the reservoir July 16, 1956.

Habits. As its name implies, the Black-crowned Night Heron is, during most of the year, largely nocturnal where its daily activities are concerned, its movements during the daylight hours being very limited. During the breeding season, however, especially when the young are well grown, it of necessity spends these daylight hours in satisfying the ever-increasing demand of its young for food.

Breeding colonies are located in the most inaccessible spots available; and in Idaho, an island is usually selected. The larger trees are preferred as nesting sites; but where these are lacking, bushes are used. This acceptance of willows and alders was the case on Blackfoot Reservoir where

Jewett found the nests on Goose Island within five or six feet of the ground. They were built of sticks and twigs, with a slight lining of finer twigs and coarse grasses.

At Bear Lake, the nests were in the open marsh and were fairly substantial platforms of dry tules one to two feet above the water. When first examined, they held eggs, usually four but occasionally three or five. These had largely hatched by June 4, and a subsequent visit on July 12 found young of varying sizes in all of the nests.

[Ixobrychus exilis (Gmelin): LEAST BITTERN]

General Distribution. Breeds from eastern Oregon, South Dakota, northern Michigan, southern Ontario and New Brunswick south through Mexico, Central America and South America to Paraguay and Brazil. Winters north to California, southern Texas, and central Florida.

Status in Idaho. Apparently of accidental occurrence in the southern part of the state. There is one sight record for the occurrence of the Least Bittern in Idaho. Lewis W. Oring (1962) reports a single bird seen on the Camas National Wildlife Refuge in Jefferson County, June 15, 1961. Although flushed at close range and satisfactorily identified, it unfortunately was not collected.

Habits. Because of its secretive existence, the Least Bittern is a difficult bird to see and is easily overlooked. It is possible, therefore, that it occurs regularly in Idaho, and future field work in the more extensive marsh areas may even reveal the fact that it nests in small numbers.

Botaurus lentiginosus (Rackett): AMERICAN BITTERN

General Distribution. Breeds from British Columbia east across the continent through Saskatchewan and northern Ontario to Newfoundland, south to southern California, southern Colorado, Missouri, western Tennessee and Maryland. Winters from the southern part of its breeding range south to the Bahamas, through Mexico and Central America to Panama, and to Puerto Rico.

Status in Idaho. A local but fairly common summer resident throughout the state.

The American Bittern was first reported for the state by Merrill (1897) who considered it common in the marshes on Lake Coeur d'Alene. Rust (1915) stated that during the interval from 1910 through 1914, he found it a rare "resident" there, a specimen being taken then.

At St. Maries, it was reported by Hand (1941) as a common summer resident occurring (1921 through 1941) from mid-April to late September. The only other records for northern Idaho are of a female that I collected at Potlatch, Latah County, May 26, 1949, and a single bird that I saw at the reservoir east of Lewiston Orchards August 21, 1956.

AN AMERICAN BITTERN IS THE SUBJECT OF THIS STUDY
IN VERTICAL LINES

Farther south in the state it has been recorded by Hand (1932) in Idaho County September 6, 1923 (on the Lochsa River at the mouth of Weir Creek), and August 22, 1929 (Long Lake); Deer Flat September 4-15, 1916 (Cantwell, in litt.); Meridian, November 16, 1912, and October 2, 1915 (Stalker, in litt.); Jerome, July 3, 1949 (Levy, 1950); Rupert, October 14, 1911 (Kenagy, in litt.); and by Davis (1935) from April 11 to September 4 (1919-21); American Falls, June 4, 1911 (Jewett, in litt.); Haden, one seen in the Teton Basin, September 14, 1910 (Cary, in litt.); Grays Lake, a common summer resident 1949-51 with arrival dates of April 28, 1950, and April 21, 1951 (Steel, 1956); Swan Lake, June 27-July 9, 1911 (Jewett, in litt.); Bear River, June 2, 1945 (Jewett, in litt.).

Habits. Inhabiting as it does swampy areas difficult of access and being by nature solitary and inclined to remain motionless for long intervals, the American Bittern is, despite its size, easily overlooked. It is probable that it breeds more commonly in Idaho than available records indicate, and there is little question that it nests in the marshes where it has been noted during the summer months. However, a nest has yet to be found in the state.

Unlike those of other herons, the nest is never in a tree or bush. Normally it is partially concealed in a wide stretch of reeds and cattails where the water is a foot or more deep and is a flat, dry platform of whatever vegetation is most readily available. The nest can rarely be found on dry ground in thick marsh grass.

Storks and Wood Ibises: *Family Ciconiidae*

Mycteria americana Linnaeus: WOOD IBIS

General Distribution. Largely resident from South Carolina, Florida and the Gulf coast south through Mexico, Central America, and South America to Peru and Argentina. Wanders north regularly to California, Arizona, and Tennessee, casually to Montana, Wisconsin, Ontario, and New Brunswick.

Status in Idaho. Of accidental occurrence in the southern part of the state.

Only once has the Wood Ibis been recorded in Idaho. Jewett (in litt.) reports a young male shot June 25, 1910, on Mores Creek, near Idaho City, Boise County. It was mounted and was at one time in the possession of a Mr. Weigle of Idaho City.

Habits. The Wood Ibis is not well named, for actually it is a stork, the only member of this widely distributed family found in this country. It is at all times an extremely wary bird; and as its flesh is also tough and unpalatable, it has suffered little at the hands of man. Since it wanders regularly during the summer months well north of its breeding range, it is possible that an occasional individual occurs at that time in Idaho.

Ibises and Spoonbills: *Family Threskiornithidae*

Plegadis chihi (Vieillot): WHITE-FACED IBIS

General Distribution. Breeds from central California east through Colorado and Nebraska to Minnesota, south to Veracruz, Mexico, and Florida. Also in South America from Peru and southeastern Brazil to central Argentina. Winters from California and southern Arizona south to El Salvador and Costa Rica. Resident within its breeding range in South America.

Status in Idaho. Of casual occurrence during the summer months in the southern part of the state. There is one record for northern Idaho. Sloanaker (1925) reports the only record to date for the northern part of the state, a specimen collected at Sandpoint, October 23, 1909.

Bureau of Sport Fisheries and Wildlife

A WELL-CAMOUFLAGED WHITE-FACED IBIS AT ITS NEST

In southern Idaho, it has been recorded at Deer Flat May 15 to 30 and June 26, 1932 (Towle, in litt.); near Rupert, in Minidoka County, rare in 1909, seen May 19, 1912, and common in 1913 (Kenagy, 1914); one bird noted June 14, 1934 (Davis, 1935); two birds seen at Lake Walcott, July 21, 1958, and one, a male collected (Burleigh); Hazelton, Jerome County, an uncommon late summer visitant in 1949; one collected at the Wilson Lake Reservoir, August 7 (Levy, 1950).

Habits. In view of its occurrence in southern Idaho in May and June, it is possible that the White-faced Ibis may nest sparingly in the state. It is rather surprising that it has never been observed at Bear Lake, for the extensive tule marshes there and the presence of a large breeding colony of Snowy Egrets would seemingly offer inducements to such a species as this. The nest is always built in the tules within a foot of the water, and unlike that of any of the herons it is compact and well cupped. Usually three or four pale blue eggs are laid.

ORDER ANSERIFORMES

Ducks, Geese, and Swans: *Family Anatidae*

Olor columbianus (Ord): WHISTLING SWAN

General Distribution. Breeds largely north of the Arctic Circle from Point Barrow, Alaska, and Baffin Island south to the Alaska Peninsula and the Barren Grounds of Canada. Winters on the Pacific coast from British Columbia to California, on the Gulf coast of Texas and Louisiana, and on the Atlantic coast from Maryland to North Carolina.

Status in Idaho. A regular and fairly common transient, both in the spring and in the fall.

In northern Idaho, the Whistling Swan was reported by Merrill (1897) as common in the spring at Fort Sherman (Coeur d'Alene); by Hand (1941) as a regular spring transient at St. Maries, Benewah County, flocks of 15 to 75 individuals being seen from late March to late April (1921-41); he states that it has been reported from Chatcolet and Coeur d'Alene in open winters. Levy (1959) saw flocks totalling over 150 birds on the Kootenai River at Copeland, Boundary County, October 23, 1951.

Because of the absence of bodies of water of any size, I rarely noted this species in Latah County. At Moscow I have but one record, April 23, 1952, while at Potlatch it was observed on the mill pond April 4, 1954 (three birds), and April 19 and 25, 1955 (two birds). At Lewiston, small flocks were found on the Snake River from time to time, while on the reservoir east of Lewiston Orchards, similar flocks were frequently seen. My extreme dates of occurrence for Nez Perce County, for the spring migration, are March 24 (1956) and June 4 (1954), and for the fall migration, October 23 (1951) and November 28 (1954).

Farther south in the state it has been recorded in Idaho County, six being seen October 28, 1925, on the Lochsa River, between the mouths of Fish and Sherman creeks (Hand, 1932); at Payette Lake, March 21 and 30, and October 20 to November 22, 1915 (Cottingham, in litt.); Lardo, October 20 to November 5, 1914 (Cottingham, in litt.); Deer Flat, April 14-17, 1912 (Dille, in litt.); September 19, 1913, November 27, 1914, to January 16, 1915, March 29 and April 3 and 4, 1915 (Cooper, in litt.); November 11-13, 1915 (Cantwell, in litt.); Minidoka, March 22 to April 3, 1915 (Cantwell, in litt.); Idaho Falls, flocks totalling 150 birds, November 7, 1926 (MacKenzie, in litt.); Grays Lake, eight seen November 3, 1949 (Burleigh).

Habits. The Whistling Swan is at all times a wary bird, ever alert and suspicious. Flocks seen on the reservoir east of Lewiston Orchards would remain most of the day well out of gunshot range until thoroughly satisfied that it was safe to feed near the shore. Their food, largely vegetable matter,

WHISTLING SWANS PROMENADING

is never obtained by diving, but by submerging their heads and long necks in water shallow enough to reach the bottom without difficulty. I noticed that when so engaged, one or more birds in a flock would remain in deeper water watching for any dangers that might threaten.

Despite their large size, they can, when alarmed, leave the water with ease and once in the air are fast and powerful flyers.

Olor buccinator Richardson: TRUMPETER SWAN

General Distribution. Breeds and is largely a resident in southern Alaska, British Columbia, Alberta, eastern Idaho, southwestern Montana, and Wyoming.

Status in Idaho. Breeds in small numbers in the extreme southeastern edge of the state, and is of casual occurrence there in migration. There is one record for northern Idaho.

The Trumpeter Swan was first recorded in the state by Dr. C. Hart Merriam, who collected an adult male on the Snake River in southern Idaho on September 23, 1873 (Coale, 1915).

A MAJESTIC TRUMPETER SWAN FAMILY

Bureau of Sport Fisheries and Wildlife

Photo by David B. Marshall

Merriam (1891) states that Bendire found this species nesting at Henrys Lake, in Fremont County, in 1877. Several broods of young were seen in August, and two were collected. Many years later, Rust (1917) reported it as occurring "sparingly" at Henrys Lake during the summer of 1916. Marshall (in litt.) reports two Trumpeter Swans confiscated by game wardens at Rexburg, Madison County, about November 1, 1941. I personally had the experience of putting up as a study skin for the collections of the Cooperative Wildlife Research Unit at the University of Idaho at Moscow, a male that was confiscated by federal game agents at Island Park, Fremont County, November 21, 1950.

The one record for the northern part of the state is that of a single bird seen on Lake Chatcolet, October 30, 1914 (Rust, 1915).

Habits. At one time facing extinction, the Trumpeter Swan, through adequate protection, is now gradually increasing in numbers within its present limited range. Although the nest has never actually been found, it is said on reliable authority that scattered pairs now breed in Fremont County where there is suitable marsh habitat.

There is still an unfortunate tendency on the part of an occasional "sportsman" to shoot a swan that is unwary enough to come within range, but otherwise this magnificent bird has few enemies. The flesh of adult birds is said to be tough and unpalatable, only the young of the year being fit for the table.

Branta canadensis (Linnaeus): CANADA GOOSE

General Distribution. Breeds from western Alaska east across the Arctic mainland and southern Arctic islands to Labrador and Newfoundland, south to northeastern California, Kansas, and Massachusetts. Winters south to Mexico and the Gulf states.

Status in Idaho. A common transient throughout the state, wintering in small numbers where conditions are suitable. Nests in small numbers in northern Idaho, and commonly in the southern part of the state.

The Canada Goose is another species that has the distinction of appearing on the first list of birds for the state. In his Journal, written during the famous Lewis and Clark expedition across the continent, Clark (*Original Journals*, III, 25, 49) states that the Canada Goose was seen on the Salmon River (at Salmon) August 23 and 31, 1805 (Jollie, 1953). It was next reported for the state by Merriam (1891) who states that is was observed by J. K. Townsend in eastern Idaho "near the Snake River" in July 1834.

Merrill (1897) considered it common in the spring and rare in the fall at Fort Sherman (Coeur d'Alene), his earliest spring arrival date being February 22. He stated that a few pairs nested each year on the Lake. Rust (1915) reported its numbers decreasing in Kootenai County, the once numerous large flocks being absent in 1913 and 1914. At St. Maries, in Benewah County, Hand (1932) found this species a common transient in March and November (1921-41), but also noted a decrease in numbers "in recent years."

It was also observed in migration at Rathdrum, March 8, 9, and 20, 1899, February 25, 1900, February 3 to March 1, 1901, February 23 to March 1, 1905, February 27, 1906, and March 20, 1907 (Danby, in litt.).

It is known to nest commonly on the Snake River, in eastern Washington, and it is probably largely from this area that small flocks appear in northern Idaho during the summer months. Snyder (1900) reports a small flock on Kaniksu Lake, Kootenai County, on July 26, and Johnston (1949) a flock of five at Moscow June 1, 1947. At Lewiston, I observed small flocks at intervals during the summer months both on the Snake River and on the reservoir east of Lewiston Orchards. Since it is common here in migration, especially in late April and May and again in November and early December, it can be considered a resident species in Nez Perce County. Yocom (1965) states that in 1953 at least six pairs of geese nested along the Clearwater River "upstream a few miles from its mouth," and that the same year another pair nested on a Snake River island one mile upstream from Lewiston.

Farther south in the state it has been reported in migration from Idaho County along the Lochsa River in April and November (Hand, 1932); Adams County, common October 23 through December 3, 1957 (Newhouse, 1960); Payette, August to October, 1884-86 and April 18-27, 1910 (Jewett, in litt); Deer Flat, September 19, December 11 and 15, 1913, November 27, 1914, to April 5, 1915 (A. C. Cooper, in litt.); October 29 to November 1, 1914, March 22 to April 3, October 5 to November 12, 1915 (Cantwell, in litt.); May 15-30, 1932 (Towle, in litt.); Minidoka, March 22 to April 3, 1915, September 16-29, 1916 (Cantwell, in litt.); Rupert, March 23, October 30 to November 4, 1919, March 23 to April 6, 1920 (Davis, 1935); Pocatello, March 18 to April 18, 1917 (R. H. Palmer, in litt.); Montpelier, common April 10-13, 1912 (Jewett, in litt.); Paris, first observed March 15, common April 4, 1930 (Hayward, in litt.); Grays Lake, a common summer resident, arrival dates being March 21, 1950, and March 20, 1951 (Steel, 1956).

Scattered pairs possibly nest on the Snake River south of Nampa, for Wyman (in litt.) states this species was seen there from May, 1909, to July, 1912, under conditions that suggested breeding.

Jewett (in litt.) found twenty nests on Goose Island, in the Blackfoot Reservoir, May 15, 1943. One held five newly-hatched young, the others from three to six eggs. Two years later, on May 30, 1945, he examined fifty nests on this same island, all holding from three to seven eggs. There was also one brood of five young that were one day out of the nest. Numerous nests were found at Grays Lake in 1950 and 1951 (Steel, 1956).

Yocom (1965) considers the most important water area for nesting geese in southern Idaho to be the Snake River, particularly where it flows through southwestern Idaho.

Habits. The Canada Goose is a sociable bird, occurring in flocks of varying sizes throughout much of the year. Even during the breeding season, this trait is noticeable; for where conditions are suitable, pairs nest in close proximity to each other. The site of the nest varies considerably and is

Bureau of Sport Fisheries and Wildlife

Photo by R. C. Twist

A CANADA GOOSE NESTING COMFORTABLY ON THE TOP OF A MUSKRAT HOUSE

influenced to a large extent by the character of the area selected for rearing the young. The nests found by Jewett on Goose Island, in Blackfoot Reservoir, were built on dry ground and were substantial beds of grasses, weed stems, and similar material. At Grays Lake, where these geese nested in the wide stretch of marsh vegetation covering much of the water, a common nesting site was the top of an old muskrat house. In eastern Washington, the nest is built on the ledge of a cliff fronting the Snake River; while in other parts of the country, it is not uncommon to find these birds utilizing an old hawk's or crow's nest well up from the ground in a large tree. Pairs are said to remain mated for life, and both birds are devoted parents, aggressively defending their young against any danger that threatens.

Branta canadensis moffitti Aldrich

Specimens taken in 1954 at the reservoir east of Lewiston Orchards, a female on October 28 and a male on November 14, represent *moffitti*, the breeding race in Idaho. Yocom (1965) estimates a breeding population of approximately 1,010 pairs of Canada Geese in the state at the present time.

Branta canadensis fulva Delacour

A female taken at the reservoir on September 24, 1957, has been identified by Aldrich as *fulva*, the dark race breeding on the coast of Alaska and British Columbia. Another female taken at the reservoir on October 28, 1956, was intermediate in its characters, being identified as *fulva*, but approaching *parvipes* in the lighter color of the underparts.

Branta bernicla hrota (Muller): BRANT

General Distribution. Breeds in the Arctic regions of eastern North America (Ellesmere Island, Southampton Island, Baffin Island), northern Greenland, and Spitsbergen. Winters on the Atlantic coast from Massachusetts to Florida and on the Pacific coast from British Columbia to northern California.

Status in Idaho. Of accidental occurrence in the northern part of the state.

There is a single record for the occurrence of this species in Idaho. Jewett (1948) reports a bird in immature plumage shot by a hunter on Lake Pend Oreille at the mouth of the Clark Fork River in Bonner County, October 7, 1947. As there was some question as to its identity, it was sent to Alden H. Miller at the Museum of Comparative Zoology, Berkeley, California, who identified it as the American Brant, *Branta bernicla hrota*.

Habits. In its migrations, the Brant follows the coasts, and relatively few individuals occur in the interior of the country. Consequently, it will rarely be found in Idaho. In appearance, it suggests a small Canada Goose; but in flight, a flock has a loose formation quite unlike the v-shaped pattern so characteristic of its larger relative.

Branta nigricans (Lawrence): BLACK BRANT

General Distribution. Breeds in the Arctic maritime regions of eastern Asia and western North America, east to northern Alaska and northwestern Canada, south to northeastern Mackenzie. Winters on the Pacific coast from British Columbia to Baja California and inland in Oregon, California, and Nevada.

Status in Idaho. A rare transient both in the spring and in the fall.

Danby (in litt.) reports this species at Rathdrum in Kootenai County on March 28 and 29, 1899. At Rupert, in Minidoka County, it was noted by Davis (1935) from March 21 to May 7 and on October 27, 1919, and on October 13, 1920. Apparently no specimen from the state exists at the present time.

Habits. The Black Brant is essentially a maritime species and only of infrequent occurrence away from salt water. It is an abundant bird on the coast, large flocks spending much of their time well off shore and feeding on the mud flats when exposed by the low tide. Hunters consider this small goose extremely wary at all times; despite their abundance within their relatively limited range in the fall, the number shot each year is never large.

Anser albifrons frontalis Baird: PACIFIC WHITE-FRONTED GOOSE

General Distribution. Breeds in northern Alaska and east to Mackenzie and Keewatin. Winters from British Columbia to Baja California, and from southern Illinois to Mexico and the Gulf coast.

Status in Idaho. A rather uncommon transient; rarely noted either in the spring or in the fall.

Wyman (in litt.) reports several taken by hunters at Nampa in the fall of 1909. Jones (1943) records an immature male that was collected in Bingham County, ten miles north of Pocatello, on December 6, 1942. Steel (1956) considered it a rare transient at Grays Lake. One bird was noted there May 11, 1950, and two on April 10, 1951.

I personally observed three birds on the reservoir east of Lewiston Orchards on October 1, 1953, and two days later, on October 3, succeeded in collecting a female that was resting on a mud flat in the Palouse River, one mile east of Potlatch.

Habits. In view of its abundance on the Pacific coast both in migration and during the winter months, it is surprising that the White-fronted Goose does not occur in larger numbers in Idaho. Its plumage is distinctive enough to be readily recognized at a reasonable distance, so it should not be easily overlooked. In common with other geese, it is sociable by nature and throughout much of the year occurs in flocks of varying sizes.

Chen hyperborea hyperborea (Pallas): SNOW GOOSE

General Distribution. Breeds in the Arctic from Point Barrow, Alaska, east to Southampton Island and southern Baffin Island and south of Eskimo

Point, Keewatin. Winters on the Pacific coast from British Columbia south to California and on the Gulf coast from Veracruz to western Florida.

Status in Idaho. A common transient both in the spring and in the fall.

In the extreme northern part of the state, the Snow Goose is apparently a rare transient. The one record for its occurrence is that of a single bird collected at Rathdrum in Kootenai County, April 11, 1902 (Danby, in litt.).

At Lewiston I found it a common transient, numerous flocks being seen on the Snake River and on the reservoir east of Lewiston Orchards. Normally the flocks seen were small, comprising from three to eight individuals, but at times quite large flocks were noted. The largest flock seen was that of approximately one hundred birds, April 21, 1956, others recorded being one of forty birds April 4, 1953, one of fifty September 30, 1953, one of sixty April 4 1955 and one of ninety April 16, 1956. My extreme dates of occurrence in Nez Perce County for the spring migration are March 19 (1953) and May 16 (1955), and for the fall migration September 16 (1955) and November 14 (1954). A male taken at the reservoir April 21, 1956, was found to represent this small race that has such a wide distribution as a breeding bird in the Arctic.

In Idaho County Hand (1932) reported seeing "thousands" on the Lochsa River (from Pete King to Sherman Creek) October 27-28, 1925. They were in flocks varying in size from 25 to 150 birds. At Payette Lake, Cottingham (in litt.) found this species a common transient, flocks being seen November 4, 1914, and March 22 to April 7 and October 21 to December 15, 1915. Newhouse (1960) noted flocks totalling "several thousand" at Council, Adams County, April 4-8, 1958.

Farther south in the state, it has been recorded at Deer Flat November 12-25, 1915 (Cantwell in litt.); Meridian, November 9, 1915 (Stalker, in litt.); Midvale, five hundred seen in early April, 1945 (R. S. Boch, in litt.).

Habits. The relative abundance of the Snow Goose during the spring months at the reservoir east of Lewiston Orchards has become a matter of concern to the farmers of this area. A considerable acreage of the open rolling prairie characteristic of much of Nez Perce County is planted to wheat each year, and the geese have developed the habit of feeding in the nearby wheat fields during their sojourn at the reservoir. Nipping off each stalk at the ground, a flock will devastate that part of the field in which they feed, but the actual damage that is done is probably not serious since their activities are limited to a relatively few acres.

Chen rossii (Cassin): Ross' Goose

General Distribution. Breeds in the Arctic in northeastern Mackenzie, on Queen Maud Gulf, and on Southampton Island. Winters in California, chiefly in the Sacramento and San Joaquin valleys.

Status in Idaho. Apparently largely of accidental occurrence in the state.

William D. Rush (in litt.) states that a Ross' Goose, wounded by a hunter, was picked up at Mud Lake, Jefferson County, on October 25, 1961, by Kenneth MacKenzie, District Conservation Officer of the Idaho Fish and Game Department. Elwood Bizeau (in litt.) reports another bird killed illegally by a hunter at Cascade Reservoir, Valley County, October 26, 1961, and confiscated by Monte Richards, Fisheries Biologist, Idaho Fish and Game Department. There are no other records.

Habits. During the winter months, Ross' Goose commonly associates with the flocks of Snow Geese that feed in the stubble fields in the central valleys of California. Its small size, not much larger than that of a Mallard, readily distinguishes it then. For many years, the breeding range of this small goose was entirely unknown, and it was not until 1940 that its well-guarded secret was revealed. Within its limited range, it is a common bird; even so, however, it can be considered the rarest and least known of our geese.

Anas platyrhynchos platyrhynchos Linnaeus: MALLARD

General Distribution. The Mallard has a wide distribution in the northern hemisphere. In North America it breeds from the Aleutian Islands east through Alaska, northern Manitoba and James Bay to southern Ontario, south to Baja California, southern New Mexico, southeastern Illinois and northern Virginia. It winters as far north as central Alaska, central Alberta and southern Ontario, south to southern Mexico and the Bahamas.

Status in Idaho. Resident and common throughout the larger part of the state most of the year. Its occurrence during the winter months is dependent on weather conditions; but wherever streams or ponds remain unfrozen, this familiar duck can usually be found.

The Mallard is the most common and most widely distributed duck in Idaho. It occurs wherever there is any open water, even the smaller creeks and ponds seeming to offer sufficient inducements for one or more pairs.

It was first reported for the state by Merriam (1891) who states that about the middle of July, 1872, he collected young of the year on the Henrys Fork of the Snake River. He also found it nesting commonly on Birch Creek, in south-central Idaho, in 1890 young still unable to fly being seen there the first week in August.

It has since been recorded from numerous localities by many observers, all local lists that have been published commenting on the presence of this species not only as a breeding bird but as a resident during the winter months as well.

In Latah County I noted it in largest numbers during late February and early March, when for an interval of several weeks northward-bound migrants appeared in large numbers in fields flooded by the melting snow. Flocks of one hundred to five hundred individuals were not uncommon then. By the end of March mated pairs were frequently observed, and by the middle of April most of the females were incubating their eggs.

"MALLARD CITY"

Actual breeding records are not numerous. Snyder (1900) frequently noted broods of young in the Hoodoo Valley in August. On Ice House Creek in Fremont County, Rust (1917) saw a female with four young able to fly on August 26, 1916. Davis (1935) reported May 2 (1919-21) as the earliest date for eggs in Minidoka County, and July 7 as the latest date for small young. At the upper end of Lake Coeur d'Alene in Kootenai County, Yocom (1946) observed two broods of young, July 1-10, 1943. In Latah County, my earliest breeding record is that of a nest found at Moscow on April 21, 1950, that held ten incubated eggs. At Potlatch, broods of newly hatched young were seen May 12, 1951, and May 10, 1953. I found a nest at Grays Lake on May 29, 1952, that held six eggs and one at New Meadows in Adams County on May 18, 1955, with five fresh eggs.

Habits. Usually the nest of a Mallard is built on dry ground near water, and is well concealed in thick grass and similar vegetation. However, some females show considerable originality in their choice of a nesting site. The nest found at Moscow on April 21, 1950, was on a slight slope within three

Bureau of Sport Fisheries and Wildlife   Photo by R. C. Twist

MALLARDS HUDDLING ON THE ICE SEEM MORE INTERESTED IN FINDING
WARMTH THAN IN ENJOYING THEIR EXCITING SURROUNDINGS

feet of a well-traveled highway, and was at least two miles from the nearest
water. One can only wonder what difficulties the female must have encountered in leading her brood of downy young to the closest stream and how
successful she was. At Grays Lake, the female had selected an old crow's
nest up eight feet from the ground in the top of a small willow in underbrush at the edge of Eagle Creek. The six eggs were lying in a bed of down
that almost concealed them from view.

Because of the high altitude (6,400 feet), Grays Lake is completely
frozen over during the winter months, so here the Mallard is a summer
resident only. Steel (1956) gives as an arrival date in the spring February 15, 1950.

Anas strepera Linnaeus: GADWALL

General Distribution. Breeds in North America from southern Alaska
east through Alberta and Manitoba to Quebec, south to California, northern

Texas, southern Wisconsin and North Carolina. Winters from the southern part of its breeding range south to Baja California, Mexico, the Gulf coast, and northern Florida.

Status in Idaho. A common summer resident in the southern part of the state, but scarce and rarely seen north of Nez Perce County.

The Gadwall was first recorded for the state by Merriam (1891) who noted it in 1872 at Marsh Creek and at Market Lake, Jefferson County. At the latter locality, eggs were taken in June. Hand (1932) reports a flock of twelve on Fish Lake, Idaho County, July 28, 1926. In Minidoka County, it was found nesting by Davis (1935), his earliest date for eggs being May 19 (1919-21). Levy (1950) considered it a common breeding bird at Cary Lake, Blaine County, in 1949, and Steel (1956) gives it this same status for Grays Lake in 1950 and 1951, his arrival dates being April 19 and April 13.

My own experience with the Gadwall has been rather limited. I saw a pair at Shoup, Lemhi County, on the Middle Fork of the Salmon River June 4, 1949, and another pair on the reservoir east of Lewiston Orchards May 16, 1953.

Habits. As there is suitable habitat in the northern part of the state, it is rather surprising that the Gadwall is such a scarce bird there. Such competent field ornithologists as R. L. Hand, H. S. Rust, and J. C. Merrill failed to record it at any time at St. Maries or Coeur d'Alene, so it would appear that in migration it avoids this rugged mountainous area. Because of its feeding habits, it is partial to shallow water, for it rarely dives, but secures its food by standing on its head with only its tail visible and probing in the soft mud at the bottom of a pool or stagnant stream. It is one of the less hardy of the ducks, migrating north late in the spring and departing from its breeding grounds early in the fall.

Anas acuta Linnaeus: PINTAIL

General Distribution. Breeds in North America from northern Alaska east across the continent to eastern Quebec, south to southern California, southern Colorado, Iowa and Illinois. Winters from the southern part of its breeding range south throughout Mexico and Central America to Colombia and to the Bahamas and Cuba.

Status in Idaho. A common summer resident in the southern part of the state and a fairly common transient in northern Idaho.

Merrill (1897) reported the Pintail as common in migration at Fort Sherman (Coeur d'Alene). At St. Maries, Hand (1941) noted it only during the spring months, finding it a fairly common transient from March until May.

In Latah County, I found this species a fairly common transient both in the spring and in the fall, being seen then wherever there was sufficient open water to afford protection and a food supply. In late February and throughout March, small flocks were frequently observed with Mallards in the flooded fields. A few small flocks are usually seen during the winter months, but their presence then depends to a large extent on the open water available.

It is said to breed in small numbers in northern Idaho, but a nest has never actually been found. I noted it but once during the summer, two birds being seen August 8, 1949, on a gravel bar in the Snake River at Lewiston.

In the southern part of the state, it was reported by Kenagy (1914) as common in Minidoka County in 1907 and "abundant" in 1913. Davis (1935) considered it a common breeding bird at Rupert, giving as extreme dates of occurrence March 20 and November 30 (1919-21) and May 19 as the average date for fresh eggs. Levy (1950) reports it common in south-central Idaho June through August, 1949. At Grays Lake, Steel (1956) found it to be an abundant summer resident from 1949 through 1951; he gives as an arrival date in the spring, April 11, 1950.

Habits. The Pintail is one of the so-called "puddle" ducks, securing its food by tipping up in shallow water. Flocks noted on the reservoir east of Lewiston Orchards would rest in a compact group well offshore most of the day, but sooner or later would be found feeding, well scattered, close to the shore. Always wary and ever on the alert, the slightest sign of danger would, however, cause them to return to the safety of the deep water.

The nest is always on dry ground, frequently half a mile or more from the nearest water, and is usually fairly well concealed in thick grass. It is a slight hollow in the ground, lined with grasses and an increasing amount of down as incubation progresses. In common with the other ducks, the female does not begin to incubate until the eggs are all laid, so the down is important both from the standpoint of concealment and of warmth for the eggs.

Anas carolinensis Gmelin: GREEN-WINGED TEAL

General Distribution. Breeds from northern Alaska east through Mackenzie and Manitoba to Newfoundland, south to southern California, northern New Mexico, northern Nebraska and northern Ohio. Winters from British Columbia, Nebraska, southern Illinois and northern Pennsylvania south to Baja California, British Honduras, and the Bahamas.

Status in Idaho. At present a fairly common transient throughout the state both in the spring and in the fall, and an uncommon summer resident in southern Idaho.

The Green-winged Teal is apparently not as common in the state today as it was in past years. Merriam (1891) considered it abundant in 1890 in south-central Idaho, recording it on Birch Creek, the Lemhi River, Big and Little Lost rivers and the Pahsimeroi, Big Wood and Salmon rivers. He stated that on September 12 fifteen were shot on Bullberg Creek at the head of Pahsimeroi Valley, and three on the Snake River October 10. Merrill (1897) found it almost as common at Fort Sherman (Coeur d'Alene), but noted it only in migration there.

Recent records indicate a perceptible decrease in the numbers of these little ducks occurring in Idaho. Rust (1915) reports one flock on Lake Coeur d'Alene August 18, 1910, and an occasional flock on the St. Joe marshes during the fall months (1910 through 1914). At St. Maries, in Benewah County, Hand (1941) found it a fairly common transient in April and May and again from September through November. Mated pairs seen in early June indicated possible breeding but no nest was ever found. I likewise found it a fairly common transient in Latah and Nez Perce counties both in the spring and in the fall. A few were noted each winter on the Clearwater River at Lewiston, and it apparently nested in small numbers at the reservoir. However, I was never able to verify this supposition.

Farther south in the state it has been reported from Idaho County, present at Fish Lake in September and October, average dates of occurrence being September 1 to October 12, and extreme dates August 12, 1926, and October 26, 1928 (Hand, 1932); Adams County, noted at the Ben Ross Reservoir April 25, 1958 (Newhouse, 1960); Riddle, Owyhee County, one pair noted and a nest with seven eggs found (May 28 to June 3, 1934) (Davis, 1934); Rupert, Minidoka County, earliest date of occurrence in the fall October 30, latest in the spring May 2 (1919-21) (Davis, 1935); south-central Idaho, fairly common and widely distributed, June through August, 1949 (Levy, 1950); Fremont County, fairly common on the small streams and on Henrys Lake in 1916 (Rust, 1917); Grays Lake, a rare summer resident, 1949 through 1951; arrival date in the spring April 13, 1950 (Steel, 1956).

Habits. The Green-winged Teal is one of the hardier of the ducks and winters as far north as there is any open water. So during mild winters, small flocks linger as far north as Nez Perce County, appearing then on the reservoir east of Lewiston Orchards and also above the dam on the Clearwater River at Lewiston. Although adept at diving, this little duck prefers to feed in shallow water, and a sudden freeze-up in late December or January will cause the abrupt departure of the small flocks that otherwise remain until spring.

The nest is always on dry ground and is a hollow lined with grasses and down from the incubating bird. It is usually close to water, but a female will at times select a site some distance away from the nearest stream. Davis states that the nest found at Riddle, in Owyhee County, was in a depression at the base of a sage bush and was fully a quarter of a mile from the nearest water.

Anas discors discors Linnaeus: BLUE-WINGED TEAL

General Distribution. Breeds from British Columbia east through northern Saskatchewan, Manitoba, and Ontario to southern Quebec, south to southern Quebec, south to southern California, southern New Mexico, central Texas, Louisiana, and Tennessee. Winters from southern California, Texas, and North Carolina south through Central America and the West Indies to Ecuador and Brazil.

Status in Idaho. A fairly common transient and an uncommon summer resident throughout the state.

The Blue-winged Teal was first recorded in the state by Merriam (1891) who in 1890 took specimens in south-central Idaho on Little Lost River on July 27, on Sawtooth Lake October 1, and on the Snake River, near Shoshone Falls, October 9-11. In this same general area, Levy (1950) found it a fairly common summer resident in 1949.

Elsewhere in southern Idaho it has been reported from Fremont County, several on Ice House Creek August 17, 1916 (Rust, 1917); Rupert, noted June 10, 1919 (Davis, 1935); Grays Lake, an uncommon summer resident, 1949 through 1951, date of arrival in the spring April 22, 1950 (Steel, 1956); Adams County, one pair seen in Indian Valley May 6, 1958 (Newhouse, 1960); Burley, Cassia county, several pairs noted June 10, 1960, in marshy areas bordering the Snake River, and a nest found that day that held nine eggs (Burleigh).

In the northern part of the state it was reported by Hand (1941) as fairly common in the spring at St. Maries, Benewah County, being seen from late April or early May until June. There was a possibility that it nested in small numbers, but a nest was never actually found.

In both Latah and Nez Perce counties, I found this species a common spring and fall transient and an uncommon summer resident. A few pairs nest each year at the reservoir east of Lewiston Orchards, and here I succeeded, on June 2, 1957, in flushing a female from nine eggs. My earliest date of arrival in the spring is April 21 (1956).

Habits. The Blue-winged Teal is one of the least hardy of the ducks, migrating north late in the spring and leaving its summer home quite early in the fall. In Idaho, if the weather is mild, it lingers in small numbers until early October; but the southward movement normally begins in late August and by the end of September few individuals remain in the state.

The nest is always on dry land and is seldom far from water. The one that I found at the reservoir was approximately one hundred feet from the water and was so well concealed in thick grass that it would have remained undiscovered had the female not flushed when almost stepped on. At Burley, the nest was equally well concealed in thick grass bordering an open marsh, and was one hundred yards from the bank of the Snake River.

Anas cyanoptera septentrionalium Snyder and Lumsden: CINNAMON TEAL

General Distribution. Breeds from British Columbia, Alberta, Saskatchewan, eastern Montana and eastern Wyoming, south to Baja California, northern Mexico, and western Texas. Winters from southern California, Arizona, New Mexico, and southern Texas to Panama and northern Colombia.

Status in Idaho. A fairly common to abundant summer resident over most of the state.

On the basis of available records, it would appear that the Cinnamon Teal has increased in numbers in Idaho in recent years. Merrill (1897) considered it rare at Fort Sherman (Coeur d'Alene) and Rust (1915) reported it uncommon in Kootenai County from 1910 through 1914, a specimen being taken then in the St. Joe marshes. However, Hand (1941) found it a common summer resident at St. Maries, Benewah County, from 1921 through 1941. A nest found there held eight eggs on May 16, 1937, and eleven eggs on May 29 (Hand, 1939).

I personally found it an uncommon summer resident in Latah and Nez Perce counties, but this was due to lack of suitable habitat. Marsh areas bordering open water are scarce in this part of the state so only a few scattered pairs were noted. They appeared in late April or early May, my earliest record for the spring migration being two birds seen at Moscow April 22 (1956).

Farther south in the state it has been recorded in Idaho County, one seen on the Lochsa River (at Lochsa Station) May 7, 1928 (Hand, 1932); Riddle, Owyhee County, two pairs noted May 28 through June 3, 1934 (Davis, 1934); Rupert, Minidoka County, extreme dates of occurrence (1919-21), April 6 and October 30, with the earliest date for fresh eggs May 19 (Davis, 1935); south-central Idaho, a fairly common summer resident in 1949 (Levy, 1950); southeastern Idaho, a nest with nine eggs collected at Marsh Creek June 29, 1872 (Merriam, 1891); Grays Lake, an abundant summer resident in 1950 and 1951, arrival dates in the spring April 17, 1950, and April 13, 1951 (Steel, 1956).

Habits. The Cinnamon Teal is unique in that it is the only duck found in North America that is limited in its distribution to the western United States. I rarely observed it in northern Idaho after midsummer, so gained the impression that as with the Blue-winged Teal, it was one of the less hardy of the ducks. There seemed little justification for this apparent early departure. Wintering as it does in the southern part of its breeding range, the distance traveled by this species in migration is relatively short both in the spring and in the fall.

Unlike those of the other teal, the nest is built either over water or on dry ground, and it is generally well concealed in thick vegetation. The one found by Hand at St. Maries was in a rather unusual situation, being but eight feet from the tracks of the Chicago, Milwaukee, St. Paul and Pacific Railroad. Each time a train passed the ground would shake, but the incubating bird seemed quite unconcerned.

[**Mareca penelope** (Linnaeus): EUROPEAN WIDGEON]

General Distribution. Breeds in Iceland, the British Isles, northern Europe, and east across Siberia to Kamchatka. Of regular occurrence in North

America both in migration and during the winter months, being recorded then on the Pacific coast from Alaska to Baja California, in the interior, and on the Atlantic coast from Newfoundland to Florida.

Status in Idaho. Recorded once in the northern part of the state.

Levy (1959) reports an adult male seen at Moscow March 18, 1950, feeding in a wheat field with Mallards and Pintails. He was unable to collect it but was able to identify it satisfactorily as a European Widgeon. As no specimen of this rather uncommon duck has been taken in the state, it seems desirable at this time to place it in the hypothetical list; although under the circumstances there is no reason to question the identification.

Mareca americana (Gmelin): AMERICAN WIDGEON

General Distribution. Breeds from Alaska, southern Manitoba, and Wisconsin, south to northern California, Colorado, and Nebraska. Winters from the southern part of its breeding range south to Costa Rica, the Bahamas, and Puerto Rico.

Status in Idaho. A common transient both in the spring and in the fall, and an uncommon summer resident in the southern part of the state.

In northern Idaho, it was reported by Merrill (1897) as common at Fort Sherman (Coeur d'Alene) the latter part of September; by Rust (1915) as fairly common in the fall on the St. Joe marshes, Kootenai County, from 1910 through 1914; and by Hand (1941) as a common transient (1921 through 1941) at St. Maries, but varying in abundance from year to year. It was observed from late March until May, and again in October and November.

I personally found it a common transient in Latah and Nez Perce counties, small flocks being frequently seen in the spring and in the fall. As with the Pintail, it can be found in late February and throughout March feeding with Mallards in the flooded fields. It winters in small numbers, its abundance at this season of the year being governed by the amount of open water available. It was never recorded during the summer months.

Farther south in the state it was reported by Hand (1932) as being noted each fall on Fish Lake, in Idaho County, from 1925 through 1929. He gives as average dates of occurrence September 20 to October 7, with extreme dates August 24 (1928) and October 18 (1929). His largest flock was one of forty birds seen October 3, 1925. In Adams County, a pair was noted by Newhouse (1960) on the Ben Ross Reservoir April 20, 1958.

In south-central Idaho, Merriam (1891) recorded a specimen taken on the Lemhi River August 31, 1890, two on Sawtooth Lake October 2, and three on the Snake River, near Shoshone Falls, October 9. In this same general area, Snyder (1900) reports young in Hoodoo Valley August 18; Davis (1935) observed it at Rupert from 1919 through 1921, with extreme dates of occurrence March 20 and November 15; and Levy (1950) found it common from June through August, 1949.

At Woods Reservoir, on the West Fork of Camas Creek, in Fremont County, "several" were seen July 17, 1916 (Rust, 1917). Steel (1956) considered it a rare summer resident at Grays Lake (1949 through 1951). He gives as arrival dates April 15, 1950, and April 13, 1951.

Habits. The American Widgeon is another of the so-called "puddle" ducks which feed in water shallow enough to eliminate the need of diving to reach the bottom. Flocks noted at the reservoir east of Lewiston Orchards were commonly seen close to the shore, although when not feeding they remained for long intervals resting in compact groups in the center of the reservoir. Fields flooded by melting snow in the early spring afforded ideal feeding grounds, and it was in such spots that this species was commonly observed at Moscow during the early spring months.

Although occurring locally during the summer months, a nest has yet to be found in Idaho. It is always built on dry ground, often at some distance from the nearest water and well concealed in thick grass and weeds. In common with other ducks, the incubating bird uses down to cover the eggs when she is away feeding, and this aids in effectively protecting the nest from any harm.

Spatula clypeata (Linnaeus): SHOVELER

General Distribution. Widely distributed in North America, Europe, and Asia. In North America it breeds from western Alaska east through central Alberta and Saskatchewan to southern Ontario, south to California, New Mexico, Kansas, Iowa, Alabama, and North Carolina. Winters from British Columbia, New Mexico, the Gulf Coast and the coast of South Carolina, south to Panama and the West Indies.

Status in Idaho. A fairly common transient and an uncommon summer resident over most of the state.

Jollie (1953) has summarized the observations of Lewis and Clark as contained in the journals they kept during their famous expedition to the Pacific coast, and lists twenty-four species of birds that were seen in Idaho. Among these is the Shoveler, a male being reported killed on the Camas Prairie May 8, 1806 (Lewis, *Original Journals,* V: 3). It was next recorded in the state by Merriam (1891) who states that it was noted on the Bear River by Townsend in 1838.

Merrill (1897) considered it common at Fort Sherman (Coeur d'Alene), stating that twenty-five were seen on June 1. Rust (1915) found it fairly common in the St. Joe marshes, in Kootenai County, from 1910 through 1914, especially in the fall. He suspected that it nested in small numbers, but he never succeeded in finding a nest. At St. Maries it was reported by Hand (1941) as a common spring transient in April and May (1921 through 1941), although there were years when relatively few flocks were seen.

I also noted it only in the spring in Latah and Nez Perce counties, but it was fairly common then, small flocks being frequently observed from early April until June. My earliest record for the spring migration is that of a pair seen at Moscow April 3 (1952), my latest record a flock of twelve birds at the reservoir June 19 (1958).

Farther south in the state it was recorded at Fish Lake, Idaho County, a flock of eight, October 26 and 27, 1928, and a flock of six October 7-11, 1929 (Hand, 1932); Adams County, a flock of four on the Ben Ross Reservoir April 20, 1958 (Newhouse, 1960); Rupert, Minidoka County, noted April 11 through June 10, and September 1 through November 4, 1919, March 21 through May 31 and October 13, 1920, and May 19, 1921 (Davis, 1935); Cary Lake, Blaine County, young noted June 4, 1949 (Levy, 1950); Grays Lake, an uncommon summer resident, 1949 through 1951, dates of arrival in the spring being April 21, 1950, and April 13, 1951 (Steel, 1956).

Habits. The Shoveler is another of the ducks that apparently is averse to cold weather, for it appears in the spring with the first flocks of Blue-winged Teal, and in the fall begins its southward movement in late August and early September. Although noted from time to time on the reservoir east of Lewiston Orchards it showed a definite preference for shallow ponds and marshes where it could feed without submerging much of its body. I have never known it to dive, and it is doubtful if it does so. As with the other ducks the nest is built on dry ground and is often at some distance from the nearest water. From nine to eleven eggs are normally laid, and until incubation begins they are well concealed with down from the incubating bird when she is away feeding.

Aix sponsa (Linnaeus): Wood Duck

General Distribution. Breeds locally over most of the United States south to central California, the Gulf coast and Florida, and in Cuba, and north to British Columbia, Manitoba, and southern Quebec. Winters from southern British Columbia to central Mexico and from Missouri, southern Illinois and Virginia to Jamaica.

Status in Idaho. A common summer resident in the northern part of the state. There are no records for southern Idaho, although it doubtless occurs there, at least sparingly, in migration.

The Wood Duck was first recorded for the state by Merrill (1897) who considered it common during the summer months at Fort Sherman (Coeur d'Alene).

Rust (1915) noted an apparent decrease in numbers in Kootenai County in 1912; two specimens were taken by him September 22 in the St. Joe marshes. Yocom (1946) observed one pair with two young at the upper end of Lake Coeur d'Alene July 1-10, 1943. Moody (1903) reports a nest found on Lake Pend d'Oreille that held eight eggs, but gives no specific date or locality.

At St. Maries it was found by Hand (1941) to be a common summer resident on the St. Joe River, being seen there from April until October (1921 through 1941). Levy (1959) likewise considered it common at St. Maries. He observed a female there with a brood of half-grown young June 19, 1951.

In Latah County I found this species fairly common during the summer months on the Palouse River at Potlatch. It usually appeared in late March and was rarely seen after the latter part of September. My earliest date of arrival in the spring is March 21 (1951). At Lewiston, in Nez Perce County, a single bird was seen on Hatwai Creek October 8, 1956. This is my latest record in the fall.

Habits. Where North American ducks are concerned, the Wood Duck is unique in many respects. It is entirely North American in its distribution, and in fact is largely confined to the United States, for it does not go very far north into Canada during the summer months or far south into Mexico during the winter. Although seen occasionally on ponds, and rarely on the larger bodies of water, it is essentially a bird of swift-flowing wooded streams. For this reason, it is rather local in its distribution in northern Idaho and is absent from the southern part of the state where suitable habitat is lacking. The nest is built in a tree either in a natural cavity or in an old woodpecker's hole large enough to hold the incubating bird and the ten to fifteen eggs that are normally laid. It is often well up from the ground.

Aythya americana (Eyton): REDHEAD

General Distribution. Breeds from British Columbia east through Alberta, Mackenzie, Saskatchewan, and Manitoba to northern Minnesota, south to southern California, northern New Mexico, northern Iowa, and Pennsylvania. Winters over much of its breeding range, south to central Mexico, the Bahamas, Cuba, and Jamaica.

Status in Idaho. A fairly common transient and an uncommon winter resident in the northern part of the state, and a locally common summer resident in southern Idaho.

At St. Maries Hand (1941) reported this species to be an irregular spring transient (1921 through 1941), being common some years and scarce others. He noted it on the St. Joe River from April until the middle of May. It was observed once in the fall, in late September.

I personally found the Redhead a fairly common transient in Latah and Nez Perce counties, both in the spring and in the fall. It was most frequently seen the last two weeks in April and in October and early November. It wintered in small numbers on the Clearwater River east of Lewiston, and appeared infrequently on the Snake River.

In south-central Idaho, a specimen was taken on Sawtooth Lake September 27, 1890 (Merriam, 1891); and in this same general area it was reported by Levy (1950) as a common summer resident in 1949. Davis (1935) noted it at Rupert in Minidoka County April 15, 1919, April 14 through May 31, 1920, and May 19, 1921; and Hamerstrom (in litt.) collected a male at Grandview, Owyhee County, November 6, 1943.

At Grays Lake, it was considered by Steel (1956) to be an abundant summer resident in 1950 and 1951. He gives as arrival dates in the spring April 15, 1950, and April 13, 1951.

Habits. The Redhead is an excellent diver; and although it commonly feeds in shallow water, the bulk of its food is roots and stems of aquatic plants that it secures by diving in water many feet in depth. On the Clearwater River at Lewiston, I never observed it close to the shore, and this was likewise true of the flocks that lingered for days on the reservoir east of Lewiston Orchards.

Its nest is never built on dry ground, but always in reeds and cattails standing in several feet of water, and it is usually substantial and well constructed. Open water that is not bordered by thick stretches of aquatic vegetation offers no suitable breeding habitat for this species and for this reason it has a rather restricted distribution in Idaho during the summer months.

Aythya collaris (Donovan): Ring-necked Duck

General Distribution. Breeds from British Columbia east through Canada to Newfoundland, south to eastern Oregon, Colorado, northern Iowa, and Pennsylvania. Winters from British Columbia, northern Texas, southern Illinois, and Massachusetts south to Panama, the Bahamas, Cuba, and Puerto Rico.

Status in Idaho. A scarce and rather local transient throughout the state. Merrill (1897) considered it a fairly common transient at Fort Sherman (Coeur d'Alene), but it apparently rarely occurs there in migration at the present time, for there are no recent records.

At St. Maries, Hand (1941) found it an irregular transient, noting it at infrequent intervals (1921 through 1941) in April and early May and in November and early December.

At Grays Lake, it occurred as a rare transient in 1950 and 1951 (Steel, 1956), although its presence in June suggested the possibility that on occasion it nested there. In 1950 it was first seen April 19.

Habits. It is doubtful if the Ring-necked Duck will ever be other than an uncommon transient in Idaho, for its center of distribution during the summer months is in the interior of the continent. It is not a common bird either on the Atlantic coast or the Pacific coast.

Although it closely resembles the Scaup Duck in appearance, its habits are not the same. It is far less gregarious, and its nest, unlike that of the Scaup, is not on dry ground but in thick marsh vegetation over water.

It dives well; and while it commonly feeds close to the shore, it also secures its food as much as forty feet below the surface of the water.

Aythya valisineria (Wilson): Canvasback

General Distribution. Breeds from central Alaska, Mackenzie, and Manitoba south to northern California, northern Colorado, and northern Minnesota. Winters from British Columbia, northern Colorado, Lake Erie, and Massachusetts south to Mexico and the Gulf states.

Status in Idaho. An uncommon transient both in the spring and the fall over most of the state, wintering in small numbers where conditions are suitable. A local summer resident in southern Idaho, its abundance is governed by the amount of nesting habitat available.

Rust (1916) reported it a rare fall transient at Coeur d'Alene from 1910 through 1914. His one spring record is that of a male taken on Lake Coeur d'Alene March 10, 1915. At St. Maries, Hand (1941) considered it an uncommon spring transient, seeing it in small numbers in April and early May (1921 through 1941).

At Lewiston, in Nez Perce County, I likewise found it an uncommon transient, small flocks appearing in April and again in October. Three birds were seen on the Clearwater River east of Lewiston December 21, 1952, so it apparently winters here at least sparingly.

Farther south in the state it was noted by Hand (1932) at Fish Lake, in Idaho County, of casual occurrence in October, 1926, and not uncommon October 17-25, 1928; at Rupert, Minidoka County (Davis, 1935), dates of occurrence March 20, 1919, May 31, 1920, and April 11, 1921; Grandview, Owyhee County, male taken December 19, 1943 (Hamerstrom, in litt.).

Levy (1950) reported it an uncommon summer resident in south-central Idaho in 1949, nesting in small numbers in the larger marshes.

At Grays Lake, it was found to be a common summer resident by Low and Nelson (1945). On July 21, 1943, they noted two broods of young, and from May 12 to 17, 1944, they saw an estimated 150 birds. A nest found May 13 held eight eggs plus two of the Redhead. Steel (1956) considered it an abundant summer resident there in 1950 and 1951. He gives as arrival dates in the spring April 20, 1950, and April 13, 1951.

Habits. The Canvasback is, in migration, essentially a bird of the larger bodies of water, for it obtains its food largely by diving to depths of twenty feet or more. The occasional small flocks that I saw on the reservoir east of Lewiston Orchards never came close to the shore, but remained well toward the middle where they were frequently observed feeding under water.

The nest is always built over water; although it is a substantial structure of reeds and marsh grass, it is usually well concealed. The one found by Low and Nelson at Grays Lake was described as built of "hardstem bulrush" and was eight inches across and three inches deep. It was barely above the surface of the water, which here was fifteen inches in depth.

Aythya marila nearctica Stejneger: GREATER SCAUP

General Distribution. Breeds from Arctic Alaska and Canada east to Quebec, south to British Columbia, North Dakota, and Michigan. Winters on the Pacific coast from the Aleutian Islands to southern California, on Lake Ontario and Lake Erie, on the Gulf coast, and on the Atlantic coast from Quebec to Cuba and the Bahamas.

Status in Idaho. Apparently of accidental occurrence in the state. There is but a single record for the occurrence of this species of Idaho. Davis

(1935) reports a specimen taken at Rupert, Minidoka County, March 28, 1920, that was identified as the Greater Scaup.

Habits. Although closely resembling the Lesser Scaup in appearance, this species is quite different in its habits. It is a hardy bird, wintering by preference on the open ocean where it appears quite at home in the roughest waters. In migration it occurs on the larger bodies of water in the interior of the country, but during the winter it is largely a maritime species. It is doubtful if it has ever been of more than casual occurrence in Idaho.

Aythya affinis (Eyton): LESSER SCAUP

General Distribution. Breeds from central Alaska east to the west shore of Hudson Bay, south to British Columbia, Idaho, Colorado, Nebraska, and Iowa. Winters from southern British Columbia, Colorado, Illinois and eastern Maryland, south through Mexico and Central America to Ecuador, and to the Bahamas and the Greater Antilles.

Status in Idaho. A common transient throughout most of the state, and a locally common summer resident in southern Idaho. Winters in small numbers where conditions are suitable.

At St. Maries, Hand (1941) reported the Lesser Scaup a common transient (1921 through 1941), flocks being observed on the lower St. Joe River in March and April, and again in November and December. He states that it was "occasional" in mild winters.

In Latah and Nez Perce counties, I likewise found it a common transient both in the spring and in the fall, being most frequently seen in April and early May and again in October and November. May 8 (1951) is my latest spring date for Moscow, a flock of thirty birds being noted that day. An occasional small flock was seen during the winter months on the Clearwater River east of Lewiston.

In Idaho County, Hand (1932) found it common on Fish Lake from October 16 to October 28, 1928. The following year a single bird was seen on the lake October 10. Newhouse (1960) noted a "large flock" on the Ben Ross Reservoir, in Adams County, April 23, 1958.

In southern Idaho Davis (1935) reported this species a fairly common winter resident at Rupert, in Minidoka County, from 1919 through 1921, his extreme dates of occurrence being October 30 and May 31. Levy (1950) considered it an uncommon and local summer resident in south-central Idaho in 1949. He noted it at Cary Lake, Blaine County, on June 4, and at Grays Lake on July 17. Steel (1956) reported it a very common summer resident at Grays Lake in 1950 and 1951. His arrival dates are April 15, 1950, and April 14, 1951.

Habits. Unlike the Greater Scaup, the Lesser Scaup is largely a bird of the interior of the continent, with an evident preference for the smaller bodies of water. Like its larger relative, however, it is an excellent diver and can and does secure its food from a depth of 20 feet or more. While it can be found in salt water in migration, it apparently has little liking for the open ocean and seldom lingers there for very long.

The nest is usually on dry ground and rarely far from water. An occasional pair will nest in an open marsh, and here the nest will be over water and well built of the vegetation available close by.

Bucephala clangula americana (Bonaparte): COMMON GOLDENEYE

General Distribution. Breeds from western Alaska, northern Mackenzie, northern Ontario, northern Quebec and Newfoundland south to southern British Columbia, northern Montana, northern Michigan, northeastern New York and Maine. Winters over much of its breeding range, south to Baja California, the Gulf coast, and Florida.

Status in Idaho. A fairly common transient and winter resident over most of the state.

At St. Maries, Hand (1941) reported it a fairly common transient and winter resident, being seen from December through April (1921-41).

Because of the lack of large bodies of water, I did not record it in Latah County, but I found it fairly common both in migration and during the winter at Lewiston, in Nez Perce County. It appeared there in October and was rarely noted after early March, my latest record in the spring being that of a single bird, a female, seen on the Clearwater River east of Lewiston March 28 (1957).

Davis (1935) considered it a regular winter resident at Rupert in Minidoka County (1919 through 1921), his extreme dates of occurrence being October 30 and May 19. At Grandview in Owyhee County, a male was collected December 14, 1943 (Hamerstrom, in litt.). At Grays Lake (Steel, 1956) it was a rare transient. It was first noted in the spring April 20, 1950, and April 14, 1951.

Habits. The Goldeneye is a hardy bird, wintering as far north as it can find open water. Consequently it is one of the few ducks that winter commonly in Idaho. At Lewiston, small flocks lingered throughout the winter in the stretch of deep water above the dam on the Clearwater River. At infrequent intervals it was also seen then on the Snake River and on the reservoir east of Lewiston Orchards. It secures its food by diving, and being wary at all times, it will never linger on the smaller shallow bodies of water.

The nest is a cavity in a tree large enough to hold the incubating bird, and not infrequently it is as high as 60 feet from the ground. The downy young, soon after they have left the egg, tumble to the ground regardless of the height, and apparently suffer no ill effects from this precarious method of reaching the nearest water.

Bucephala islandica (Gmelin): BARROW'S GOLDENEYE

General Distribution. Breeds from southern Alaska and Mackenzie south to central California and southern Oregon, in Colorado, and in Quebec, northern Labrador, and Greenland. Winters on the Pacific coast south to southern California, on the Atlantic coast to South Carolina, and in the interior to Missouri.

Status in Idaho. An uncommon transient and winter resident. There are very few published records for this species in the state; but because of its similarity to the Common Goldeneye, it has probably been largely overlooked.

Merrill (1897) considered it "abundant" during the winter at Fort Sherman (Coeur d'Alene), but it is possible that many of the flocks he observed were of the preceding species.

I satisfactorily identified *islandica* but once in Nez Perce County, having seen a pair on the reservoir east of Lewiston Orchards April 4, 1955.

Davis (1935) recorded it at Rupert, in Minidoka County, between the dates of October 7 and May 7 (1919 through 1921).

Fichter (in litt.) reports one bird seen by McQueen on a small tributary of the Snake River, in Bingham County, January 25, 1960.

Habits. So closely do the two Goldeneyes resemble each other that they are often difficult to distinguish in the field. Consequently, *islandica* is possibly more common as a winter resident in Idaho than the few records would indicate. In actions, the two species are also quite similar. Neither is to any extent gregarious and rarely will more than two or three be seen together. During the summer months, Barrow's Goldeneye shows a preference for mountain streams and seems to delight in feeding in turbulent water. The nest is either in a natural cavity or an old woodpecker's hole, and while usually near water may on occasion be some distance away. The height from the ground is apparently of little concern.

Bucephala albeola (Linnaeus): BUFFLEHEAD

General Distribution. Breeds from southern Alaska, Mackenzie, and Ontario south to northern California and northern Montana. Winters from the Aleutian Islands, the Great Lakes, and New Brunswick south to Mexico, the Gulf coast, and northern Florida.

Status in Idaho. A fairly common transient over most of the state; it possibly winters sparingly where conditions are suitable.

Merrill (1897) considered the Buffllehead common in winter at Fort Sherman (Coeur d'Alene), but it would appear that it now occurs in northern Idaho as a spring and fall transient only. Rust (1915) reported it "not common" in Kootenai County (1910 through 1914), noting it each fall in small numbers on Lake Coeur d'Alene. At St. Maries it was an uncommon spring transient (1921-41), being noted at infrequent intervals in April and early May (Hand, 1941). Both in Latah and Nez Perce counties, I found it a fairly common transient, being most frequently seen the latter part of April and early May, and again in late October and November. My extreme dates of occurrence in the spring are April 4 (1955) on the reservoir east of Lewiston Orchards and May 21 (1949) at Moscow.

In Idaho County it was noted in 1928 on Fish Lake, October 16 and 17, and at frequent intervals on the Lochsa River in late October and early November (Hand, 1932). Newhouse (1960) saw a pair on the Ben Ross Reservoir in Adams County April 23, 1958.

In southern Idaho, it was recorded at Rupert, Minidoka County, May 6 and October 30, 1919, November 15, 1920, and May 19, 1921 (Davis, 1935); Grandview, Owyhee County, a female collected December 15, 1943 (Hamerstrom, in litt.); Grays Lake, an uncommon transient, 1949 through 1951, dates of arrival in the spring being April 17, 1950, and April 13, 1951 (Steel, 1956).

Habits. Because of its small size, the Bufflehead is not much sought after by the average hunter. It is not especially wary, but since its food is to a large extent secured by diving it will be found in migration mainly on the larger bodies of water, and only infrequently on the small shallow ponds and streams. It is an expert diver, rivaling a grebe in this respect. When alarmed, however, it prefers to seek safety by flying rather than by diving.

The nest is in a cavity of either a living or dead tree; and since this species is one of the smallest of our ducks, an old Flicker's hole is generally found quite acceptable. It is rather surprising, however, through what a small opening the female can squeeze if the nesting site proves otherwise acceptable. Steel (1956) considers it possible that the Bufflehead breeds rarely at Grays Lake, but if so the nest would be some distance from the nearest water, as the willows at the edge of the lake are not large enough to afford a cavity a Bufflehead could use.

Clangula hyemalis (Linnaeus): OLDSQUAW

General Distribution. Circumpolar. In North America the Oldsquaw breeds in arctic Alaska and along the Arctic coast of Canada south to the Aleutian Islands, Churchill, and the Straits of Belle Isle. Winters on the Pacific coast south to California, on the Great Lakes and on the Atlantic coast to South Carolina.

Status in Idaho. A rare transient in the northern part of the state. It was first recorded in Idaho by Yocom (1950), who observed one bird at New Meadows, Adams County, on April 1, 1950. It was feeding with a flock of Goldeneyes, and was readily identified as a male in winter plumage.

Jollie (1955) states that a female was collected on the Pend Oreille River by Gerald Madsen on November 25, 1950.

The most recent record (Fichter, in litt.) is that of a female collected on December 24, 1966, at the head of Spring Creek, in Bingham County.

Habits. The Oldsquaw is one of the hardiest of the ducks, wintering as far north as it can find open water. It is to a large extent a maritime species during the winter months occurring in largest numbers on both coasts of the United States. It is doubtful if many individuals reach Idaho in migration; it is unquestionably one of the scarcest of the ducks occurring in the state.

Compared to most of its near relatives, it is a noisy and rather loquacious bird, this characteristic being the reason for the name by which it is commonly known. Its notes are loud and distinctive, and during the winter months the duck is a conspicious feature of the coast areas where it occurs.

Histrionicus histrionicus (Linnaeus): HARLEQUIN DUCK

General Distribution. Breeds in Siberia and Manchuria, and in North America from central Alaska, Baffin Island, and northern Quebec south to central California, Colorado, and central Labrador. Winters on the Pacific coast from the Aleutian Islands south to southern California, on Lake Ontario and Lake Erie, and on the Atlantic coast from Newfoundland to Massachusetts.

Status in Idaho. An uncommon summer resident in the northern part of the state.

Merrill (1897) considered the Harlequin Duck a rare summer resident at Fort Sherman (Coeur d'Alene), where it was observed on the "St. Joseph" and Coeur d'Alene rivers. Rust (1915) gave it this same status for Kootenai County (1910 through 1914). He states that a specimen was taken on the St. Joe River.

In Benewah County, Hand (1941) likewise found it uncommon during the summer months (1921-41), seeing it then on the upper St. Joe River and the Little North Fork of the Clearwater. He reports a nest with the female incubating that was found at the mouth of Malin Creek between Avery and Red Ives Ranger Station.

The farthest south that this species is known to occur in the state is along the upper Lochsa River in Idaho County where Hand (1932) noted it in pairs in May and June. Although he has no records later than July 12, he states that it probably breeds there.

Habits. In many respects this small handsome duck is unique in regard to its habits. Throughout most of the year it is essentially a bird of the seacoast, spending its life offshore where it seems to delight in feeding in the roughest waters. It comes inland in the spring, however, and until the young are safely reared it can be found in northern Idaho on turbulent roaring mountain streams. Calm placid waters are not to its liking, and are largely avoided. It has been rarely observed after midsummer, so apparently the females take their broods of young to the coast as soon as they are well enough developed to make this long flight. The males spend but a very short time in Idaho, for they desert the females as soon as the eggs are laid and gather in small flocks off the coasts of British Columbia and Washington.

The nest is a slight hollow in the ground lined with grasses, and is rarely far from water.

Melanitta deglandi deglandi (Bonaparte): WHITE-WINGED SCOTER

General Distribution. Breeds from the Mackenzie Delta, central Manitoba and northern Ontario south to northeastern Washington and North Dakota. Winters south to Colorado, Nebraska, Louisiana, and Alabama, on the Great Lakes, and on the Atlantic coast from the Gulf of St. Lawrence to South Carolina.

Status in Idaho. Known only as an uncommon fall transient in the northern part of the State.

Rust (1915) recorded it on Lake Coeur d'Alene October 20 through December 1, 1913, and stated that "specimens examined were young females." Levy (1959) observed a single bird, a female, on the Kootenai River at Copeland, Boundary County, November 2, 1951.

Habits. Of the three scoters found in North America, this species is most commonly observed away from the coast. In Idaho it should be looked for on the larger bodies of water, for it is an expert diver and secures its food well below the surface of the water.

On the coast, its food is almost entirely mollusks, and its ability to digest oysters and mussels as much as two inches in length, and swallowed whole, is quite amazing. Apparently it possesses the unusual ability to disintegrate the shells in its gizzard chemically, and so enjoys the succulent morsels that this procedure makes available.

Melanitta perspicillata (Linnaeus): SURF SCOTER

General Distribution. Breeds from western Alaska east to the Anderson River in northern Canada, south to northern British Columbia, Great Slave Lake, James Bay, and central Labrador. Winters on the Pacific coast from the Aleutian Islands to the Gulf of California, on the Great Lakes, and on the Atlantic coast from the Bay of Fundy to Florida.

Status in Idaho. Of accidental occurrence in the northern part of the state.

There is but a single record for this species in Idaho. Rust (1913) states that he "examined" an adult male Surf Scoter that was shot at Coeur d'Alene October 9, 1912.

Habits. Although it winters regularly on the Great Lakes, the Surf Scoter, as its name implies, is largely a bird of the seacoast. Throughout the interior of the country, it is a rare and irregular transient, and such being the case will always be of rare occurrence in Idaho. Probably its food dictates this avoidance of inland waters; for it is only on the submerged reefs lying off the coast that the mollusks on which it largely feeds, mussels, scallops, and clams are numerous and easily accessible.

Oxyura jamaicensis rubida (Wilson): RUDDY DUCK

General Distribution. Breeds from central British Columbia, Alberta, and Manitoba, south to Guatemala, central Texas, northern Iowa and Illinois. Winters south to Costa Rica, southern Louisiana, and the Bahamas.

Status in Idaho. A fairly common transient, a scarce and rather local summer resident in the northern part of the state, and a common summer resident in the southeastern corner of Idaho.

In Kootenai County, it was considered by Merrill (1897) as a fairly common spring and fall transient at Fort Sherman (Coeur d'Alene), and by Rust (1915) as a common fall transient (1910 through 1914).

Hand (1941) noted it only in the spring at St. Maries, Benewah County, seeing it at infrequent intervals in May (1921 through 1941).

I found it a fairly common transient in Latah and Nez Perce counties, seeing it most frequently in May and again in October. A few pairs nested each year at the reservoir east of Lewiston Orchards. My extreme dates of occurrence are April 26 (1957) and November 4 (1953).

At Council in Adams County, Newhouse (1960) collected a specimen November 24, 1957, and noted it on the Ben Ross Reservoir April 28, 1958.

In southern Idaho it was reported by Davis (1935) at Rupert, Minidoka County, between the dates of April 11 and September 16 (1919 through 1921). A specimen was taken at Grandview, Owyhee County, November 10, 1943 (Hamerstrom, in litt.). Levy (1950) considered it common and widely distributed in south-central Idaho during the summer of 1949. At Grays Lake Steel (1956) found it a common summer resident in 1950 and 1951. He gives as arrival dates April 23, 1950, and April 25, 1951.

Habits. Ruddy Ducks build their nests over water, and a lack of suitable habitat undoubtedly limits their distribution in the northern part of the state during the summer months. At the reservoir east of Lewiston Orchards small isolated areas of reeds and marsh grass growing in shallow water afforded the right environment, and here a few pairs of Ruddys nested in association with Coots and Yellow-headed Blackbirds. It was of interest to note that unlike other ducks the males did not desert the females once they began to incubate, but remained close by, and eventually accepted their share of the responsibility for caring for the downy young.

Lophodytes cucullatus (Linnaeus): HOODED MERGANSER

General Distribution. Breeds from eastern Alaska east through Mackenzie, Manitoba, Ontario, and southern Quebec to New Brunswick, south to Oregon, Wyoming, central Nebraska, Arkansas and western Tennessee. Winters over much of its breeding range and south to Mexico, the Gulf coast and northern Florida.

Status in Idaho. At present an uncommon transient over most of the state; possibly breeds sparingly both in northern and southern Idaho.

Apparently the Hooded Merganser was at one time much more common in Idaho than it is today, for Merrill (1897) reported it "abundant" as a transient at Fort Sherman (Coeur d'Alene), seeing flocks of forty and fifty birds during the fall migration. Rust, on the other hand (1915), considered it uncommon, seeing an occasional small flock (March, 1910, through December, 1914) on the St. Joe River and Chatcolet Lake. At St. Maries, Benewah County, Hand (1941) noted it from late March to September (1921 through 1941), and stated that an occasional pair possibly nested there.

I found it a rather scarce transient. A single bird, a female, was seen on the Palouse River at Potlatch, Latah County, October 23, 1949, while at Lewiston it was noted on the Snake River March 4, 1949, and on the reservoir April 12 and November 1, 1957.

CASSIN'S FINCH

PLATE I

Hand (1932) found it equally scarce in Idaho County, noting it on Fish Lake October 18, 1928, and October 10 and 11, 1929.

In southern Idaho Davis (1935) recorded it at Rupert, Minidoka County, between the dates of November 6 and May 19 (1919 through 1921). Levy (1950) considered it a rare and very local summer resident in south-central Idaho in 1949.

Habits. This handsome little duck is like the Wood Duck, essentially a bird of the wooded streams and flooded bottomlands. However, in migration it can be found on open bodies of water where it associates with such species as the Lesser Scaup and Redhead that also secure their food by diving. Fish is a regular part of its diet, but during the summer months it feeds in shallow water where it secures aquatic insects, frogs and tadpoles, crawfish, and, to a less extent, aquatic vegetation. It rarely occurs on salt water either in migration or during the winter months.

The nest is a cavity in a tree large enough to hold the incubating bird, and preferably near water. No nesting material is used. The eggs are laid on fragments of rotted wood and such debris as dead leaves that may have accumulated during the fall and winter. Height is apparently immaterial, the downy young being able to tumble to the ground without injury to themselves.

Mergus merganser americanus Cassin: COMMON MERGANSER

General Distribution. Breeds from southern Alaska, Manitoba, Ontario, and Newfoundland south to central California, Chihuahua, South Dakota, Wisconsin, central New York and Nova Scotia. Winters over much of its breeding range south to Sonora, the Gulf coast and Florida, and in Bermuda.

Status in Idaho. Largely resident in northern Idaho, nesting on many of the mountain streams and varying in abundance during the winter months according to the severity of the weather. An uncommon transient and winter resident in the southern part of the state.

The Common Merganser is another species that was first recorded in Idaho by the Lewis and Clark expedition on its way to the Pacific coast. In the journal that he kept, Lewis (*Original Journals,* IV: 148-49) states that it was seen on the Clearwater River, being common "to every part of the river" (Jollie, 1953).

Merrill (1897) reported it common during the fall and winter at Fort Sherman (Coeur d'Alene), and Rust (1915) also noted it there at this time of the year. He states that two adult males were "examined" at Hayden Lake November 19, 1914. In Benewah County, Hand (1941) considered it a common summer resident along St. Joe River (1921-41), where it was likewise frequently seen during open winters.

I found it largely resident in both Latah and Nez Perce counties, seeing it throughout most of the year on the larger streams and lakes. Verner (1953) noted two broods of young on the Palouse River near Harvard

(Latah County), one of nine on August 7, 1951, and another of fifteen on June 23, 1952.

In Idaho County Hand (1932) found it breeding commonly along the Lochsa River (1923 through 1929) and also observed it on Fish Lake from the middle of August to late October. Orr (1951) recorded it as common along the middle branch of the Clearwater River between Kooskia and Selway Falls September 5, 1941; two were seen near Selway Falls September 8.

In southern Idaho, Davis (1935) reported it at Rupert between the dates of October 12 and April 14 (1919 through 1921). Levy (1950) noted a single bird at Jerome July 2, 1949. At Grays Lake Steel (1956) considered it a rare transient. He gives as arrival dates in the spring April 19, 1950, and April 16, 1951.

Habits. The presence of broods of young during the summer months eliminates any doubt as to this Merganser nesting in northern Idaho, but a nest has never actually been found. One can only theorize, therefore, as to the breeding habits of this species in the state. Over much of its breeding range, it commonly nests in cavities in trees; but it is also known to nest on the ground, the eggs being laid in a hollow between or partially under large boulders.

Its food is largely fish, and these it has no difficulty in securing, for it is an expert diver and adept at swimming under water. It is equally at home both on fresh-water lakes and streams in the interior and on the coast, large numbers wintering on salt water well offshore where an adequate food supply is always at hand.

Mergus serrator serrator Linnaeus: RED-BREASTED MERGANSER

General Distribution. Widely distributed in the northern hemisphere. In North America breeds from the Arctic coast of Alaska, Mackenzie, Baffin Island and Labrador south to British Columbia, southern Manitoba, Michigan, Ontario and northern New York. Winters over much of its breeding range south to Baja California, New Mexico, the Gulf coast and Florida.

Status in Idaho. A rather scarce transient, and a rare winter resident.

There are but a few records for the occurrence of this species in the state. Merrill (1897) took a single specimen at Fort Sherman (Coeur d'Alene) and Rust (1915) reports it rare there (March, 1910, to December, 1914). He states that he "examined" a specimen shot on Lake Coeur d'Alene.

In south-central Idaho several small flocks were seen on Sawtooth Lake in the fall of 1890 (Merriam, 1891), and it was reported as occurring sparingly on Henrys Lake in Fremont County (Rust, 1917).

Davis (1935) recorded it at Rupert, Minidoka County, between the dates of September 4 and May 27 (1919 through 1921). At Grays Lake it occurred as a rare transient (Steel, 1956). He gives as arrival dates April 19, 1950, and April 16, 1951.

Habits. The Red-breasted Merganser is, except during the breeding season, largely a maritime species, so it will never be seen in any numbers in Idaho. It occurs to some extent on the Great Lakes during the winter months, but it is only off the coast that it is really abundant. Its food is largely fish; and being a skillful diver and adept at swimming under the water, it has little difficulty in satisfying its voracious appetite. Because of its liking for fish, its flesh is rather unpalatable, and consequently it is not a popular bird with the more experienced duck hunter.

Unlike the other mergansers, its nest is always built on the ground and is usually within a short distance of water. It is so well concealed under the drooping branches of a spruce or a willow that its presence is revealed only when the female flushes from underfoot.

The Red-breasted Merganser is one of the few species of ducks in which the male remains with the female while she incubates and later helps care for the young.

ORDER FALCONIFORMES

American Vultures: *Family Cathartidae*

Cathartes aura teter Friedmann: TURKEY VULTURE

General Distribution. Breeds from southern British Columbia east through Alberta, Saskatchewan, and Manitoba to western Ontario, south to Baja California, southern Mexico, and eastern Texas. Winters from California and Nebraska south to Ecuador.

Status in Idaho. Of general distribution over the state during the summer months, but common only in southern Idaho. The first birds appear in early April, and by late September only an occasional individual remains in the state.

The Turkey Vulture was first recorded in Idaho by the Lewis and Clark expedition. On June 13, 1806, Lewis comments in his Journal (*Original Journals*, V:133) that on the Weippe Prairie "Buzzards had eaten up a deer which had been killed, butchered and hung up this morning." (Jollie, 1953.)

It was next reported in south-central Idaho by Merriam (1891). He states that it was observed by Ridgway in the City of Rocks on October 3, 1868, and that he personally found it common on the Snake River in July, 1890. That same year he also saw three on the Big Lost River near Arco July 25, found it common on Birch Creek in early August, and also noted it at the Lemhi Indian Agency, in the Pahsimeroi and Challis valleys.

Merrill (1897) states that a few were seen during the summer months at Fort Sherman (Coeur d'Alene), arriving about the middle of April and leaving in September. Rust (1915) gives it this same status for Kootenai County, an occasional bird being seen during the summer (1910 through 1914).

In Benewah County it was considered by Hand (1941) an uncommon straggler in the summer. He saw one bird east of Monumental Buttes July 15, 1931, and nine on St. Maries Peak July 9, 1935.

Levy (1959) reports a single bird seen at Copeland, Boundary County, April 7, 1950, and a female collected from a flock of six at Bonners Ferry September 25, 1951. He also cites the only record for Latah County, one bird seen at Bovill in May, 1949.

Farther south in the state it has been reported from Grangeville, Idaho County, one bird June 29, 1949 (Burleigh); Adams County, one bird in Indian Valley April 12, 1958 (Newhouse, 1960); Weiser, Washington County, one bird August 14, 1957 (Burleigh); Owyhee County, two birds at Riddle May 28 to June 3, 1934 (Davis, 1934); two at Homedale June 23, and three at Marsing June 25, 1949 (Burleigh); Cassia County, nine birds at Almo June 21, 1949, and three at Oakley (Goose Creek) June 23,

1950 (Burleigh); Fremont County, two seen in Little Dry Creek Canyon July 31, 1916 (Rust, 1917); Bonneville County, one bird at Grays Lake June 8, 1957 (Burleigh).

Habits. Although a nest has never actually been found, the presence of the Turkey Vulture in Idaho during the summer months would indicate that it nests wherever conditions are suitable. The eggs, almost invariably two in number, are laid on the bare ground, and are well concealed under an overhanging rock, in a cave at the base of a cliff, or in dense underbrush at the base of an old rotten stub.

On the ground the Turkey Vulture, with its bare head and neck and awkward movements, presents a rather unattractive picture, but in the air the effect is quite the opposite. Few birds approach it in its powers of flight. Taking advantage of all air currents, it soars overhead for long intervals with hardly a movement of its wings; and in its search for food, it covers a large area each day with apparently little effort. On several occasions in Owyhee County, I observed Turkey Vultures feeding with Ravens on a dead cow; and although there was a certain amount of squabbling over the choicer morsels, the two species seemed to accept each other's presence as a matter of course.

Hawks: *Family Accipitridae*

Accipiter gentilis atricapillus (Wilson): GOSHAWK

General Distribution. Breeds from northwestern Alaska east across the continent to Labrador and Newfoundland, south to California, southern Arizona, Michigan, Pennsylvania and western Maryland. Winters over much of its breeding range south to central Mexico (Jalisco), Missouri, Kentucky, and Virginia.

Status in Idaho. Of general distribution over much of the state during the summer months, but in small numbers. Fairly common and equally well distributed during the winter months.

The Goshawk was first recorded in Idaho by Merriam (1891), who noted it in the Salmon River and Sawtooth Mountains in the south-central part of the state.

Merrill (1897) found it common at Fort Sherman (Coeur d'Alene) in migration and during the winter, seeing it in the spring as late as May 30. He states that it was especially abundant during the early winter of 1896-97.

Hand (1933) reported it in the Clearwater Mountains, "on the St. Joe and Little North Fork drainage," during the summer months, giving the following dates on which it was observed: July 6, 1921, June 6, 1922, July 27 and 28 and August 13, 1930, July 27, 1931, August 8, 10 and 20, 1932. He states that it was usually common in September and October, and that it was also noted during the winter.

In Latah County one bird was seen by Johnston (1949) on Little Sand Creek, thirty miles northeast of Moscow, on June 5, 1947. I personally found it of irregular occurrence at Moscow during the late winter, seeing an occasional bird in January when the snow on the ground was at its greatest depth and minimum temperatures were zero or lower. My latest date of occurrence then is January 23 (1955).

In the Boise National Forest it was noted on nine different occasions during the winter of 1938-39, and twice from November 7, 1939, to February 1, 1940. It was also seen near Swanholm Creek, in Elmore County, March 29, 1940 (Marshall, 1945).

One pair of Goshawks was found nesting in 1950 in thick woods part way up Hyndman Peak (at an altitude of approximately 9,000 feet). Hyndman Peak is fifteen miles east of Ketchum, in Blaine County. The nest, on June 27, held two half-grown young (Burleigh) (Jollie, in litt.); collected an adult female June 30, 1949, and a nestling female July 2, at Heglar Pass in Power County.

Steel (1956) considered it a rare transient (1949-51) at Grays Lake.

Habits. The Goshawk is one bird that is thoroughly disliked by both sportsmen and farmers. Birds form a large source of its food, and there is no question but that it is a destructive species where grouse, pheasants, and birds of similar size are concerned. Worcester (1928) states that at St. Maries it was very destructive to game birds, the remains of twelve pheasants being found on December 12, 1927, that had apparently been killed by Goshawks. He estimates the average kill to be two such species a day. Marshall (1945) studied the food habits of the Goshawk on the Boise National Forest during the winter months (1938-40), and was interested to find that snowshoe rabbits were an important source of food at this season of the year. Of eleven individuals that were observed, six were feeding on grouse and five on rabbits.

The nest found on Hyndman Peak was large and substantially built of sticks and twigs with a slight lining of strips of bark and fresh fir sprays. It was forty feet up and six feet out on the limb of a large fir. Both parents were present, and while showing concern over the intrusion of their privacy they remained at a safe distance while the nest was examined. It must be admitted that this was a decided relief, for there are numerous instances where the female Goshawk has savagely defended her nest, and actually inflicted injury on the individual interested in its contents.

Accipiter striatus velox (Wilson): SHARP-SHINNED HAWK

General Distribution. Breeds from Alaska east across the continent to Labrador and Newfoundland, south to California, Texas, Louisiana, Alabama, and South Carolina. Winters from British Columbia, Minnesota, Ontario, and Nova Scotia south to the Gulf coast and southern Florida and through Mexico and Central America to Panama.

Status in Idaho. A common transient throughout the state, and an uncommon and rather local winter resident; breeds in small numbers in northern Idaho and possibly in the southern part of the state where conditions are suitable.

At Coeur d'Alene it was reported by Merrill (1897), a specimen taken May 15; by Rust (1915), a fairly common summer resident (1910 through 1914), a specimen taken December 2; and by Yocom (1946), an occasional bird noted at the upper end of Lake Coeur d'Alene July 1 to 10, 1943.

At Clark Fork, Bonner County, one bird was seen on Trestle Creek August 25, 1917, and another that same day at the top of a nearby ridge (Burleigh, 1923).

Hand (1941) found it common in migration and occasional in winter at St. Maries, Benewah County (1921 through 1941). He states that it possibly "breeds in the mountains."

In Latah County Johnston (1949) reports a specimen taken by Engler on Moscow Mountain August 16, 1938 (Olson, MS). I personally found the Sharp-shinned Hawk a fairly common transient at Moscow both in the spring and in the fall, and of regular occurrence, but in small numbers, during the winter months. In the fall the first birds usually appeared in early September, rarely in late August, while in the spring an occasional bird was frequently seen through the first week in May, but rarely thereafter. My extreme dates of occurrence are August 25 (1951) and May 30 (1950). At Lewiston, Nez Perce County, it was less often noted both in migration and in the winter, my extreme dates of occurrence there being September 8 (1954) and February 9 (1956).

Specimens referable to *velox* were taken at Moscow February 6 and 20, 1955, and November 6, 1956, and at Lewiston November 11, 1953, and February 9 and November 24, 1956.

In Idaho County Orr (1951) reports a specimen taken two miles south of Selway Falls September 6, 1941, and another bird seen there on September 9.

In south-central Idaho Merriam (1891) considered this species "tolerably common" in 1890; a specimen was taken in the Salmon River Mountains August 28. He also noted it at Shoshone Falls, on the Snake River, October 10. Jewett (1912) saw one bird at Ketchum November 13, 1910. In Fremont County Rust (1917) reports one pair of these little hawks in Little Dry Creek Canyon in late June and July, 1916.

At Rupert, Minidoka County, Davis (1935) noted this species between the dates of October 30 and January 13 (1919 through 1921).

I saw a single bird at Triangle, Owyhee County, June 25, 1949.

Habits. Although rodents, frogs, lizards, and even large insects such as locusts and grasshoppers are eaten by the Sharp-shinned Hawk, small birds are its principal food. As a migrant, it appears both in the spring and in the fall when small birds are moving to and from their summer haunts, and it exacts a daily toll from their ranks. Merriam (1891) states that a Wilson's

Warbler was found in the stomach of the specimen taken in the Salmon River Mountains.

A nest found by Rust at Coeur d'Alene June 15, 1913, held five eggs that hatched on July 3. It was thirty-four feet from the ground in a Douglas fir, and was built entirely of small dry fir twigs. Both parents were very aggressive in defense of their young, attacking viciously when the nest was examined and actually striking Rust's back on one occasion (Rust, 1914).

Accipiter cooperii (Bonaparte): COOPER'S HAWK

General Distribution. Breeds from southern British Columbia east through Manitoba and southern Quebec to Nova Scotia, south to Baja California, central Texas, the northern half of the Gulf states and central Florida. Winters over much of its breeding range south throughout the United States and Mexico to Costa Rica.

Status in Idaho. An uncommon summer resident in the mountainous areas of the state, and an equally uncommon transient and winter resident, occurring after the breeding season in the more open arid country.

At St. Maries, Benewah County, it was considered by Hand (1941) to be an uncommon summer resident (April to October, 1921 through 1941), occasionally appearing in numbers in the fall.

In Latah County it was reported by Johnston (1949) as being frequently seen on Moscow Mountain June 1 to August 16, 1947. An adult male was collected on July 15. I personally found it a rather uncommon transient and winter resident. It was noted at Moscow October 4, 1950, September 17, 1951, and January 19, 1952, and at Potlatch February 12, 1955, October 31, 1956, and April 19, 1957. I also noted it at Lewiston, Nez Perce County, September 13, 1950, and December 28, 1951. Merriam (1891) states that according to Bendire it nested at Fort Lapwai.

In Idaho County (Orr, 1951) a specimen was taken two miles south of Selway Falls September 8, 1941, and one bird was seen six miles south of Lolo Pass July 20, 1944.

There are not many records for southern Idaho. Merriam (1891) states that in 1890 the Cooper's Hawk was seen in the mountains in the south-central part of the state, and also in the valley of Birch Creek, and on the Lemhi River. Rust (1917) reports two records for Fremont County in 1916, single birds being noted at Spencer July 18, and near Small August 11. One bird was seen at Rupert, Minidoka County, April 11, 1919 (Davis, 1935).

Habits. Because of its wide distribution in the United States, the Cooper's Hawk can be considered one of the most common of our hawks. Its food consists to a large extent of birds; and being bold and audacious in its actions, it has earned the cordial dislike of both sportsmen and farmers. Its forays in the farmyard result in the loss of many chickens, and its activities in this respect are unquestionably a major factor in the antipathy that exists towards even the most beneficial hawks. It is doubtful, however, if sportsmen are justified in their attitude, for it is small birds that suffer from the depredations of the Cooper's Hawk, species larger than the Flicker or Meadowlark being seldom attacked.

The nest is large and substantially built of sticks and twigs and is generally in a crotch of a large tree from thirty to forty-five feet from the ground. Thick woods are preferred as a nesting site, but the nest is easily found for its presence is soon revealed by the actions of the birds. Their loud cackling notes show their resentment at any invasion of their privacy, but they are not aggressive in their defense of their eggs or young, and remain at a safe distance even when the nest is examined.

Buteo jamaicensis calurus (Cassin): RED-TAILED HAWK

General Distribution. Breeds from central Alaska, Mackenzie, and Saskatchewan south to Baja California and western New Mexico. Winters from British Columbia and southern Minnesota south to Guatemala and Nicaragua and east to Louisiana.

Status in Idaho. Resident and common throughout the year except in the extreme northern counties, where it has not been recorded during the winter months.

In northern Idaho, the Red-tailed Hawk has been reported from the following localities: Kootenai County, one collected at Blue Lake in 1894 (Snyder, 1900); a rare summer resident (1910-14); one collected March 14, 1913 (Rust, 1915).

Bonner County, one pair noted during the summer of 1917 at the Trestle Creek Lookout Station north of Clark Fork (Burleigh, 1923).

Benewah County, a fairly common summer resident at St. Maries from March to late October (1921 through 1941) (Hand, 1941).

Latah County, common "in forested areas" June 1–August 16, 1947 (Johnston, 1949); noted almost daily near Harvard during the summers of 1951 and 1952 (Verner, 1953); resident, and fairly common throughout the year at Moscow; in March and again in late October, there is a perceptible increase in the number of birds seen, indicating the presence of individuals that breed farther north; a specimen taken April 2, 1949, proved typical of the western race, *calurus* (Burleigh).

Idaho County, frequently noted in September, 1941, near Selway Falls; not uncommon in July, 1944, in the vicinity of Lolo Pass (Orr, 1951).

Farther south in the state it has been reported as follows:

Fremont County, one pair seen in Little Dry Creek Canyon June 19, 1916 (Rust, 1917).

Butte County, common in late July, 1890, on the Big Lost River below Arco (Merriam, 1891).

Bonneville County, a common summer resident; arrival dates April 6, 1950, and April 6, 1951 (Steel, 1956).

Gooding County, a common breeding bird in 1949 of the Snake River "breaks," a nest found June 10 held four young (Levy, 1950).

Adams County, common at Council throughout the year (1957-58) (Newhouse, 1960).

Owyhee County, a nest found at Riddle June 3, 1934, that held three heavily-incubated eggs (Davis, 1934).

Habits. The Red-tailed Hawk is a very beneficial bird, and deserves better treatment than it gets from the average farmer. The ground squirrel is often a serious problem to the farmer in the western states, and this is true in Idaho wherever farming is an important source of income. The Red-tailed Hawk is largely a rodent eater, and the ground squirrel that is so destructive to farm crops is a favored source of food and preyed upon extensively. It is interesting to note that the first reference to the occurrence of this species in the state (Merriam, 1891) commented on the fact that there was a ground squirrel in the stomach of a bird collected near Arco in July, 1890. Birds are rarely, if ever, molested, but snakes are frequently eaten, rattlesnakes seemingly being captured with no ill effects to these hawks.

The site of the nest varies according to the character of the country, although the upper crotch of a large tree seems to be preferred where available. The nest found by Davis at Riddle, in Owyhee County, was in an area where vegetation was sparse, so of necessity the site selected was the top of an alder but fifteen feet from the ground. Along the Snake River in south-central Idaho, ledges of cliffs are commonly used, and it was in such a situation that Levy located a nest near Gooding. Regardless of where situated, the nests are substantial structures of sticks and twigs, the hollow in the top being lined with shreds and strips of bark.

Buteo harlani (Audubon): HARLAN'S HAWK

General Distribution. Breeds in Alaska, northern British Columbia, and Alberta. Winters in Kansas, Missouri, and Arkansas south to Texas and Louisiana.

Status in Idaho. Recorded once in the northern part of the state.

Levy (1961) reported a female taken near Genesee, Latah County, on November 27, 1938. It is now in the collection of the Zoology Department of the University of Idaho at Moscow.

Habits. In appearance and actions, this species is very similar to the Red-tailed Hawk. Since its food is also very largely rodents it is highly beneficial with regard to agriculture, and its presence during the winter months should be encouraged by the farmer. Unfortunately this is rarely the case at the present time. Because of its limited range, its numbers are likewise limited, and it is doubtful if it will ever be other than of casual occurrence in Idaho.

Buteo platypterus platypterus (Vieillot): BROAD-WINGED HAWK

General Distribution. Breeds from central Alberta east through Manitoba and northern Ontario to southern Quebec, south to southern Texas, the

Gulf coast states and Florida. Winters in Florida, and south through Central America to Peru and Brazil.

Status in Idaho. Of accidental occurrence in the state.

There is one record. Davis (1936) reports a specimen in immature plumage taken at Castle Creek, eight miles south of Oreana, Owyhee County, on May 23, 1935.

Habits. The Broad-winged Hawk is another beneficial species, its food being to a very large extent rodents. Reptiles and large insects are eaten to some extent, and on occasion small birds. It deserves protection at all times, but being less wary than other hawks, its numbers have suffered from indiscriminate shooting on the part of those having an antipathy to all birds of prey.

Buteo swainsoni Bonaparte: SWAINSON'S HAWK

General Distribution. Breeds from Alaska east through Mackenzie, Saskatchewan, and Manitoba to western Minnesota, south to Baja California, Durango, and southern Texas. Winters in Argentina.

Status in Idaho. A common summer resident in the southern part of the state; breeds in small numbers in northern Idaho except in the extreme northern counties where it occurs as an uncommon fall transient.

In Kootenai County Merrill (1897) reports a bird in immature plumage taken at Fort Sherman (Coeur d'Alene) September 14, and Rust (1915) states that it was infrequently seen in the fall at Coeur d'Alene (1910 through 1914); three fully grown young of the year were collected in September, 1913.

In Benewah County Hand (1941) found it a rare straggler at St. Maries in August (1921 through 1941).

In Latah County it was an uncommon summer resident, a few scattered pairs nesting in the stream bottoms and on the wooded hillsides. Johnston (1949) states that a nest with young was found by Engler (MS) on Paradise Ridge, southeast of Moscow, May 31, 1937. In early May, 1950, I found a nest with the female incubating in a wooded ravine four miles south of Moscow. An adult female was collected at Genesee August 4, 1955, and another at Moscow July 21, 1957.

In southern Idaho Merriam (1891) reports a nest at Fort Hall July 9, 1872, that held one young bird and one egg. In 1890 he collected a specimen on July 22 fifteen miles south of Arco, noted a pair with young on Birch Creek in early August, and saw one bird in adult plumage at Fort Lemhi in September. Jewett (1912) recorded this species at Ketchum, Blaine County, in 1910 and states that a specimen was taken on October 31. In Fremont County Rust (1917) found it fairly common from June through August, 1916. Steel (1956) considered it a common summer resident at Grays Lake (1949 through 1951); a nest found there May 20, 1951, held two eggs. At Pocatello, Bannock County, I saw one pair of these hawks on Buckskin Creek June 9, 1955. Levy (1950) reports this species a common summer resident in south-central Idaho in 1949. Davis (1935) noted it at Rupert, Minidoka County, as late as October 30, 1919.

Habits. Swainson's Hawk is essentially a bird of open country. Its preference is for sparsely wooded prairies and even deserts, so it is not surprising that it is uncommon even as a transient in the extreme northern part of Idaho.

In common with the other buteos, it consumes rodents as a large proportion of its food, although it appears equally fond of large insects and is known to feed exclusively on grasshoppers wherever they are abundant. Birds are rarely if ever attacked, so this hawk can be considered one of our most beneficial species.

The nest is usually built in a tree within twenty feet of the ground, but lacking such a site it may be in a thick bush or even on the ground. The one found at Grays Lake was on the top of a rock on an island in the open marsh; and being substantially constructed of sticks and twigs, it was conspicious some distance away. The two eggs that this nest held is the number usually laid.

Few other hawks are known to winter consistently so far south of the normal breeding range. It is doubtful if it ever occurs in the United States during the winter months, or even as far north as Central America.

Buteo lagopus s. johannis (Gmelin): ROUGH-LEGGED HAWK

General Distribution. Breeds from the Aleutian Islands and the interior of Alaska east through northern Mackenzie and Baffin Island to northern Labrador, south to Manitoba, southern Quebec, and Newfoundland. Winters from southern British Columbia, Saskatchewan, southern Ontario, and Maine south to California, Oklahoma, Tennessee, and Virginia.

Status in Idaho. A fairly common winter resident throughout the state.

In Kootenai County it was recorded by Merrill (1897) as "occasionally seen in early spring and late autumn" at Fort Sherman (Coeur d'Alene); and by Rust (1915), an occasional bird noted in the late fall on the St. Joe River (1910 through 1914), and one specimen taken December 20, 1912.

In Benewah County Hand (1941) considered it an occasional migrant and winter visitor at St. Maries, occurring from October to late March.

I found it a fairly common winter resident in Latah County, seeing one or two birds almost daily from early November until the end of March. It was noted then at Potlatch, Viola, Moscow, and Genesee. My extreme dates of occurrence are November 1 (1952) and March 29 (1950). A specimen was collected by Seymour Levy at Genesee December 15, 1949.

In southern Idaho Davis (1935) reports this species at Rupert in Minidoka County between the dates of November 7 and May 11 (1919 through 1921). I saw one bird at Oreana in Owyhee County on February 21, 1950.

Steel (1956) found it a common winter resident at Grays Lake (1949 through 1951). He stated that it "leaves by last of April."

In extreme southern Idaho, near the Utah state line, Porter (1951) noted it as follows: Standrod, three seen October 30, 1949; one on December 27, 1950; Almo, two on December 4, 1950; one on December 26, 1950; two on January 28, 1951; Strevell, three on December 3, 1950.

Habits. The Rough-legged Hawk is another very beneficial species, for its food consists almost entirely of rodents. Grasshoppers, where abundant, are eaten in large numbers, but as far as is known birds are never molested. In Idaho, this is a hawk of the more open country. It is usually seen soaring low over the open fields or perched on the top of a telephone pole at the side of a road. For a large bird, it is relatively unsuspicious and not difficult to approach, and as a result many are killed in the fall by hunters. In view of its value to the farmer, it deserves protection at all times.

Buteo regalis (Gray): FERRUGINOUS HAWK

General Distribution. Breeds from eastern Washington, southern Saskatchewan, and Manitoba south to eastern Oregon, Nevada, New Mexico and northern Texas. Winters south to Baja California and northern Mexico.

Status in Idaho. An uncommon and rather local summer resident in the southern part of the state.

There are very few published records for the occurrence of this species in Idaho.

Porter (1951) reports a nest found in Cassia County that on May 27, 1950 held two downy young and an infertile egg. The site was twelve miles west of Strevell and two miles west of Standrod. He expressed the opinion that this hawk was probably a common summer resident in this part of the state. Jollie (1952), however, was convinced that quite the contrary was true. He spent a week in the field in Cassia County in 1949 and failed to see a single bird. My own experience was similar to this.

Donald J. Nicholson (in litt.) states that a nest found May 11, 1961, north of Camas, in Jefferson County, held eight well incubated eggs, an unusually large number for this species to lay.

Habits. It is possible that the Ferruginous Hawk was more plentiful in past years in Idaho than it is today. It is a bird of the "wide open spaces" and much of southern Idaho would seem ideally suited to its needs. Being unsuspicious by nature, however, it was probably approached and shot with little difficulty as it perched on a fencepost, or, as was a common habit, on the ground. Throughout much of its range, it has become noticeably scarcer in recent years, and this is undoubtedly due to the unjustified persecution to which it has been subjected. As with the other buteos it prefers rodents to any other food, and as it is especially fond of ground squirrels, it is a very beneficial species for the farmer. Its usual method of securing its prey consists of remaining motionless in the top of a bush or small tree, or even on the ground, and then making a sudden pounce when a ground squirrel is some distance from its burrow.

The nest found by Porter in Cassia County was described as being twelve feet from the ground in a juniper, while the one found by Nicholson was in a crotch of a cottonwood.

Aquila chrysaetos canadensis (Linnaeus): Golden Eagle

General Distribution. Breeds from northern Alaska east through Mackenzie, Saskatchewan, and Manitoba to Quebec, south to Baja California, northern Mexico, Texas, western Nebraska, New York, and Maine. Winters south to the Gulf states and northern Florida.

Status in Idaho. Uncommon and of local occurrence throughout the year over much of the state; possibly breeds sparingly, although there is no record of a nest having actually been found.

In Kootenai County it was reported by Snyder (1900) as "not common" in 1894 at the Kaniksu and Blue lakes; by Merrill (1897) as occurring sparingly throughout the year at Fort Sherman (Coeur d'Alene); by Rust (1916) as rare (1910 through 1914) at Coeur d'Alene. He states that a specimen was taken there October 11, 1915.

Hand (1941) saw a mounted bird at Moscow in 1935 that had been shot at Elk River in Clearwater County. He was advised that in the late 1920s the Golden Eagle was reported to have nested on Shefoot Mountain, near Avery, in Shoshone County.

The one record for Latah County is that of a bird in immature plumage seen June 16, 1947, twenty miles northeast of Moscow (Johnston, 1949).

One bird was seen at Lewiston, Nez Perce County, on May 8 and again on May 16, 1953 (Burleigh).

In Idaho County Orr (1951) noted this species near Selway Falls on September 18 and 25, 1941.

In Adams County Newhouse (1960) reports eleven seen from twelve miles north of Council to Indian Valley, July 15, 1957, to April 2, 1958.

On the Boise National Forest two were noted in February, 1939, on Swanholm Creek, in Elmore County, and two in December of that year at the Deer Park Guard Station (Marshall, 1945).

Farther east in the state it was reported by Merriam (1891) as being noted during the summer of 1890 in the Salmon River Mountains and in the Lemhi and Birch Creek Valleys. In this same general area, I saw two birds at Shoup, Lemhi County, June 4, 1949.

Jewett (1912) noted one bird at Ketchum, Blaine County, October 29, 1910. In Fremont County Rust (1917) reported this species as occurring sparingly at the higher altitudes (June through August, 1916). Steel (1956) considered it a rare "visitant" at Grays Lake (1949-51).

In extreme southern Idaho it was noted at Grandview, Owyhee County, specimen taken December 10, 1943 (Hamerstrom, in litt.); Marsing, Owyhee County, two birds February 19, 1950 (Burleigh); at the Silent City of Rocks, Cassia County, one pair June 19, 1949 (Levy, 1950); at Rupert, Minidoka County, one bird April 11, 1919 (Davis, 1935).

THE GOLDEN EAGLE

Habits. The Golden Eagle is a majestic bird that, from an aesthetic viewpoint, well deserves protection. Unfortunately it is considered rather destructive to the young of such species as deer, antelope, and mountain goat, so it is shot at every opportunity. That it is so destructive, however, is open to question. Studies made of its food habits have failed to show with any degree of certainty that it habitually, or even commonly, preys on these game species. On the other hand it is an important factor in reducing the numbers of ground squirrels, prairie dogs, and marmots, so it is probable that the good it does at least balances the bad.

In the western states the nest is almost always built on the ledge of a cliff, and it is in such a situation that it should be looked for in Idaho. The most inaccessible spot is always chosen, and while height is apparently not important the nest is usually well up from the ground. It is a massive structure of sticks, twigs, grasses, shreds of bark and similar material, and where unmolested it is used year after year by the same pair of birds. Two eggs are normally laid, but one not infrequently.

Haliaeetus leucocephalus alascanus Townsend: BALD EAGLE

General Distribution. Breeds from the Aleutian Islands, Mackenzie, Ontario, Quebec, and Newfoundland south to southern Oregon, Colorado, Wisconsin, Ohio, and Maryland. Winters as far north as Alaska, northern Mackenzie and southern Quebec.

Status in Idaho. A scarce and rather local summer resident throughout the state.

The Bald Eagle was one of the twenty-four species mentioned in the journals of Lewis and Clark as being seen in Idaho. Lewis (*Original Journals*, V:119) states that at Kamiah, on May 18, 1806, he took "the part of a salmon from an Eagle," and that on June 9, 1806, two nearly grown young "of the gray kind" were brought in by an Indian (Jollie, 1953).

Merrill (1897) states that at Fort Sherman (Coeur d'Alene) "a few pairs breed about the lake" and that a bird in adult plumage was seen as early as February 5.

Rust (1915) reports it rare in Kootenai County, an occasional bird in immature plumage being noted in the fall.

Hand (1941) also considered it rare in Benewah County. He found a pair nesting in 1930 and 1931 along the Little North Fork of the Clearwater River, and saw one bird at Chatcolet Lake on February 24, 1939.

I have but one record for Latah County, seeing one bird in adult plumage at Troy on April 4, 1949. At Lewiston, in Nez Perce County, I recorded it twice. On October 21, 1950, a bird in immature plumage, apparently killed that day by a duck hunter, was picked up at the edge of the Snake River, and on April 6, 1955, an adult was noted soaring over the reservoir east of Lewiston Orchards.

Orr (1951) reports an adult seen four miles southwest of Selway Falls, in Idaho County, on September 16, 1941, and Newhouse (1960) recorded one bird in Indian Valley, Adams County, April 12, 1958.

Farther south in the state it has been recorded by Merriam (1891) at Sawtooth Lake October 1, 1890, and at Shoshone Falls, on the Snake River, October 10; by Marshall (1945) on the Boise National Forest, in Elmore County, one bird at Swanholm Creek in February, 1939, and one in March in Middle Fork Canyon; and by me at Soda Springs, Caribou County, one adult on November 11, 1957.

The most recent breeding record (Fichter, in litt.) is that of a nest found in 1969 by Walter L. Bodie, Conservation Officer with the Idaho Fish and Game Department, two miles north of Irwin in Bonneville County. Two young that were successfully reared left this nest between the eighth and the twentieth of June. The nest was described as being "six feet high and five feet across at the top," and was fifty feet from the ground in a large cottonwood.

Habits. The food of the Bald Eagle varies according to season, but where available fish is preferred; consequently it is about the larger bodies of water in Idaho that it can be found during the summer months. It is en-

CALLIOPE HUMMINGBIRD

PLATE II

tirely capable of capturing its prey alive, but it appears equally fond of dead fish that have been washed up on the shore of a lake or river, and in this respect it is a valuable scavenger. As our national emblem, it is now protected by federal law, and in view of its decrease in numbers in recent years this protection comes at an opportune time. To a large extent it is a beneficial species, for while birds form a certain part of its diet it also destroys such injurious rodents as ground squirrels and rats.

Unlike the Golden Eagle, the Bald Eagle rarely builds its nest on the ledge of a cliff, preferring the top of the largest tree available. The material used is large sticks, the slight cavity in the top being lined with grasses and shreds of bark. As it is often used year after year, and constantly added to, the nest is often a massive structure four feet or more in height. Two dull white eggs are normally laid.

Circus cyaneus hudsonius (Linnaeus): MARSH HAWK

General Distribution. Breed from northern Alaska, Mackenzie, Manitoba, Ontario, central Quebec, and Labrador south to Baja California, New Mexico, Kansas, and Virginia. Winters from British Columbia, Saskatchewan, southern Ontario, and Massachusetts south through Mexico and Central America to Colombia and to Cuba.

Status in Idaho. Resident and locally common throughout all of the state except in the extreme northern counties, where its status is that of an uncommon transient and summer resident.

In Kootenai County it was recorded by Merrill (1897) at Fort Sherman (Coeur d'Alene) as a "not uncommon" fall transient, by Rust (1915) as an uncommon summer resident and transient, and by Yocom (1946) as occurring at the upper end of Lake Coeur d'Alene July 1-10, 1943.

Hand (1941) noted an occasional bird at St. Maries, Benewah County, from late March to May and again in September and October (1921 through 1941); he states that "immatures" were seen at the tops of the open ridges in August and early September.

In Latah County Johnston (1949) noted it frequently at Moscow "feeding over the larger fields" June 1 through August 16, 1947, and Verner (1953) reported it uncommon at Harvard, where it was seen August 8, 1951, and July 7, 1952. I found it fairly common throughout the year at Moscow. During the winter months, regardless of the depth of the snow, it was frequently observed flying low over the open fields. Two nests were found, one with five small young on May 28, 1949, and the other with two fresh eggs April 21, 1957.

At Lewiston, in Nez Perce County, I also found it fairly common throughout the year. Merriam (1891) states that Bendire found a nest with eggs near Fort Lapwai June 15, 1871.

At Council, Adams County, Newhouse (1960) considered it a common summer resident. He gives as his latest date in the fall October 15 (1957), his earliest date of arrival in the spring March 19 (1958).

In south-central Idaho, it was reported by Merriam (1891) as common in 1890 along the Lemhi and Birch Creek valleys, and in the valleys of the Little Lost, Pahsimeroi, Salmon and Snake rivers. He collected a male in immature plumage in the Lemhi Valley September 6. In this same general area Levy (1950) found this species a common summer resident during the summer of 1949.

At Mountain Home in Elmore County, Evenden (1946) found a nest that on May 2, 1944, held five fresh eggs. Davis (1935) gives May 19 as his earliest date for eggs at Rupert, Minidoka County (1919 through 1921).

In Fremont County Rust (1917) reports several seen July 18, 1916, in the Camas Meadows near Kilgore. Steel (1956) considered this species a common summer resident at Grays Lake (1949 through 1951). He gives as arrival dates in the spring April 10, 1950, and April 7, 1951.

Habits. The Marsh Hawk is essentially a bird of open country, spending its days flying low over open fields and marshes searching for the rodents that form the bulk of its food. Forested areas are consistently shunned, so it is not surprising that it is scarce in the extreme northern part of the state. Its mastery of the air is such that the daylight hours are largely spent on the wing. On rare occasions I have seen one perched on a fence post, and I have flushed an occasional bird from the ground, but I have never known this hawk to perch in a tree or bush. It is another highly beneficial species, for while it eats birds, it is the rodents that are so destructive to farmers' crops that it preys upon most consistently. In Idaho ground squirrels are a favorite source of food, but rats, mice, and rabbits are also taken at every opportunity. Merriam (1891) comments on the fact that the stomach of a Marsh Hawk collected in the Lemhi Valley contained a chipmunk.

As might be suspected the nest is always on the ground, and a marshy spot is apparently always selected if it is available. This was the case at Moscow where both nests that were found were in the middle of open marshy fields. They were fairly well built of marsh grass, and while there was no attempt at concealment they were by no means conspicious.

The nest found by Evenden at Mountain Home in 1944 was in a dense clump of weeds in an abandoned pasture. It was partially completed on April 17, and held one egg on April 24. On May 2 the male was flushed from five fresh eggs. On June 2 there were newly hatched young in this nest, so in this one instance the incubation period was thirty days.

Ospreys: *Family Pandionidae*

Pandion haliaetus carolinensis (Gmelin): OSPREY

General Distribution. Breeds from Alaska, Mackenzie, northern Manitoba, northern Ontario, central Quebec, and Labrador south to Baja California, Arizona, the Gulf coast and Florida. Winters from central California, southern Texas, and the Gulf coast south to Chile and Argentina.

Status in Idaho. A fairly common but local summer resident in the northern part of the state, breeding in eastern Idaho as far south as Fremont County.

In Bonner County a pair of Ospreys nest each year on a piling in Lake Pend Oreille that is within a hundred yards of the bridge on Highway 95 that crosses the lake to Sandpoint (Burleigh).

In Kootenai County this species was reported by Merrill (1897) as being frequently noted during the summer months on Lake Coeur d'Alene; his earliest date of arrival in the spring was April 28. Snyder (1900) states that in 1894 it was observed "on all the lakes" in the county. Rust (1915) considered it an uncommon summer resident. Yocom (1946) noted it at the upper end of Lake Coeur d'Alene July 1 to 10, 1943, as many as four being seen daily. One nest was found in the top of a dead tree at the edge of the lake. I personally saw a single bird on Lake Coeur d'Alene May 4, 1950.

At St. Maries in Benewah County, Hand (1941) reported it as nesting on the larger streams (1921 through 1941), being present from April until September. I observed one bird at St. Maries April 25, 1956.

In Nez Perce County it was found breeding at Fort Lapwai by Bendire in 1870 (Merriam, 1891). I noted it on only a few occasions on the Snake River at Lewiston, my dates of occurrence being October 21, 1950, April 28, 1951, and April 16, 1956.

At Orofino, in Clearwater County, one bird was seen June 13, 1951, in the top of a dead tree at the edge of the Clearwater River (Burleigh). On the Selway Fork "of the middle branch of the Clearwater River," in Idaho County, two birds were noted September 5, 1941 (Orr, 1951).

At McCall, in Valley County, several pairs of Ospreys nest each year on the Payette Lakes. A nestling male, not long out of the egg, was collected there June 27, 1949 (Burleigh).

In south-central Idaho Merriam (1891) reports a nest found on the Henrys Fork of the Snake River in 1872. He states that in 1890 three birds were seen on Birch Creek in late August, several on the Salmon River, "between Challis and the mouth of the Pahsimeroi," September 18 to 20, and several on Sawtooth Lake the last week of September. Rust (1917) states that it occurs sparingly on the North Fork of the Snake River, in Fremont County, and on Henrys Lake. He saw one bird on Henrys Lake August 25, 1916.

Habits. The Osprey is commonly known throughout the country as the Fish Hawk, and this is a good name for it, for its food consists entirely of fish. These it catches in relatively shallow water, for it lacks the ability to dive in deep water. Unlike the Bald Eagle it is not a scavenger and will not touch dead fish that have washed up on the shore. There exists a general antipathy towards hawks and owls, but this is not the case where the Osprey is concerned. Many are unquestionably killed by ignorant sportsmen, but over much of its breeding range it is afforded protection by landowners who appreciate the fact that only fish are eaten and who enjoy the presence of these birds on their property. The nest is built of sticks, twigs, pieces of sod, and almost any material that is readily available, and since, where the birds are unmolested, it is used for many years and constantly added to, it is often a massive structure. The height from the ground is apparently immaterial, the main requirement being that it be close to water where the food supply exists.

Caracaras and Falcons: *Family Falconidae*

Falco rusticolus Linnaeus: Gyrfalcon

General Distribution. In Europe breeds from Iceland, Scandinavia, and northern Russia south to Kamchatka and the Bering Sea. Winters south to France, northern Germany, southern Russia, and Japan. Also breeds in Alaska, Ellesmere Island, and northern Greenland, wintering south to Montana, southern Manitoba, New York, and Massachusetts.

Status in Idaho. Recorded once in the southern part of the state. Ligon (1968) reports the capture of a Gyrfalcon by R. L. Siler and T. N. Smith on February 26, 1968, "in open farming country eight miles east of American Falls Power County, Idaho." It was in the gray phase, and was "in first basic (first winter) plumage."

Habits. The Gyrfalcon is the largest of the falcons, being twenty-two inches in length. It is essentially a bird of the Arctic tundra, preying largely on grouse and ptarmigan, but also to some extent on such far northern rodents as the lemming. Only when exceptionally severe winters make existence precarious does it come very far south, and records for its occurrence anywhere in the United States during any one winter are not numerous. This is probably just as well, considering the destruction to our grouse and pheasants that would otherwise result.

This was one of the favorite birds of medieval falconers. Bold and fierce by nature and capable of attaining an estimated speed of 180 miles an hour, it was the exceptional bird that could escape when attacked.

Falco mexicanus Schlegel: Prairie Falcon

General Distribution. Breeds from British Columbia, southern Alberta, southern Saskatchewan, and North Dakota south to Baja California, southern Arizona, southern New Mexico, and northern Texas. Winters from the northern part of its breeding range south into Mexico.

Status in Idaho. A scarce transient in the northern part of the state, where it possibly breeds sparingly. In southern Idaho it occurs throughout the year, but is uncommon and local in its distribution.

At Coeur d'Alene it was reported rare by Merrill (1897), one specimen being "taken in September." Rust (1913) likewise considered it rare in Kootenai County. He states a specimen was "examined" at Coeur d'Alene November 6, 1912. In Benewah County it was noted by Hand (1941) at Snow Peak June 16, 1930, and near Taft Tunnel July 27, 1940, so despite its rarity an occasional pair may nest in these northern counties. My one record for Latah County is that of a single bird seen at Genesee February 28, 1950.

In south-central Idaho it was reported by Merriam (1891) as nesting in the Blackfoot Mountains in early July, 1890. He also noted several birds on Big Lost River July 22, and one on Birch Creek August 7.

Farther south in the state it was recorded in the Preuss Range, Bear Lake County, where a juvenile male was collected in Home Canyon July 18, 1934 (Brodkorb, in litt.), at Rupert October 31, 1919 (Davis, 1935), at the Silent City of Rocks, near Almo, June 21, 1945 (Burleigh), and at Homedale, Owyhee County, June 23, 1943, and February 22 (Sage Creek Canyon) and February 24 (Poison Creek Canyon), 1950 (Burleigh).

Habits. The nesting site of the Prairie Falcon is the ledge of a cliff, preferably well up from the ground, and in my experience it is only near sheer cliffs that this species will be seen during the summer months. The few cliffs that I have had an opportunity to investigate in southern Idaho have always been found to harbor a pair of these falcons, so it is probable that the actual breeding population is larger than the limited number of records would indicate. It is largely a bird of the plains, even deserts, having apparently little liking for heavily wooded areas; thus its scarcity in the northern part of the state is more or less to be expected. A suitable nesting site has been known to tempt an occasional pair to spend the summer months in rather limited open country, so its presence in Benewah County in June and July could mean that there was a nest in the vicinity.

No attempt is made to build a nest, the eggs being laid on the bare rock or on such debris that normally accumulates in such a spot.

Such mammals as the rabbit, the prairie dog and the ground squirrel are preyed upon to some extent, but the food of this falcon is largely birds, both large and small. It does not seem to bother poultry much, but that may be due to the isolated country in which much of the year is spent. A specimen taken by Merriam on Birch Creek in August had a Horned Lark in its stomach. Were it more plentiful, it could be a rather destructive species, but its numbers are not large enough to justify any concern in this respect.

Falco peregrinus anatum Bonaparte: PEREGRINE FALCON

General Distribution. Breeds from northern Alaska, Mackenzie, Baffin Island, and Greenland south to Baja California, southwestern Texas, Colorado, northeastern Louisiana, and northwestern Georgia. Winters as far north as British Columbia, Nebraska, Indiana, Massachusetts, and New Brunswick, and south through Mexico, Central America, and the West Indies to northern Chile and Argentina.

Status in Idaho. Of rare occurrence throughout the year.

There are few records for the occurrence of this falcon in Idaho. In the southern part of the state it was noted at Pocatello, Bannock County, February 16, 1946 (Webster, 1946), and at Wilson Lake, in Jerome County, July 7, 1949 (Levy, 1950).

I personally recorded it at Cataldo, Kootenai County, May 21, 1949, and at Lewiston, Nez Perce County, September 24, 1955.

Habits. The food of the Peregrine Falcon consists almost entirely of birds, and its mastery of the air is such that once a victim is selected it rarely, if ever, escapes. It is unquestionably the swiftest of our birds of prey and can easily overtake any bird that it pursues. Species known to be eaten vary in size from the large ducks to sparrows and even warblers. The one seen at Pocatello was watched by Webster as it killed a female Mallard, while at Wilson Lake the bird noted there by Levy was preying on shore birds. At Cataldo I was watching Black Terns feeding over an open marsh when suddenly a Peregrine Falcon appeared, seized one of the terns and carried it to the top of a nearby snag, and soon devoured it. Although widely distributed in North America this falcon is nowhere plentiful, and because of its limited numbers it will never be a serious threat to the welfare of our bird life.

As with the Prairie Falcons, the nest is a ledge of a sheer cliff, usually well near the top, the eggs lying on the bare rock. Since such nesting sites are frequently in river gorges or on the seacoast, water fowl are consistently preyed upon, and for this reason this species has for many years been commonly known as the Duck Hawk.

Falco columbarius Linnaeus: PIGEON HAWK

General Distribution. Breeds from northern Alaska, Mackenzie, northern Manitoba, northern Quebec, and Labrador south to Oregon, North Dakota, Michigan, and Nova Scotia. Winters south to Peru and central Venezuela, and through the West Indies to Trinidad.

Status in Idaho. A regular but uncommon winter resident in the northern part of the state, frequently appearing in August and lingering in the spring until late April. There are no records for southern Idaho.

In Kootenai County the Pigeon Hawk has been recorded in Hoodoo Valley, in August, 1894 (Snyder, 1900), at Fort Sherman (Coeur d'Alene), specimens taken August 20 and October 1 (Merrill, 1897), and at Echo Bay on Lake Coeur d'Alene, one specimen taken (Rust, 1915).

Hand (1941) reports one seen at St. Maries, Benewah County, October 3, 1936, and states that it was noted on a few occasions in August at "the higher altitudes."

In Latah County, I found this little falcon a regular and not uncommon winter resident at Moscow, seeing an occasional bird each year regardless of the depth of the snow or of subzero temperatures. My extreme dates of occurrence are October 3 (1950) and April 24 (1953). It was noted once at Genesee on March 19, 1953.

I have but two records for Lewiston, Nez Perce County, September 24, 1949, and September 28, 1951.

I saw one bird at Headquarters, Clearwater County, March 25, 1953.

Habits. It is generally recognized that falcons are essentially bird eaters, and my own impression based, it must be admitted, on rather limited experience, was that the Pigeon Hawk preyed almost entirely on small birds. It was, therefore, somewhat of a surprise to me, on examining the stomach contents of the specimens taken at Moscow, to find mice in practically all of them. In fact the only bird remains I identified were those of a Robin in the stomach of the female I collected December 26, 1951. Apparently the Pigeon Hawk, to some extent at least, a beneficial species, although its actual numbers are so limited that it will never jeopardize the existence of our small birds.

Unlike the other falcons this species commonly selects a large spruce or fir as a nesting site, building a substantial nest of sticks, twigs, and shreds of bark or, as is often the case, utilizing an old nest of a crow. On rare occasions a hollow in the ground, concealed by overhanging brush, is used.

Falco columbarius suckleyi Ridgway

On the basis of specimens critically examined, this dark form that breeds in western British Columbia is the race that occurs most commonly in migration and during the winter months in northern Idaho. Five specimens were taken as follows: Moscow, a male December 7, 1956, and females March 7, 1952, February 27, 1953, and February 17, 1956; Genesee, a female March 19, 1953.

Falco columbarius bendirei Swann

This noticeably paler race that occurs during the summer months in northwestern North America is apparently rather scarce both as a transient and winter resident. Two specimens referable to *bendirei* were taken at Moscow, females December 26, 1951, and April 24, 1953.

Falco sparverius Linnaeus: SPARROW HAWK

General Distribution. Of wide distribution in the Americas. In North America breeds from northern Alaska east across the continent to southern Quebec, south to northern Mexico, the Gulf coast, and southern Florida. Winters north to British Columbia, Colorado, Illinois, Ontario, and Nova Scotia.

Status in Idaho. A fairly common transient and summer resident throughout the state; winters in small numbers except in the extreme northern counties.

At the Trestle Creek Lookout Station forty miles north of Clark Fork, in Bonner County, one bird was seen July 20, 1917, and three on August 23. The altitude here was approximately seven thousand feet (Burleigh, 1923).

In Kootenai County it was reported by Merrill (1897) as a common summer resident at Fort Sherman (Coeur d'Alene), arriving in early April and being common by the fifteenth to the twentieth of the month; by Snyder

(1900) as common in the Hoodoo Valley in late August; by Rust (1915) as a fairly common summer resident in Kootenai County; by Yocom (1946) as noted daily at the upper end of Lake Coeur d'Alene July 1 to 10, 1943.

Hand (1941) considered it a common summer resident at St. Maries, Benewah County, being present from April until October (1921 through 1941).

In Latah County it was reported by Johnston (1949) as common from June 1 to August 16, 1947, being seen along the roads on fence posts or telephone poles. Verner (1953) recorded it at Harvard June 29, 1952. At Moscow I found it a fairly common summer resident, and an uncommon winter resident. An occasional bird was seen from late October until April, but it was late April or early May before it was present in any numbers; and by the middle of October there was a noticeable decrease in the numbers seen.

Its status at Lewiston in Nez Perce County was much the same as that at Moscow. It was fairly common during the summer months, and despite the lack of snow and infrequent low temperatures, it was noted only in small numbers throughout the winter.

I have two records for Clearwater County, single birds observed at Weippe November 6, 1952, and at Headquarters April 21, 1953.

In Idaho County it was noted by Orr (1951) at Selway Falls, three birds being seen September 6, 1941. Newhouse (1960) reported it a common summer resident at Council in Adams County, his extreme dates of occurrence being April 4 (1958) and December 28 (1957).

In south-central Idaho Merriam (1891) found it "common everywhere" in 1890. He states that adults were watched feeding young in late July in the Lost River Mountains. In Lemhi County I saw two birds, apparently a mated pair, at Shoup, in the Bitterroot Mountains, June 4, 1949. Rust (1917) considered it fairly common during the summer of 1916 in Fremont County; breeding pairs were noted in Little Dry Creek Canyon June 19, and in Beaver Creek Canyon June 26. Steel (1956) considered it a common summer resident at Grays Lake (1949 through 1951), giving as dates of arrival in the spring April 13, 1950, and April 19, 1951.

In extreme southern Idaho Davis (1935) reported it as breeding in Minidoka County (1919-21), giving as the earliest date for eggs May 2. Levy (1950) found it an uncommon breeding bird in the summer of 1949 in an area that included Minidoka, Jerome, Twin Falls, and Cassia counties. I noted an occasional bird in the vicinity of Marsing, Owyhee County, June 24, 1949.

Although a difference of opinion exists among taxonomists as to the validity of a western race of the Sparrow Hawk, a critical examination of a small series of these hawks taken throughout the year in Idaho indicated the presence of two recognizable forms. The nominate race *sparverius* can be distinguished from the breeding bird of the northwestern United States by its smaller size and darker coloration, and these characters were readily apparent in specimens taken in migration and during the winter months.

Ten specimens out of a total of thirty-six were typical of birds representing the nominate race and were distinct from the noticeably paler population that breeds and is to some extent resident in Idaho. At first glance the number of specimens identified as *sparverius* might seem rather large, but it should be borne in mind that this form breeds north of Idaho in Alaska and Mackenzie, and it is logical to assume that transients from this area would appear in the northwestern United States in migration.

Falco sparverius sparverius Linnaeus

Specimens identified as *sparverius* are as follows:
Moscow, males February 7, 1950, and January 8 and December 1, 1956, and a female December 7, 1956; Potlatch, a female October 5, 1957; Genesee, a male March 12, 1950; Lewiston, males December 18, 1947; October 12, 1949, November 13, 1952, and February 21, 1956.

Falco sparverius phalaena Lesson

Breeding specimens identified as *phalaena* were taken as follows:
Moscow, males July 30, 1948, and July 1, 1953; Potlatch, males July 17, 1955, and July 4, 1958; New Meadows, a female June 15, 1955; Oreana, Owyhee County, a female June 25, 1949.

Specimens taken as transients and during the winter months included the following:
Moscow, males November 10, 1947, December 26, 1948, January 21, 1950, February 13, 1953, and March 9, 1956, and females November 21, 1955, and January 24, 1956; Potlatch, males October 16, 1949, February 28, 1953, and May 1, 1955; Genesee, males October 30, 1947, November 12, 1949, December 8, 1951, February 12, 1952, and February 13, 1953; Weippe, a male November 6, 1952.

Habits. Wherever there is open country one will find the Sparrow Hawk in Idaho. Thick woods are consistently shunned, although slashings that result from logging operations sooner or later attract these little falcons. The top of a telephone pole or a fence post is a favorite spot from which to watch for an unwary mouse or large insect, and it is in such a spot that they are usually seen. Although small birds are preyed on to a limited extent, especially during the winter months, the food of the Sparrow Hawk consists largely of rodents. Where available grasshoppers are eaten to the exclusion of all other food. Thus this species can be considered highly beneficial and worthy of protection at all times.

Unlike those of other falcons the nest is never in the open, the site selected being either a natural cavity or an old woodpecker's hole, preferably in a dead tree standing well out from the nearest woods. Height from the ground is apparently not important, although the average nest is usually well toward the top of the tree selected. No attempt is made to line the cavity, the eggs, four or five in number, lying on fragments of rotted wood.

ORDER GALLIFORMES

Grouse and Ptarmigan: *Family Tetraonidae*

Dendragapus obscurus (Say): Blue Grouse

General Distribution. Resident from southeastern Alaska, Mackenzie, and western Alberta south to southern California, northern Arizona, and New Mexico.

Status in Idaho. Common in all heavily timbered areas throughout the state.

The Blue Grouse is another species that was first recorded in Idaho by the Lewis and Clark expedition. In his Journal Lewis (*Original Journals,* III:76) reports it, under date of September 20, 1805, as occurring in the state, and later (*Original Journals,* V:161) states that one was killed June 26, 1806 (Jollie, 1953).

The one record for Boundary County is that of a pair that I saw well toward the top of Harrison Peak, at an altitude of six thousand feet, on June 25, 1957. One, the female, was collected.

In Kootenai County it was reported by Snyder (1900) as abundant at Blue Lake July 12 to 30, 1894, and equally common in the Hoodoo Valley the latter part of August; by Merrill (1897) as fairly common at Fort Sherman (Coeur d'Alene) from the lake to the tops of the surrounding mountains, a brood of nearly grown young was seen July 1, and a female with a "brood of chicks" on Mica Peak July 2; and by Rust (1915) as a "fairly common resident in the mountains" (1910 through 1914).

In Benewah County Hand (1941) found it common "in the high mountains" (1921 through 1941); fully 150 were noted in August, 1934, on a mountain slope on the St. Joe–Clearwater divide.

Johnston (1949) reports one bird seen June 30, 1947, on West Twin Mountain in Latah County. Bendire (1889) noted this species at Fort Lapwai, in Nez Perce County, in 1870 and 1871. I saw a single bird near the top of a ridge (altitude 5,000 feet) at Headquarters, Clearwater County, November 7, 1952.

In Idaho County Orr (1951) considered it abundant in September, 1941, "in the western part of the Clearwater Mountains" above an altitude of 4,500 feet. The birds were in coveys, apparently family groups of four to eight individuals. Twelve specimens were taken September 11-27. In July, 1948, he found the Blue Grouse very scarce in the northern part of the Bitterroot Mountains and "adjacent Clearwater." It was noted but once, a female with half-grown young on July 12.

Marshall (1945) considered it "rather common" in the Boise National Forest from September, 1938, to September, 1940.

At Shoup, Lemhi County, in the Bitterroot Mountains, six pairs of these birds were seen June 4, 1949, in open woods at the head of Cramer Creek (altitude 5,000 feet); two broods of young were approximately a week old (Burleigh).

Arvey (1949) reported this species unusually plentiful in the vicinity of the Loon Creek Ranger Station and Indian Springs, in Custer County, August 12 through September 3, 1948. Numerous family groups were noted, the young by that date being well grown. He also found it unusually plentiful then at Perkins Lake and Prairie Creek in Blaine County as compared to numbers recorded from 1938 to 1949. Four young comprised the average brood, the extreme being two and seven.

At Ketchum in Blaine County Jewett (1912) reported it common during the late fall and winter of 1910. In October several small flocks were noted along Spring Creek at an altitude of 6,500 feet, and on November 5 a flock comprising fully one-hundred individuals was seen at an altitude of 8,000 feet on Boyle Mountain. During December it was common at this altitude on "pine covered ridges." None were noted then in the valleys. Near the foot of Easley Peak north of Ketchum, at approximately 7,000 feet, a male was flushed in open woods June 25, 1950 (Burleigh).

Merriam (1891) found this species common in early August, 1872, on the Henrys Fork of the Snake River. He also states that it was abundant in 1890 in the Sawtooth, Pahsimeroi, and Salmon River mountains.

In Fremont County Rust (1917) noted a male in Little Dry Creek Canyon July 8, 1916, and a female with three young on August 10.

At Grays Lake in Bonneville County, I saw several birds on a wooded ridge, at approximately 6,600 feet, June 12, 1949. Steel (1956) reports a brood of three young "about 3 weeks old" July 13, 1951.

Brodkorb (in litt.) reports specimens taken in August, 1935, in Bear Lake County, on Fiddle Creek in the Preuss Mountains.

Levy (1950) considered the Blue Grouse fairly common "in the higher mountain areas" of south-central Idaho during the summer of 1949.

Habits. This species is unique in that it spends the summer months in the valleys and on the lower slopes of the ridges, and the winter months at the tops of the ridges. Marshall (1946) states that on the Boise National Forest broods of fully grown young begin to move upward by the middle of August, and within a month all "were in subalpine country." The movement to a lower altitude usually begins in March, but from early October until March no Blue Grouse were found below six thousand feet. After the middle of November when an increasing depth of snow covered the ground, the birds spent most of the time in the tops of the thickest conifers, rarely leaving the tree that had been selected. Their food then consisted almost entirely of the needles and buds of conifers, and in this connection it was of interest to note that gravel was retained in the stomach throughout the winter months. During the spring and early summer the flowering parts of various plants were eaten to a large extent, while in late summer insects, especially grasshoppers, were given preference.

Stewart (1944) made a detailed study of the food of the Blue Grouse in Idaho and found that needles of the Douglas fir comprised 78.2 per cent of the food eaten in the winter. The remainder included needles of the spruce and pine, the buds of the cherry and willow. During the summer months the diet was considerably more varied and consisted of green leaves, fruits and seeds, flowers, animal matter, and coniferous needles.

Orr (1951) examined the stomach contents of specimens taken in September in the Clearwater Mountains and found that the birds were eating the needles of larch and fir, alder buds, and grasshoppers.

Dendragapus obscurus richardsonii (Douglas)

Specimens representing this northern race were taken by W. L. Pengelly in Bonner County September 27, 1950, by Paul D. Dalke in the Nez Perce National Forest August 11, 1950, by Seymour H. Levy at Copeland, Boundary County, November 3, 1951, and by me on Harrison Peak, Boundary County, June 25, 1957. On the basis of these specimens it would appear that the range of *richardsonii* in Idaho is limited to the extreme northern part of the state.

Dendragapus obscurus pallidus Swarth

Blue Grouse over the greater part of Idaho are typical of *pallidus*, characterized by being distinctly paler than *richardsonii*. In a series of specimens examined, a total of fifty-five were found to represent this race. They were taken throughout the state and included the following localities: Kootenai County, Idaho County (Riggins, Whitebird, Seven Devils Mountains), Gem County (Big Butte), Boise County (Scott Mountain, Hunter Creek, Horseshoe Bend), Elmore County (Atlanta), Lemhi County (Pattec Creek, Perreau Creek, Color Creek, Shoup), Custer County (Dickey, Lost River Mountains), Blaine County (Ketchum).

Dendragapus obscurus oreinus Behle and Selander

This race, described from Utah, is the form occurring in the extreme southern part of Idaho. Specimens were taken by S. G. Jewett at Albion, Cassia County, August 7, 1910, and by L. J. Goldman at Grays Lake, Bonneville County, October 15, 1916. It would appear that Bonneville County is an area of integration between *oreinus* and *pallidus*, specimens taken by Paul D. Dalke at Gray May 13, 1950, and by Seymour H. Levy east of Alpine, Wyoming, May 28, 1951, approaching *pallidus* in their characters.

Canachites canadensis franklinii (Douglas): SPRUCE GROUSE

General Distribution. Resident from southeastern Alaska, British Columbia, and central Alberta south to northeastern Oregon, south-central Idaho, western Montana, and northwestern Wyoming.

Status in Idaho. Fairly common in the more heavily timbered areas of the state as far south as Blaine County in south-central Idaho.

The Spruce Grouse is another species that was first recorded in the state by the Lewis and Clark expedition. Lewis (*Original Journals,* V:138) states that a female was shot for food on the Lolo Trail, above Weippe, June 16, 1806, and that another was shot "on the eastern end of the Lolo Trail" June 28, 1806 (Jollie, 1953).

In Bonner County this grouse was found to be fairly plentiful in 1917 in open timber on the higher ridges north of Clark Fork. A female with two half-grown young was seen August 14, and on September 8 five were noted feeding together on huckleberries (Burleigh, 1923).

Rust (1916) considered it uncommon at Coeur d'Alene, in Kootenai County (1910 through 1915), being observed infrequently in the heavier timber. An adult female was collected October 10, 1915.

In Benewah County Hand (1941) reported it "usually quite common" (1921 through 1941), noting it on the mountainsides from 4,000 to 6,000 feet. Jollie (1955) states that a male collected six miles "south southwest" of Emida on November 12, 1950, was a hybrid between this species and the Blue Grouse. It was intermediate in size, and the plumage, while suggestive of *Dendragapus obscurus,* was more like that of *Canachites canadensis.*

In Shoshone County it was found to be fairly plentiful in 1951 on the higher ridges south of Avery. On June 21 three males were seen in the course of the morning (Burleigh).

It apparently has never been common in Latah County, the only record for its occurrence being that of a female collected by Ray Brooks July 18, 1899 (Johnston, 1949).

On the Boise National Forest Marshall (1945) reported it "infrequently observed" (1938 through 1940).

In Blaine County Jewett (1912) recorded it at the head of Wood River and on Baker Creek. Arvey (1949) noted it at Perkins Lake, stating that from August 12 to September 3, 1948, fifteen roosted there each night in a grove of conifers. He also found this species unusually common then in the vicinity of the Loon Creek Ranger Station in Custer County; it was observed daily the latter part of August and early September.

Habits. Bendire (1892) considered the Spruce Grouse a common bird in northern Idaho in 1881, occurring, in his experience between an altitude of 5,000 and 9,000 feet. He described their favored haunts as "along the edges of wet or swampy mountain valleys, the so-called 'Camas prairie,' or the borders of the numerous little streams found in such regions among groves or thickets of spruce and tamarack." The one exception was a "covey" of ten birds that he encountered that summer "in the low flat and densely timbered region between the southern end of Pend Oreille Lake and Lake Coeur d'Alene, at an altitude not exceeding 3,500 feet."

Although there is no altitudinal migration in the fall as is the case with the Blue Grouse, the individuals comprising the resident population separate when the snow covers the ground and hunt out the tops of the thickest firs where they remain inactive during the winter months. During this period their food consists almost entirely of fir needles.

Bonasa umbellus (Linnaeus): RUFFED GROUSE

General Distribution. Resident from central Alaska east across the continent through central Saskatchewan, northern Ontario, and southern Quebec to southern Labrador, south to northern California, southern Idaho, northern Colorado, western South Dakota, central Arkansas, northern Georgia, western South Carolina, and northern Virginia.

Status in Idaho. Resident and common in all forested areas throughout the state.

The Ruffed Grouse was first recorded in Idaho by the Lewis and Clark expedition, being mentioned from time to time in the journals that Lewis kept (*Original Journals,* III:76; IV:128; V:161) (Jollie, 1953).

In Kootenai County it was recorded by Merrill (1897) as "exceedingly abundant"; by Snyder (1900) as common at Hoodoo Lake in August, 1894; by Rust (1915) as common (1910 through 1914) in "coniferous timber"; by Yocom (1946) as common, July 1-10, 1943, at the upper end of Lake Coeur d'Alene, one brood of young was seen.

In Benewah County it was considered by Hand (1941) as common "at low to moderate altitudes" (1921 through 1941).

In Latah County Johnston (1949) reported it common (June 1 to August 16, 1947). Verner (1953) found a nest at Harvard June 21, 1951, that held eight eggs, just hatching, and saw a brood of at least six young there, nearly grown, July 18, 1952. Hungerford (1953) reported it common on the University of Idaho Experimental Forest, on Flat Creek, near Deary. I personally found it common and well distributed.

An interesting record was that of a bird I flushed October 11, 1957, from willows bordering the reservoir east of Lewiston Orchards. The nearest wooded ridge was approximately five miles south of the reservoir, so this was clearly a case of fall wandering frequently observed in this species.

Orr (1951) found it abundant in September, 1941, in the Selway area in Idaho County, occurring from an altitude of 1,900 feet to the tops of the ridges (6,000 feet).

Farther south in the state it has been recorded in Adams County, common in 1957 and 1958 (Newhouse, 1960); in the Boise National Forest, fairly common, 1938 through 1940 (Marshall, 1945); in the Salmon River Mountains, several collected September 4, 1890 (Merriam, 1891); in Fremont County, two males seen in Little Dry Creek Canyon July 8, 1916, and a female with ten well-grown young on the North Fork of the Snake River August 26, 1916 (Rust, 1917); and at Grays Lake, "resident" (Steel, 1956); three birds seen in a ravine part way up an open ridge (6,000 feet) November 3, 1949 (Burleigh).

Habits. Hungerford (1953) has studied in detail the life history of the Ruffed Grouse on the University of Idaho Experimental Forest near Deary, and has given us a good picture of its activities throughout the year. According to his findings the birds are solitary during the winter. The first drumming occurs in early March, continues through May and persists sporadically until late June. Laying starts in late April or early May. At an altitude of 2,000 to 3,000 feet activities may be a week or ten days ahead of those 1,000 to 2,000 feet higher. Incubation is generally underway by early May, and hatching occurs during the first half of June. Females with young (from three to nine) remain together through most of August, not infrequently until the end of September, and rarely until late October. Roosting in the snow is common throughout the winter. Serviceberry is the most important source of buds for winter food, and there are usually a morning and an afternoon feeding periods. In the spring, catkins of the willow, alder, and poplar are eaten, in the summer, clover, grass, and small ground cover plants, and in the fall, fruits and berries.

Bonasa umbellus phaia Aldrich and Friedmann

This race is the breeding bird of extreme northern Idaho. It was described by Aldrich and Friedmann (1943), the type being a male collected by R. T. Young at Priest River October 9, 1897. Specimens representing this subspecies have been collected as follows: Bonner County, Sandpoint, female, October 1, 1950 (Robert Salter); Shoshone County, Dismal Lake, female, October 1, 1951 (S. H. Levy); Latah County, six miles northeast of Harvard, male, July 11, 1947 (D. W. Johnston); Deary, female, October 2, 1948; 2 males, October 8, 1949 (Burleigh). Two specimens taken farther south in the state, a male from McCall, Valley County, April 18, 1949, and a female from Whitebird, Idaho County, October 9, 1948, approach *affinis* in their characters, but are closer to *phaia*.

Bonasa umbellus affinis Aldrich and Friedmann

This race occurs in western Idaho, its range, based on specimens taken, extending north to Latah County and south to Boise County. Specimens personally collected and referable to *affinis* are as follows: Latah County, Moscow, male, November 30, 1947; Juliaetta, female, November 10, 1949; Nez Perce County, Lake Waha, male, October 7, 1949; Clearwater County, Headquarters, females November 11, 1951, October 22, 1952, March 31, 1954. Four specimens, all males, collected in the Boise National Forest in Boise County by W. A. Marshall are also referable to *affinis*. They were taken on March 2 and November 27, 1939, and January 15 and 22, 1940.

Bonasa umbellus incana Aldrich and Friedmann

Incana is a gray race that is found in extreme southeastern Idaho. Two specimens taken by L. J. Goldman in 1916 at Pegram in Bear Lake County, a female January 14 and a male February 2, are referable to *incana.* I personally collected two males at Gray, in Bonneville County, November 3, 1949, that are also typical of this pale subspecies.

Pedioecetes phasianellus columbianus (Ord): Sharp-tailed Grouse

General Distribution. Resident from northern British Columbia and western Montana south to eastern Oregon, northern Utah, and northern New Mexico.

Status in Idaho. Once common over much of the state, occurring wherever there was suitable habitat; now extremely scarce and rarely observed.

Merrill (1897) reported it at Fort Sherman (Coeur d'Alene) as "quite common, particularly on the extensive prairie north of the fort." In the winter it was found "in the pine woods for considerable distances."

Rust (1915), however, stated that it was becoming rare in Kootenai County, only a few small flocks being seen on the prairie north of Coeur d'Alene (1910 through 1914).

At Moscow in Latah County where it was once common in the open Palouse country, it has not been noted since October 27, 1920, when "a covey of five birds" was seen at the base of Moscow Mountain (Hand, 1941).

Merriam (1891) states that Bendire reported "flocks of from one to two hundred in the winter in the vicinity of Ft. Lapwai." There are no recent records for Nez Perce County.

Rust (1917) found it rare in Fremont County, his one record being that of a small flock seen near Kilgore August 26, 1916.

In south-central Idaho it was noted in 1872 near Fort Hall and on the Portneuf and Snake Rivers. One bird was taken August 31, 1890, near the Lemhi Indian Agency (Merriam, 1891).

Habits. The Sharp-tailed Grouse is a bird of the open prairie, and in Idaho it was at one time abundant in the bunch-grass country which is characteristic of large areas of the state. With the advent of man and the inevitable change in much of its preferred habitat, it gradually became scarce and today is absent over the larger part of its original range. Wheat fields are unsuitable as nesting sites, and this factor, as well as uncontrolled hunting pressure, resulted in its rapid disappearance from areas where it once was common.

Bendire (1892) states that "a bunch-grass covered hillside, with a southerly exposure, seemed to be a favorite nesting site with this Grouse at Fort Lapwai. The nest, like that of all the Grouse, is always placed on the ground, usually close alongside some tall bunch of coarse grass, which hides it completely from view. Even if it did not, the female harmonizes in color so thoroughly with her surroundings that she is apt not to be noticed unless she should leave her nest which she does not do very readily, as she is a very close sitter. A slight hollow, usually scratched out on the upper side of a bunch of grass, if the nest is placed on a hillside, is fairly lined with dry grass of which there is ordinarily an abundance to be found in the vicinity, and this constitutes the nest."

Centrocercus urophasianus (Bonaparte): SAGE GROUSE

General Distribution. Resident from central Washington, southern Idaho, Montana, southern Alberta, southern Saskatchewan and western North Dakota south to eastern California, Nevada, Utah, western Colorado, and northwestern Nebraska.

Status in Idaho. Locally common in suitable habitat in the southern part of the state.

The Sage Grouse was first recorded in Idaho by the Lewis and Clark expedition. In his Journals (*Original Journals,* II:386; III:33) Clark comments on the presence of this species in the Lemhi Valley, and in the valley of the Salmon River (Jollie, 1953).

Merriam (1891) states that in 1872 he noted it in the Teton Basin, along the Henrys Fork of the Snake River and at Henrys Lake. In 1890 he found it abundant in south-central Idaho in "the sage plains and valleys." In this same general area Levy (1950) reported it common "in sagebrush areas" during the summer of 1949.

In Fremont County Rust (1917) noted it in 1916 at Spencer July 31, near Highbridge August 10, at Sheridan Creek August 17, and at Kilgore August 26. Steel (1956) considered it a common resident at Grays Lake (1949 through 1951). He observed a brood of five young, about half grown, on July 25, 1949.

In Minidoka County Kenagy (1914) reported it becoming noticeably scarcer. He considered it "tolerably common" in 1907, found it rare in 1911, and recorded none in 1913. Davis (1935) noted it at Rupert March 29, 1919, but made no comment as to the number seen.

At Riddle in Owyhee County Davis (1934) saw a female with a brood of young May 30, 1934. He stated that it was once common, was now scarce, but was apparently increasing in numbers due to adequate protection. Excessive hunting pressure was given as the cause for its scarcity, for he was told that a single hunter was known to have killed as many as three hundred birds in one day.

Habits. This bird is well named for only where there is sage brush in Idaho will one find the Sage Grouse. With its gray coloration it matches perfectly its surroundings, and only during the spring months when the male indulges in its spectacular courtship display is it at all conspicious.

It spends life on the ground, and unless unduly alarmed it prefers to escape any danger that threatens by running rather than by flying. Throughout most of the year its food consists of the leaves of the sage, but during the summer months it varies its diet by eating such insects as ants, beetles and grasshoppers. The stomach of a specimen collected by Merriam in south-central Idaho in 1890 contained sage leaves, seeds, and a single ladybird beetle (*Coccinellidae*) (Judd, 1905). It is largely resident wherever

Bureau of Sport Fisheries and Wildlife

Photo by David B. Marshall

STRUTTING—THE TRADITIONAL COURTSHIP RITE PERFORMED BY A MALE SAGE GROUSE FOR TWO ADMIRING ONLOOKERS

it occurs in the state, although deep snows at the higher altitudes force it at times to seek the valleys when the sage is completely buried and its food supply has temporarily disappeared.

Quails, Pheasants, and Peacocks: *Family Phasianidae*

Colinus virginianus (Linnaeus): BOBWHITE

General Distribution. Resident from eastern South Dakota, Wisconsin, southern Ontario and southern Maine south to Guatemala, the Gulf coast of the United States, and Cuba.

Status in Idaho. Introduced into the state as early as 1877 and now of local occurrence where there is suitable habitat.

Apparently the first successful introduction of the Bobwhite into Idaho was made at Boise in 1877 (Newton Hibbs, in the *American Field* of February 16, 1889). It was considered common there in 1890 (Merriam, 1891). T. E. Wilcox (in litt.) likewise states that it was successfully introduced in the Boise Valley prior to 1885.

Rust (1915) states that it was introduced in the "Spokane Prairie, Washington" and that he found it (1910 through 1914) nesting in meadows about Coeur d'Alene.

Hand (1941) considered it rare at St. Maries; he heard a male calling there July 1, 1934.

In Latah County Johnston (1949) reports a single bird seen June 3, 1947, at Viola. I personally flushed a covey of eight birds from the edge of a field north of Moscow December 14, 1947.

Aldrich (1946) examined specimens taken at Nampa, in Canyon County, and found that birds introduced there came from widely separated areas and represented three races, *virginianus* of the southeastern United States, *mexicanus* of Mexico, and *taylori* of Kansas and Oklahoma.

Habits. Although a hardy bird, the Bobwhite is vulnerable to long cold winters and especially deep snows; consequently at the extreme northern limits of its range survival is often precarious. In Idaho its numbers are materially reduced during severe winters, and for this reason it is questionable if it will ever be a successful game species over much of the state.

Lophortyx californicus (Shaw): CALIFORNIA QUAIL

General Distribution. Resident from southern Oregon and western Nevada south to Baja California.

Status in Idaho. Introduced into the western part of the state and locally common where conditions are suitable.

Hand (1941) noted this species in small numbers at Clarkia, in Shoshone County (1921 through 1941).

At Lewiston, in Nez Perce County, I found it abundant and well distributed, due probably to the mild winters and the infrequent snowfall there. It was especially numerous on Hatwai Creek, four miles east of Lewiston, where during the fall and winter months, flocks totalling forty or more birds were encountered. South of Lewiston on the Snake River it has been reported locally common almost to the Nevada line.

Newhouse (1960) reports a covey on the Weiser River in Adams County in September, 1958.

Habits. The California Quail, within its normal range, rarely experiences any snowfall or low temperatures. For this reason in Idaho it is only in those parts of the state where the winters are mild that it has been successfully introduced. At Lewiston, the lowest point in the state at an altitude of 860 feet, this species has prospered, finding conditions comparable to those in areas where it is indigenous. Introductions at higher altitudes have resulted in the disappearance of these quail after a winter of deep snows and subfreezing temperatures.

Lophortyx gambelii Gambel: GAMBEL'S QUAIL

General Distribution. Resident from southern Nevada, southern Utah, and western Colorado south to Baja California and western Texas.

Status in Idaho. The Gambel's Quail was introduced into the state in 1921, in Lemhi County, in the vicinity of the junction of the Lemhi River with the Salmon. It still occurs here in limited numbers, but this is the only area in Idaho where it can be found at the present time.

Habits. "Quail cover along the Lemhi where these birds live is of a tight impenetrable quality that defies the trampling of livestock. This explains how these birds have survived through the years in a habitat so far north of the normal range of the Gambel's Quail. Creek banks and bottom edges are lined with bunchgrass, willow thickets, brush piles, brambles and vines in which quail are able to find sanctuary at all seasons. When the snow is deep the birds find dry passageway through these tangles. Grazing livestock are not able to reach all the forage in such tangles, so that during the winter season ample weed seed is assured the quail.

"The nest is the usual lined hollow with a clutch numbering ten to twelve eggs, whitish blotched with brown. The striped-backed chicks are alert youngsters which may be flushed with their mothers at the edge of the tangled thickets which are always found in the home territory." *Educational Leaflet* of the Idaho Fish and Game Department.

Oreortyx pictus pictus (Douglas): MOUNTAIN QUAIL

General Distribution. Resident from southeastern Washington south through eastern Oregon and western Idaho to California and western Nevada.

Status in Idaho. Locally common in suitable habitat in the western part of the state as far north as Latah County.

The Mountain Quail reaches its northern limits in the state on the open ridges along the Clearwater River in Latah County. At Juliaetta Johnston (1949) noted an adult and fifteen young July 4, 1947. I personally flushed a small covey of three birds here February 13, 1950, from underbrush in a ravine, and succeeded in collecting two of them, a male and a female.

In Idaho County, a male was collected by D. Arvey ten miles south of Riggins May 14, 1939, a female four miles northwest of Pollock July 8, 1940; and a male by me at Lucile on February 27, 1950.

Wyman (1912) reported this species common at Nampa, in Canyon County, and stated that it occurred as far east as Shoshone and Twin Falls. Farther south he found it equally common in the Owyhee foothills, forty miles south of Nampa, where he was told that on one occasion two hunters shot forty-four in two hours.

In 1950 I found it common and well distributed in the northern part of Owyhee County. Coveys of from six to twenty-four birds were noted at Oreana February 21, at Marsing (in Squaw Creek Canyon) February 22, and at Homedale (in Poison Creek Canyon) February 24. Specimens were taken at Oreana and Marsing.

Habits. The Mountain Quail is well named, for it is a bird of the mountain slopes, occurring in thickets and stretches of underbrush where it is inconspicuous and often difficult to find. In those parts of its range where the higher ridges are covered with deep snow during the winter months, it has an altitudinal migration, retreating to lower altitudes during the late fall. In Idaho, however, the winters are relatively mild in the western edge of the state, so the birds are resident wherever they are found.

The nest is a slight hollow in the ground, well concealed by fallen brush or thick vegetation, and the incubating bird sits so tightly that she must be stepped on before she flushes. Normally ten or twelve eggs are laid, but as many as twenty-two have been found in one nest.

This is not a popular bird with the sportsman, for it prefers to escape when danger threatens by running rather than flying, and in the thickets it frequents it is very difficult to see.

Phasianus colchicus Linnaeus: RING-NECKED PHEASANT

General Distribution. Native to Russia, Mongolia, Japan, Afghanistan, southern China and Formosa.

Status in Idaho. The Ring-necked Pheasant was first introduced into Idaho on the Clearwater River drainage near the town of Kamiah in 1903. In succeeding years there were other introductions in various parts of the state, and by 1930 it was common and well established in all agricultural areas. "Areas of greatest concentration today are the irrigated lands of Canyon, Ada, Gem, and Washington counties in southwestern Idaho, and Lincoln and Gooding counties on the Snake River plains. It is estimated that fall populations in these areas have reached fifty birds per one-hundred acres in some years" *Educational Leaflet* of the Idaho Fish and Game Department.

Definite records where it has been recorded are: Kootenai County, Worley, common in July, 1943 (Yocom, 1946); Fernan Lake, specimen taken in December, 1913 (Rust, 1915); Benewah County, common (1921 through 1941) "in the lower St. Joe and St. Maries Valleys" (Hand, 1941); Latah County, common in open country in 1947 (Johnston, 1949); Moscow, nest found May 1, 1949, that held thirteen fresh eggs (Burleigh); Nez Perce County, Lewiston, nest found July 31, 1950, that held eight incubated eggs (Burleigh); Adams County, common in 1957-58 (Newhouse, 1960); south-central Idaho, common to abundant June through August, 1949 (Levy, 1950); Grays Lake, introduction unsuccessful, a single male seen 1949 through 1951 (Steel, 1956).

Habits. "Pheasants are polygamous. Cocks begin to display rivalry during February as the winter flocks start to break up. By early March the roosters have established individual 'crowing territories' to which hens are attracted. A cock is often observed in company with several hens. The hens conceal their nests in weed patches, along weedy fencerows, or in alfalfa, clover, or grain fields. Nests may contain ten to fourteen olive-brown unspotted eggs. The peak of the hatch usually occurs in June. Pheasants produce only one brood a year.

"Young pheasants require a large proportion of insect food, and at any age seek some green 'salad' foods in their diet. Mature birds take any available vegetable food, weed seeds, grains, and tender plant parts. Most grain utilized is waste gleanings from stubble fields after the grain harvest." *Educational Leaflet* of the Idaho Fish and Game Department.

Alectoris graeca (Meisner): Chukar

General Distribution. Native to France, Switzerland, Germany, Hungary, Yugoslavia, Bulgaria, Turkey, Italy, Greece, India, Nepal, Tibet, and inner Mongolia.

Status in Idaho. This partridge was first introduced into Idaho in Nez Perce County in 1933. Other introductions have been made in twenty-three counties of the state, but with only partial success. According to the Idaho Fish and Game Department, "the greatest success was attained in Gem County, particularly in the Squaw Butte area."

Habits. "The nest is a depression in the ground with a lining of dried grass and a few feathers. It is usually located under low-growing vegetation. Chukars seem to prefer south-facing slopes for nesting. The average number of eggs in the clutch is about fifteen. The incubation period is twenty-four days. Egg laying usually starts about the middle of April with the young hatching in the first ten days of June. The cocks usually leave the hens sometime after the egg clutch is complete, although some may remain in the vicinity until the brood is nearly hatched. The young are led from the nest immediately after the hatch and are quick in movement and proficient at hiding. They usually can fly at two weeks of age.

"The Chukar's main diet consists of grass, leaves and seeds, particularly those of cheatgrass. They also utilize weed seeds and small fruits. Chukars are capable of scratching through rather deep snow in search of food. The range of the Chukar is limited by the availability of water in summer months. They tend to congregate in large flocks at watering sites when other water holes and streams dry up in late summer. Chukars prefer a living area with cheatgrass, bunchgrass, and sagebrush. They like rock outcroppings, cliffs and bluffs with brushy stream bottoms and swales." *Educational Leaflet* of the Idaho Fish and Game Department.

Perdix perdix (Linnaeus): GRAY PARTRIDGE

General Distribution. Native to England, Ireland, Scotland, Norway, Sweden, Belgium, Switzerland, Austria, Hungary, and western Rumania.

Status in Idaho. As far as can be determined, the Gray Partridge moved into Idaho from Oregon and Washington when they were introduced in those states about 1900. Since then additional introductions have been made in Idaho and it is now well distributed throughout the agricultural areas of the state.

Definite localities where it has been recorded are: Kootenai County, Worley, two coveys noted in July, 1943 (Yocom, 1946); Benewah County, St. Maries, found in moderate numbers (1921 through 1941) (Hand, 1941); Latah County, fairly common in 1947 (Johnston, 1949); Adams County, common, 1957-58 (Newhouse, 1960); south-central Idaho, locally common June through August, 1949 (Levy, 1950).

Habits. "Huns pair in late January and early February. Courtship display before the females includes strutting and a spreading of the chestnut tail feathers. Alfalfa stubble, wasteland or grassy fencerows are selected for nesting sites. A well-concealed depression lined with dry grass and feathers may contain up to eighteen eggs. The male accompanies the female and the young birds and remains a member of the family group. During the growth period young Huns require large amounts of insect food and green vegetation. Weed seeds and waste grains become important to their diet later in the summer, but Hungarian partridges relish green plant food as a part of the diet at all times." *Educational Leaflet* of the Idaho Fish and Game Department.

ORDER GRUIFORMES

Cranes: *Family Gruidae*

Grus americana (Linnaeus): WHOOPING CRANE

General Distribution. Formerly bred in southern Mackenzie, Alberta, Saskatchewan, Manitoba, North Dakota, Minnesota, Iowa, and Louisiana. Now known to breed only in south-central Mackenzie and to winter in southern Texas and Louisiana.

Status in Idaho. The few records would indicate that at one time the Whooping Crane occurred as a scarce transient in the state. It has not been recorded in recent years.

Townsend (1839) states that it was seen on the Bear River July 8 or 9, 1834.

Allen (1952) reports a record in the distribution files of the Fish and Wildlife service to the effect that this species was noted by Danby at Rathdrum, in Kootenai County, April 8, 1899.

A tibial fragment from the upper Pliocene, found on the Snake River thirteen miles northwest of Grandview, in Owyhee County, has been identified as *Grus americana* (Miller, 1944). Feduccia (1967) reports tibiotarsus fragments also from the Upper Pliocene, that he considers as representing *Grus americana*, that came from Glenns Ferry, Elmore County.

Habits. Because of its impressive appearance and the wholehearted effort on the part of state and federal agencies to save it from extinction, the Whooping Crane is a bird known at least by name to a large segment of the general public. Once abundant and widely distributed, it has disappeared over the larger part of its original range, and its numbers have been reduced to a point where there seemed little hope of its surviving for very long. Rigid protection and wide publicity through the medium of newspapers and current periodicals have had encouraging results, but the ultimate outcome is still in doubt. A careful count in 1952 showed that there were twenty-five of these magnificent birds still in existence, all of them concentrated during the winter months on the Aransas National Wildlife Refuge in eastern Texas. At the present time they have increased to thirty-eight, but this number is still much too small to justify undue optimism concerning their future survival.

Grus canadensis tabida (Peters): SANDHILL CRANE

General Distribution. Breeds from British Columbia, Alberta, Saskatchewan, Manitoba, Minnesota, and Michigan south to northern California, eastern Nevada, northern Utah, Montana, and Wyoming. Winters in California and northern Baja California, and in southern Texas, southern New Mexico, and northern Mexico.

Status in Idaho. Originally a common summer resident with a wide distribution over the state; now much reduced in numbers and limited as a breeding bird to the southeastern corner of Idaho.

The Sandhill Crane was first recorded in the state in 1806 by the Lewis and Clark expedition. Lewis (*Original Journals,* VI:217) reported it common May 14 on the Clearwater River, a mile and a half north of the mouth of Lawyer Canyon (in Idaho County). A nest with young just leaving the egg was found May 20. Clark (*Original Journals,* V:54) stated that it was reported to be abundant in this part of the state and that on May 21 a young bird five or six days old was brought into camp. Lewis (V:122) reported many seen on the Weippe Prairie June 10 (Jollie, 1953).

Merriam (1891) found it common on the Henrys Fork of the Snake River in early August, 1872. He stated that young were reported by Bendire near Fort Lapwai in June, 1871, and eggs on an island in the Snake River near Olds Ferry in May, 1877. In 1890 he observed several on Sawtooth Lake September 26.

At Fort Sherman (Coeur d'Alene) it was considered by Merrill (1897) as a not uncommon transient. Although no nests were located he suspected that a few pairs bred each year at the southern end of Lake Coeur d'Alene.

In his summary of breeding localities for the Sandhill Crane in Idaho, Walkinshaw (1949) cites the following early records: "Bonner County (egg, May 6, 1860); Custer County (nest, June, 1940); Blaine County (Alturas Lake, nest, 1936); Fremont County (Warm River, eggs, May 4, 1912); Teton County (Driggs, young, June 21, 1938); Bannock County (eggs, May 16, 1900)."

At the present time this species is limited as a breeding bird to a few areas in the southeastern edge of the state, but there it is still common. At Grays Lake, in Caribou County, Walkinshaw (1949) found it in 1941, well distributed in the open marsh comprising the larger part of the lake. His estimate was seven pairs to each seven hundred acres of marsh. He also noted it in small numbers at Henry, north of Soda Springs, where young were seen May 24. Steel (1956) considered it an abundant summer resident at Grays Lake (1949-51); he gives as arrival dates April 3, 1950, and April 1, 1951.

In June, 1957, I found this crane common at Henrys Lake, in Fremont County, and was told that an estimated fifty pairs nested here each year. On June 10, pairs, apparently with young, were frequently noted, and a breeding male was collected.

Measurements of two breeding males from Idaho were: Grays Lake, May 26, 1951, wing chord 540 mm., tail 208, culmen 101; Henrys Lake, June 10, 1957, wing chord 525 mm., tail 200, culmen 116.

Habits. Walkinshaw (1949) states that a total of thirteen nests were found at Grays Lake in 1941. Two of these were in shallow water, another

SANDHILL CRANES HAVING AN ARGUMENT

Bureau of Sport Fisheries and Wildlife

Photo by David B. Marshall

on a small island. He gives as extreme dates for nests with eggs May 6 and June 20, the average date being May 26.

The usual nest is a mass of dried tules, reeds, marsh grass and such vegetation that is in the immediate vicinity. It is generally at least five feet in diameter and a foot or more in height. The site selected is generally well toward the center of the open marsh, and in water several feet in depth.

Grus canadensis canadensis (Linnaeus)

As a transient this subspecies is only infrequently recorded in the state. A single bird, found feeding in a small pond in a pasture near Genesee, March 2, 1953, was collected and identified as this small northern race (Jollie, 1955). Although this is the only definite record for Idaho it is possible that one or more of the following sight records refer to *canadensis*: Rupert, Minidoka County, November 11, 1911 (Bent, 1926); March 3, 1919, and March 13, 1920 (Davis, 1935); Meridian, Ada County, November 1, 1914 (Bent, 1926); Copeland, Boundary County, two seen October 28, 1951 (Levy, 1959); Lewiston, Nez Perce County, a flock of eight birds seen at the reservoir east of Lewiston Orchards September 21, 1955, and another flock of nine at this same spot October 2, 1957 (Burleigh).

William S. Huey of the New Mexico Department of Game and Fish states (in litt.) that a crane marked during the winter with a colored band on the Bosque del Apache National Wildlife Refuge in New Mexico was noted the following summer at Grays Lake.

Rails, Gallinules, and Coots: *Family Rallidae*

Rallus limicola limicola Vieillot: Virginia Rail

General Distribution. Breeds from British Columbia east through Saskatchewan, Ontario and southern Quebec to Nova Scotia, south to Baja California, northern New Mexico, Missouri, northern Alabama, and the coast of North Carolina. Winters from southern British Columbia south along the coast to Baja California, on the Gulf coast, on the Atlantic coast from North Carolina to central Florida and south through Mexico to Guatemala.

Status in Idaho. A locally common summer resident where there is suitable habitat both in the northern and southern part of the state.

Because of its secretive habits, making it a rather difficult bird to see, the Virginia Rail has been recorded in but a few spots in the state. It undoubtedly has a much wider distribution than the few records indicate.

Hand (1941) considered it a common summer resident at St. Maries, in Benewah County (1921 through 1941), although he stated that it was noted most commonly "between April 25 and June 6."

Levy (1950) noted young of the year August 1, 1949, at Greene's Trout Farm east of Twin Falls.

At Grays Lake Steel (1956) reported it a fairly common summer resident (1949-51). He found a nest with nine eggs June 10, 1950, and saw newly hatched young June 15, 1951.

Habits. Few birds are harder to see than the Virginia Rail. Only when taken unawares will it fly, and then it will go but a short distance, legs dangling, its movements slow and with the appearance of weakness, before it drops into the thick marsh grass. That it is capable of long sustained flight, however, is evidenced by the long journeys it makes between its summer and winter homes.

It is probable that it occurs as a breeding bird in many of the marsh areas in the state, but only careful study will determine its actual abundance during the summer months.

Cattails are preferred as a nesting site, and here the nest, well built of marsh grass and fragments of the cattails, is well concealed and difficult to find. The number of eggs laid varies from seven to twelve.

Porzana carolina (Linnaeus): SORA

General Distribution. Breeds from British Columbia east through Mackenzie and northern Ontario to Prince Edward Island, south to Baja California, southern New Mexico, Oklahoma, Indiana, and Pennsylvania. Winters from California, southern Texas, the Gulf coast and Florida south through Mexico and Central America to Peru, Venezuela and British Guiana.

Status in Idaho. A fairly common but local summer resident in suitable habitat throughout the state.

In Kootenai County it was reported by Merrill (1897) as "not rare" in the marshes at Fort Sherman, Coeur d'Alene, and breeding; by Snyder (1900) as common at Hoodoo Lake, downy young being taken August 13; by Rust (1915) as a "rare resident of the marshes" in the county (1910 through 1914).

In Benewah County it was found by Hand (1941) to be a fairly common summer resident at St. Maries, occurring from April to September (1921 through 1941).

In Latah County it nests in small numbers at Potlatch, in the marshes bordering the Palouse River, being seen there at infrequent intervals between the extreme dates of April 30 (1949) and August 16 (1949). At Moscow, where there are no marshes where this rail could nest, it was noted but once, a single bird being flushed May 2, 1953, from thick marsh grass fringing a pool in an open, marshy field. It was also noted but once at Lewiston, in Nez Perce County, one bird being flushed August 2, 1949, from a stretch of reeds fringing the Snake River.

Specimens were taken at Potlatch, males April 30 and August 16, 1949, and a female May 22, 1955; at Moscow, a male May 2, 1952; and at Lewiston, a male August 2, 1949 (Burleigh).

Newhouse (1960) reports one bird seen at Council, Adams County, July 25, 1958.

Rust (1917) noted one bird, apparently a transient, at Henrys Lake, in Fremont County, August 25, 1916.

At Grays Lake it was considered by Steel (1956) to be a common summer resident (1949 through 1951). He gives as arrival dates June 1, 1950, and May 6, 1951.

In south-central Idaho Merriam (1891) reports several seen in a marsh on Big Lost River, eight miles above Arco, July 26, 1890. Levy (1950) states that in this same general area it is said to be a common summer resident. He collected a specimen at Greene's Trout Farm, east of Twin Falls, August 1, 1949. A late record for the fall is that of a bird seen at Rupert September 16, 1911 (Bent, 1926).

Habits. The Sora is a common and widely distributed species, but because of the nature of its haunts and its secretive habits it is not often seen. My experience with it in Idaho is probably more or less typical. More often than not my efforts to find it in a stretch of open marsh proved unsuccessful, the few I did see being largely accidental. As with the Virginia Rail it is extremely reluctant to fly, preferring to esacpe any danger that threatens by running.

The nest is usually in cattails and always over water, often knee-deep. Although substantially built of fragments of cattails and marsh grass, it is well concealed and frequently rather difficult to find. From six to eighteen eggs are laid, the usual number being ten to twelve.

Fulica americana americana Gmelin: AMERICAN COOT

General Distribution. Breeds from British Columbia east through central Saskatchewan and southern Ontario to New Brunswick, south to Baja California, Nicaragua, the Gulf coast, Florida, Cuba, and Jamaica. Winters widely across the continent in much of its breeding range and south to Panama, the Greater Antilles and the Bahama Islands.

Status in Idaho. A common but local summer resident over the larger part of the state. Of irregular occurrence during the winter months in northern Idaho, its presence then being governed by the severity of the weather.

In Kootenai County it was reported by Merrill (1897) as common, especially in the fall, at Fort Sherman (Coeur d'Alene); by Snyder (1900) as abundant on Hoodoo Lake, young being collected there August 13, 1894; by Rust (1915) as fairly common in the fall, especially on Lake Chatcolet where (1910 through 1914) large numbers were frequently seen.

At St. Maries, in Benewah County, it was considered by Hand (1941) to be an abundant transient and common summer resident. It was usually present from April to November, although on occasion it was observed during the winter months.

In Latah County I found it to be an uncommon spring transient, seeing it both at Moscow and at Potlatch at infrequent intervals and in small numbers. It doubtless occurs in the fall, although I never recorded it then. My extreme dates of occurrence at Moscow are April 23 (1950) and May 19 (1949), and at Potlatch April 19 (1957) and May 2 (1951).

At Lewiston in Nez Perce County, it was a common transient both in the spring and in the fall. Normally only small flocks were seen, but on one occasion, October 16, 1953, fully two hundred Coots were found on the reservoir east of Lewiston Orchards. During the winter months, single birds, rarely small flocks, were noted on the Clearwater and Snake rivers, and from time to time on the reservoir. In 1956 unusually high water on the reservoir in the late spring flooded an area thickly overgrown with small willows, and for the first time this species nested here in small numbers. On July 8, I searched these willows and succeeded in finding two broods of newly hatched young and a nest with eight eggs.

In Idaho County Hand (1932) noted one bird on Long Lake October 19, 1927, and another on Fish Lake October 17, 1928.

Newhouse (1960) found it common in April, 1958, on the Ben Ross Reservoir near Council, in Adams County, "several flocks of over one hundred birds" being seen then.

At Homedale, in Owyhee County, I saw a flock of approximately forty birds on the Snake River November 5, 1949.

In Fremont County a small flock was noted on the Camas Meadows, near Kilgore, August 26, 1916 (Rust, 1917).

Steel (1956) considered the Coot a very abundant summer resident at Grays Lake (1949 through 1951). He gives as arrival dates April 19, 1950, and April 13, 1951, and as dates when the first nests were observed May 12, 1950, and May 15, 1951. I likewise found this species common at Grays Lake in June, 1949, and collected one of a brood of newly hatched young on June 10.

In south-central Idaho Merriam (1891) reported taking two specimens in Sawtooth Lake October 2, 1890. Davis (1935) found it a common summer resident in Minidoka County (1919-21). He gives as extreme dates of occurrence at Rupert April 11 and November 4, and as the earliest date for eggs May 31. Levy (1950) found it equally common during the summer of 1949 in Jerome County. A nest found July 2 at Jerome held eight eggs.

Habits. Although the Coot winters in small numbers in northern Idaho, its existence then is somewhat precarious. Tempted by mild weather during the early winter, birds that remain in the state instead of going farther south fail at times to survive the severe weather that is normally experienced in late December and January. This was the case in January, 1957, with a flock of five birds that lingered on the reservoir east of Lewiston Orchards. A sudden and rather unexpected interval of unusually cold weather resulted in the reservoir being completely frozen over by the middle of the month, an occurrence rarely observed here. I visited the reservoir on January 16 and found this flock of five birds huddled on the ice well offshore and apparently dead. It is only with great difficulty that the Coot can fly into the air when on solid ground, and this difficulty was probably increased to the point where it proved impossible to leave the ice, the birds under these circumstances either starving or freezing to death.

The birds that had used the flooded willows at the reservoir as a suitable spot to rear their young had selected a rather unusual nesting site, for normally the nests are built in cattails and rushes. Otherwise the one nest found was quite typical, being a substantial bed of grasses and other marsh vegetation, floating in water three feet in depth. No attempt was made at concealment, and this also was characteristic.

ORDER CHARADRIIFORMES

Plovers, Turnstones, and Surfbirds: *Family Charadriidae*

Charadrius semipalmatus Bonaparte: SEMIPALMATED PLOVER

General Distribution. Breeds from Alaska, northern Mackenzie, southern Baffin Island and northern Labrador south to northern British Columbia, southern Mackenzie, Hudson Bay, Newfoundland and southern Nova Scotia. Winters from central California, Sonora, the Gulf coast, and South Carolina south to Colombia and Chile, and through the West Indies to Patagonia.

Status in Idaho. Now known as a scarce spring transient and a common fall transient in the northern part of the state. There is one record for southern Idaho.

The Semipalmated Plover was first recorded in Idaho by Seymour H. Levy, who collected a female at the Wilson Lake Reservoir near Hazelton, in Jerome County, July 22, 1949 (Levy, 1950). He (Levy, 1950) also noted a flock of six at Rose Lake, in Kootenai County, August 29, 1949, and a flock of fifteen at Medicine Lake, in Kootenai County, August 28, 1951 (Levy, 1959).

I personally found this species a scarce spring transient and a common fall transient at Potlatch, in Latah County, and at Lewiston, in Nez Perce County.

In the spring it was noted only in 1954, low water that year both in the Palouse River at Potlatch and at the reservoir east of Lewiston Orchards, producing shore bird habitat that rarely exists at this time of the year. On the mud flats in the Palouse River two birds were seen May 4, one bird May 5, and two May 7 and May 8. At the reservoir single birds were seen May 10 and May 16. I also collected a female April 30, 1954, at Salmon, in Lemhi County, as it fed with other shore birds at the edge of a pool in a partially flooded field.

In the fall the first birds usually appeared shortly after the middle of July, and were seen almost daily then, singly or in small flocks comprising three or four individuals, until the end of September. Only rarely was this species recorded in October. My extreme dates of occurrence at Potlatch are August 1 (1953) and October 6 (1953), and at Lewiston July 14 (1956) and September 24 (1955).

In view of the fact that this species had apparently been completely overlooked in the state until recorded by Levy in 1949, it was felt desirable to collect a sufficient number of specimens both to verify the identification of the individuals seen and to show the relative abundance of the Semi-palmated Plover as a transient in Idaho. Accordingly, a total of twenty-four specimens were taken as follows: Potlatch, males May 7 and 8, 1954, August 30, 1955; females August 23 and October 6, 1953, May 4 and 5, and August 11, 1954, September 2 and 10, 1955, August 20, 1956, August 25, 1957; Lewiston, males July 26, 1953, May 10 and 16, and August 13, 1954, August 2, 1955, July 27, 1958; females, August 19 and 26, 1953, August 28, 1954, September 4 and 24, 1955, August 16, 1956.

Habits. The scarcity of the Semipalmated Plover as a spring transient in Idaho would appear to be caused by a lack of suitable habitat at this time of the year. Melting snow at the higher altitudes after the first of May results in high water on the rivers, and even the smaller streams, that persists into early summer. As the water drops in July, gravel bars and mud flats are exposed, and here shore birds find ideal feeding grounds. Such conditions are almost totally lacking during the spring months, so it is not surprising that shore birds are few and far between at that time.

At Potlatch, the Semipalmated Plover fed on the mud flats exposed by low water on the Palouse River, while at Lewiston it was equally common on gravel bars in the Snake River, and on recently exposed mud flats at the reservoir.

Charadrius alexandrinus nivosus (Cassin): SNOWY PLOVER

General Distribution. Breeds on the Pacific coast from southern Washington to southern Baja California, and in the interior through western Nevada, Utah, eastern Colorado, Kansas, and Oklahoma to southern Texas. Winters on the Pacific coast south of northern Oregon, and on the Gulf coast from Texas east to Mississippi.

Status in Idaho. Largely of accidental occurrence in the southern part of the state; the only definite record is that of two specimens taken by Downing and Fichter (1968) on May 1, 1966, "on the northwest shore of American Falls Reservoir four miles east of Aberdeen, Bingham County, Idaho." There are previous records unconfirmed by specimens of birds seen in 1964 at the Minidoka Wildlife Refuge, and at the Bruneau Sand Dunes area.

Habits. In common with the other shore birds, this species, when seen, will be found feeding on exposed mud flats or gravel bars in the larger streams. It is possibly more common than the few records indicate for it closely resembles the Semipalmated Plover, differing from this latter species in being smaller and paler.

Charadrius vociferus vociferus Linnaeus: KILLDEER

General Distribution. Breeds from northern British Columbia, Mackenzie, northern Ontario, and Quebec south to Baja California, northern Mexico, the Gulf coast and central Florida. Winters from southern British Columbia, northern Utah, Oklahoma, the Ohio Valley and Long Island, south through Mexico and central America to Colombia and Ecuador, and in Bermuda, the Bahamas, and the Antilles.

Status in Idaho. Common and well distributed during the summer months over much of the state. Winters in the northern part of the state, but of irregular occurrence then except at Lewiston, where it is common.

In Kootenai County, the Killdeer was reported by Merrill (1897) as occurring during the summer months at Fort Sherman (Coeur d'Alene), a few pairs nesting on the prairie near the Spokane River; by Rust (1915) as a not common summer resident (1910 through 1914), being seen between the dates of March 9 and September 1; by Yocom (1946) as being noted at the upper end of Lake Coeur d'Alene July 1 to 10, 1943 (one breeding pair).

At Clark Fork, in Bonner County, it was found to be fairly plentiful during the summer of 1917 in the open fields about the town (Burleigh, 1923).

Hand (1941) considered it a common summer resident (1921 through 1941) at St. Maries, in Benewah County, occurring from March until October. On rare occasions it was noted during the winter.

In Latah County Johnston (1949) recorded it as common in the vicinity of Moscow June 1 to August 16, 1947. Verner (1953) reported it rare at Harvard, his one record being a single bird seen July 18, 1952. I personally found it common and well distributed as a breeding bird wherever there were open fields or pastures, noting it at Potlatch, Viola, Moscow, Troy, and Genesee. Being a hardy species, the first spring transients usually appeared by the middle of February (earliest date of arrival February 8, 1952, small flocks seen both at Moscow and at Genesee), and it was late October before there was any noticeable decrease in numbers. A flock of thirty birds seen at Moscow November 12, 1947, is my latest record for fall transients. During the winter it was of irregular occurrence and noted then in small numbers, my dates of occurrence then being as follows: Moscow, January 5 and 6, 1949, one bird; December 27, 1949, one bird; December 24, 1951, through January 6, 1952, a flock of five; December 20, 1953, a flock of twelve; December 31, 1954, a flock of eight; January 4, 1957, a flock of five; Potlatch, December 7, 1952, one bird; December 13, 1956, three birds; Troy, December 13, 1947, one bird; Genesee, December 30, 1947, three birds.

At Lewiston in Nez Perce County, the Killdeer is resident and common throughout the year, occurring, except during the breeding season, in small noisy flocks.

At Weippe, in Clearwater County, I found this species a common summer resident. Because of the altitude, three thousand feet, snow frequently covers much of the open country until late in March. However, as early as February 28 (1954), a flock of twelve birds appeared, and on March 28, 1952, and March 24, 1953, small flocks were present in many of the open fields and pastures.

Hand (1932) reported single birds at Fish Lake in Idaho County, September 19 and 25, 1929.

At Council, in Adams County, this species was considered by Newhouse (1960) to be a common summer resident, being noted in 1958 between the dates of March 3 and December 1.

A MELANCHOLY KILLDEER ON ITS NEST IN A GRAVEL PIT

Photo by Ray C. Erickson

Bureau of Sport Fisheries and Wildlife

At Shoup, in Lemhi County, I noted an occasional bird on June 4, 1949, feeding at the edge of the Salmon River.

In Fremont County it was reported by Rust (1917) as "common along the streams" in 1916.

Steel (1956) reported the Killdeer a common summer resident at Grays Lake (1949 through 1951). He gives as arrival dates April 5, 1950, and April 5, 1951.

In south-central Idaho it was reported by Merriam (1891) as common in 1890 on the Snake and Blackfoot Rivers, in the Lemhi and Birch Creek valleys, and also in the valley of the Big Wood River. He observed several on the Snake River near Shoshone Falls, October 9 to 11. In this same general area Levy (1950) found it "abundant" from June through August, 1949.

In the extreme southern part of the state, it has been noted in Minidoka County, a summer resident (1919 through 1921), with May 6 the earliest date for eggs (Davis, 1935); at Almo, in Cassia County, several birds seen June 19, 1949 (Burleigh); and at Riddle, Owyhee County, several birds noted daily, May 28 through June 3, 1934 (Davis, 1934).

Specimens, representing breeding populations, have been taken in various parts of the state as follows: Kootenai County (Hauser), Benewah County (St. Maries), Latah County (Potlatch, Moscow, Troy, Genesee), Nez Perce County (Lewiston), Clearwater County (Weippe, Headquarters), Lemhi County (Salmon), Blaine County (Headwaters of the Salmon River), Jefferson County (Terreton), Bonneville County (Gray), Caribou County (Soda Springs), Cassia County (Burley).

Habits. The Killdeer is one of the earliest birds to nest in the northern part of the state, a brood of young already out of the nest for several days being seen at Moscow April 24, 1949. At Grays Lake at an altitude of 6,386 feet, snow normally covers the ground until early April and not infrequently until the end of the month, so this species breeds much later, Steel (1956) giving April 22, 1951, as his earliest date for a nest that held two fresh eggs.

It is possible that at Lewiston (altitude 840 feet) two broods are occasionally reared, for on July 4, 1955, I found a brood of newly-hatched downy young on a gravel bar at the edge of the Snake River.

Both male and female incubate and are equally solicitous in caring for the young.

Pluvialis dominica (Müller): AMERICAN GOLDEN PLOVER

General Distribution. Breeds on the Arctic coasts of Siberia and Alaska south to central Mackenzie, northeastern Manitoba, and Baffin Island. Winters from Bolivia and southern Brazil south to central Argentina and in India, China, the Hawaiian Islands, and Australia.

Status in Idaho. Known only from the northern part of the state where it is a rare spring transient, and scarce but of more or less regular occurrence in the fall.

The Golden Plover was first reported for Idaho by Merrill (1897) who stated that "a large flight" was noted at Fort Sherman (Coeur d'Alene) from the fifteenth to the twentieth of September, 1896.

Sloanaker (1925) collected one bird from a flock of four at Lake Chactolet, Benewah County, October 1, 1923.

Levy (1959) saw a single bird, which he collected at Hauser, Kootenai County, May 14, 1950.

In Latah County, I noted it once at Moscow, a single bird September 15, 1952, and once at Potlatch, one bird May 20, 1954.

At Lewiston, in Nez Perce County, the Golden Plover was not observed during the spring, but was recorded at infrequent intervals in the fall, both on the Snake River and at the reservoir east of Lewiston Orchards. Dates of occurrence then are: 1952, two birds September 28 and two October 5; 1953, two birds September 12; 1955, one bird September 12; 1956, one bird September 13 and one bird September 22; 1957, one bird September 4, a flock of five October 9, a flock of seven October 12.

Habits. In migration, the Golden Plover is commonly found in open prairie country or in large fields and pastures, where the grass is short and it can find its favorite food of grasshoppers and other large insects. In Idaho, however, its behavior has invariably been quite different. At Lewiston it was seen on gravel bars in the Snake River or on exposed mud flats at the reservoir, and at no time at any distance from water. A possible explanation is that the recently cutover wheat fields, characteristic of this part of the state during the fall months, do not furnish the insect food necessary to attract this large plover.

At all times a wary bird, it discourages a close approach; but even at a distance it can be distinguished from the Black-bellied Plover by the absence of the white upper tail coverts.

Pluvialis dominica dominica (Müller)

On the basis of specimens taken, the nominate race is the one that commonly occurs in Idaho, eight out of nine critically examined being referable to *dominica*. These were as follows: Hauser, Kootenai County, female May 14, 1950 (Levy); Moscow, male September 15, 1952, Lewiston, female September 13, 1956, male September 22, 1956, female September 4, 1957, female October 9, 1957, two females October 12, 1957 (Burleigh).

Pluvialis dominica fulva (Gmelin)

The specimen taken by Sloanaker on Lake Chactolet October 1, 1923, has been identified as *fulva*, the race breeding in Siberia and extreme western Alaska. There are no other records for the state.

Squatarola squatarola (Linnaeus): BLACK-BELLIED PLOVER

General Distribution. Breeds in Russia and northern Siberia, and in northern Alaska, Mackenzie and Banks Island south to southwestern Alaska,

Southampton Island, and Baffin Island. Winters on the coasts of southern Europe and Asia south to southern Africa and Australia, and from British Columbia south to Chile, on the Gulf coast, and from New Jersey south through the West Indies to southern Brazil.

Status in Idaho. A rare spring transient, and scarce and of irregular occurrence in the fall.

There are but two records for the occurrence of the Black-bellied Plover in Idaho in the spring. Steel (1956) recorded it at Grays Lake May 13, 1951, and I saw a single bird on a mud flat in the Palouse River at Potlatch May 11, 1954.

Fall records are more numerous. In Kootenai County Merrill (1897) reported four taken on the "St. Joseph" marshes September 12, and Rust (1915) stated that it was a rare transient (1910 through 1914); he took one specimen on the "St. Joe" marshes.

Levy (1959) noted four birds on Lake Pend Oreille, near Sandpoint, Bonner County, September 28, 1950.

At St. Maries, Benewah County, it was considered by Hand (1941) a rare fall transient. He observed from one to three individuals there September 19 through October 4, 1936.

I have but one fall record for Latah County, a single bird being seen on the Palouse River, at Potlatch, October 5, 1957.

At Lewiston, in Nez Perce County, I noted the Black-bellied Plover at infrequent intervals from August until October, my extreme dates of occurrence being August 8 (1958) and October 13 (1957). Normally but one or two individuals would be seen throughout the fall months, the one exception being 1957 when this species was almost plentiful. It was not until September 18 that two birds were noted for the first time that fall at the reservoir, but it was recorded almost daily thereafter, both at the reservoir and on the Snake River until October 13. Usually one or two birds were seen, the largest number observed at any one time being a flock of five birds on October 1, and a flock of nine on October 9.

To verify the identification of this scarce shore bird in Idaho, nine specimens were taken at Lewiston as follows: males September 21, 1954, September 21, 1955, September 18 and October 2, 9, and 12, 1957; females September 18 and October 4 and 5, 1957.

Habits. It is generally agreed that this large plover is an extremely wary bird, and as it likewise never migrated in the large flocks so characteristic of many of the other shore birds it was never subject to the slaughter suffered by such species as the Golden Plover. Consequently it has always been a relatively common bird throughout its normal range. In migration it occurs commonly in the interior of the country, and it is probably a lack of suitable habitat that makes it a scarce transient in Idaho. The melting snow on the higher ridges causes flood conditions on the rivers that persist from March until into July, and it is not until the mud flats and gravel bars are exposed in early summer that conditions are favorable for such species as this.

[Arenaria interpres (Linnaeus): RUDDY TURNSTONE]

General Distribution. Breeds in northern Alaska, Ellesmere Island, Greenland, Iceland, and northern Scandinavia south to the delta of the Yukon River, Southampton Island, and Baffin Island. Winters from central California, the Gulf coast and South Carolina south to central Chile and southern Brazil and in the Hawaiian Islands, Africa, India, the East Indies and Australia.

Status in Idaho. Of accidental occurrence in the southern part of the state.

There is but one record for the occurrence of the Ruddy Turnstone in Idaho. A single bird, in partial breeding plumage, was seen by Lewis W. Oring July 19, 1961, on the Camas National Wildlife Refuge two miles west of Hamer, in Jefferson County (Oring, 1962).

Habits. The Turnstone is, on the Pacific coast, a bird of the ocean beaches, rarely occurring far inland. It is doubtful, therefore, if in Idaho its presence can be considered other than merely accidental.

Woodcock, Snipe, and Sandpipers: *Family Scolopacidae*

Capella gallinago delicata (Ord): COMMON SNIPE

General Distribution. Breeds from northern Alaska east across the continent to Newfoundland, south to northern California, northern Colorado, central Iowa, northern Ohio, and southern New York. Winters from southern British Columbia, northern Utah, central Nebraska, Kentucky, and Virginia south through Mexico, Central America and the West Indies to southern Brazil.

Status in Idaho. A common summer resident over much of the state, wintering in small numbers where conditions are suitable.

In Kootenai County it was reported by Merrill (1897) as abundant in the fall of 1896 at Fort Sherman (Coeur d'Alene), being most numerous from late August until the middle of September, and again from October 22 to November 5. Snyder (1900) noted its presence at Blue Lake and took specimens there in 1894. Rust (1915) considered it a rare fall transient; he saw one bird on Lake Coeur d'Alene September 13, 1913, and collected two on Chatcolet Lake in September, 1914. On April 30, 1955, I flushed six birds, spring transients, from the edge of a stream in an open field north of Hauser.

At St. Maries, in Benewah County, Hand (1914) reported it a common summer resident (1921 through 1941), occurring from April until October. I personally flushed sixteen birds from the edge of an open marsh at St. Maries April 1, 1953.

In Latah County, Johnston (1949) collected a breeding male on the Palouse River at Harvard June 23, 1947. It also nests in marshes bordering the Palouse River at Potlatch. I noted it there in the spring as early as March 26 (1952), and in late May and June I saw males giving their courtship flight high overhead. At Moscow it was a common transient both in the spring and in the fall, small flocks being frequently seen in late March and April, and again in October and early November. It wintered in small numbers, but was noted then only on Paradise Creek west of town, warm water from the sewage disposal plant keeping the stream from freezing over even during the coldest weather. Actual records for the winter months are as follows: 1949, one bird collected on Paradise Creek, January 5, several seen January 14; December 28, five birds flushed at the edge of the stream; 1950, the same five birds seen January 6, and at intervals throughout the month; 1951, one bird seen and collected, December 24; 1952, one bird seen January 4; 1957, one bird seen February 1.

At Lewiston, in Nez Perce County, I likewise found it a common transient, and noted it in small numbers during the winter months. Of interest was the presence of an occasional bird with flocks of sandpipers in late July and August feeding on exposed mud flats at the edge of the reservoir. One was seen as early as July 26, 1957, and July 27, 1958. Whether these were very early transients, or represented an undetected breeding population in the rather limited open marsh on the Snake River, can only be surmised.

In Idaho County Hand (1932) reported six birds on Fish Lake September 16, 1924, and an occasional bird "along the Lochsa" in April, and again in September and October.

At New Meadows in Adams County, I found it breeding commonly in the open marshy meadows at an altitude of 4,200 feet; "winnowing" males were seen as early as April 18, 1949, and April 22, 1954, and in late May and June in 1955, 1957, and 1958. Newhouse (1960) considered it a common summer resident at Council, occurring in 1958 between the dates of March 31 and October 1.

In Valley County, I noted this species in 1955 in open marsh at McCall on May 19 and at Donnelly May 20. Apparently it breeds commonly there.

Rust (1917) reported a single bird on Ice House Creek, in Fremont County, August 26, 1916, and several that same day at Camas Meadows.

At Ketchum, in Blaine County, Jewett (1912) flushed several birds along the Wood River in December, 1910, but it is very doubtful if this species actually winters at this altitude (6,000 feet).

Steel (1956) found it a very common summer resident at Grays Lake (1949 through 1951) and succeeded in locating a nest that on July 9, 1951, held four eggs. He gives as arrival dates April 11, 1950, and April 19, 1951.

In south-central Idaho Merriam (1891) reported one bird collected and others seen on the Salmon River, near Challis, September 20, 1890. Farther south in the state it was reported by Kenagy (1914) as rare in Minidoka County in 1909 but "abundant" in 1913; by Davis (1935) as resident (1919 through 1921) at Rupert; by Levy (1950) as a common breeding bird in the south-central counties during the summer of 1949. He collected a specimen at Twin Falls August 13. I personally noted "winnowing" males in 1954 in open marsh at Burley, Cassia County, April 23, and at Montpelier, Bear Lake County, April 27, and in 1955 at Hagerman, Gooding County, June 2, and at American Falls, Power County, June 9.

Habits. The courtship or "winnowing" flight of the Common Snipe is a familiar sight in the open marshes where this species nests, and this action on the part of the males has been used in determining breeding populations. However, the question has arisen as to whether "winnowing" ever occurred in migration, before the birds reached their breeding grounds, for this factor would have a definite bearing on the date when reliable censuses could be made. I was interested, therefore, in an experience I had at Moscow, that to my mind definitely answered this question. On April 24, 1957, I flushed eight birds in an open field that was temporarily flooded by heavy rains. They circled high overhead in a rather compact group for a minute or so, and then one bird separated from the others and gave its "winnowing" flight several times before dropping to the ground.

The hardiness of this species was dramatically shown by the occurrence of one or more birds on Paradise Creek, at Moscow, during the winter months. Although the winters varied they were normally characterized by deep snow and low temperatures, but the open water below the sewage disposal plant apparently offered a sufficient food supply for the successful survival of the snipe that were found there. On January 14, 1949, the snow had reached a depth of three feet, and the minimum temperature was five degrees below zero, but even under these conditions snipe flushed in their characteristic manner from the edge of the stream.

Numenius americanus Bechstein: Long-billed Curlew

General Distribution. Breeds from southern British Columbia, Alberta, Saskatchewan, and Manitoba south to Utah, New Mexico, and Texas. Winters from California, western Nevada, Texas, and Louisiana south to Oaxaca and Guatemala, and from South Carolina to Florida.

Status in Idaho. The Long-billed Curlew originally nested in the northern part of the state, but is now a rare transient there. In southern Idaho it is still a fairly common breeding bird, but local in its distribution.

The only evidence that this species once nested in northern Idaho is a statement by Bendire (Merriam, 1891) that it was found breeding near Fort Lapwai. Merrill (1897) stated that it was not uncommon on the "prairie" at Fort Sherman (Coeur d'Alene), arriving the latter part of March, but he made no comment as to whether it actually nested there.

I have a single record for Lewiston, seeing one bird at the reservoir east of Lewiston Orchards August 24, 1954.

Bent (1929) gives as early arrival dates Grangeville, March 14 and Neeley, March 15, and as a late date of departure Neeley, October 1.

Newhouse (1960) saw two in Indian Valley, Adams County, April 14, 1958.

In the southern part of the state it was first reported by Merriam (1891) who noted it in 1872 "on the Sage Plains from southern Idaho to the Henry Fork of the Snake River"; and in 1890 he saw three adults and young on the Blackfoot River in the middle of July.

Oberholser (1918) reported specimens taken at American Falls, Power County, May 27, 1911, and at Dickey, Custer County, June 8, 1912.

At Grays Lake Steel (1956) found it a common summer resident (1949 through 1951). He gives as arrival dates April 10, 1950, and April 6, 1951, and states that a nest was found May 9, 1951. While at Grays Lake June 8 to 17, 1949, I likewise found this species common. A young bird out of the nest at least several days was collected June 15, and an adult male June 16.

Elsewhere in southern Idaho it was noted by Davis (1935) at Rupert May 31, 1920; and by me at Homedale, Owyhee County, one pair June 23, 1949; at Terreton, Jefferson County, one bird April 29, 1954, and a flock of twelve April 30; at Malad City, Oneida County, one pair June 8, 1955; and at Montpelier, Bear Lake County, three birds April 13, 1958 (one, a male, collected).

Habits. The Long-billed Curlew is apparently a hardy bird, for it often appears in the spring on its breeding grounds while snow and low temperatures characterize the days. The three birds that I saw at Montpelier April 13, 1958, were feeding in an open marsh that was covered with six inches of frozen snow, and they seemed reasonably content in such surroundings. On the other hand, the departure in the fall is quite early, the majority of the birds leaving as soon as the young are fully grown. Late July sees the first southward movement, and by the latter part of August the breeding population is invariably gone.

At one time this species was an abundant bird over much of the continent, and doubtless it was common then in northern Idaho where there was suitable habitat. With the settlement of the northern counties, however, wheat fields gradually replaced the open grasslands, and as the grasslands disappeared, so probably did the curlew.

Numenius americanus americanus Bechstein

The nominate race is the breeding form in southern Idaho, specimens examined from Dickey, Grays Lake, Montpelier, Malad City, and American Falls being referable to *americanus*.

[Numenius americanus parvus Bishop]

Specimens are necessary before *parvus* can be accepted as occurring in the state, but on the basis of geographic probability the records for Coeur d'Alene, Lewiston, Lapwai, Grangeville and Indian Valley are referable to this northern race of the Long-billed Curlew.

Bartramia longicauda (Bechstein): UPLAND PLOVER

General Distribution. Breeds from southern Alaska, central Saskatchewan, southern Ontario and southern Quebec south to eastern Washington, southern Montana, central Colorado, northern Texas, southern Indiana, Tennessee, central Virginia, and Maryland. Winters from northern Argentina, Uruguay, and southern Brazil to southern Argentina.

Status in Idaho. An uncommon summer resident in the open prairie between Hauser and Rathdrum, in Kootenai County. Not noted elsewhere in the state.

Merrill (1897) recorded this species for the first time in Idaho. He stated that it nested "not uncommonly" on the prairie north of Fort Sherman (Coeur d'Alene), and that it "left for the south" about the twentieth of July.

Levy (1959) reported a small breeding colony at Hauser in 1950. He collected a female on May 14 that held a fully developed egg.

On June 17, 1950, May 15, 1952, and July 2, 1956, I searched the open prairie between Hauser and Rathdrum and on each occasion noted breeding pairs of these birds. Three pairs was the maximum number I recorded on any one day. A pair I observed July 2 apparently had young close by, judging from their excited actions.

Habits. Both in migration and on its breeding grounds the Upland Plover is a bird not easily overlooked. On the Rathdrum Prairie it commonly perched on the top of a fence post or telephone pole, and if disturbed its emphatic alarm notes at once revealed its presence.

In migration it frequently flies so high that it is barely visible, but even then its prolonged mellow whistle can be easily heard. It has never been recorded in Idaho south of its breeding range, so it would appear that it leaves the state by a route that takes it directly east to the open prairie country, and that it returns in the spring by the same pathway. In view of the long journey it makes each year to and from its winter home on the pampas of southern South America, it is surprising what a relatively short interval it spends on its breeding grounds. Although no arrival dates are available it apparently does not reach northern Idaho in the spring until early May, for on April 30, 1955, I was unsuccessful, despite a two-hour search, in finding a single bird. And I have been equally unsuccessful in recording this species at any time after the last of July.

Actitis macularia rava (Burleigh): SPOTTED SANDPIPER

General Distribution. Breeds from northwestern Alaska, Yukon and western Mackenzie south through British Columbia, Washington, Oregon, and Idaho. Winters in the West Indies and Central America south to Venezuela and Peru.

Status in Idaho. A common summer resident throughout the state.

In Kootenai County the Spotted Sandpiper was reported by Merrill (1897) as a common summer resident at Fort Sherman (Coeur d'Alene), and he succeeded in finding several nests; by Rust (1915) as a fairly common summer resident (1910 through 1914), he took a specimen at Coeur d'Alene on May 17, and found a nest there on June 27, 1914, that held four eggs; by Yocom (1946) as noted at the upper end of Lake Coeur d'Alene July 1 to 10, 1943, several birds being seen then. Bent (1929) gives May 1 as the earliest date it was observed at Rathdrum.

At Clark Fork, in Bonner County, it was found to be fairly plentiful during the summer of 1917 in the more open country along the Pend Oreille River (Burleigh, 1923). Bent (1929) gives September 19 as the latest date it was observed at Priest River.

Hand (1941) considered it a common summer resident at St. Maries in Benewah County, occurring from May until September (1921 through 1941). I noted one breeding pair at Clarkia, in Shoshone County, July 5, 1948.

In Latah County Johnston (1949) reported several birds seen on the Palouse River at Harvard June 11, 1947. Verner (1953) found it a common breeding bird at Harvard in 1951 and 1952. He noted a brood of four downy young July 5, 1951, and a similar brood at the same spot July 2, 1952. I found it common and well distributed during the summer months, noting it at Princeton, Potlatch, Viola, and Moscow. It usually appeared in the spring, the middle of May, and was rarely observed after the middle of September, my extreme dates of occurrence for Potlatch being May 2 (1954) and October 7 (1957), and for Moscow May 5 (1951) and September 10 (1952).

In Nez Perce County, it was reported by Bendire as breeding near Fort Lapwai (Merriam, 1891). I found it a common summer resident at Lewiston, where it usually was noted in early May, and was rarely seen after the middle of September. My earliest record in the spring is April 28, 1952, while in the fall it has been noted as late as November 4, 1953, a single bird at the reservoir east of Lewiston Orchards.

At Headquarters, in Clearwater County, a single bird, apparently a transient, was seen May 17, 1953, feeding at the edge of a stream in a clearing deep in the woods (Burleigh).

Hand (1932) considered it a common summer resident along the Lochsa and Selway rivers in Idaho County in 1924. He also noted it at Fish **Lake** in August and early September.

In Adams County I noted a breeding pair at New Meadows June 28, 1949, and Newhouse (1960) reported it at Council July 17 and August 7, 1958.

Rust (1917) found it common along the streams in Fremont County during the summer of 1916, and observed downy young July 16 at Woods Reservoir, on the west fork of Camas Creek.

In south-central Idaho Merriam (1891) reported it "tolerably common along Birch Creek and Lemhi River" in 1890. Levy (1950) found it a common summer resident in this part of the state during the summer of 1949.

Oring (1962) gives it this same status (1961) for the Camas Refuge and Mud Lake in Jefferson County.

At Grays Lake Steel (1956) considered it an uncommon summer resident (1949 through 1951). He gives as an arrival date May 22, 1951.

In extremely southern Idaho it was reported by Kenagy (1941) as "tolerably common" in 1910 in Minidoka County and "abundant" in 1913. Davis (1935) noted it during the summer months at Rupert (1919 through 1921), and gives as extreme dates of occurrence May 6 and September 4. His earliest date for fresh eggs was June 7. Bent (1929) gives as extreme dates of occurrence at Rupert May 3 and October 2.

At Burley, in Cassia County, I noted one breeding pair in a marshy field on the Snake River June 10, 1960.

Davis (1934) observed two birds at Riddle, in Owyhee County, May 28 through June 3, 1934.

Specimens identified as *rava* were taken at the following localities in the state: Boundary County, Bonners Ferry; Bonner County, Sandpoint and Clark Fork; Shoshone County, Clarkia; Clearwater County, Headquarters; Latah County, Potlatch and Moscow; Nez Perce County, Lewiston; Adams County, New Meadows; Washington County, Weiser; Owyhee County, Silver City; Ada County, Boise; Blaine County, Sun Valley; Custer County, Challis; Caribou County, Henry; Cassia County, Burley; Power County, American Falls; Oneida County, Juniper.

This northwestern race of the Spotted Sandpiper can be distinguished in adult plumage by the dark gray rather than grayish brown upperparts, and in the young of the year by the brownish gray rather than dark brown upperparts.

Habits. Unlike most of the other sandpipers this species is, in Idaho at least, never seen in flocks. When it appears in the spring single birds, then pairs, gradually occupy suitable habitat along the streams or ponds. Its disappearance in the fall is just as inconspicuous. Broods of young remain with their parents until fully grown, but by late summer young of the year can be found feeding alone.

The nest is a slight hollow in the ground, lined with grasses, weed stems and any similar material that is available in the vicinity, and is usually close to water. It is always well concealed. Both male and female incubate, and are equally concerned with the welfare of their young. But one brood is reared each year, and occasional pairs would appear to nest rather late in the spring, for young still unable to fly were seen at Lewiston, August 8, 1949.

Tringa solitaria Wilson: Solitary Sandpiper

General Distribution. Breeds from central Alaska east through northern Manitoba and northern Ontario to central Labrador, south to central British Columbia, southern Manitoba, and central Quebec. Winters from the coast of the Gulf of Mexico and Florida south to southern Argentina.

Status in Idaho. A common transient in the northern part of the state where there is suitable habitat, but apparently of rare occurrence in southern Idaho.

In Kootenai County Merrill (1897) records a single specimen taken at Fort Sherman (Coeur d'Alene) on August 26.

In Benewah County Hand (1941) reported it an uncommon transient at St. Maries (1921 through 1941), noting it in May, and again in August and September.

In Latah County one bird was observed by Johnston (1949) at Potlatch August 11, 1947. It was at Potlatch that I personally found this species most common as a transient both in the spring and in the fall. Shallow pools along the Palouse River provided suitable spots in which to feed and rest, and here one or more birds could be seen almost daily in late April and early May, and again in August and early September, my extreme dates being April 21 (1954) and May 12 (1955), and July 30 (1949) and September 12 (1954). At Moscow it was a regular transient both in the spring and in the fall, but was never numerous, an occasional bird being seen feeding at the edges of shallow pools in open marshy fields. My extreme dates of occurrence are April 23 (1953) and May 10 (1951), and August 12 (1950) and September 12 (1952).

At Lewiston high water in the spring both on the rivers and at the reservoir eliminated any suitable shorebird habitat, and no Solitary Sandpipers were observed then. As a fall transient, however, this species was fairly plentiful, although with one exception, a single bird on the Snake River August 13, 1950, it was noted only at the reservoir. My extreme dates of occurrence there are July 4 (1953) and September 4 (1955).

In Idaho County Hand (1932) considered it a "not common but regular fall migrant" at Fish Lake. He gives as average dates of occurrence July 31 and August 20, and as extreme dates July 23 (1927) and August 26 (1928). He also saw an occasional bird on the larger streams. I noted one bird at New Meadows, in Adams County, August 14, 1957.

In south-central Idaho Merriam (1891) reported "a few seen" in 1890 on the Lemhi River and on Birch Creek, and one on a beaver pond in the Salmon River Mountains. I saw one bird at Salmon April 30, 1954.

Oring (in 1962) states that in 1961 he found this species an uncommon fall transient on the Camas National Wildlife Refuge in Jefferson County, his extreme dates of occurrence being July 19 and August 29.

At Grays Lake Steel (1956) found it a rare transient (1949 through 1951). His one record is that of a single bird seen May 30, 1950.

In extreme southern Idaho it has been observed on but one occasion, a single bird at Rupert, in Minidoka County, April 9, 1920 (Davis, 1935).

Habits. As its name implies, the Solitary Sandpiper is one of the least gregarious of the shore birds, and rarely will more than one bird be seen at any one spot. At Potlatch, where in the late summer months the shallow pools along the Palouse River afford ideal habitat for this species, as many as eight individuals have been noted in the course of an afternoon in mid-

August, and it was not uncommon to see from four to six then. At no time, however, would more than two birds be found at any one pool, and even this was exceptional, my usual experience being the sight of one bird feeding at the water's edge ahead of me, and eventually another under similar circumstances.

Were conditions suitable in the spring it is probable that this species would be much more numerous in Idaho than it now is. With the melting of the snow on the higher ridges in May and early June the water in the streams consistently floods the areas where shore birds would normally feed, and as a result there is too often little inducement for the Solitary Sandpiper to linger even briefly in its journey to its northern breeding grounds.

It is apparently a hardy species, for not infrequently in late April and early May I have seen it at Potlatch when the day was characterized by a steady snowfall and a blustery cold wind.

Tringa solitaria solitaria Wilson

On the basis of specimens taken in Idaho the nominate race of the Solitary Sandpiper, heretofore unrecorded in the state, would appear to be a common transient. In a series of specimens taken and critically examined, 50 per cent were typical of *solitaria*. These were collected at Potlatch, between the dates of August 8 (1951) and September 8 (1950), at Moscow, between the dates of April 25 (1952) and May 9 (1951) and August 17 (1948) and September 12 (1952), and at Lewiston between the dates of July 28 (1958) and August 21 (1953). Seven additional specimens were intermediate in their characters, being closer to *solitaria* in size but approaching *cinnamomea* in the color of the upper parts.

Tringa solitaria cinnamomea (Brewster)

This western race of the Solitary Sandpiper does not occur as a breeding bird east of southern Mackenzie and northeastern Manitoba. It can be distinguished from *solitaria* by its larger size, lighter upper parts, and the presence of white mottling on the inner web of the outer primary. As with the nominate race, 50 per cent of the specimens collected in Idaho were found to be typical of *cinnamomea*, so this race is apparently equally common as a transient in the state, both in the spring and in the fall. These specimens were taken at Potlatch between the dates of April 25 (1955) and May 12 (1955), and July 30 (1949) and September 12 (1954), at Moscow between the dates of April 26 (1951) and May 7 (1951) and August 12 (1950) and September 12 (1952), at Lewiston between the dates of July 4 (1953) and August 13 (1950), at New Meadows August 14, 1957, and at Salmon April 30, 1954. Two additional specimens were intermediate in their characters, being closer to *cinnamomea* in respect to the white mottling of the outer primary, but approaching *solitaria* in size.

Catoptrophorus semipalmatus inornatus (Brewster): WILLET

General Distribution. Breeds from eastern Oregon, Idaho, Alberta, southern Saskatchewan and southern Manitoba south to northern California, central Utah, northern Colorado and eastern South Dakota. Winters from northern California to Chile, in South Carolina and Florida, on the Gulf coast and from Central America to northern Colombia.

Status in Idaho. A common but local summer resident in the southern part of the state.

Merriam (1891) reported taking a specimen on the Henrys Fork of the Snake River July 16, 1872. At Chilly, in Custer County, I noted one breeding pair in an open marsh June 29, 1950. At Mud Lake, north of Terreton, in Jefferson County, I saw scattered pairs April 29, 1954, so this species probably nests fairly commonly here. Oring (1962) found it in 1961 an "abundant summer resident until August 22" at the Camas National Wildlife Refuge in Jefferson County.

At Grays Lake Steel (1956) considered it (1949 through 1951) a common summer resident, giving as arrival dates April 19, 1950, and April 19, 1951. A nest found May 26, 1951, held four eggs. I was at Grays Lake April 28, 1954, and noted willets at frequent intervals during the morning, usually in pairs.

I saw two pairs at Soda Springs in Caribou County, April 26, 1954. While at Montpelier, in Bear Lake County, I noted several May 26, 1952, and two April 13, 1958. The latter date is the earliest this species has been recorded in Idaho in the spring; the open marsh that day was still covered with six inches of frozen snow.

In Minidoka County Davis (1935) reported it a summer resident at Rupert, with extreme dates of occurrence (1919 through 1921) May 1 and September 18. He gives as the earliest date for fresh eggs May 21. Bent (1929) cites October 20 as a late fall date for Rupert. Levy (1950) reported "large flocks" at the Wilson Lake Reservoir in Jerome County in August, 1949, and stated that it is a common summer resident in south-central Idaho.

In Owyhee County Davis (1935) reported seeing four pairs at Riddle May 28 through June 3, 1934.

Specimens identified as *inornatus* were taken by Pierce Brodkorb (in litt.) as follows: Seven at Malad City, Oneida County, April 9, 10, and 13, 1930; eleven at Montpelier, Bear Lake County, May 10-19, 1930; a male at Roberts, Jefferson County, May 13, 1931, and a female at Mud Lake, Jefferson County, May 16, 1931.

Other specimens of this western race, collected by me, are as follows: a male at Gray June 9, 1949, and females at Chilly June 29, 1950, Soda Springs April 26, 1954, and Montpelier April 13, 1958. This western race can be distinguished from *semipalmatus* by its larger size, longer, slenderer bill, and paler upperparts.

Kodachrome by Donald J. Obee, Boise, Idaho

LEWIS'S WOODPECKER

PLATE III

Habits. To one familiar with the Willet as a bird of the coastal marshes it comes as rather a surprise to find this large conspicuous shore bird common in the open marshes in the interior of the country. On its breeding grounds it is a noisy bird, greeting the intruder with its loud ringing notes that are uttered as long as one is in sight. It is, therefore, not easily overlooked, and this is especially true because of its large size and its habit of commonly alighting on the top of a fence post, or even a thick bush, when alarmed.

The nest is a hollow in the ground, lined with grasses and usually well concealed and difficult to find. The incubating bird will almost invariably leave the eggs when the marsh is entered by an intruder, and its excited outcry gives no indication whatsoever of the spot where the nest might be. In fact its actions are so misleading that the result is often a fruitless search in the wrong spot.

After the young are fully grown the southward movement is soon under way, and by early September the Willets that have reared their young in Idaho are on the coastal beaches where they will remain until the following spring.

Totanus melanoleucus (Gmelin): GREATER YELLOWLEGS

General Distribution. Breeds from southern Alaska east through central Alberta to Labrador, south to southeastern Quebec and Newfoundland. Winters from British Columbia, southern Nevada, central New Mexico, the Gulf coast and South Carolina south through Mexico, Central America and the West Indies to southern South America.

Status in Idaho. A fairly common transient both in the spring and in the fall, although at times less numerous in the spring when, as frequently happens, high water on the streams eliminates a suitable shorebird habitat.

In Kootenai County Merrill (1897) reported this species a common fall transient at Fort Sherman (Coeur d'Alene). He observed it once in the spring, on June 20. I noted it on two occasions at Hauser, a single bird April 30, 1955, and a flock of four May 6, 1957.

Hand (1941) apparently never recorded it at St. Maries in Benewah County, but he stated that a specimen was taken there by Victor Jones, from a flock of twenty-five, on August 4, 1938.

I found it a fairly common transient in Latah County both in the spring and in the fall, but less numerous in the spring when its distribution was limited to the few pools that persisted until late May in open marshy fields. Usually only one or two birds would be seen at any one spot, although it was not uncommon for small flocks comprising from four to eight individuals to appear. The maximum number noted at one time was a flock of twelve, observed at Moscow April 20, 1952. At Moscow my extreme dates of occurrence in the spring are April 20 (1952) and May 14 (1953), while in the fall I recorded it but once, a flock of three birds July 7, 1950. At Potlatch it was extremely scarce in the spring, high water in the Palouse

River in April and most of May flooding bottomlands that, when the water receded in late June, became ideal shorebird habitat. I have but three spring records, seeing one bird April 21, 1949, a flock of six April 25, 1955, and two April 23, 1957. In the fall it was frequently noted along the Palouse River from the latter part of July until early October, my extreme dates of occurrence being July 19 (1951) and October 18 (1953). At Genesee it was noted on a few occasions feeding at the edges of pools in open fields, a single bird July 1, 1952, a flock of five April 16, 1954, and two birds April 21, 1955.

At Lewiston, in Nez Perce County, I found this species a fairly plentiful transient both in the spring and in the fall. In the spring it was usually the middle of April before the first small flock appeared, an unusually early record being that of three birds seen on Hatwai Creek February 24, 1958. Normally no Greater Yellowlegs were noted after the middle of May (my latest date in May, the sixteenth, in 1953), or in the fall migration before early July, so two records for late June at the reservoir east of Lewiston Orchards, June 26, 1955, and June 19, 1958, doubtless represented nonbreeding birds. Exposed gravel bars in the Snake River were favorite feeding spots during the fall months, and here these Yellowlegs were frequently noted until late October or early November. A rather late record for the fall migration is that of a single bird seen on a gravel bar December 1, 1954.

In Idaho County Hand (1932) reported two birds at Fish Lake July 30, 1928.

In the southern part of the state it was noted at Rupert, in Minidoka County, September 4, 1919, April 11 through April 17, 1920, and September 4, 1920 (Davis, 1935), and was considered by Levy (1950) as fairly common, June through August, 1949, in this same general area. Oring (1962) states that it was a common transient June 18 to August 22, 1961, on the Camas National Wildlife Refuge in Jefferson County. Steel (1956) found it an uncommon transient at Grays Lake (1949 through 1951). He gives as arrival dates April 20, 1950, and April 17, 1951. I saw one bird at Grays Lake June 16, 1949, apparently another nonbreeding individual that was lingering south of its normal range at this time of the year.

Bent (1927) gives as early arrival dates Meridian, April 14, and Rupert, April 20, and as a late departure date Meridian, November 12.

Specimens were collected to determine whether there was any geographic variation in birds occurring in western North America, but all were found undistinguishable from specimens taken in the eastern United States. These were as follows: Moscow, males April 20, 1952, and April 23, 1953; Potlatch, males April 21, 1949, April 23, 1957, July 19, 1951, and August 1, October 13 and October 18, 1953, and a female October 4, 1953; Lewiston, males October 5 and October 27, 1952, and April 16, 1954, and females September 24, 1949, September 28 and October 4, 1951, October 1, 1952, July 5 and November 1, 1953, November 24, 1954 (two), and February 24, 1958 (two).

Habits. The Greater Yellowlegs is a wary bird and one easily alarmed when danger, real or fancied, threatens. As a result its loud ringing cries immediately reveal its presence if its haunts are invaded, and this can prove rather disconcerting if one wishes to remain inconspicuous. On more than one occasion other shore birds feeding with or near a flock of Yellowlegs have responded to their alarm notes and taken flight before I had even satisfactorily identified them. As might be suspected, duck hunters, who frequently have this same experience, have little liking for a bird that adds to their difficulties in getting their bag limit.

Totanus flavipes (Gmelin): LESSER YELLOWLEGS

General Distribution. Breeds from north-central Alaska, east through Mackenzie, Manitoba and northern Ontario to northern Quebec, south to central British Columbia, Alberta, central Saskatchewan and central Quebec. Winters on the Gulf coast, on the Atlantic coast north to South Carolina, and south through Central America and the West Indies to Chile and Argentina.

Status in Idaho. A rather scarce spring transient in the northern part of the state, but fairly common there in the fall, from the latter part of July until the middle of September. Unrecorded in southern Idaho in the spring but of common occurrence there in the fall.

At St. Maries, in Benewah County, Hand (1941) found this species a rare transient, citing as his one record several birds noted between April 19 and May 11, 1935.

In Latah County it was only at Potlatch, on the mud flats and at the edges of the scattered pools along the Palouse River, that this Yellowlegs was observed in any numbers. It was rarely noted in the spring, my few records being of single birds seen May 5 and 8, 1954, and April 25, 1955. In the fall the first individuals appeared the latter part of July, and were of frequent occurrence then until the middle of September. Usually one or two birds would be seen feeding with other shorebirds, although on occasion small flocks were noted, the largest recorded being one of twelve July 31, 1953, and another of ten August 18, 1957. My extreme dates of occurrence for the fall migration here are July 28 (1951) and October 3 (1953).

At Moscow there was little suitable habitat for a species such as this, and consequently it was only infrequently seen. My few records are of single birds observed September 10, 1952, May 7, 1953, May 3, 1954, and a flock of three April 29, 1955.

At Lewiston, in Nez Perce County, it was noted but once in the spring, a single bird being seen at the reservoir east of Lewiston Orchards on the unusually late date of June 4, 1954. In the fall, however, it was fairly common and was observed at frequent intervals from late July until the middle of September, both on exposed gravel bars in the Snake River and at the reservoir. My extreme dates of occurrence are July 17 (1956) and September 22 (1956).

In the southern part of the state it was noted at Rupert in Minidoka County from September 1 to September 4, 1919, and on August 25, 1920 (Davis, 1935), and was found to be an uncommon and early fall transient in this same general area in 1949 (Levy, 1950). Oring (1962) reported it a common fall transient in 1961 on the Camas National Wildlife Refuge in Jefferson County, being observed there from July 2 through August 29; Fichter (in litt.) reports it common in the fall on mud flats at the American Falls Reservoir, Bingham County.

Specimens verifying the identification of this species were taken as follows: Lewiston, males August 2, 1949, September 16, 1951, August 28, 1953, September 21, 1954, and July 29, 1956, and females July 24, 1953, June 4, 1954, and July 19, 1955; Moscow, males September 10, 1952, May 7, 1953, May 5, 1954, and April 29, 1955; Potlatch, males July 28, 1951, July 31, 1953, and August 15, 1954, and a female October 3, 1953.

Habits. In both appearance and actions this species is a smaller edition of the Greater Yellowlegs, and size being often rather deceptive in the field, it is probable that the Lesser Yellowlegs has been largely overlooked in past years. This could account for the few published records for a species that has been found to be a fairly common transient in the northern part of the state, and possibly is equally common in southern Idaho. In the spring it migrates to a large extent up the Mississippi Valley, so it will always occur in small numbers in Idaho at this season of the year.

Erolia melanotos (Vieillot): PECTORAL SANDPIPER

General Distribution. Breeds in eastern Siberia, and from northern Alaska east through northern Yukon and northern Mackenzie to Southampton Island, south to central Mackenzie, Keewatin, and the south coast of Hudson Bay. Winters from Peru, southern Bolivia, northern Argentina, and Uruguay south to Chile and Patagonia.

Status in Idaho. A fairly common fall transient in the northern part of the state, and a scarce fall transient in southern Idaho. There are no spring records.

In Kootenai County Merrill (1897) reported this species to be common in 1896 "from the last of August until early in October." He stated that it was abundant on September 12, seeing flocks "of considerable size." I saw a single bird at Hauser July 16, 1957, feeding at the edge of a pool in an open field.

Hand (1941) reported it fairly common at St. Maries, in Benewah County, September 17 to 30, 1934. He observed a single bird here September 26, 1936.

Levy (1959) saw a single bird at Copeland, Boundary County, October 29, 1951, "apparently the latest fall record for the state."

It was only at Potlatch that I recorded the Pectoral Sandpiper in Latah County, but here it was fairly plentiful on the Palouse River from the latter part of August until early October. Usually one or two birds would be found feeding with other shorebirds on exposed mud flats in the river, the largest number noted at one time being a flock of twenty on September 14, 1955, and a similar sized flock on September 30, 1956. My extreme dates of occurrence are August 15 (1956) and October 13 (1953).

At Lewiston, in Nez Perce County, I found this species also fairly plentiful in the fall, noting it both on exposed gravel bars in the Snake River and at the reservoir east of Lewiston Orchards from the latter part of July until the middle of October. As at Potlatch one or two birds were usually seen feeding with other shorebirds, the largest number noted at one time being a flock of approximately forty at the reservoir September 14, 1955.

In southern Idaho Oring (1962) reported this species as an uncommon fall transient in 1961 on the Camas National Wildlife Refuge in Jefferson County, being observed from July 20 through August 14. Bent (1927) gives as a late date of departure in the fall Deer Flat, November 1.

Specimens verifying the identification of this species were taken as follows: Potlatch, males August 26, 1951, August 23 and October 13, 1953, and September 24, 1956; females September 1 and September 8, 1955; Lewiston, males September 28, September 30, and October 1, 1953, August 28, 1954, September 16 and September 28, 1955; females, August 19 and September 17, 1949, August 16, August 24, September 16, September 24 and October 3, 1953, August 28, 1954, and October 6, 1957; Hauser, male July 16, 1957.

Habits. In the eastern United States the Pectoral Sandpiper is a common transient both in the spring and in the fall, and it is familiarly known as a Grass Snipe because of its actions and its seeming preference for marshy meadows. In Idaho, however, this name would not be very appropriate, for here it associates with other shorebirds on the exposed mud flats and gravel bars. While its actions are somewhat deliberate, it is rarely observed to be motionless. It is unsuspicious on most occasions, and can be approached without much difficulty and readily identified; so it is rather surprising that there are so few published records for the state.

Erolia fuscicollis (Vieillot): WHITE-RUMPED SANDPIPER

General Distribution. Breeds from northern Alaska, northern Yukon, and northern Baffin Island south to Mackenzie, the coast of Hudson Bay and Southampton Island. Winters in southern South America from Paraguay and southern Brazil to Tierra del Fuego and the Falkland Islands.

Status in Idaho. Apparently of accidental occurrence in the state. There is but a single record for the occurrence of this species in Idaho. Levy (1959) reports collecting a female at Hauser, Kootenai County, May 26, 1950. This specimen is now in the Charles E. Conner Museum on the campus of the Washington State University, Pullman, Washington.

Habits. In the spring the White-rumped Sandpiper migrates through the interior of the country, but in the fall it is scarce there, the southward movement taking these little shorebirds to the Atlantic coast and then apparently over the ocean to South America. Under these circumstances this species will never be other than of accidental occurrence in Idaho. It is one of the least suspicious of the sandpipers, permitting a close approach without showing much alarm.

Erolia bairdii (Coues): BAIRD'S SANDPIPER

General Distribution. Breeds in Siberia, and from the Arctic coast of Alaska, northern Yukon, Ellesmere Island and Greenland south to northern Mackenzie and southern Baffin Island. Winters in northern Ecuador and Chile, and from southern Bolivia south through western Argentina to Santa Cruz.

Status in Idaho. A scarce spring transient, and a fairly common but local fall transient over much of the state.

Although apparently largely overlooked by ornithologists who in past years have kept more or less detailed records of the bird life of Idaho, the Baird's Sandpiper would nevertheless appear to be fairly plentiful and of regular occurrence in the state. Such at least is my impression regarding northern Idaho.

In the spring it was extremely scarce, and over an interval of eleven years I recorded it on but three occasions, a single bird at Moscow May 7, 1953, a flock of three at Potlatch May 4, 1954, and one bird at Hauser May 6, 1957.

In the fall it was noted at frequent intervals, both at Potlatch and at Lewiston, from the latter part of July until the middle of September, but it was most numerous in August and early September. Usually from one to three birds would be found feeding with other shorebirds, the maximum number noted at one time being a flock of eleven at the reservoir east of Lewiston Orchards September 1, 1957, and a flock of eighteen at the reservoir July 31, 1958. My extreme dates of occurrence at Potlatch are July 21 (1951) and September 28 (1956), and at Lewiston July 14 (1956) and October 9 (1957).

Specimens verifying the status of this species as a fairly common transient in northern Idaho were taken as follows: Potlatch, males July 21 and 28 and August 8, 24, and 29, 1951, May 4 and September 15, 1954, September 28, 1956, and September 1, 1957; females August 8, 1951, August 2 and 6, 1953, August 30 and September 10 and 14, 1955, and August 18, 1956; Lewiston, males July 19 and 28 and September 4, 12, 24, and 28, 1953, August 8 and 13, and September 4 and 10, 1954, August 2, 1955, August 1, 1956, October 4, 1957, and July 3, 1958; females August 19 and September 1 and 16, 1953, July 28 and August 16, 21, and 31, 1954, September 24, 1955, July 14 and September 11, 1956, July 26, September 4 and October 9, 1957, and August 12, 1958; Moscow, male May 7, 1953; Hauser, male May 6, 1957.

Brodkorb (in litt.) collected seven specimens at Fish Creek Reservoir, Blaine County, August 15, 1929, and eight at Mackay Dam, Custer County, August 30, 1931.

Oring (1962) reported it an "abundant transient" on the Camas National Wildlife Refuge, in Jefferson County, August 10 through August 29, 1961. He collected one specimen, an immature male, on August 20.

Habits. The Baird's Sandpiper is considered a difficult bird to identify, since it so closely resembles the other small sandpipers and has no distinguishing characteristic by which it can be readily recognized. Even so, it is rather surprising that it has been so completely overlooked in past years.

At Moscow it was observed on but one occasion, but this was because of lack of suitable habitat. The one bird seen was feeding with a flock of Least Sandpipers at the edge of a pool in an open, partially flooded field. It was in a similar situation that the one bird was noted at Hauser, in Kootenai County. At Lewiston it was found both on exposed gravel bars in the Snake River and on mud flats at the edge of the reservoir east of Lewiston Orchards.

Erolia minutilla (Vieillot): LEAST SANDPIPER

General Distribution. Breeds from central Alaska east through northern Mackenzie to northern Labrador, south to northeastern Manitoba, eastern Quebec, Nova Scotia, and Newfoundland. Winters from Oregon, central New Mexico, the Gulf coast, and North Carolina south through Mexico and Central America to Peru and Brazil.

Status in Idaho. A fairly common transient, both in the spring and in the fall, over most of the state.

In Kootenai County Merrill (1897) reported three specimens taken August 15 at Fort Sherman (Coeur d'Alene). I noted a small flock of four birds at Hauser May 6, 1953, and another flock of six May 6, 1957.

In Latah County I found this species a fairly common transient. In the spring small flocks appeared in late April and early May, while in the fall similar flocks were present from the latter part of July until the end of September. Usually two or three birds would be seen feeding with other shorebirds, the maximum number noted at any one time being a flock of sixteen at Moscow May 7, 1953, and one of twenty at Potlatch May 4, 1954. My extreme dates of occurrence at Potlatch are May 2 (1954) and May 11 (1954), and July 19 (1951) and October 3 (1953); and at Moscow April 24 (1953) and May 15 (1953), and August 10 (1950) and September 17 (1950). At Genesee a single bird was seen May 13, 1949.

At Lewiston, in Nez Perce County, the Least Sandpiper was equally plentiful in the spring and in the fall, single birds or small flocks being frequently seen both on gravel bars in the Snake River and at the reservoir. My extreme dates of occurrence are April 28 (1953) and May 12 (1953) and July 4 (1953) and October 4 (1957).

In Idaho County Hand (1932) noted one bird at Fish Lake August 11 and 16, 1926.

In southern Idaho this species was seen at Rupert, in Minidoka County, July 7 to September 4, 1919, and on August 1, 1920 (Davis, 1935). Levy

(1950) considered it an uncommon fall transient in south-central Idaho in 1949. Oring (1962) found it a common fall transient in 1961 on the Camas National Wildlife Refuge in Jefferson County, noting it between the dates of July 31 and August 22.

Specimens verifying the identification of this species were taken as follows: Potlatch, males July 19, 1951, and May 2, 1954, and a female October 3, 1953; Moscow, males April 24 and May 10, 1953, and females August 10 and September 17, 1950; Genesee, a female May 13, 1949. Lewiston, males August 24, 1949, April 28, July 8, and September 16, 1953, and July 7 and October 4, 1957, and females August 13, 1953, September 13, 1954, July 4, 1955, and July 8, 1956.

Habits. Unlike other of the shorebirds, the Least Sandpiper does not vary its migration route at different times of the year, being equally plentiful both in the spring and in the fall on the Atlantic coast, in the interior of the country, and on the Pacific coast. The published records of its occurrence in Idaho, therefore, point out the scarcity of suitable habitat in the state, especially in the spring. Its preference is for wet meadows, and here it feeds in the short grass, and at the edges of pools and sloughs. Where such are lacking it will accept open beaches, and it showed little reluctance in feeding on gravel bars in the Snake River and on mud flats both on the Palouse River at Potlatch, and at the reservoir east of Lewiston Orchards.

Erolia alpina pacifica (Coues): DUNLIN

General Distribution. Breeds from northern Alaska, northern Mackenzie, and Somerset Island south along the west coast of Alaska and Mackenzie to Southampton Island and on Hudson Bay. Winters on the Pacific coast from British Columbia to Baja California, on the Gulf coast, and on the Atlantic coast from Massachusetts to Florida.

Status in Idaho. Apparently largely of accidental occurrence in the state.

There are but a few records for the occurrence of the Dunlin in Idaho. It was first noted on April 30, 1954, when I collected a male in full breeding plumage at Salmon, in Lemhi County, as it fed with other shorebirds in a partially flooded field.

On April 4, 1955, two birds were found at the reservoir east of Lewiston Orchards and one of them, a male, was collected.

Downing and Fichter (1968) report five Dunlins seen and one collected "on the northwest shore of American Falls Reservoir four miles east of Aberdeen, Bingham County, Idaho" April 30 and May 1, 1966, and a single bird April 21, 1967, twelve miles northeast of Aberdeen, "in a backwater of the Snake River."

Habits. The Dunlin is essentially a bird of the seacoast, occurring only in small numbers in the interior of the country. It is abundant in migration both on the Atlantic coast and on the Pacific coast, so it is not surprising that it is frequently recorded east or west of its accustomed route. It is doubtful, however, if it will ever be recorded in Idaho other than as a rare straggler.

Limnodromus griseus (Gmelin): SHORT-BILLED DOWITCHER

General Distribution. Breeds in the coastal region of southern Alaska, southern Mackenzie, northern Alberta, northern Saskatchewan, and northern Manitoba. Winters from central California, southern New Mexico, the Gulf coast and South Carolina south through Central America and the West Indies to Peru and central Brazil.

Status in Idaho. An uncommon and irregular transient in the northern part of the state.

Because of the similarity between this species and the Long-billed Dowitcher, *Limnodromus scolopaceus,* specimens are necessary for satisfactory identification. It is probable, therefore, that it is more plentiful as a transient in Idaho than the relatively few records would indicate, and further collecting is desirable to determine this point. On the basis of actual specimens I recorded it once at Potlatch in the fall, while at Lewiston I noted it once in the spring and on six occasions in the fall. Two races were represented.

Habits. Unlike the other shorebirds this dowitcher apparently has no liking for the exposed gravel bars on the Snake River, and on just one occasion was found there, two birds, both of which were collected September 10, 1954. Otherwise one or two birds would be found feeding with other shorebirds on the extensive mud flats in the Palouse River, or at the Reservoir. They were normally unsuspicious and easily approached, but even under the most favorable conditions their identity as to species could only be surmised.

Limnodromus griseus hendersoni Rowan

Males were taken at Lewiston August 19, 1953, and at Potlatch September 26, 1956, and a female at Lewiston September 10, 1954.

Limnodromus griseus caurinus Pitelka

Males were taken at Lewiston May 6 and August 24, 1954, and July 13, 1956, and females September 24, 1953, September 10, 1954, and July 28, 1956.

Limnodromus scolopaceus (Say): LONG-BILLED DOWITCHER

General Distribution. Breeds in Siberia, in the coastal region of Alaska, and in Mackenzie. Winters from central California, southern New Mexico, and the Gulf coast south through Mexico to Guatemala.

Status in Idaho. A fairly common spring transient in northern Idaho, and a common but local fall transient throughout the state.

In Kootenai County Merrill (1897) reported five specimens taken at Fort Sherman (Coeur d'Alene) on September 12; he did not comment on the status of this species. At Hauser I noted a flock of seven birds April 30, 1955, and a smaller flock of five May 6, 1957.

At St. Maries, in Benewah County, Hand (1941) observed flocks of six to fifteen birds between September 7 and October 10, 1936.

In Latah County I found this species a common fall transient at Potlatch, seeing single birds or small flocks at frequent intervals on the exposed mud flats in the Palouse River from the latter part of July until early October. My extreme dates of occurrence then are July 19 (1951) and October 4 (1953). Because of lack of suitable habitat it was not noted in the spring. For this same reason it was largely of accidental occurrence at Moscow, my one record being that of a single bird seen May 18, 1953, feeding at the edge of a pool in an open marshy field.

At Lewiston, in Nez Perce County, it was a common transient both in the spring and in the fall, being seen both on the Snake River and at the reservoir. My extreme dates of occurrence are May 6 (1954) and May 23 (1955) and July 8 (1956) and October 6 (1953).

In south-central Idaho Levy (1950) reported the Dowitcher a fairly common fall transient in 1949, flocks containing as many as twenty-five individuals being seen. Specimens identified as *scolopaceus* were taken at Wilson Lake July 22 and at Twin Falls August 13.

Steel (1956) considered it an uncommon transient at Grays Lake (1949 through 1951). He cites no actual dates of occurrence.

On the Camas National Wildlife Refuge, in Jefferson County, Oring (1962) found it a common fall transient in 1961, being seen between the dates of July 4 and August 22. Two specimens identified as *scolopaceus* were taken July 6.

In order to verify the identification of the Dowitchers occurring as transients in the northern part of the state forty-seven specimens were taken between July 19, 1951, and July 27, 1958. Of this number thirty-eight were found to represent *scolopaceus* and were collected as follows: Potlatch, males July 28 and August 18, 1951, and September 24, 1956, and females July 19, 1951, October 3, 1953 (two), and August 12 and September 24, 1956 (two) Lewiston, males September 16, 1951, May 21; (two), July 13, and August 16, 1953, May 16 and July 28, 1954, August 2, 1955, July 24, August 4, and August 8, 1956, July 21, July 26 (two), and October 2, 1957, and July 27, 1958 (two), females July 12, July 16, July 19, and August 16, 1953, July 21, 1954, May 17, and August 2, 1955, July 8, July 19, and July 28, 1956, and September 12, 1957; Hauser, a female April 30, 1955, and a male and female May 6, 1957.

Habits. In migration dowitchers seem to prefer open beaches and mud flats, so in Idaho, especially in the spring, it is extremely local in its distribution. Were conditions more suitable it would probably be much more numerous. Birds seen in the spring at Moscow, and at Hauser, were feeding at the edges of pools in open fields, and such spots, the result of melting snow, are rather limited in number and frequently of short duration. On the coast it occurs in large flocks, but in Idaho, single birds or small flocks comprising three to five individuals are normally seen feeding with other shorebirds. The maximum number noted at any one time was a flock of fourteen at the reservoir east of Lewiston Orchards July 21, 1954, and a flock of sixteen on the Palouse River at Potlatch September 14, 1955.

Micropalama himantopus (Bonaparte): STILT SANDPIPER

General Distribution. Breeds in northern Alaska east through northern Mackenzie, southeastern Keewatin, northeastern Manitoba, and northern Ontario. Winters in South America from Bolivia south to Uruguay and central Argentina.

Status in Idaho. A rather scarce fall transient in the northern part of the state. There are two records for southern Idaho.

The Stilt Sandpiper was first recorded in northern Idaho by Levy (1959) who collected a female at Rose Lake, Kootenai County, August 29, 1949.

At Potlatch, Latah County, I recorded it on two occasions in 1955, taking a female August 30, and another female September 8.

For Lewiston, Nez Perce County, I have three records. A male was collected September 10, 1954, a single bird seen September 11, 1955, and a female taken August 21, 1957.

In southern Idaho Davis (1935) noted it at Rupert, Minidoka County, May 13, 1919, and Oring (1962) saw a single bird "in breeding plumage" on the Camas National Wildlfe Refuge, in Jefferson County, August 13, 1961.

Habits. The Stilt Sandpiper is one of the less common of the shorebirds, and apparently only in the Mississippi Valley is it of more than casual occurrence in migration. The relatively few records for Idaho invariably involved single birds, and it is doubtful if its status in this respect will ever change.

Both at Potlatch and at Lewiston it was found on exposed mud flats with other shorebirds, but it always fed alone in the shallow water a short distance from the shore where it probed for food in the wet mud. Its movements then were rather deliberate, and in noticeable contrast to the restless actions of the other sandpipers in its vicinity.

Ereunetes pusillus (Linnaeus): SEMIPALMATED SANDPIPER

General Distribution. Breeds from northern Alaska, northern Mackenzie, Baffin Island, and northern Labrador south to the mouth of the Yukon in Alaska, central Mackenzie, the south coast of Hudson Bay and northern Quebec. Winters from the Gulf coast and South Carolina south through eastern Mexico and the West Indies to southern Brazil.

Status in Idaho. A rare spring transient, and a fairly common fall transient in the northern part of the state. There is one sight record for southern Idaho.

The Semipalmated Sandpiper was first recorded for the state by Earl J. Larrison who collected a male at Rose Lake, in Kootenai County, August 24, 1949 (Levy, 1959). The following year Levy (1959) collected two females at Hauser, Kootenai County, May 26, 1950, and saw a single bird at Sandpoint, Bonner County, September 28, 1950.

Both in Latah and in Nez Perce counties I found this species a fairly common transient in the fall, seeing one or two birds, rarely small flocks, frequently from the latter part of July until early September.

Because of lack of suitable habitat at Moscow it was rarely observed there, my only records being those of a small flock of six birds seen from August 9 through August 11, 1950, and a single bird August 13, 1952.

My extreme dates of occurrence for Potlatch are July 28 (1951) and August 18 (1957), and for Lewiston July 27 (1958) and September 10 (1954).

Only once was this little sandpiper noted in the spring, a single bird at Moscow May 29, 1953.

Oring (1962) reports one bird seen on the Camas National Wildlife Refuge, in Jefferson County, July 31, 1961.

Because of the close similarity between this species and the Western Sandpiper it was considered desirable to collect a sufficient number of specimens to verify its status as a transient in Idaho. In all, twenty-nine specimens were taken as follows: Potlatch, males July 28 and August 13, 1951, August 1 and August 2, 1953, August 15, 1956, August 18, 1957, and August 2, 1958; females August 13, 1951, August 2, 1953, August 15 and 17, 1956, and August 1 and 4, 1957; Moscow, males August 9 and 10, 1950, August 13, 1952, and May 29, 1953; females August 10 and 11, 1950; Lewiston, males August 16 and 24, 1957, and August 4, 1958; females September 10, 1954, August 4 and August 31, and September 6, 1956, August 21, 1957, and July 27 and 31, 1958.

Habits. There are very few records for the occurrence of the Semipalmated Sandpiper anywhere in the western United States, even on the coast, but in view of its regular occurrence in northern Idaho in the fall it is quite possible that it has been largely overlooked in past years. In immature and winter plumage it resembles very closely the Western Sandpiper, so fall transients are often difficult to identify satisfactorily in the field. Its rarity in the spring, however, would suggest that in migration it is largely confined then to the eastern half of the country. On the Atlantic coast it is abundant, large flocks being commonly observed, but in northern Idaho even small flocks were infrequently noted. Maximum numbers seen at any one time were flocks of six birds at Moscow August 10, 1950, and at Potlatch August 13, 1951, and August 18, 1957.

Ereunetes mauri Cabanis: WESTERN SANDPIPER

General Distributon. Breeds on the coasts of western and northern Alaska. Winters from the coast of California, the Gulf coast, and North Carolina south on both coasts of Mexico and Central America to Peru, and in the West Indies.

Status in Idaho. A common fall transient throughout the state. Recorded once in the spring in northern Idaho.

In Kootenai County Merrill (1897) reports a specimen taken at Fort Sherman (Coeur d'Alene) on August 15.

In Latah County I found the Western Sandpiper a common fall transient at Potlatch, seeing flocks of varying size on mud flats in the Palouse River from the latter part of July until early September. My extreme dates of occurrence are July 19 (1951) and September 5 (1955). I have one record for the spring migration, a single bird being seen May 18, 1954. At Moscow, lack of suitable habitat limited materially the abundance of this little sandpiper, and it was noted on only a few occasions in the fall feeding at the edges of ponds in open fields. My actual dates of occurrence are August 9 and 11, 1950, and August 5, 1951.

At Lewiston, in Nez Perce County, it was an abundant fall transient, numerous flocks being seen from early July, rarely late June, until the first of October. My extreme dates of occurrence are June 30 (1955) and October 1 (1957).

Newhouse (1960) reports a specimen taken at Indian Valley, Adams County, August 15, 1957. Rust (1917) saw a small flock at Henrys Lake, and another on an irrigation ditch near Spencer, both in Fremont County, August 27, 1916.

Oring (1962) considered this species an "abundant" fall transient in 1961 on the Camas National Wildlife Refuge in Jefferson County, noting it from July 3 through August 29. Two specimens were collected on July 4.

In south-central Idaho Merriam (1891) reported a flock of fifteen on Big Lost River near Arco, July 25, 1890, several specimens being taken. In this same general area Levy (1950) found the Western Sandpiper an abundant fall transient from June through August, 1949.

In order to verify the status of this species as a common fall transient in the northern part of the state specimens were taken as follows: Potlatch, a male August 18, 1951, and females July 19 and 31, 1951, May 18, 1954, and August 2, 1958; Moscow, females August 9, 1950, and August 5, 1951; Lewiston, males September 16, 1951, July 12, 1952, September 21, 1953, July 21, 1954, September 21, 1955, and August 8, 1958, and females August 21, 1950, July 5, August 24 and September 19, 1953, September 10, 1954, June 30, September 11, and September 16, 1955, July 1 and October 1, 1957, and August 4, 1958.

Habits. In view of its abundance in migration the Western Sandpiper must be a very common and widely distributed bird within its rather limited breeding range in northern Alaska. It is unquestionably the most common of the shorebirds occurring in migration in Idaho. Flocks of thirty to forty birds were not uncommon in August, the largest number noted at any one time being approximately 150 at the reservoir east of Lewiston Orchards on August 24, 1953.

Migration in the spring is apparently almost entirely along the coast, for it is then exceedingly abundant there, and very rare in the interior. In fact, considering my one spring record at Potlatch and none for Lewiston over a period of eleven years, it might be considered largely of accidental occurrence at this season of the year.

It is a gentle, unsuspicious little bird that is easily approached as it feeds along the water's edge, but because of its close resemblance to the Semipalmated Sandpiper it is not easily identified in the field.

Tryngites subruficollis (Vieillot): BUFF-BREASTED SANDPIPER

General Distribution. Breeds in northern Alaska, northern Yukon, and northern Mackenzie. Winters in central Argentina.

Status in Idaho. A rare fall transient.

There is but a single record for the occurrence of this species in Idaho. A specimen was taken by Seymour H. Levy in Jerome County September 5, 1951.

Habits. The Buff-breasted Sandpiper migrates in the spring through the Mississippi Valley, and it is unknown at that time on both the Atlantic coast and the Pacific coast. In the fall it follows much the same route, but is more widely spread out; while rare, it has been noted from time to time in the western United States. There is little question but that it will always occur in extremely limited numbers in Idaho.

Limosa fedoa (Linnaeus): MARBLED GODWIT

General Distribution. Breeds from central Alberta, southern Saskatchewan, and southern Manitoba south to Montana, northern South Dakota, and Minnesota. Winters from central California, southern Texas, and South Carolina south on the coast of Mexico to Guatemala and British Honduras.

Status in Idaho. An uncommon and local transient both in the northern and southern part of the state.

In northern Idaho I noted this species only at the reservoir east of Lewiston Orchards, seeing single birds at rather infrequent intervals. My dates of occurrence are: May 13 and 19, 1954, June 26, 1955, August 16, 1956, and July 28, 1958. Three specimens were taken, a male May 13, 1954, and females June 26, 1955, and July 28, 1958.

In southern Idaho a specimen was taken at Rupert, Minidoka County, August 1, 1920 (Davis, 1935). Levy (1950) reports a single bird seen at Wilson Lake, Jerome County, July 18, 1949, and (in litt.) one bird September 5, 1951. Oring (1962) observed several at the Camas National Wildlife Refuge, Jefferson County, June 29 to July 31, 1961.

Habits. The Marbled Godwit was once an abundant bird, but its numbers have been so reduced in recent years that it has become a relatively scarce transient over most of the country. It nests to a large extent in the Canadian prairie provinces, and here the original prairie has been gradually but steadily replaced by farms and settlements that have destroyed the natural habitat of these large shorebirds. In migration it frequents the tide flats on the coast, so the exposed mud flats at the reservoir would appear to offer it a similar suitable area in which to feed and rest.

[**Limosa haemastica** (Linnaeus): HUDSONIAN GODWIT]

General Distribution. Breeds locally from northwestern Mackenzie to northeastern Manitoba. Winters on the coast of Chile, and from Paraguay south to Tierra del Fuego and the Falkland Islands.

Status in Idaho. Largely of accidental occurrence in the state.

There is but a single record for the Hudsonian Godwit in Idaho. Davis (1935) reported it at Rupert, Minidoka County, July 7, 1919.

Habits. The Hudsonian Godwit is not a common bird anywhere, and in view of the route it follows in migration it will always be of accidental occurrence in Idaho. In the spring it follows the Mississippi Valley, while in the fall migrating flocks gather on the Atlantic coast and then apparently fly over the ocean to South America where they spend the winter months. There are spring records as far west as Montana, but the Rocky Mountains would appear to be an effective barrier where stragglers are concerned.

Crocethia alba (Pallas) SANDERLING

General Distribution. Breeds on the Arctic coast from Point Barrow, Alaska, to Greenland, south to northern Mackenzie and the coast of Hudson Bay. Winters from southern British Columbia, the Gulf coast, and Massachusetts south to Chile and southern Argentina.

Status in Idaho. A rare spring transient, and a regular and not uncommon fall transient in the northern part of the state. Recorded twice in southern Idaho.

At Sandpoint, Bonner County, I saw a single bird August 20, 1958, feeding at the water's edge on Lake Pend Oreille.

At Lewiston, Nez Perce County, I found this species a regular and fairly common transient in the fall, seeing single birds, rarely small flocks, at frequent intervals from the latter part of July until early October. It was in late August and in September that this species was most plentiful; for July I have but one record and for October two. My extreme dates of occurrence are July 24 (1953) and October 8 (1951). My one record for the spring migration is that of a single bird, in winter plumage, seen May 10, 1954.

In order to verify the status of the Sanderling as a transient in Idaho the following specimens were taken at Lewiston: males September 21, 1953, August 31, 1956, September 8, 15, 18, and 22, and October 6, 1957. Females July 24 and September 24, 1953, May 10, 1954, September 7 and 21, 1955, August 24, September 24 and October 8, 1957.

In southern Idaho Davis (1935) took a specimen at Rupert, Minidoka County, May 19, 1921. Oring (1962) reported this species an uncommon fall transient in 1961 on the Camas National Wildlife Refuge, in Jefferson County. He took one specimen, an adult female, on July 16.

Habits. Although it occurs in migration in the interior of the country, the Sanderling is characteristically a bird of the open ocean beaches. Probably for this reason I never noted it on the exposed mud flats in the Palouse River at Potlatch. At the reservoir, on the other hand, the bare soil at the water's edge at least suggested the sandy beach this little sandpiper prefers, and here it was found feeding with other shorebirds. On the coast it occurs in large flocks, but in northern Idaho single birds most frequently appeared. The largest number observed at any one time was a flock of three on September 18, 1957.

Avocets and Stilts: *Family Recurvirostridae*

Recurvirostra americana Gmelin: AMERICAN AVOCET

General Distribution. Breeds from central Washington, northern Montana, southern Saskatchewan, and southern Manitoba south to southern California, northern Utah, southern New Mexico and southern Texas. Winters from California and southern Texas south through Mexico to Guatemala.

Status in Idaho. A common transient and rare summer resident in the northern part of the state, and a common but local summer resident in southern Idaho.

In Kootenai County Merrill (1897) reported a pair seen and one bird collected in September at Fort Sherman (Coeur d'Alene). Moody (1903) cited the only breeding record for the northern part of the state, a nest with four eggs found on Lake Pend Oreille. Rust (1915) considered this species a rare transient in Kootenai County (1910 through 1914). One specimen was taken by him on the St. Joe marshes.

In Latah County I found the Avocet a scarce transient, largely because of the scarcity of suitable habitat, and noted it only during the fall migration. Actual records of occurrence are: Moscow, July 12, 1951, and July 10, 1952; Potlatch August 11, 1954, and July 15, 1956.

At Lewiston, in Nez Perce County, it was a common transient both in the spring and in the fall, flocks of varying sizes being seen at the reservoir from April until June, and again from early July until the middle of September. My extreme dates of occurrence are April 10 (1956) and June 21 (1955) (average date of departure June 13), and July 1 (1956) and November 10 (1953) (average date of departure September 10).

In Clearwater County a flock of four birds was seen at Elk River May 4, 1950 (Hale Ebling, in litt.).

In south-central Idaho Merriam (1891) noted this species on the Henrys Fork of the Snake River in July, 1872, and on Sawtooth Lake in late September, 1890. Rust (1917) reports a flock of eight at Small, in Fremont County, June 20, 1916. Oring (1962) found it an "abundant summer resi-

VIOLET-GREEN SWALLOW

PLATE IV

A GRACEFUL AVOCET WITH ITS HANDSOME EGGS

dent" in 1961 on the Camas National Wildlife Refuge in Jefferson County. Steel (1956) considered the Avocet an uncommon summer resident at Grays Lake (1949 through 1951). Three nests were found May 14, 1951, two with four eggs each, and one with five. He gives as dates of arrival April 22, 1950, and April 16, 1951.

At Rupert, in Minidoka County, Davis (1935) gives as extreme dates of occurrence (1919 through 1921) March 21 and September 20, and as the earliest date for fresh eggs June 7. Bent (1927) cites as a late date of departure at Rupert October 21. Arvey (1947) reports a specimen taken at Hagerman, Gooding County, June 16, 1940. Levy (1950) considered this species a common summer resident in 1949 in this same general area. He states that a flock of over fifty birds was seen at Wilson Lake, in Jerome County, July 22. I saw a flock of twelve birds at Twin Falls May 30, 1951.

At Boise, on June 22, 1949, I noted three breeding pairs about a large pond. Bent (1927) gives February 15 as an early date of arrival at Deer Flat, Canyon County.

Specimens verifying the identification of this species were taken as follows: Boise, a female June 22, 1949; Moscow, a female July 12, 1951; Lewiston, a male April 25, 1953, and females July 12, July 24, and August 21, 1953, and July 1, 1956.

Habits. The Avocet is a sociable bird, single birds appearing only rarely at the reservoir or on the Palouse River at Potlatch. Usually flocks comprising from eight to sixteen individuals were noted, although it was not uncommon to see as many as thirty feeding together. The maximum number observed at any one time was forty-six at the reservoir July 19, 1955. In view of the relative abundance of this species in migration it is rather surprising that it does not nest more commonly in the northern part of the state, especially since there are areas apparently well suited to this large wader for breeding purposes.

The Avocet possesses one trait that sets it apart from its near relatives. It swims well, and often flocks seen at the reservoir were resting in a compact group on the water well offshore, rather than on the shore itself, as might be expected.

Nests found in Idaho were slight hollows in the ground meagerly lined with fine grasses, and were in the open, with no concealment whatsoever.

Himantopus mexicanus (Müller): BLACK-NECKED STILT

General Distribution. Breeds from southern Oregon, southern Saskatchewan, southern Colorado, the Gulf coast of Texas and southern Louisiana, and South Carolina south through Mexico and Central America to northern Brazil. Winters north to central California, the Rio Grande Valley in Texas, and the Mississippi Delta.

Status in Idaho. An uncommon and rather local summer resident in the southern part of the state.

According to Merriam (1891) the stilt was seen by Bendire on the Snake River, near Olds Ferry, in July, 1877.

Davis (1935) found it nesting in small numbers near Rupert, in Minidoka County, 1919 through 1921. He gives as extreme dates of occurrence April 13 and September 28. A nest with fresh eggs was found May 31.

I noted three birds at Lake Walcott, on the Minidoka National Wildlife Refuge, July 21, 1958. Oring (1962) found it "an uncommon summer visitor" in 1961 on the Camas National Wildlife Refuge, noting it from July 17 to August 2.

Habits. Stilts are birds of open marshes and wet meadows, where their long legs permit them to wade in water a foot or more in depth as they feed. They are able to swim, but unlike the Avocet they avoid deep water, their activities being limited to shallow pools. Southern Idaho is at the northern limit of the breeding range of this species; therefore the Black-necked Stilt will probably never be a common bird in the state, and will always be rather local in its distribution.

Phalaropes: *Family Phalaropodidae*

Phalaropus fulicarius (Linnaeus): RED PHALAROPE

General Distribution. Circumpolar, breeding in North America in northern Alaska, Mackenzie, Southampton Island, Baffin Island, northern Quebec, and northern Labrador. Winters at sea, chiefly in the southern hemisphere.

Status in Idaho. Largely of accidental occurrence in the fall in the northern part of the state.

The Red Phalarope was first recorded in Idaho by Hand (1935) who saw one bird on the St. Joe River, near St. Maries, October 13 and 14, 1934. He stated that he was able to approach within fifteen feet of it as it fed at the edge of the river, and so was able satisfactorily to identify it.

On September 22, 1957, this species was recorded in the state for the second time when I collected a male at the reservoir east of Lewiston Orchards. It was feeding in shallow water near the shore, and was unsuspicious and easily approached.

Habits. The Red Phalarope is essentially a bird of the open ocean, for except during the breeding season it is found so far offshore that only during severe storms does it appear near land. During migration stragglers occur in the interior of the country, but it is nowhere a common bird except on the coast.

Steganopus tricolor Vieillot: WILSON'S PHALAROPE

General Distribution. Breeds from British Columbia east through central Saskatchewan, central Minnesota and southern Michigan to southern Ontario, south to central California, northern Utah, central Kansas, and northern Indiana. Winters in Chile and Argentina.

Status in Idaho. A fairly common transient and an uncommon summer resident in the northern part of the state, and a fairly common but local summer resident in southern Idaho.

At Hauser, in Kootenai County, I noted this species twice in the spring, a single bird on May 6, 1953, and two on May 6, 1957. For the fall migration I have one record, a small flock of four birds July 16, 1957.

Hand (1941) considered this species a rather uncommon spring transient at St. Maries, in Benewah County, seeing it singly or in small flocks in May (1921 through 1941).

In Latah County two birds were noted by Johnston (1949) at Potlatch, on the Palouse River, August 11, 1947. For some obscure reason, I found this phalarope a very scarce transient at Potlatch, my only records there being that of four birds seen July 31 and two August 1, 1953.

At Moscow it was a fairly common transient both in the spring and in the fall, my extreme dates of occurrence being April 25 (1952) and May 25 (1953), and July 9 (1951) and July 26 (1951). In 1952 one pair was seen June 12 in a stretch of open marsh, and although no nest was found, there is little question but that they were nesting there.

At Lewiston, in Nez Perce County, I noted this species only at the reservoir east of Lewiston Orchards, but here it was a fairly common transient, seeing flocks of varying sizes in May and again in July and the first half of August. For two years, 1954 and 1955, the water level was unusually high, resulting in open marsh where these phalaropes nested in small numbers. Six apparently mated pairs were noted June 6, 1954, while on June 21, 1955, approximately thirty birds, largely fully grown young of the year, were seen. My extreme dates of occurrence at the reservoir for transient flocks are May 12 (1953) and May 21 (1953), and July 8 (1953) and August 19 (1956).

At New Meadows, in Adams County, I saw one pair June 5, 1951, in a large open marsh, and although no nest was found it is probable that they reared young there.

Two apparently mated pairs that I saw at McCall, in Valley County, May 19, 1955, also probably nested in the open marsh where they were feeding, but I had no opportunity to verify this supposition.

In Southern Idaho it was first recorded by Merriam (1891) who took a specimen in Marsh Valley June 30, 1872. Levy (1950) considered it, in 1949, a common summer resident in the south-central part of the state, while at Grays Lake Steel (1956) gave it this same status (1949 through 1951). He cites as arrival dates, males April 25, 1950, and April 19, 1951, and females May 9, 1951. He found a nest on May 28, 1950, that held four eggs.

Davis (1935) reported this phalarope at Rupert, in Minidoka County, May 13, 1919. I noted scattered pairs in open marsh on the Snake River, at Burley, Cassia County, June 18, 1949. Bent (1927) gives May 14 as an early date of arrival at Meridian, Ada County.

At Riddle, in Owyhee County, Davis (1934) observed "at least twelve pairs" from May 28 through June 3, 1934. He collected a female on May 29.

A HURRYING WILSON'S PHALAROPE

Photo by R. C. Twist

Bureau of Sport Fisheries and Wildlife

I collected the following specimens to verify the occurrence of this species in the state: Grays Lake, Caribou County, female, June 14, 1949; Moscow, male, July 9, 1951, females, May 8 and 14, and July 26, 1951, April 25, 1952; Potlatch, female, August 1, 1955; Lewiston, males August 4, 1953 and August 19, 1956; McCall, Valley County, male, May 19, 1955; Hauser, Kootenai County, male, July 16, 1957.

Habits. Like the other phalaropes this species swims well, but in my experience it is not often seen in deep water. An occasional small flock in migration at the reservoir will rest for a time well offshore, but sooner or later it will be found feeding, well scattered out, in shallow water bordering marshy areas. At Lewiston it consistently avoided the gravel bars in the Snake River.

The nest is a slight hollow in the ground, lined with fine grasses; and although in short grass where concealment is difficult, it is very hard to find. Apparently only the male incubates, and he sits so tightly that only when almost stepped upon will he flush and reveal the nest. The Wilson's Phalarope unquestionably breeds over much of the state where there is suitable habitat, but only at Grays Lake has a nest actually been found.

Lobipes lobatus (Linnaeus): Northern Phalarope

General Distribution. Breeds from northern Alaska, northern Mackenzie, central Keewatin and Baffin Island south to northern British Columbia, northern Manitoba, James Bay and the coast of Labrador. Winters at sea, from Ecuador to southern Argentina.

Status in Idaho. A scarce spring transient, and a not uncommon fall transient over most of the state.

In Kootenai County it was reported by Merrill (1897) as being "abundant" in late August and early September on Lake Coeur d'Alene. Rust (1915), however, found it a rare fall transient (1910 through 1914) on the lake.

In Latah County there was little suitable habitat, so this species was noted on only a few occasions. For Moscow I have but two records, seeing single birds August 10, 1950, and May 14, 1955. The mud flats in the Palouse River at Potlatch apparently offered this little phalarope few inducements, and I noted it but twice. One bird was seen August 10, 1956, and a flock of ten noted August 26, 1956.

At Lewiston, in Nez Perce County, it was a scarce transient in the spring, but fairly common in the fall, being most numerous in August when small flocks were frequently seen at the reservoir east of Lewiston Orchards. For the spring migration I have the following records: two birds seen June 1, 4, and 6, 1954, and single birds, in full breeding plumage, May 17 and June 18, 1955. For the fall migration my extreme dates of occurrence are July 24 (1955) and September 12 (1957).

In order to verify the status of this species as a transient in northern Idaho I collected the following specimens: Moscow, males August 10, 1950, and May 14, 1955; Potlatch, females August 10 and 26, 1956; Lewiston, males June 1, 4, and 6, and August 8, 1954, August 27, 1956, and September 12, 1957, and females August 24, 1953, May 17 and June 18, 1955, August 29, 1956, and September 4, 1957.

This species was first recorded in the southern part of the state by Merriam (1891) who saw two and collected one September 5, 1890, "on a small alpine lake at timber line in the Salmon River Mountains."

Rust (1917) noted two June 20, 1916, on a small pond near Small, Fremont County.

Davis (1935) recorded it but once at Rupert, in Minidoka County, a single bird May 13, 1919.

Levy (1950) found it an uncommon fall transient in south-central Idaho in 1949. He saw a flock "of more than thirty" at Wilson Lake, in Jerome County, July 27 and collected three.

Oring (1962) considered it a common fall transient in 1961 on the Camas National Wildlife Refuge in Jefferson County, noting it from August 13 through August 29. An immature male was collected August 13 and four immature females August 19.

Habits. Like the Red Phalarope this species migrates commonly well off-shore on both coasts; however, it is not uncommon in the interior of the country, especially in the fall. At the reservoir east of Lewiston Orchards flocks comprising five to twelve individuals were frequently seen in August. A rather unusual occurrence was the presence of a flock of fully three hundred of these little phalaropes that in midmorning, on August 27, 1956, were resting in a compact group in the center of the reservoir. They remained there until noon, when they began to leave in small groups, flying directly west (toward the coast) and fading soon out of sight. Within fifteen minutes from the time this movement began none was left.

Although this species normally secures its food in shallow water near the shore, it was not unusual to find an occasional bird feeding with other shorebirds on an exposed mud flat.

Jaegers and Skuas: *Family Stercorariidae*

Stercorarius pomarinus (Temminck): POMARINE JAEGER

General Distribution. Breeds from western Alaska, Mackenzie, Southampton Island, and northern Quebec to western Greenland, and across northern Russia. Winters at sea, in the Atlantic from Cape Hatteras to the West Indies, and in the Pacific from southern California to Peru, also off the coast of Africa and of eastern Australia.

Status in Idaho. Of accidental occurrence in the southern part of the state. There is a single record for this species in Idaho. Davis (1935) reports a specimen taken on the Snake River, near Rupert, Minidoka County, September 4, 1919.

Habits. Being a bird of the open ocean much of the year, it is doubtful if this jaeger occurs often in Idaho. It secures its food to a large extent by harassing gulls and terns and robbing them of the fish they have succeeded in catching, so it should be looked for on the lakes and larger streams during the fall months.

[**Stercorarius parasiticus** (Linnaeus): PARASITIC JAEGER]

General Distribution. Circumpolar; in North America breeds from northern Alaska, Northwest Territories and northern Ellesmere Island, south to Kodiak Island, Manitoba, Ontario, Quebec, and Labrador. Winters off-shore, in the Pacific from southern California to southern Chile, in the Atlantic from Maine to Argentina.

Status in Idaho. Of accidental occurrence in the northern part of the state.

There is one record for this species in Idaho. Hand (1941) reports one bird seen, and "carefully identified" at St. Maries, Benewah County, September 23, 1936.

Habits. As with the other jaegers this species is a bird of the open ocean, coming inland only during the summer months to rear its young on the Arctic tundra. In migration, especially in the fall, an occasional individual has been recorded often enough in the interior of the country to indicate that such a route apparently is followed regularly by a limited number of these birds. It is well named, for it satisfies its voracious appetite by robbing gulls and terns of food that is rightfully theirs.

Stercorarius longicaudus Vieillot: LONG-TAILED JAEGER

General Distribution. In North America, breeds from western Alaska, northern Yukon, Melville Island and Ellesmere Island south to Southampton Island and northern Quebec. Winters at sea, both in the Atlantic Ocean and in the Pacific Ocean off South America.

Status in Idaho. Of accidental occurrence in the southern part of the state.

There is one record for this species in Idaho. In November 10, 1956, a dead bird was picked up on the shore of Mud Lake, Jefferson County, by Kenneth Mackenzie, District Conservation Officer of the Idaho Fish and Game Department. It was saved as a specimen, and is now in the collections of the United States National Museum, Washington, D.C.

Habits. In all respects this species is similar to the other jaegers. It comes ashore to nest on the Arctic tundra, but otherwise it spends its life on the open ocean harassing the gulls and terns. In the fall it is frequently recorded in the interior of the country, so it is possible that it occurs more frequently in Idaho than the one record would indicate.

Gulls and Terns: *Family Laridae*

Larus hyperboreus Gunnerus: GLAUCOUS GULL

General Distribution. Cosmopolitan; in North America breeds from northern Alaska, Northwest Territories, Greenland, and Iceland south to Hudson Bay and Labrador. Winters south to southern California, the Great Lakes, and on the Atlantic coast to Georgia.

Status in Idaho. Apparently of casual occurrence in the northern part of the state.

Recorded in Kootenai County by LaFave (1965) who states: "Three immatures were noted at Coeur d'Alene Lake and the Spokane River at Coeur d'Alene, Idaho, on 22 February 1963 whereupon photographs were taken at close range by J. Acton. Another immature was noted at Coeur d'Alene on 16 February 1964."

Habits. This hardy gull winters as far north as it can find any open water, and as the open ocean offers it the food and security from molestation that it desires, it is rarely found inland. It is rather surprising therefore that it is of more than accidental occurrence in Idaho, and it will be of interest to see if in future years it again appears in the state during the winter months.

Larus glaucescens Naumann: GLAUCOUS-WINGED GULL

General Distribution. Breeds from western Alaska south to northwestern Washington. Winters south along the coast to southern Baja California.

Status in Idaho. Recorded once at Coeur d'Alene, and possibly of casual occurrence in the northern part of the state.

LaFave (1965) reported the occurrence of this species at Coeur d'Alene in 1963. He states: "Two immatures were noted at Spokane on 16 February 1961, and another immature along the Spokane River at Coeur d'Alene 22 February 1963 which was photographed by J. Acton."

Habits. Like the preceding species, this gull has rarely been observed away from the coast, but since 1956 it has been found to be of casual occurrence in eastern Washington (LaFave, 1965). It is possible therefore that it is commoner in northern Idaho than the one record would indicate. Because of its large size and voracious appetite it should be looked for on the larger bodies of water.

Larus argentatus smithsonianus Coues: HERRING GULL

General Distribution. Circumpolar; in North America breeds from central Alaska, northern Mackenzie, Baffin Island, northern Quebec and northern Labrador south to British Columbia, eastern Montana, northern Wisconsin, northern Ohio and Long Island. Winters from the southern part of its breeding range south on the Pacific coast to El Salvador, on the Great Lakes, on the Gulf of Mexico, and on the Atlantic coast to Cuba.

Status in Idaho. A rare fall transient and winter visitant in the northern part of the state.

Merrill (1897) reports several specimens taken during the fall and winter at Fort Sherman (Coeur d'Alene).

My one record is that of two birds, in immature plumage, seen August 13, 1951, at Potlatch, Latah County, resting on a mud flat in the Palouse River.

Habits. In view of the fact that the Herring Gull is the most widely distributed and best known of the gulls in the northern hemisphere, it is rather surprising that it is such a scarce bird in Idaho. Because of its large size only the larger lakes and rivers would attract it in migration, and it is possible that in such spots it has been largely overlooked in past years. As opportunity offered, however, I have carefully scrutinized the gulls that I have seen on both Lake Pend Oreille and Lake Coeur d'Alene, and I have yet to see this species on either of these bodies of water.

It is a notable scavenger, and recognizing the benefits to be derived from the proximity of man, it can be found in the harbors on both coasts during much of the year. Here it is unsuspicious and easily approached, although normally it is a wary bird that does not tolerate a close acquaintance.

Larus californicus Lawrence: CALIFORNIA GULL

General Distribution. Breeds from central Mackenzie south through Saskatchewan and Manitoba to northern California, northern Utah and central North Dakota. Winters from southern Washington and southwestern Idaho south along the Pacific coast to Guatemala.

Status in Idaho. A scarce summer visitant and fall transient in the northern part of the state, and a common summer resident in southern Idaho.

For some obscure reason the California Gull rarely occurs in northern Idaho, although conditions on the larger lakes and streams would seem well suited to its needs. Yocom (1946) noted it at the upper end of Lake Coeur d'Alene in Kootenai County July 1-10, 1943, stating that it was noted daily then. I have three records for the Snake River at Lewiston, one bird being collected August 13, 1954, while another was seen September 30, 1954, and two October 24, 1955.

Hand (1932) reports one bird on the Lochsa River, at the Lochsa Ranger Station in Idaho County, May 29-31, 1923. I saw nine birds at New Meadows, Adams County, June 21, 1950, feeding over a large flooded field.

Oring (1962) found this gull a common "summer resident" in 1961 in Jefferson County, both at Mud Lake and on the Camas National Wildlife Refuge.

At Grays Lake Steel (1956) found it a common spring visitant (1949 through 1951), none being seen after the third week in May. He gives as an arrival date April 6, 1950. He states that on a few occasions birds in immature plumage appeared in midsummer.

Davis (1935) considered this species a common summer resident (1919 through 1921) at Rupert, in Minidoka County, although there was no evidence of breeding. He cites as extreme dates of occurrence March 28 and November 4. Levy (1950) gives it this same status for south-central Idaho in 1949, stating that although it was noted daily on the Snake River he knew of no nesting colonies.

On June 23, 1949, at Homedale, in Owyhee County, I found this gull fairly plentiful on the Snake River. Thirty birds were seen at Nampa, in Canyon County November 4, 1949, feeding in a recently plowed field. It is said to winter commonly on the Deer Flat National Wildlife Refuge, six miles southwest of Nampa.

As far as is now known it nests in three widely separated spots in the southern part of the state. There is a breeding colony of several thousand pairs on a small island in Lake Lowell, on the Deer Flat National Wildlife Refuge (Research Leaflet 163-R, Fish and Wildlife Service). Steel (1956) states that it nests on the Blackfoot Reservoir in Caribou County. On June 9, 1955, Edson Fichter showed me a breeding colony of possibly five hundred pairs at the American Falls Reservoir in Power County. Many of the nests held eggs, although there were numerous young varying in age from just hatched to fully a week old.

Habits. Banding records indicate that at least a portion of the population of California Gulls in southern Idaho during the fall months are transients from Canada. Robertson (1928) states that among the gulls of this species that were banded in June, 1927, at Bittern Lake, ten miles west of Camrose, Alberta, one was recovered on October 2 of that year at Caldwell, in Canyon County, and another on November 1 at Idaho Falls, Bonneville County.

The breeding colony that I saw at the American Falls Reservoir had selected a stretch of open ground on an isolated spot bordering the water, and here the nests were concentrated in a rather limited area. Normally an island is selected, as far offshore as possible, but apparently when such a site is not available the mainland is used. The nests at the reservoir were fairly well built of grasses, weed stems, and small twigs, and in many instances they were so close together that they almost touched. As the ground was bare for a considerable distance, there was no attempt at concealment.

Larus delawarensis Ord: RING-BILLED GULL

General Distribution. Breeds from central Washington, Alberta, northern Saskatchewan and southern Manitoba south to northern California, southern Colorado, and northern South Dakota, and from central Quebec and Newfoundland south to Michigan and northern New York. Winters from Oregon south along the Pacific coast to southern Mexico, on the Great Lakes, on the Gulf coast, and on the Atlantic coast from the Gulf of St. Lawrence to southern Florida and Cuba.

Status in Idaho. An uncommon spring transient and a common fall transient in the northern part of the state, a few individuals occurring during the winter months when there is open water on the lakes and rivers. An uncommon and rather local summer resident in southern Idaho.

In Kootenai County Merrill (1897) reported an adult taken January 6, and several in immature plumage in September, on Lake Coeur d'Alene. He considered it "not rare" in the winter, but did not record it in the summer. Rust (1915) reported this species uncommon on Lake Coeur d'Alene in the fall and during the winter months (March, 1910, through December, 1914). On October 16, 1956, I saw approximately 120 of these gulls feeding at a garbage dump at the edge of the lake. The following spring two birds were seen on the lake on March 13, when it was still largely frozen over, and on March 21 twelve were found at the garbage dump where this species had been observed the previous fall. On March 19, 1958, I noted two birds at Hauser, feeding in a newly-plowed field.

At St. Maries, in Benewah County, Hand (1941) reported this species a common transient both in the spring and in the fall, seeing it from March to May, and again from September to December (1921 through 1941). An occasional bird was noted during the winter.

In Latah County there are no large bodies of water, so this species was rarely noted. My few records are of single birds seen at Potlatch September 4, 1951, and July 4, 1956, and at Moscow May 12, 1952, and April 26, 1955.

At Lewiston in Nez Perce County, it was a scarce spring transient, but common in the fall when small flocks were frequently seen both on the Snake River and on the reservoir from late July until the latter part of October. My few records for the spring migration are: a single bird May 4, 1951, a flock of thirteen April 28, 1953, and a flock of ten May 10, 1954. My extreme dates of occurrence in the fall are July 24 (1952) and October 21 (1949). During the winter of 1951-52 several birds appeared on the Snake River November 16 and were noted at frequent intervals thereafter through February 21.

At Council, in Adams County, this species was observed by Newhouse (1960) from May 31 to August 13, 1958. He stated that a flock of "nearly 1200" was seen on July 9.

Steel (1956) considered this gull an uncommon transient at Grays Lake (1949 through 1951), while Levy (1950) reported it an uncommon summer resident in 1949 in south-central Idaho, but with no evidence of breeding.

Oring (1962) found it common during the summer of 1961 on Mud Lake and on the Camas National Wildlife Refuge, in Jefferson County.

As far as now known the Ring-billed Gull nests in Idaho only on the Minidoka National Wildlife Refuge, eight miles northeast of Rupert. Two small breeding colonies have occupied islands in Lake Walcott for some years now, and here nesting activities are apparently well under way by late May or early June. I was at the Refuge on July 21, 1958, and that day saw numerous fully grown young of the year resting in a more or less compact group well offshore. One male in immature plumage was collected to verify the identification.

Habits. The Ring-billed Gull would probably be a commoner breeding bird in Idaho if there were more suitable nesting habitat. Without exception breeding colonies are located on islands where protection is afforded from the attacks of predatory mammals, and such sites are extremely scarce in the state.

The nests are fairly well built of grasses, weed stems, and similar material, and no attempt is made at concealment. As is customary with most of the gulls, the nests are concentrated within a limited area, usually within a few feet of each other.

During the late fall and winter months, this species occurs on the coast, and it is common then in the harbors where its ability as a scavenger is well known.

Larus pipixcan Wagler: FRANKLIN'S GULL

General Distribution. Breeds from southern Alberta, Saskatchewan and Manitoba, south to central Oregon, northern Utah, northern South Dakota and northern Iowa. Winters on the Pacific coast from Guatemala to Chile, and on the Gulf coast from Texas to Louisiana.

Status in Idaho. A local summer resident in the southern part of the state; apparently of accidental occurrence in northern Idaho.

The one record for the northern part of the state is that of a single bird, a female in subadult plumage, that appeared at the reservoir east of Lewiston Orchards on July 14, 1956. It was collected to verify the identification.

Slipp (1942) summarized the occurrence of this species in southern Idaho through 1941, his records indicating that its status then was merely that of a straggler. He states that two were seen July 28, 1910, by Stanley G. Jewett at the Minidoka Dam; two were collected in April, 1937, at Meridian, Ada County, by Buck Cherry; a flock of fifty was noted May 24, 1941, at Henry, Caribou County, by Victor E. Jones and L. H. Walkinshaw; and it was recorded November 11, 1941, at Springfield, Bingham County, by Victor E. Jones.

The first definite evidence of breeding in the state was reported by Levy (1950) who stated that in June, 1949, he found a "large colony—established" at Grays Lake. This was later verified by Steel (1956) who found this little gull an abundant summer resident (1949 through 1951) at Grays Lake. He gives as arrival dates April 1, 1950, and April 12, 1951. On April 28, 1954, I was at Grays Lake for part of the day and found this species again plentiful here, seeing scattered flocks feeding in the open fields.

On July 21, 1958, I was shown a small breeding colony on Lake Walcott, on the Minidoka National Wildlife Refuge. As with the Ring-billed Gull, apparently nesting activities were well under way by late May, for young of the year, already fully grown, were seen that day feeding over the lake. Two years later, on June 17, 1960, I was again at the Minidoka Refuge, and was interested to note a considerable increase in the number of Franklin's Gulls nesting there. Because of the depth of the water it proved impracticable to search the wide stretch of reeds for nests, but I estimated that close to one thousand pairs were breeding on the Refuge that year. A probable explanation of this sudden increase suggested itself when I visited Grays Lake several days later, on June 23. Much to my surprise I found the lake almost dry, and the marsh vegetation that had previously covered so much of the lake bed almost completely gone. No Franklin's Gulls were seen, and as the disappearance of their natural habitat had obviously forced them to seek another area, it appeared logical to me that this breeding population had moved to the Minidoka Refuge.

Oring (1962) found this species an "abundant summer resident" in 1961 on the Camas National Wildlife Refuge in Jefferson County, but he observed none after July 29.

Habits. In some respects the Franklin's Gull differs radically from its near relatives. Much of the year is spent away from the coast, and its food then is almost entirely insectivorous. Birds that I watched at Grays Lake showed a preference for recently plowed fields, and here they followed the furrows picking up insects and larvae that had been unearthed. Before the spring plowing began, fields and pastures were given preference over the open water in the lake. It is only to a very limited degree a scavenger, and does not frequent the harbors during the winter months.

The nest is never built on dry ground, but in stretches of reeds growing in water two or more feet in depth. It is a substantial floating mass of dead reeds, and no effort is made at concealment.

Larus philadelphia (Ord): BONAPARTE'S GULL

General Distribution. Breeds from central Alaska, northern Mackenzie, and central Ontario south to central British Columbia, southern Alberta, and western Saskatchewan. Winters on the Pacific coast from Washington to Baja California, on the Gulf coast, and on the Atlantic coast from Massachusetts to Florida and Cuba.

Status in Idaho. A scarce spring transient and an uncommon fall transient throughout the state.

In Kootenai County Merrill (1897) reported one taken and several seen in November, at Fort Sherman (Coeur d'Alene). Rust (1915) found it an uncommon fall transient on Lake Coeur d'Alene (March, 1910, to December, 1914).

At Copeland, in Boundary County, Levy (1959) noted "flocks of from ten to thirty birds" on the Kootenai River October 16 to 29, 1951.

At Moscow, in Latah County, I have but two records, both for the spring migration, single birds being seen May 8, 1951, and May 3, 1954. Levy (1959) observed one bird at Moscow May 16, 1950.

At Lewiston, in Nez Perce County, I found this little gull a rather uncommon transient both in the spring and in the fall, seeing it on the reservoir east of Lewiston Orchards and, less frequently, on the Snake River. My records for the spring migration are: three birds seen April 25, 1953, and a single bird June 30, 1955; and for the fall migration: one bird November 1,

1953, two on October 28, 1954, a flock of five October 24, 1955, a flock of nine October 28, 1956, and two birds November 1, 1956.

Hand (1932) reported eight birds on the Lochsa River in Idaho County October 28, 1925.

Newhouse (1960) collected one bird in immature plumage at Indian Valley in Adams County, December 3, 1957.

In southern Idaho it has been rarely observed. Davis (1934) reported a female collected at Riddle, Owyhee County, May 30, 1934, and Steel (1956) stated that it was a rare transient at Grays Lake, his one record being that of four birds seen May 4, 1951.

Habits. In its flight and general actions this little gull, when watched at the reservoir east of Lewiston Orchards, resembled closely a tern, but its square rather than forked tail readily identified it. As with the Franklin's Gull its food is largely insectivorous, but the flocks seen in Idaho always fed over water. I have never observed it on the ground in recently plowed fields, and if it ever acquires its food in this way it must be an uncommon occurrence. In no sense of the word is it a scavenger, as are its larger relatives, although in migration and during the winter months it can be found in the harbors.

It is the only gull that does not build its nest on the ground, the usual location being on a thick branch of a conifer several feet from the trunk and from four to fifteen feet from the ground.

Sterna forsteri Nuttall: FORSTER'S TERN

General Distribution. Breeds from southern Alberta, Saskatchewan, and Manitoba south to southern California, Utah, eastern Colorado, and northern Iowa, in Texas and Louisiana, and in eastern Maryland and Virginia. Winters from central California south to southern Mexico, on the Gulf coast, and from Virginia to northern Florida.

Status in Idaho. A fairly common but rather local summer resident in the southern part of the state, and of casual occurrence during the summer months as far north as Adams County.

Forster's Tern was first recorded in southern Idaho by Merriam (1891), who reported two specimens taken on Marsh Creek June 30, 1872.

Davis (1935) found it a summer resident at Rupert, in Minidoka County (1919 through 1921). He cites as extreme dates of occurrence May 1 and September 9, and as the earliest date for eggs June 7.

Levy (1950) considered this tern in 1949 widely distributed during the summer months in southern Idaho, but apparently saw no breeding colonies. He collected one specimen at Wilson Lake, in Jerome County, on July 7.

Steel (1956) found it a fairly common summer resident at Grays Lake (1949 through 1951). He gives as arrival dates May 24, 1950, and May 8, 1951. A nest found June 22, 1950, held two fresh eggs.

Oring (1962) reported it a common summer resident in 1961 at Mud Lake and on the Camas National Wildlife Refuge, in Jefferson County.

Bureau of Sport Fisheries and Wildlife   *Photo by David B. Marshall*

A FORSTER'S TERN MIRRORED ON ITS WATERY NEST

I saw four birds at Marsing, Owyhee County, on June 24, 1949, feeding over the Snake River, two at Twin Falls May 31, 1951, and six at Hazelton, Jerome County, June 20, 1960. I collected the following specimens to verify the occurrence of this species in the southern part of the state: two males and a female at Grays Lake June 11, 1949, a male at Twin Falls May 31, 1951, and two males and a female at Hazelton June 20, 1960.

The farthest north that the Forster's Tern has been recorded in Idaho is New Meadows, Adams County, where, on June 5, 1951, I saw two birds feeding over open pools in a large marsh. It is possible that this was a breeding pair, although no nest was found to support this supposition.

Habits. Forster's Tern is essentially a bird of the open marsh, its food being secured over water where both small fish and the larger insects, such as the dragonfly, are successfully pursued. Lack of suitable habitat is apparently responsible for its absence during the summer months in the northern half of the state, and this factor doubtless also accounts for the fact that it has never been recorded there in migration.

The nest is usually substantially built of dead reeds and marsh grass, and the normal situation is in open marsh where no attempt is made at concealment. Breeding colonies occupy a rather limited area, the nests being so close together as to almost touch at times.

Sterna hirundo hirundo Linnaeus: COMMON TERN

General Distribution. Breeds in North America from southern Mackenzie east through central Manitoba and Quebec to Newfoundland, south to southern Alberta, Montana, northern South Dakota, northern Indiana, northern Ohio and North Carolina, and on the coast of Texas. Winters from Baja California to Ecuador, and from South Carolina to northern South America.

Status in Idaho. A rare spring transient, and an irregular and scarce fall transient in the northern part of the state.

Rust (1915) found the Common Tern a rare transient on Lake Coeur d'Alene (1910 through 1914). He stated that one specimen was collected.

With one exception I noted this species only at Lewiston, in Nez Perce County where I saw it at infrequent intervals on the Snake River, and rarely on the reservoir east of Lewiston Orchards. My one spring record is that of three birds seen resting on a gravel bar in the Snake River June 8, 1950. In the fall, single birds or small flocks appeared in late August or early September and were present from time to time until well into October, my extreme dates of occurrence being August 24 (1953) and October 21 (1950). Maximum numbers observed were two small flocks, totalling sixteen birds, on the Snake River September 12, 1949, and a flock of six birds at the reservoir August 27, 1956. Specimens verifying the identification of this tern were taken at Lewiston as follows: males September 12, 1949, September 21, 1951, August 24, 1953, and August 27, 1956, and females September 30, 1953, and August 27, 1956.

I have one record for Potlatch, in Latah County, a single bird being seen feeding over the Palouse River August 26, 1954.

Habits. The lack of records for the Common Tern in southern Idaho is possibly due to the very close resemblance of this species to the Forster's Tern, for during much of the year the grayish underparts and somewhat shorter tail of *hirundo* are the only characters distinguishing it from *forsteri*. This is often difficult to determine satisfactorily in the field, so transient Common Terns could easily be overlooked.

In actions, however, the two species differ somewhat. The food of the Common Tern is largely small fish, and these it secures by diving into the water, usually being completely submerged before reappearing with its prey in its bill. On the other hand, Forster's Tern seldom dives, taking its food from the surface of the water.

[Sterna albifrons Pallas: LEAST TERN]

General Distribution. Breeds on the Pacific coast from central California to southern Baja California. Winters south to Guatemala.

Status in Idaho. Of accidental occurrence in the southern part of the state.

The only record for the occurrence of the Least Tern in Idaho is that of a single bird seen by Davis (1934) at Riddle, Owyhee County, May 30 and June 1, 1934.

Habits. In the western United States this little tern is confined entirely to the ocean beaches, and its presence in the interior is merely accidental.

Hydroprogne caspia (Pallas): CASPIAN TERN

General Distribution. Cosmopolitan; breeds in North America in widely separated localities, from central Mackenzie east across the continent to Newfoundland, south to Baja California, northern Utah, southern Texas, and South Carolina. Winters north to central California, on the Gulf coast, on the Atlantic coast north to North Carolina, and in the West Indies.

Status in Idaho. A regular but not common summer visitant in the southern part of the state; recorded once in northern Idaho.

The one record for the northern part of the state is that of two birds that I saw on the reservoir east of Lewiston Orchards July 31, 1958.

In southern Idaho this large tern is rather local in its distribution, being limited to the larger bodies of water. Its presence throughout the summer months would suggest that it may nest in small numbers in some isolated spot, although as yet no breeding colonies have been found.

Davis (1935) gives as arrival dates at Rupert, Minidoka County, May 6, 1919, May 1, 1920, and April 29, 1921.

Levy (1950) reported it seen "in limited numbers" during the summer of 1949, noting it "at almost every lake visited."

I saw one bird at Marsing, Owyhee County, June 24, 1949, feeding over the Snake River, and two at the Blackfoot Reservoir, in Caribou County, May 25, 1951. One of the latter, a male, was collected.

Oring (1962) recorded it in small numbers during the summer of 1961 at Mud Lake and on the Camas National Wildlife Refuge in Jefferson County.

Habits. The food of the Caspian Tern is almost entirely small fish. The birds that I have watched in southern Idaho secured their prey by plunging into the water, usually being completely submerged for a brief interval.

This species is said to breed in small numbers at the Blackfoot Reservoir, but there is no record of a nest having actually been found. The usual site is an island where the eggs and young are safe from predators, and here a hollow is scraped in the sand and lined with any material such as twigs and bits of shell available in the vicinity.

Chlidonias niger surinamensis (Gmelin): BLACK TERN

General Distribution. Breeds from central British Columbia east through Saskatchewan and Manitoba to northern Ontario, south to central California, Colorado, Missouri, western Kentucky, and western New York. Winters on the Pacific coast from Panama to Peru, and on the Atlantic coast from Panama to Surinam.

Status in Idaho. A fairly common but local summer resident over much of the state.

In Kootenai County Rust (1915) noted a single bird at Hayden Lake in June, 1914, and stated that in June of that year he found this species fairly common as a breeding bird in "the St. Joe marshes."

I was in Kootenai County May 21, 1949, and that day found three small breeding colonies comprising eight to ten pairs in open marshes at Rose Lake, Cataldo, and Harrison. At Hauser on May 6, 1951, I saw a single bird, an early spring transient, feeding over a flooded field.

Hand (1941) considered the Black Tern a common summer resident near St. Maries, in Benewah County, occurring from May 10 to mid-August (1921-41). He stated that it nested in "the marshes of the lower St. Joe."

In Latah County there is no suitable nesting habitat, so I recorded this species there only as a rather scarce transient. It was seen at Moscow July 31, 1949, May 23, 1950, and May 13, 1952, and at Potlatch August 8, 1951, and July 31, 1953.

At Lewiston, in Nez Perce County, there are likewise no open marshes, but while the Black Tern occurred only as a transient it was fairly common in the spring and again in the fall, both on the Snake River and on the reservoir east of Lewiston Orchards. In the spring it was usually seen from early May until early June, my extreme dates for transients in breeding plumage being May 8 (1953) and June 8 (1950). Single birds still in winter plumage were noted at the reservoir June 18 and 21, 1955, and June 19, 1958, and were very probably nonbreeding birds with no incentive to reach their nesting grounds. In the fall the first transients appeared in late July and were noted at intervals until early September, my extreme dates of occurrence being July 28 (1954) and September 16 (1954).

In southern Idaho Davis (1935) reported it at Rupert, Minidoka County, May 19, 1921, and fifteen miles south of Riddle, Owyhee County (1934), May 28 through June 3, 1934. At this latter locality these terns were "quite common" and were apparently nesting in a large open marsh.

Levy (1950) found this species a common summer resident in south-central Idaho in 1949, and it was given this same status by Steel (1956) at Grays Lake (1949 through 1951), and by Oring (1962) at Mud Lake and on the Camas National Wildlife Refuge in 1961.

Habits. The food of the Black Tern in Idaho is apparently entirely insectivorous. Birds watched at the reservoir were picking up insects in flight, both in the air and from the surface of the water, and at no time were seen to plunge into the water for the small fish that, during the winter months, are said to form part of their diet. These same feeding habits were observed in Kootenai County and at Grays Lake.

The usual nesting site is over water two or more feet in depth, the nest being built of fragments of reeds and cattails, and placed on the matted dead growth of the previous year. The site, however, frequently varies according to the locality. At Harrison, in Kootenai County, the nests were on small islands in the open water, almost within reach of the shore, and with no attempt made at concealment. Three that were examined held one, two, and three eggs each. At Rose Lake, these terns were nesting on the top of muskrat houses, an incubating bird being noted on every house that could be seen from the shore.

Auks, Murres, and Puffins: *Family Alcidae*

Synthliboramphus antiquum (Gmelin): ANCIENT MURRELET

General Distribution. Breeds in North America on the Aleutian and Kodiak Islands south to the Queen Charlotte Islands in British Columbia, and casually to northwestern Washington. Winters south to northern Baja California.

Status in Idaho. Of accidental occurrence in the northern part of the state.

There is a single record for the occurrence of this species in Idaho. Hedges (1941) states that a female in adult plumage was found dead on the shore of Hayden Lake, in Kootenai County, by John C. Lindgren on December 29, 1929. It was prepared as a specimen, and identified as the Ancient Murrelet.

Habits. The Ancient Murrelet is a bird of the open ocean, its presence on or near land being restricted to the interval in the spring and early summer when it is rearing its young. There are very few instances of its occurrence inland, and in each case this was during the late fall months. Thus, apparently, it is during the fall migration that an occasional individual strays from the long-established route that would take it away from the mainland. Under these circumstances, it will always be one of the rarest species known to occur in Idaho.

ORDER COLUMBIFORMES

Pigeons and Doves: *Family Columbidae*

Columba fasciata monilis Vigors: BAND-TAILED PIGEON

General Distribution. Breeds from southern British Columbia south through Washington, Oregon, and California to northern Baja California. Winters north to northern California.

Status in Idaho. Of accidental occurrence in the state.

Although reported by Merrill (1897) as being noted by Cooper in what is now northern Idaho, it was not until 1947 that this species was definitely recorded for the state. In the course of field work that year, two specimens of the Band-tailed Pigeon were taken by Arthur C. Twomey in southern Idaho. One, a female (Carnegie Museum, 131818), was collected on June 20 on Reynolds Creek, five miles south of Reynolds, Owyhee County. The other, a male (Carnegie Museum, 132402), on October 5 at Bogus Basin, eight miles north of Boise, in Boise County. "The October bird is immature, with only a few iridescent feathers showing on the nape. The June bird I would judge to be a yearling; it is rather dull in color, and has several remiges very worn, apparently retained juvenile feathers—I would not be surprised if this were a non-breeding individual." (Kenneth C. Parkes, personal communication.)

Habits. In the northwestern United States the Band-tailed Pigeon is confined to the coast region west of the Cascades. There are extremely few records east of its normal range, so it is doubtful if it occurs in Idaho other than as a rare straggler. The food eaten consists largely of nuts and berries, and acorns are given preference wherever available. It is probable that the absence of oaks throughout all of Idaho is an important factor where the rarity of this species, even in migration, is concerned.

Columba livia Gmelin: ROCK DOVE

General Distribution. Native to Europe and Asia.

Status in Idaho. Now occurs in small numbers in the feral state in Owyhee County, and possibly elsewhere in southern Idaho.

Habits. Although never actually introduced into this country, the escape of numerous individuals from captivity has resulted in the Rock Dove being now common and widely distributed in North America. In June, 1949, I noted occasional pairs of these birds in rugged canyons south of Homedale, where they were apparently nesting on inaccessible ledges well toward the tops of high cliffs. They doubtless occur in similar situations elsewhere in the southern part of the state.

Zenaidura macroura (Linnaeus): MOURNING DOVE

General Distribution. Breeds from Alaska east through Alberta, Manitoba, Ontario, and Quebec to New Brunswick, south through Mexico and Central America to Panama, and in the Bahama Islands, Cuba, and Puerto Rico. Migrant in the northern part of its range.

Status in Idaho. A common summer resident throughout the state. Winters commonly at Lewiston, in Nez Perce County, and irregularly and in small numbers in Latah County.

This is another of the species of birds recorded for the first time in Idaho by the Lewis and Clark expedition. Clark (*Original Journals,* III:44) stated that it was noted along the Salmon River August 26, 1805, and Lewis (*Original Journals,* VI: 217) said that doves were heard "cooing" at Kamiah May 27, 1806 (Jollie, 1953).

It is doubtful if any other bird occurs in greater numbers or has as wide a distribution in the state. It is found during the summer months as far north as Boundary County (on the British Columbia line), south to Riddle, Owyhee County (on the Nevada state line, and Bear Lake County (on the Utah state line), and from Washington and Oregon in the western part of the state to Montana and Wyoming in eastern Idaho. Localities where it has been reported as a common summer resident include the following: Boundary County, Bonners Ferry and Porthill (Burleigh); Kootenai County, Coeur d'Alene (Merrill, 1897; Rust, 1915; Yocom, 1946); Benewah County, St. Maries (Hand, 1941); Latah County, Potlatch, Viola (Burleigh), Harvard (Verner, 1953), Moscow (Johnston, 1949; Burleigh); Nez Perce County, Lewiston (Burleigh); Clearwater County, Weippe (Burleigh); Adams County, Council (Newhouse, 1960); Owyhee County, Riddle (Davis, 1934), Homedale (Burleigh); Ada County, Boise (Burleigh); Minidoka County, Rupert (Davis, 1935); Lemhi County, Shoup (Burleigh), Custer County, Willow Creek Summit (Burleigh); Fremont County, Spencer (Rust, 1917); Bingham County, Blackfoot (Merriam, 1891); Jefferson County, Camas Refuge and Mud Lake (Oring, 1962); Bonneville County, Grays Lake (Steel, 1956); Power County, American Falls (Fichter, 1959).

It is usually the latter part of April before the Mourning Dove appears in the spring, and the last small flocks are generally gone by the end of October. Each year there is a perceptible decrease in numbers after the middle of September, but although the majority of the birds disappear at that time a few small flocks invariably linger for another month. Extreme dates of occurrence are: Coeur d'Alene, April 19, 1950 (Burleigh); Potlatch, April 25 (1955) and November 6 (1948) (Burleigh); Moscow, April 21 (1950) and October 31 (1948) (Burleigh); Weippe, April 20, 1953 (Burleigh); Council, April 14 to October 23 (1957-58) (Newhouse, 1960); Meridian, April 6 to November 4 (Bent, 1932); Rupert, May 1 to November 14 (1919 through 1921) (Davis, 1935); Grays Lake, May 1, 1951 (Steel, 1956); Pocatello, April 22 (Bent, 1932).

At Lewiston I found this species common throughout the year. Numbers present during the winter months vary, but the scattered small flocks that occur from late fall until early spring along both the Snake and the Clearwater rivers usually total about eighty individuals.

At infrequent intervals it has been noted in Latah County during the winter, and it is suspected that the birds seen then were venturesome individuals that temporarily left Lewiston. It is felt that this assumption is especially true in February and early March, for it is almost two months later before Mourning Dove transients appear in the spring anywhere in Idaho. Records that can be considered as referring to wintering individuals are as follows: Moscow, single birds seen December 28, 1950, January 19, 1951, and March 5, 1953; Viola, a flock of sixteen birds February 13, 1955; Potlatch, a single bird March 4, 1957.

Habits. The Mourning Dove in Idaho apparently has no preference regarding a suitable habitat other than that it be fairly open country. It has no liking for, nor will it be found in, dense forest, but otherwise is at home in the arid desert country characteristic of Owyhee County, in the cottonwood groves fringing the Snake River, in the wheat fields of the Palouse, or in cutover areas left by logging operations in the northern Panhandle. It also disregards altitude, for it nests commonly at Lewiston, the lowest point in the state (860 feet), and, as far as my own experience is concerned, to 7,300 feet at Willow Creek Summit, in Custer County.

Two and possibly three broods are reared each year, the first in May and early June, the last in late August and early September. At Potlatch my earliest nest was one that held two fresh eggs on May 22, 1955, my latest one that held one half-grown nestling on September 4, 1951. At Moscow a nest found August 15, 1950, held two well-fledged young. As might be expected, my latest breeding records are for Lewiston, where I found a nest with two half-incubated eggs on September 4, 1950, and another with one almost fully fledged young bird on September 17, 1957. Considering the altitude, 7,300 feet, a nest found at Willow Creek Summit July 14, 1958, with two fresh eggs may have represented a first brood.

The site of the nest varies considerably, although the usual situation is in a thick bush or sapling from three to ten feet from the ground. Merriam (1891) reports three nests, each on the ground and holding two eggs, at Blackfoot in mid-July; and Rust (1917) reports one at Spencer, in Fremont County, that held two eggs on June 16, 1916, and was also on the ground under a sage bush. A nest I found at Boise on June 22, 1949, with two well-incubated eggs, was two feet from the ground on the top of a stump, while another found the following day, June 23, near Homedale, Owyhee County, was on a lower ledge of a cliff in a rugged canyon.

Fichter (1959) gives an interesting account of a study he made of a breeding concentration of Mourning Doves at American Falls, Power County, in 1953. The area concerned comprised four orchards that totaled 13.4 acres. Summarized briefly, he estimated one hundred pairs of doves used these orchards; 208 nests were found of which 177 were successful, 324 young being reared. The nesting season extended from the first week in May to September 6. The peak of nesting activity was the latter two thirds of July, ninety-two nests being found July 11-15 and July 22-27.

Zenaidura macroura carolinensis (Linnaeus)

A male collected at Lewiston January 24, 1952, was found to represent this dark eastern race, the one record to date for Idaho. While rather unexpected, it is, of course, not surprising that an occasional individual should straggle west of its normal range that extends west to Wisconsin and eastern Texas.

Zenaidura macroura marginella (Woodhouse)

This distinctly pale race is the form that occurs commonly throughout the state. Specimens identified as *marginella* were taken as follows: Latah County, Potlatch, males October 18, 1953, and March 3, 1957, and an immature female September 5, 1954 (Burleigh), Moscow, males May 27, 1948 (Burleigh), and May 12, 1950 (S. H. Levy); Nez Perce County, Lewiston, males November 16 and December 28, 1951, January 19, August 19, and November 24, 1954, and females November 11 and December 13, 1948, December 13, 1950, October 14, 1951, and September 17, 1957 (Burleigh); Elmore County, Glenns Ferry, male July 4, 1910 (S. G. Jewett); Bingham County, Blackfoot, male July 8, 1898 (C. P. Streator); Franklin County, Swan Lake, male July 7, 1911 (S. G. Jewett).

Ectopistes migratorius (Linnaeus): PASSENGER PIGEON

General Distribution. Now extinct. Formerly occurred as a breeding bird from central Montana east across the continent to Nova Scotia, south to eastern Kansas, Oklahoma, and the Gulf states.

Status in Idaho. Of accidental occurrence in the northern part of the state.

According to Merrill (1897) Cooper reported this species in what he then considered Montana, but is now accepted as northern Idaho. This is verified by Allen J. Duvall (in litt.) who states that "I find that a specimen of the Passenger Pigeon, collected June 17, 1860, at Pack River, by C. B. Kennerly, was listed by Ridgway for both Montana and Oregon. However, Ridgway was in error as Pack River is in Idaho, and the specimen was collected by one of the Northwestern Boundary Survey. It is given as 48° 22′ lat., 116° 28′ long. by Marcus Baker, Bull. 174, U.S. Geological Surveys."

Habits. Few birds were known to be more gregarious than the Passenger Pigeon, for throughout the year, even during the nesting season, it occurred in large compact flocks. Such being the case, it is probable that only infrequently did an occasional individual stray west of the normal range of this species, and that it was always a rare bird in Idaho.

ORDER CUCULIFORMES

Cuckoos, Roadrunners, and Anis: *Family Cuculidae*

Coccyzus americanus occidentalis Ridgway: YELLOW-BILLED CUCKOO

General Distribution. Breeds from southern British Columbia, northern Utah, central Colorado and western Texas south into northwestern Mexico. Winters in South America.

Status in Idaho. A rare and rather local summer resident.

This species was first recorded in Idaho by Merrill (1897) who reported one bird seen July 30, 1895, at Fort Sherman (Coeur d'Alene).

Davis (1935) collected a specimen at Rupert, Minidoka County, May 16, 1918, and states that occupied nests were found there by Dr. Fayre Kenagy.

There are no other records.

Habits. The Yellow-billed Cuckoo is a quiet, rather retiring bird that could be easily overlooked were it not for its loud, prolonged "song." This is uttered as the bird sits motionless in dense foliage, where even though its presence is known it is difficult to see. Its movements are swift and stealthy, but on the whole, it is not a very shy bird.

It has no liking for dense woods, and open arid country offers few inducements to a species such as this; its scarcity in Idaho may therefore be partially due to a lack of suitable habitat.

Coccyzus erythropthalmus (Wilson): BLACK-BILLED CUCKOO

General Distribution. Breeds from southern Saskatchewan east through Manitoba, northern Minnesota and southern Ontario to Nova Scotia, south to southern Wyoming, Kansas, Tennessee, and South Carolina. Winters in northern South America.

Status in Idaho. A rare summer resident in the southern part of the state.

Arvey (1941) recorded this species for the first time in Idaho, collecting a female with enlarged ovaries July 10, 1941, at Slide Gulch, on the Middle Fork of the Boise River (Boise County). He later (Arvey, 1947) observed this cuckoo on two occasions during the summer months at Boise, Ada County.

Hudson (1952) collected a female at Grays Lake on June 20, 1952, and heard another that day and on the following day.

Habits. In practically all respects, haunts, habits, and behavior, the Black-billed Cuckoo resembles the preceding species. Its notes are also quite similar, so that unless the bird is seen there is often some doubt as to its identity. In the United States it is not known to nest farther west than eastern Montana, but its presence in Idaho during the summer months would indicate that it breeds at least sparingly in the southern part of the state.

ORDER STRIGIFORMES

Barn Owls: *Family Tytonidae*

Tyto alba pratincola (Bonaparte): BARN OWL

General Distribution. Resident from southern British Columbia east through North Dakota, Michigan, and southern Ontario to Massachusetts, south through Mexico to Guatemala, to the Gulf coast, and on the Atlantic coast to southern Florida.

Status in Idaho. Known only from a single specimen taken in the northern part of the state.

There is a mounted specimen of the Barn Owl in the collections of the Zoology Department, University of Idaho, that was taken near Moscow, in Latah County (Arvey, 1947). More complete information is unfortunately lacking, but there would appear to be no question as to the actual locality involved.

It has not been recorded otherwise in the state.

Habits. Although it has a wide distribution in this country, it is only in the southern part of the United States that the Barn Owl is a common bird. Idaho is at almost the extreme northern limit of its range and it is doubtful if, in view of the length and severity of the winters, it is of more than casual occurrence in the state. Its food consists almost entirely of rodents, and when, as is not infrequently the case, the ground is covered for much of the winter with deep snow, securing an adequate food supply must be extremely difficult for this species. It is entirely nocturnal in its habits, and easily overlooked, so its actual status in Idaho has yet to be determined.

Typical Owls: *Family Strigidae*

Otus asio (Linnaeus): SCREECH OWL

General Distribution. Resident from southern Alaska east through southern Manitoba and southern Ontario to Maine, south to northern Mexico and southern Florida.

Status in Idaho. Occurs throughout the wooded areas of the state and is probably fairly common, although further study is needed to determine its actual status.

Because of its nocturnal habits, the Screech Owl can be easily overlooked, and there are not many records for its occurrence in Idaho.

In Kootenai County Merrill (1897) considered it rare at Fort Sherman (Coeur d'Alene), stating that it was occasionally heard "in and about the fort." Rust (1916) gives it this same status for Coeur d'Alene. He collected a specimen there on January 18, 1916.

In Latah County I found this owl fairly common around Moscow, but did not note it elsewhere. Johnston (1949) collected an immature specimen there July 9, 1947, and I took two in the city limits in 1949, a male on January 10 and a female on August 11.

Hasbrouck (1893) reported it as occurring on the Nez Perce Indian Reservation (Lapwai, Nez Perce County), but he did not give any details as to its relative abundance. Arvey (1947) took a specimen at Lapwai December 25, 1938.

Orr (1951) frequently heard it at night, in September, 1941, "in the Selway region" in Idaho County. He saw one bird on September 5 two miles south of Selway Falls.

There are two records for southern Idaho. Arvey (1947) took a specimen at Boise, Ada County, April 11, 1942, and Levy (1962) one at Oakley, Cassia County, on June 10, 1951.

Habits. Because it is active only after nightfall and remains well hidden during the daylight hours, it is difficult to determine how common the Screech Owl is over much of Idaho. In eleven years residence at Moscow, I observed but two individuals, and in each instance their presence was revealed by the excitement displayed by Robins, House Finches, and other small birds when this small owl was discovered roosting in the open during the daytime. It is in the early spring that its presence can be most easily detected, for it is at this time of the year that its tremulous call can be heard after dark.

In the eastern United States the Screech Owl has two color phases, one red, the other gray, but this apparently is not the case in Idaho. I have not had the opportunity to examine many specimens, but those I have seen have been similar in appearance and could be considered the gray phase.

Otus asio macfarlanei (Brewster)

The specimens taken at Moscow, in the northern part of the state, have been found referable to this large dark race described from Walla Walla, Washington. It is resident in the northern Great Basin, from southern British Columbia south to northern California and east to western Montana, west of the Continental Divide.

Otus asio inyoensis Grinnell

The specimen taken by Levy in Cassia County in 1951 has been identified by Alden H. Miller as approaching *macfarlanei* but referable to *inyoensis.* He states that southern Idaho appears to be an area of intergradation between *macfarlanei* and *inyoensis,* but that this specimen from Oakley "makes a very distinct and quite close approach to *inyoensis.*" John W. Aldrich has also examined this specimen and states that in his opinion "there is no resemblance at all between it and the much darker and more brownish *macfarlanei*."

The range of *inyoensis*, as given in the 1957 A.O.U. *Check-List*, is central Nevada and northwestern Utah south to Inyo County, California.

Otus flammeolus flammeolus (Kaup): FLAMMULATED OWL

General Distribution. Breeds from southern British Columbia, Idaho, and northern Colorado south through the mountains to southern California, western Texas, and the northern half of Mexico. Winters north to southern California.

Status in Idaho. Apparently an uncommon summer resident in the more heavily wooded areas in the state.

This species was first recorded in Idaho by Merriam (1891) who reported an adult male taken by himself and Vernon Bailey on Big Wood River north of Ketchum, in Blaine County, September 22, 1890. Rust (1915) considered it rather uncommon in Kootenai County (1910 through 1914). He took a specimen at Fernan Lake on September 28, 1914.

There are no other records.

Merriam (1891) thought that the specimen collected at Ketchum represented a new and unrecognized race, being "similar to *M. flammeolus* but smaller and paler," and named it *Megascops flammeolus idahoensis*. It has never been recognized, however, by the A.O.U. Committee on Classification and Nomenclature.

Habits. As with the other owls that are active only after nightfall, it is rather difficult to determine just how common the Flammulated Owl is as a breeding bird in Idaho. Only rarely will one be seen in an exposed situation during the daytime, a thick spruce or fir offering the desired concealment during the hours of inactivity. While not at all timid, it is not known to frequent the shade trees in the towns as the Screech Owl does, its preference at all times being heavily wooded areas usually at the higher elevations. As a result it is seldom observed, and throughout its range it is generally considered one of the rarest of the owls.

Bubo virginianus (Gmelin): GREAT HORNED OWL

General Distribution. Resident from the limit of trees in the Arctic to the Straits of Magellan.

Status in Idaho. Fairly common over the entire state; of general distribution in the forested areas, but of local occurrence in the open arid country where tree growth is limited to the stream bottoms.

The Great Horned Owl was first recorded in Idaho by the Lewis and Clark expedition. Lewis (*Original Journals*, IV:129-30) stated in his journal that it was seen at Kamiah, and (*Original Journals*, V:76) that one was killed May 28, 1806 (Jollie, 1953).

Numerous observers have reported it at various places throughout the state, consensus being that it is a relatively common species wherever found. Localities where noted are as follows: Bonner County, Clark Fork (Trestle Creek, September 11, 1917) (Burleigh 1923); Kootenai County, Coeur d'Alene, occurs commonly (Merrill, 1897); frequently seen (Rust, 1912, 1917); upper end of Lake Coeur d'Alene, heard "nightly" July 1 to 10, 1943 (Yocom, 1946); Benewah County, St. Maries, fairly common, 1921 through 1941 (Hand, 1941); Latah County, twenty-five miles northeast of Moscow, three seen, June 4, 1947, and one in immature plumage collected there a week later (Johnston, 1949); Harvard, often heard at night the latter part of July and early August, 1952; one seen on August 4 (Verner, 1953); Potlatch, Genesee, Moscow, Deary frequently noted, 1947-58 (Burleigh); Nez Perce County, Lapwai, reported by Bendire as taken at Fort Lapwai in 1871 (Merriam, 1891); Lewiston, noted, 1941-58, on Hatwai Creek and in cottonwoods on both the Snake and the Clearwater rivers (Burleigh); Idaho County, frequently heard at night, in September, 1941, "in the Selway region" (Orr, 1951); Boise County, Boise National Forest, frequently heard, 1938-40, one collected February 4, 1940 (Marshall, 1945); Owyhee County, Riddle, one bird seen May 28-June 3, 1934 (Davis, 1934); south-central Idaho, common in the Salmon River and Sawtooth Mountains in 1890; one collected on September 30 at Sawtooth Lake (Merriam, 1891); Clark County, one seen July 14, 1961, on Signal Peak (Oring, 1962); Fremont County, occurs sparingly, one shot at Henrys Lake (Rust, 1917); Jefferson County, common during the summer of 1961 on the Camas National Wildlife Refuge (Oring, 1962); Blaine County, fairly common at Ketchum, one collected November 21, 1910 (Jewett, 1912); one seen July 31, 1949, below Magic Dam on the Wood River (Levy, 1950); Bonneville County, Grays Lake, fairly common, 1949-51 (Steel, 1956); Big Elk Creek, three heard August 6, 1961 (Oring 1962); Caribou County, Soda Springs, nest found May 12, 1944 (Low, 1945).

Habits. Although it hunts its prey only after nightfall, this species is noticeably less secretive in its actions than the smaller owls, for it can commonly be seen during the daylight hours perched in an open situation where it is frequently rather conspicuous. It is usually easily approached then, for at Moscow I have often been able to walk almost beneath an individual as it perched on an upper limb of a cottonwood or box elder before it became uneasy and flew.

It is one of the earliest species to nest in the spring, but in Idaho the date when the eggs are laid would appear to be influenced by the altitude. On Reynolds Creek west of Murphy, in Owyhee County, I found a bird, on February 26, 1950, incubating on a nest sixty feet from the ground in the top of a large cottonwood. I was unable to ascertain its contents but it unquestionably held eggs. In direct contrast was a nest found at Grays Lake on May 14, 1951 (Steel, 1956), that held "one young just hatching and the

A SOBER GREAT-HORNED OWL DEEP IN ITS NEST

other egg not yet pipped." The altitude at Murphy is approximately 4,000 feet, whereas at Grays Lake it is 6,300 feet. The usual situation for the nest is the top of the largest tree that is available, but in Idaho ledges of cliffs are commonly used in areas where vegetation is sparse. Low (1945) states that in May, 1944, a pair was found at Soda Springs nesting in a clay bank.

Although it commonly feeds on birds, both large and small, it prefers mammals; its reputation for destructiveness is probably far from justified. Merriam (1891) collected a specimen in the Sawtooth Mountains in September, 1890, and found in its stomach two gophers and three mice.

Bubo virginianus wapacuthu (Gmelin)

This northern race of the Great Horned Owl, occurring from the tree limit in Mackenzie Valley to Hudson Bay, is to some extent migratory and is found in Idaho in small numbers in the fall and winter months. Specimens identified as *arcticus* (a synonym of *wapacuthu*) were reported by Bendire as taken at Ft. Lapwai, Nez Perce County, in 1871, and at Ft. Sherman

(Coeur d'Alene) in 1880 (Merriam, 1891), by Rust (1913) at Coeur d'Alene October 8, 1912, and by Rust (1917) at Henrys Lake, Fremont County. Other specimens identified as *subarcticus* (another synonym of *wapacuthu*) were reported by Merrill (1897) as taken at Coeur d'Alene, where he states this northern race was not uncommon during the winter months. I collected one specimen, a female, at Potlatch September 6, 1952.

Bubo virginianus occidentalis Stone

This relatively pale race is the resident breeding form occurring in the southern half of the state. Specimens identified as *occidentalis* have been taken in Washington County, Weiser, November 22, 1951; Owyhee County, Bruneau, February 6, 1930, Homedale, February 24, 1950, Murphy, February 26, 1950; Elmore County, Glenns Ferry, February 8, 1930; Blaine County, Ketchum, November 21, 1910; Fremont County, Henrys Lake, June 25, 1960; Bonneville County, Caribou Mountain, July 5, 1930; Oneida County, Malad City, April 4, 1930. It apparently wanders to some extent during the winter months, for I collected two male specimens at Moscow on February 1 and February 15, 1950, that were typical of this race.

Bubo virginianus lagophonus (Oberholser)

This is the resident breeding form of the northern half of the state, its range extending north to the interior of Alaska and the Yukon, and south to eastern Washington and Oregon, and northwestern Montana. Specimens identified as *lagophonus* have been taken as follows: Latah County, twenty-five miles northeast of Moscow, female, im., June 12, 1947; Moscow, male, im., July 3, 1948, female September 27, 1950; Viola, male September 19, 1949; Genesee, female November 27, 1948; Coyote Grade, female November 11, 1948; Nez Perce County, Lewiston, male, im., July 31, 1950; Idaho County, Riggins, September 15, 1939; Elmore County, Thurman, male March 12, 1923; Boise County, Sawtooth Lake, male September 30, 1890.

Bubo virginianus saturatus Ridgway

This is the darkest of the races occurring in the northwestern United States. It is largely resident on the Pacific coast from southern Alaska south to central California, but an occasional individual is found during the winter months east of the coast ranges. Two specimens that I took at Moscow, both males, one on November 20, 1947, the other on January 24, 1955, have been identified as *saturatus*.

Nyctea scandiaca (Linnaeus): SNOWY OWL

General Distribution. Circumpolar. Breeds in North America on the Barren Grounds from the islands of the Bering Sea, the Yukon Delta, Melville Island, and northern Greenland south to central Mackenzie, central Keewatin and northern Ungava. Winters from the Arctic coast south to the southern Canadian provinces and irregularly to California, Texas, Louisiana, and Georgia.

Status in Idaho. Of uncommon occurrence in the state during the winter months. Merrill (1897) found it not uncommon in winter at Fort Sherman, but "irregular and uncertain" in its appearance. He states that it was unusually abundant in December, 1896.

Rust (1915) reported it rare in Kootenai County (1910 through 1914). One specimen was taken at Coeur d'Alene.

Hand (1941) examined a specimen at Emida, Benewah County, in 1931 that was shot there the winter before.

My one record for Latah County is that of a bird seen at Genesee on February 8, 1951.

In south-central Idaho two mounted specimens were examined by Merriam (1891) that had been shot on Birch Creek. Bent (1938) cites November 23 as an early date of arrival at Meridian, Ada County.

Habits. The scarcity of records would indicate that the Snowy Owl is never a common bird in Idaho. Active during the daylight hours and frequenting open prairie country or the larger fields and pastures in wooded areas, it is a conspicuous bird wherever found. The one individual I saw at Genesee was on a fence post at the edge of a field, and although it was the middle of the day it was wide awake, and so alert that it would not permit a close approach. This wariness is apparently characteristic of this large owl, even on its breeding grounds in the far north where it rarely encounters man.

Where available, the preferred food is rodents, so it can be considered a beneficial species during its sojourn in the state.

Surnia ulula caparoch (Müller): Hawk Owl

General Distribution. Breeds from northern Alaska, central Mackenzie, northern Manitoba, northern Quebec and Newfoundland south to northern British Columbia, northern Idaho, northern Montana, Michigan, central Ontario and New Brunswick. Winters casually south to Nebraska, Illinois, northern Ohio, and New Jersey.

Status in Idaho. Apparently a rare breeding bird in the state. There are no records for the winter months.

Hand (1953) first recorded this species for Idaho when, on August 27, 1923, he noted a single individual on the Lolo Trail (in Idaho County) between the Lochsa River and the North Fork of the Clearwater. Two years later, on November 3, 1925, he collected an immature male at Stanley Butte, twelve miles south of the Lochsa. There are no other records.

Habits. Like the preceding species, this medium-sized owl is active during the daylight hours, hunting its rodent prey even in bright sunshine during the middle of a clear day. It frequents open woods or the edges of clearings, perching in the top of a tall tree or old snag from which vantage point it watches the ground for an unwary mouse or chipmunk. Under these circumstances, it is far from inconspicuous, so the fact that it has been so seldom observed would indicate that it is a rare bird in Idaho. Both in appearance and actions it suggests a hawk rather than an owl, so it is well named.

Glaucidium gnoma pinicola Nelson: PYGMY OWL

General Distribution. Resident in the Rocky Mountain region of the United States from Idaho and western Montana south to extreme eastern California, the mountains of southern Arizona and New Mexico.

Status in Idaho. Fairly common throughout the year in the northern half of the state.

In Kootenai County the Pygmy Owl was reported by Merrill (1897) as not uncommon at Fort Sherman (Coeur d'Alene), and by Rust (1915) as frequently noted in September and October (1910 through 1914). Arvey (1947) lists a specimen taken at Priest River, Bonner County, January 3, 1939.

Hand (1941) considered it common during the fall and winter at St. Maries, in Benewah County (1921 through 1941).

In Latah County Johnston (1949) noted an occasional bird from June 1 through August 16, 1947. My own experience with this little owl was limited to the open valleys, and here I found it fairly common and well distributed during the fall and winter months. It was observed at Moscow between the dates of October 30 (1957) and March 14 (1956), and specimens were taken there February 15, 1950, November 7 and December 12, 1951, March 14, 1956, and October 30, 1957. Specimens were also taken at Viola December 20, 1947, Troy January 7, 1948, and Princeton December 12, 1951.

In Nez Perce County I noted single birds at Culdesac and at Spalding November 13, 1949.

I likewise have two records for Clearwater County, Weippe, February 14, 1952, and Greer, January 9, 1956.

In Idaho County Orr (1951) recorded this species in 1941 four miles southwest of Selway Falls, one bird being seen September 16, and another heard September 21. I collected a male at Grangeville November 20, 1951. In the collections of the Museum of Comparative Zoology at Berkeley, California, there is a female taken October 8, 1957, by W. C. Russell, five miles northeast of the junction of Whitecap Creek and the Selway River.

Rust (1917) reports a mounted specimen that he examined in Fremont County that was taken at Henrys Lake, the southernmost point that this species has been recorded in the state.

A critical examination of specimens taken in the state has shown that *pinicola* is a valid race, with characters readily separating it from *californicum*. From *californicum* it differs in being grayer and darker; and no specimens of *pinicola* examined approached the extreme reddish phase common in the California race. Actually the so-called grayish phase of *californicum* closely resembles the reddish phase of *pinicola*, but is not as dark.

Habits. During the summer months, the Pygmy Owl is found in the thick fir and spruce woods, and is inconspicuous and rarely observed then. In the late fall, however, depending to some extent on the first heavy snowfall, it appears in the open valleys, and can frequently be seen perched on the top of a telephone pole or on a fence post at the edge of a field. It is apparently more diurnal than the other small owls, its actions during the daylight hours giving the impression that it is ever on the alert for an unwary mouse or small bird. It is easily approached then, and shows little or no fear of the observer. Although rodents and large insects are preferred for food, small birds are taken as opportunity offers. Johnston (1949) states that a specimen collected in Latah County during the summer of 1947 had the remains of an empidonax flycatcher in its stomach.

Speotyto cunicularia hypugaea (Bonaparte): BURROWING OWL

General Distribution. Breeds from southern British Columbia, Alberta, Saskatchewan and southern Manitoba south to Baja California and central Mexico and east to Minnesota, Iowa, and central Kansas. Winters south to the Gulf coast of Mississippi and western Florida, and through western Central America to Panama.

Status in Idaho. A locally common summer resident in the southern part of the state. Reported as occurring at one time in northern Idaho.

The Burrowing Owl has been reported from the following localities: Parma, Canyon County, two pairs noted June 4, 1951, and one male collected (Burleigh); Ada County, Boise, a specimen taken April 2, 1939 (Arvey, 1947); Meridian, extreme dates of occurrence March 5 and December 14; Deer Flat Refuge, March 18 and November 1 (Bent, 1938); Riddle, Owyhee County, a single bird seen May 28 through June 3, 1934 (Davis, 1934); Minidoka County, "tolerably common" in 1907, rare in 1913 (Kenagy, 1914), Rupert, 1919 through 1921, earliest date of arrival March 21, latest record in the fall September 28, fresh eggs April 20 (Davis, 1935); Twin Falls County, common in 1949, twelve noted at one spot near Filer on August 4 (Levy, 1950); south-central Idaho, 1890 "rare"; noted at Blackfoot in July; one taken at Big Butte July 18; specimens taken in 1872 "in Malade Valley and Portneuf Canyon and at Fort Hall" (Merriam, 1891); Jefferson County, one bird seen at Terreton April 29, 1954 (Burleigh), Camas National Wildlife Refuge, a locally common summer resident, two "colonies" noted on the Refuge, and another five miles southeast of Hamer (Oring, 1962).

The only evidence that it ever occurred in the northern part of the state is a statement by Merriam (1891) that it was reported by Bendire as nesting at Fort Lapwai (Nez Perce County).

Habits. Although largely nocturnal in its activities, the Burrowing Owl can be seen during the daylight hours perched on a fence post or standing at the edge of its burrow in the open country it frequents. In the southern part of its range, it is largely nonmigratory; but in Idaho it is usually the latter part of March before the first birds appear in the spring and only an occasional individual is noted after the end of October. With the increasing use of irrigation and the growing importance of agriculture in the state, the natural habitat of this owl has decreased in recent years, but locally it is still a common bird over much of its original range. It is one of the most beneficial species to agriculture, for its food consists largely of such large insects as grasshoppers, locusts and beetles, and rodents. Fortunately, this fact seems to be realized by the average farmer or rancher, and on the whole it suffers little persecution.

Strix nebulosa nebulosa Forster: GREAT GRAY OWL

General Distribution. Breeds in boreal forests from central Alaska, northern Mackenzie, northern Manitoba and northern Ontario south to California, northern Idaho, Wyoming, and northern Minnesota. Winters south to Nebraska, Indiana, Ohio, and New Jersey.

Status in Idaho. Resident in small numbers in the northern part of the state; apparently occurs occasionally in southern Idaho during the winter months.

This large owl is another species first recorded in the state by the Lewis and Clark expedition. Clark (*Original Journals,* V:59-60) states in one of his journals that a specimen was taken at Kamiah, on the Clearwater River, May 23, 1806 (Jollie, 1953).

Hand (1941) cites two records for Shoshone County; he states that in the summer of 1924 an adult and an immature were reported shot between the Roundtop Ranger Station and Fishhook Peak, and that on June 24, 1931, he was shown the wings and claws of an adult and of a half-grown immature that were reported shot the day before at "Forty-nine Meadows" west of Roundtop Ranger Station.

Rust (1915) considered it rare in Kootenai County. He collected an adult female at Mica Bay on Lake Coeur d'Alene on December 4, 1914.

The one record for Benewah County is that of a mounted specimen reported to have been shot at Santa in the fall of 1924 or 1925 (Hand, 1941).

Arvey (1947) was given a specimen on December 8, 1938, that was shot that day nine miles northeast of Grangeville, in Idaho County.

The one record for the southern part of the state is that of a specimen taken at St. Anthony in Fremont County, in December, 1910 (Bent, 1938).

Habits. Despite its size, almost that of the Great Horned Owl, this species is noticeably different in temperament from its near relative. It lacks its ferocity and savageness, and is one of our more beneficial birds of prey. Although small birds are part of its normal diet, the smaller mammals, squirrels, rabbits, and rats, form the bulk of its food. In the northern part of its range, where the days in midsummer are twenty-four hours long, it is, of necessity, diurnal in its activities, and this trait has been found to be characteristic of individuals occurring much farther south. This species is said to be very unsuspicious and easily approached without showing any alarm, but too little is known of its habits in Idaho to justify any definite conclusions in this respect.

Asio otus tuftsi Godfrey: Long-eared Owl

General Distribution. Breeds from southern Mackenzie and Saskatchewan south to northern Baja California, southern Arizona, New Mexico, and western Texas. Winters over much of its breeding range in the United States and south to Sonora and Durango.

Status in Idaho. A fairly common but local summer resident over much of the state, wintering irregularly and in small numbers in the more open country.

Apparently in the extreme northern part of Idaho the Long-eared Owl is a rare bird, and it possibly occurs as a fall transient only. In Kootenai County it was recorded by Merrill (1897) who stated that a single specimen was taken at Fort Sherman (Coeur d'Alene); by Snyder (1900) who collected a specimen in the Hoodoo Valley August 18, 1894; and by Rust (1915) who took a specimen on Lake Coeur d'Alene September 13, 1913.

In Latah County Arvey (1947) reported this species fairly common, taking a specimen five miles southwest of Moscow April 29, 1940. Johnston (1949) noted a "group" of six birds at Harvard July 2, 1947. I also found this owl fairly common and well distributed during the summer months in the open Palouse country about Moscow, appearing in the spring on or shortly after the middle of March (March 14, 1949, March 19, 1950, March 23, 1952) and being rarely observed after the latter part of October. Regardless of deep snows and low temperatures, an occasional individual remains throughout the winter, my records for this time of the year being as follows: December 25, 1948 (three birds), January 19, 1951 (one bird), January 12, 1955 (two birds), December 23 and 30, 1956 (two birds), February 3, 1957 (one bird).

Bendire (1892) reported the Long-eared Owl a common bird in 1871 in the vicinity of Fort Lapwai, in Nez Perce County; he succeeded in finding sixteen occupied nests that year between the dates of April 16 and June 6.

In Fremont County, a single bird was noted by Rust (1917) at Highbridge June 26, 1916. Oring (1962) found this species a common summer resident in 1961 on the Camas National Wildlife Refuge in Jefferson County. He collected an immature male on Camas Creek August 17.

Merriam (1891) saw an occasional bird in the course of field work in south-central Idaho, taking specimens on Devil Creek June 28, 1872, and at Blackfoot, Bingham County, July 17, 1890.

Davis (1935) reported this owl as resident in Minidoka County, giving as the earliest date for eggs (1919 through 1921) April 17, and the latest date for young in the nest June 10.

To determine the race occurring in Idaho both during the breeding season, and as a transient and winter resident, I collected a series of thirteen specimens as follows: Moscow, males December 25, 1948, March 23, 1949, January 19, 1951, April 12, 1952, February 22, 1955, December 30, 1956, February 3 and April 21, 1957; females October 15, 1949, June 16, 1953, February 6, 1955; Genesee, male July 13, 1953; Lapwai, female January 13,

1955. Examined critically, they were found to be paler below than *wilsonianus*, but darker above than typical *tuftsi*. However, although intermediate in their characters they are closer to *tuftsi*, and accordingly the population of *Asio otus* in Idaho can be considered as representing this western race.

Habits. In Idaho the Long-eared Owl is a bird of the more open country, shunning the heavy timber and occurring in thickets and underbrush in the stream bottoms. It is one of the least diurnal of the owls, and except during the nesting season it is rarely seen, remaining well hidden throughout the day in a dense thicket. In the vicinity of Moscow, there are abandoned apple orchards here and there, and these are favored spots for this species during much of the year.

At Moscow the usual nest site is an old and often rather delapidated Magpie's nest, the eggs being laid in a hollow in the top and never concealed from view. There is apparently some irregularity in the time that individual pairs nest, for in 1948 I found a nest on May 19 that held two well-grown young, while another held five partially incubated eggs on May 23. Bendire (1882) states that three nests that he found on April 16, 1871, at Fort Lapwai, held respectively six slightly incubated eggs, five fresh eggs, and three fresh eggs. They were in each case old crows' nests, averaging twelve feet from the ground, and although relined to some extent with grasses, dead leaves, and feathers, were rather delapidated looking.

Asio flammeus flammeus (Pontoppidan): SHORT-EARED OWL

General Distribution. Cosmopolitan. In North America breeds from northern Alaska, Baffin Island, Labrador and Newfoundland south to southern California, Utah, Kansas, northern Indiana, and Virginia. Winters over much of its breeding range south to Baja California, Texas, the Gulf coast and Florida.

Status in Idaho. Resident throughout the state, breeding locally, and in small numbers, where there is suitable habitat, and common during the winter months when its numbers are augmented by transients from the northern part of its range.

In Bonner County one bird was seen at the top of an open ridge north of Clark Fork August 15, 1917 (Burleigh, 1923).

In Kootenai County, it was reported by Merrill (1897) as frequently seen at Fort Sherman (Coeur d'Alene) in the fall, and by Rust (1915) as "not common"; two specimens were taken by him.

In Shoshone County Hand (1941) noted a single bird July 26, 1935, between Avery and the Roundtop Ranger Station.

Worcester (1928) stated that on December 6, 1927, "hundreds" of short-eared owls were seen near St. Maries, in Benewah County, feeding on rodents that flood conditions had driven to a limited area of high ground.

In Latah County Arvey (1947) reported it common; he collected a specimen five miles southwest of Moscow April 29, 1940. Johnston (1949) noted one bird south of Moscow June 28, 1947. I personally found this owl rather scarce during the summer months in the open Palouse country, but this was doubtless due to the fact that wheat fields had replaced large areas that originally were suitable nesting habitat. In the winter it was most plentiful from late December until early February when one or more birds were seen daily flying low over the snow-covered fields. The largest number noted during any one day was twelve, on January 24, 1951, in the open country between Moscow and Genesee.

In Nez Perce County it was reported by Bendire as breeding in 1871 at Fort Lapwai, two occupied nests being found there in early May (Merriam, 1891). I noted an occasional bird each winter in Coyote Canyon, northeast of Lewiston, and observed what was apparently a family party at the reservoir east of Lewiston Orchards August 2, 1957.

The larger part of Clearwater County is heavily wooded, and only at Weippe is there open prairie acceptable to the Short-eared Owl. Here I saw a single bird on December 24, 1952, and again a single bird June 27, 1955.

In Adams County there is an extensive stretch of open marshy meadow north of New Meadows where one or more pairs of these owls nests each year. Six birds were seen there November 20, 1951, resting on fence posts at the side of a road, and two were observed feeding over the marsh May 18 and again on June 1, 1955. Newhouse (1960) noted one bird at Council July 14, 1958.

Owyhee County is largely open arid desert, but Herbert E. Salinger (in litt.) reports a small marshy area at Homedale where a Short-eared Owl's nest holding five well-incubated eggs was found June 12, 1950.

In Fremont County Rust (1915) took a specimen at Henrys Lake. Oring (1962) found this species a "common summer resident" in 1961 on the Camas National Wildlife Refuge in Jefferson County. Steel (1956) considered it a fairly common summer resident at Grays Lake (1949 through 1951); he gives as an arrival date in the spring April 19, 1951. A nest with one fresh egg was found May 8, 1951.

In south-central Idaho it was reported by Kenagy (1914) as abundant in Minidoka County 1910-11, but rare 1912-13; by Davis (1935) as nesting in the vicinity of Rupert (1919 through 1921), with May 19 as the earliest date for eggs; by Levy (1950) as uncommon during the summer of 1949. I noted two birds at Twin Falls June 19, 1949.

In order to verify the occurrence of this species in the state, a small series of fifteen specimens was taken as follows: Moscow, males January 8, 25, and 30, 1950, January 29, 1956; female January 6, 1950; Troy, female January 24, 1950; Genesee, male June 4, 1957, female January 24, 1951; Coyote Grade, males October 16 and 19, 1949, female January 12, 1950; Lewiston, female August 2, 1957; Weippe, male December 24, 1952; New Meadows, males November 20, 1951, and June 1, 1955.

Habits. Despite its resemblance to the Long-eared Owl, the Short-eared Owl is quite different in many respects. In Idaho it was noticeably diurnal in its activities, and as it frequented open country rather than woods and thickets, it was at times a conspicuous part of the landscape. This was especially true during the winter months when it could be seen flying low over the snow-covered fields searching for an unwary rodent. Its numbers varied during the winter, and while always present then there were years when it was almost abundant. At this season of the year it showed a tendency to assemble in small groups, one such daytime roost being found at Genesee in 1955 where on January 24 fourteen birds were flushed from a thick growth of tall weeds in a ditch in the middle of an open field.

The nest is always built on the ground, and where available a marshy area is selected. The two nests found by Bendire at Fort Lapwai May 6, 1871 (Bendire, 1892), were "slight depressions not more than two inches deep lined with pieces of dry grass and a few feathers from the birds." Both were well concealed in thick grass. One held four slightly incubated eggs, and the other three fresh eggs. Levy (1950) found this species nesting in hayfields in the south-central part of the state, and this is possibly a common practice where there is no open marsh.

Aegolius funereus richardsoni (Bonaparte): Boreal Owl

General Distribution. Breeds from northern Alaska, central Saskatchewan, northern Ontario and Labrador south to northern British Columbia, central Alberta, southern Manitoba, and New Brunswick. Winters over much of its breeding range and south to southern Oregon, Idaho, Colorado, Nebraska, Illinois and New York.

Status in Idaho. Apparently of rare occurrence during the winter in the extreme northern part of the state.

The Boreal Owl has been recorded but twice in Idaho, each time in Kootenai County. Merrill (1897) reported two specimens taken at Fort Sherman (Coeur d'Alene) in the early spring of 1894, and Rust (1915) states that it was rare in winter in Kootenai County and that one specimen was collected.

Habits. This little owl is largely resident wherever it is found, occurring south of its breeding range only during winters when unusually deep snows and low temperatures make existence rather precarious. The smaller rodents and large insects form the bulk of its food, so it is one of our more beneficial birds of prey. It is to a large extent nocturnal in its habits, and as it normally remains quietly concealed in thick vegetation during the daylight hours it can be easily overlooked. It is, therefore, possibly more common in Idaho than the few records indicate.

Aegolius acadicus acadicus (Gmelin): Saw-whet Owl

General Distribution. Breeds from southern Alaska, central Alberta, southern Manitoba, northern Ontario and Nova Scotia south to southern California, Mexico (Veracruz), central Missouri, Ohio, and Maryland. Win-

A SAW-WHET OWL IN AN ARTISTIC SETTING

ters over much of its breeding range, and south to Louisiana, Georgia, and Florida.

Status in Idaho. Resident in small numbers in the northern part of the state, and of uncommon occurrence during the winter months in southern Idaho.

In Kootenai County Merrill (1897) reported a specimen taken January 19 at Fort Sherman (Coeur d'Alene), and Rust (1915) stated that it was rarely observed in the county (1910 through 1914). He also collected one specimen.

Levy (1959) cited one record for Shoshone County, a male taken October 22, 1950, on Thor Mountain, near Dismal Lake.

In Latah County I observed this little owl at infrequent intervals in the vicinity of Moscow from late fall until early spring (February 1 and October 21, 1949, November 14, 1955, January 10, 1956, March 9, 1958), and on one occasion at Princeton (January 20, 1949). It doubtless breeds in the heavy timber on the nearby mountain slopes, but I have no actual evidence to that effect.

That it leaves the wooded ridges during the winter months, at least in small numbers, is further indicated by the presence then of an occasional individual in willows bordering the Snake River at Lewiston. Single birds were noted under such circumstances on December 7, 1949, and December 2, 1956.

In Idaho County Orr (1951) reported a specimen taken September 14, 1941, four miles southwest of Selway Falls.

Rust (1917) noted this species in Fremont County, stating that a specimen was taken at Henrys Lake.

According to Davis (1935) it occurred as a winter resident in the vicinity of Rupert, in Minidoka County (1919 through 1921), his extreme dates of occurrence being December 18 and April 17.

Habits. The actual status of the Saw-whet Owl in Idaho cannot be definitely stated without a more detailed study throughout the state.

It is entirely nocturnal in its activities; and as it normally remains well concealed during the day in a dense thicket, its presence could go entirely undetected even when searched for. The few individuals that I have seen were noted quite by accident, the bush selected for a daytime retreat being open enough to reveal this little owl dozing away the hours of bright sunlight. It was possible then to almost touch it before it showed any alarm, and even then it flew but a short distance before seeking the seclusion of another thicket. There is little question that it nests in the state, but a nest has yet to be found to verify this supposition.

It is another of our beneficial birds of prey, for while small birds are occasionally eaten, the bulk of its food consists of small rodents.

ORDER CAPRIMULGIFORMES

Goatsuckers: *Family Caprimulgidae*

Phalaenoptilus nuttallii nuttallii (Audubon): POOR-WILL

General Distribution. Breeds from southern British Columbia, Alberta, northern South Dakota and Nebraska south to southeastern California and northern Mexico (Sonora and Coahuila). Winters north to California, southern Arizona, and southern Texas.

Status in Idaho. A fairly common but local summer resident in the southern part of the state. Apparently of accidental occurrence in northern Idaho.

The one record for the northern part of the state is that of a bird that I flushed in a ravine four miles south of Moscow on May 14, 1949.

Rust (1917) reported a bird heard after dark at the mouth of Little Dry Creek Canyon, in Fremont County, on August 11, 1916.

In south-central Idaho Merriam (1891) stated that in 1890 one was taken on the lava beds west of Blackfoot July 17, that one was heard in a canyon in the Lost River Mountains the last week in July, and that one was seen in the Birch Creek Valley in early August. In this same general area it was reported by Levy (1950) as fairly common during the summer of 1949.

I saw a single bird on East Brownlee Creek, west of Cambridge in Washington County, June 7, 1952.

Davis (1934) heard this species "nightly" May 28 through June 3, 1934, at Riddle, in Owyhee County. A specimen was taken by Malcolm Jollie on Mary's Creek, eight miles east of Riddle, June 18, 1949. At the Museum of Veterate Zoology at Berkeley, California, there are specimens taken by Alden H. Miller on Cuddy Mountain, Washington County, July 1, 1932, and by W. B. Davis six miles west of Murphy, Owyhee County, May 24, 1935, and twenty miles northeast of Preston, Franklin County, July 12, 1937. In Bear Lake County a specimen was taken by Pierce Brodkorb at Joe's Gap in the Preuss Range, September 3, 1934, and by Malcolm Jollie at Bloomington Lake, ten miles west of Bloomington, July 9, 1949.

Habits. Were it not for its liking for dirt roads, the Poor-Will would merely be a sound in the night to the average person. Active only during the night, it dozes throughout the day on the ground, and its plumage blends so perfectly with its surroundings that even a few feet away it would not be noticed. After dark, however, it commonly rests in the middle of a dirt road, if one is available, and it was in such a situation that I encountered the few individuals that I saw in Idaho. If approached in an automobile, it at once attracts attention for its eyes have a pink gleam that in the headlights of the car reveal it even at a distance.

Throughout its breeding range it seems to prefer the higher altitudes, and this is certainly true in Idaho. Although there was suitable habitat at Lewiston it has never been noted there, and only above four thousand feet has it been found to be at all plentiful. The specimen taken by W. B. Davis north of Preston, in Franklin County, was at an altitude of 6,700 feet.

Chordeiles minor (Forster): COMMON NIGHTHAWK

General Distribution. Breeds from southern Yukon, northern Saskatchewan, northern Ontario and Quebec south to southern California, northern Mexico (Sonora, Durango, and Chiapas), the Bahama Islands, Jamaica and Puerto Rico. Winters in South America from Colombia and Venezuela south to central Argentina.

Status in Idaho. A common summer resident throughout the state.

Few birds in Idaho have a wider distribution or are less local in their occurrence than the Nighthawk, for wherever there is any open country at least one pair can be found. Altitude is apparently no limiting factor, for it breeds commonly at Lewiston, at 840 feet, and on the higher ridges to at least 7,000 feet. Localities from which it has been reported are: Bonner County, Clark Fork, three feeding overhead July 3, 1917 (Burleigh, 1923); Kootenai County, Fort Sherman, common summer resident (Merrill, 1897); Blue Lake, nest with "downy young" July 20, 1894 (Snyder, 1900); Coeur d'Alene, common summer resident, 1911-47 (Rust, 1947); Benewah County, St. Maries, common summer resident, 1921-41 (Hand, 1941); Latah County, Harvard, uncommon, two seen on July 2, 1952 (Verner, 1953); Moscow, fairly common, June 1-August 16, 1947 (Johnston, 1949), a local and not common summer resident, 1948-58 (Burleigh); Bovill, three seen July 5, 1948, feeding over an open slashing (Burleigh); Potlatch, a flock of eight birds, apparently late transients, seen June 24, 1953, feeding over an open hillside (Burleigh); Nez Perce County, Lewiston, common summer resident, 1948-58 (Burleigh); Idaho County, frequently seen in July, 1948, over the canyons of Brushy Creek and Crooked Fork four miles southwest of Lolo Pass (Orr, 1951); Whitebird, one breeding pair noted June 24, 1958 (Burleigh); Adams County, Council, common June 7 to August 29, 1958 (Newhouse, 1961); Ada County, Boise, noted June 11, 1942 (Selander, 1954); Owyhee County, Marsing, fairly common summer resident, specimens taken June 3, 1951, June 25, 26, 27, 1958, July 16, 1960 (Burleigh); Riddle, fairly common May 28-June 3, 1934 (Davis, 1934); Canyon County, Melba, large roost noted August 1, 1950, in cottonwoods at the edge of the Snake River (Selander and Preece, 1951); Blaine County, Hailey, specimen taken on Wood River June 25, 1939 (Arvey, 1947); Ketchum, fairly common June 24-28, 1950 (Burleigh); Fremont County, several noted June 8, 1916, in Little Dry Creek Canyon, fairly common by July 1, seldom observed after August 20 (Rust, 1917); Jefferson County, Camas National Wildlife Refuge, common summer resident in 1961 (Oring, 1962); Bonneville County, Gray, uncommon summer resident (Steel, 1956); south-central Idaho, "tolerably common" in 1890, eggs taken at Blackfoot, Bingham County July 14, and downy young at Arco, Butte County, July 25 (Merriam, 1891); common summer resident in 1949 (Levy, 1950); Minidoka County, Rupert, common summer resident, 1919-21 (Davis, 1935).

Habits. The Nighthawk was the subject of a thorough study by Rust at Coeur d'Alene (1911-47), and he summarized briefly (1947) the results of his observations as follows: Spring arrival dates May 29, June 18 (average June 9). The female arrives in advance of the male, from one or two days to a week occasionally. Egg-laying extends from the middle of June to the middle of July (27 nests, June 16 to July 15—average June 30). Incubation period, entirely by female, eighteen days. Food consists of insects, and includes various beetles, ants, and grasshoppers; feeding is done just before dark and throughout the night, rarely in the daytime. The fall migration begins from the fifteenth to the thirty-first of August; the latest date of departure is October 9.

At Moscow this species was never noted before early June, and it was often the middle of the month before the first bird appeared. My earliest date of arrival is June 7 (1948 and 1953). In the fall only an occasional bird was seen after the middle of September, but one or two frequently lingered within the city limits through the first week in October, appearing at dusk and feeding over the buildings comprising the business section. My latest dates of departure are October 5, 1953, October 13, 1955, and October 10, 1957.

An interesting and rather unusual contribution to our knowledge of the life history of the Nighthawk was made by Selander and Preece (1951) who in 1950 discovered what they called "cock roosts" in southern Idaho. On July 31 at Buhl, in Twin Falls County, fifty males were found roosting together, and on August 1 fully one hundred males were observed under similar circumstances in cottonwoods at the edge of the Snake River five miles southwest of Melba, in Canyon County. It was suggested that this may be a "normal behavior pattern," but further study is necessary to verify this assumption.

Chordeiles minor minor (Forster)

Since the nominate race occurs during the summer months north of Idaho, in southern Yukon, it is not improbable that it is a regular transient in the state, both in the spring and in the fall. A specimen taken at Boise June 11, 1942, has been identified as *minor* (Selander, 1954), and I personally took two specimens of this race at Moscow in 1950, a male on June 15, and a female September 16.

Chordeiles minor hesperis Grinnell

Hesperis is the race that occurs as a breeding bird over all of the state except the extreme southwestern corner. Specimens critically examined that were found to represent *hesperis* are as follows: Coeur d'Alene, female, July

29, 1948; St. Maries, female, August 8, 1955; Potlatch, male, June 24, 1953; Moscow, male, June 19, 1947, immature male, September 1, 1951; Lewiston, male, July 12, 1952, female July 16, 1952; Whitebird, male, June 24, 1958; Marsing, female, June 27, 1958; Pocatello, male, June 11, 1955.

Selander (1954) states that specimens taken in 1942 in southern Idaho, and identified as *hesperis* were from the following localities: Weiser, Montour (Gem County), Ashton, Big Butte and Birch Creek (Butte County), Pocatello, Idaho Falls, Elba, Stanrod, Lowman, Riddle, Hammett, Glenns Ferry, Mountain Home, Nampa, Melba, Buhl, Hagerman, Red Fish Lake (Custer County).

Chordeiles minor sennetti Coues

A female taken at Lewiston September 11, 1956, was found to represent this Great Plains race. This is the only record for the state. It was resting at noon on a fence post at the side of a road, and even before it was collected, its pale coloration caused me to suspect its identity.

Chordeiles minor howelli Oberholser

The one record for the occurrence of this race in Idaho is that of a male taken at Potlatch June 24, 1953. It was one of eight birds, obviously transients, that were noted that day, feeding late in the morning over an open hillside.

Chordeiles minor twomeyi Hawkins

This recently described race is the breeding Nighthawk of the extreme southwestern corner of the state. In appearance it suggests *sennetti*, but the upperparts are darker, and the underparts have little or no brown wash, with the barring darker and more distinct. Specimens identified as *twomeyi* have been taken as follows: Owyhee County, Riddle, male June 2, 1934 (W. B. Davis); Marsing, males June 3, 1951, June 25, 26, 27, 1958, July 16, 1960 (Burleigh); Canyon County, Melba, male, August 1, 1950 (R. K. Selander); Elmore County, King Hill, male, June 4, 1935 (Davis), Glenns Ferry, male, July 3, 1950 (Selander).

ORDER APODIFORMES

Swifts: *Family Apodidae*

Chaetura vauxi vauxi (Townsend): Vaux's Swift

General Distribution. Breeds from southern Alaska, northern British Columbia and western Montana south through Washington and Oregon to central California. Winters from southern Mexico to Guatemala.

Status in Idaho. A fairly common summer resident in the northern half of the state.

I found this little swift a common summer resident in Bonner County in 1917, noting it on both Lightning Creek and Trestle Creek north of Clark Fork. It was last observed in the fall on September 11, three birds being seen on Trestle Creek (Burleigh, 1923). Bent (1940) cites September 10 as a date of departure for Priest River.

In Kootenai County it was reported by Merrill (1897) as occurring during the summer months at Fort Sherman (Coeur d'Alene), arriving early in May, and disappearing after August 31. Bent (1940) gives May 6 as an early date of arrival at Coeur d'Alene, and for Rose Lake, May 11.

Hand (1941) reported it a summer resident at St. Maries, in Benewah County, appearing in May and leaving in early September (1921 through 1941).

In Latah County it was noted by Johnston in 1947 on Moscow Mountain in early June, and at Potlatch on August 11 (Johnston, 1949). I found it a fairly common but local summer resident (1947 through 1958), its occurrence during the summer months being limited to areas where there were suitable nesting sites. At Moscow it was observed between the dates of May 3 (1953) and September 20 (1950), while at Potlatch a single bird was seen as early as April 30, 1950. A bird observed at Bovill July 19, 1948, was apparently nesting in the vicinity.

As far as my own experience went, Vaux's Swift occurred at Lewiston, on the Snake River, only as an uncommon fall transient, small flocks appearing in early September and at irregular intervals then until the end of the month. My extreme dates of occurrence are September 4 (1957) and October 1 (1954). I have no records for the spring months.

In Idaho County Orr (1951) noted it "almost daily" in July, 1948, four miles southwest of Lolo Pass.

At New Meadows in Adams County, I observed single birds June 26, 1949, and June 5, 1951, and two birds at McCall, Valley County, May 5, 1952. A specimen was taken by Malcolm Jollie on Little Payette Lake, three miles northeast of McCall, on July 29, 1949.

The farthest south this species is known to nest in the western part of the state is on East Brownlee Creek, west of Cambridge, in Washington County.

Here I saw two birds on June 6, 1952, whose actions indicated clearly that they were a breeding pair.

In eastern Idaho its southern limits as a breeding bird are apparently on Signal Peak northeast of Spencer, in Clark County, where Oring (1962) noted one bird on June 19, 1961.

Habits. Unlike the Chimney Swift of the eastern United States, Vaux's Swift has not taken advantage of the favorable environment resulting from the settlement of the state. Chimneys as nesting sites have as yet been completely ignored in Idaho, and this is also the case with late summer **roosts**. This is difficult to understand, for logging operations have unquestionably limited suitable nesting sites to some extent at least, and have forced the birds to abandon areas otherwise suitable in every way. As a result this species is rather local in this occurrence in the state, and nowhere is it very common during the summer months. The one spot where I have observed it in any numbers is in a wooded ravine at Robinson's Lake, four miles east of Moscow. Here in early September each year these swifts gather from apparently a wide area, and roost each night for three weeks or more in an old fir stub at the edge of a clearing. The largest number I have observed at this spot was approximately one hundred, on September 20, 1950. Earlier in the month fewer were seen, while after that date they were always gone.

Aeronautes saxatalis saxatalis (Woodhouse): WHITE-THROATED SWIFT

General Distribution. Breeds from southern British Columbia, Idaho, western Colorado, New Mexico and western Texas south to Baja California and Sinaloa. Winters from central California, central Arizona and New Mexico south to southern Mexico.

Status in Idaho. Of local occurrence in the southern part of the state during the summer months.

There are few actual records for the occurrence of this swift in Idaho.

Apparently the first specimens to be taken in the state are a male and a female collected by W. B. Davis May 14, 1935, on Salmon Creek, eight miles west of Rogerson, in Twin Falls County.

Levy (1950) states that it is an uncommon summer resident in south-central Idaho, nesting in small numbers along the Snake River.

My own experience with this species is limited to two localities. On June 19 and 21, 1949, I watched four birds entering crevices of a high cliff north of Almo, in Cassia County, where judging from their actions, they were feeding young. Nine years later, on July 11, 1958, I found eight pairs nesting near the top of a sheer two-hundred-foot cliff ten miles south of Challis, in Custer County. They were also feeding young, as they were continually entering crevices for brief intervals that were without exception entirely inaccessible. A male was collected that day.

Habits. Because of the isolated and frequently relatively inaccessible areas of the state where this species nests, it is difficult to do otherwise than merely hazard a guess as to its actual abundance. The site chosen for nesting is a sheer and usually high cliff that more often than not walls in a rugged mountain canyon; as such a situation is not uncommon over much of southern Idaho, it is probable that the White-throated Swift is common and well distributed. Altitude is apparently disregarded.

Hummingbirds: *Family Trochilidae*

Archilochus alexandri (Bourcier and Mulsant): BLACK-CHINNED HUMMINGBIRD

General Distribution. Breeds from southern British Columbia and Montana south through Idaho, Colorado, New Mexico and southern Texas to Baja California, Sonora, and Chihuahua. Winters from southern California south through western Mexico to Michoacan.

Status in Idaho. An uncommon summer resident in the northern part of the state, rare and seldom recorded in southern Idaho.

In Kootenai County this hummingbird was reported by Merrill (1897) to be a common transient in May at Fort Sherman (Coeur d'Alene), but only a few pairs remained to nest; by Snyder (1900) as being uncommon at Blue Lake, he collected a female there July 10, 1894; by Rust (1915) as an uncommon summer resident (1910 through 1914) at Coeur d'Alene, he found a nest June 8 on Fernan Creek that held two eggs; by Yocom (1946) as being noted daily, July 1-10, 1943, at the upper end of Lake Coeur d'Alene.

In Benewah County Hand (1941) considered it an uncommon summer resident at St. Maries (1921-41), occurring from May to July.

It was first recorded in Latah County by Johnston (1949), who collected a male at Harvard July 14, 1947. At Moscow I found this species a rather scarce summer resident (1948 through 1958), seeing an occasional bird from early June until the middle of July. My extreme dates of occurrence are June 5 (1950) and July 13 (1950). I have one record for Potlatch, a male being collected in woods bordering the Palouse River July 12, 1956.

In southern Idaho it has been recorded on but two occasions. Arvey (1950) noted it in 1948 along the Portneuf River, in Bannock County, and Levy (1950) saw a single bird, a male, at the Silent City of Rocks, in Cassia County, June 21, 1949.

Habits. Because of its diminutive size and the rapidity of its movements, this hummingbird could be easily overlooked, so it is possibly more common than the relatively few records indicate. Satisfactory identification requires an unobstructed view at reasonably close range, and too often this is not possible when one of these minute birds darts by overhead. At Moscow the majority of the individuals I recognized were perched on telephone wires at the side of a road, and under such circumstances there was no question as to their identity.

STELLER'S JAY

PLATE V

The middle of July is rather early for the fall migration, so it is not improbable that in midsummer this hummingbird leaves the valleys and goes to the higher ridges where the winter snows have finally melted and there are flowers in profusion.

Selasphorus platycercus platycercus (Swainson): BROAD-TAILED HUMMINGBIRD

General Distribution. Breeds from Oregon, Idaho and northern Wyoming south to southern California, northern Mexico, and western Texas. Winters in central and southwestern Mexico.

Status in Idaho. A rather local and uncommon summer resident in all but the extreme northern part of the state.

As yet this species has not been recorded in Idaho north of Latah County, where there are two records for its occurrence. Johnston (1949) saw two birds at Harvard July 9, 1947, and Jollie (in litt.) collected a female on Moscow Mountain, seven miles northeast of Moscow, May 25, 1949.

In south-central Idaho Merriam (1891) reported a specimen taken at Big Butte July 19, 1890, and Bent (1940) states that one was seen at Spencer, in Clark County, July 9, 1916. Steel (1956) considered it a summer resident at Grays Lake (1949 through 1951) but made no comment as to its actual abundance there. I saw two males on Eagle Creek, north of Gray, June 14, 1949; one was collected to verify the identification.

In Minidoka County this species was reported by Kenagy as "tolerably common" in 1909, and rare in 1913. Davis (1935) recorded it at Rupert May 27, 1920.

In the Museum of Vertebrate Zoology, Berkeley, California, there are two males collected by W. B. Davis July 12 and 13, 1937, on Strawberry Creek twenty miles northeast of Preston, Franklin County.

Habits. The Broad-tailed Hummingbird reaches the extreme northern limits of its breeding range in Idaho, and thus it is more or less to be expected that its numbers during the summer months are small. It is considered, however, to be the common hummingbird of the Rocky Mountains, and one that during the summer months is rarely seen away from the mountain ridges. The birds that I saw at Gray revealed their presence by the shrill buzz of their wings as they darted by overhead, a sound characteristic of this species alone, and one that will always readily identify it.

Selasphorus rufus (Gmelin): RUFOUS HUMMINGBIRD

General Distribution. Breeds from southeastern Alaska, Alberta and western Montana south through Washington and Oregon to northwestern California and central Idaho. Winters in Mexico south to Veracruz.

Status in Idaho. A common summer resident in the northern half of the state, and a common fall transient in southern Idaho.

In Bonner County a male was observed in a wooded ravine east of Clark Fork July 4, 1917 (Burleigh, 1923).

In Kootenai County this species was reported by Merrill (1897) as a common spring migrant, "probably breeding" at Fort Sherman (Coeur d'Alene). Snyder (1900) found a nest with two young at Blue Lake July 17, 1894. Rust (1915) stated that this hummingbird was occasionally seen at Coeur d'Alene during May and June. Bent (1940) cites May 5 as an early date of arrival at Rathdrum.

At St. Maries, in Benewah County, it was considered by Hand (1941) a common summer resident (1921-41), occurring from the first of May until early September.

At Moscow, in Latah County, it was reported by Johnston (1949) as common June 1-August 16, 1947. I likewise found it a fairly common summer resident there (1948-58), appearing in late April or early May and being rarely observed after the first of September. My extreme dates of occurrence are April 27 (1949 and 1953) and September 9 (1950). Verner (1953) reported it a common resident at Harvard during the summer of 1952.

At Weippe, in Clearwater County, a male was seen June 13, 1951 (Burleigh).

Orr (1951) reported this species "fairly abundant" in July, 1948, in the Lolo Pass region in Idaho County, noting it from 4,000 to 7,000 feet. An adult female was taken July 8.

A male that I saw at New Meadows, in Adams County, May 21, 1955, could have been a breeding bird, and if so this would represent the extreme southern breeding limits of the Rufous Hummingbird in the state.

In southern Idaho Davis (1935) recorded it only as a fall transient in Minidoka County, observing it at Rupert from August 20 to September 7, 1919, and from August 14 to September 5, 1920.

Oring (1962) reported it a common fall transient in 1961 on the Camas National Wildlife Refuge in Jefferson County, seeing it there from July 25 through August 28. An immature male was collected July 25.

Habits. The Rufous Hummingbird is unique in that it breeds much farther north than any other hummingbird, being the only species that can be found during the summer months in Alaska. In Idaho it is rarely observed south of Idaho County, but its appearance in late May in Adams County suggests the possibility that it may nest sparingly at New Meadows and at McCall.

The fall migration begins early, the adult males beginning to disappear after the first of July. Very few are seen in August, and this is apparently true even in the southern part of the state. Oring (1962) states that on the Camas Refuge, where this species was a common transient in late July and August, "only one adult male was observed, while as many as fifteen females and/or immatures were seen in a single day."

Stellula calliope (Gould): CALLIOPE HUMMINGBIRD

General Distribution. Breeds from central British Columbia and southern Alberta south to Baja California and east to Utah and western Colorado. Winters in Mexico south to Guerrero.

Status in Idaho. A fairly common summer resident throughout the state.

At Clark Fork, in Bonner County, this species was found to be a common summer resident in 1917, occurring both in the valleys and to the tops of the higher ridges. It was noted for the last time in the fall on August 29 (Burleigh, 1923). Bent (1940) cites August 24 as a departure date at Priest River.

In Kootenai County is was considered by Merrill (1897) as the most common "of the Hummers" at Fort Sherman (Coeur d'Alene), both "in migration and nesting," its arrival in spring "coinciding with the first blossoming of the wild "hawthorne." Rust, however, (1915) found it an uncommon summer resident at Coeur d'Alene (1910-14). Bent (1940) gives May 20 as an arrival date for Coeur d'Alene. In the Museum of Vertebrate Zoology, Berkeley, California, there is a juvenile male taken by R. T. Orr at Coeur d'Alene July 25, 1932.

Hand (1941) reported this species a fairly common summer resident at St. Maries, in Benewah County (1921-41), occurring from May to late August or early September.

In Latah County Arvey (1947) reported it a common summer resident. He collected a specimen ten miles northeast of Moscow May 10, 1940. Johnston (1949) likewise considered it a fairly common summer resident in the vicinity of Moscow, noting it from June 1 to August 16, 1947. I personally found it fairly common and well distributed during the summer months (1948-58) and equally numerous in the valleys and on the mountainsides. My earliest date of arrival, at Moscow, is April 23 (1949); my latest date of departure, at Potlatch, September 3 (1955). Normally, however, it was early May, even later, before the first bird appeared, and the latter part of August when the last one was seen.

In south-central Idaho Levy (1950) reported it common from June until August, 1949.

Steel (1956) reported it a summer resident at Grays Lake (1949-51), but made no comment as to its relative abundance. I noted an occasional bird in the vicinity of Gray June 9-17, 1949. Oring (1962) noted a female feeding, "a full-grown immature," at Big Elk Creek in Bonneville County, August 6, 1961. In the Museum of Vertebrate Zoology, Berkeley, California, there are two specimens, both females, taken by W. B. Davis July 16, 1936, in the Big Hole Mountains, eight miles northeast of Swan Valley in Bonneville County.

Habits. One normally associates hummingbirds with the warm days of late spring and summer, so it was an interesting experience to witness the arrival of the Calliope Hummingbird in northern Idaho under rather adverse weather conditions. May 13, 1955, was a cold, gloomy day, with an almost steady light snowfall, but two birds were seen that morning at Moscow, the first to be recorded that spring. It must be admitted that they seemed decidedly out of place under such wintry conditions.

The height of the nest from the ground varies considerably throughout the breeding range of this species, but my rather limited experience would indicate that in Idaho an upper limb of one of the larger trees available is given preference. A nest found at Clark Fork, in Bonner County, that held two almost fully fledged young on July 4, 1917, was thirty feet from the ground at the outer end of a limb of a large Douglas fir. Another almost completed nest at Moscow, a female was seen to be working on May 28, 1948, was also thirty feet from the ground, and it was near the outer end of a limb of a large ponderosa pine.

Oring (1962) has contributed a rather unusual observation where the life history of the Calliope Hummingbird is concerned. He states that on Big Elk Creek, in Bonneville County, he watched a female feeding a young bird while both were in the air, the female "poking her bill down the young's mouth just as is often done with young before they leave the nest." He apparently is the first to witness an occurrence of this kind involving any hummingbird, and the question arises as to how common this practice actually is.

ORDER CORACIIFORMES

Kingfishers: *Family Alcedinidae*

Megaceryle alcyon (Linnaeus): BELTED KINGFISHER

General Distribution. Breeds from northeastern Alaska east across the continent to Newfoundland, south to southern California, New Mexico, southern Texas, the Gulf coast, and southern Florida. Winters over much of its breeding range and south to Panama, the West Indies and Bermuda.

Status in Idaho. A fairly common summer resident throughout the state, wintering in small numbers wherever any open water exists.

At Bonners Ferry in Boundary County, one bird was seen November 23, 1948, the late date indicating the possibility that this species occurs during the winter months in the extreme northern edge of the state (Burleigh).

A rather unexpected record for Bonner County is that of a bird seen September 4, 1917, flying over the top of a high ridge north of Clark Fork (Burleigh, 1923).

In Kootenai County this species was reported by Merrill (1897) as being "common in summer" at Fort Sherman (Coeur d'Alene), an occasional bird being noted during the winter months. It was usually the middle of April before the first transients appeared. Rust (1915) likewise reported it a common summer resident at Coeur d'Alene (1910-14). Yocom (1946) noted a breeding pair at the upper end of Lake Coeur d'Alene July 1-10, 1943. I saw one bird on Lake Coeur d'Alene January 1, 1954. Snyder (1900) found it uncommon at Blue Lake during the summer of 1894. Bent (1940) cites April 9 as an arrival date at Rathdrum.

In Benewah County it was considered by Hand (1941) a common summer resident at St. Maries (1921-41), appearing in April and being rarely observed after the first of November. An occasional bird was seen during the winter.

In Latah County it appeared during the summer months only on the Palouse River, scattered pairs occurring where there were high banks suitable as nesting sites. Arvey (1947) reported it common; he took one specimen April 19, 1940. Johnston (1949) noted it at Potlatch June 1 to August 16, 1947, and considered it uncommon there. Verner (1953) found it fairly common at Harvard during the summer of 1952; three well-grown young were seen August 1. I noted it in small numbers between Potlatch and Princeton, my earliest record in the spring being April 30 (1949), my latest in the fall December 7 (1952). At Moscow it was observed at rare intervals during the winter months on Paradise Creek, my few records for its occurrence then being January 7, 1948, and January 14 and December 24, 1951. I have one record for the fall migration, September 12, 1952.

At Lewiston, in Nez Perce County, it was seen daily on both the Snake River and the Clearwater River, and there was little fluctuation in numbers throughout the year. It unquestionably nested where conditions were suitable, but I never succeeded in finding a nest. I have one record for Culdesac, November 13, 1949.

I noted it on infrequent occasions in Clearwater County, seeing single birds at Ahsahka January 7, 1951, at Pierce July 1, 1952, at Headquarters August 26 and December 24, 1952, at Weippe September 15, 1951, and February 7, 1953, and at Orofino February 8, 1954.

In Idaho County Orr (1951) reported it common along the larger streams in the Clearwater and the Bitterroot Mountains in September, 1941, and July, 1948. Newhouse (1960) observed an occasional bird in Indian Valley, Adams County, from April through August, 1958. I saw one bird on the Snake River at Weiser, in Washington County, November 22, 1951.

At Boise, in Ada County, several were noted during the winters of 1938-39, and 1939-40 (Marshall, 1945).

In Fremont County Rust (1917) reported it common from June through August, 1916. Jewett (1912) saw several birds along the Wood River at Ketchum, Blaine County, in November and December, 1910. At Grays Lake this species was considered by Steel (1956) to be a rare summer resident (1949 through 1951). He gives as arrival dates April 28, 1950, and May 6, 1951. Oring (1962) noted one bird on Big Elk Creek, in Bonneville County, August 6, 1961. Low (1945) found a pair nesting in a clay bank at Soda Springs, Caribou County (May 12-17, 1944).

In south-central Idaho Merriam (1891) reported it common on the Snake River in 1890 and "on the beaver ponds and the lakes at the east foot of the Sawtooth Mountains." In this same general area Levy (1950) found it fairly common during the summer of 1949.

At Rupert, in Minidoka County, it was noted during the summer months (1919-21), and a nest with eggs was found on May 27 (Davis, 1935).

Habits. The Belted Kingfisher is a hardy bird, its presence in Idaho during the winter months being governed by the severity of the weather. As long as there is open water on the larger streams, insuring an adequate food supply, it apparently sees no reason to go farther south and seems unaffected by blizzards and low temperatures. It is a solitary bird, so while generally distributed over the state it is actually nowhere common as far as numbers are concerned.

Megaceryle alcyon alcyon (Linnaeus)

A male taken on the Snake River at Lewiston January 19, 1957, had the following measurements: wing, 158 mm., tail, 86. These are smaller than the minimum for *caurina,* so this specimen would appear to represent the nominate race of the Belted Kingfisher that breeds as far west as British Columbia and Mackenzie. Ridgway (1914) gives the following measurements for males of the two recognized races of *Megaceryle alcyon: Alcyon—*

wing 145-161 (156.3) mm.; tail 82-93.5 (87.7). *Caurina*—wing 159-169 (163.1); tail 88-96.5 (92.1).

Megaceryle alcyon caurina (Grinnell)

This western race of the Belted Kingfisher, breeding north to central Alaska and east to the Black Hills of South Dakota, is the form occurring throughout the state where conditions are suitable. Specimens identified as *caurina* have been taken as follows: Males, Moscow, September 12, 1952, Lewiston, September 28, 1951, and April 13, 1953, Weippe, September 15, 1951, Orofino February 8, 1954; females, Clarkia, Shoshone County, August 7, 1948, Potlatch, September 4, 1951, and August 1, 1955, Pierce, July 1, 1952, Headquarters, August 26, 1952.

ORDER PICIFORMES

Woodpeckers and Wrynecks: *Family Picidae*

Colaptes auratus (Linnaeus): YELLOW-SHAFTED FLICKER

General Distribution. Breeds from the limit of trees in central Alaska, northern Manitoba, central Quebec and Newfoundland south to southern Texas, the Gulf coast and southern Florida. Winters over much of its breeding range, south to southern California and Arizona, and to Cuba.

Status in Idaho. Of casual occurrence both in the northern and in the southern part of the state during the late fall and winter months.

It would appear that in past years the Yellow-shafted Flicker has been overlooked in Idaho, for while uncommon it is apparently present in small numbers each winter. In Latah County I have noted it as follows: Moscow, males November 14, 1949, January 3, 1950, February 13, 1956; females January 29, 1951, February 23, 1953. Genesee, female March 4, 1956. I have one record for Lewiston, a female seen January 21, 1951.

There are two sight records for southern Idaho. Hoskins (1953) observed one bird September 27, 1952, on Elk Mountain, six miles south of Three Creek, Owyhee County. Throckmorton (1953) likewise observed one bird December 13, 1952, in the Snake River Valley near the Hagerman Wildlife Refuge, Gooding County.

Habits. The presence of this woodpecker in northern Idaho during the winter months is probably the result of the presence in the towns of ornamental shrubs and trees that bear edible fruit. During much of the year flickers commonly feed on the ground, for they are especially fond of ants, which they eat in large numbers. In the winter, however, the snow that covers the ground necessitates a change in their feeding habits, and in Moscow, as well as other towns of similar size, the fruit of the Russian olive and the mountain ash are eaten as long as any remains. To a lesser degree this is true also of apples that are not picked in the fall and often remain on the tree, unless eaten by the birds, until early spring. Since such food was not available before the state was settled, it would be interesting to know the status then of species such as this.

Colaptes auratus borealis Ridgway

Two females taken at Moscow on January 29, 1951, and February 23, 1953, and another female taken at Genesee March 4, 1956, were found to represent this northern race of the Yellow-shafted Flicker that breeds from Alaska south to central British Columbia. A male taken at Moscow February 13, 1956, was an interesting hybrid between *borealis* and *Colaptes cafer,* and could not be allocated to either species. Except for the head it was typical of *auratus*, both the tail and wings being yellow; on the head, however, it lacked the red nuchal band, and the "mustache" (malar stripe) was red.

Colaptes auratus luteus Bangs

A male taken at Moscow November 14, 1949, is typical of this race that breeds as far north and west as Montana. It is probably largely of accidental occurrence in the state.

Colaptes cafer (Gmelin): RED-SHAFTED FLICKER

General Distribution. Breeds from southern Alaska, southern Alberta, and southern Saskatchewan south to Baja California, northern Mexico and western Texas, and east to the western edge of the Great Plains. Winters north to British Columbia, Montana, and South Dakota.

Status in Idaho. A common summer resident throughout the state. Winters locally in varying numbers, its relative abundance being governed by the severity of the weather and the available food supply.

In Bonner County this familiar woodpecker was found to be common in the vicinity of Clark Fork during the summer of 1917, occurring from the valleys to the tops of the ridges. On August 6 sixteen were noted feeding together (Burleigh, 1923). On November 25, 1948, I noted a single bird within the town limits of Clark Fork.

In Kootenai County it was reported by Merrill (1897) as common in summer at Fort Sherman (Coeur d'Alene), nesting from the lake to the summit of Mica Peak. A few birds remained each winter but it was late March before the first transients appeared. Rust (1915) likewise considered it a common summer resident at Coeur d'Alene (1910 through 1914); he cites as dates of winter occurrence November 28, December 8, February 10 and 22. Yocom (1946) found it common at the upper end of Lake Coeur d'Alene July 1 to 10, 1943. I noted a single bird, a female, at Coeur d'Alene on December 16, 1950.

At St. Maries, in Benewah County, it was reported by Hand (1941) as common during the summer months, and of regular occurrence in winter, being widely distributed from the valleys to the tops of the higher ridges.

In Latah County Johnston (1949) considered it common in the vicinity of Moscow June 1 through August 16, 1947. An adult male was collected on June 1. Verner (1953) also reported it common at Harvard during the summer of 1952. I personally found this woodpecker common and well distributed during the summer months in Latah County (1947 through 1958). It was of regular occurrence during the winter, but its numbers varied in that season depending on the food supply available. There were years when from early November until March only an occasional bird was seen, and other years when, singly or in small flocks, it was noted almost daily.

At Lewiston, in Nez Perce County, it was a common resident species. There was, however, a perceptible increase in numbers in the late fall due to the appearance of transients from farther north, and there was a corresponding decrease in early spring.

In Clearwater County I noted it only as a fairly common summer resident, my one winter record being that of a single bird seen, and collected, at Weippe December 24, 1952. At Headquarters the first birds appeared in the spring on April 10, 1952, March 25, 1953, and February 28, 1954, in each instance when the ground was still covered with a foot or more of snow.

In Idaho County Orr (1951) found this species common in September, 1941, and July, 1948, in the Clearwater and Bitterroot mountains.

Newhouse (1961) reported it common at Council, in Adams County, from March until December, 1958. I saw one pair of these flickers at the top of Cuddy Mountain (at an altitude of 7,600 feet) in Washington County, June 6, 1952. At this date the snow was still in wide drifts five and six feet deep.

At Shoup, in Lemhi County, I found the Red-shafted Flicker fairly common June 4 to 6, 1949, on the wooded slopes of the Bitterroot mountains, frequently seeing it daily. Arvey (1947) took one specimen on Owl Creek, in Blaine County, September 8, 1940.

Rust (1917) reported it fairly common in Fremont County from July through August, 1916. Oring (1962) gave it the same status on the Camas National Wildlife Refuge, in Jefferson County, during the summer of 1961.

At Grays Lake Steel (1956) found it a common summer resident only (1949 through 1951), seeing it from early April until late fall. He cites as an arrival date April 6, 1950. I saw a single bird at Gray November 3, 1949.

In south-central Idaho Merriam (1891) reported this species in 1890 on the Snake River near Blackfoot, in July; at Big Butte, on the Big Lost River in the Big Lost River mountains; in the Salmon River and Sawtooth mountains (until early October); and on the Snake River near Shoshone Falls, October 9 to 11. Levy (1950) considered it a common breeding bird in this same general area during the summer of 1949.

At Rupert, in Minidoka County, Davis (1935) reported it present during the summer months (1919-21), but did not comment on its relative abundance. He gives May 20 as the earliest date for eggs.

Habits. At Moscow I found the Red-shafted Flicker common throughout the year, but apparently while resident as a species, the breeding population is to some extent at least migratory. This was shown by specimens taken during the winter months that in frequent instances showed hybridism between this species and *auratus*. The most common character was the presence of a red crescent on the back of the neck, although an occasional individual had the red of the wing or tail replaced by yellow. Under these circumstances it would appear that at least a portion of the breeding population is replaced in the fall by birds from such an area as southern British Columbia where the two species meet.

In view of the severe winters so often experienced in northern Idaho, it seems strange that the Red-shafted Flicker does not go farther south in the late fall. Subzero temperatures and snow to a depth of three feet or more are not uncommon in January, and at times characterize late December and early February. The only food available then consists of fleshy fruits such as the Russian Olive, the mountain ash, and unpicked apples still on the tree, but it would appear that this woodpecker is sufficiently hardy to survive under these circumstances.

Colaptes cafer cafer (Gmelin)

Two specimens from northern Idaho were found to be typical of the nominate race that breeds on the Pacific coast from Alaska to northern California. Both were males, and were collected as follows: Deary, Latah County, November 13, 1948, and Lewiston, January 28, 1956. A third specimen, taken at Moscow December 16, 1951, was referable to *cafer* but showed traces of hybridism with *auratus*, there being an inconspicuous red crescent on the back of the neck. Although *cafer* is considered largely resident throughout its range, there is apparently a casual movement east during the late fall months.

Colaptes cafer collaris Vigors

This is the race that occurs throughout all of Idaho. Specimens personally taken, and identified as *collaris*, are as follows: Males, Moscow, November 5, December 1, and December 6, 1947, December 10 and 27, 1949, January 6, 1952, January 24 and February 12, 1954, March 10, 1956; Genesee, December 1, 1951; Potlatch, December 13, 1956; Headquarters, April 11, 1952, February 28, 1954; Gray, May 28, 1952. Females, Moscow, November 18, 1947, November 21, December 7 and 18, 1948, January 3 and 9, 1950, January 19, 1951, January 19, 1952, January 4, 1954, February 24, 1955, February 22, 1956, January 24 and December 1, 1957; Coeur d'Alene, December 16, 1950; Lewiston, February 1, 1950; Gray, May 28, 1952.

Three additional specimens referable to *collaris* showed varying degrees of hybridism with *auratus*. All were males and were taken at Moscow January 2, 1949, and February 13, 1956, and at Lewiston February 24, 1952.

[Colaptes cafer canescens Brodkorb]

This race was described by Pierce Brodkrob (1935) as being grayer above than *collaris*, and with the underparts "more pinkish." His type is a male taken at Bear Lake Outlet (5,900 feet) four miles southwest of Montpelier, Bear Lake County, August 30, 1934. This would be the form occurring in southeastern Idaho, but it has not been recognized as valid by the A.O.U. Committee on Nomenclature.

Dryocopus pileatus picinus (Bangs): PILEATED WOODPECKER

General Distribution. Resident from northern British Columbia south through Washington and Oregon to California, and east to Idaho and western Montana.

Status in Idaho. Fairly common in all but the extreme southern part of the state, and resident wherever found.

The Pileated Woodpecker is another species that was first recorded in Idaho by the Lewis and Clark expedition. In one of his journals, Lewis (*Original Journals,* V:136) stated that it was observed June 15, 1806, on the Lolo Trail above Weippe (Jollie, 1953).

In Bonner County two birds were seen September 14, 1917, in a wooded valley north of Clark Fork (Burleigh, 1923). A single bird, a female noted at Sandpoint November 26, 1948, was collected.

In Kootenai County Merrill (1897) reported this species common at Fort Sherman (Coeur d'Alene). Rust (1915) considered it uncommon at Coeur d'Alene (1910 through 1914), noting it only in "heavy timber." Yocom (1946) observed it at the upper end of Lake Coeur d'Alene July 1-10, 1943, reporting it "often seen."

Hand (1941) reported it fairly common at St. Maries, in Benewah County (1921 through 1941), nesting in the valleys and wandering in the fall to the tops of the higher ridges.

In Latah County Arvey (1947) reported a specimen taken ten miles northeast of Moscow November 18, 1939. Johnston (1949) found it uncommon (June 1 through August 16, 1947), and limited in its distribution to the "more heavily timbered areas." He noted family groups in early July. Verner (1953) reported one bird seen at Harvard July 2, 1951, and stated that in 1952 it was uncommon there. I found it fairly common in Latah County (1947 through 1958) but rather local in its distribution, for it was largely confined to the thicker stretches of woods. A female was taken at Deary December 13, 1947, and a male at Moscow January 4, 1951.

At Headquarters, in Clearwater County, I noted two birds October 27, 1951, and on subsequent visits to this area one or two birds could be seen or heard on the wooded ridges in the course of a day's field work.

In Idaho County Orr (1951) found this species "relatively common" in September, 1941, in the Selway mountains, observing it from 1,900 to 6,000 feet. Specimens were taken September 13 and 17 four miles southwest of Selway Falls.

The farthest south it has been recorded in the western part of the state is in the Boise National Forest, in Boise County. Here Marshall (1945) noted it on Hunter Creek in January, 1930, and on February 22, 1939, and on Swanholm Creek February 18 and March 4, 1939.

In south-central Idaho Merriam (1891) reported it rare, his one record being that of a specimen taken August 19, 1890, near Birch Creek, in the Salmon River Mountains. Jewett (1912), however, considered it fairly common along Spring Creek near Ketchum, in Blaine County, from October through December, 1910.

In the eastern part of the state it has not been recorded south of Signal Peak, in Clark County. Here Oring (1962) observed "several" June 19 and July 15, 1961.

Habits. Although resident wherever it occurred, this large woodpecker would appear to wander to some extent during the fall months, and my rather limited experience would suggest that this involved an altitudinal migration. On two occasions, October 16, 1951, and October 19, 1952, single birds were seen on Hatwai Creek, four miles east of Lewiston, but otherwise there are no records for Nez Perce County.

Despite the relatively few localities where it has been recorded in the state, it undoubtedly occurs wherever there are stretches of heavy timber extensive enough to afford an ample food supply and nesting sites. One would suppose that so large and conspicuous a bird would attract the attention of even the most casual observer, but actually it is quiet much of the year, and so shy that it usually must be searched for to be seen. Consequently it is surprisingly easy to overlook, and probably for this reason it has not been recorded in areas where it doubtlessly can be found throughout the year.

[Melanerpes erythrocephalus (Linnaeus): RED-HEADED WOODPECKER]

General Distribution. Southern Saskatchewan, southern Manitoba, southern Ontario, and southern Quebec south to northern New Mexico, central Texas, the Gulf coast, and Florida.

Status in Idaho. Recorded once in the southern part of the state. Fichter (1960) reports a single bird seen in Craters of the Moon National Monument, Butte County, June 24, 1957. While it was not collected, the distinctive plumage of this woodpecker, and Edson Fichter's reputation as a competent and experienced field ornithologist, leave no doubt as to the presence of this species in Idaho.

Habits. In view of the fact that the Red-headed Woodpecker breeds, and is relatively common, as far west as central Montana and Wyoming, one might logically expect it to be at least of casual occurrence in Idaho. However, the Continental Divide has proven an effective barrier to other species and is probably the factor responsible for the rarity of this species in the state. It is essentially a bird of the more open country, avoiding the thicker stretches of woods, and showing a preference for the small woodlots that are found on so many of the farms in this country.

Asyndesmus lewis (Gray): LEWIS' WOODPECKER

General Distribution. Breeds from southern British Columbia, Alberta, Montana, and South Dakota south to southern California, central Arizona, and southern New Mexico, and east to northern Nebraska and eastern Colorado. Winters from northern Oregon south to Baja California and northern Sonora, and from Colorado to western Texas.

Status in Idaho. A fairly common but local summer resident in all but the extreme southern part of the state, where it has been recorded in but two widely separated localities.

Lewis' Woodpecker was one of the species "discovered" by the Lewis and Clark expedition. It was observed for the first time in Idaho on September 20, 1805, on the Lolo Trail above Weippe (Lewis, *Original Journals*, III:76). The first specimen was taken May 16, 1806, at Kamiah (Clark, *Original Journals*, V:43), but it was first described in detail May 27, 1806, by Lewis in one of his journals (*Original Journals*, V:70-71) (Jollie, 1953).

The A.O.U. *Check-List* (1957) gives Gray (Gen. Birds, Vol. 3, 1849, App., p. 22) as the accepted authority for the original designation of the type, the type locality being stated as follows: "No locality mentioned = Montana, about lat. 46° N." However, Davis and Stevenson (1934) point out that the original description specified "the headquarters of the Clearwater River, in the Bitterroot Mountains, Idaho," and suggest that the type locality should be "two miles north of Kamiah, Idaho County, Idaho" with the probable date May 17, 1806 (Lewis).

In view of the fact that this distinctive woodpecker shuns thick woods and is found in slashings and open groves of large trees, and is, therefore, not easily overlooked, it is rather surprising that there are so few published records for its occurrence in the state.

I noted one pair at Bonners Ferry, Boundary County, June 22, 1957, in open woods bordering the Kootenai River, and the following day, June 23, I saw an occasional pair in old slashings west of Clark Fork, Bonner County.

In Kootenai County Merrill (1897) considered it common and generally distributed at Fort Sherman (Coeur d'Alene). He stated that it appeared each year in early May. I noted one pair in an open slashing at Hauser May 15, 1952.

Hand (1941) found it a common summer resident at St. Maries, Benewah County (1921-41), being present from May until September.

In Latah County Johnston (1949) reported it locally common June 1 through August 16, 1947, noting it then on "Moscow Mountain and on Potlatch Creek." I personally found it fairly common, and also quite local in its occurrence. I observed it at Moscow between the dates of May 1 (1952) and October 2 (1950) (average date of departure September 12), and at Potlatch from May 1 (1957) until late August.

In Nez Perce County it was reported by Bendire as nesting commonly at Fort Lapwai (Merriam, 1891). At Lewiston it was limited in its distribution to the large cottonwoods along the rivers and the smaller streams, but it was a not uncommon summer resident there. My extreme dates of occurrence are May 1 (1953) and September 12 (1949). On June 30, 1949, I noted three birds at Culdesac, in large cottonwoods at the edge of a stream.

My one record for Clearwater County is that of three birds seen August 1, 1952, in an open slashing west of Weippe.

Newhouse (1960) reported this species common at Council and at Indian Valley, Adams County, May 14 to September 13, 1958.

Although not definitely known to winter in the state, it may do so in small numbers. On November 23, 1951, I saw two birds within the city limits of Payette, Payette County, and this late date suggests the possibility that they would remain there throughout the winter.

The one record for the extreme southwestern part of the state is that of one bird that I observed at Triangle, Owyhee County, June 25, 1949. Elsewhere in the state it has been noted at Shoup, Lemhi County, three birds seen in open pine woods at the head of Cramer Creek June 4, 1949 (Burleigh); Ketchum, Blaine County, fairly plentiful in the valley (6,000 feet) June 24-28, 1950 (Burleigh); Grays Lake, a rare summer resident, 1949-51 (Steel, 1956). Merriam (1891) stated that it was seen by J. K. Townsend on the Bear River, in extreme southeastern Idaho, in July, 1834.

Habits. In appearance and actions the Lewis' Woodpecker is quite unlike the other woodpeckers indigenous to Idaho. In my experience, it spends its days in the top of a dead or partly dead tree, from which vantage point it sallies forth for the insects that form a large part of its food, which it is quite expert at catching. I have never seen it on the ground, or removing insects or their larvae from the trunk and branches of a tree in the orthodox woodpecker manner. In the late summer and fall such berries as are available are eagerly eaten.

A nest that I found at Potlatch on July 13, 1952, held noisy young, and was forty feet from the ground in the trunk of a large dead cottonwood standing at the edge of the Palouse River.

Sphyrapicus varius nuchalis Baird: YELLOW-BELLIED SAPSUCKER

General Distribution. Breeds from southern British Columbia and Alberta south to northern California, Nevada, northern New Mexico, and western Texas. Winters from the southern part of its breeding range south to Baja California and northern Mexico.

Status in Idaho. A fairly common summer resident throughout the state.

At Clark Fork, in Bonner County, this sapsucker was found, in 1917, to be fairly plentiful during the late summer about the open mountain meadows at the tops of the ridges. It was first noted on July 29, and daily then until early September (Burleigh, 1923). I saw one bird in open woods west of Clark Fork on September 29, 1957.

In Kootenai County Merrill (1897) stated that a few pairs nested in the cottonwoods bordering Lake Coeur d'Alene. Rust (1915) reported a nest with young in French Gulch June 6, 1914.

At St. Maries, in Benewah County, Hand (1941) considered this species a fairly common summer resident (1921-41) "in Canadian Zone forests," being present from April until late September.

In Latah County Johnston (1949) reported it "breeding sparingly" (June through August, 1947). Verner (1953) saw a bird entering a nest at Harvard July 2, 1951, and located another nest with young in this same general area July 2, 1952. I personally found this species rather local in its distribution, and except as a transient in the spring and in the fall, by no means common. My earliest dates of arrival in the spring are: Deary, April 12 (1949) and Moscow April 7 (1951), and for departure in the fall: Moscow, October 7 (1950) and Potlatch September 24 (1951).

At Headquarters, in Clearwater County, where it was fairly common during the summer months, my dates of arrival in the spring are April 10, 1952, and April 21, 1953. In Idaho County Arvey (1947) reported a specimen taken ten miles southwest of Riggins September 15, 1939. Orr (1951) reported one seen July 6 and an immature female collected July 21, 1948, four miles southwest of Lolo Pass.

At New Meadows, Adams County, I noted one breeding pair in an open slashing at the foot of a ridge June 28, 1949.

At Triangle, Owyhee County, I saw one bird, apparently representing a breeding pair, June 25, 1949, in aspens at the edge of a stream.

Oring (1962) found this species "common" on Signal Peak, Clark County, June 19 and July 14-15, 1961. He observed one bird at Hamer, Jefferson County, on June 24.

Steel (1956) considered it a common summer resident at Grays Lake (1949 through 1951). I saw a male on Eagle Creek, north of Gray, June 13, 1949, and three birds in aspen groves south of Gray May 23, 1951.

At Ketchum, in Blaine County, I found this sapsucker fairly common June 24-28, 1950, in aspen groves fringing Big Wood River.

Levy (1950) reported it a common summer resident in 1949 in south-central Idaho. At Almo, in Cassia County, I noted an occasional bird June 19-21, 1949, in aspen groves on the lower ridges. Jollie (in litt.) took two breeding males July 2, 1949, at Heglar Pass, twenty miles south of American Falls, Power County.

Davis (1953) reported it a transient and possible winter resident at Rupert, in Minidoka County, his extreme dates of occurrence (1919-21) being October 3 and April 10.

In the Museum of Vertebrate Zoology, Berkeley, California, there are specimens taken by W. B. Davis on Cottonwood Creek, two miles west of the Craters of the Moon, Blaine County, July 8, 1937, and on Strawberry Creek, twenty miles northeast of Preston, Franklin County, July 15, 1937; and by R. W. Smith, four miles north of Ashton, Fremont County, August 15 and 18, 1939.

Habits. Throughout its range in the western United States the Yellow-bellied Sapsucker is largely limited in its distribution to the large aspen groves that characterize the higher ridges, and it is in such a situation that I have usually encountered it in Idaho. I have never noted it during the summer months below an altitude of 3,000 feet, and in my experience it is most common between 5,000 and 7,000 feet. The nest, as might be expected, is usually in a large aspen, but occasional pairs show an individuality in this respect. The one found by Rust in Kootenai County was in "a tall hemlock stub," while the two found by Verner in Latah County were fifty feet up "in dead fir snags."

Sphyrapicus thyroideus nataliae (Malherbe): WILLIAMSON'S SAPSUCKER

General Distribution. Breeds from southern British Columbia south in the mountains to northern New Mexico and central Arizona. Winters from Baja California and western Texas south to Jalisco and Durango.

Kodachrome by Donald J. Obee, Boise, Idaho

CLARK'S NUTCRACKER

PLATE VI

Status in Idaho. An uncommon and local summer resident throughout the state.

Although northern Idaho is well within its breeding range, Williamson's Sapsucker is practically unknown north of Idaho County. Merrill (1898) reported it at Coeur d'Alene in August, 1895, but subsequent observers have failed to record it anywhere in Kootenai County.

The farthest north in the state that I have personally recorded it is at Whitebird Summit, south of Grangeville, Idaho County, where I saw a male at the edge of an open slashing May 21, 1955.

At New Meadows, Adams County, June 27, 1949, and the following day, June 28, at McCall, Valley County, I watched two adults as in each instance they fed young in nests in open slashings. Jollie (in litt.) collected a male in juvenal plumage at Payette Lake, north of McCall, July 25, 1949.

On June 6, 1949, I noted two pairs of these sapsuckers, one of them feeding young in a nest in an old pine stub in open pine woods west of Shoup, Lemhi County.

At Ketchum, Blaine County, I saw a single bird, a female, on June 25, 1950, in open woods halfway up Easley Peak (8,500 feet).

Oring (1962) noted one pair (which he collected) on Signal Peak, Clark County, July 14, 1961.

Apparently this species is more common in Bear Lake County than elsewhere in Idaho, for it has been recorded there by three different observers. At the Museum of Vertebrate Zoology, Berkeley, California, there are two specimens taken by W. B. Davis in the Copenhagen Basin, Wasatch Mountains, Bear Lake County, July 17, 1937. Jollie (in litt.) collected two specimens at Bloomington Lake, ten miles west of Bloomington, July 9, 1949, and John B. Hurley (in litt.) collected a female in Emigration Canyon, twelve miles west of Montpelier, June 15, 1959.

Habits. Unlike the Yellow-bellied Sapsucker, this species shows little interest in the aspen groves, and while found in Idaho in thick fir and spruce woods its preference seems to be for ridges covered with open stretches of Ponderosa pine. It is characteristically a bird of the higher altitudes, and in my experience it does not nest below 5,000 feet, and is most common between 6,000 and 8,000 feet.

The few nests that I have seen in Idaho were in old rotten stubs in slashings, and were from twenty to sixty feet from the ground. Both sexes incubate, and the male shows as much concern over the welfare of the young as does the female.

Dendrocopos villosus monticola (Anthony): Hairy Woodpecker

General Distribution. Resident in the Rocky Mountain region from southern British Columbia, Alberta, Montana, South Dakota, and western Nebraska south to northern Nevada, central Utah, and northern New Mexico.

Status in Idaho. Resident and fairly common in all the forested areas of the state.

The Hairy Woodpecker has a wide and uniform distribution over the state, and has been reported in all published lists dealing with the avifauna of Idaho.

Boundary County. Several birds seen and a male collected on Harrison Peak, September 28, 1957 (Burleigh).

Bonner County. Fairly plentiful in 1917 in the vicinity of Clarks Fork, occurring in the valleys and to the tops of the higher ridges (Burleigh, 1923).

Kootenai County. "Abundant" in the winter at Fort Sherman (Coeur d'Alene); breeds sparingly; two nests with young on June 15 (Merrill, 1897); one bird in immature plumage collected in Hoodoo Valley in 1894 (Snyder, 1900); common at Coeur d'Alene, 1910-14 (Rust, 1915); common at the upper end of Lake Coeur d'Alene July 1-10, 1943 (Yocom, 1946).

Benewah County. Common and widely distributed at St. Maries, 1921 through 1941 (Hand, 1941).

Latah County. Noted in cutover areas June 1–August 16, 1947 (Johnston, 1949); fairly common at Harvard during the summers of 1951 and 1952 (Verner, 1953); fairly common, 1947 through 1958, and noted in all the wooded areas in the county; at Moscow, a female was seen May 24, 1949, carrying food to young in a nest at the edge of a clearing at the top of Paradise Ridge (Burleigh).

Nez Perce County. An uncommon winter resident at Lewiston, an occasional bird being seen on Hatwai Creek, or in cottonwoods along the Snake River, from October until early April. Extreme dates of occurrence October 13 (1957) and April 6 (1952) (Burleigh).

Idaho County. Specimen taken four miles northwest of Pollock July 1, 1940 (Arvey, 1947); "Numerous" in the Selway region in September, 1941; specimens taken September 10-23 four miles southwest of Selway Falls (Orr, 1951).

Adams County. Noted at Indian Valley October 15, 1958 (Newhouse, 1960).

Boise County. Noted on the Boise National Forest from January through March, 1939, and also in January, 1940 (Marshall, 1945).

Lemhi County. Noted on Colson Creek, north of Shoup, June 5, 1949 (Burleigh).

Fremont County. Fairly common June through August, 1916 (Rust, 1917).

Clark County. Noted on Signal Peak June 19, 1961 (Oring, 1962).

Blaine County. Common in the vicinity of Ketchum October through December, 1910 (Jewett, 1912).

Bonneville County. Uncommon resident at Grays Lake, 1949 through 1951 (Steel, 1956). One bird seen June 13, 1949, in the fir woods near the top of Caribou Mountain (8,500 feet) (Burleigh).

South-central Idaho. "Tolerably common" in 1890 in the Salmon River and Sawtooth mountains and "in the upper part of Wood River Valley" (Merriam, 1891).

Power County. Specimen taken June 29, 1949, at Heglar Pass, twenty miles south of American Falls (Jollie, in litt.).

Minidoka County. One seen at Rupert April 17, 1920 (Davis, 1935).

Cassia County. Fairly common in 1949 "in the higher forested areas"; a pair noted at a nest in the Silent City of Rocks on June 21 (Levy, 1950).

In order to determine the possibility of geographic variation in the Hairy Woodpeckers resident in Idaho sixteen specimens were taken in various parts of the state. All were found to be typical of the Rocky Mountain race *monticola*. These specimens are as follows: Males, Boundary County, Harrison Peak, September 28, 1957; Latah County, Moscow, October 30 and November 27, 1947, March 26, 1949, October 27, 1950, November 4, 1951; Deary, December 13, 1951; Nez Perce County, Lewiston, October 28, 1951, October 13 and November 1, 1957, March 28, 1958; Lake Waha, March 1, 1954. Females, Moscow, November 16, 1947, October 2, 1952, November 4, 1957; Lemhi County, Shoup, November 1, 1949.

Habits. Wherever found throughout its wide range in North America, the Hairy Woodpecker is rather a solitary bird, and this trait is at once apparent in Idaho. Invariably only a single bird will be seen feeding alone in a wooded area, only during the breeding season two being observed together.

Although considered a resident species, there is a noticeable altitudinal migration in the fall, the birds leaving the higher ridges and appearing then in the valleys. At Moscow they have appeared in the Arboretum on the University campus, within the city limits, as early in the fall as August 25 (1949). It is doubtful if, during the summer months, they occur below an altitude of 3000 feet.

The one nest that I found at Moscow, to which, on May 24, 1949, both adult birds were carrying food to their young, was twelve feet from the ground in an old rotten fir stub.

When available fleshy fruits are eaten, but insects, their eggs and their larvae, comprise fully 80 per cent of the food of this woodpecker. Rust (1915) states that at Coeur d'Alene it frequently eats frozen apples during the winter months.

Dendrocopos pubescens (Linnaeus): DOWNY WOODPECKER

General Distribution. Resident from southeastern Alaska, southern Mackenzie, James Bay, southern Quebec and Newfoundland south to southern California, northern New Mexico, the Gulf coast and southern Florida.

Status in Idaho. Fairly common but rather local in its distribution throughout the state; least numerous in southern Idaho, where it has been noted in but a few widely separated localities.

Bonner County. Noted on Lightning Creek, north of Clark Fork, where a nest with almost fully fledged young was found July 8, 1917 (Burleigh, 1923).

Kootenai County. An uncommon resident at Fort Sherman (Coeur d'Alene) (Merrill, 1897); "not common," (1910-14); two specimens taken at

Fernan Lake (Rust, 1915); one bird seen at the upper end of Lake Coeur d'Alene July 1-10, 1943 (Yocom, 1946); one bird seen in cottonwoods at the edge of Lake Coeur d'Alene February 14, 1950 (Burleigh).

Benewah County. A fairly common resident at St. Maries, 1921 through 1941, in the cottonwoods in the valleys (Hand, 1941).

Latah County. Common resident; specimen taken at Potlatch November 3, 1939 (Arvey, 1947); noted but once during the summer of 1947, one bird June 20 on the "State Game Refuge" (Johnston, 1949); fairly common, but rather local in its distribution in the county (1947 through 1958) (Burleigh).

Nez Perce County. Uncommon at Lewiston (1947 through 1958); noted on Hatwai Creek, and in cottonwoods and willows fringing the Snake River; a female in immature plumage taken July 12, 1952 (Burleigh); a male collected at Myrtle Beach February 16, 1954 (Burleigh).

Clearwater County. A male collected at Weippe February 8, 1954, feeding on apples in an old abandoned orchard (Burleigh).

Idaho County. Females taken September 25 and 26, 1941, four miles southwest of Selway Falls (Orr, 1951).

Adams County. Noted throughout the year (1957-58) at Council and at Indian Valley (Newhouse, 1960).

Boise County. Noted occasionally on the Boise National Forest during the winters of 1938-39 and 1939-40 (Marshall, 1945).

Owyhee County. A single bird, a female, noted at Oreana February 21, 1950 (Burleigh).

Blaine County. One seen in 1890 "in the upper part of Wood River Valley" (Merriam, 1891); common in aspens and cottonwoods on the Wood River, in the vicinity of Ketchum, October through December, 1910 (Jewett, 1912).

Fremont County. Occurred sparingly in willows and in aspen groves, June through August, 1916 (Rust, 1917).

Jefferson County. An "uncommon summer resident" in 1961, on the Camas National Wildlife Refuge (Oring, 1962).

Bonneville County. A single bird, a male, seen November 11, 1957, in willows at the edge of Grays Lake (Burleigh).

Habits. Because of the partiality of this species for deciduous timber, it is rather local in its distribution in Idaho, and probably also for this same reason it is nowhere a very common bird.

Altitude apparently has an appreciable influence on its occurrence in the state, and my limited experience has largely convinced me that it is most common above 2,000 feet, and below 6,000 feet. Although I noted it throughout the year at Lewiston (altitude 860 feet, the lowest point in the state), it was by no means a common bird there. On the other hand, Steel failed to record it at Grays Lake (6,400 feet) despite suitable habitat at the edge of the lake. I noted a single bird in November in willows on Eagle Creek, two miles north of Gray, so it would appear that it occurs in small numbers but is a rare bird at this altitude.

A nest that I found at Moscow June 19, 1948, held small young, and was eighteen feet from the ground in an old rotten pine stub at the edge of an open slashing on Paradise Ridge.

Dendrocopos pubescens parvirostris (Burleigh)

This recently described race of the Downy Woodpecker (Burleigh, 1960) occurs throughout all of Idaho except the extreme eastern edge of the state. It can be distinguished from *leucurus,* occupying the larger part of the Rocky Mountain region, by its short slender bill, deep black upper parts, and the limited amount of spotting on the wings. Specimens typical of this race have been taken at Cocolalla (Bonner County), St. Maries, Potlatch, Moscow, Helmer (Latah County), Lewiston, Myrtle Beach, Weippe, Gray, Murphy (Owyhee County) and Oreana.

Dendrocopos pubescens leucurus (Hartlaub)

This race, characteristic of the Rocky Mountain region, occurs in the extreme eastern edge of the state, specimens typical of *leucurus* having been taken in Fremont County (Ashton and Henrys Lake), Bonneville County (Swan Lake), and Bannock County (Inkom). An immature male from Challis, Custer County, suggests *parvirostris* in the small size of the bill, but otherwise has the characters of *leucurus.*

Dendrocopos albolarvatus albolarvatus (Cassin): WHITE-HEADED WOODPECKER

General Distribution. Resident from northern Washington and northern Idaho south through Oregon and western Idaho to northern California and Nevada.

Status in Idaho. A scarce and rather local resident species in the western part of the state.

Merrill (1897) considered the White-headed Woodpecker a rare resident at Fort Sherman (Coeur d'Alene).

In Latah County it was recorded by Verner (in litt.) at the east end of Moscow Mountain, one-half mile east of the lookout November 23, 1952, and on the west slope of Crumarine Creek, five miles north of Moscow, March 22, 1953.

In Nez Perce County it was reported by Levy (1959) as "a local and rare breeding bird." He collected a male on Craig Mountain, near Zaza, June 15, 1951. I noted a single bird in open pine woods at Lake Waha March 6, 1953.

Arvey (1947) collected a specimen ten miles southwest of Riggins, Idaho County, May 14, 1939.

Levy (in litt.) states that "three birds were seen in different areas and on different dates during July, 1947, in the immediate vicinity of New Meadows," Adams County.

Marshall (1945) noted this species on the Boise National Forest, in Boise County, single birds being seen on Swanholm Creek February 13, 1939, and on Hunter Creek January 15, 1940.

Habits. In Idaho the White-headed Woodpecker reaches the northern and eastern limits of its range, and under these circumstances it is not surprising that it is not a common bird. Its distinctive plumage renders it easily recognizable, so where it occurs its presence should be at once apparent. Unlike its near relatives, its preference is for mountain slopes covered with open Ponderosa pine, and so partial is it to such a site that it is almost useless to look for it elsewhere. During the summer months it can be found at the tops of the higher ridges, but in the late fall it makes a gradual altitudinal migration to the valleys, and here it remains until early spring.

Picoides arcticus (Swainson): BLACK-BACKED THREE-TOED WOODPECKER

General Distribution. Largely resident from central Alaska, northern Manitoba, northern Quebec and Newfoundland south to northern California, northern Wyoming, Minnesota, the upper peninsula of Michigan, and northern New York.

Status in Idaho. Resident, but apparently uncommon and of local occurrence in the northern half of the state. There is a single record for southern Idaho.

In Kootenai County Merrill (1897) reported this species fairly common, "especially at higher altitudes." Rust (1915) stated that a male and a female were taken near Garwood September 29, 1914.

Hand (1941) found this three-toed woodpecker (1921-41) a rather uncommon resident "in Canadian Zone forests" in Benewah and Shoshone counties. Levy (1959) reported one seen at Dismal Lake, in Shoshone County, October 16, 1950.

In Latah County it has been noted only at Harvard. Here one breeding pair was seen by Johnston (1949) during the summer of 1947, while Verner (1953) observed two birds here on April 15 and August 8, 1951, and June 23, 1952.

I have one record for Clearwater County, a female with a well-pronounced brood patch being taken at Bungalow June 19, 1952.

In Idaho County a pair was seen (and the male collected) on July 13, 1948, six miles southwest of Lolo Pass (Orr, 1951).

At New Meadows in Adams County, one bird, a female, was noted August 28, 1955 (Burleigh).

The one record for southern Idaho is that of a male taken at Sawtooth Lake in Custer County, October 3, 1890 (Merriam, 1891).

Habits. Judging from my rather limited experience with this species in Idaho it is, compared with other woodpeckers, quiet and inconspicuous;

and as it frequents the heavier timber it can be easily overlooked. It is probably, therefore, more common than the relatively few records would indicate. Economically, it is an extremely beneficial bird, for its food consists largely of wood-boring beetles that are so destructive to living conifers.

In two respects it is unique in comparison with other woodpeckers. It has three toes instead of four, and in the male the crown patch is yellow rather than red.

Picoides tridactylus (Linnaeus): NORTHERN THREE-TOED WOODPECKER

General Distribution. Resident from the limit of trees in Alaska, Yukon, Mackenzie, Manitoba, and Quebec south to Oregon, Arizona, New Mexico, Minnesota, Ontario, and northern New York.

Status in Idaho. Resident over much of the state, but apparently uncommon, and rather local in its distribution.

Actual records for the occurrence of this species in Idaho, while relatively few in number, include to a large extent the timbered areas of the state, and are as follows:

Boundary County. A specimen taken four miles west of Meadow Creek, July 29, 1932 (Museum of Vertebrate Zoology, Berkeley); two specimens taken in thick fir woods halfway up Harrison Peak (altitude approximately 5,000 feet) September 28, 1957 (Burleigh).

Bonner County. Three specimens taken by Charles F. Hedges at Coolin, on Priest Lake, August 27 and September 10, 1929 (Museum of Vertebrate Zoology).

Shoshone County. Fairly plentiful in the vicinity of Dismal Lake June 20 and 21, 1951; a nest with the female incubating was found, and three specimens, all males, were taken (Burleigh).

Latah County. One bird noted in a wooded ravine east of Deary April 12, 1949; collected (Burleigh).

Clearwater County. Three specimens taken by D. H. Blanchard at Weippe July 20, 1932 (Museum of Vertebrate Zoology); at Headquarters a breeding pair was collected June 15, 1951, and a female February 8, 1953 (Burleigh).

Idaho County. Noted four miles southwest of Selway Falls September 29, 1941, and six miles southwest of Lolo Pass July 13 and 20, 1948; males collected July 13 and 20 (Orr, 1951).

Salmon River Mountains. One taken and several others seen in 1890 (Merriam, 1891).

Bitterroot Mountains. One specimen taken on the west slope of the mountains (Bangs, 1900).

Blaine County. Three seen in the vicinity of Ketchum, October through December, 1910; one taken November 3 at an altitude of 7,500 feet (Jewett, 1912).

Clark County. A male taken on Signal Peak June 19, 1961, and another seen July 15 (Oring, 1962).

Bear Lake County. Specimens in the Museum of Vertebrate Zoology were taken on the west rim of the Copenhagen Basin (altitude 8,400) in the Wasatch Mountains (Arvey, 1947).

Habits. Except during the breeding season, this three-toed woodpecker, like the preceding species, is quiet and inconspicuous and, in my experience, must be looked for to be seen. It rarely utters a note of any kind during the fall and winter months, and when feeding it remains motionless for long intervals after its hunger has been satisfied. Consequently, it may be present in many areas where it has been unrecorded, and may be more common in Idaho than is generally realized.

The two nests that I succeeded in finding were both in old rotten fir stubs, the one at Headquarters being ten feet from the ground, the other at Dismal Lake eight feet up. Both were in open slashings, a site commonly chosen by this species throughout its range.

Picoides tridactylus fasciatus Baird

Specimens taken in northern Idaho, from Boundary County south to the Salmon River Mountains, have been critically examined and found to represent this northern race that breeds from northern Alaska south to southern Oregon and northern Montana. The chief characters that distinguish it from *bacatus* of eastern North America are the more extensive white of the back, and the white barring of the upper tail coverts and lower rump.

Picoides tridactylus dorsalis Baird

This, the most southern race of *Picoides tridactylus,* occurs from central Montana south to central Arizona and New Mexico. It resembles *fasciatus* but is larger, and the sides and flanks are less barred with black. Specimens taken in the Wasatch Mountains in Bear Lake County, and on Signal Peak in Clark County, have been identified as *dorsalis,* so its range in Idaho would appear to be limited to the southeastern corner of the state.

ORDER PASSERIFORMES

Tyrant Flycatchers: *Family Tyrannidae*

Tyrannus tyrannus hespericola Oberholser: EASTERN KINGBIRD

General Distribution. Breeds from northern British Columbia, southern Mackenzie, and central Saskatchewan south to northeastern California, northern Utah and Colorado. Winters in South America from Peru to Bolivia.

Status in Idaho. A common summer resident in suitable habitat throughout the state, although less numerous and local in its distribution in southern Idaho.

The Eastern Kingbird is another species having the distinction of being first recorded in the state by the Lewis and Clark expedition, Lewis noting in one of his Journals (*Original Journals,* V:136) that it was seen on the Lolo Trail above Weippe June 15, 1806.

Subsequent observers have all reported its presence in Idaho, published annotated lists emphasizing the wide distribution of this familiar species. Summarized briefly, the localities where the Eastern Kingbird has been noted in the state are as follows:

Boundary County. Fairly plentiful at Porthill June 26, 1957 (Burleigh).

Bonner County. Fairly plentiful summer resident at Clark Fork in 1917 (Burleigh, 1923).

Kootenai County. Fairly common summer resident at Fort Sherman (Coeur d'Alene) (Merrill, 1897); uncommon summer resident (1910-14) on the St. Joe and Spokane rivers (Rust, 1915); noted at the upper end of Lake Coeur d'Alene July 1-10, 1943 (Yocom, 1946).

Benewah County. Common summer resident (1921 through 1941) at St. Maries (Hand, 1941).

Latah County. Common in open country June 1–August 16, 1947 (Johnston, 1949); noted at Harvard July 23, 1951, and July 30, 1952 (Verner, 1953); common and well distributed throughout the county during the summer months (1948 through 1958); noted at Potlatch, Viola, Moscow, Troy, Deary, Kendrick, Genesee (Burleigh).

Nez Perce County. A common summer resident at Lewiston (Burleigh).

Clearwater County. Three birds seen at Orofino August 28, 1949, and a single bird at Headquarters August 27, 1952 (Burleigh).

Adams County. One pair noted at New Meadows June 27, 1949 (Burleigh); one pair noted at Council June 8, 1952 (Burleigh); a common summer resident at Council in 1958 (Newhouse, 1960).

Valley County. A specimen taken at Copeland Flats July 25, 1929 (Brodkorb).

Washington County. One pair seen at Weiser June 4, 1952 (Burleigh); this species a common summer resident at the western edge of the state, eight breeding pairs being noted, June 8, 1952, between the Brownlee Ranger Station and Cambridge (Burleigh).

Boise County. One pair seen at Horseshoe Bend June 21, 1950 (Burleigh).

Owyhee County. Specimens taken on the Bruneau River June 7 and 9, 1932 (Brodkorb); one pair noted at Marsing June 24, 1949 (Burleigh).

Lemhi County. An occasional bird noted at Salmon June 29, 1950 (Burleigh).

Custer County. One pair seen at Challis July 15, 1958 (Burleigh).

Fremont County. Found to be fairly plentiful at St. Anthony June 10, 1957, four breeding pairs being noted during the morning; specimen taken at Henrys Lake June 25, 1960 (Burleigh).

Jefferson County. Specimen taken at Mud Lake May 28, 1931 (Brodkorb); found to be a common summer resident on the Camas National Wildlife Refuge, two miles west of Hamer, in 1961 (Oring, 1962).

Bonneville County. A rare summer resident at Grays Lake (1949-51) (Steel, 1956); single birds seen at Gray May 30, 1952, and June 7, 1957 (Burleigh).

Caribou County. One bird seen at Soda Springs June 15, 1949 (Burleigh).

Bear Lake County. Specimens taken at Montpelier June 9 and 14, 1930 (Brodkorb).

Bannock County. This species found to be a fairly plentiful summer resident at Pocatello in 1955, an occasional breeding pair being seen June 9 (Burleigh).

South Central Idaho. Common in 1872 at Fort Hall, "along the Snake River, and Henry Fork"; also common in July, 1890, along the Snake River near Blackfoot, along Cedar Creek in the Blackfoot Mountains, and on Big Lost River, and in August on Birch Creek (Merriam, 1891).

Minidoka County. A rare summer resident, 1911 through 1913 (Kenagy, 1914); found to be a summer resident at Rupert (1919-21) (Davis, 1935); several birds seen on the Minidoka National Wildlife Refuge July 21, 1958 (Burleigh).

Twin Falls County. Specimens taken at Twin Falls July 11, 1932 (Brodkorb); and August 1, 1949 (Levy, 1950).

Gooding County. One breeding pair noted at Hagerman June 19, 1960 (Burleigh).

In order to determine the validity of *hespericola* described by Harry C. Oberholser from southern Oregon in 1932, but to date not recognized by the A. O. U. Committee on Nomenclature, a series of specimens was taken throughout the state. These included adults in fresh spring plumage and in worn fall plumage, and immatures of various ages. Compared with a similar series from the eastern United States it was at once apparent that *hespericola* was a well-marked race with characters that readily separated it from *tyrannus*. It is characterized by being larger, and paler above (blue-gray with little suggestion of black), the gray of the chest paler, and the white edging of the coverts and secondaries more extensive and clearer white.

Habits. When one bears in mind the fact that this species winters in South America, it seems strange that it should travel such a long distance to reach Idaho and then remain in the state just long enough to rear its young. I never recorded it in Latah County before the middle of May, and not infrequently it was the latter part of that month before the first bird appeared. By the middle of August there was a noticeable decrease in the number seen, and only rarely was it noted after the first of September. My extreme dates of occurrence (1948 through 1958) are: Potlatch—May 21 (1948) and September 1 (1957); Moscow—May 14 (1949) and September 4 (1953); Genesee—May 21 (1955) and September 4 (1952). At Lewiston it was observed between the dates of May 13 (1949) and September 7 (1953). Merrill (1897) cites the last week in May as the time of arrival in the spring at Coeur d'Alene, and Hand (1941) states that it was present at St. Maries (1921 through 1941) from May 20 to late August. Farther south in the state Newhouse (1960) noted it at Council, in 1958, between the dates of May 17 and September 5, and Davis (1935) observed it at Rupert from June 12 to September 7 (1919 through 1921).

In view of its late arrival in the spring it is doubtful if this Kingbird nests before the middle of June, and the average date for fresh eggs is possibly even later than this. Merriam (1891) reports a nest with nearly fledged young on the Blackfoot River July 12, 1872, and another on the Snake River that held three fresh eggs on July 14. A nest that I found in Nez Perce County on July 14, 1957, with four slightly incubated eggs was in a rather unusual situation, being built on a beam of a small dock extending out over the reservoir east of Lewiston Orchards, up ten feet from the water.

Tyrannus verticalis Say: WESTERN KINGBIRD

General Distribution. Breeds from southern British Columbia east through southern Saskatchewan, southern Manitoba and southern Michigan to northern Ohio, south to Baja California, Chihuahua, central Texas and northern Missouri. Winters from Guerrero and Morelos, in southern Mexico, to northern Nicaragua, and in small numbers on the coast of South Carolina and Florida.

Status in Idaho. In northern Idaho restricted to a few localities possessing the desired habitat requirements, but fairly common there during the summer months. A common summer resident over much of the southern part of the state.

The Western Kingbird is characteristically a bird of open prairie country, so it is not surprising that it is extremely local in its occurrence in northern Idaho.

In Kootenai County it is found only in the open Spokane Valley, but here it is common and well distributed. Merrill (1897) reported the presence of "a pair or two" each year at Fort Sherman (Coeur d'Alene).

Rust (1915) stated that a nest with young was found at Post Falls July 5, 1913, and I personally noted two pairs of these Kingbirds at Post Falls May 15, 1952. Two months later, on July 21, I found this species fairly plentiful in the vicinity of Hauser, seeing three broods of well-grown young that day. The following year I spent May 6 in the field between Hauser and Rathdrum; that day I noted seven Western Kingbirds there, in each case around farm houses in the open prairie country. Yocom (1946) considered this species common "in the agricultural country" about Coeur d'Alene July 1-10, 1943.

In Latah County Johnston (1949) noted this species on two occasions during the summer of 1947, collecting an adult male at Moscow on June 28 and seeing young of the year at Juliaetta August 12. I found it of regular occurrence but by no means common in the open Palouse country at Moscow (1948 through 1958), but as a breeding bird I observed it nowhere else in the county. I have two records for transients at Genesee, seeing single birds July 16, 1948, and May 20, 1950; and I have one record for Potlatch, August 26, 1951.

At Lewiston, in Nez Perce County, it was a common and well-distributed summer resident, scattered pairs occurring about the ranch houses and in the cottonwoods on the Snake River. Its relative abundance is best illustrated by the fact that on May 13, 1949, during a morning that I spent in the field in the vicinity of Lewiston, seven breeding pairs were noted. According to Merriam (1891) several pairs were reported by Bendire as breeding at Fort Lapwai in 1871.

The one record for Idaho County is that of one pair that I noted in open country east of Grangeville June 8, 1952.

At New Meadows, in Adams County, where it does not occur during the summer months, a single bird, a fall transient, was seen August 14, 1957. At Council, however, in open country farther south in the county, this species was reported by Newhouse (1960) as a common summer resident.

In the southern part of the state, it was considered common during the summer months in Minidoka County by Kenagy (1914) and Davis (1935), in south-central Idaho by Merriam (1891) and Levy (1950), and in 1961 on the Camas National Wildlife Refuge, in Jefferson County, by Oring (1962). Steel (1956) found it a rare summer resident (1949-51) at Grays Lake. I noted a single bird at Gray May 28, 1952. Specimens were taken by Arvey (1947) at Arrowrock Reservoir, Boise County, June 15, 1941, and by Malcolm Jollie at American Falls, Power County, July 3, 1949.

Transients were observed at Henrys Lake, Fremont County, August 25, 1916 (Rust, 1917), at Montpelier May 26, 1952 (Burleigh), and at Soda Springs August 25, 1955 (Burleigh).

Habits. The Western Kingbird is apparently a hardier bird than the preceding species, for it arrives in the state in the spring almost a month earlier; it departs in the fall, however, at practically the same time. Extreme dates of occurrence are: Moscow, May 4 (1957) and September 6 (1954); Lewiston, April 20 (1950) and September 8 (1951); Council, April 28 to September 1 (1958); Rupert, May 9 to October 10 (1919-21).

Although always present in Idaho by early May, it would appear that this bird makes no attempt to rear a brood of young before the middle of June, and it does so probably often later than this. Merriam (1891) states that two nests with eggs were collected June 28, 1872, on Devil Creek, in the south-central part of the state, and Davis (1935) cites July 1 as the date for fresh eggs at Rupert, in Minidoka County. A nest that I found at Moscow July 6, 1950, held three well-fledged young. Where available, a tree is usually selected as a nesting site, but individual pairs show considerable originality in this respect. A nest found by Bendire at Fort Lapwai was "built on the sill of one of the attic windows of my quarters," while the one found by Rust at Post Falls was on a "cross bar of a telephone pole."

[**Muscivora forficata** (Gmelin): Scissor-tailed Flycatcher]

General Distribution. Breeds from southern Colorado, Nebraska, and western Arkansas south to southern Texas and western Louisiana. Winters from southern Mexico (Chiapas) to western Panama.

Status in Idaho. Of accidental occurrence in the state.

The one record for this species in Idaho is that of a bird seen August 6, 7, and 16, 1955, on the Wood River, fifteen miles from Sun Valley, Blaine County (Thornburg, 1956).

Habits. In view of its breeding range in the south-central part of the United States, it is doubtful if the Scissor-tailed Flycatcher will ever be of other than accidental occurrence in Idaho. However, it has appeared casually as far west as California, and as far north as Manitoba, so it is not too surprising that this one individual appeared in Blaine County. As distinctive a bird as this could hardly be misidentified, but it is unfortunate that it was not collected in order to verify the identification.

Myiarchus cinerascens cinerascens (Lawrence): Ash-throated Flycatcher

General Distribution. Breeds from southern Oregon, southern Idaho, Colorado and central Texas south to Baja California and southern Mexico (Guerrero). Winters from northern Baja California, central Arizona, and Tamaulipas south to Guatemala and El Salvador.

Status in Idaho. A fairly common summer resident in the extreme southern part of the state.

Although actually recorded in but a few localities in southern Idaho, this species is probably fairly common and well distributed in suitable habitat bordering both Nevada and Utah.

It was apparently first recorded in the state by Arvey (1947) who took a specimen at the head of Taylor Creek, on the Boise National Forest in Boise County, August 7, 1941. This record is of special interest, as this is the farthest north that this species has been found in Idaho.

Three miles south of Oakley, in Cassia County, the ridges are covered with a fairly open stand of junipers, and this habitat would appear to satisfy the rather exacting requirements of the Ash-throated Flycatcher. Over a period of years field work carried on in the vicinity of Goose Creek has always revealed its presence on these juniper-covered ridges, and specimens verifying its occurrence have been taken as follows: three males, 2 females, June 25-27, 1949 (Jollie); male, female, August 11, 1950 (Levy); two males, July 19-20, 1958; male, June 13, 1960 (Burleigh).

At Massacre Rocks, twelve miles west of American Falls, Power County, a male was taken June 21, 1960 (Burleigh).

It is reported as breeding at Pocatello, in Bannock County, and doubtless does so as conditions there are similar to those in Cassia County.

Habits. Throughout its wide range in the western United States the Ash-throated Flycatcher occurs in quite varied habitat, but in Idaho is restricted to the arid juniper-covered ridges that occupy a rather limited area on the southern edge of the state. Here it is a fairly common bird during the summer months, but in my experience it is so quiet and inconspicuous that it can be easily overlooked.

Although an old woodpecker hole is commonly used as a nesting site, in Idaho, due to the complete absence of woodpeckers during the breeding season in the junipers, a natural cavity is utilized. Fortunately this presents no problem as many of the trees are old and gnarled, and there is no scarcity of suitable cavities.

Sayornis saya (Bonaparte): SAY'S PHOEBE

General Distribution. Breeds from northern Alaska, northern Alberta, and southwestern Manitoba south to central Mexico (Durango and Zacatecas). Winters from northern California, southern New Mexico and southern Texas south to southern Baja California and Veracruz.

Status in Idaho. A local but fairly common summer resident throughout the state. Possibly of casual occurrence during the winter months at Lewiston, in Nez Perce County.

In Kootenai County Merrill (1898) considered this species a common summer resident at Couer d'Alene. Rust (1915), however, found it uncommon during the summer months (1910 through 1914). Yocom (1946) noted one pair at the upper end of Lake Coeur d'Alene July 1-10, 1943.

In Latah County Johnston (1949) reported a specimen taken thirteen miles south of Moscow June 28, 1947. I found it an uncommon and local summer resident in the county (1948-58), noting it at Potlatch, Moscow, and Genesee.

At Lewiston, however, in Nez Perce County, it was common and well distributed during the summer months. Bendire (1895) likewise found it a common summer resident at Fort Lapwai and at the Nez Perce Indian Agency.

A specimen was taken by Arvey (1947) at Pollock, in Idaho County, but he failed to cite the date of collection.

In Owyhee County I noted the Say's Phoebe at Oreana June 25, 1949, and February 21, 1950, at Murphy February 21, 1950, and at Homedale February 24, 1950.

Merriam (1891) considered it common in 1890 in the lower Lemhi Valley. I noted it at North Fork, in Lemhi County, June 7, 1949.

Davis (1935) reported it a summer resident at Rupert, in Minidoka County, occurring there between the dates of March 23 and September 29 (1919-21).

In Cassia County Levy (1950) found it a fairly common breeding bird "of the canyons" in 1949. One pair had a nest "on the rafters of an occupied store" in Almo June 21.

Habits. The Say's Phoebe is one of the earliest migrants to appear in northern Idaho in the spring. Its arrival is influenced to some extent by the weather, and while noted in Latah County in late February it was usually early March before the first bird was seen. My earliest dates of arrival are: Potlatch, March 21 (1950); Moscow, March 7 (1954); Genesee, February 28 (1958). In the fall this species was rarely seen after late August, my latest date of departure being a single bird noted at Genesee, September 8 (1952).

At Lewiston it could almost be considered a resident species, for I have records for every month of the year. It was invariably present from late February until the middle of September, and I have also noted single birds as follows: October 31 (1951), November 16 (1951), December 21 (1953), January 28 (1954), February 10 (1953).

Bendire (1895) comments as follows on the breeding habits of the Say's Phoebe in Nez Perce County. "I have taken a full set of eggs containing small embryos on April 17, 1871. Here (Fort Lapwai) they nested mostly under the eaves of outhouses and stables; but one pair selected the plate or rail over the main door of my quarters, and another a corner on the hospital porch. In this vicinity I also found a pair occupying an old Cliff Swallow's nest attached to an overhanging ledge of rock in Soldier's Canyon, on the road to Lewiston, Idaho, and another in a very unusual position in the same canyon, in an old Robin's nest, placed in a syringa bush, about four feet from the ground."

Sayornis saya saya (Bonaparte)

This southern race of the Say's Phoebe is the breeding form throughout all of Idaho. A series of seventeen specimens taken from 1948 through 1958 in various parts of the state were found to be typical of *saya* both in respect to size and color.

Sayornis saya yukonensis Bishop

In view of the fact that *yukonensis* is the breeding form in Washington and as far south in Oregon as Umatilla, it is not surprising that both in Latah County and Nez Perce County both races of *saya* occur, and that in this western edge of the state there is a noticeable intergradation between the two. Six specimens taken at Lewiston are typical of *yukonensis,* and while they possibly represent transients it is not improbable that one or more would have nested here. These specimens are as follows: males March 4, 1949, February 10, 1953, January 28, 1954, March 16, 1955, and April 26, 1957; and a female March 16, 1950. Eight additional specimens were intermediate in their characters, and while approaching *yukonensis* in the grayer coloration of the upperparts were closer to *saya* and were so identified. These were as follows: males, Lewiston, April 24, 1950, July 4, 1955; Genesee, April 21, 1951; Moscow, May 2, 1948; females, Lewiston, April 24 and September 13, 1950, April 6, 1952; Moscow, April 30, 1951.

Yukonensis has been recorded once in southern Idaho, a specimen having been taken by F. Hamerstrom at Grand View, Owyhee County, November 16, 1943.

Yukonensis can be distinguished from the nominate race *saya* by its darker grayer upperparts and by its smaller bill.

Empidonax traillii (Audubon): TRAILL'S FLYCATCHER

General Distribution. Breeds from central Alaska east through northern Mackenzie, northern Ontario and Quebec to Newfoundland, south to southern California, western Texas, Missouri, and Maryland. Winters from southern Mexico to Argentina.

Status in Idaho. A common summer resident in suitable habitat throughout the state.

Because of the similarity in appearance of the Empidonax flycatchers, and the difficulty of identifying them in life, even during the breeding season, they appear on very few of the local lists of the avifauna of Idaho. It seems advisable under these circumstances to cite only those localities where specimens have been taken and identified as *traillii*. Further field work will undoubtedly reveal the presence of this species in areas throughout the state where as yet it has not been recorded, and verify the few sight records that have been published. (St. Maries, Benewah County—Hand, 1941; Rupert, Minidoka County—Davis, 1935; Hamer, Jefferson County—Oring, 1962.)

On the basis of actual specimens the Traill's Flycatcher has been recorded as a breeding bird in the following localities in Idaho:

South Central Idaho. Specimens taken June 28, 1872, on Devil Creek, in July, 1890, on Big Lost River, and on August 4 and 15, 1890, on Birch Creek (Merriam, 1891).

Valley County. Specimens taken in 1929 in Long Valley July 19, and on the Payette River, at Lake, July 21.

Owyhee County. Bruneau River, June 6, 1932.

Lemhi County. Leadore, July 3 and 4, 1931; Salmon, July 8 and 10, 1931.

Custer County. Challis, August 6, 1931.

Clark County. Spencer, June 6 and 11, 1931.

Fremont County. Big Springs, August 21, 1930.

Jefferson County. Mud Lake, May 26 and 27, 1931.

Blaine County. Lava Lake, August 19 and 20, 1929; Ketchum, August 22, 1931.

Bonneville County. Grays Lake, July 1, 1930.
Caribou County. The Narrows, June 28 and 29, 1930.
Bear Lake County. Montpelier, July 21, 1930.
Cassia County. Burley, September 3, 1932 (Brodkorb, in litt.).

Boundary County. Porthill (single pair, June 26, 1957).
Bonner County. Clark Fork (occasional bird, July 26, 1960).
Shoshone County. Clarkia (breeding pair noted July 19, 1948).
Latah County. Common summer resident (1948-58); noted at Harvard, Princeton, Potlatch, Moscow, Troy, Genesee.
Nez Perce County. Lewiston (common summer resident (1948-58); Lapwai (occasional bird seen July 12, 1950).
Clearwater County. Breeding pairs noted at Weippe June 13, 1951; Headquarters June 15, 1951, and June 17, 1952; Bungalow June 19, 1952.
Adams County. New Meadows (scattered breeding pairs noted in 1958 and 1959).
Washington County. Weiser (several breeding pairs noted June 4, 1952, at the edge of the Snake River).
Ada County. Boise (several breeding pairs noted June 22, 1949, and July 15, 1960).
Owyhee County. Silver City (an occasional breeding pair noted July 13, 1960, at an altitude of seven thousand feet).
Lemhi County. Salmon (several breeding pairs noted June 7, 1949).
Custer County. Challis (fairly plentiful July 14-15, 1958); Stanley (occasional breeding pair noted July 16, 1958).
Blaine County. Ketchum (fairly plentiful June 26, 1950, and July 3, 1960, on the Big Wood River).
Fremont County. Targhee Pass (several breeding pairs noted June 27, 1960, at an altitude of seven thousand feet).
Bonneville County. Gray (fairly plentiful June 17, 1949, at the edge of Grays Lake and on Eagle Creek).
Bannock County. Pocatello (several breeding pairs noted June 18, 1949).
Cassia County. Almo (several breeding pairs noted June 13, 1955); Burley (fairly plentiful June 9, 1960, along the Snake River) (Burleigh).

Owyhee County. Specimens taken at Riddle June 17, 1949 (Jollie), and at Delamar August 8, 1950 (Levy).
Habits. The Traill's Flycatcher is the latest migrant to appear in Idaho in the spring. It is possible that an occasional individual may appear after the middle of May, but on the basis of actual specimens it is the end of the month before this species is normally present in the state; my earliest records are of males taken at Princeton, in Latah County, May 30, 1949, and in Caribou County, two miles west of Freedom, Wyoming, May 31, 1952. Its departure in the fall is rather early, for there is a noticeable decrease in numbers by the middle of August, and only rarely is this little flycatcher recorded after the last of the month. My extreme dates of departure for northern Idaho are: Moscow August 31 (1948), Potlatch September 8

(1950), Genesee September 8 (1952), and Lewiston September 8 (1957). A male taken in willows on Eagle Creek, north of Gray, on August 26, 1955, represents a somewhat late date of occurrence for this species at this altitude (6,300 feet).

A nest found at Moscow July 15, 1950, held three slightly incubated eggs, and was six feet up in a bush in underbrush at the edge of a dry stream bed. Verner (1953) reports two nests found at Harvard. One held four well-grown young on August 7, 1951, and was four feet up in a ninebark (*Opulaster pauciflorus*). The other held three newly hatched young on July 17, 1952, and was three feet up in a hawthorne (*Cretaegus brevispina*).

Empidonax traillii adastus Oberholser

The distribution of the races of *Empidonax traillii* in Idaho is rather puzzling. An analysis of available specimens would indicate that *adastus* is the breeding form in the northern part of the state, its range extending from Boundary County (Porthill) to Clearwater County (Bungalow, Headquarters). However, there are specimens of this race taken in June at Salmon (June 7, 1949), Pocatello (June 18, 1949), Weiser (June 4, 1952) and Targhee Pass (June 27, 1960). This at first glance would not agree with the range outlined above. The probable explanation here is that these are belated transients, who actually, despite the late date, do not represent the breeding population of these areas.

Empidonax traillii extimus

This race is the breeding form over the larger part of the state, breeding specimens identified as *extimus* having been taken as far north as Clearwater County (Weippe—June 13, 1951). Clearwater County and Nez Perce County would appear to be the area of intergradation between *extimus* and *adastus*, specimens taken at Lapwai (July 12, 1950), and Headquarters (June 17, 1952), being intermediate in their characters between these two races, but closer to *extimus*.

Empidonax traillii campestris

Breeding specimens representing this race were taken in Caribou County, two miles west of Freedom, Wyoming, May 31 and June 1, 1952.

Empidonax minimus (Baird and Baird): LEAST FLYCATCHER

General Distribution. Breeds from southern Yukon east through central Mackenzie and northern Ontario to central Quebec, south to northern British Columbia, northern Wyoming, Kansas, eastern Tennessee and northern Georgia. Winters from northern Mexico (Tamaulipas) south through central America to Panama.

Status in Idaho. Now known as a rare fall transient.

There are two records for the occurrence of *Empidonax minimus* in Idaho.

It was first recorded in the state on September 3, 1952, when I collected a male in fresh fall plumage at Moscow.

Some years later a female was taken by Oring (1962) on Signal Peak, in Clark County, July 14, 1961. In view of the fact that this species is known to nest at Missoula, in western Montana, it is not improbable that this specimen represents a breeding bird, although it is realized that the middle of July is not too early for the southward movement of these small flycatchers to be under way.

Habits. During the spring months the Least Flycatcher is a noisy bird, its distinctive note, an emphatic two-syllabled "chebec," being uttered constantly throughout the day. It is conspicuous then and not easily overlooked; so if it does nest in Idaho it must occur in rather small numbers and in relatively isolated areas. In late summer it becomes silent, and as in appearance and actions it so closely resembles the other *empidonax* flycatchers it must be collected for satisfactory identification.

In the northern part of its range it shows a preference during the summer months for open aspen groves, and it is in such a situation that it may ultimately be found nesting in Idaho.

Empidonax hammondii (Xantus): HAMMOND'S FLYCATCHER

General Distribution. Breeds from southern Alaska, British Columbia, central Alberta and western Montana south to central California, northern Nevada, Utah, and northern New Mexico. Winters from southern Arizona and northern Mexico (Nuevo Leon and Tamaulipas) south to northern Nicaragua.

Status in Idaho. A fairly common summer resident in suitable habitat throughout the state.

Although of general distribution in Idaho Hammond's Flycatcher is so difficult to distinguish in life from the other *empidonax* flycatchers that it appears on few local lists. This is just as well, for sight records where these species are concerned have little or no value. Based on actual specimens *Empidonax hammondii* has been recorded in but a few localities in the state, but additional collecting should reveal its presence during the summer months wherever there is suitable habitat.

Rust (1915) reported a specimen taken at Coeur d'Alene August 1, 1914; and Jollie (in litt.) noted four breeding males at Heglar Pass, twenty miles south of American Falls, Power County, June 30–July 1, 1949.

I have personally taken specimens representing the breeding population as follows:

Latah County. Moscow, June 4 and 5, 1948, May 29, 1950, June 13, 1952; Harvard, July 21, 1953, August 22 and September 23, 1957, August 16, 1958; Potlatch, July 13, 1957.

Lemhi County. Shoup, June 6, 1949.
Blaine County. Sun Valley, June 28, 1950.
Fremont County. Henrys Lake, June 13, 1957.
Additional specimens whose status could be considered as transients are:
Latah County. Deary, May 7, 1948; Viola, May 18, 1948.
Valley County. McCall, September 18, 1955.

Habits. On the basis of specimens taken, Hammond's Flycatcher arrives in Idaho in the spring in early May, rarely the latter part of April, and usually lingers in the fall until early October. My extreme dates of occurrence at Moscow are April 22 (1950) and October 12 (1955). At Potlatch my latest date of occurrence in the fall is October 2 (1949). I noted it at Lewiston only as a rather scarce fall transient, specimens being taken there September 8, 1951, September 6, 1953, and September 6 and October 8, 1956.

The one definite breeding record for the state is that of a nest found by Verner (1953) at Harvard, Latah County, July 1, 1952. The female was apparently incubating that day, but on July 9 it was watched as it fed young. The usual nesting site of this little flycatcher is on an upper limb of a large conifer, and this nest was no exception, being seventy-five feet from the ground in a dead grand fir.

Empidonax oberholseri Phillips: DUSKY FLYCATCHER

General Distribution. Breeds from southern Yukon, southern Alberta, southern Saskatchewan and Wyoming south to southern California, central Arizona and northern New Mexico. Winters from southern Arizona south through Mexico to Guerrero and Oaxaca.

Status in Idaho. A fairly common summer resident in suitable habitat throughout the state.

The difficulty of distinguishing this species in life from the other *empidonax* flycatchers has caused it to be omitted from all but a very few of the local lists that have been published. In only a few instances has it been listed and then on the basis of specimens taken, as follows:

Kootenai County. One specimen taken at Fort Sherman (Coeur d'Alene) on May 17 (Merrill, 1897); specimens taken at Coeur d'Alene May 25 and September 1 (Rust, 1915).

Latah County. One specimen taken June 27, 1947, one mile east of Moscow, and another on June 30 on "West Twin Mountain" (Johnston, 1949).

South Central Idaho. One specimen taken on Birch Creek August 4, 1890 (Merriam, 1891).

Minidoka County. Reported by Davis (1935) at Rupert on the following dates: May 5, 1919, May 6 through May 20, 1920, and May 19, 1921.

Jollie (in litt.) reports specimens taken in 1949 on Mary's Creek, eight miles east of Riddle, Owyhee County, June 19 and 20; ten miles west of Bloomington, Bear Lake County, July 10; and three miles northeast of McCall, Valley County, July 25. Levy (in litt.) took specimens in 1951 at

Silver City, Owyhee County, June 2, and at the Silent City of Rocks, Cassia County, June 6.

I have personally taken specimens representing the breeding population as follows:

Bonner County. Clark Fork, June 23, 1957; Sandpoint, June 24, 1957, and August 20, 1958.

Kootenai County. Coeur d'Alene, July 28, 1948.

Latah County. Viola, July 18, 1950; Moscow, June 6 and 19, and July 4 and 25, 1948, May 16, and July 7, 1949, and June 4 and July 15, 1950; Deary, July 24, 1948; Potlatch, May 19, 1957.

Idaho County. Whitebird Summit, July 1, 1951.

Washington County. Cambridge, June 6, 1952.

Custer County. Willow Creek Summit, July 13 and 14, 1958.

Fremont County. Targhee Pass, June 12, 1957.

Bonneville County. Gray, June 12, 13, and 15, 1949, May 27 and June 2, 1952, and June 7, 1957.

Cassia County. Almo, June 19, 1949.

Owyhee County. Triangle June 25, 1949; Silver City, August 8, 1950, and June 2, 1951.

Habits. Although the Dusky Flycatcher has a wide distribution in the state, it has not been recorded during the breeding season below an altitude of 2,500 feet, and it would appear to occur in greatest numbers between 5,000 and 6,000 feet. The highest altitude at which I have noted it is 7,500 feet, at Willow Creek Summit south of Challis. At Lewiston it was an uncommon transient (1948 through 1958), my extreme dates of occurrence in the spring being April 24 (1950) and May 28 (1957), and in the fall September 14 (1952) and September 23 (1951). It was fairly common during the summer months at Moscow and Potlatch, my extreme dates of occurrence at Moscow being April 26 (1953) and September 14 (1950), and at Potlatch April 30 (1949) and September 13 (1949).

At Coeur d'Alene Rust also found this little flycatcher a fairly common summer resident. He found numerous nests there, and stated (Bent, 1942): "On brushy hillsides nests are usually located in low shrubs, and on wooded flats in small pines from seven feet up." The average pair were nesting by the middle of June, and by early July the young were on the wing. A nest I found at Troy in Latah County on June 2, 1949, held four fresh eggs, and was three feet from the ground in an alder in underbrush bordering a stream. I also encountered one pair at Harvard on July 21, 1953, with a brood of bobtailed fledglings barely able to fly on that date.

Empidonax wrightii Baird: GRAY FLYCATCHER

General Distribution. Breeds from central Oregon, southern Idaho and southern Wyoming south to central California, central Arizona, and central New Mexico. Winters from southern California and Arizona south through Mexico to Michoacan and Puebla.

Status in Idaho. A not uncommon summer resident in the extreme southern part of the state.

The Gray Flycatcher has been recorded from but two counties in Idaho, but further field work should reveal its presence during the summer months from Owyhee County east along the southern edge of the state to Bear Lake County. In Idaho its distribution is limited to the juniper-covered ridges that enter the state for a short distance from both Nevada and Utah; where this habitat occurs this species should be found.

In Owyhee County specimens have been taken at Riddle June 3, 1934 (Davis, 1934); on Mary's Creek, eight miles east of Riddle, June 18, 1949 (Jollie, in litt.); and at Silver City August 9, 1950 (Levy, 1962).

In Cassia County it has been recorded only in the vicinity of Goose Creek, ten miles south of Oakley, but here it is fairly plentiful in the junipers that characterize this area. Specimens have been taken by Jollie (in litt.) on June 27, 1949; by Levy (1962) on August 12, 1950, and September 12, 1951; and by me on June 22, 1950, June 5, 1957, and July 19 and 20, 1958.

Habits. In migration the Gray Flycatcher is so similar in appearance and actions to the other *empidonax* flycatchers that except under unusual circumstances it is impractical to attempt to identify it in life. In Idaho, however, it is the only small flycatcher found during the summer months on the arid juniper-covered ridges in the extreme southern edge of the state, so at this season of the year it should be readily recognized. A nest has yet to be found, but in other parts of its breeding range a juniper is commonly used as a nesting site, and this is doubtless the case in Idaho. Extreme dates of occurrence elsewhere are April 24 (Colorado) and September 11 (Nevada), and this is probably true also of Idaho.

Empidonax difficilis hellmayri Brodkorb: WESTERN FLYCATCHER

General Distribution. Breeds from eastern Washington, southern Montana and western South Dakota south to northern Mexico (western Chihuahua and northern Coahuila). Recorded in winter only in Mexico (Durango and Hidalgo).

Status in Idaho. Now known as a rare summer resident in the northern part of the state.

Hand (1941) reported this species as a rather uncommon summer resident in Benewah County (1921 through 1941), being infrequently noted from May through August "along the larger streams in the mountains."

It is possible that it breeds at least sparingly in Latah County, for in recent years it has been found nesting along the Palouse River in Whitman County, Washington.

I have two records for Moscow, specimens being taken there in 1951 on August 23 and September 26.

Davis (1935) reported the Western Flycatcher at Rupert, Minidoka County, May 15, 1919, May 27 and 31, 1920, and May 21, 1921, but did not comment on whether specimens were actually taken to substantiate these records.

Habits. Although closely resembling in appearance the other *Empidonax* flycatchers, the Western Flycatcher differs remarkably in its way of nesting. It shows a decided preference for deciduous woods, and here the nest, usually substantially built of green moss, fragments of dead leaves, and shreds of bark, can be found in quite a variety of situations. It may be in an old woodpecker's hole, or in a natural cavity well up from the ground, in the upturned roots of a fallen tree, on the side of a steep bank, or, not infrequently, on a beam inside a shed or barn. It seems to like the vicinity of water, and in Idaho it should be looked for in moist ravines and thick swampy woods.

Contopus sordidulus Sclater: WESTERN WOOD PEWEE

General Distribution. Breeds from central Alaska, southern Yukon and southern Mackenzie south to northern Baja California and northern Mexico (Sonora and Chihuahua) and east to North Dakota, South Dakota, and western Texas. Winters from central Panama to Venezuela, Peru, and Bolivia.

Status in Idaho. A fairly common summer resident throughout the state.

The Western Wood Pewee has a wide distribution in Idaho, occurring as a breeding bird from an altitude of 840 feet at Lewiston (the lowest in the state) to 8,795 feet at Galena Summit, in Blaine County. It appears on all the local lists that have been published, and at the present time it has been reported from the following localities:

Bonner County. Clark Fork, an occasional pair noted in July, 1917 (Burleigh, 1923); specimen taken July 26, 1960 (Burleigh).

Kootenai County. Coeur d'Alene, a common summer resident (Merrill, 1897); common summer resident, 1910 through 1914 (Rust, 1915); specimen taken July 28, 1960 (Burleigh).

Benewah County. St. Maries, a common and widely distributed summer resident (1921 through 1941), occurring from late May until early September (Hand, 1941); specimen taken July 30, 1960 (Burleigh).

Latah County. Only infrequently noted, June 1–August 16, 1947 (Johnston, 1949); a fairly common but local summer resident, 1948-58; most frequently observed at Moscow and at Potlatch (Burleigh).

Nez Perce County. Lewiston, a fairly common summer resident (Burleigh).

Idaho County. Two seen September 6, 1941, three miles southeast of Selway Falls (Orr, 1951).

Adams County. Council, observed from May 28 to August 18, 1958 (Newhouse, 1960).

Valley County. Specimens taken in 1929 at Upper Payette Lake July 16, and at Tamarack Swamp, Long Valley, July 19 (F. C. Hibben).

Owyhee County. Riddle, frequently noted May 28–June 3, 1934; specimen taken on Indian Creek June 2 (Davis, 1934); Triangle, one breeding pair found in an open aspen grove in a ravine June 25, 1949 (Burleigh).

Custer County. Specimens taken at Challis August 4, 6, and 7, 1931 (Brodkorb), and July 6, 1960 (Burleigh), Little Redfish Lake August 15, 1931 (Brodkorb), and Mackay July 13, 1958 (Burleigh).

Blaine County. Specimens taken at Carey August 17, 1929 (A. B. Fuller), and at Galena Summit June 26, 1950, Sun Valley July 1, 1960, and Ketchum July 3, 1960 (Burleigh).

Fremont County. Noted at Spencer June 23, 1916 (Rust, 1917); specimens taken eight miles north of Warm River August 12 and 14, 1930 (Paul E. Trapier), four miles north of Ashton August 20, 1939 (R. W. Smith), and at Henrys Lake June 25, 1960 (Burleigh).

Teton County. Specimens taken on Horseshoe Creek July 30, 1930 (Trapier).

Jefferson County. Common summer resident, in 1961, on the Camas National Wildlife Refuge; specimen taken August 22 (Oring, 1962).

Bonneville County. An uncommon summer resident (1949-51) at Grays Lake (Steel, 1956); specimens taken on Eagle Creek, north of Gray, June 23, 1960 (Burleigh); a common summer resident in 1961 on Big Elk Creek (Oring, 1962).

Caribou County. Specimen taken at Soda Springs June 24, 1960 (Burleigh).

South Central Idaho. Specimens taken in "Teton Canyon, eastern Idaho" on July 27, 1872; noted in 1890 in the Salmon River Mountains until the middle of August (Merriam, 1891); a common breeding bird "in the stream bottoms" of the south-central counties (Levy, 1950).

Minidoka County. Noted for the first time in the spring at Rupert May 6, 1919, May 9, 1920, and May 19, 1921 (Davis, 1935).

Cassia County. Specimen taken seven miles west of Burley August 25, 1932 (Brodkorb).

Habits. The Western Wood Pewee is one of the latest migrants to arrive in Idaho in the spring. It is only infrequently seen before the middle of May and is largely of casual occurrence until the last of the month. In the fall there is a noticeable decrease in numbers in early September, and few individuals are noted after the middle of the month. At Potlatch my extreme dates of occurrence are May 19 (1952) and August 31 (1949), at Moscow May 9 (1949) and September 19 (1949). At Lewiston my latest date of departure is September 1 (1949).

Nesting activities are apparently delayed until well into June, judging from the few nests I have seen. The first, found at Clark Fork on July 4, 1917, held four young, and was thirty feet up in a large white pine. Another found at Lewiston on July 24, 1950, held two well-fledged young, and was eighteen feet from the ground in a cottonwood, in open woods at the edge of the Snake River. Still another, found at Moscow on the unusually late date of September 2, 1957, held three almost fully fledged young. It was ten feet from the ground on a dead limb of a large maple in the yard of a house in the residential section of the city.

Contopus sordidulus veliei Coues

A female taken by W. B. Davis (University of California Museum of Vertebrate Zoology, No. 67698) on Indian Creek, two miles southwest of Riddle, Owyhee County, June 2, 1934, was found to represent this race. Further collecting is necessary to determine its actual distribution in the state. It is characterized by fuscous-olive upperparts and yellow belly.

Contopus sordidulus siccicola Burleigh

This is the form occurring over the larger part of the state, being the breeding Wood Pewee of the western slopes of the northern Rocky Mountains. Specimens, as indicated above, and identified as *siccicola,* have been taken at Clark Fork, Coeur d'Alene, St. Maries, Potlatch, Moscow, Lewiston, Valley County (upper Payette Lake and Tamarack Swamp), Challis, Mackay, Galena Summit, Sun Valley, Ketchum, Ashton, Teton County (Horseshoe Creek), Gray, Soda Springs, and Burley. It is characterized by the gray wash of the upperparts and the pale yellow of the belly.

Nuttallornis borealis (Swainson): OLIVE-SIDED FLYCATCHER

General Distribution. Breeds from northern Alaska east across the continent through central Mackenzie, northern Manitoba and central Quebec to Newfoundland south to Baja California, central Arizona, northern New Mexico, northern Wisconsin, northern Ohio and Massachusetts, and in the mountains from New York to western North Carolina. Winters in South America from Colombia and northern Venezuela to Peru.

Status in Idaho. A fairly common but local summer resident, occurring throughout the state on the forested mountain slopes.

In Boundary County one pair was seen July 5, 1957, in open woods well toward the top of Harrison Peak (6,000 feet). The female was collected (Burleigh).

In Bonner County scattered pairs were noted in 1917, north of Clark Fork, in the mountain meadows at timberline; they were conspicuous and much in evidence after early August (Burleigh, 1923).

In Kootenai County this species was considered by Merrill (1897) as breeding sparingly at Fort Sherman (Coeur d'Alene). Rust (1915) reported it an uncommon summer resident at Coeur d'Alene (1910 through 1914). I noted one bird at Harrison May 21, 1949.

In Benewah County Hand (1941) reported it a common summer resident in the mountains, occurring from late May until September. He observed it at lower altitudes in migration.

In Latah County Johnston (1949) found it "common in coniferous forest areas" from June 1 through August 16, 1947. Verner (1953) considered it uncommon at Harvard during the summer of 1952, a single bird being seen on July 11. In the vicinity of Moscow I found it breeding on Moscow Mountain, and on Tomer's Butte, while in August and early September (1948 through 1958) it was a fairly common transient in the valleys. A specimen representing the breeding population was taken on Tomer's Butte May 24, 1949, while at Moscow transients were collected August 17, 1948, July 26, August 10 and September 2, 1949, September 18, 1950, June 9, August 20 and September 7, 1951, and August 14, 1952. A fall transient was seen at Potlatch September 13, 1952.

At Lewiston, in Nez Perce County, I noted it twice in migration; a male was collected on Hatwai Creek August 28, 1951, and another individual was seen September 6, 1954.

In Idaho County it was reported by Orr (1951) as "relatively uncommon" in July, 1948, in the Clearwater and Bitterroot mountains.

In Valley County a specimen was taken by Jollie (in litt.) on Little Payette Lake, three miles northeast of McCall, July 26, 1949.

In Boise County a specimen was taken by Arvey (1947) at Idaho City May 23, 1941.

In Blaine County I noted breeding pairs on Easley Peak (8,000 feet) June 25, 1950, at Galena Summit (8,795 feet) June 26, and near the top of Hyndman Peak (10,000 feet) June 27.

In Fremont County it was reported by Rust (1917) as occurring "sparingly" in 1916, and as being seen July 9 in Little Rock Creek Canyon.

In Teton County two specimens were taken by Merriam (1891) in Teton Canyon July 27, 1872.

Oring (1962) reported several birds seen on Signal Peak, Bonneville County, June 19, 1961, and a specimen taken that day. It was noted once, August 28, on the Camas National Wildlife Refuge in Jefferson County.

In Bear Lake County specimens were taken by Jollie (in litt.) ten miles west of Bloomington July 9, 1949.

Davis (1935) cites one record for Minidoka County, September 7, 1919.

Habits. The Olive-sided Flycatcher is another species that, in spite of its long journey each year to and from its winter quarters in northern South America, remains in Idaho only long enough to rear its young. My earliest record in the spring is May 21, 1949, at Harrison, in Kootenai County, while at Moscow my earliest record is May 24 (1949). The southward movement in the fall apparently begins in July, for a bird seen on July 26, 1949, in the Arboretum on the University of Idaho campus at Moscow, was unquestionably a fall transient. Throughout August (1948 through 1958) this species was frequently seen in and about the city, but after early September it was rarely observed. My latest record in the fall is September 18 (1950).

Larks: *Family Alaudidae*

Eremophila alpestris (Linnaeus): Horned Lark

General Distribution. Cosmopolitan; in North America breeds from Alaska and the Arctic coast of Canada south to Baja California, southern Mexico, southern Louisiana, northern Mississippi, northern Georgia and North Carolina. Winters in all but the more northern parts of its range.

Status in Idaho. A common summer resident throughout the state, occurring wherever there is suitable habitat. Fairly common also during the winter months, although the flocks that are present then are composed of one or more of the races breeding farther north, individuals of the breeding population being rarely observed from late October until February.

Bonner County. There are no definite breeding records for the county. Small flocks were noted in 1917 on the open ridges north of Clark Fork, six birds appearing August 30, and similar sized flocks being present daily then until the middle of September (Burleigh, 1923).

Kootenai County. A common summer resident on the "prairie" north and west of Fort Sherman (Coeur d'Alene), returning in March each year (Merrill, 1897); a common summer resident, 1910 through 1914, on the "prairie" north of Coeur d'Alene (Rust, 1915); a common summer resident in the open prairie country in the Spokane Valley east of the Washington line, being noted at Hauser, Rathdrum, and Post Falls (Burleigh).

Shoshone County. Flocks noted on open ridges and in alpine meadows in September and early October (1921 through 1941) (Hand, 1941); two males taken from a large flock on Three Sisters Peak, in the St. Joe National Forest, October 8, 1949 (Levy, 1959). Not known to breed in the county.

Latah County. Common and generally distributed, June 1 through August 16, 1947; a female collected on Paradise Ridge (Johnston, 1949); a common breeding bird (1948-58) in suitable habitat throughout the county; noted at Potlatch, Viola, Moscow, Troy, Genesee, and Deary; flocks observed at infrequent intervals during the winter months (Burleigh).

Nez Perce County. Common throughout the year at Lewiston; flocks varying in size from twenty to fully two hundred birds of common occurrence during the winter months (Burleigh).

Clearwater County. Found to be breeding in small numbers (1952) in the open prairie country south of Weippe; one flock of twelve birds seen at Headquarters September 20, 1952 (Burleigh).

Idaho County. Scattered breeding pairs noted (1949-58) on the Camas Prairie west of Grangeville, and on the lower slopes of the open ridges between White Bird and Riggins (Burleigh).

Adams County. A "large flock" seen at Indian Valley January 28, 1958 (Newhouse, 1960).

Gem County. Small flocks seen in the open fields in the vicinity of Emmett November 23, 1951 (Burleigh).

Ada County. Common and well distributed, April 15-17, 1949, in the arid desert country east of Boise (Burleigh).

Owyhee County. Common at Riddle May 28 through June 3, 1934 (Davis, 1934); common and of general distribution, February 19-25, 1950, in the arid desert country between Marsing and Riddle (Burleigh).

Fremont County. Common in suitable habitat, June through August, 1916 (Rust, 1917).

Jefferson County. An "abundant" summer resident in 1961 on the Camas National Wildlife Refuge (Oring, 1962).

Bonneville County. A fairly common summer resident (1949-51) at Grays Lake, appearing in the spring in early April (April 6, 1950) (Steel, 1956).

South Central Idaho. Abundant in 1890 "throughout the sage plains and valleys" (Merriam, 1891); "common to abundant in sagebrush areas" June through August, 1949 (Levy, 1950).

Minidoka County. "Common to abundant," 1907 through 1913 (Kenagy, 1914); a common breeding bird at Rupert, 1919-21; young noted May 2 (Davis, 1935).

Cassia County. Common in June (1950, 1955, 1957, 1960) in the open fields and arid desert country between Burley and Oakley (Burleigh).

Habits. The Horned Lark is a hardy bird, frequenting areas where there is little or no vegetation, seemingly unaffected by the most adverse weather conditions. Thus it was rather unexpected to find that the breeding population in northern Idaho departed in October, and that, except at Lewiston, it was rarely observed during the winter months. *Merrilli* was last recorded in the fall at Hauser on October 9 (1952), and at Moscow on October 13 (1951). It was, however, the first migrant to appear in the spring, arriving in late January or early February when the open fields were still covered with snow, and low temperatures were the rule rather than the exception. Usually the males appeared first in the fields where they would eventually nest, but within a few days pairs could be seen, and courtship displays were much in evidence.

Nesting is early. At Moscow a female with a conspicuous brood patch was collected April 5, 1949, and well-grown young of the year out of the nest for some time were seen May 12, 1951. Young approximately this same age were noted at Lewiston April 19, 1952.

Eremophila alpestris arcticola (Oberholser)

This northern race is uncommon during the winter months in the northern part of the state, but it is apparently a common winter resident in southern Idaho. Small flocks appear in the fall the latter part of September, and it is early March before they are recorded for the last time. The first record for the state is that of a specimen taken by Merrill (1897) at Fort Sherman (Coeur d'Alene) September 28, 1890, and identified at the time as *leucolaema*. Hand (1941) stated that flocks of Horned Larks seen in Shoshone County on open ridges and in alpine meadows in September and early October (1921-41) were large and pale, and undoubtedly represented this race. This assumption is verified to some extent by the fact that two males collected by Levy (1959) on October 8, 1949, from a large flock on Three Sisters Peak, in Shoshone County, were *arcticola.*

On the basis of specimens taken I have recorded *arcticola* in the state on the following dates: Moscow, February 4, 1950, March 4, 1952; Genesee, December 6, 1953; Lewiston, December 6, 1952; Headquarters September 20, 1952; Emmett, November 23, 1951.

In the collections of the Colorado Museum of Natural History at Denver, there are 109 specimens of the Horned Lark taken by Brodkorb in southern Idaho that were identified by Harry C. Oberholser as *arcticola.* Localities and dates include the following: Boise, Ada County, January 30 and February 1, 1930; Mud Lake, Jefferson County, November 4, 1931; Wapello, Bingham County, December 16 and 23, 1931; Pocatello, Bannock County, January 5 and 12, 1932; American Falls, Power County, January 13, 19, 20, 21, 22, 23, 25, and 26, 1932; Burley, Cassia County, January 29 and February 2, 1932; Twin Falls, Twin Falls County, January 22 and February 9, 10, 11, and 13, 1932; Gooding, Gooding County, February 19 and 20, 1932.

Eremophila alpestris enthymia (Oberholser)

Although unrecorded from the northern part of the state, this race of the Horned Lark is apparently a common winter resident in southern Idaho. In the collections of the Colorado Museum of Natural History there are numerous specimens of this species taken by Brodkorb in southern Idaho that were identified by Harry C. Oberholser as *enthymia.* Localities and dates include the following: Montpelier, Bear Lake County, January 23 and 26, and February 15, 1931; Soda Springs, Caribou County, February 15 and 20, 1931; Mackay, Custer County, September 3, 1931; Mud Lake, Jefferson County, October 6 and November 4, 1931; Pocatello, Bannock County, January 5, 1932; American Falls, Power County, January 13 and 20, 1932.

Eremophila alpestris utahensis (Behle)

This is the race that breeds commonly in the southern part of Idaho. Specimens representing the breeding population, and identified as *utahensis,* have been taken as follows: Custer County, Dickey, June 12, 1912, Challis, July 15, 1958; Jefferson County, Terreton, April 29, 1954; Bonneville County, Idaho Falls, May 28, 1951, June 29, 1960, Gray, June 16, 1949, May 20, 1951; Caribou County, Soda Springs, April 13, 1958; Bingham County, Blackfoot, July 15, 1890; Power County, American Falls, May 30, 1911, June 12, 1955; Lincoln County, Shoshone, April 25, 1954; Jerome County, Jerome, June 20, 1949; Cassia County, Oakley, June 23, 1950.

Eremophila alpestris alpina (Jewett)

This race, found during the summer months in the coast ranges of western Washington, resembles *arcticola* but is smaller, and the brown of the upper parts has a grayish wash. It is apparently not uncommon during the winter months in northern Idaho, but in my experience one or more individuals are almost without exception associated with flocks of *arcticola*. I have no records of flocks composed entirely of *alpina*. Specimens identified as *alpina* have been taken as follows: Viola, February 4, 1949; Moscow, March 4, 1952, February 26, 1954, January 16, 1955; Genesee, February 1, 1952, December 6, 1953, February 8, 1956; Lewiston, February 1, 1950, September 21, 1953; Headquarters, September 20, 1952; Emmett, November 23, 1951.

Eremophila alpestris lamprochroma (Oberholser)

This race of the Horned Lark breeds commonly in the southwestern corner of the state, but on the basis of specimens taken it does not occur during the summer months north of Ada County or east of Owyhee County. Further collecting may modify this statement somewhat, but there is little question but that it has a rather restricted breeding range in Idaho. Specimens identified as *lamprochroma* have been taken as follows: Ada County, Boise, April 15, 1949; Owyhee County, Marsing, February 19, 1950, Murphy, February 21, 1950, Riddle, February 25, 1950. In the northern part of the state it has occurred at irregular intervals throughout the year, but as this is the breeding race in the arid sagebrush plains of eastern Washington it is logical to assume that specimens taken were stragglers from this area. Specimens from northern Idaho identified as *lamprochroma* by John W. Aldrich are as follows: Viola, February 4, 1949; Moscow, May 28, 1948, December 22, 1949, April 2 and June 16, 1950, February 10 and 22, and March 9, 1952; Genesee, February 13, 1951, March 8, 1952, February 4, 1954, January 24, 1955; Lewiston, December 21, 1951, March 13, 1952, January 28 and February 10, 1955.

Eremophila alpestris merrilli (Dwight)

This race is a common breeding bird in northern Idaho, occurring wherever there is suitable habitat. At Lewiston it is resident and plentiful throughout the year, occurring, except during the breeding season, in flocks varying in size from twenty to fully two hundred individuals. Elsewhere it is a summer resident only, being present from late January or early February until the middle of October. My one definite record for the winter months is that of two specimens taken at Moscow on December 22, 1949, from a flock of six birds that as far as I could determine were all *merrilli*. A series of specimens collected from 1948 through 1958, and in most instances representing the breeding population, are from the following localities: Kootenai County, Hauser, Rathdrum, Post Falls; Latah County, Viola, Moscow, Genesee, Deary; Nez Perce County, Lewiston, Coyote Canyon; Clearwater County, Weippe; Lewis County, Nez Perce; Idaho County, Grangeville; Washington County, Midvale.

Swallows: *Family Hirundinidae*

Tachycineta thalassina lepida Mearns: VIOLET-GREEN SWALLOW

General Distribution. Breeds from Alaska, southern Yukon, southern Alberta, central Montana and southern South Dakota south to Baja California, southern Arizona, and southern New Mexico. Winters from central California and northern Mexico south to Honduras and El Salvador.

Status in Idaho. A common summer resident throughout the state.

During the breeding season the Violet-green Swallow is commonly found about high sheer cliffs, and is a close associate of the White-throated Swift at this time of the year. Such nesting sites are frequently in rather isolated and relatively inaccessible parts of the state; for this reason this species is more plentiful and more widely distributed than the available information would indicate.

Kootenai County. Common in summer at Fort Sherman (Coeur d'Alene), in cottonwoods along the lake; arrives from the middle to the end of March (Merrill, 1898); "very numerous," July 1-10, 1943, at the upper end of Lake Coeur d'Alene (Yocom, 1946); plentiful about the lake April 19, 1950 (Burleigh).

Benewah County. A common summer resident (1921 through 1941); widely distributed from the valleys to the higher ridges; present from late March until August (Hand, 1941); two small flocks noted at St. Maries April 1, 1953 (Burleigh).

Latah County. Found nesting at Moscow, about the town and on the University campus, in June, 1947; small flocks common in late summer (Johnston, 1949); common at Harvard through the middle of July, 1952 (Verner, 1953); fairly common during the summer months, and well distributed throughout the county (1948 through 1958), occurring about the farms and at the edges of the towns (Burleigh).

Nez Perce County. A common summer resident at Lewiston (1948-58), appearing in March and frequently lingering in the fall until early October; first arrivals noted at Myrtle Beach March 28, 1952, Peck March 25, 1953, and Spalding April 8, 1953 (Burleigh).

Clearwater County. Found breeding in small numbers (1952-58) at Weippe, Pierce, and Headquarters (Burleigh).

Idaho County. Specimen taken at Pollock June 27, 1940 (Arvey, 1947).

Valley County. A fairly common summer resident at McCall, and about the Payette Lakes (1949-58) (Burleigh).

Adams County. Noted at Indian Valley April 17, 1958 (Newhouse, 1960).

Owyhee County. Common at Riddle May 28-June 3, 1934 (Davis, 1934).

Fremont County. Observed in small numbers in Little Dry Creek Canyon June and July, 1916 (Rust, 1917).

Jefferson County. Noted on the Camas National Wildlife Refuge July 4 and 12, 1961; two specimens taken (Oring, 1962).

Bonneville County. A fairly common summer resident at Gray's Lake 1949-51 (Steel, 1956); common at Big Elk Creek August 6, 1961; one specimen in immature plumage collected (Oring, 1962).

South Central Idaho. Abundant on the Snake River and on Big Lost River in July, 1890; common in the Birch Creek Valley until the middle of August (Merriam, 1891); a common breeding bird in this same general area in 1949 (Levy, 1950).

Minidoka County. Noted at Rupert May 11, 1919 (Davis, 1935).

Cassia County. Three pairs found nesting at the Silent City of Rocks June 19, 1949 (Burleigh).

Habits. The Violet-green Swallow is a hardy bird, for it frequently appears in the spring in northern Idaho when snow is still on the ground and the temperature at night drops well below freezing. It was observed at Moscow March 25, 1955, when the ground was covered with two inches of snow and a minimum temperature of eleven degrees was recorded the previous night, while at Headquarters it was noted as early as April 9 (1952) when there was still a foot of snow on the ground. My earliest date of arrival at Moscow is March 20 (1949); at Potlatch it has been seen as late in the fall as September 12 (1951). My extreme dates of occurrence at Lewiston are March 8 (1954) and March 9 (1958) and October 4 (1949 and 1951).

The nesting site is a cavity, and individual pairs apparently accept whatever is available in this respect. Merrill (1898) found this species nesting in the cottonwoods at the edge of Lake Coeur d'Alene. Yocom (1946) stated that it was "very numerous" at the upper end of the lake July 1-10, 1943, and that the nests were "in bird houses, in knotholes in the sides of the cabins, under the eaves and in the buildings themselves." While I was at Moscow (1948-58), two or three pairs nested each year under the eaves of the forestry building on the University campus. At the Silent City of Rocks in Cassia County, on June 29, 1949, and again in a canyon south of Challis on July 11, 1958, I found this swallow nesting in crevices of cliffs, the sites selected being as inaccessible as those of the White-throated Swifts that were using similar crevices.

Iridoprocne bicolor (Vieillot): TREE SWALLOW

General Distribution. Breeds from northern Alaska, southern Yukon, central Mackenzie, northern Quebec and Newfoundland south to southern California, central Utah, northern Kansas, northern Tennessee and Virginia. Winters from southern California, northern Mexico, the Gulf coast, and on the Atlantic coast from Massachusetts south to Honduras and Cuba.

Status in Idaho. A fairly common but local summer resident throughout the state.

Bonner County. A flock of eight birds, adults and young of the year, seen at Clark Fork July 3, 1917 (Burleigh, 1923).

Kootenai County. A common summer resident at Coeur d'Alene (1910-14), nesting in cottonwoods at the edge of the lake (Rust, 1915); noted at the upper end of Lake Coeur d'Alene July 1-10, 1943; one pair nesting in a woodpecker hole in a cottonwood; an occasional small flock seen feeding over the lake (Yocom, 1946); noted May 21, 1949, at numerous spots between Harrison and Cataldo where dead trees, with suitable cavities as nesting sites, occurred in open marshes (Burleigh).

Benewah County. A common summer resident at St. Maries, occurring from the middle of March until August; noted on the St. Joe River as far east as Avery (Hand, 1941).

Latah County. Several pairs found nesting in cavities in pilings at the edge of the Palouse River at Potlatch (1951-56); noted but once at Moscow, a flock of six birds March 19, 1956 (Burleigh).

Valley County. A common summer resident at McCall (Little Payette Lake); specimen taken July 25, 1949 (Jollie in litt.).

Adams County. Noted at Indian Valley May 28, 1958 (Newhouse, 1960).

Fremont County. Fairly plentiful June 26, 1960, in Targhee Pass (7,000 feet), cavities in the larger aspens being used as nesting sites (Burleigh).

Clark County. Frequently observed on Signal Peak June 19 and July 14 and 15, 1961; a specimen taken June 19 (Oring, 1962).

Bonneville County. A common summer resident at Grays Lake (1949-1951) (Steel, 1956); an occasional bird seen feeding over the open fields at Gray June 8-17, 1949 (Burleigh); specimen taken July 12, 1949 (Jollie).

Bear Lake County. Observed at Bloomington Lake, ten miles west of Bloomington, July 10 and 11, 1949 (Jollie in litt.).

Minidoka County. Noted at Rupert May 27, 1921 (Davis, 1935).

Cassia County. One breeding pair noted at the Silent City of Rocks June 21, 1949; abundant in late summer "about reservoirs and lakes" (Levy, 1950).

In order to determine the possibility of geographic variation in the Tree Swallows of the western United States a small series of fourteen specimens was collected in various parts of Idaho, as follows: Cataldo, male, May 21, 1949; Coeur d'Alene, female, April 19, 1950, immature male, July 22, 1952; St. Maries, female, April 1, 1953; Potlatch, males, April 21 and 30, 1949, immature males, August 29, 1951, August 23, 1953, immature female, July 21, 1953; Lewiston, female, April 8, 1949, males, April 1, 1952, March 16, 1955, March 16, 1956; Targhee Pass, male, June 26, 1960. Examined critically, only one noticeable difference was noted where eastern specimens were concerned. In eastern North America there are two distinct color phases, the upper parts of the Tree Swallow being either steel-blue or steel-green. Both phases are equally common. In Idaho all specimens examined without exception had steel-blue upperparts, none having even a suggestion of the steel-green so common farther east.

Habits. Like the Violet-green Swallow, the Tree Swallow is a hardy bird, although in the spring it usually appears several weeks later than the preceding species, and in the fall it has never been recorded later than the end of August. At Lewiston it has been noted as early as March 16 (1955 and 1956), but it is usually the first of April, even later, before the first small flocks are seen. The six birds observed at Moscow on March 19, 1956, seemed oddly out of place as they fed over open fields still covered with several inches of snow. In the late summer this species gradually disappears; while still plentiful at Coeur d'Alene on July 22, 1952, it was not recorded there a month later. My latest records in the fall are for Potlatch, fully grown young of the year being seen feeding with other swallows on August 29, 1951, and August 23, 1953.

Riparia riparia riparia (Linnaeus): BANK SWALLOW

General Distribution. Cosmopolitan; in North America breeds from northern Alaska, southern Yukon, southern Mackenzie, southern Quebec and Newfoundland south to southern California, northern Utah, Texas, Arkansas, northern Alabama and eastern Virginia. Winters from Colombia and British Guiana to northern Argentina.

Status in Idaho. A common but rather local summer resident throughout the state.

In Kootenai County it was reported by Merrill (1898) as being found nesting, July 16, 1890, along the Coeur d'Alene River. Rust (1915) considered it an uncommon summer resident in the county.

In Latah County it occurred only as an uncommon transient. Arvey (1947) took a specimen "four and one-half miles southwest of Moscow" May 26, 1930, and Johnston (1949) saw a single bird at Juliaetta July 4, 1947. I noted it but once at Moscow, on August 22, 1950, while at Potlatch it occurred as a rather scarce fall transient, being seen between the dates of July 21 (1953) and September 8 (1953).

In Nez Perce County I found it a common summer resident at Lewiston, colonies comprising from forty to possibly one hundred pairs nesting in banks along the Snake River.

At Marsing, in Owyhee County, I observed numerous individuals June 24, 1949, feeding over the Snake River, but I did not find the nesting site that was undoubtedly somewhere in the vicinity.

In Fremont County a small nesting colony was found at Henrys Lake August 17, 1916 (Rust, 1917).

Steel (1956) considered it an uncommon summer resident at Grays Lake, in Bonneville County (1949-51); I observed two birds there August 26, 1955; Oring (1962) noted several at Big Elk Creek August 6, 1961.

Low (1945) found a large colony of approximately 150 pairs nesting in a clay bank at Soda Springs, Caribou County, May 12-17, 1944.

In Jefferson County Oring (1962) found this species a common summer resident in 1961 on the Camas National Wildlife Refuge.

In south-central Idaho Merriam (1891) reported a colony breeding in July, 1872, on the Henry Fork of the Snake River. In this same general area it was considered by Levy (1950) to be a common summer resident in 1949.

In Power County a specimen was taken at American Falls July 4, 1949 (Jollie, in litt.).

Davis (1935) reported it breeding at Rupert, Minidoka County (1919-21), but did not comment otherwise on its status there; he cites May 19 as the earliest date for eggs.

Habits. Because of its rather exacting requirements for a nesting site the Bank Swallow, while widely distributed in Idaho, is rather local in its distribution. Its nest is a burrow in a steep dirt bank, and such a bank must be large enough to accommodate the numerous pairs that are always found nesting together. It is possible that under certain circumstances as few as one or two pairs may be found utilizing a limited area, but in my experience this extremely sociable species has never accepted such conditions. The other swallows have without exception accepted the advantages man has to offer, and modified their manner of nesting to conform to the new environment, but the Bank Swallow nests today as it did when this country was virgin wilderness.

It is not as hardy a bird as the two preceding species, for it is usually the latter part of April before it appears in the spring, and the middle of August sees a noticeable decrease in the numbers present. My extreme dates of occurrence at Lewiston are April 12 (1954) and September 24 (1954). Davis (1935) gives as his extreme dates of occurrence at Rupert (1919-21) April 6 and September 5.

Stelgidopteryx ruficollis aphractus (Oberholser): ROUGH-WINGED SWALLOW

General Distribution. Breeds from southern British Columbia, east of the coast ranges, and southern Alberta south through eastern Washington east of the Cascades to southern Oregon and southern Idaho and east to western Montana west of the Continental Divide.

Status in Idaho. A fairly common but local summer resident throughout the state.

Although the Rough-winged Swallow has a wide distribution in Idaho, its dependence to a very large extent on dirt banks in which to nest has limited it to those localities where such nesting sites are available. Consequently it can apparently be easily overlooked, and appears on relatively few of the local lists that have been published.

Bonner County. A single pair noted July 4, 1917, at Clark Fork (Burleigh, 1923); several breeding pairs noted at Sandpoint July 27, 1960 (Burleigh).

Kootenai County. Noted daily, July 1-10, 1943, at the upper end of Lake Coeur d'Alene (Yocom, 1946).

Benewah County. Fairly common summer resident about St. Maries (1921 through 1941), being observed from late April to August on both the St. Joe and St. Maries rivers (Hand, 1941).

Latah County. Found nesting in 1947 north of Moscow, and at Harvard (Johnston, 1949); seen entering a nest in a bank at the edge of the Palouse River at Harvard, July 1, 1951; last observed in 1952 on July 22 (Verner, 1953); found to be a fairly common breeding bird in the country (1948-58), occurring wherever there was a suitable nesting site (Burleigh).

Nez Perce County. A fairly common summer resident at Lewiston, nesting in banks along the Snake River (Burleigh).

Adams County. First noted at Indian Valley April 17, 1958; later seen during May and June (Newhouse, 1960).

Canyon County. Breeding specimens taken at Nampa from nesting colonies June 24, 1949, and July 14, 1960 (Burleigh).

Owyhee County. Common at Riddle May 28-June 3, 1934 (Davis, 1934); noted at Marsing April 16, 1949, and at Murphy June 3, 1951 (Burleigh).

Blaine County. Several breeding pairs observed at Ketchum July 2, 1960 (Burleigh).

Bonneville County. An uncommon summer resident at Grays Lake (1949-51) (Steel, 1956); two pairs found nesting June 11, 1949, in a bank at the side of a road on Eagle Creek; an occasional bird noted June 2, 1952 (Burleigh).

Caribou County. A small colony found nesting in a clay bank at Soda Springs May 12-17, 1944 (Low, 1945); breeding specimen taken at Soda Springs June 8, 1949 (Burleigh).

Jefferson County. A common summer resident in 1961 on the Camas National Wildlife Refuge (Oring, 1962).

South Central Idaho. "Not too common" but well distributed as a breeding bird in 1949 (Levy, 1950).

Cassia County. A colony of approximately twenty pairs found at Burley June 18, 1949, nesting in a bank at the edge of the Snake River; several birds in immature plumage seen at this same spot August 27, 1955 (Burleigh).

A series of specimens taken in various parts of the state, on dates varying from early April until early September (1948-60), were compared with specimens from the eastern United States, and were found to represent *aphractus*, the race described by Oberholser from Oregon. The characters of this race, separating it from *serripennis*, are its larger size and the paler underparts and upperparts (grayer, less rufescent). Localities where specimens were taken were Sandpoint, Potlatch, Moscow, Genesee, Lewiston, Nampa, Marsing, Murphy, Ketchum, Gray, Soda Springs, Burley.

Habits. Unlike the Bank Swallow which it so closely resembles, the Rough-winged Swallow is apparently not too socially inclined, single pairs being usually found nesting alone in a dirt bank large enough to accommodate the burrow. The one exception, in my experience in Idaho, is the small colony of approximately twenty pairs that has nested year after year in the same high bank on the Snake River at Burley. The nest found at Clark Fork on July 4, 1917, held six well-incubated eggs, and was in the site normally chosen, in a bank at the edge of the stream. Another nest that I found at Moscow on June 27, 1949, holding five fully fledged young, was in a quite different situation, being on a beam under a wooden bridge crossing a small stream.

This species usually does not appear in the spring until after the middle of April, and is only infrequently observed after the middle of August. My earliest dates of arrival in northern Idaho are: Potlatch, April 14 (1954),

Moscow April 22 (1951 and 1956), Genesee April 19 (1949), Lewiston April 6 (1956). Dates of departure in the fall are: Potlatch, September 3 (1955), Moscow August 31 (1948), Lewiston September 11 (1955).

Hirundo rustica erythrogaster Boddaert: BARN SWALLOW

General Distribution. Breeds from northern Alaska, southern Yukon, Mackenzie, central Ontario, and Labrador south to Baja California, southern Mexico (Michoacan, Puebla), western Texas, Arkansas, northern Alabama, and North Carolina. Winters from Panama and northern South America south to central Chile and Argentina.

Status in Idaho. A fairly common but local summer resident throughout the state, occurring wherever there are suitable nesting sites.

Kootenai County. Noted "about ranches" on the prairie northwest of Fort Sherman (Coeur d'Alene) (Merrill, 1898); a fairly common summer resident at Coeur d'Alene (1910-14), occurring from late May until the first week in September (Rust, 1915); noted "occasionally" at the upper end of Lake Coeur d'Alene July 1-10, 1943 (Yocom, 1946).

Benewah County. A rather uncommon summer resident at St. Maries (1921-41), occurring from May to early September (Hand, 1941).

Shoshone County. An uncommon summer resident at Clarkia (Hand, 1941).

Latah County. A "common breeder" in 1947 (Johnston, 1949); an occasional bird noted at Harvard in June, 1952 (Verner, 1953); a not uncommon summer resident (1948-58), occurring largely about farms (Burleigh).

Nez Perce County. A fairly common summer resident (Burleigh).

Adams County. Common at Council in 1958 from May 1 to September 19; abundant in late August and early September (Newhouse, 1960).

Valley County. Three birds observed at McCall September 17, 1955, feeding overhead over the town (Burleigh).

Owyhee County. Common at Riddle May 28 through June 3, 1934 (Davis, 1934).

Fremont County. A nest found near Spencer August 1, 1916, on a rafter in a barn, held three fully grown young and one infertile egg (Rust, 1917).

Jefferson County. A common summer resident in 1961 on the Camas National Wildlife Refuge (Oring, 1962).

Bonneville County. A common summer resident at Grays Lake (1949-51); arrival date May 14, 1951 (Steel, 1956).

South Central Idaho. Common at Fort Hall in early July, 1872; 1890; one seen at the foot of the Blackfoot Mountains on July 12; one pair found breeding on a ranch at Big Butte; noted almost daily in August "in Birch Creek and Lemhi Valleys"; found breeding near Nicholia and at the Lemhi Indian Agency (Merriam, 1891); found to be a common breeding bird in 1949 in "south central Idaho" (Levy, 1950).

Minidoka County. A rare breeding bird (1911-13) (Kenagy, 1914); a summer resident at Rupert, extreme dates of occurrence (1919-21) being May 2 and September 8; earliest date for eggs June 6 (Davis, 1935).

Habits. The Barn Swallow is the last of the swallows to appear in the spring in Idaho; it is usually early May before the first birds are seen feeding overhead, and the middle of the month before this species is relatively plentiful. My earliest dates of arrival in the northern part of the state (1948 through 1958) are: Potlatch, May 1 (1957), Moscow April 23 (1953), Lewiston April 25 (1953). In the fall, however, it is the last to depart; in northern Idaho it is present throughout September, and is frequently seen in early October. My latest dates of departure are: Moscow September 28 (1951 and 1952), Genesee October 4 (1951), Lewiston October 9 (1957).

Originally this species nested in caves, and on ledges of cliffs, but I know of no instance in Idaho where in recent years the nest has not been built in a barn or shed or, less frequently, on a beam under a bridge. An unusually late nest that I found at Lewiston on August 21, 1952, held four partially incubated eggs, and was plastered against a beam under a bridge crossing a small stream.

Petrochelidon pyrrhonota (Vieillot): CLIFF SWALLOW

General Distribution. Breeds from central Alaska, central Yukon, western Mackenzie, central Saskatchewan, southern Manitoba, Ontario and southern Quebec south to central Mexico, west-central Texas, the Gulf coast, northern Georgia and western North Carolina. Winters in South America from southern Brazil south to central Chile and central Argentina.

Status in Idaho. A common summer resident throughout the state.

Bonner County. A common summer resident in 1917 at Clark Fork (Burleigh, 1923).

Kootenai County. "Common in summer" at Fort Sherman (Coeur d'Alene), from the last of April to the middle of August (Merrill, 1898); a common summer resident at Coeur d'Alene, 1910-14 (Rust, 1915); noted daily at the upper end of Lake Coeur d'Alene July 1-10, 1943 (Yocom, 1946); a breeding colony of possibly twenty pairs seen at Hauser May 6, 1953, working on half-completed nests under the eaves of a large water tank (Burleigh).

Benewah County. A locally common summer resident, 1921-41, at St. Maries; present from late April to late July (Hand, 1941).

Shoshone County. A locally common summer resident at Clarkia (Hand, 1941).

Latah County. A specimen taken at Troy May 6, 1939 (Arvey, 1947); "common throughout the county" June 1-August 16, 1947 (Johnston, 1949); noted at Harvard in late June and July, 1952 (Verner, 1953); a fairly common but locally distributed summer resident throughout the county (1948-58 (Burleigh).

Nez Perce County. A common summer resident at Lewiston (Burleigh).

Idaho County. Nesting colonies noted in June (1949 through 1958) on cliffs along the Salmon River between White Bird and Riggins (Burleigh).

Adams County. Fairly common in 1958 at Council, May 28 through July 20 (Newhouse, 1960).

Owyhee County. Common at Riddle May 28 through June 3, 1934 (Davis, 1934).

Custer County. A nesting colony noted on a cliff south of Challis July 11, 1958 (Burleigh).

Fremont County. Common June through August, 1916, nesting under eaves of houses and on cliffs (Rust, 1917).

Jefferson County. A flock of "approximately 300 birds" noted on the Camas National Wildlife Refuge July 4, 1961 (Oring, 1962).

Bonneville County. Very common summer resident at Grays Lake (1949-51); arrival date April 30, 1951 (Steel, 1956); common on Big Elk Creek August 6, 1961 (Oring, 1962).

Caribou County. A large colony of approximately one hundred pairs found nesting on a clay bank at Soda Springs May 12, 1944 (Low, 1945).

South Central Idaho. Common at Fort Hall in July, 1872; a nest with two eggs was collected on Ross Fork July 3, "fastened to the bank of the stream eight feet above the water"; found nesting in July, 1890, on the Blackfoot River; also south of Nicholia, and in the Birch Creek Valley (Merriam, 1891); an "abundant" breeding bird in southern Idaho in 1949, nesting in large colonies on cliffs along the Snake River; a specimen taken at Buhl, Twin Falls County, on June 16 (Levy, 1950).

Minidoka County. A common summer resident at Rupert (1919-21), occurring between the dates of April 20 and September 10; earliest date for eggs May 7 (Davis, 1935).

Habits. The Cliff Swallow is unquestionably the most plentiful of the seven species of swallows known to occur in Idaho. Extremely sociable, it nests in large colonies, and as it has willingly accepted the proximity of man it is well distributed throughout the state. Originally a cliff was the accepted nesting site, and such a situation is still favored by numerous colonies. However, buildings have been found to be equally acceptable, and the flask-shaped nests can now be commonly seen plastered in long rows under the eaves of barns, schoolhouses, churches, sheds, and even occupied houses.

Apparently weather is an important factor in determining the appearance of this species in the spring. The first flocks are not infrequently seen in early April, but there are years when, because of adverse weather conditions farther south, it is late that month before the Cliff Swallow appears in northern Idaho. My extreme dates of occurrence at Lewiston are April 6 (1956) and September 27 (1953), and at Moscow April 23 (1950) and September 17 (1950). At Potlatch my latest date in the fall is August 29 (1951).

Petrochelidon pyrrhonota hypopolia Oberholser

A critical examination of specimens of the Cliff Swallow taken throughout the state, from early April until late September, showed that *hypopolia* is the breeding race in Idaho. This is the extreme northwestern form of this species, breeding north to central Alaska and Mackenzie, and south to California and northern Utah. Specimens collected were from the following localities: Kootenai County, Hauser; Latah County, Princeton, Potlatch, Moscow, Joel, Genesee; Nez Perce County, Lewiston; Adams County, New Meadows; Washington County, Weiser; Lemhi County, Salmon; Custer County, Challis; Bonneville County, Gray; Twin Falls County, Twin Falls; Cassia County, Oakley.

Petrochelidon pyrrhonota pyrrhonota (Vieillot)

As far as now known the nominate race of the Cliff Swallow occurs as a casual fall transient in the northern part of the state. It was taken at Moscow on August 22 and September 6, 1950, and at Lewiston on September 7, 1952, and September 12, 1957. An adult male collected from a nesting colony on the Salmon River south of White Bird on June 24, 1958, was typical of *pyrrhonota,* and was apparently a straggler that had lingered east of its normal breeding range.

[Progne subis (Linnaeus): PURPLE MARTIN]

General Distribution. Breeds west of the Cascades, from British Columbia to Baja California, and east of the Rockies from eastern British Columbia, central Alberta, central Saskatchewan, southern Manitoba, southern Ontario, southern Quebec and Nova Scotia south to the Gulf coast and southern Florida. Winters in South America from Venezuela to southern Brazil.

Status in Idaho. Apparently of accidental occurrence in the northern part of the state.

There is a single sight record for northern Idaho. On July 20, 1948, a "small group" was seen feeding over the canyon at the junction of Crooked Fork and Brushy Creek, four miles southwest of Lolo Pass (Orr, 1951).

Habits. It would appear that altitude is a contributing factor in the presence of the Purple Martin during the summer months. Few birds have a wider distribution on the North American continent, so its absence even in migration from the eastern edge of the Rocky Mountains to the Cascades is rather significant. Under the circumstances it is doubtful if it will ever be of more than accidental occurrence in Idaho.

Jays, Magpies, and Crows: *Family Corvidae*

Perisoreus canadensis (Linnaeus): GRAY JAY

General Distribution. Resident from northern Alaska, northern Yukon, Mackenzie, Keewatin, northern Quebec and Newfoundland south to northern California, central Arizona, northern New Mexico, northern Minnesota, northern Michigan and northeastern New York.

Status in Idaho. A fairly common resident species in the more heavily forested areas of the state.

The Gray Jay was first recorded in Idaho by the Lewis and Clark Expedition. Lewis (*Original Journals,* III:76) states in one of his journals that it was seen September 20, 1805, on the Lolo Trail above Weippe, and that it was reported "common" there (Jollie, 1953).

Boundary County. Specimens in the Museum of Vertebrate Zoology at Berkeley taken four miles west of Meadow Creek by D. H. Blanchard and R. T. Orr August 29, 1932; two birds seen, and one collected, at Eastport November 24, 1948 (Burleigh).

Bonner County. Specimen taken on Blue Creek, eight miles northeast of Priest Lake, March 5, 1939 (Arvey, 1947); three birds seen July 4, 1917, at Clark Fork, and three July 21 at the Trestle Creek Lookout north of Clark Fork (Burleigh, 1923); a flock of five birds seen at Nordman, on Priest Lake, July 22, 1960 (Burleigh).

Kootenai County. A "common resident"; a pair seen collecting nesting material near Hoodoo Lake on April 17, 1895 (Merrill, 1897); a "not common" resident (1910-14) (Rust, 1915).

Shoshone County. A locally common resident on the St. Joe National Forest (1921-41) "in densely timbered areas" in the Canadian zone (Hand, 1941); fairly plentiful at Avery June 20 and 21, 1951, small flocks (adults and fully grown young) being seen each day in thick woods at the tops of the ridges; a specimen taken by Seymour Levy at Dismal Lake on June 21 (Burleigh); specimen taken at Clarkia September 22, 1951 (Jollie).

Benewah County. Three birds seen in thick fir woods at Santa July 17, 1948 (Burleigh).

Latah County. "Fairly common in forested areas" June 1-August 16, 1947 (Johnston, 1949); noted at Deary May 7, 1948, and October 13, 1949, and at Troy March 12, 1953 (Burleigh); specimen taken on Bald Mountain September 23, 1949 (E. Larrison); specimens in the Museum of Vertebrate Zoology, Berkeley, taken by Jollie at Helmer November 11, 1951, at Harvard October 16, 1955, and at Bovill November 5, 1955; common on the higher ridges at Harvard during the summer of 1951 and 1952; a "group of five" seen July 26, 1952 (Verner, 1953).

Nez Perce County. Specimen taken in the Craig Mountains June 15, 1951 (Levy).

Clearwater County. Specimens in the Museum of Vertebrate Zoology, Berkeley, taken by A. H. Miller at Weippe July 19, 1932; noted at Headquarters October 27 and November 11, 1951, and June 18, 1952 (Burleigh).

Idaho County. Specimen taken June 14, 1939, by E. Williams ten miles south of Riggins (Jollie, in litt.); "not uncommon" on the higher ridges "of the Selway region" in September, 1941; five males and three females collected September 11-25 four miles southwest of Selway Falls (Orr, 1951); specimen taken by W. C. Russell October 7, 1957, five miles northeast of the junction of Whitecap Creek and the Selway River.

Valley County. Small flocks noted on Brundage Mountain, north of McCall, August 28, 1955, and June 28, 1958 (Burleigh).

South Central Idaho. Common in July, 1872, in Teton Canyon; 1890: "tolerably common" in the Salmon River Mountains, and in "the divide" between Big Lost River and Trail Creek; "half a dozen caught in marten traps" in the Sawtooth Mountains (Merriam, 1891).

Blaine County. Uncommon at Ketchum October through December, 1910; specimens taken November 3 and 5 (Jewett, 1912).

Fremont County. Specimens in the Denver Museum of Natural History in Colorado taken at Big Springs by Paul E. Trapier August 20, 1930.

Custer County. Specimens in the Denver Museum of Natural History taken at Big Redfish Lake by F. C. Hibben August 2, 1929; a specimen in the Museum of Vertebrate Zoology, Berkeley, taken at the head of the Pahsimeroi River by J. A. Donohoe July 25, 1936.

Clark County. Two "juveniles" seen and one collected on Signal Peak July 14, 1961 (Oring, 1962).

Habits. During the larger part of the year the Gray Jay, although an inhabitant of the more heavily forested areas of the state, is a bird not easily overlooked. Anyone entering the woods for any purpose whatsoever is the object of immediate interest on the part of these inquisitive jays, and they show no fear of the intruder as they appear overhead, and with characteristic sailing flight move from tree to tree as they satisfy their curiosity. In the nesting season, however, the story is quite different. They retire then to the most isolated areas, as far as possible from any human habitation, and until the young are fully grown this jay is silent and secretive, and practically never seen. Nesting is very early, usually while the snow is deep on the ground and temperatures at night well below freezing, but even so it is June before it is possible to encounter family parties consisting of adults and dark plumaged young.

Perisoreus canadensis bicolor Miller

This is the race occurring in northern and west-central Idaho, from Boundary County south to McCall in Valley County. Thirteen specimens that I collected in this part of the state (1948 through 1958) were found to be typical of *bicolor,* and are as follows: Boundary County, Eastport, male, November 24, 1948; Shoshone County, Avery, immature male, June 20, 1951; Benewah County, Santa, female, July 17, 1948; Latah County, Deary, male, May 7, 1948; Troy, male, female, March 12, 1953; Clearwater County, Headquarters, males, June 18 and November 7, 1952, females, October 27, 1951, and November 7, 1952; Valley County, McCall, male, June 28, 1958, females, August 28, 1955, and June 28, 1958.

Perisoreus canadensis capitalis Ridgway

This Rocky Mountain race, distinguished from *bicolor* by its larger size and paler coloration, is limited in its distribution to the southeastern corner of the state. Specimens examined that were found to represent *capitalis* are as follows: Fremont County, Big Springs, male, female, August 20, 1930 (Paul E. Trapier); Clark County, Signal Peak, juvenile, July 14, 1961 (Lewis W. Oring); Custer County, Big Redfish Lake, two males, August 2, 1929 (F. C. Hibben); head of the Pahsimeroi River, female, July 25, 1936 (J. A. Donohoe).

[Cyanocitta cristata (Linnaeus): BLUE JAY]

General Distribution. Central Alberta, Saskatchewan, southern Manitoba, Ontario, southern Quebec and Newfoundland south through the Dakotas, eastern Wyoming, Nebraska, eastern Colorado and the Texas Panhandle to southeastern Texas, the Gulf coast and southern Florida.

Status in Idaho. Of accidental occurrence in the northern part of the state.

There is one record for the occurrence of the Blue Jay in Idaho. Arvey (1944) reports one bird seen on Moscow Mountain by Dr. R. F. Daubenmire September 20, 1942.

Habits. Although generally considered a resident species, the Blue Jay is to some extent migratory in the northern part of its range. It is not surprising therefore that, occurring as it does as far west as Alberta, it should appear in Idaho in the fall. A specimen identified as *cyanotephra* was taken at Pullman, in eastern Washington, January 4, 1951, so it is possible that it is present in Idaho more often than the one record would indicate.

Cyanocitta stelleri annectens (Baird): STELLER'S JAY

General Distribution. Resident from the interior of British Columbia and southwestern Alberta south to northeastern Oregon, southern Idaho, and northwestern Wyoming.

Status in Idaho. Resident and fairly common in the forested areas throughout the state.

The Steller's Jay is another species that was first recorded in Idaho by the Lewis and Clark expedition. Lewis states in one of his journals (*Original Journals*, III:75-76) that it was seen on the Lolo Trail, above Weippe, September 19 and 20, 1805 (Jollie, 1953).

Boundary County. Noted at Eastport November 24, 1948 (Burleigh).

Bonner County. Frequently seen in July, 1917 at Clark Fork, and in cutover areas on Trestle Creek, but not in the heavy timber on Lightning Creek (Burleigh, 1923).

Kootenai County. Fairly common at Fort Sherman (Coeur d'Alene) in spring and fall; a few in winter; seen in July on Mica Peak (Merrill, 1897); noted at Blue Lake, "at the higher altitudes," in 1894; not common (Snyder, 1900); common at Coeur d'Alene, 1910 through 1914 (Rust, 1915); frequently seen at the upper end of Lake Coeur d'Alene July 1-10, 1943 (Yocom, 1946).

Shoshone County. Specimen taken "ten miles downstream from Avery" August 26, 1949 (Jollie); common on the St. Joe National Forest, 1921 to 1941 (Hand, 1941).

Latah County. Specimens taken on Moscow Mountain by S. E. Piper July 30, 1898 (Johnston, 1949), and November 25, 1938, and October 14, 1939 (Arvey); common at Harvard during the summers of 1951 and 1952 (Verner, 1953); fairly common and generally distributed in the wooded areas of the county (1947-58); specimens taken at Potlatch, Moscow, Genesee, Juliaetta, Deary (Burleigh).

Nez Perce County. Uncommon; noted at Lake Waha May 27, 1949, and at Culdesac November 16, 1957 (Burleigh).

Clearwater County. Fairly common (1951-56) in the vicinity of Headquarters (Burleigh).

Idaho County. Specimen taken on the Lochsa River at Van Camp November 5, 1938 (Arvey); fairly common in the "Lolo Pass region" in July, 1948; common in the "Selway region" in September, 1941; eight specimens taken September 7-27 south of Selway Falls (Orr, 1951).

Adams County. Rarely seen (1957-58) in the valley in the vicinity of Council, but common on the higher ridges (Newhouse, 1960).

Washington County. Noted in open woods halfway up Cuddy Mountain (altitude 6,100 feet) on June 6, 1952 (Burleigh).

Boise County. Common during the winter months, 1938-40, on the Boise National Forest; usually noted in pairs (Marshall, 1945).

Lemhi County. Noted on Colson Creek, north of Shoup, June 4, 1949 (Burleigh).

Fremont County. Noted "sparingly" June through August, 1916 (Rust, 1917).

Blaine County. Noted in the vicinity of Ketchum October through December, 1910; several on Rook's Creek; common at the Boston Mine (Jewett, 1912).

South Central Idaho. Common in the Teton Basin in 1872; infrequently seen in the Salmon River Mountains, at the Lemhi Indian Agency, in the Wood River Valley, and near Sawtooth Lake in 1890 (Merriam, 1891).

Bonneville County. Uncommon at Grays Lake 1949-51 (Steel, 1956); one pair noted near the top of a ridge at Gray (6,600 feet) May 23, 1951 (Burleigh).

Bear Lake County. Four specimens taken at Bloomington Lake, ten miles west of Bloomington, July 9 and 10, 1949 (Larrison and Jollie).

Habits. Although resident throughout its range in Idaho, there is apparently, to some extent at least, an altitudinal migration in the late fall, and the Steller's Jay appears at that time away from the wooded areas where it is normally found. A characteristic example of this fall "wandering," if it can be so called, was the presence on November 4, 1956, of five birds in underbrush at the side of a road south of Genesee. At this spot large open wheat fields dominated the landscape, with the nearest thick woods possibly twenty miles away. It is at this time of the year that this species is occasionally found in the Arboretum on the campus of the University at Moscow.

Aphelocoma coerulescens nevadae Pitelka: Scrub Jay

General Distribution. Resident from southeastern Oregon, southern Idaho and western Utah south to southeastern California and northern Mexico (Sonora and Chihuahua).

Status in Idaho. Locally fairly common in the extreme southern part of the state.

Merriam (1891) states that Ridgway found the Scrub Jay "abundant" at the "City of Rocks" in Cassia County October 3, 1868.

It was reported by Levy (1962) as fairly common in the "Goose Creek Mountains" in Cassia County. He took specimens there, a female and a juvenile male, June 11, 1951.

I personally noted this species on Mink Creek, south of Pocatello, Bannock County, June 12, 1955, and November 10, 1957, and on Goose Creek November 9, 1957. A specimen, a female, was collected on Mink Creek on November 10.

Habits. The habitat requirements of this species in Idaho would appear to be rather exacting, for the Scrub Jay occurs only on low ridges covered with a rather open growth of juniper. Its distribution therefore is limited to a very small area in the state; and under these circumstances it will probably never exist in larger numbers than at the present time.

A characteristic that proved rather surprising was the extreme shyness of these jays. In my experience they were very difficult to approach, or even see, and it took the better part of a morning before I succeeded in collecting the one specimen on Mink Creek.

Pica pica hudsonia (Sabine): Black-billed Magpie

General Distribution. Resident from central Alaska, southern Yukon, central Alberta, central Saskatchewan and western Manitoba south to central eastern California, northern Arizona, northern New Mexico and western Oklahoma.

Status in Idaho. Resident and common throughout the state. In the extreme northern counties the magpie as a breeding bird apparently was rather scarce at one time, but it has increased in recent years and is now fairly plentiful.

This is still another species that was recorded for the first time in Idaho by the Lewis and Clark expedition. In one of his journals (*Original Journals*, VI:217) Lewis states that young magpies, fully fledged, were seen at Kamiah May 20, 1806 (Jollie, 1953).

Judging from published records the magpie has only in recent years become a fairly common breeding bird in the northern part of the state. At Clark Fork, in Bonner County, I did not record it at any time during the summer of 1917, my one record being that of a single bird seen September 14. In Kootenai County its status would appear to have been originally that of a winter resident. Merrill (1897) considered it not uncommon in the winter at Fort Sherman, but rarely saw it after March. Snyder (1900) found it common in the winter, and noted it once during the summer at Hoodoo Lake, on August 16, 1894. Rust (1915) states that it was common during the winter months (1910-14) at Coeur d'Alene, being present from early September to early spring. He cites August 27, 1914, as his "earliest record of arrival." In view of these facts it is of interest that Yocom (1946) reported the magpie "very common" July 1-10, 1943, at the upper end of Lake Coeur d'Alene.

At St. Maries, in Benewah County, Hand (1941) reported it an "irregularly common resident" (1921-41); he states that in the fall it was noted on the higher ridges.

In Latah County this species was reported by Johnston (1949) as common "in the open country" June 1 through August 16, 1947. I found it common in the county throughout the year (1947-58), and well distributed both during the summer months and in the winter.

It was equally common then at Lewiston, in Nez Perce County.

In the southern part of the state it was reported common at Council, Adams County, 1957-58 (Newhouse, 1960); on the Boise National Forest, Boise County, 1938-40 (Marshall, 1945); at Riddle, Owyhee County, May 28-June 3, 1934 (Davis, 1934); at Shoup, Lemhi County, June 4-6, 1949 (Burleigh); on the Camas National Wildlife Refuge, Jefferson County, June 6-August 29, 1961 (Oring, 1962); at Grays Lake, Bonneville County, 1949-51 (Steel, 1956); at Rupert, Minidoka County, 1919-21 (Davis, 1935); at Sawtooth Lake, Custer County, in October, 1890, and at Shoshone Falls, Jerome County, October 9-11, 1890 (Merriam, 1891); at Ketchum, Blaine County, October through December, 1910 (Jewett, 1912).

In the collections of the Department of Zoology, University of Idaho, Moscow, there are specimens of the magpie taken by Arvey at Driggs, Teton County, December 25, 1938, and by Larrison on Goose Creek, Cassia County, June 25, 1949.

Habits. Magpies nest early in Idaho, for in the northern part of the state snow is frequently on the ground in early April when the females are incubating full sets of eggs. At Moscow my earliest nest is one that held five fresh eggs on April 10, 1949. It was eight feet from the ground in the top of a red haw (*Cretaegus*) in underbrush bordering a stream. Another nest held three fully fledged young on May 23, 1948. At Lewiston I found a nest on April 8, 1949, with nine fresh eggs that was ten feet from the ground in the top of a cottonwood sapling in underbrush bordering the Snake River.

Evenden (1947) made a study of the nesting habits of this species at Mountain Home, Elmore County, in April, 1944. Summarized briefly, a total of twenty-one nests were found, two on the twelfth, sixteen on the seventeenth, two on the twenty-second, and one on the twenty-seventh. Eggs varied in number from five to eight, and as seven is the number usually laid the assumption was that some of the females had not completed their clutches. The nests were all within five feet of the ground, sixteen being in willows, two in hawthorns, two in rosebushes, and one in sagebrush.

Davis (1935) gives as his earliest date for eggs in Minidoka County (1919-21) April 11, and the latest date for young still in the nest June 6.

In view of the bad reputation the magpie has for eating the eggs and young of other birds a report by Fichter (1959) on the nesting habits of the Mourning Dove at American Falls, in Power County, is of unusual interest. With the immediate objective of banding the nestlings, a careful search was made, from early spring until late summer, of four large orchards, and a total of 208 dove nests were found, in which 324 young were successfully reared. In not a single instance was predation by magpies noted.

Corvus corax sinuatus Wagler: COMMON RAVEN

General Distribution. Resident from central British Columbia, northern Idaho, western Montana and southwestern South Dakota south to southern California, Arizona, and Mexico, and through Guatemala, Honduras, and El Salvador to Nicaragua.

Status in Idaho. Fairly common throughout the state, but rather local in its distribution.

The Raven is another species that was recorded for the first time in Idaho by the Lewis and Clark expedition. In their journals Lewis (*Original Journals*, III:76) and Clark (*Original Journals*, III:74) state that it was observed on the Lolo Trail September 19 and 20, 1805, and Lewis (*Original Journals*, III:83) reports one killed on September 22 just before reaching the Weippe Prairie (Jollie, 1953).

Kootenai County. Merrill (1897) states that it was seen occasionally at Fort Sherman (Coeur d'Alene), and Rust (1915) reports three birds observed at Coeur d'Alene April 20, 1913.

Shoshone County. Hand (1941) considered this species a "not uncommon resident" in the St. Joe National Forest (1921-41), although limited in its distribution to "the high mountains." I saw two birds in a wooded ravine at Clarkia August 8, 1948. Jollie (in litt.) noted a flock of twenty-six at Avery August 26, 1949.

Latah County. Johnston (1949) saw four birds three miles east of Harvard June 14, 1947; Verner (1953) noted a flock of twelve at Harvard July 5, 1951, and again at intervals during the rest of that summer; the following year he saw three birds on July 31; in the open Palouse country, characterized by large wheat fields, it was of casual occurrence after the nesting season; it was noted at Potlatch February 12, 1949, and at Moscow October 10, 1949, August 27, 1950, and January 25, 1957 (Burleigh).

Nez Perce County. At Lewiston, on the Snake River, it was noted at rather infrequent intervals, and was merely a straggler in the open country there. A single bird was seen November 18, 1948, and pairs were noted January 29, 1949, and February 8, 1951 (Burleigh).

Clearwater County. Two birds observed at Ahsahka January 7, 1951. At Headquarters it was possible throughout the year (1951-58) to find Ravens feeding about the town's garbage dump in a clearing in the woods; they were present in smallest numbers during the nesting season, and most numerous during the winter, the largest number observed at any one time being twenty on February 8, 1954. One specimen, a male, was collected at this spot September 18, 1954 (Burleigh).

Idaho County. Noted occasionally in September, 1941, and July, 1948, at Lolo Pass and in the Selway region (Orr, 1951).

Owyhee County. Two birds seen daily at Riddle May 28-June 3, 1934 (Davis, 1934); two specimens in juvenile plumage collected at Riddle June 20 and 22, 1949 (Jollie, in litt.).

Clark County. Several birds seen on Signal Peak June 19 and July 15, 1961 (Oring, 1962).

Bonneville County. Uncommon at Grays Lake, 1949-51 (Steel, 1956); noted on Big Elk Creek August 5, 1961 (Oring, 1962).

South Central Idaho. Noted as common by Ridgway at the "City of Rocks" October 3, 1868; noted along the Snake River, on the "Snake Plains," in Birch Creek Valley, in the valleys of the Pahsimeroi and Salmon rivers, at Castle Rock south of Snake River, and along the north base of the Bruneau and Elk Mountains in 1890 (Merriam, 1891); uncommon and generally distributed during the summer of 1949 in this same general region (Levy, 1950).

Minidoka County. Reported by Davis (1935) as a winter resident (1919-21) in the vicinity of Rupert, extreme dates of occurrence being given as October 27 and May 19.

Habits. In my experience the preferred nesting site of a pair of Ravens in Idaho is a crevice in a sheer cliff where eggs and young are safe from any molestation. In other parts of its range it is known frequently to nest in the upper branches of large trees, and there is one instance of this practice occurring in southern Idaho. Fichter (in litt.) states that on June 17, 1958, he found a nest with young "near fledgling age" in a juniper tree near the Cassia-Oneida County line. Cliffs affording nesting sites are not numerous, especially in the northern part of the state, so this species is nowhere a common bird, and in many localities it is merely a straggler in the fall and winter months.

Like the Crow, with which it is often confused by the casual observer, it has the reputation of being rather fond of the eggs and young of other birds, but being always wary and difficult to approach it suffers little at the hands of hunters. Actually it is of economic value as a scavenger, for it will eat practically anything it can digest, and it is also known to be beneficial in the destruction of injurious rodents and insects.

MOUNTAIN CHICKADEE

PLATE VII

Corvus brachyrhynchos hesperis Ridgway: COMMON CROW

General Distribution. Largely resident from British Columbia, central Alberta and central Saskatchewan south to northern Baja California, central Arizona, and northern New Mexico.

Status in Idaho. A fairly common but local summer resident over most of the state, and a common winter resident in the extreme southwestern counties.

Boundary County. Two specimens taken at Porthill by Musgrove and Larrison November 20, 1949 (Jollie, in litt.); a specimen taken by Levy at Copeland April 7, 1950; fairly plentiful at Bonners Ferry June 22, 1957; a brood of well-grown young noted in woods bordering the Kootenai River (Burleigh).

Bonner County. Fairly plentiful in the vicinity of Clark Fork in the summer of 1917 (Burleigh, 1923); an occasional bird noted at Priest River June 29, 1957; an adult male collected that day (Burleigh).

Kootenai County. Common in migration at Fort Sherman (Coeur d'Alene); a few pairs breed at the "edge of the prairie" (Merrill, 1897); noted at the upper end of Lake Coeur d'Alene July 1-10, 1943 (Yocom, 1946); two birds seen March 19, 1958, in the open prairie at Hauser (Burleigh).

Benewah County. An uncommon summer resident (1910-14) in "the St. Joe Valley" east of St. Maries (Rust, 1915); a common summer resident (1921-41) in the vicinity of St. Maries; present from March to October (Hand, 1941).

Latah County. Of irregular occurrence during the spring migration in the open Palouse country. At Potlatch it was seen between the dates of March 13 (1949) and May 1 (1948), at Moscow between the dates of March 24 (1950) and May 19 (1948), and at Genesee on April 10, 1953. Usually one or two birds would be found feeding in the wheat fields the third week in April; at no times were flocks of any size noted. My one record for the fall is that of four birds seen at Genesee August 21, 1950 (Burleigh).

Nez Perce County. Bendire (1895) reported this species as breeding at Fort Lapwai in 1870-71, and common during the winter months. Its status has apparently changed in recent years, for in my experience it does not occur during the winter, and is extremely scarce during the summer. At Lewiston my extreme dates of occurrence are February 24 (1958) and September 16 (1954). It apparently breeds sparingly, for two birds were seen July 8, 1953, in cottonwoods at the edge of the Snake River.

Clearwater County. Three birds, summer stragglers, noted in the prairie south of Weippe August 1, 1952.

Valley County. A noisy flock of sixteen birds noted well within the town limits of McCall March 19, 1967; ground that day covered with several feet of snow (Burleigh).

Adams County. New Meadows, birds found to be plentiful here April 15, 1949; scattered pairs seen in the open meadows; three small flocks, totalling thirty birds, seen February 27, 1950; none was noted ten days earlier (on the seventeenth); snow still a foot deep; scattered pairs again seen in the open meadows May 18, 1955; nest found that held two fresh eggs (Burleigh); this species common at Council February 18 to December 18, 1958; most numerous during March and April (Newhouse, 1960).

Washington County. Birds abundant at Weiser February 18, 1950; numerous noisy flocks noted during the morning (Burleigh).

Payette County. Small flocks noted at Payette November 23, 1951 (Burleigh).

Ada County. This species apparently resident at Boise, and fairly common both as a breeding bird and during the winter months; on April 17, 1949, scattered pairs or single birds were frequently noted, their actions indicating that they were nesting at that time while on November 7, 1957, numerous flocks were seen in the open fields (Burleigh).

Owyhee County. Numerous small noisy flocks seen daily, February 19-26, 1950, at Homedale (Burleigh).

Lemhi County. Common in 1890 "in the Lemhi Valley" in August and early September (Merriam, 1891); noted in small numbers at Shoup, on the Salmon River, June 6, 1949 (Burleigh).

Custer County. A few noted in 1890 at Sawtooth Lake in late September (Merriam, 1891).

Clark County. Found to be uncommon breeding bird in 1916; one noted at Spencer July 15, and three at Kilgore August 26 (Rust, 1917).

Jefferson County. "Abundant" on the Camas National Wildlife Refuge June 6 to August 29, 1961 (Oring, 1962).

Bonneville County. A common summer resident at Grays Lake, 1949-51 (Steel, 1956); nest with four small young found May 29, 1952, in an aspen grove on Eagle Creek, two miles north of Gray (Burleigh).

Minidoka County. Reported by Davis (1935) as a winter resident only at Rupert (1919-21), his extreme dates of occurrence being October 27 and April 7.

South Central Idaho. Found to be a common summer resident in 1949 (Levy, 1950).

Habits. As in other parts of its range in the western United States the Crow is largely restricted in its distribution in Idaho during the summer months to the vicinity of cottonwood and aspen groves. Here the nest is built, usually within twenty feet of the ground; and while altitude is a factor in the date when nesting activities begin, it is doubtful if anywhere in the state the females are incubating full sets of eggs before the first of May. Coniferous woods are consistently shunned, and as this limits, often radically, the availability of nesting sites there is a noticeable tendency to colonize that is quite at variance with the habits of this species in the east. This is true also of the height of the nest from the ground. The one found at New Meadows on May 18, 1955, with two fresh eggs, was but seven feet up in the top of a rather thick red haw (*Cretaegus*), and this is not unusually close to the ground for this western population.

Gymnorhinus cyanocephala Wied: Piñon Jay

General Distribution. Resident from central Oregon, central Montana, and western South Dakota south to northern Baja California, central Arizona, central New Mexico, and western Oklahoma.

Status in Idaho. Apparently resident, and common in the extreme southern edge of the state. There are no actual breeding records, but in view of the presence of this species in Cassia County in June it is quite possible that the fully grown young observed were reared somewhere in the vicinity.

The Piñon Jay was first recorded in Idaho by Merriam (1891) who stated that Ridgway reported it abundant at the "City of Rocks" in Cassia County, on October 3, 1868.

Davis (1935) found it a winter resident in the vicinity of Rupert, Minidoka County (1919-21), noting it between the dates of August 12 and May 20.

Levy (1962) considered it a common "late summer visitant" on Goose Creek, south of Oakley, in Cassia County. There he noted a flock of thirty birds on June 12, 1951, and another flock of fifty on September 12. He collected a female on this latter date. In this same area I observed a flock of approximately sixty of these jays on June 3, 1955, and a smaller flock of twenty on November 8, 1957.

At Pocatello, Bannock County, this species is equally common on the juniper-covered ridges that characterize this southeastern corner of the state. I noted two birds on Buckskin Creek June 11, 1955, and a flock of one hundred or so on Mink Creek November 12, 1957.

Habits. Although recorded at the present time from only a few localities in the state, further field work should reveal the presence of the Piñon Jay along the entire southern edge of Idaho. Its distribution is restricted to areas where either the piñon pine or the juniper, or both, are found; so, while common where it occurs, it will never have an extensive range. It is one species not easily overlooked. Highly gregarious, it remains in flocks throughout the year; even during the breeding season when individuals comprising a flock nest together in a rather limited area, several pairs often build their nests in the same tree. As long as available the edible seeds of the piñon pine or the berries of the cedar are the preferred food; in their search for a sufficient quantity to satisfy their appetites the restless flocks, always noisy, cover long distances each day. Under such circumstances these jays may be present one day, and not be seen again for weeks, so their actual abundance is not easy to determine.

Nucifraga columbiana (Wilson): Clark's Nutcracker

General Distribution. Resident from central British Columbia, southwestern Alberta and central Montana south through the mountains to northern Baja California, eastern Arizona, and western New Mexico.

Status in Idaho. A common resident species throughout the mountain areas of the state.

Clark's Nutcracker has the distinction of being one of the species "discovered" by the historic Lewis and Clark expedition to the Pacific coast. It was mentioned in one of Clark's journals (*Original Journals,* III:17) as being observed near the mouth "of the North Fork," twenty miles northwest of Salmon, August 22, 1805, and this is apparently the first actual record for this species (Jollie, 1953). The type locality is based on a specimen taken by Lewis on May 28, 1806, and is generally accepted as two miles north of Kamiah, in Idaho County (Davis, 1934).

Bonner County. Common during the summer of 1917 on the higher ridges north of Clark Fork; noisy and much in evidence (Burleigh, 1923).

Kootenai County. Common at Fort Sherman (Coeur d'Alene) during the winter of 1894-95; rare in 1895-96; common again in 1896-97; apparently dependent on pine seed for food; several family parties seen on Mica Peak in early July (Merrill, 1897); of irregular occurrence at Coeur d'Alene during the fall and winter (1910-14); presence dependent on "pine-cone crop"; abundant October, 1911, to December, 1912; noted on August 11, 1914 (Rust, 1915); a flock of ten birds seen February 14, 1950, in pine woods bordering Lake Coeur d'Alene, and a male collected (Bureigh).

Shoshone County. A common resident "of the high mountains" on the St. Joe National Forest (1921-41); noted at lower altitudes in the fall and winter (Hand, 1941).

Latah County. Of irregular occurrence from late fall until early spring on the wooded ridges north and east of Moscow; noted on Tomer's Butte November 8, 1948; and on Moscow Mountain from September 26 through December 24, 1950, on March 20 and April 27, 1951, and on December 16, 1956; specimens taken September 26 and October 10, 15, 24, and 29 and December 24, 1950, and March 20, 1951 (Burleigh).

Nez Perce County. A family party, the adults and two fully grown young, seen May 27, 1949, at Lake Waha, south of Lewiston, in open woods at the top of a ridge (altitude approximately 4,300 feet); the male collected (Burleigh).

Idaho County. Specimens taken by C. Engler on June 26, 1938, one-half mile east of Two Lakes, and by D. Croghan on May 14, 1939, ten miles southwest of Riggins (Jollie, in litt.); a flock of fifteen seen September 17, 1941, at Selway Falls, and "a few" September 20 in the Crags Mountains; common near timberline in the Bitterroot Mountains in July, 1948; a male taken July 16 eight and a half miles southeast of Lolo Pass (Orr, 1951).

Valley County. Specimen taken June 6, 1949, on Little Payette Lake, three miles northeast of McCall (Jollie, in litt.); one small flock noted at McCall June 28, 1949 (Burleigh).

Boise County. Noted "commonly" on the Boise National Forest during the winter (1938-40), from 4,000 to 7,000 feet (Marshall, 1945); two birds seen at Bogus Basin (6,400 feet) on February 23, 1950 (Burleigh).

Owyhee County. A flock of approximately twenty birds seen at Three Creek May 31, 1951, feeding in junipers in a wooded ravine (Burleigh).

Lemhi County. This species found to be plentiful June 4-6, 1949, on the wooded ridges north of Shoup, being observed daily on Cramer Creek, Colson Creek, and Color Creek; especially numerous on Cramer Creek, where flocks totalling thirty birds were seen (Burleigh).

Fremont County. Occurs sparingly; fully grown young seen in Little Dry Creek Canyon June 18, 1916 (Rust, 1917).

Clark County. Common on Signal Peak July 14-15, 1961; a male collected July 15 (Oring, 1962).

Blaine County. Common from October through December, 1910, on the Wood River at Ketchum, and on the nearby ridges to an altitude of 8,000 feet (Jewett, 1912).

Bonneville County. Three birds seen north of Gray June 13, 1949, in fir woods near the top of Caribou Mountain (altitude approximately 9,000 feet) (Burleigh).

South central Idaho. Reported by Townsend as occurring in July, 1834, in the mountains near Bear River; common in 1890 "on all the mountains visited" (Merriam, 1891).

Cassia County. Uncommon; two birds seen on Mt. Harrison June 21, 1949 (Levy, 1950).

Habits. Although largely resident throughout its range in Idaho the Clark's Nutcracker wanders widely during the fall and winter months. Regardless of the severity of the weather it can be found in midwinter at the tops of the higher ridges, and small noisy flocks are apt to be seen then at almost any spot in the valleys. Its movements at this season of the year are to some extent unpredictable, being apparently governed by the presence or absence of the seed of such conifers as the pine and the fir. Pine seed especially is favored, and where there is a heavy cone crop in the fall a flock of Nutcrackers will linger until this source of food is completely gone. Like other members of its family this species is to a large extent omnivorous. It frequents human habitations during the winter months for any scraps of food it can find, and is under these circumstances fearless and easily approached.

Titmice, Verdins, and Bushtits: *Family Paridae*

Parus atricapillus Linnaeus: BLACK-CAPPED CHICKADEE

General Distribution. Resident from central Alaska, southern Yukon, southwestern Mackenzie, central Saskatchewan, central Manitoba, Ontario, southern Quebec and Newfoundland south to northern California, northern Nevada, northern New Mexico, northern Oklahoma, central Missouri, eastern Tennessee and western North Carolina.

Status in Idaho. A common resident species in suitable habitat throughout the state.

Bonner County. Found to be fairly plentiful in 1917 at Clark Fork (Burleigh, 1923).

Kootenai County. Common at Fort Sherman (Coeur d'Alene), in willows in the open marsh (Merrill, 1898); a common resident at Coeur d'Alene (1910-14) (Rust, 1915); frequently noted at the upper end of Lake Coeur d'Alene July 1-10, 1943 (Yocom, 1946).

Shoshone County. Specimen taken by C. Engler on Nine Mile Creek, four miles northeast of Wallace, July 15, 1938 (Jollie, in litt.).

Benewah County. A common resident at St. Maries (1921-41), occurring from the "Transition Zone" to 4,000 feet (Hand, 1941).

Latah County. Infrequently noted in the "forested areas" (June 1-August 16, 1947); young birds seen in July and August; an immature male collected at Harvard June 25 (Johnston, 1949); seen almost daily at Harvard during the summers of 1951 and 1952 (Verner, 1953); common and well distributed throughout the county (1947-58), occurring largely in the valleys in deciduous underbrush bordering streams (Burleigh).

Nez Perce County. Reported by Bendire as common at Fort Lapwai (Merriam, 1891); noted as a rare fall straggler only at Lewiston where it was recorded twice in 1951 on Hatwai Creek, a single bird on September 23, and a flock of eight on October 21 (Burleigh).

Clearwater County. Noted as an uncommon resident at Headquarters; three birds seen there November 11, 1951 (Burleigh).

Idaho County. Frequently observed in September, 1941; in "the Selway region" from 1,900 to 5,800 feet; two females taken September 6 southeast of Selway Falls (Orr, 1951); a flock of eight birds seen at Riggins November 20, 1951, in underbrush at the edge of the Salmon River (Burleigh).

Adams County. Common "at higher elevation"; noted in the valleys March 3 to December 3, 1958 (Newhouse, 1960).

Washington County. Found to be fairly common in 1951 at Cambridge, being noted in deciduous woods bordering the Weiser River on June 4 and again on November 21; noted at Weiser on June 4, 1952, in willows at the edge of the Snake River (Burleigh).

Lemhi County. Common in 1890 along the streams "in the Lemhi and Birch Creek Valleys" (Merriam, 1891); two adults with a brood of fully fledged young seen at North Fork July 10, 1958 (Burleigh).

Fremont County. Found to be fairly common in 1916, but limited in its distribution to areas where there were willows or aspen groves (Rust, 1917).

Clark County. A female in immature plumage taken on Signal Peak July 15, 1961 (Oring, 1962).

Jefferson County. Common June 6-August 29, 1961, on the Camas National Wildlife Refuge (Oring, 1962).

Blaine County. Common in the vicinity of Ketchum October through December, 1910, being observed then in willows at the edge of the Wood River (Jewett, 1912); a breeding male taken at Sun Valley June 28, 1950 (Levy, 1962).

Bonneville County. A common resident (1949-51) at Grays Lake (Steel, 1956); noted in 1949 in willows on Eagle Creek, north of Gray, June 9-17, and November 3 (Burleigh).

Minidoka County. Recorded as a winter resident only (1919-21) in the vicinity of Rupert, extreme dates of occurrence being January 1 and March 25 (Davis, 1935).

Cassia County. One small flock noted at Burley November 13, 1957, in underbrush at the edge of the Snake River (Burleigh).

Habits. Although considered resident within its breeding range the Black-capped Chickadee apparently wanders to some extent during the winter months. At Lewiston, where it has never been noted during the summer, small flocks have appeared on Hatwai Creek as early as September 23 (1951) and have been seen at irregular intervals there as late as March 4 (1953). The small flock noted at Salmon on November 2, 1949, where the breeding race is *garrinus*, would indicate that, to some extent at least, this species travels long distances in the late fall months.

Unlike the other chickadees *atricapillus* is limited in its distribution in Idaho to deciduous underbrush bordering streams and open marshes. Conifers are largely shunned, even during the winter. Altitude, however, is apparently no factor, provided there is suitable habitat available. I found this species as common at Gray, at 6,300 feet, as it was at Moscow, at 2,500 feet.

Breeding activities begin in late April, but it is the latter part of May before the majority of these chickadees are incubating full sets of eggs. A nest found by Rust (1915) in French Gulch, near Coeur d'Alene, was in a birch stub, and held seven eggs on May 30.

Parus atricapillus nevadensis (Linsdale)

This pale race of the Black-capped Chickadee is limited in its range in Idaho to the south-central part of the state. There are specimens identified as *nevadensis* from the following localities: Elmore County, Glenns Ferry (February); Cassia County, Howell's Canyon, eight miles southeast of Albion (December), Elba (June), Burley (November), Goose Creek Mountains (August); Blaine County, Bellevue (January), Sun Valley (June), Trail Creek (August), Corral Creek (August), Deer Creek (September).

Parus atricapillus garrinus Behle

This recently described race has a less restricted range than the preceding, occurring in eastern Idaho from Lemhi County south to the Utah line. There are specimens identified as *garrinus* from the following localities: Lemhi County, Salmon (July), North Fork (July), Lemhi (September); Custer County, Challis (June), Garden Creek (August), Mackay (July and September); Fremont County, St. Anthony (June), Big Falls (August), Mount Sawtelle (Yale Creek) (August), Stewart Ranch (November); Clark County, Beaver Creek (June), Medicine Lodge Creek (June), Signal Peak (July); Jefferson County, Rigby (May), Mud Lake (October and November); Madison County, Moody Creek, three miles west of Rexburg (December); Teton County, Horseshoe Creek, Big Hole Mountain (July); Bonneville County, Gray (May, June and November); Butte County, Arco (September); Bingham County, Blackfoot (March, April, December); Bannock County, Portneuf River (January); Oneida County, Malad City (April); Franklin County, Preston (March and April); Bear Lake County, Montpelier (January), Bloomington (January), St. Charles (January), Dingle (February), Fish Haven (May), Paris (September).

Parus atricapillus fortuitus (Dawson and Bowles)

This race, with its darker coloration, is readily distinguished from the preceding two, its appearance suggesting the Black-capped Chickadee of the eastern United States. It has quite an extensive range in Idaho, occurring in the northern third of the state and along the western border south to the Snake River that forms the boundary with Oregon. There are specimens identified as *fortuitus* from the following localities: Bonner County, Cocolalla (July), Priest Lake (July), Hunt Creek, Selkirk Mountains (August); Kootenai County, Coeur d'Alene (February, March, May, October, November); Latah County, Harvard (December), Princeton (October), Potlatch (January, November), Viola (March, November), Moscow (January, March, October, November, December), Troy (January), Deary (November), Genesee (January); Nez Perce County, Lewiston (March, October); Idaho County, Selway Falls (September), Riggins (November); Washington County, Cambridge (June, November), Weiser (June); Ada County, Boise (March). Two specimens taken at Salmon, in Lemhi County, November 2, 1949, are referable to *fortuitus*, and apparently represent winter stragglers from the range of this race farther north and west in the state.

Parus gambeli Ridgway: MOUNTAIN CHICKADEE

General Distribution. Resident in the Rocky Mountains, the Sierra Nevada, and the inner coast ranges from northern British Columbia and southwestern Alberta to northern Baja California, southeastern Arizona, southeastern New Mexico and southwestern Texas.

Status in Idaho. A common resident in the forested areas of the state.

Bonner County. Fairly common during the summer of 1917 in the fir woods on the higher ridges north of Clark Fork; a female noted feeding stubby-tailed young on August 28 (Burleigh, 1923); the type specimen of *Parus gambeli grinnelli* taken by C. F. Hedges at Priest Lake August 15, 1927 (Van Rossem, 1928).

Kootenai County. An "abundant" resident at Fort Sherman (Coeur d'Alene) (Merrill, 1898); an "abundant" resident, 1910-14, at Coeur d'Alene (Rust, 1915); one small flock seen in pine woods bordering Lake Coeur d'Alene February 14, 1950 (Burleigh).

Benewah County. A common resident (1921-41) at "higher elevations;" at lower altitudes in winter (Hand, 1941).

Latah County. Fairly common, June 1-August 16, 1947, especially at higher altitudes (Johnston, 1949); common and of general distribution (1947-58) on the higher ridges during the spring and summer months, and in the valleys in the fall and winter (Burleigh).

Nez Perce County. Of irregular occurrence at Lewiston from September until March (1952-57), small flocks being noted on Hatwai Creek, and in willows and cottonwoods at the edge of the Snake River (Burleigh).

Clearwater County. One family group, adults and fully grown young, seen at Headquarters August 27, 1952 (Burleigh).

Idaho County. Noted in September, 1941, and July, 1948, in "the Lolo Pass and Selway regions"; two males taken, September 10 (Selway Falls, 1,900 feet) and July 16 (eight and a half miles southeast of Lolo Pass, 7,000 feet) (Orr, 1951).

Washington County. Two mated pairs seen June 6, 1952, in fir woods at the top of Cuddy Mountain (7,600 feet) (Burleigh).

Boise County. Abundant during the winter months (1938-40) in the Boise National Forest (Marshall, 1945); scattered small flocks noted February 23, 1950, in the fir woods at Bogus Basin (6,400 feet) (Burleigh).

Owyhee County. Winter stragglers noted in 1950 as follows, in each instance in willows bordering streams: De Lamar, three birds February 19; Homedale, two birds February 24; Bruneau, a single bird February 25 (Burleigh). Levy (1962) reported a specimen taken at De Lamar August 7, 1950.

Lemhi County. Small flocks noted in 1949 in the Bitterroot Mountains, north of Shoup, at the head of Cramer Creek on October 31, and on Colson Creek on November 1 (Burleigh).

Custer County. An occasional bird noted on Mount Borah, at an altitude of eight thousand feet, July 12, 1958 (Burleigh).

South Central Idaho. Abundant in 1890 in the Salmon River and the Sawtooth mountains (Merriam, 1891).

Fremont County. Common in 1916 in fir woods on the higher ridges (Rust, 1915); an occasional bird noted in Targhee Pass (7,000 feet) June 12, 1957 (Burleigh).

Clark County. Several seen on Signal Peak on June 19 and again on July 14, 1961; an adult male taken on June 19 (Oring, 1962).

Blaine County. Common in 1910 on the higher ridges in the vicinity of Ketchum; approximately one hundred noted October 31 on Boyle Mountain (altitude 8,000 feet) (Jewett, 1912); an occasional bird noted July 10, 1960, on Trail Creek Summit (altitude 7,800 feet) (Burleigh).

Bonneville County. A common resident species at Grays Lake, 1949-51 (Steel, 1956); one small flock noted June 13, 1949, near the top of Caribou Mountain (8,500 feet) (Burleigh); several seen August 6, 1961, in Mike Spencer Canyon, six miles east of Swan Valley (Oring, 1962).

Minidoka County. Recorded as a winter resident at Rupert (1919-21), extreme dates of occurrence being January 13 and March 25 (Davis, 1935).

Cassia County. Noted in the City of Rocks June 19, 1949; one small flock, winter stragglers, seen at Burley November 13, 1957, in underbrush at the edge of the Snake River (Burleigh).

Habits. The Mountain Chickadee is well named, for in Idaho it is found throughout the year in thick woods on the higher ridges. It is doubtful if it nests below 4,000 feet, and during the summer months breeding pairs have been found as high as 7,600 feet on Cuddy Mountain in Washington County, and at 8,500 feet on Caribou Mountain in Bonneville County. While largely resident within its range this species makes a noticeable altitudinal migration in the fall, and during the winter small flocks can be seen in the valleys, feeding in the cottonwoods and willows along the streams. At Moscow this chickadee has appeared in the Arboretum on the University campus as early as August 29 (1952), and has been noted at this same spot as late in the spring as April 15 (1953). Usually, however, the first small flocks are seen in late October or early November, and the last only infrequently after the middle of March. At Potlatch extreme dates of occurrence are December 31 (1949) and February 12 (1950), while at Genesee one small flock was noted April 4, 1953. At Lewiston small flocks were seen at irregular intervals on Hatwai Creek, and rarely in cottonwoods at the edge of the Snake River, my extreme dates of occurrence being September 16 (1953) and March 16 (1953).

Parus gambeli grinnelli (Van Rossem)

This race of the Mountain Chickadee has an extensive range in the state, occurring throughout much of the northern half of Idaho. Behle (1956) made a critical study of this species and states that specimens representing *grinnelli* have been taken "at Coeur d'Alene, Coolin (Bonner County), Priest Lake, Lost Creek (Bonner County), Hunt Creek (Bonner County), Horseheaven Creek (Elmore County), Hunter Creek (Elmore County), North Fork of the Boise River (Elmore County), Selway Falls (Idaho County), Beaver Ridge, eight and a half miles southeast of Lolo Pass (Idaho County), Castle Creek Ranger Station, South Fork of the Clearwater River (Idaho County), Bald Mountain (Latah County), Dickey (Custer County), Summit, Smith Mountain (Adams County)." Additional specimens identified as *grinnelli* were personally taken as follows: Kootenai County, Coeur d'Alene (February); Benewah County, St. Maries (October); Latah County, Princeton (December), Potlatch (February), Moscow (January, March, April, September, November), Deary (October); Nez Perce County, Lewiston (March, October, December); Clearwater County, Headquarters (August, November); Washington County, Cambridge (June).

Parus gambeli inyoensis (Grinnell)

This race has a rather limited distribution in the southeastern edge of the state. Specimens identified as *inyoensis* have been taken in Owyhee County, De Lamar (February), Homedale (February), Bruneau (February); Cassia County, Mount Harrison, ten miles south of Albion (June), Corner Canyon, four miles north of Elba (June), Oakley (November), Burley (November).

Parus gambeli wasatchensis (Behle)

This recently described race occurs in central and southeastern Idaho. In his original description Behle (1956) cites specimens from Valley County, five miles east of Warm Lake, and five miles west of Cape Horn, Sawtooth Range, and from Adams County, three miles west of Payette Lake. Additional specimens of *wasatchensis* have been taken in Valley County, McCall (June and September); Adams County, New Meadows (November); Boise County, Bogus Basin (February and July); Lemhi County, Canyon Creek (July), Shoup (October and November); Custer County, Mount Borah (July), Garden Creek (August), Little Redfish Lake (August), Lower Cedar Creek (September), Mackay (September); Blaine County, Trail Creek Summit (July), Basset Gulch, Trail Creek (August), Deer Creek, six miles northwest of Hailey (September); Clark County, Grouse Canyon (June), Signal Peak (June); Bonneville County, Gray (November); Butte County, Arco Peak (September); Power County, Havenor's, seven miles northwest of Pocatello (April); Bear Lake County, Home Canyon (February); Franklin County, Wasatch Range (June), Joe's Gap, Preuss Range (July).

Parus gambeli gambeli Ridgway

The nominate race of the Mountain Chickadee has an extremely limited range in Idaho, for it has been recorded only in Fremont County at the eastern edge of the state. Behle (1956) reports a specimen taken in August seventeen miles east and four miles north of Ashton, and there are additional specimens taken in Targhee Pass (7,000 feet) in June, and at Big Spring, Sawtelle, and Macks Inn in August.

Parus rufescens levyi Burleigh: CHESTNUT-BACKED CHICKADEE

General Distribution. Resident in southern British Columbia east of the coast ranges, northern Washington east of the Cascades, northern Idaho, northeastern Oregon, and western Montana west of the Continental Divide.

Status in Idaho. A fairly common resident species in the forested areas in the northern part of the state, occurring as far south as Idaho County.

Bonner County. Fairly common in 1917 in heavy timber in the valleys north of Clark Fork; frequently noted on Lightning Creek (Burleigh, 1923).

Kootenai County. Resident and fairly common at Fort Sherman (Coeur d'Alene) (Merrill, 1898); a "not common" resident, 1910-14, at Coeur d'Alene (Rust, 1915).

Benewah County. A common resident, 1921-41, "in the Canadian and Upper Transition Zones"; at lower altitudes in winter (Hand, 1941).

Latah County. Common June 1-August 16, 1947, in the forested areas of the county (Johnston, 1949); a flock of approximately fifteen, adults and young, seen at Harvard August 5, 1952 (Verner, 1953); fairly common (1947-58), but local in its distribution in the county during the summer months, occurring then in the more heavily forested areas; noted in the open valleys in the late fall and winter (Burleigh).

Nez Perce County. Noted on Hatwai Creek, east of Lewiston, during the winter of 1952-53 (Burleigh).

Clearwater County. Fairly common, 1952-56, on the wooded ridges at Headquarters (Burleigh).

Idaho County. Common in July, 1948, "along the upper parts" of the Lolo Trail (4,000 to 6,000 feet) (Orr, 1951).

The Chestnut-backed Chickadees of Idaho can be distinguished from the nominate race by their darker coloration. Specimens typical of *levyi* have been taken in Kootenai County, Coeur d'Alene (April); Benewah County, St. Maries (October); Latah County, Moscow (November), twenty miles northeast of Moscow (June), Harvard (July), East Fork Meadow Creek (June), Deary (February, May, December); Nez Perce County, Lewiston (February, March, December); Clearwater County, Headquarters (February, March); Idaho County, Castle Creek Ranger Station, south fork of the Clearwater River (July, August).

Habits. This species shows, in common with the other chickadees, a definite tendency to wander during the late fall months. At Moscow it was not uncommon in November to see small flocks feeding in the shade trees well within the city limits, a radical departure from the thick fir woods frequented in the summer. At Lewiston it was apparently largely of accidental occurrence, for it was only during the winter of 1952-53 that small flocks were noted feeding in the deciduous underbrush on Hatwai Creek. Extreme dates of occurrence were December 21 and March 16.

In view of the fact that the range of this species is to a very large extent on the Pacific coast, where the winters are mild and characterized by heavy rainfall, it is interesting that it has adapted itself to the severe winters commonly experienced in northern Idaho. Deep snows and low temperatures, not infrequently below zero, are the rule rather than the exception, but the Chestnut-backed Chickadees would appear to be unaffected by this inhospitable weather.

Parus inornatus ridgwayi Richmond: PLAIN TITMOUSE

General Distribution. Resident from northern Nevada, southern Idaho, southern Wyoming, southern Colorado and western Oklahoma south to southeastern California, northern Arizona, central New Mexico and western Texas.

Status in Idaho. A fairly common resident in the extreme southern edge of the state.

At present the Plain Titmouse has been recorded from but two localities in Idaho, but further field work should reveal its presence from Owyhee County in the western corner of the state to Bear Lake County on the Wyoming line.

Cassia County. Reported as fairly plentiful on Goose Creek, ten miles south of Oakley, and specimens taken, by Jollie (in litt.) June 26, 1949; by Levy (1962) June 23, 1950, and August 3, 1951; and by myself November 8 and 9, 1957, and July 19 and 20, 1958.

Bannock County. Arvey (1947) found this species fairly plentiful on Pocatello Creek, three miles east of Pocatello, April 2, 1939; a specimen was taken on that date; I noted it in small numbers on Buckskin Creek June 11, 1955, and on Mink Creek June 12, 1955, and November 10 and 12, 1957.

Twelve specimens taken in southern Idaho are typical of *ridgwayi*, and are from the following localities: Cassia County, Goose Creek, males November 8 and 9, 1957; immature males July 19 and 20, 1958, females June 23, 1950, November 8, 1957; Bannock County, Pocatello, males June 11, 1955 (Buckskin Creek), and November 10 and 12, 1957 (Mink Creek), females June 12, 1955, and November 10 and 12, 1957 (Mink Creek).

Habits. In common with such species as the Ash-throated Flycatcher and the Scrub Jay, the Plain Titmouse is limited in its distribution to the juniper-covered ridges in the extreme southern part of the state. Its range therefore occupies a rather small area in Idaho, and, in view of this habitat preference, it will never be more numerous than it is at the present time. In my experience it is a rather quiet bird, and one that in most instances must be looked for to be seen. Throughout most of the year it occurs in small restless flocks; these are doubtless family groups that remain together until the nesting season.

Psaltriparus minimus plumbeus (Baird): COMMON BUSHTIT

General Distribution. Resident from southern Oregon, southern Idaho, Wyoming, western Colorado, and western Oklahoma south to southern California, northern Sonora, southern New Mexico, and central Texas.

Status in Idaho. A fairly common resident in the extreme southwestern edge of the state.

In Owyhee County the Bushtit has been reported from Oreana, specimen taken May 22, 1935 (Davis); specimen taken "S. Fork Owyhee River 12 mi. N. Nevada line" (Arvey, 1947); Marsing, several small flocks totalling thirty birds noted in Squaw Creek Canyon February 22, 1950 (Burleigh); Murphy, one small flock of three birds seen February 26, 1950 (Burleigh); Reynolds Creek, several pairs noted and nest with seven fresh eggs found June 3, 1951 (Burleigh).

In Cassia County a specimen was taken eight miles southeast of Albion December 24, 1935 (Davis), and three birds were seen on Goose Creek, ten miles south of Oakley June 6, 1957 (Burleigh).

Six specimens personally taken, and found to be typical of *plumbeus,* are as follows: males, Marsing, February 22, 1950, Murphy, February 26, 1950, Reynolds Creek, June 3, 1951, Oakley (Goose Creek), June 6, 1957; females, Marsing, February 22, Oakley (Goose Creek), June 6.

Habits. The distribution of the Bushtit in Idaho is apparently, as with the preceding species, limited to the juniper-covered ridges in the southern edge of the state. However, while it feeds in the junipers it seems to prefer the deciduous underbrush in the stream bottoms, and it is here that the small flocks are normally seen throughout much of the year. The nest found on Reynolds Creek on June 3, 1951, was five feet from the ground in a greasewood bush at the edge of the stream, and was the usual pendant structure composed of bark fiber, fragments of dead leaves, moss, plant down and spiders' webs.

While unrecorded from the eastern part of the state it is probable that in suitable habitat it occurs there, at least in small numbers.

Nuthatches: *Family Sittidae*

Sitta carolinensis tenuissima Grinnell: WHITE-BREASTED NUTHATCH

General Distribution. Resident from southern British Columbia, eastern Washington, northern Idaho and western Wyoming south to eastern California, southern Nevada, and northern Utah.

Status in Idaho. An uncommon and local resident in the forested areas of the state.

Bonner County. One bird seen August 11, 1917, at the Trestle Creek Lookout Station north of Clark Fork (Burleigh, 1923).

Kootenai County. Uncommon at Fort Sherman (Coeur d'Alene); breeds sparingly (Merrill, 1898); a "not common" resident (1910-14) "of coniferous timber" (Rust, 1915).

Shoshone County. Uncommon on the St. Joe National Forest, 1921-41, occurring in the yellow pines of the Transition Zone, and in the whitebark pines of the Hudsonian Zone (Hand, 1941).

Latah County. Fairly common; a specimen taken at Princeton November 20, 1938 (Arvey, 1947); recorded but once during the summer of 1947, a specimen being taken on June 16 twenty miles northeast of Moscow (Johnston, 1949); uncommon 1948-58, and noted at rather infrequent intervals; it was recorded on Tomer's Butte, southeast of Moscow, June 19, 1948, on Moscow Mountain October 29 and December 25, 1950, and in the city limits of Moscow October 20, 1955 (Burleigh).

Nez Perce County. Two birds seen at Lake Waha March 1, 1954, in open pine woods partway up a ridge (Burleigh).

Adams County. A female seen in an open slashing at New Meadows June 27, 1949, feeding a fully grown young bird of the year (Burleigh).

Boise County. An occasional bird noted on the Boise National Forest during the winter months (1938-40) (Marshall, 1945).

Lemhi County. Two birds seen November 1, 1949, at the head of Colson Creek, north of Shoup (Burleigh).

Custer County. A specimen taken in 1890 at Sawtooth Lake, and an occasional bird seen in the Salmon River and Lost River mountains (Merriam, 1891); two birds seen July 12, 1958 in open pine woods on the south slope of a ridge possibly halfway up Mount Borah (altitude approximately 8,500 feet) (Burleigh).

Blaine County. An occasional bird noted at Ketchum October through December, 1910 (Jewett, 1912).

Jefferson County. One bird, a fall straggler, seen on the Camas National Wildlife Refuge August 22, 1961 (Oring, 1962).

Bear Lake County. Noted "above Bloomington Lake" June 10, 1949 (Jollie, in litt.).

Ten specimens, taken at various times of the year, and over much of the state, were found to be typical of *tenuissima*. They are as follows: Kootenai County, Dudley, female October 8, 1950; Latah County, Meadow Creek, male June 16, 1947, Moscow, males October 29 and December 25, 1950, female December 31, 1950; Nez Perce County, Lake Waha, female March 1, 1954; Adams County, New Meadows, immature female June 27, 1949; Lemhi County, Shoup, two females November 1, 1949; Custer County, Mount Borah, male July, 1958.

Habits. Few birds in Idaho are more exacting in their requirements than is the White-breasted Nuthatch. In my experience it frequents only the open pine woods that characterize the southern slopes of the mountain ridges. The northern slopes, with their thick stands of spruce and fir, are consistently shunned, and while an occasional individual may venture into such an area it is so unusual that I personally never noted such an occurrence. Altitude would appear to be no factor in determining the distribution of this species, for it has been found in ponderosa pine at 2,500 feet, and at 8,500 feet in open stretches of whitebark pine; at these extremes in elevation the primary consideration, open pine woods, was apparently the controlling factor.

In common with other resident species there is a tendency to wander in the late summer and fall months, but this is not as pronounced as with the chickadees. Other than the one bird that appeared in the city limits of Moscow, there is only one additional record for the occurrence of this nuthatch at any distance from its normal haunts—the individual observed in late August on the Camas National Wildlife Refuge.

Sitta canadensis Linnaeus: RED-BREASTED NUTHATCH

General Distribution. Breeds from southeastern Alaska, southern Yukon, southern Mackenzie, northern Ontario, southern Quebec and Newfoundland south to southern California, southeastern Arizona, southern Colorado, southwestern South Dakota, central Minnesota, Wisconsin, northern Michigan, and southern New York, and in the Appalachians to eastern Tennessee and western North Carolina. Winters over much of its breeding range and south to southern Texas, and the Gulf coast.

Status in Idaho. A common resident in the forested areas of the state, although some years less numerous during the winter months.

Bonner County. Common during the summer of 1917 on the wooded ridges north of Clark Fork (Burleigh, 1923).

Kootenai County. Common in winter at Fort Sherman (Coeur d'Alene); breeds (Merrill, 1898); a common resident species at Coeur d'Alene, 1910-14 (Rust, 1915); an occasional bird seen at the upper end of Lake Coeur d'Alene July 1-10, 1943 (Yocom, 1946); noted in small numbers at Coeur d'Alene February 14 and December 16, 1950, and January 8, 1957 (Burleigh).

Benewah County. Common and widely distributed (1921-41); noted at St. Maries every month of the year; also noted at 6,000 feet and higher in midwinter (Hand, 1941).

Latah County. Common "in the forested areas" June 1-August 16, 1947 (Johnston, 1949); seen daily at Harvard during the summers of 1951 and 1952 (Verner, 1953); common and of general distribution throughout much of the year in the forested areas of the county (1947-58); noted each winter, but in varying numbers, being abundant some years, and scarce others (Burleigh).

Nez Perce County. Several birds seen in thick fir woods at Lake Waha (altitude 4,300 feet) May 27, 1949; noted once at Lewiston, on the Snake River, a single bird September 6, 1953 (Burleigh).

Clearwater County. Three birds seen at Ahsahka January 7, 1951, in fir woods at the top of a ridge; found to be fairly plentiful at Headquarters June 14 and 15, 1951, being noted daily both in the valleys and well toward the tops of the wooded ridges; an occasional bird seen here January 13, 1952, and December 25, 1956 (Burleigh).

Idaho County. Frequently seen in September, 1941, "in the Selway region"; fifteen noted September 6; common in July, 1948, "in the Lolo Pass region"; a pair seen July 8 carrying food to young in the nest (Orr, 1951).

Boise County. Noted occasionally during the winter months, 1938-40, in the Boise National Forest (Marshall, 1945); two birds seen at Bogus Basin February 23, 1950, in fir woods at the top of a ridge (altitude approximately 6,400 feet) (Burleigh).

Owyhee County. Noted in June, 1951, at De Lamar and Silver City (Levy, 1962).

Lemhi County. One taken and two others seen in 1890 "in the Salmon River Mountains near Junction" (Merriam, 1891); noted in small numbers on Colson Creek, north of Shoup, on June 5 and again on November 1, 1949 (Burleigh).

Kodachrome by Donald J. Obee, Boise, Idaho

DIPPER

PLATE VIII

Blaine County. Common in the vicinity of Ketchum October through December, 1910 (Jewett, 1912); seen at Galena in June, 1950 (Levy, 1962).

Clark County. Several noted on Signal Peak June 19 and July 14, 1961 (Oring, 1962).

Jefferson County. A "common transient" on the Camas National Wildlife Refuge August 22-29, 1961 (Oring, 1962).

Bonneville County. A fairly common summer resident at Grays Lake, 1949-51 (Steel, 1956).

Minidoka County. Reported by Davis (1935) as an irregular fall transient at Rupert, being observed from August 12 through September 7, 1919, and on September 10, 1920.

Cassia County. Noted at the City of Rocks in June, 1949 (Levy, 1962).

Habits. Although the Red-breasted Nuthatch can be considered a resident species in Idaho, its presence during the winter months is apparently dependent to a large extent on the cones of the spruce and fir that ripen in the fall. Some years these conifers have an abundant cone crop and this little nuthatch is plentiful; other years there are few or no cones, and few nuthatches are encountered during the winter months.

Unlike the White-breasted Nuthatch which uses a natural cavity for its nest, this species excavates its own cavity, usually in an old rotten stub. The average height from the ground varies from twelve to fifteen feet. A consistent habit is the smearing of pitch around the entrance of the hole, the wood for a distance of several inches around the opening being carefully covered with globules of pitch brought by both birds from the time the nest is started until the young have flown. It is possible that this is done to discourage any curiosity on the part of a squirrel, and it may save the eggs and young from molestation by this recognized enemy of cavity nesting birds.

Sitta canadensis clariterga Burleigh

This western race is distinct from *canadensis* in that the upperparts are lighter and more bluish, and lack to a large extent the grayish wash characteristic of *canadensis*. This character is clearly evident in a series of species personally taken in Idaho at various times of the year. These are as follows: Kootenai County, Coeur d'Alene, male February 14, 1950, females February 14, 1950, and January 8, 1957; Latah County, Potlatch, males January 13 and April 4, 1954, female October 2, 1949, Princeton, female December 12, 1951, Moscow, males October 22, November 17 and December 4, 1949, March 6, 1950, December 8, 1952, December 12 and 16, 1956, November 28, 1957, females January 24, 1948, November 11, 1949, November 3, 1951, immature male, July 25, 1948, July 13, 1950, immature female, August 10, 1949, August 9, 1951; Nez Perce County, Lake Waha, male April 20, 1950; Clearwater County, Headquarters, males June 15, 1951, and March 18 and December 25, 1956; Lemhi County, Shoup, males June 5 and November 1, 1949.

Additional specimens have been taken in the state as follows: Latah

County, Troy, male May 6, 1939, Paradise Ridge, male October 9, 1938 (Arvey); Shoshone County, Clarkia, female September 29, 1941; Bonner County, fifteen miles northeast of Priest River, male October 5, 1941 (A. Olson) (Jollie, in litt.).

Boise County, specimen taken eleven miles southwest of Idaho City October 20, 1946 (Arvey, 1947).

Fremont County, Sawtelle Peak, 9,500 feet (August); Custer County, Challis, Little Redfish Lake (August); Clark County, Grouse Canyon (June); Franklin County, Emigration Canyon (June) (Brodkorb).

Sitta canadensis canadensis Linnaeus

The nominate race, breeding north and east of the range of *clariterga,* is apparently of casual occurrence in Idaho during the late fall and winter months. A female taken at Moscow November 11, 1949, and a male at Coeur d'Alene December 16, 1950, were found to be typical of the breeding population of the eastern United States.

Sitta pygmaea melanotis Van Rossem: PIGMY NUTHATCH

General Distribution. Resident from southern British Columbia, northern Idaho, western Montana and southwestern South Dakota south to central California, northern Sonora, southern New Mexico and northern Coahuila.

Status in Idaho. Locally a common resident in the northern part of the state; reported from but a few localities in southern Idaho where apparently it occurs in rather limited numbers.

Kootenai County. The "most abundant resident bird" at Fort Sherman (Coeur d'Alene); occurs in flocks in winter; nests in buildings in the fort, entering through knotholes (Merrill, 1898); an abundant resident at Coeur d'Alene, 1910-14; noted nesting in telephone poles (Rust, 1915); specimens taken at Coeur d'Alene by H. Carey April 4-5, 1939 (Jollie, in litt.).

Latah County. Infrequently noted during the summer of 1947; specimens taken at Princeton June 18, and at Kendrick August 12 (Johnston, 1949); locally common 1947-58, in suitable habitat in the vicinity of Moscow, being seen throughout the year on Tomer's Butte and on Moscow Mountain; equally common in open pine woods on the Palouse River at Potlatch (Burleigh).

Lemhi County. Seen in small numbers on Colson Creek, north of Shoup, June 4-6 and October 31, 1949 (Burleigh).

A small series of eleven birds personally taken in the state were found to be typical of *melanotis,* and are as follows: Latah County, Moscow, male November 12, 1947, females November 15 and December 22, 1947, and November 8, 1948, Potlatch, males November 18 and December 31, 1949, and November 18, 1951, females January 21, 1949, and January 22, 1950; Lemhi County, Shoup, two males October 31, 1949.

Norris (1958) states that specimens of *Sitta pygmaea* are recorded from Bonner County (Coolin), Kootenai County (Coeur d'Alene), Latah County

(Moscow, Troy), Idaho County (Castle Creek Ranger Station), Adams County (New Meadows, Tamarack), Boise County (Hunter Creek, Boise National Forest), Cassia County (Albion).

Habits. The Pygmy Nuthatch is another species whose habitat requirements in Idaho are so exacting that, while locally common, it has as yet been reported from a relatively few localities in the state. Open ponderosa pine woods are apparently essential for the well-being of this little nuthatch. Elsewhere over its wide range in the western United States it accepts various species of pines, but in Idaho, in my experience, it consistently shuns even the whitebark pine, which is acceptable to the White-breasted Nuthatch. Consequently the Pygmy Nuthatch has never been recorded on the higher ridges, and is limited in its distribution to the southern slopes of the mountains between an altitude of 2,000 and 3,500 feet. Here it is resident in every sense of the word, for I have never at any time observed any tendency on the part of the small flocks to leave the areas they show such a liking for. Even in nesting this preference is noticeable. The nest cavity is excavated by the birds themselves, and while it may be in an old stub or in the dead limb of a large tree, a pine is almost invariably selected.

During the fall and early winter months pine seed is eaten as long as it is available. Otherwise small insects, their eggs and larvae, are the main sources of food of the Pygmy Nuthatch.

Creepers: *Family Certhiidae*

Certhia familiaris montana Ridgway: BROWN CREEPER

General Distribution. Breeds from southern Alaska, central British Columbia, western Alberta and central Saskatchewan south to eastern Oregon, northern Nevada, northern Arizona, southern New Mexico, and western Texas. Winters within its breeding range, and south to southern California.

Status in Idaho. A fairly common resident in the forested areas throughout the state.

Kootenai County. Abundant in winter at Fort Sherman (Coeur d'Alene); disappears in April and reappears the middle of September; noted once in the summer (Merrill, 1898); a not-common resident at Coeur d'Alene "in coniferous timber," 1910-14; one taken December 29; occasional in summer (Rust, 1915); observed at the upper end of Lake Coeur d'Alene July 1-10, 1943, apparently "rather common" (Yocom, 1946).

Shoshone County. Uncommon resident on the St. Joe National Forest; breeds in Canadian Zone, and winters at lower altitudes; seen at St. Maries (Benewah County) in winter (Hand, 1941); one breeding pair noted on a wooded ridge south of Avery June 19, 1951 (Burleigh).

Latah County. Fairly common in the forested areas June 1-August 16, 1947 (Johnston, 1949); seen occasionally at Harvard during the summers of

1951 and 1952, but not very common (Verner, 1953); fairly common throughout the year and of general distribution (1947-58) in the larger stretches of woods in the county (Burleigh).

Nez Perce County. An irregular and rather uncommon winter visitant at Lewiston, being noted on Hatwai Creek October 21, 1951, March 4 and December 24, 1953, and December 4, 1957 (Burleigh).

Clearwater County. A fairly common resident species on the wooded ridges about Headquarters (1952-58), although only infrequently noted during the winter months (Burleigh).

Idaho County. Noted several times in September, 1941, "in the Selway region"; also observed July 4, 1948, four miles southwest of Lolo Pass (Orr, 1951).

Boise County. Only infrequently observed on the Boise National Forest, single birds being seen on Swanholm Creek February 13, 1939, and on Trail Creek February 12, 1940 (Marshall, 1945).

Washington County. Noted at Weiser, in woods bordering the Weiser River, November 22, 1951, and November 15, 1957 (Burleigh).

Lemhi County. One bird seen on Cramer Creek, north of Shoup, October 31, 1949 (Burleigh).

Custer County. One specimen taken and several others seen at Sawtooth Lake in 1890 (Merriam, 1891).

Blaine County. "Not common" in the vicinity of Ketchum October through December, 1910; one taken on Rook's Creek (at an altitude of 7,500 feet) on November 3 (Jewett, 1912); one bird seen on Alder Creek, north of Ketchum, June 24, 1950, and three the following day in open woods halfway up Easley Peak (altitude approximately 9,000 feet) (Burleigh); noted at Galena June 26, 1950 (Levy, 1962).

Fremont County. Five specimens taken at Yellowstone by L. L. Sandridge in August, 1949 (Arvey, 1950).

Clark County. One bird seen on Signal Peak July 15, 1961 (Oring, 1962).

Bonneville County. An uncommon summer resident, 1949-51 (Steel, 1956).

Specimens personally taken in Idaho at various times of the year were found to represent the Rocky Mountain race *montana*. They are as follows: Kootenai County, Coeur d'Alene, female February 14, 1950; Shoshone County, Avery, male June 19, 1951; Latah County, Potlatch, males September 29, 1949, February 12, 1950, females April 12, 1951, November 22, 1956, immature female July 31, 1949; Moscow, males January 2 and 24, 1948, April 23, September 9, November 9 and 14, 1949, January 23, March 11 and 31, 1950, February 11 and December 2, 1951, September 23, 1952, December 12, 1956, females November 7, 1947, November 8, 1948, August 14 and October 22, 1949, March 1, 1950, November 8, 1951, October 14 and December 2, 1952, November 28, 1953, April 15, 1956, March 2, 1958, immature male July 23, 1948, immature female July 25, 1948, Deary, two males May 14, 1948; Nez Perce County, Lewiston, male December 4, 1957, females March 4 and December 24, 1953, January 12, 1954; Clearwater County, Headquarters, males June 27, 1951, November 7, 1952, female January 31, 1954; Washington County, Weiser, male November 22, 1951, female November 15, 1957; Blaine County, Ketchum, male June 24, 1950.

Additional specimens have been reported from: Shoshone County, St. Joe National Forest, July 3, 1937 (H. Carey); Idaho County, Lochsa River at Van Camp, November 5, 1938 (D. Arvey); Custer County, Little Redfish Lake, August (Brodkorb).

Habits. Although the Brown Creeper can be found in Idaho throughout the winter months, its appearance in late October on Hatwai Creek at Lewiston, and in November on the Weiser River at Weiser, would suggest an altitudinal migration on the part of this species. At Moscow (altitude 2,500 feet) there was no noticeable decrease in numbers seen in the late fall, nor during the winter regardless of the severity of the weather. However, creepers have been found during the summer to an altitude of 9,000 feet in the Sawtooth Mountains, and they possibly occur even higher elsewhere in the state. It is probable that this breeding population retreats to a less rigorous climate with the advent of the first cold weather.

Dippers: *Family Cinclidae*

Cinclus mexicanus unicolor Bonaparte: DIPPER

General Distribution. Resident from northern Alaska, central Yukon, central Alberta, northern Montana and southwestern South Dakota south to southern California, southeastern Arizona, and central New Mexico.

Status in Idaho. A fairly common resident in suitable habitat throughout the state.

Boundary County. One pair, feeding young in nest, seen June 25, 1957, on a small stream well toward the top of Harrison Peak, altitude approximately 6,300 feet (Burleigh).

Bonner County. Noted twice in 1917 on streams north of Clark Fork, single birds on Lightning Creek August 29, and on Trestle Creek September 12 (Burleigh, 1923); two birds, one singing, seen on Lightning Creek November 25, 1948 (Burleigh).

Kootenai County. Fairly common in the vicinity of Fort Sherman (Coeur d'Alene) (Merrill, 1898); not common, but of regular occurrence (1910-41); one noted on Fernan Creek October 25 (Rust, 1915).

Shoshone County. A common resident (1921-41) on the mountain streams in the St. Joe National Forest (Hand, 1941).

Clearwater County. One bird seen south of Orofino January 12, 1952, feeding at the edge of the Clearwater River; another observed the following day north of Pierce, feeding at the edge of open water on a small stream then largely frozen over (Burleigh).

Idaho County. Frequently noted in September, 1941, "in the Selway region," and in July, 1948, "in the Lolo Pass region"; nests with large young found July 6 and July 12 on Brushy Creek, five miles southwest of Lolo Pass (Orr, 1951).

Washington County. Noted on the Weiser River north of Council November 20, 1951 (Burleigh), and on the Little Weiser River May 17, 1958 (Newhouse, 1960).

Boise County. Fairly common resident in the Boise National Forest; none seen above 4,400 feet during the winter of 1938-39; below this altitude average occurrence was two birds per mile of stream; noted in early March, after the spring thaw, on Swanholm and Trail creeks; the following winter, with no freeze-up, noted on North Fork and on Hunter Creek (Marshall, 1945).

Owyhee County. One bird seen at Three Creek May 31, 1951 (Burleigh).

Fremont County. An adult with three well-grown young seen on the West Fork of Camas Creek July 16, 1916 (Rust, 1917).

South Central Idaho. Observed in 1890 on many of the streams in the Pahsimeroi and Sawtooth Mountains; nest found on the West Fork of the Pahsimeroi; also noted on the Snake River in October; several seen on Trail Creek and on Wood River (Merriam, 1891).

Blaine County. Common from October through December, 1910, on all the streams in the vicinity of Ketchum; singing in zero weather (Jewett, 1912); noted on Hyndman Creek June 27, 1950 (Levy, 1962).

Bonneville County. An uncommon resident, 1949-51, at Grays Lake (Steel, 1956); one bird seen on Eagle Creek, north of Gray, May 21, 1951 (Burleigh), fully grown young of the year noted on Big Elk Creek August 5, 1961 (Oring, 1962).

Specimens of the Dipper have been taken in Idaho as follows: Bonner County, Clark Fork (November) (Burleigh); Shoshone County, Quartz Creek, St. Joe National Forest (July) (H. Carey); Lemhi County, Carmen Creek (July); Blaine County, Warfield Canyon (August); Butte County, Arco Peak (September); Caribou County, Soda Springs (February) (Brodkorb); Bonneville County, Gray (May) (Burleigh), Big Elk Creek (August) (Oring).

Habits. The Dipper is a hardy bird, for it remains on its preferred swift mountain streams throughout the severest winters, retreating to lower altitudes only if the stream completely freezes over. The bird I watched near Pierce in mid-January was taking advantage of openings in the stream then almost completely frozen over, entering the water at one point and reappearing again where there was open water possibly fifty yards away. The food it was seeking under these conditions was the larvae and adults of aquatic insects, and it was securing them as it searched among the numerous small rocks covering the bottom of this stream.

The nest is a compact ball of moss with the entrance on one side, and it is either at the edge of or over the swift roaring stream that the birds frequent. Orr (1951) stated that one nest that he found near Lolo Pass was attached to the sheer face of a rock ten feet above the "deep swift-flowing water" of Brushy Creek. Another found on this same stream a few days later was attached to a log overhanging the water. While near the top of Harrison Peak in late June I watched a pair of Dippers feeding young in a nest that was on a ledge behind a waterfall on this sheer mountainside; to reach the nestlings required a quick plunge through the water that concealed the nest from view.

Wrens: *Family Troglodytidae*

Troglodytes aedon parkmanii Audubon: HOUSE WREN

General Distribution. Breeds from central British Columbia, central Alberta, southern Saskatchewan, southern Manitoba and central Ontario south to northern Baja California, southeastern Arizona, central New Mexico, central Oklahoma, northern Arkansas, and western Kentucky. Winters from the southern part of its breeding range south to southern Mexico (Oaxaca and Veracruz) and along the Gulf coast to southern Florida.

Status in Idaho. A common summer resident throughout the state.

Bonner County. Found to be common during the summer of 1917 in and about the town of Clark Fork; a brood of five fully grown young seen July 4 (Burleigh, 1923).

Kootenai County. Common "in summer" at Fort Sherman (Coeur d'Alene) (Merrill, 1898); an uncommon summer resident at Coeur d'Alene, 1910-14 (Rust, 1915); several breeding pairs noted at the upper end of Lake Coeur d'Alene July 1-10, 1943 (Yocom, 1946).

Shoshone County. A common summer resident on the St. Joe National Forest, occurring from late April to the middle of September; often noted at high altitudes (Hand, 1941).

Latah County. Common in the cutover areas, June 1-August 16, 1947 (Johnston, 1949); found to be a common breeding bird at Harvard during the summers of 1951 and 1952; two nests found on July 1, 1951, one with four eggs, and the other with four young (Verner, 1953); common and well distributed throughout the county during the summer months (1948-58), usually appearing in early May and being only infrequently seen after the middle of September (Burleigh).

Nez Perce County. A fairly common summer resident at Lewiston, 1948-58, scattered pairs nesting in the willows and cottonwoods at the edge of the Snake River (Burleigh).

Idaho County. Noted once in 1941, two birds being seen September 20 at Canteen Meadow in the Crags Mountains (Orr, 1951).

Owyhee County. One breeding pair noted at Triangle June 25, 1949 (Burleigh).

Fremont County. A nest with young found July 16 on the West Fork of Camas Creek (Rust, 1917).

Clark County. One pair found nesting in an old building at Spencer June 15, 1916 (Rust, 1917); several birds observed on Signal Peak June 19, 1961 (Oring, 1962).

Blaine County. Birds found to be fairly plentiful in the vicinity of Ketchum, June 24-28, 1950, both in the valleys and in the aspen groves on the mountainsides to an altitude of 8,000 feet (Easley Peak) (Burleigh).

South Central Idaho. Common in 1872 on the Henry Fork of the Snake River; nest found on the Middle Fork that held five young on July 20; in 1890 a nest with fully grown young was found at Blackfoot on July 10, and specimens taken that month on Big Lost River (Merriam, 1891); Levy (1950) considered this species a fairly common breeding bird in this same general area in 1949.

Jefferson County. One breeding pair noted on the Camas National Wildlife Refuge in 1961 (Oring, 1962).

Bonneville County. A common summer resident, 1949-51, at Grays Lake (Steel, 1956).

Minidoka County. Davis (1935) reported the House Wren as occurring at Rupert, but made no comments on its relative abundance there.

Cassia County. One breeding pair noted June 21, 1949, at the Silent City of Rocks north of Almo (Levy, 1950).

Specimens of the House Wren taken in various parts of Idaho were examined critically, and found to represent this western race, *parkmanii*. They came from the following localities: Latah County, Potlatch (April, May, July, September) (Burleigh), Moscow (April, May, June, July, August, September, October) (Burleigh), Troy (September) (C. Engler); Nez Perce County, Lewiston (May, July, September, October) (Burleigh); Idaho County, Riggins (May) (Arvey); Boise County, Bogus Basin (July) (Brodkorb); Owyhee County, Florida Mountain (June) (Bordkorb); Custer County, Mackay (September) (Brodkorb); Blaine County, Ketchum (July), Sun Valley (July) (Burleigh); Fremont County, Targhee National Forest (July) (Brodkorb); Jefferson County, Rigby (May) (Brodkorb); Teton County, Horseshoe Creek, Big Hole Mountains (August), Victor (August) (Brodkorb); Bonneville County, Caribou National Forest (July) (Brodkorb); Caribou County, The Narrows, Blackfoot River (June) (Brodkorb); Franklin County, Emigration Canyon (June) (Brodkorb); Bear Lake County, Snowdrift Mountains, Preuss Range (June) (Brodkorb); Cassia County, Malta (September) (Brodkorb).

Habits. Although the House Wren frequently appears in the spring in Idaho in late April, it is influenced to some extent then by weather conditions, and it is just as often early May before the first individual is seen. In 1955 it was May 13 before one bird was noted for the first time at Moscow, but as that day was characterized by a steady light snowfall the one bird seen could possibly be considered an early and hardy migrant! At Potlatch my extreme dates of occurrence are April 29 (1953) and September 24

(1952), at Moscow April 26 (1952) and October 5 (1951), and at Lewiston May 4 (1957) and October 8 (1956). Davis (1935) gives April 29, 1920, as an arrival date at Rupert, and Steel (1956) June 4, 1950, and May 27, 1951, as the dates on which this species was first observed in the spring at Grays Lake.

The House Wren originally nested in natural cavities and old woodpecker holes, and over much of Idaho it still rears its young as its forebears did. However, it willingly accepts the proximity of man, and takes advantage of nesting sites that barns and unoccupied buildings furnish. Rust (1917) states that a nest found at Spencer in 1916, in Clark County, was in an old building. Verner (1953) records two nests found at Harvard in 1951 under similar conditions. One was under the eaves of a building, the other on a window ledge.

Royall and Pillmore (1968) give an interesting account of a male House Wren that, over an interval of a week (July 11 through July 18, 1967,) carried food to three young flickers. The woodpecker's nest (in the Sawtooth National Forest in Camas County) was in an aspen snag, while fifteen inches directly above it was the wren's nest. The time and frequency of feeding the young flickers varied considerably each day, but on July 12 the wren fed these nestlings sixty-two times in 124 minutes of observation.

Troglodytes troglodytes salebrosus Burleigh: WINTER WREN

General Distribution. Breeds in southern British Columbia east of the coast ranges, southwestern Alberta, northern Washington east of the Cascades, Idaho, northeastern Oregon and western Montana west of the Continental Divide. Winters at lower altitudes at the southern edge of its breeding range, and casually farther south.

Status in Idaho. A fairly common summer resident in the northern half of the state; winters in small numbers where conditions are suitable; reported during the summer from one locality in south-central Idaho.

Boundary County. One bird seen in a wooded ravine at Bonners Ferry November 23, 1948 (Burleigh).

Bonner County. Singing males noted during the summer of 1917 in thick woods on Lightning Creek, north of Clark Fork (Burleigh, 1923); one bird seen at Sandpoint November 26, 1948 (Burleigh).

Kootenai County. A common "resident" at Fort Sherman (Coeur d'Alene) (Merrill, 1898); fairly common, 1910-14, "in coniferous timber" (Rust, 1915).

Shoshone County. A fairly common summer resident, 1921-41, "in Canadian Zone forests" on the St. Joe National Forest; frequently noted in winter (Hand, 1941); fairly plentiful June 20-21, 1951, on the wooded ridges south of Avery (Burleigh).

Latah County. Common in the "densely forested regions" June 1-August 16, 1947 (Johnston, 1949); noted at Harvard April 13, 1952, and at intervals during the following summer (Verner, 1953); a fairly common summer resident, 1947-58, in the wooded ravines on the mountainsides; noted at infrequent intervals during the winter (Burleigh).

Nez Perce County. One record, a single bird being seen December 24, 1953, on Hatwai Creek, east of Lewiston (Burleigh).

Clearwater County. A fairly common summer resident, 1951-58, on the thickly wooded ridges in the vicinity of Headquarters, appearing in the spring the middle of April, and being present then until the middle of November (Burleigh).

Boise County. Noted on Hunter Creek, on the Boise National Forest, February 5 and 14, 1939 (Marshall, 1945).

Idaho County. A specimen taken September 21, 1941, four miles southwest of Selway Falls; found to be a common "resident" in July, 1948, in the Lolo Pass region; noted from 4,000 to 7,000 feet; nest with four small young found July 24, five miles southwest of Lolo Pass (Orr, 1951).

Blaine County. One bird seen October 1, 1890, in the Sawtooth Mountains (Merriam, 1891).

Clark County. Several seen on Three Mile Creek, at the base of Signal Peak, July 15, 1961 (Oring, 1962).

Bannock County. Noted on Pocatello Creek, near Pocatello, May 2, 1961 (Fichter, in litt.).

Salebrosus is similar to *Troglodytes troglodytes pacificus* but decidedly darker, both above and below (Burleigh, 1959). Specimens taken in the northern part of Idaho were examined critically, and were found to have the characteristics distinguishing this northern Rocky Mountain race. They are as follows: Boundary County, Bonners Ferry, female November 23, 1948; Bonner County, Priest Lake, male October 2, 1897, Hope, immature female June 13, 1903, Sandpoint, female November 26, 1948; Shoshone County, Avery, male June 20, 1951, Dismal Lake, male June 21, 1951; Latah County, Moscow, males October 6, 1948, October 27, 1950, March 26 and September 29, 1952, April 10 and October 4, 1954, March 7 and November 2, 1957, females October 25, 1951, October 19, 1953, April 17, 1954, May 2 and October 13, 1955, immature female September 7, 1956, Deary (Flat Creek), males May 7 and November 13, 1948, December 13, 1951, females May 7, 1948, December 13, 1951, Harvard, immature male June 30, 1953; Clearwater County, Headquarters, males June 14, October 27 and November 11, 1951, females November 7, 1952, April 21, 1953.

Additional specimens have been taken in Shoshone County, Quartz Creek, St. Joe National Forest, July 24, 1937 (H. Carey), and Clarkia September 29, 1941 (A. Olson); Benewah County, St. Maries, April 17, 1942 (A. Olson) (Jollie, in litt.); Idaho County, Lochsa River, at Van Camp, November 5, 1939 (Arvey, 1947).

Habits. Despite its diminutive size the Winter Wren is a hardy bird, small numbers successfully surviving the severe winters that normally characterize northern Idaho. On Flat Creek, east of Deary, I saw an occasional bird on December 13, 1947, and again on December 13, 1951, when the snow was a foot deep on the ground, and the temperature was well below freezing. At Headquarters, in Clearwater County, at an altitude of 3,000 feet, I never observed it later in the fall than November 11 (1951), and my earliest record in the spring is April 18 (1954). On this latter date the ground in the thick fir woods was still covered with the deep drifts of snow that usually persist until early May.

The nest of this little wren is a ball of green moss intermixed with fine twigs, the entrance being on the side. It is usually on or near the ground, and the site given preference is in the upturned roots of a fallen tree. Orr (1951) states that the nest found in 1948 five miles southwest of Lolo Pass was "beneath the exposed roots of a blueberry bush on a road bank."

Telmatodytes palustris (Wilson): LONG-BILLED MARSH WREN

General Distribution. Central British Columbia, northern Alberta, southern Saskatchewan, southern Manitoba, southern Ontario and southern Quebec south to northern Baja California, southern Mexico, the Gulf coast and southern Florida.

Status in Idaho. A scarce fall transient in the northern part of the state, and a common but local summer resident in southern Idaho.

Kootenai County. Rare in the fall in the marshes on Lake Coeur d'Alene (Merrill, 1898); a single bird noted October 6, 1951, in open marsh bordering Lake Coeur d'Alene (Burleigh).

Benewah County. Noted in open marsh at St. Maries October 3 and 4, 1936 (Hand, 1941).

Nez Perce County. An uncommon but regular fall transient at the reservoir at Lewiston Orchards, frequenting cattails in the marshy areas at the edge of the open water; in 1954, and again in 1955, it lingered until after the middle of January, but as it has never been recorded in February its status as a winter resident is open to question (Burleigh).

Jefferson County. An "abundant" summer resident in 1961 on the Camas National Wildlife Refuge (Oring, 1962).

Bonneville County. An abundant summer resident, 1949-51, at Grays Lake; arrival dates in the spring April 20, 1950, and May 14, 1951 (Steel, 1956).

Minidoka County. A common summer resident at Rupert (1919-21); extreme dates of occurrence March 13 and October 2; earliest date for fresh eggs May 20 (Davis, 1935).

Jerome County. Common in early October, 1890, at Shoshone Falls (Merriam, 1891).

Twin Falls County. A breeding colony noted at Greene's Trout Farm, east of Twin Falls, August 1, 1949 (Levy, 1950).

Cassia County. Found to be fairly plentiful at Burley April 24, 1954, in cattail marshes at the edge of the Snake River; males singing throughout the morning; an occasional bird noted in this same area November 13, 1957 (Burleigh).

Habits. The status of the Long-billed Marsh Wren in northern Idaho presents an interesting problem. Within its rather extensive breeding range it can normally be found wherever there is suitable habitat—cattail marshes bordering stretches of open water. Such areas exist in many localities in the northern part of the state, notably along the Palouse River at Potlatch, and on Lake Coeur d'Alene, but for some reason they are consistently ignored by these wrens during the summer months. These marshes would appear to be suitable in every way for breeding colonies, but even in migration only an occasional bird has been noted in the fall.

At the reservoir east of Lewiston Orchards this species usually appears each fall in early October and lingers until late December or early January. A rather unexpected record was the appearance of one bird, in immature plumage, on August 28, 1958. Otherwise my earliest date of arrival is October 1 (1955). I have two records for January, seeing single birds January 13, 1954, and January 28, 1955.

Telmatodytes palustris pulverius Aldrich

This race is the breeding Long-billed Marsh Wren of the northwestern portion of the Great Basin region, occurring from east-central Washington south to northeastern California. It is characterized as being the dullest colored of all the interior forms of this widely distributed species, being relatively pale, with rufescence at a minimum. Specimens of *pulverius* personally taken, and with one exception from northern Idaho, are as follows: Kootenai County, Coeur d'Alene, female October 6, 1951; Nez Perce County, Lewiston Orchards, males October 6 and 16 and December 1, 1953, January 28, 1955, October 28, November 11, and December 19, 1956, November 21, 1957, immature male August 28, 1958; Cassia County, Burley, male November 13, 1957.

Telmatodytes palustris plesius (Oberholser)

Plesius is the race of the Long-billed Marsh Wren breeding throughout the Rocky Mountain region; it occurs as a common but rather local summer resident in southern Idaho. Two specimens I took at Grays Lake, males on June 10, 1949, and two at Burley, males on April 24, 1954, are typical of *plesius*.

Additional specimens now in the Denver Museum of Natural History in Colorado have been taken by Brodkorb as follows: Jefferson County, Mud Lake (May, October); Bear Lake County, Montpelier (May), Turnpike (May), Fish Haven (May); Twin Falls County, Hagerman (July).

Catherpes mexicanus griseus Aldrich: CANON WREN

General Distribution. Resident in eastern Washington, eastern Oregon, and Idaho.

Status in Idaho. A fairly common resident in the southwestern part of the state, and along the Snake River as far north as Nez Perce County.

The actual distribution of the Cañon Wren in Idaho is imperfectly known, for much of the state where it doubtless occurs is so inaccessible that no field work has been carried on there. This is true of much of the Snake River from Weiser to Lewiston, and also of the Wilderness Area lying between the Snake and the Salmon rivers in the central part of the state. Where there are canyons with suitable nesting sites this wren should be found, so in spite of the few records for the occurrence of this species in Idaho it probably is well distributed and not uncommon.

Latah County. One bird, heard singing by Lowell Adams in the city limits of Moscow July 7, 1947 (Johnston, 1949); another "woke me early one morning (January 26, 1955) singing on my windowsill in Moscow" (Verner, in litt.).

Nez Perce County. Birds resident and fairly common at Lewiston, 1948-58, frequenting the low cliffs and rocky slopes on the ridges fronting both the Clearwater and the Snake rivers (Burleigh).

Idaho County. Specimen taken by Arvey (1947) four miles northwest of Pollock July 15, 1940.

Owyhee County. Birds found to be fairly plentiful in 1950 south of Homedale, being seen on February 22 in Sage Creek Canyon (one bird), and on February 24 in Poison Creek Canyon (two birds) and Jump Creek Canyon (four birds) (Burleigh).

Jerome County. Noted early in October, 1890, on the Snake River near Shoshone Falls (Merriam, 1891).

Twin Falls County. Specimen taken in August by Brodkorb (in litt.) in "the Salmon Falls Creek Canyon."

A comparison of specimens personally taken in Idaho with a comparable series from the range of *conspersus,* the race having a wide distribution in the Rocky Mountain region, showed that *griseus* is a valid race, easily distinguished by its grayish upperparts and darker underparts. Specimens from Idaho critically examined in this connection are as follows: Nez Perce County, Lewiston, males July 16 and November 1, 1948, March 12, 1958; Owyhee County, Homedale, males February 22 and 24, 1950.

Habits. Elsewhere in its extensive range in the western United States the Cañon Wren is becoming a familiar bird in the cities and larger towns, and in view of its appearance on two occasions in Moscow it is not improbable that eventually this may be the case in Idaho. At the present time, however, it is limited in its distribution to rocky canyons and the cliffs that characterize the mesas in the southern part of the state. Here it finds a congenial home which throughout the year offers it the environment it prefers, and which it leaves only on rare occasions for any length of time.

Salpinctes obsoletus obsoletus (Say): ROCK WREN

General Distribution. Breeds from southern British Columbia, southern Alberta, southwestern Saskatchewan, and western North Dakota south, east of the coast ranges, to southern Baja California and central Mexico

(Zacatecas and San Luis Potosi). Winters north to northern California, Idaho, southern Utah, northern New Mexico and southern Texas.

Status in Idaho. A fairly common summer resident in suitable habitat throughout the state; recorded in winter at Moscow and at Lewiston.

Kootenai County. One pair, "nesting," seen July 2 on Mica Peak (Merrill, 1898).

Shoshone County. A common summer resident (1921-41) on the St. Joe National Forest, occurring from mid-June until early September "on high open ridge tops" (Hand, 1941); observed by Levy "during the summer" on Grassy and Cougar peaks, north of Kingston (Jollie, in litt.).

Benewah County. Two birds noted June 4, 1936, on the outskirts of St. Maries; seen almost daily until early July "in a brushy cutover timber tract"; one noted June 13 singing "atop a piece of piling on the edge of the mill-pond" (Hand, 1937).

Latah County. Observed during the summer of 1947 on East Moscow Mountain and on Paradise Ridge; adults seen carrying food (Johnston, 1949); noted at the top of Tomer's Butte June 28, 1953, and a single bird in the city limits of Moscow from early January until March 27, 1955 (Burleigh).

Nez Perce County. Fairly plentiful at Lewiston and to a large extent resident, on the rocky slopes at the edge of the Clearwater and Snake Rivers; frequently noted there during the winter months (November through January).

Valley County. Two birds seen September 11, 1958, on an open ridge north of McCall (Burleigh).

Washington County. One bird seen June 6, 1952, on a rocky slope at the top of Cuddy Mountain (altitude 7,600 feet) (Burleigh).

Owyhee County. Common at Riddle May 28 through June 3, 1934 (Davis, 1934); several birds noted in Sage Creek Canyon, south of Homedale, February 22, 1950 (Burleigh).

Fremont County. Several seen July 31, 1916, in Little Dry Creek Canyon (Rust, 1917).

Jefferson County. Common in the vicinity of Hamer during the summer of 1961; "about" ten pairs recorded there; an adult female collected July 23 (Oring, 1962).

Bonneville County. A fairly common summer resident, 1949-51, at Grays Lake (Steel, 1956) .

Caribou County. Noted at Soda Springs May 25, 1951 (Burleigh).

South Central Idaho. Common in 1890 "on the rocky summits of most of the mountains visited"; seen on the Snake River in October (Merriam, 1891); a common breeding bird in 1949 in this same general area, occurring "in rocky canyons and outcrops" (Levy, 1950).

Minidoka County. Noted at Rupert May 19 and 27, 1921 (Davis, 1935).

Cassia County. One pair seen on an open rocky ridge north of Almo (altitude 6,800 feet) June 19, 1949; found to be fairly plentiful on Goose

Creek, south of Oakley, June 23, 1950; singing males noted at intervals during the morning (Burleigh).

Specimens verifying the occurrence of this species in Idaho were taken as follows: Nez Perce County, Juliaetta, July 28, 1938 (C. Engler), Lewiston, males November 1, 1948, December 28, 1951, December 1, 1954, females November 11 and 18, 1948, January 1, 1951 (Burleigh); Valley County, McCall, male September 11, 1958 (Burleigh); Washington County, Cuddy Mountain (7,600 feet), male June 6, 1952 (Burleigh); Canyon County, Caldwell (April) (Brodkorb); Ada County, Boise, June 24, 1941 (Arvey); Owyhee County, Mary's Creek, eight miles east of Riddle, June 17, 1949 (Jollie), Duck Valley, June (Brodkorb); Custer County, Mackay Dam (August), Crow's Nest (September) (Brodkorb); Blaine County, Hailey, June 27, 1939 (Arvey); Clark County, Small (June) (Brodkorb); Jefferson County, Hamer, female July 23, 1961 (Oring); Teton County, Big Hole Mountains (August) (Brodkorb); Butte County, Whiz Canyon (September) (Brodkorb); Caribou County, Soda Springs, male May 25, 1951 (Burleigh); Power County, Massacre Rock, male June 21, 1960 (Burleigh); Jerome County, Eden, two males, one female June 16, 1960 (Burleigh); Twin Falls County, Salmon Falls Creek (July, August) (Brodkorb).

Habits. The actual status of the Rock Wren over much of the state is probably that of a summer resident, although it may occur occasionally in winter in southern Idaho. Birds seen south of Homedale in Owyhee County, in late February, were rather early for spring transients, so it would appear that this species winters, at least in small numbers, in this southwestern corner of the state. Bent (1948) cites April 22 as an arrival date at Pocatello; at Twin Falls I noted a single bird on a rocky slope at the edge of the Snake River April 15, 1964.

Unlike the Cañon Wren, the Rock Wren shows no interest in the inducements that man might offer. As its name implies, rocky slopes offer it the environment it demands, and it is in such a site, regardless of altitude, that it can be found over much of Idaho. The nest is built in most instances in a crevice in the rocks, and almost without exception the entrance is lined with small flat stones.

Mockingbirds and Thrashers: *Family Mimidae*

Mimus polyglottos leucopterus (Vigors): MOCKINGBIRD

General Distribution. Largely resident from southern Oregon, northern Nevada, northern Utah, southeastern Wyoming and southwestern South Dakota south to southern Baja California, southern Mexico (Oaxaca), and the Gulf coast of Texas.

Status in Idaho. Apparently of accidental occurrence in the southern part of the state.

There are three records for the occurrence of the Mockingbird in Idaho. One was seen at the south end of Grays Lake July 11, 1949, and a male was collected December 31, 1950, in an orchard at Lake Lowell, four miles northeast of Marsing, in Canyon County (Jollie, 1951). One bird was seen at and near Horse Heaven Pass, Custer County, May 31 and June 1, 1961 (Fichter, in litt.).

Habits. In recent years this familiar bird has been gradually extending its range northward, and it is possible that eventually it may occur regularly in at least the southern part of Idaho. There are now records for British Columbia, Alberta, and Saskatchewan, and while they are relatively few in number they indicate a definite movement north of the normal breeding range.

Dumetella carolinensis ruficrissa Aldrich: Catbird

General Distribution. Breeds from southwestern British Columbia, Montana and northern North Dakota south to northern Oregon, eastern Arizona, and northern New Mexico. Winters, as far as now known, in the West Indies.

Status in Idaho. A common and well-distributed summer resident in the northern part of the state; fairly common but rather local in its distribution in southern Idaho.

Boundary County. Birds found to be fairly plentiful at Porthill June 26, 1957 (Burleigh).

Bonner County. Found to be a fairly plentiful summer resident in 1917 in thickets and underbrush in the vicinity of Clark Fork (Burleigh, 1923); fairly plentiful June 21, 1957, at Sandpoint, in deciduous underbrush bordering the streams (Burleigh).

Kootenai County. Common in summer at Fort Sherman (Coeur d'Alene) (Merrill, 1898); a "not common" summer resident, 1910-14, at Coeur d'Alene; young able to fly seen July 10 (Rust, 1915); one pair noted at the upper end of Lake Coeur d'Alene July 1-10, 1943 (Yocom, 1946); two pairs seen July 4, 1949, in alders bordering Lake Coeur d'Alene (Burleigh).

Shoshone County. Several birds seen in Mullan June 30, 1950, in alder thickets at the edge of a stream (Burleigh).

Benewah County. A common summer resident at St. Maries, 1921-41, from late May through September, being found in underbrush along the streams (Hand, 1941).

Latah County. Noted in small numbers, June 1-August 16, 1947, along the streams (Johnston, 1949); a common summer resident (1951-52) at Harvard; young seen August 8, 1952 (Verner, 1953); found to be a common and well distributed summer resident throughout the county (1948-58), occurring from the middle of May until the latter part of September (Burleigh).

Nez Perce County. Lewiston, an extremely scarce summer resident; one definite breeding record, three young of the year seen July 28, 1953, with the two adult birds, in underbrush at the edge of the Snake River; noted in small numbers on Hatwai Creek in late August and early September. Culdesac, several birds seen June 30, 1949, in alders fringing a stream. Lapwai, birds found to be fairly plentiful here July 12, 1950, being frequently seen in thickets and stretches of underbrush (Burleigh).

Clearwater County. Noted in small numbers at Orofino June 12, 1951, at Weippe June 13, 1951, at Elk River June 25, 1951, and at Headquarters June 9, 1952 (Burleigh).

Lewis County. One breeding pair noted at Nez Perce June 20, 1952 (Burleigh).

Idaho County. A single bird seen September 8, 1941, two miles southeast of Selway Falls (Orr, 1951).

Adams County. Several birds noted at Council June 5, 1951 (Burleigh); common at Council from late May through September 5, 1958 (Newhouse, 1960).

Washington County. Three birds seen at Weiser June 26, 1949, in alders fringing a stream (Burleigh).

Ada County. One bird seen in "the Boise river bottoms" August 1, 1909; the only record; apparently rare here (Wyman, 1911); two birds seen at Boise July 15, 1960, the female was collected, and found to have a conspicuous brood patch (Burleigh).

Common in the Snake River Valley from Nampa east to Pocatello, and in the foothills north of Boise (Jewett, 1912).

Custer County. Birds found to be fairly plentiful at Challis July 6, 1960, being frequently seen in underbrush at the edge of the Salmon River; a single bird seen at Mackay July 7, 1960, in alders fringing the Big Lost River (Burleigh).

Blaine County. Noted at Ketchum June 24, 1950, in underbrush at the edge of the Big Wood River (Burleigh).

Fremont County. Several pairs noted in late June, 1916, in willow thickets on Little Dry Creek (Rust, 1917).

Clark County. Several birds seen June 19 and July 15, 1961, at the foot of Signal Peak (Oring, 1962).

Jefferson County. Noted near Hamer August 22 and 24, and on the Camas National Wildlife Refuge August 28, 1961 (Oring, 1962).

Bonneville County. A fairly common summer resident at Grays Lake, 1949-51 (Steel, 1956); an occasional pair noted at Gray June 11 and 12, 1949, in the stream bottoms, and about thickets on the open ridges to an altitude of approximately 6,600 feet (Burleigh); "large numbers" seen on Big Elk Creek August 5, 1961 (Oring, 1962).

Bannock County. Birds found to be fairly plentiful at Pocatello June 10, 1955 (Burleigh).

Power County. A single bird seen at Massacre Rocks June 21, 1960, in dense underbrush at the edge of a stream (Burleigh).

South Central Idaho. A few seen on the Snake River, near Blackfoot, and in Cedar Creek Canyon (in the foothills of the Blackfoot Mountains) in early July, 1890; two specimens taken; one seen on Big Lost River fifteen miles below Arco in late July (Merriam, 1891); found to be fairly common in south-central Idaho during the summers of 1950 and 1951, frequenting "brush and thickets along water courses" (Levy, 1962).

Cassia County. A singing male noted at Burley June 9-11, 1960, in underbrush at the edge of the Snake River (Burleigh).

Although as yet not recognized by the A. O. U. Committee on Nomenclature, *ruficrissa* is a valid race that should be accepted by taxonomists. The chief characters as given in the original description are the paler underparts and lighter crissum. The latter is not a good character, there being considerable variation in individual specimens, the crissum of some being noticeably paler, while in others it is indistinguishable from examples of the eastern population, *carolinensis*. The upper parts of *ruficrissa* however are paler, more gray, and lacking the brown wash characteristic of *carolinensis*, and the pileum is dull black, in contrast to the deep black of *carolinensis*.

Specimens, personally collected throughout the state, were critically examined in determining the validity of this western race of the Catbird. They were taken at the following localities: Bonner County, Sandpoint; Kootenai County, Coeur d'Alene; Benewah County, St. Maries, Plummer; Shoshone County, Mullan, Clarkia; Latah County, Moscow, Potlatch, Viola, Bovill, Troy, Kendrick; Nez Perce County, Lewiston, Lapwai; Clearwater County, Elk River, Headquarters, Weippe, Orofino; Lewis County, Nezerce; Adams County, Council; Washington County, Weiser; Ada County, Boise; Custer County, Challis, Mackay; Bonneville County, Gray; Caribou County, two miles west of Freedom, Wyoming; Bannock County, Pocatello; Cassia County, Burley.

Habits. The Catbird is one of the last birds found in Idaho in the spring, frequently not being seen until the later part of May, and never being of more than casual occurrence until the end of the month. At Potlatch my extreme dates of occurrence are May 21 (1948) and September 25 (1955), at Moscow May 16 (1949) and September 26 (1955). At Lewiston, although there was suitable habitat along both the Snake and the Clearwater rivers, it was extremely scarce during the summer months, but it was a fairly plentiful transient in the fall. Apparently late August sees the height of the fall migration, for on August 26, 1958 this species was found to be fairly plentiful on Hatwai Creek, being seen frequently that morning in thickets and underbrush bordering the stream. Newhouse (1960) gives May 28 as the date of arrival at Council in 1958. At Gray, altitude 6,300 feet, I saw a single bird, possibly because of the date an early spring transient, on May 27, 1951.

[**Toxostoma rufum** (Linnaeus): Brown Thrasher]

General Distribution. Breeds from southern Alberta east across the continent to southern Maine, south through central Montana, eastern Wyoming, eastern Colorado, and eastern Texas, to the Gulf coast and southern Florida. Winters north to eastern Oklahoma, southern Tennessee, and southern Maryland.

Status in Idaho. Of accidental occurrence in the southern part of the state.

There is one sight record for this species in Idaho: Wilbur (1965) states that a Brown Thrasher was seen on the Minidoka National Wildlife Refuge near Rupert in 1963. "It was first seen September 4 by Robert G. Nelson, then manager of the refuge, who tentatively identified it as this species. I went to the area on the following day and confirmed his observation. It was still present on September 9."

Habits. In view of the fact that the Brown Thrasher is of regular occurrence during the summer months in southern Alberta, it possibly is more common in Idaho than this one record would indicate. Frequenting thickets and underbrush as it does, it could be overlooked during the early fall months when vegetation has reached its maximum density, affording optimum concealment for a species such as this.

Oreoscoptes montanus (Townsend): Sage Thrasher

General Distribution. Breeds from central British Columbia, southern Idaho, southern Montana and southeastern Wyoming south to southern California, southern Nevada, Utah, northern New Mexico, and northwestern Texas. Winters over much of its breeding range and south to southern Baja California and northern Mexico (Sonora, Chihuahua and Tamaulipas).

Status in Idaho. A common summer resident in the southern part of the state.

In northern Idaho it occurs only as a scarce transient, there being no suitable habitat to induce it to remain during the summer months. Here the Sage Thrasher has been recorded only in Nez Perce County where it has been noted on two occasions at Lewiston. I saw one bird September 1, 1949, and two May 8, 1953; a female was collected in each instance.

Farther south in the state it is found as a breeding bird as far north as Idaho County, but it is common and of general distribution only in the extensive sagebrush plains south of the mountains.

It has been recorded in Washington County, three seen at Council "during most of August," 1958 (Newhouse, 1960); Owyhee County, found to be a common breeding bird at Riddle May 28-June 3, 1934 (Davis, 1934); fairly plentiful and frequently noted at Triangle June 25, 1949 (Burleigh); Custer County, noted in sagebrush at Willow Creek Summit (altitude approximately 7,200 feet) May 25, 1952 (Burleigh); Clark County, a common summer resident in 1916 in the vicinity of Spencer, where a nest with four eggs was found June 19 (Rust, 1917); Jefferson County, common on the Camas National Wildlife Refuge June 6 through August 29, 1961 (Oring, 1962); Bonneville County, a fairly common summer resident at Grays Lake, 1949-51 (Steel, 1956); Bannock County, noted in sagebrush at Pebble June 8, 1949, a male collected (Burleigh); south-central Idaho, common in 1890 "throughout the sage-covered plains and valleys"; specimens taken at Junction, in the Lemhi Valley, and in Birch Creek Valley on September 7 (Merriam, 1891); a common breeding bird in 1949 "on sagebrush plains" in south-central Idaho (Levy, 1950); Minidoka County, abundant in the county in 1907, but scarce and rarely seen by 1913 (Kenagy, 1914); a common summer resident at Rupert, 1919-21; fresh eggs June 4 (Davis, 1935).

Specimens, now in the Denver Museum of Natural History in Colorado, have been taken by Brodkorb as follows: Custer County, Mount McCaleb (September); Clark County, Grouse Canyon (June), Birch Creek (June); Jefferson County, Mud Lake (May); Butte County, Deadman Canyon (September); Caribou County, Soda Springs (May); Oneida County, Malad City (April); Jerome County, Jerome (August); Twin Falls County, Rogerson (July); Cassia County, Oakley (August), Malta (September).

Habits. Although the Sage Thrasher occurs during the summer months well north of Idaho, it is a scarce transient only in the northern part of the state. This is due to its rather exacting requirements. As its name implies its distribution is limited to areas where the sagebrush predominates; where there is no sagebrush there are no Sage Thrashers. It is apparently a summer resident only in southern Idaho, for there are no records for the winter months. Davis (1935) gives as extreme dates of occurrence for Rupert (1919-21) April 11 and September 20. Bent (1948) cites March 31 as an early date of arrival at Rupert, and September 21 as a late date of departure at Meridian.

Thrushes, Solitaires, and Bluebirds: Family Turdidae

Turdus migratorius Linneaus: ROBIN

General Distribution. Breeds from the limit of trees in northern Alaska, northern Canada, and Newfoundland south to southern Mexico and the Gulf of Mexico. Winters south to Baja California, Guatemala, and southern Florida.

Status in Idaho. A common summer resident throughout the state. Recorded during the winter months in Kootenai County (Coeur d'Alene), Benewah County (St. Maries), Latah County (Moscow, Genesee), and Nez Perce County (Lewiston).

The Robin is unquestionably the most common and most widely distributed bird in Idaho. It shuns the thicker stretches of woods, and only in migration will it be found in the open, sparsely-vegetated desert country of the southern part of the state; otherwise it can be encountered during the summer months from the cottonwood groves on the Snake River to the fir woods on the higher ridges, to an altitude of 10,000 feet or more. It has benefited by the settlement of the state, and is now a common bird in the towns and larger cities that have replaced the original wilderness.

Bonner County. A common summer resident in 1917 in and about Clark Fork; noted about the Trestle Creek Lookout Station in August (Burleigh, 1923).

Kootenai County. Arrives at Fort Sherman (Coeur d'Alene) the last week in February; abundant during the summer (Merrill, 1898); an abundant summer resident at Coeur d'Alene 1910-14; a few in mild winters; earliest in spring February 11; "fall migration in October" (Rust, 1915); common at the upper end of Lake Coeur d'Alene July 1-10, 1943 (Yocom, 1946); an occasional small flock noted in the open prairie at Hauser February 21, 1953 (Burleigh).

Shoshone County. An abundant summer resident on the St. Joe National Forest (1921-41), from the valleys "to 6,500 feet or higher"; winters regularly "but in varying numbers" (Hand, 1941).

Latah County. Common and well distributed June 1-August 16, 1947 (Johnston, 1949); a very common breeding bird at Harvard 1951-52 (Verner, 1953); a common summer resident and of general distribution throughout the county (1947-58); winters regularly at Moscow, but there were years when it was unusually plentiful, and others when only a few scattered flocks were seen (Burleigh).

Nez Perce County. A common resident species at Lewiston, 1947-58; numerous flocks usually present each winter (Burleigh).

Clearwater County. A fairly common summer resident at Headquarters (1952-58); extreme dates of occurrence February 28 (1954) and October 17 (1955); a flock of possibly one hundred birds noted April 21, 1953, and another of possibly sixty April 18, 1954; a common summer resident at Weippe (1952-58), usually appearing the latter part of February and being rarely seen after the end of October; noted in the spring as early as February 8, 1954 (a flock of forty birds), and as late in the fall as December 10, 1952 (a flock of thirty birds).

Idaho County. Abundant in September, 1941, in "the Selway area," and in July, 1948, in "the Lolo Pass Region" (Orr, 1951).

Valley County. Birds found to be fairly plentiful at McCall April 12, 1958, although at this altitude, 5,000 feet, the ground was still covered with fully three feet of hard snow. A single bird noted at McCall March 19, 1967 (Burleigh).

Adams County. Common "most of the year" (1958) at Council; none seen from November through January; large flocks noted in March, April, and October (Newhouse, 1960).

Washington County. One small flock of twelve birds seen at Cambridge November 21, 1951, in woods bordering the Weiser River (Burleigh).

Owyhee County. Common at Riddle May 28-June 3, 1934; young of the year seen (Davis, 1934); a few small scattered flocks noted at Homedale February 20-26, 1950 (Burleigh).

Lemhi County. Birds found to be fairly plentiful June 4-6, 1949, in the open pine woods covering the mountain slopes north of Shoup (Burleigh).

Fremont County. Common in the summer of 1916; nest with three eggs found June 11 on Little Dry Creek (Rust, 1917).

Clark County. Common on Signal Peak June 19 and July 15, 1961 (Oring, 1962).

Jefferson County. "Small groups" seen on the Camas National Wildlife Refuge July 26 and 29, 1961 (Oring, 1962).

Bonneville County. A common summer resident at Grays Lake, 1949-51; in 1950 first noted in the spring on April 5 (Steel, 1956); found to be common at Grays Lake June 8-17, 1949, being seen daily from the willows at the edge of the lake (6,400 feet) to the top of Caribou Mountain (9,800 feet) (Burleigh); common at Big Elk Creek August 6, 1961 (Oring, 1962).

Blaine County. Noted in the vicinity of Ketchum October 27, 1910 (Jewett, 1912); an occasional bird seen April 14, 1964, in the open valley between Ketchum and Sun Valley (6,000 feet) (Burleigh).

South Central Idaho. "Tolerably common" in July 1890, along the Snake River, near Blackfoot, in the Lost River Mountains, and on Big Lost River; noted in small numbers in August and September in the Lemhi and Birch Creek Valleys, and in the Wood River Valley; a small flock seen in late September at Sawtooth Lake (Merriam, 1891); a common breeding bird in south-central Idaho in 1949; noted in river bottoms and on farms (Levy, 1950).

Minidoka County. Rare in 1909; common in 1913 (Kenagy, 1914); a common summer resident at Rupert, 1919-21; extreme dates of occurrence February 27 and November 1, eggs May 6 (Davis, 1935).

Cassia County. Birds fairly plentiful June 19, 1949, in arid rugged country west of Almo (Burleigh).

Habits. Although the Robin now occurs commonly at Moscow during the winter months, it is doubtful if it was originally found in Latah County except as a summer resident. Few other birds have accepted so readily the advantages offered by the proximity of man; the planting of such ornamental trees as the Russian olive and the mountain ash made available a food supply during the late fall and winter that this species was quick to take advantage of. An additional source of food are the orchards that supply frozen but apparently palatable apples that are eagerly eaten by the Robins until the last one is gone.

At Moscow breeding activities begin early in the spring. On March 17, 1949, a female was seen carrying material to a nest already well built, up fifteen feet from the ground in the crotch of a pine, and several weeks later, on April 6, another female was seen incubating on a nest that was eight from the ground in the crotch of a maple. At Lewiston a nest was found on April 13, 1957, that held four partially incubated eggs, and was six feet from the ground in a crotch of a willow at the edge of the Clearwater River. Hand (1939) reports a nest found at Monumental Buttes, on the St. Joe National Forest, that held eggs on June 19, 1934, and was eight feet up in a hemlock. It apparently had been built while the sapling was bent by the weight of the snow deposited during the previous winter. Melting of the snow had caused the tree to straighten, tilting the nest until, when found, the eggs were in rather a precarious position. Verner (1953) states that at Harvard a pair of Robins used the same nest for two years. On June 27, 1951, and again on July I, 1952, this nest held four young.

Turdus migratorius migratorius Linnaeus

On the basis of specimens taken, the nominate race of the Robin that occurs during the summer months north of Idaho in Alaska, Yukon, and Mackenzie can be found in small numbers in the northern part of the state during the winter months. I have collected thirteen specimens identified as *migratorius* at Moscow between the dates of October 15 (1949) and February 22 (1949); they are as follows: males December 10, 1947, February 22 and October 15, 1949, January 4 and 27, 1950, October 31, 1952, February 4, 1955, January 31 and December 23, 1956; females December 25, 1949, January 15, 1950, December 31, 1951, January 26, 1954. There is one record for the occurrence of *migratorius* in southern Idaho, a male taken at Cambridge, in Washington County, November 21, 1951.

Turdus migratorius caurinus (Grinnell)

This extreme western race of the Robin, occurring as a breeding bird from southeastern Alaska to northern Oregon, is characterized by its noticeably darker underparts. There apparently is either a well-defined movement inland in the late fall, or this race has a wider breeding range than is now recognized, for *caurinus* was found to be a regular and fairly common winter resident in northern Idaho. From 1947 through the winter of 1957 I collected numerous Robins typical of this dark coast race, and I soon came to the conclusion that *caurinus* was the common winter Robin of the northern part of the state. These specimens were taken at Moscow between the dates of October 5 (1948) and March 28 (1951), at Potlatch September 29, 1949, and February 14, 1954, at Viola November 23, 1952, at Lewiston November 27, 1948, and February 13, 1954, at Peck, Nez Perce County, December 10, 1952, and at Weippe December 10, 1952, and April 8, 1953.

Turdus migratorius propinquus Ridgway

This western race of the Robin, breeding from central eastern British Columbia south to southern California and east to western Nebraska, is characterized by its large size, paler coloration both above and below, and the absence of the white tip at the end of the tail feathers. It is a common and widely distributed summer resident throughout Idaho, and a fairly common winter resident in the northern part of the state. In order to verify its occurrence both as breeding and as wintering in the state, specimens, all found to be typical of *propinquus*, were taken from 1947 to 1958 as follows: Bonner County, Clark Fork (June), Priest Lake (June); Kootenai County, Spirit Lake (June), Coeur d'Alene (February, April), Post Falls (May), Hauser (February); Latah County, Moscow (every month of the year but

September), Potlatch (February, March, April, May, September, October, November), Viola (March, October, November), Troy (March), Genesee (January, March), Juliaetta (November), Deary (April, July); Nez Perce County, Lewiston (January, February, March, April, May, August, September, November, December), Myrtle Beach (February, March); Clearwater County, Headquarters (March, April, October), Weippe (February, March, April, October, November); Valley County, McCall (April); Washington County, Cambridge (May, November); Owyhee County, Murphy (February); Bonneville County, Gray (June); Butte County, Arco (May).

There are also, in the collections of the Denver Museum of Natural History, specimens of *Turdus migratorius*, identified as *propinquus*, that were taken by Pierce Brodkorb from February until November in many localities throughout southern Idaho.

Ixoreus naevius (Gmelin): VARIED THRUSH

General Distribution. Breeds from north-central Alaska, central Yukon and northwestern Mackenzie south to northwestern California, northern Idaho, and northwestern Montana; in winter south to northern Baja California.

Status in Idaho. A common summer resident in the northern part of the state. Winters in small numbers at Moscow, but rarely recorded elsewhere in Latah County from the latter part of November until the middle of February.

The Varied Thrush is one of the species first reported in Idaho by the famous Lewis and Clark expedition. In one of his journals Lewis (*Original Journals*, III:75) states that it was seen September 2, 1805, on the upper west fork of Fish Creek (North Fork of the Salmon River), and again on September 20, 1805, at the west end of the Lolo Trail, above Weippe (Jollie, 1953).

Boundary County. A single bird, a female, noted at Bonners Ferry November 23, 1948 (Burleigh).

Bonner County. Found to be a common breeding bird in 1917 in heavy timber in the valleys north of Clark Fork (Burleigh, 1923); November 8 cited by Bent (1949) as a departure date for Priest River.

Kootenai County. First noted at Fort Sherman (Coeur d'Alene) during the first week of March; in 1896 this species arrived on April 3; none seen in the fall; possibly breeds (Merrill, 1898); fairly common at Coeur d'Alene during the summer months (1910-14) (Rust, 1915); noted at Fourth of July Summit, twenty miles east of Coeur d'Alene, May 21, 1949; a flock of ten birds seen in open woods at the edge of Lake Coeur d'Alene March 13, 1957 (Burleigh); March 8 cited by Bent (1949) as an early arrival date for Coeur d'Alene.

Shoshone County. A common summer resident on the St. Joe National Forest (1921-41) "in Canadian Zone forests" (Hand, 1941); this species found to be quite plentiful, June 19-21, 1951, on the mountain slopes south of Avery, being frequently seen each day in the thick woods on the higher ridges (Burleigh).

Benewah County. Noted at St. Maries (1921-41) in March and October (Hand, 1941); apparently now breeds at St. Maries in at least small numbers, several birds being seen there (and a male collected) on July 31, 1960 (Burleigh).

Latah County. Fairly common June 1-August 16, 1947; most frequently observed at the higher altitudes; noted as low as 2,500 feet (Johnston, 1949); seen at Laird Park, north of Harvard, April 13 and July 3, 1952; possibly breeds on the mountain slopes (Verner, 1953); a fairly common but rather local breeding bird in the county (1947-58); observed during the summer months in wooded ravines on Moscow Mountain, at Robinson's Lake, east of Moscow, and on Flat Creek, east of Deary; of regular occurrence each winter at Moscow, and noted once then at Potlatch, a single bird on January 13, 1955 (Burleigh).

Nez Perce County. The Varied Thrush was found to be an irregular and rather uncommon transient at Lewiston, being seen in small numbers in woods bordering Hatwai Creek. Actual dates of occurrence are as follows: February 21, 1952, January 9 and 10, and February 21 through March 26, 1955, April 16, 1956, October 31, 1957 (Burleigh).

Clearwater County. A fairly common summer resident (1951-54) at Headquarters; an occasional male noted at Bungalow June 19, 1952 (Burleigh).

Idaho County. Abundant in the northeastern Clearwater and northern Bitterroot Mountains in July, 1948; found in dense forests of spruce, fir, and western red cedar; noted carrying nesting material the middle of July; a female collected July 10 and a male July 18, southwest of Lolo Pass; specimens also taken September 28, 1941, six miles southwest of Selway Falls (Orr, 1951).

Valley County. A male was collected on Brundage Mountain, two miles north of McCall, on June 29, 1958. It was in thick woods almost at the top of the mountain (at an altitude of approximately 7,300 feet), and showed so much concern over my presence that it was suspected at the time of having young close by. In the collections of the Denver Museum of Natural History there are three specimens of the Varied Thrush taken by Brodkorb on Brundage Mountain in July. This is the farthest south that this species is now known to occur in Idaho during the summer months.

Habits. In view of the fact that the average winter in northern Idaho is characterized by deep snow and subzero temperatures, the Varied Thrush must be considered one of our more hardy species. Temperatures as low as sixteen degrees below zero are not uncommon in January, and on one occasion the thermometer in my backyard registered thirty-three degrees below zero. Snow then frequently reaches a depth of three feet or more; sudden thaws do occur, but bare ground at this time of the year is almost noteworthy. Like the Robin, the Varied Thrush eats mainly the fruit of the mountain ash and the Russian olive, as well as frozen apples found on many of the trees; under these circumstances it is not surprising that the small flocks encountered are largely within the city limits of Moscow.

At Headquarters, in Clearwater County, this species is a summer resident only, disappearing in late October and usually not reappearing again until the middle of March. My earliest record is that of a male noted on February 28, 1954. The snow then was still fully two feet deep on the ground, but it had melted at the base of the larger trees, and it was on these patches of exposed ground that this bird was feeding.

Breeding activities begin early in the spring, often while snow is still on the ground. On May 26, 1950, a brood of young, already out of the nest several days, was seen in a thickly wooded ravine at Robinson's Lake. It is possible that two broods are reared each year, for on August 7, 1917, I found a nest in heavy timber north of Clark Fork, in Bonner County, that held three well-incubated eggs. It was fifteen feet from the ground at the outer end of a limb of a large hemlock at the side of a stream, and it was substantially built of hemlock twigs and moss, lined chiefly at the bottom with soft crushed fragments of weed stems.

Ixoreus naevius naevius (Gmelin)

The nominate race of the Varied Thrush breeds on the Pacific coast, west of the coast ranges, from southern Alaska to northern California. Based on actual specimens taken it occurs as a rare winter resident in northern Idaho, although it may be more common than the few records indicate. Males identified as *naevius* were collected at Lewiston February 21, 1955, and at Moscow October 7, 1957, and females at Moscow January 4, 1955, and October 23, 1956.

Ixoreus naevius meruloides (Swainson)

In the original description of *meruloides* the female is characterized as having the upperparts gray and lacking the brown wash typical of the nominate race, but no character is given separating the males. However, a critical study of these two races revealed the fact that in the males of *meruloides* the blue of the upperparts is noticeably lighter than in the males of *naevius*, this character readily separating the two races regardless of season.

In connection with this taxonomic study specimens were collected (1947-58) at various times of the year, and throughout the breeding range of this species in the northern part of the state. These were taken as follows: Kootenai County, Fourth of July Summit, May 21, 1949, Coeur d'Alene, March 13, 1957; Shoshone County, Avery, June 20 and 21, 1951; Benewah County, St. Maries, July 31, 1960; Latah County, Potlatch, one winter specimen, January 13, 1955, in the spring between the dates of February 17

(1952) and March 21 (1951), one fall specimen, November 23, 1952, Moscow, numerous specimens between the dates of October 17 (1951) and April 22 (1953), Deary, May 7, 1948; Nez Perce County, Lewiston, February 21, 1952, January 9, February 21, and March 13, 20, and 26, 1955, April 16, 1956; Clearwater County, Headquarters, June 14, 1951, March 29, April 10, and October 22, 1952, March 25, 1953, February 28, 1954, Bungalow, June 19, 1952; Valley County, Brundage Mountain, June 29, 1958.

[**Hylocichla mustelina** (Gmelin): WOOD THRUSH]

General Distribution. Breeds from eastern South Dakota, central Wisconsin, southern Ontario and southern Quebec south to southeastern Texas, the Gulf coast, and northern Florida. Winters from southern Texas south through eastern Mexico and Central America to Panama.

Status in Idaho. Of accidental occurrence in the southern part of the state.

There is one record for the occurrence of this species in Idaho, near Rupert, in Minidoka County.

Wilbur (1965) states that "On October 8, 1963, a Wood Thrush (*Hylocichla mustelina*) was seen at the Minidoka Refuge headquarters. It was observed on and off during the day, during which time it scratched in the duff at the edge of my lawn or perched silently in a nearby tree."

Habits. This species has not heretofore been recorded anywhere in the northwestern part of the United States, so it is unfortunate that the individual observed on the Minidoka National Wildlife Refuge was not collected to verify the identification. Idaho is so far west of its normal breeding range that its appearance in the state must be considered accidental, regardless of season.

Hylocichla guttata (Pallas): HERMIT THRUSH

General Distribution. Breeds from central Alaska, southern Yukon, southern Mackenzie, southern Manitoba, northern Ontario, central Quebec and Newfoundland south to southern California, northern New Mexico, central Wisconsin, and Maryland. Winters south to Baja California, Guatemala, the Gulf of Mexico and southern Florida.

Status in Idaho. A common summer resident on the higher forested ridges throughout the state; noted from 4,300 feet (Lake Waha) to 10,000 feet (Hyndman Peak); a common transient in the valleys both in the spring and in the fall; recorded twice during the winter in northern Idaho.

Boundary County. An occasional bird noted north of Porthill July 4, 1957, in thick woods near the top of a ridge (Burleigh).

Bonner County. A fairly common summer resident in 1917 on the higher ridges north of Clark Fork; none noted below 6,000 feet; singing throughout July; a pair seen July 17 carrying food to young still in the nest (Burleigh,

1923); noted by Charles F. Hedges in June, 1929, at Priest Lake, at an altitude of 5,500 feet.

Kootenai County. An occasional bird noted at Coeur d'Alene in September (1910-14); specimens taken September 12 and 24 identified as *Hylocichla guttata guttata* (Rust, 1915).

Shoshone County. A local but common summer resident on the St. Joe National Forest (1921-41), in "the upper Canadian and Hudsonian zones," from early June until early September; two noted October 9, 1931, six miles east of Monumental Buttes (Hand, 1941).

Latah County. Noted only as a fairly common transient in the valleys (1948-58); most frequently seen from late April until the middle of May, and again from early September until the middle of September; recorded twice during the winter (Burleigh).

Nez Perce County. One breeding pair taken May 27, 1949, in open woods at the top of a ridge south of Lake Waha (altitude 4,300 feet); female with a well-developed brood patch; recorded at Lewiston on two occasions in the spring, on May 16 and again on June 4, 1953 (Burleigh).

Idaho County. Two adult females collected September 17 and 25, 1941, four miles southwest of Selway Falls; both identified as *Hylocichla guttata guttata* (Orr, 1951).

Adams County. Two breeding specimens taken in the Smith Mountains have been identified as *polionota* (McCabe, 1932); one bird seen at Indian Valley "the last week of May" (Newhouse, 1960).

Valley County. One bird noted June 28, 1958, in thick woods near the top of Brundage Mountain (altitude 6,500 feet) (Burleigh).

Lemhi County. Two breeding pairs noted in Lost Trail Pass (altitude 6,950 feet) June 30, 1950 (Burleigh).

Fremont County. Fairly common during the summer of 1916 "at the heads of the Canyons"; noted June 18 "at the head of Little Dry Creek Canyon" (Rust, 1917); found to be fairly common June 26, 1960, in open woods near the top of Targhee Pass (altitude 7,000 feet) (Burleigh).

Clark County. Several birds heard singing on Signal Peak July 14, 1961 (Oring, 1962).

Blaine County. Noted June 25, 1950, in open woods part way up Easley Peak (altitude 8,500 feet), June 26 in open fir woods at Galena (7,600 feet), and June 27 near the top of Hyndman Peak (10,000 feet) (Burleigh).

South Central Idaho. "A few" seen in the Salmon River Mountains in August, 1890, and one on the Snake River October 9 (Merriam, 1891); an uncommon summer resident in 1949 "in the higher wooded areas" in the south-central counties (Levy, 1950).

Minidoka County. Transients seen at Rupert May 12, 1919, and May 7, 1920 (Davis, 1935).

Cassia County. Several birds noted June 19, 1949, at the Silent City of Rocks, west of Almo, in thick woods composed of juniper and mountain mahogany (altitude approximately 7,000 feet) (Burleigh).

Habits. Unlike the other Thrushes, the Hermit Thrush is limited during the summer months, wherever it occurs in Idaho, to the higher ridges. I have never noted it then below 4,000 feet, in my limited experience it is most common between 6,000 and 7,000 feet. I have recorded it as high as 10,000 feet in Blaine County, and it doubtless occurs even higher where conditions are suitable. This preference is noticeable even in migration, for at Lewiston, the lowest spot in the state, I observed it on only two occasions in the spring during ten years of field work in this northwestern corner of Nez Perce County.

Hylocichla guttata guttata (Pallas)

This Alaskan race occurs as a breeding bird as far south as southern British Columbia. On the basis of specimens taken it is a scarce fall transient in the northern part of the state. In the series of specimens of the Hermit Thrush that I took at Moscow (1948 through 1958), seven were found to represent the nominate race, and are as follows: a female, September 30, 1948; two males, September 23 and October 7, 1949; a male, October 12, 1950; a female, October 8, 1951; a female, October 2, 1953; a male, December 24, 1954. There are additional specimens of this race taken by C. F. Hedges at Chase Lake, a female in immature plumage October 10, 1930, and at Priest Lake, females in immature plumage September 16 and 21, 1931; and by S. H. Levy at Fox Creek, a male October 8, 1949.

Hylocichla guttata polionota Grinnell

This race is the breeding Hermit Thrush of the southwestern part of the state. It has been recorded in but a few widely separated localities, and would appear to be rather local in its distribution. However, further field work should reveal its presence in other areas where there is suitable habitat. Breeding specimens have been taken at Lake Waha, Nez Perce County, May 27, 1949 (Burleigh); Tamarack, Adams County, July 19 and 20, 1930 (C. F. Hedges); Warm Lake, Valley County, July 5, 1932 (D. H. Blanchard), and July 9, 1932 (A. H. Miller); Brundage Mountain, Valley County, June 28, 1958 (Burleigh); Cuddy Mountain, Washington County, July 2, 1932 (A. H. Miller).

Hylocichla guttata auduboni (Baird)

This race, the breeding Hermit Thrush of the eastern part of the state, can be distinguished from *polionota* by its larger size and more rufescent, less gray, upperparts. It is also rather local in its distribution, but according to available records it would appear to be more common during the summer months in eastern Idaho than is *polionota* farther west in the state. Specimens identified as *auduboni* have been taken as follows: Lost Trail Pass, Lemhi County, June 30, 1950 (Burleigh); Head Big Lost River, Custer County, July 11, 1935 (W. B. Davis); Head Pahsimeroi River, Custer

County, July 23, 1936 (W. B. Davis); Little Redfish Lake, Custer County, August (Brodkorb); Easley Peak, Blaine County, June 25, 1950 (Burleigh); Galena, Blaine County, June 26, 1950 (S. H. Levy), and July 17, 1958 (Burleigh); Hyndman Peak, Blaine County, June 27, 1950 (Burleigh); Targhee Pass, Fremont County, June 26, 1960 (Burleigh); Heglar Pass, twenty miles south of American Falls, Power County, July 1, 1949 (M. Jollie); Bridge, Cassia County, August 16, 1910 (S. G. Jewett); Mount Harrison, ten miles south of Albion, Cassia County, June 15, 1936 (W. B. Davis); Silent City of Rocks, Cassia County, June 19, 1949 (Burleigh); one mile west of Summit, Franklin County, June (P. Brodkorb); Joe's Gap, Preuss Range, five miles northeast of Montpelier, Bear Lake County, August 17, 1934 (P. Brodkorb).

Hylocichla guttata vaccinia Cumming

This race is limited in its distribution during the summer months to Vancouver Island. It can be distinguished from the other Hermit Thrushes by its small size and dark gray upperparts. As a transient in Idaho it has never been recorded in the spring, while in the fall it occurs in rather small numbers in the northern part of the state. At Moscow I succeeded in taking six specimens that have been identified as *vaccinia*, males on September 26, October 5, and October 19, 1951, September 30, 1955, and September 14, 1957, and a female September 9, 1956.

Hylocichla guttata oromela Oberholser

This is the race that breeds in northern Idaho, where it is apparently uncommon and local in its distribution. It can be distinguished by its small size and light gray upperparts. A male taken by C. F. Hedges at Priest Lake June 24, 1929, and a female collected by me on a wooded ridge north of Porthill, Boundary County, July 4, 1957, have been identified by John W. Aldrich as *oromela*. Both represent the breeding population of this part of the state.

In the series of Hermit Thrushes that I collected in northern Idaho, 1948 through 1958, almost 75 per cent were found to represent this race. One was taken at Potlatch, a female May 16, 1948, and two at Lewiston, a male May 16, 1953, and a female June 4, 1953. The others were taken at Moscow in the spring between the dates of April 23 (1952) and May 31 (1955), in the fall between the dates of September 4 (1958) and October 25 (1956), and on January 16, 1954. There are additional specimens of *oromela* taken by C. F. Hedges at Payette May 19, 1930, and by S. H. Levy at Cow Creek September 22, 1950.

Hylocichla guttata euboria Oberholser

This race, occurring during the summer months in the Yukon, is apparently a rare fall transient in northern Idaho. I have but one record for its occurrence then, a male taken at Moscow October 8, 1951. Another specimen, a female taken at Moscow September 15, 1949, has been identified as *guttata*, but approaching *euboria* in its characters.

[Hylocichla guttata dwighti Bishop]

The type specimen of this proposed race (Bishop, 1933) is an adult male taken at Priest Lake (altitude 5,500 feet) June 23, 1929, by Charles F. Hedges. It is described as similar to *Hylocichla guttata auduboni*, the upperparts being gray, but the individual being smaller. The range as given is northern Idaho. It has not been recognized as valid by the A. O. U. Committee on Nomenclature.

Hylocichla ustulata swainsoni (Tschudi): Swainson's Thrush

General Distribution. Breeds from southern British Columbia east through central Alberta, central Manitoba and northern Ontario to southern Labrador, south to central California, central Utah, central Colorado, northern Minnesota, northern Michigan and central New Hampshire, and in the Appalachians to eastern West Virginia. Winters from El Salvador to northwestern Argentina.

Status in Idaho. A common summer resident in forested areas throughout much of the state.

Bonner County. A common summer resident in 1917 in heavy timber in the valleys north of Clark Fork (Burleigh, 1923); an occasional bird seen in thick woods bordering the Pack River north of Sandpoint, June 24, 1957 (Burleigh); noted at Priest River June 29, 1957; common in woods bordering Priest Lake June 22-24, 1960 (Burleigh).

Kootenai County. Breeds commonly at Fort Sherman (Coeur d'Alene) (Merrill, 1898); noted in late July, 1897, at Blue Lake, in Hoodoo Valley (Snyder, 1900); a common summer resident at Coeur d'Alene, 1910-14 (Rust, 1915); an occasional bird noted July 4, 1949, in woods bordering Lake Coeur d'Alene (Burleigh).

Shoshone County. A common summer resident, 1921-41, on the St. Joe National Forest, being found, from May until September, in the "upper transition and Canadian Zones" (Hand, 1941); a common breeding bird at Avery in 1951, being frequently seen June 19-21 both in the valleys and on the higher ridges (Burleigh); an occasional bird noted at Lookout Pass (altitude approximately 5,000 feet) July 9, 1958 (Burleigh).

Benewah County. Found to be fairly plentiful at St. Maries July 30-31, 1960 (Burleigh).

Latah County. Common, June 1-August 16, 1947, "in forested areas" in the county (Johnston, 1949); a common summer resident at Harvard, 1951-52 (Verner, 1953); found to be a common summer resident throughout the county, 1948-58, usually observed in the spring the latter part of May, and being rarely seen after early September (Burleigh).

Nez Perce County. A rather scarce fall transient at Lewiston, being recorded between the dates of August 12 (1952) and September 1 (1949); there are no spring records (Burleigh).

Clearwater County. A common summer resident on the wooded ridges at Headquarters, 1951-56; not noted in the fall later than August 27 (1952); common at Bungalow June 19, 1952 (Burleigh).

Idaho County. One bird collected September 11, 1941, two miles southeast of Selway Falls (altitude 1,900 feet); abundant during July, 1948, in "the upper water shed of the Lochsa Fork"; birds seen "from the canyon bottoms almost to timber line"; males taken July 6 (4,000 feet) and July 16 (7,000 feet) south of Lolo Pass (Orr, 1951); several birds noted at White Bird Summit (altitude 4,400 feet) July 1, 1951 (Burleigh).

Washington County. An occasional bird noted on Cuddy Mountain, north of Cambridge, June 5, 1952 (Burleigh).

Boise County. Fairly common at Bogus Basin, eighteen miles north of Boise, July 17, 1960 (Burleigh).

Owyhee County. Frequently noted at Silver City (altitude approximately 7,000 feet) July 13, 1960 (Burleigh).

Blaine County. Found to be a common summer resident on the lower slopes of the mountains north and east of Ketchum, occurring from the valleys to an altitude of 7,500 feet; frequently observed June 24-28, 1950, July 17, 1958 (Galena), and July 10, 1960 (Trail Creek Summit) (Burleigh).

South Central Idaho. An "abundant" summer resident of "the Transition and Canadian Zones"; especially common in June, 1950, in the Sawtooth and Challis National Forests (Levy, 1962).

Clark County. Several noted on Signal Peak June 20 and July 14, 1961 (Oring, 1962).

Teton Basin. Nest found July 21, 1872, with two fresh eggs (Merriam, 1891).

Bonneville County. A very common summer resident (1949-51) at Grays Lake; arrival date June 1, 1950 (Steel, 1956); two singing males seen on Caribou Mountain at an altitude of 8,000 feet, June 13, 1949 (Burleigh).

In order to determine what races of the Swainson's Thrush occur in Idaho, both as breeding birds and as transients, a series of specimens was taken throughout the state, from late May until early September, 1948-60. Without exception these specimens were found to represent *swainsoni*. They were taken as follows: Bonner County, Sandpoint, June 24, 1957, Priest River, June 29, 1957, Priest Lake, July 22, 1960; Kootenai County, Coeur d'Alene, July 4, 1949; Shoshone County, Avery, June 19-20, 1951, Dismal Lake, June 21, 1951, Lookout Pass, July 9, 1958; Benewah County, St. Maries, July 31, 1960; Latah County, Harvard, July 8, 1953, Princeton, July 21, 1949, August 24, 1950, Potlatch, August 13 and 16, and September 4, 1948, August 16 and 21, 1949, September 4, 1951, July 13, 1957, Moscow, thirty-five specimens between the dates of June 4, 1948, and July 29, 1960, Bovill, July 19, 1948; Nez Perce County, Lewiston, September 1, 1949; Clearwater County, Headquarters, June 14 and 27, 1951, June 18 and

August 27, 1952, Bungalow, June 19, 1952; Idaho County, White Bird Summit, July 1, 1951; Washington County, Cuddy Mountain, June 5, 1952; Boise County, Bogus Basin, July 17, 1960; Owyhee County, Silver City, July 13, 1960; Blaine County, Ketchum, June 24, 1950, Easley Peak, June 25, 1950, Trail Creek Summit, July 10, 1960; Bonneville County, Gray, June 12 and 13, 1949.

Habits. The Swainson's Thrush is one of the last species to arrive in Idaho in the spring, for only rarely has one of these thrushes been observed before the end of May. It is equally early in its departure in the fall, for there is a noticeable decrease in numbers the middle of August, and only an occasional bird has been noted after the first of September. My extreme dates of occurrence for Moscow are May 17 (1952) and September 13 (1952). At Potlatch my latest date in the fall is September 4 (1949 and 1951).

It is apparently the middle of June before breeding activities are well underway, and the last of the month before the earliest nests hold fresh eggs. Rust (1915) states that a nest found at Coeur d'Alene on June 27 held four fresh eggs. On Lightning Creek, north of Clark Fork, I succeeded in finding three nests July 6, 1917, four eggs in one, three in the other two, all well incubated. They were in hemlocks, varying in height from four to ten feet from the ground; small and compact, they were built of fine twigs, grasses, bits of rotten wood, shreds of inner bark, and moss, and lined with skeleton leaves and moss. Verner (1953) found a nest at Harvard July 14, 1951, that held three eggs and was seven feet up in an alder.

At Silver City, on July 13, 1960, I was interested to note that the Swainson's Thrush was largely limited in its distribution to the willow thickets fringing the streams, a habitat radically unlike the fir and spruce woods where this species occurs throughout the rest of the state.

Hylocichla minima minima (Lafresnaye): GRAY-CHEEKED THRUSH

General Distribution. Breeds from northeastern Siberia and northern Alaska east through northern Mackenzie and northern Quebec to central Labrador, south to northern British Columbia, northern Saskatchewan, eastern Quebec and Newfoundland. Winters from Nicaragua south to northern Peru and northwestern Brazil.

Status in Idaho. Of accidental occurrence in the northern part of the state.

There is one record for the occurrence of the Gray-cheeked Thrush in Idaho. On September 7, 1951, I collected a male in post-juvenile plumage in the Arboretum on the campus of the University of Idaho at Moscow.

Habits. In view of the route it follows in migration, both in the spring and in the fall, the Gray-cheeked Thrush will never be other than of accidental occurrence in Idaho. From its far northern summer home in Alaska and Mackenzie it travels east across the continent in the fall, and is rare then even in British Columbia and Alberta. It follows the same route on its return journey in the spring, so it is practically unknown, regardless of season, anywhere on the Pacific coast south of northern British Columbia.

Hylocichla fuscescens subpallida Burleigh and Duvall: VEERY

General Distribution. Breeds in northern Washington east of the Cascades, in Idaho, and in western Montana west of the Continental Divide. Winter range not known.

Status in Idaho. A common summer resident in the northern part of the state. Less common and of local distribution in southern Idaho.

Boundary County. An occasional bird noted in stream bottoms in the vicinity of Bonners Ferry June 22, 1957 (Burleigh).

Kootenai County. Common in the cottonwoods bordering Lake Coeur d'Alene; arrives about the twentieth of May (Merrill, 1898); common at the upper end of Lake Coeur d'Alene July 1-10, 1943 (Yocom, 1946).

Benewah County. A common summer resident, 1921-41, in the willows and cottonwoods along the lower St. Joe and St. Maries rivers, present from late May to August (Hand, 1941).

Latah County. Locally common, June to August, 1947, along the streams (Johnston, 1949); a locally common summer resident throughout the county, 1948-58, usually appearing the latter part of May, and being only infrequently seen after the middle of August (Burleigh).

Nez Perce County. One breeding pair noted at Lapwai July 12, 1950, in woods bordering a stream (altitude approximately 900 feet) (Burleigh).

Clearwater County. Several birds seen June 12, 1951, and July 1, 1952, in underbrush bordering the Clearwater River south of Orofino (Burleigh).

Idaho County. There are specimens of the Veery in the Museum of Vertebrate Zoology, Berkeley, taken at Castle Creek Ranger Station (Arvey, 1947).

Adams County. An occasional bird seen in alder thickets at New Meadows June 27-28, 1949, and at Council June 5, 1951 (Burleigh).

Washington County. This species found to be fairly plentiful at Cambridge, in woods bordering the Weiser River, June 4, 1951, and on East Brownlee Creek, west of Cambridge, June 7, 1952 (Burleigh).

Owyhee County. There are specimens of the Veery in the Museum of Vertebrate Zoology, Berkeley, taken seven miles southeast of Murphy (Arvey, 1947).

Lemhi County. A specimen of the Veery in the Denver Museum of Natural History, Colorado, was taken in July by Brodkorb at Salmon.

Custer County. An occasional bird noted in alder thickets on the Salmon River at Challis June 29, 1950, and on the Big Lost River at Mackay July 7, 1960 (Burleigh).

Blaine County. Singing males noted at Ketchum, in woods bordering the Big Wood River, June 24, 1950, and at Sun Valley, in alder thickets on Trail Creek, June 28, 1950, and July 4 and 9, 1960 (Burleigh).

Fremont County. Found in 1916 to occur sparingly in willow thickets in the canyons; noted June 25 at the outlet of Beaver Creek Canyon, and on July 16 in the Camas Meadows (Rust, 1917); noted June 11, 1957, in alder thickets at the edge of Henrys Lake (altitude 6,700 feet) (Burleigh).

Clark County. Several "heard" on Signal Peak July 14, 1961 (Oring, 1962).

Bonneville County. Noted in the Snake River Valley, nine miles southeast of Irwin, July 13, 1949 (Jollie, in litt.); a fairly common summer resident at Grays Lake, 1949-51 (Steel, 1956).

Caribou County. Two birds seen June 1, 1952, two miles west of Freedom, Wyoming, in willow thickets bordering a stream (Burleigh).

Subpallida can be readily distinguished from the other recognized races of *Hylocichla fuscescens* by the gray wash of the upper parts. The original description (Burleigh and Duvall, 1959) is based on a critical examination of fifty-seven specimens taken in Idaho, Washington, and Montana. Specimens from Idaho are as follows: Boundary County, Bonners Ferry, adult male June 22, 1957; Benewah County, St. Maries, adult male June 22, 1948; Latah County, Potlatch, adult males May 21, 1948, May 24, 1950, July 12, 1951, May 13 and July 12, 1952, immature males August 13, 1948, August 2, 1951, August 3, 1952, adult females May 26 and July 13, 1949, July 12, 1951, August 12, 1956, June 30, 1957, immature females August 16, 1948, August 26, 1951, Princeton, adult male May 30, 1949, Moscow, adult males May 25, 1948, September 2, 1950, May 16 and June 10, 1951, May 21, 1952, May 22, 1953, immature male August 18, 1949, adult females July 19, 1949, June 16, 1958, immature females August 23, 1949, September 7, 1957; Nez Perce County, Lapwai, adult male July 12, 1950; Clearwater County, Orofino, adult males June 12, 1951, July 1, 1952; Washington County, Cambridge, adult males June 4, 1951, June 7, 1952; Custer County, Challis, adult female June 29, 1950; Blaine County, Sun Valley, adult male June 28, 1950; Fremont County, Henrys Lake, adult male June 11, 1957.

Habits. Despite the few published records for the occurrence of the Veery in Idaho, it is common and widely distributed in the state. Being a shy, quiet bird, and one that remains much of the time in the alder and willow thickets it frequents, it is easily overlooked. Consequently its presence will remain undetected in areas where it is relatively plentiful.

It is one of the later migrants to arrive in the spring, rarely appearing before the middle of May; the bulk of the birds depart in the fall in late August, although an occasional individual will linger until early September. My extreme dates of occurrence for Moscow are May 15 (1951) and September 7 (1957), and for Potlatch May 13 (1952) and August 21 (1949).

In the eastern United States the nest of the Veery is built on the ground, but this apparently is not the case with the western races. Nests found in Washington and in Colorado were two and three feet from the ground, and Merrill (1898) states that those he found at Coeur d'Alene varied from two to seven feet from the ground.

Sialia mexicana occidentalis Townsend: WESTERN BLUEBIRD

General Distribution. Breeds from southern British Columbia and southern Montana south to southern California, northern Idaho, and northwestern Wyoming. Winters at lower altitudes within its breeding range.

Status in Idaho. A fairly common but local summer resident in the northern part of the state.

Kootenai County. A common summer resident at Fort Sherman (Coeur d'Alene); arrives in late February or early March (Merrill, 1898); a common summer resident at Coeur d'Alene, 1910-14, being present from the first week in March until the middle of October (Rust, 1915); a flock of six birds, the adults and four fully grown young of the year, seen at Coeur d'Alene August 14, 1948; noted at Hauser as early as March 12 (1957), and as late as October 18 (1956) (Burleigh).

Benewah County. One pair of these bluebirds seen near the mouth of the St. Maries River April 3, 1932 (Hand, 1941); a single bird, a male, seen at St. Maries April 1, 1953 (Burleigh).

Latah County. Rare; three young left their nest in a telephone pole one mile east of Harvard June 25, 1947 (Johnston, 1949); an uncommon and local summer resident, 1948-58; definitely known to breed only at Potlatch, Moscow (Moscow Mountain), and Deary (Burleigh).

Nez Perce County. A breeding male taken on Craig Mountain June 15, 1951 (Levy, 1959); an uncommon spring transient at Lewiston, small flocks being noted March 12, 1950, March 19, 1953, March 10, 1954, March 20, 1955 (Burleigh).

Clearwater County. Noted at Ahsahka April 8, 1951, and at Weippe, where it is an uncommon summer resident, between the dates of March 29 (1952) and October 26 (1951) (Burleigh).

Minidoka County. Recorded at Rupert August 14, 1920 (Davis, 1935); otherwise unreported from southern Idaho.

In order both to verify the occurrence of this species in Idaho, and to determine the race involved, specimens were taken, 1948-58, throughout its breeding range in the northern part of the state. These were found to be typical of *occidentalis*, and are as follows: Kootenai County, Coeur d'Alene, male March 13, 1957, immature male August 14, 1948, Hauser, males October 4 and 18, 1956, March 12, 1957, females October 16, 1956, March 12, 1957; Latah County, Potlatch, male March 29, 1950, immature males July 26 and September 8, 1956, Viola, male March 4, 1957, female March 4, 1957, Moscow, males May 1, 1949, March 9, 1950, March 22 and 27, 1953, female March 9, 1950, Genesee, female November 21, 1956, Deary, male April 14, 1953; Clearwater County, Ahsahka, male April 8, 1951, Weippe, males October 26, 1951, March 29, 1952, September 19, 1954, female September 19, 1954 (Burleigh).

Habits. In general appearance and actions this species closely resembles the Eastern Bluebird, but there is one very noticeable difference. Its near relative in the eastern United States has a very pleasing song, whereas, in my experience, the Western Bluebird is almost voiceless. Even during the breeding season the males that I have watched were silent for long intervals, only infrequently uttering a low note as they carried on their normal activities.

In Latah County the Western Bluebird rarely appeared in the spring before the latter part of March. A rather early record is that of two birds seen at Moscow March 9, 1950. After the broods of young are fully fledged this species soon disappears from the areas where it has nested, and it is rarely observed after the middle of August. An unusually late record for the fall is that of a single bird seen at Genesee November 21, 1956.

At Potlatch, on July 26, 1956, a brood of fully fledged young was seen with the two adult birds in an open slashing at the edge of the Palouse River.

Sialia currucoides (Bechstein): MOUNTAIN BLUEBIRD

General Distribution. Breeds from central Alaska, southern Mackenzie, and southern Manitoba south to southern California, northern Arizona, southern New Mexico, and western Oklahoma. Winters from southern British Columbia and western Montana south to Baja California, Sonora, and Nuevo Leon.

Status in Idaho. A common summer resident throughout the state. Recorded once during the winter.

Bonner County. A common summer resident in 1917 in the vicinity of Clark Fork, occurring from the valleys to the tops of the higher ridges (Burleigh, 1923).

Kootenai County. Arrives at Fort Sherman (Coeur d'Alene) in early March; more common at the higher altitudes (Merrill, 1898); a common summer resident, 1910-14, at Coeur d'Alene; present from the first week in March until October (Rust, 1915); noted at the upper end of Lake Coeur d'Alene July 1-10, 1943; common "in the agricultural country" (Yocom, 1946); a flock of twenty birds seen in the open prairie at Hauser October 9, 1952, scattered along a telephone wire at the side of a road (Burleigh).

Shoshone County. A common summer resident, 1921-41, on the St. Joe National Forest, from March until October; noted from the valleys to "near the tops of the highest peaks" (Hand, 1941).

Benewah County. Noted at Emida (a brood of fully grown young) August 8, 1948, and at Worley (one small flock) October 6, 1951 (Burleigh).

Latah County. "Abundant" June through August, 1947; noted along the highways (Johnston, 1949); a common summer resident, 1948-58; well distributed throughout the county (Burleigh).

Nez Perce County. A scarce summer resident (1948-58) at Lewiston, and an uncommon transient, being more numerous in the spring than in the fall; noted at Lake Waha March 6, 1953 (Burleigh).

Clearwater County. A fairly common summer resident (1952-56) in the open prairie at Weippe, appearing in the spring in late February or early March when the ground was still covered with snow, and lingering in the fall until the middle of October; one breeding pair noted at Headquarters June 17, 1952; what was apparently a mated pair noted at Orofino April 8, 1953 (Burleigh).

Idaho County. Many were seen "in the Crags Mountains" September 20, 1941, and a male was collected that day at Canteen Meadow, nine miles northeast of Selway Falls (Orr, 1951).

Valley County. Birds fairly plentiful in open slashings at McCall April 17, 1949 (Burleigh).

Adams County. Two birds seen at Mesa "the last few days of March," 1958 (Newhouse, 1960).

Washington County. One pair seen in open fir woods at the top of Cuddy Mountain (altitude 7,600 feet) June 6, 1952; snow still in drifts five feet deep (Burleigh).

South Central Idaho. Common in 1890 on the Salmon River, Lost River, Pahsimeroi and Sawtooth Mountains, and in the Lemhi and Birch Creek valleys; a few seen at Shoshone Falls October 9-11; young on Birch Creek August 6 (Merriam, 1891); considered by Levy (1950) to be an uncommon summer resident in 1949 "in the higher areas" in the south-central counties.

Blaine County. Several males seen at timberline near the top of Easley Peak, north of Ketchum (altitude approximately 11,000 feet) June 25, 1950 (Burleigh).

Fremont County. Found in 1916 to occur sparingly in the county (Rust, 1917).

Clark County. A nest with three fully fledged young found at Spencer June 28, 1916 (Rust, 1917); common on Signal Peak June 19 and August 14, 1961 (Oring, 1962).

Bonneville County. A common summer resident at Grays Lake, 1949-51; arrival date April 5, 1951 (Steel, 1956).

Minidoka County. Reported by Davis (1935) as a summer resident at Rupert (1919-21); earliest date of arrival March 9, latest date of departure October 3, eggs May 6.

Cassia County. An occasional bird noted June 19-21, 1949, at the City of Rocks, west of Almo (Burleigh).

In order to verify the occurrence of this species in the state, and to check the possibility of any geographic variation in Idaho, specimens were taken, 1947-58, as follows: Kootenai County, Coeur d'Alene, male April 19, 1950, Hauser, male October 9, 1952; Benewah County, Emida, male immature August 8, 1948, Worley, male October 6, 1951; Latah County, Potlatch, male and female March 8, 1949, Viola, males March 2, 1950, and February 14, 1954, Moscow, twenty-four specimens between the dates of November 14, 1947, and February 28, 1957, Troy, male February 28, 1948, Deary, male immature and female immature July 2, 1950, male March 12, 1953, Genesee, female immature June 8, 1953, male November 21, 1956; Nez Perce County, Lake Waha, male March 6, 1953, Lewiston, males March 19 and 21 and May 4, 1953, March 24, 1955; Clearwater County, Weippe, males March 29, 1952, and February 24, 1953, Headquarters, female June 17, 1952; Valley County, McCall, male April 17, 1949; Bonneville County, Gray, male June 16, 1949 (Burleigh).

In the Denver Museum of Natural History there are sixty specimens of the Mountain Bluebird taken by Pierce Brodkorb, from March until October, at the following localities in southern Idaho: Custer County, Garden Creek, Mackay; Blaine County, Ketchum, Quigley Creek; Clark County,

Medicine Lodge Creek; Jefferson County, Mud Lake; Butte County, Whiz Canyon; Teton County, Big Hole Mountain; Caribou County, Henry, The Narrows, Blackfoot River; Bear Lake County, Bennington, Snowdrift Mountains, eighteen miles east of Montpelier; Franklin County, Preston, Wasatch Range; Oneida County, Malad City; Cassia County, Goose Creek Mountains, Basin Creek, five miles east of Oakley; Gooding County, Gooding; Boise County, Bogus Basin; Owyhee County, Silver City.

Habits. The Mountain Bluebird is a hardy bird, arriving in Idaho in the spring when the ground is still covered with snow and low temperatures are the rule rather than the exception. The first small flocks appear in late February, and in the fall it is early November when this species is usually recorded for the last time. At Moscow my extreme dates of occurrence are February 21 (1951) and November 14 (1947), at Lewiston March 19 (1953) and November 11, 1948. A rather late date for the fall is that of a single bird, a male, seen at Genesee November 21, 1956. I have one record for the winter months, seeing a male in adult plumage at Moscow December 24, 1950.

Altitude is apparently no limiting factor concerning the occurrence of this species in the state. It has been found nesting at Lewiston, at an altitude of approximately 800 feet, and at timberline on Easley Peak, in Blaine County, at 11,000 feet. Its one requirement seems to be open country where there are sufficient trees large enough to provide nesting sites; where such a habitat exists the Mountain Bluebird will be found.

A nest that I found at Clark Fork July 10, 1917, with well-grown young was fifteen feet from the ground in a cavity in an old fir stub, and this is the situation usually chosen. However, individual pairs show some originality in this respect. Merrill (1898) states that a pair nested on a rafter of the hospital porch at Fort Sherman, and Hand (1939) found a nest in the St. Joe National Forest holding small young July 21, 1932, that was in a wooden box nailed to the outside of a cabin. More orthodox was a nest found by Rust (1917) at Spencer that held three fully fledged young on June 28, 1916, that was in a cavity in a fence post.

Myadestes townsendi (Audubon): TOWNSEND'S SOLITAIRE

General Distribution. Breeds from eastern Alaska, southern Yukon, and southern Mackenzie south to northern California, northeastern Arizona, and northeastern New Mexico. Winters at lower altitudes from southern British Columbia and southern Manitoba south to Baja California and central Texas.

Status in Idaho. A fairly common resident species in the northern part of the state; less numerous and of local occurrence in southern Idaho.

Boundary County. One bird seen in open fir woods near the top of Continental Mountain (altitude 6,700 feet) July 4, 1957 (Burleigh).

Bonner County. Frequently noted in August and early September, 1917, on the higher ridges north of Clark Fork (Burleigh, 1923).

Kootenai County. Not uncommon in migration; one pair found nesting on Mica Peak; arrives about April 1; a specimen taken December 22 (Merrill, 1898); an uncommon transient and winter resident at Coeur d'Alene (1910-14); one specimen taken January 10, 1913 (Rust, 1915).

Shoshone County. A not uncommon summer resident (1921-41) on the St. Joe National Forest, occurring during the summer months "in the Canadian and Hudsonian Zones" (Hand, 1941); one bird seen at Calder June 19, 1951 (Burleigh).

Benewah County. Noted at St. Maries (1921-41) during the winter months (Hand, 1941); three birds seen in open woods at St. Maries April 1, 1953 (Burleigh).

Latah County. Noted, June 1 to August 16, 1947, in forested areas above 2,500 feet; adults feeding well-fledged young seen June 20 on the Little Sand Creek road (Johnston, 1949); found to be breeding in 1951 and 1952 on "the mountain sides" north of Harvard; a nest seen July 3, 1951, held three eggs (Verner, 1953); an uncommon summer resident and a regular but uncommon winter resident (1947-58), occurring on the higher ridges during the summer months, and in the valleys from early September until early May (Burleigh).

Nez Perce County. Found to be a rather scarce transient at Lewiston (1947-58), single birds seen February 8, 1951, March 1 and March 13, 1952, and March 31, 1956 (Burleigh).

Clearwater County. Single birds seen at Headquarters April 11, 1952 and March 17, 1955 (Burleigh).

Idaho County. Noted in small groups in the Selway Falls region in September, 1941; three specimens taken September 9 and 10 at an altitude of 1,900 feet; frequently seen in July, 1948, in the Lolo Pass region (Orr, 1951).

Adams County. One bird seen at Indian Valley October 2, 1958 (Newhouse, 1960).

Valley County. One bird noted at Cascade June 15, 1955 (Burleigh); a specimen taken in July on Brundage Mountain by Pierce Brodkorb.

Lemhi County. A specimen taken in July on Canyon Creek by Brodkorb.

Bonneville County. An uncommon summer resident, 1949-51, at Grays Lake (Steel, 1956); one bird seen May 23, 1951, in open woods near the top of Caribou Mountain (Burleigh).

South Central Idaho. Common September 12 to 16, 1890, in the Pahsimeroi Mountains, a dozen noted in a day; one seen on the Snake River, near Shoshone Falls, October 10 (Merriam, 1891); "seen regularly" in June, 1950, in the Sawtooth and Challis National Forests (Levy, 1962).

Bear Lake County. A specimen taken in June by Brodkorb in the Snowdrift Mountains in the Preuss Range.

Minidoka County. Noted at Rupert May 9, 1920 (Davis, 1935).

In order to verify the occurrence of the Solitaire in Idaho, specimens were taken, 1947-58, in various parts of the state, as follows: Boundary County, Continental Mountain, male July 4, 1957; Benewah County, St. Maries, male April 1, 1953; Latah County, Harvard, male June 30, 1953, Princeton, immature male July 21, 1949, Potlatch, male November 8, 1947, Moscow, males January 2, 1948, May 1, 1949, April 25 and December 19, 1950, October 20, 1951, March 1, 1953, females April 15 and May 9, 1948, December 9, 1949, January 30 and November 14, 1951, September 9, 1952, February 16, April 17, and May 3 and 11, 1953; Nez Perce County, Lewiston, males March 1 and 13, 1952, March 31, 1956; Clearwater County, Headquarters, females April 11, 1952, March 17, 1955; Valley County, Cascade, male June 15, 1955; Bonneville County, Gray, female May 23, 1951 (Burleigh).

Habits. Townsend's Solitaire is another hardy species, for as long as there is an available food supply it apparently is unaffected by the severest winter weather. Its food during much of the year consists of the berries of such shrubs and trees as the elderberry, the serviceberry, the mountain ash, and the privet; and at Moscow, where it winters regularly, such fare enables it to survive frequent blizzards and temperatures that drop as low as thirty degrees below zero.

The nest is built on the ground, and in my limited experience a low bank or cliff is preferred as a nesting site. Hand (1939) gives an interesting account of a nest with three small young that he found July 17, 1934, in Reid's Gulch, on the St. Joe National Forest. It was on a rocky bluff, and "was removed during blasting operations, and then replaced without disturbing the birds." The nest found at Harvard (Verner, 1953) was described as being "three feet above the road in a bank."

Orr (1951) states that the Solitaires seen in the Selway Falls region in September were feeding on mountain ash and western yew berries, varying this diet with insects caught in the air.

Old World Warblers, Gnatcatchers, and Kinglets: *Family Sylviidae*

Polioptila caerulea amoenissima Grinnell: BLUE-GRAY GNATCATCHER

General Distribution. Breeds from northern California, southern Idaho, and Colorado south to Baja California, northern Sonora, Coahuila, and Nuevo Leon. Winters north to southern California, central Arizona and western Texas.

Status in Idaho. An uncommon summer resident in the extreme southeastern edge of the state.

The Gnatcatcher was first recorded in the state by Brodkorb (1935) who collected an immature female in Bear Lake County October 7, 1932, near the mouth of Sheep Creek, eight miles southwest of Raymond.

I personally noted it at three localities where it apparently nested in small numbers. In Cassia County I saw one pair June 22, 1950, fifteen miles north of Oakley; and I observed three birds, at least two of them fully grown of the year, July 19, 1958, on Goose Creek, ten miles south of Oakley. In Power County a single bird was seen June 21, 1960, at Massacre Rocks, twelve miles west of American Falls.

Habits. Elsewhere in its range in the western United States the Gnatcatcher shows a preference during the summer months for chaparral and various species of small oaks, but in southern Idaho it has been found to be limited in its distribution to the low ridges covered with an open stand of juniper. It has never been recorded in any other situation, so with such exacting habitat requirements it will always occupy a very limited area in the state. As yet it has not been noted west of Cassia County, but further field work should reveal its presence wherever conditions are suitable.

Regulus satrapa Lichtenstein: GOLDEN-CROWNED KINGLET

General Distribution. Breeds from the Kenai Peninsula, Kodiak Island, central Yukon, Lake Athabaska, northern Manitoba, Quebec and Newfoundland south to southern California, southern Arizona, New Mexico, central Minnesota and northern New York, and in the mountains to eastern Tennessee and western North Carolina. Winters from Alaska, Alberta, southern Ontario and Newfoundland to southern California, southern Texas, the Gulf coast and northern Florida.

Status in Idaho. A fairly common resident species in the northern part of the state; less numerous and of local distribution in southern Idaho.

Bonner County. Scattered pairs noted in July, 1917, along the streams in the valleys north of Clark Fork; later, in August and early September, small flocks appeared on the higher ridges (Burleigh, 1923).

Kootenai County. Resident at Fort Sherman (Coeur d'Alene); common; broods of fully fledged young seen June 19 (Merrill, 1898); a common resident at Coeur d'Alene (1910-14) (Rust, 1915); a flock of eight birds seen in woods bordering Lake Coeur d'Alene January 8, 1957 (Burleigh).

Shoshone County. A common summer resident (1921-41) on the St. Joe National Forest, "in Canadian Zone forests"; winters at lower altitudes (Hand, 1941).

Latah County. Found to be uncommon "in the forested areas" June 1-August 16, 1947 (Johnston, 1949); noted twice at Harvard in 1952, on April 13 and August 1 (at the head of Strychnine Creek) (Verner, 1953); a fairly common resident species (1947-58), occurring on the wooded ridges during the summer months, and in the valleys from early October until late April (Burleigh).

Nez Perce County. A fairly common winter resident at Lewiston (1947-58), small flocks being seen from late October until early April in woods both on the Clearwater and on the Snake rivers; extreme dates of occurrence October 21 (1950) and April 6 (1951) (Burleigh).

Clearwater County. Fairly common throughout the year (1951-56) on the wooded ridges at Headquarters; one breeding pair noted at Musselshell June 16, 1951 (Burleigh).

Idaho County. Small flocks noted in September, 1941, in the Selway region; a male collected September 12 near Selway Falls (altitude 5,500 feet); common in July, 1948, in the Lolo Pass region; two males collected July 8, six miles southwest of Lolo Pass (altitude 6,000 feet) (Orr, 1951).

Valley County. A specimen in the Museum of Vertebrate Zoology, Berkeley, an immature male, was taken by D. H. Blanchard at Payette Lake July 4, 1932.

Washington County. One small flock of four birds seen at Weiser November 22, 1951, in woods bordering the Weiser River (Burleigh).

Boise County. Small flocks noted each winter, 1938-40, on the Boise National Forest (Marshall, 1945).

Ada County. One small flock noted at Boise November 7, 1957 (Burleigh).

Fremont County. An occasional bird seen June 18, 1916, at the head of Little Dry Creek Canyon (Rust, 1917).

Blaine County. Common at Ketchum October through December, 1910 (Jewett, 1912).

South Central Idaho. A male taken and others seen in the Salmon River Mountains in August, 1890; common in early September in the Lemhi and Birch Creek valleys; a few in the Pahsimeroi Mountains the middle of September; several in the Sawtooth Mountains the first of October (Merriam, 1891).

Franklin County. A specimen in the Denver Museum of Natural History was taken by Brodkorb in Emigration Canyon in June.

Cassia County. A specimen in the Museum of Vertebrate Zoology, Berkeley, a breeding male, was taken by W. B. Davis on Mount Independence, eight miles southwest of Elba, June 8, 1935.

Habits. Despite its diminutive size the Golden-crowned Kinglet is a hardy bird, apparently having no difficulty in surviving the most severe winter weather in Idaho. I have encountered small flocks on Moscow Mountain in late December and January, when there was a foot or more of snow on the ground and the temperature registered below zero, that seemed entirely unconcerned with their bleak surroundings. At this season of the year, however, to a large extent they desert the mountain slopes where they occur during the summer months, and they are then commonly observed in the valleys.

The female was incubating on a nest at Potlatch May 22, 1955, that when found two weeks earlier was only partially built. It was thirty feet up and four feet out at the end of a limb of a Douglas fir, at the edge of a stretch of thick fir woods.

Regulus satrapa amoenus Van Rossem

A critical study of specimens collected (1947-58) in various parts of Idaho showed that the resident population of *Regulus satrapa* has the characters of *amoenus,* the race occupying all but the extreme southern edge of the Rocky Mountain region. These are as follows: Kootenai County, Coeur d'Alene, male January 8, 1957; Latah County, Harvard, male January 3, 1954, Potlatch, males December 7, 1952, and November 22, 1956, Moscow, males November 11 and 30, 1947, January 24 and June 6, 1948, September 22 and December 4, 1949, October 22 and December 2, 1951, November 18, 1952, October 4, 1954, October 19 and November 6, 1956, November 19,

1957, March 31, 1958, females October 26, 1949, December 19, 1950, October 2 and 19, 1951, March 31, 1952, Genesee, male October 28, 1948, Deary, males December 22, 1948, and February 19, 1953; Nez Perce County, Lewiston, males October 21, 1950, October 28 and December 9, 1951, March 16, 1953, January 10, 1955, female April 6, 1951; Clearwater County, Musselshell, male June 16, 1951, Headquarters, males November 11, 1951, June 18, 1952, March 18, 1956; Washington County, Weiser, male November 22, 1951; Ada County, Boise, female November 7, 1957.

Regulus satrapa satrapa Lichtenstein

The nominate race of *Regulus satrapa* breeds as far west in Canada as Lake Athabaska, and possibly occurs as an uncommon but regular transient in Idaho. A female was taken at Moscow November 16, 1949, and another female at Pullman, Washington, eight miles west of Moscow, April 23, 1948.

Regulus calendula (Linnaeus): RUBY-CROWNED KINGLET

General Distribution. Breeds from northwestern Alaska, Mackenzie, northern Ontario, southern Labrador and Newfoundland south to Baja California, southern Arizona, central New Mexico, northern Michigan, and northern New York. Winters from southern British Columbia, Idaho, Nebraska, Illinois, West Virginia, and New Jersey south to Guatemala, the Gulf coast of the United States, and Florida.

Status in Idaho. A common summer resident in the northern part of the state, wintering irregularly and in small numbers at Lewiston. Less numerous and of local distribution in southern Idaho.

Bonner County. First noted in 1917 at the Trestle Creek Lookout, north of Clark Fork, August 23, and daily thereafter (Burleigh, 1923).

Kootenai County. Arrives at Fort Sherman (Coeur d'Alene) about the middle of April; breeds commonly (Merrill, 1898); common in the spring at Coeur d'Alene (1910-14); probably nests; a specimen taken April 20, 1915 (Rust, 1916); noted daily, July 1-10, 1943, at the upper end of Lake Coeur d'Alene (Yocom, 1946); several birds noted September 23, 1948, in woods bordering Lake Coeur d'Alene (Burleigh); Bent (1949) cites April 7 as an arrival date for Coeur d'Alene.

Shoshone County. A common summer resident (1921-41) on the St. Joe National Forest, occurring "in forests of the Transition and Canadian Zones" (Hand, 1941); an occasional singing male noted at Lookout Pass (altitude 4,738 feet) June 15, 1958 (Burleigh).

Benewah County. Abundant at St. Maries in migration; noted from the middle of April until October (Hand, 1941).

Latah County. Plentiful, June 1-August 16, 1947, "in densely forested areas" (Johnston, 1949); a common summer resident at Harvard, 1951-52; young seen July 29, 1952 (Verner, 1953); common and of general distribution throughout the county (1948-58), usually appearing in the spring in early April, and being only infrequently noted after the latter part of October (Burleigh).

Nez Perce County. A fairly common transient, and an uncommon winter resident at Lewiston (1948-58); extreme dates of occurrence September 6 (1953) and May 16 (1953) (Burleigh).

Clearwater County. A fairly common summer resident (1951-56) at Headquarters, earliest date of arrival in the spring April 21 (1953) (Burleigh).

Valley County. Specimens in the Denver Museum of Natural History in Colorado were taken by Brodkorb in July on Brundage Mountain and at Payette Lake.

Washington County. An occasional bird noted at Weiser November 22, 1951, in woods bordering the Weiser River, and on November 15, 1957, in willows at the edge of the Snake River; several singing males seen partway up Cuddy Mountain (altitude 6,000 feet) June 6, 1952 (Burleigh).

Ada County. Noted December 10, 1957 and March 21, 1967, in underbrush fringing Dry Creek four miles north of Boise (Burleigh). Bent (1949) cites December 23 as a departure date for Meridian. These dates suggest the possibility that this species winters, at least in small numbers, in southern Idaho.

Owyhee County. Noted at Silver City June 2, 1951, and a male collected that day (Levy, 1962); specimens from the east slope of Florida Mountain, taken by Brodkorb in June, are in the Denver Museum of Natural History.

Fremont County. Fairly common in 1916 in canyons, and on wooded ridges (Rust, 1917).

Clark County. Several seen on Signal Peak June 19 and July 14, 1961 (Oring, 1962).

Blaine County. An occasional singing male noted June 24-28, 1950, on the mountainsides north and east of Ketchum, to an altitude of approximately 10,000 feet (Burleigh).

Bonneville County. A common summer resident at Grays Lake, 1949-51; arrival dates April 17, 1950, and April 26, 1951 (Steel, 1956); noted on Caribou Mountain May 23, and at Alpine May 28, 1951 (Burleigh).

Franklin County. There are specimens in the Denver Museum of Natural History taken in June by Brodkorb one mile west of Summit.

South Central Idaho. Common in 1890 during the fall migration in the Pahsimeroi and Salmon River Mountains; a few seen in the Sawtooth Mountains about October 1, and at Shoshone Falls October 9 to 11 (Merriam, 1891).

Minidoka County. Noted in migration at Rupert, 1919-21; arrival dates in the spring April 19, 1919, April 6, 1920, April 12, 1921 (Davis, 1935).

Habits. The Ruby-crowned Kinglet is not as hardy a bird as the preceding species; it winters in small numbers only at Lewiston, where the winters are relatively mild because of the low altitude (738 feet). At Moscow a single bird seen March 6, 1958, suggested a wintering individual, for this is a month earlier than this Kinglet usually appears in northern Idaho in the spring. A possible explanation is that it had wintered at Lewiston, and had been tempted by spring-like weather prematurely to begin its northward migration. In Latah County, where this species is a common summer resident, it is normally present from early April until the latter part of October. At Moscow my extreme dates of occurrence are April 2 (1950 and 1953) and November 8 (1956), at Potlatch March 25 (1956) and October 17 (1948).

At Potlatch I saw a female May 21, 1948, carrying nesting material, but I was unsuccessful in finding the nest. Five years later I was more fortunate at Moscow, a nest that I had found being built holding seven fresh eggs May 29, 1953. It was twenty feet from the ground at the outer end of a limb of a Douglas fir standing at the edge of a clearing in a wooded ravine.

Regulus calendula cineraceus Grinnell

This race, occurring during the summer months throughout the Rocky Mountain region, is a common summer resident and abundant transient in Idaho. Specimens verifying its occurrence in the state, and typical of *cineraceus,* were taken as follows: Kootenai County, Coeur d'Alene, female September 23, 1948; Shoshone County, Lookout Pass, male June 15, 1958; Latah County, Potlatch, males October 10, 1948, April 21, 1949, April 9 and 16, 1950, April 4, 1954, March 25 and October 7, 1956, April 14, 1957, females July 31, 1949, October 15, 1950, May 4, 1952, Viola, female May 3, 1948, Moscow, fifty-eight specimens between the dates of April 19, 1948, and August 16, 1958; Nez Perce County, Lewiston, males October 21, 1951, October 19, 1952, February 13 and April 2, 1953, January 28, 1954, January 6 and 19, October 21 and 24, November 1 and 16, December 4, 1956, March 6 and April 4, 1958, females September 24, 1949, September 28, 1952, May 16, 1953, September 13 and November 8, 1956, September 8, 1957; Washington County, Weiser, males November 22, 1951, November 15, 1957; Ada County, Boise, male December 10, 1957; Bonneville County, Gray, female May 23, 1951 (Burleigh).

Regulus calendula grinnelli Palmer

This coastal race, occurring during the summer months in Alaska and British Columbia, would appear to be a rare transient in northern Idaho. There is one record for the state, a male I took at Lewiston October 28, 1952.

Regulus calendula calendula (Linnaeus)

The nominate race of the Ruby-crowned Kinglet that breeds north of Idaho in British Columbia and Alberta apparently occurs as a rather scarce transient in the state. Over an interval of eleven years I took three specimens at Moscow, males October 20, 1951, April 8, 1955, and October 19, 1956. It is of interest in this connection to record a specimen of *calendula,* a male, that I collected at Spokane October 12, 1956.

Wagtails and Pipits: *Family Motacillidae*

Anthus spinoletta (Linnaeus): WATER PIPIT

General Distribution. Breeds from northern Alaska, northern Yukon, northern Mackenzie, northern Quebec and Newfoundland south to northern Oregon, northern Arizona, New Mexico, northern Ontario, and Maine. Winters from British Columbia, Nevada, southern Utah, Texas, Arkansas, West Virginia and Delaware south to Baja California, through eastern Mexico to Guatemala, the Gulf coast, and Florida.

Status in Idaho. An uncommon spring transient, and a common fall transient throughout the state; recorded in winter at Lewiston (in 1951 and again in 1954); reported as breeding above timberline (9,500 feet) near Mount Borah, Custer County.

Bonner County. First fall transients noted in 1917 on September 12, a flock of fifty birds on a talus slope below the Trestle Creek Lookout north of Clark Fork (Burleigh, 1923); two small flocks seen in open fields at Clark Fork September 29, 1957 (Burleigh).

Kootenai County. Rare in spring at Fort Sherman (Coeur d'Alene); seen the middle of May; abundant in the fall from the first of September until early November (Merrill, 1898); an uncommon fall migrant (1910-14) at Coeur d'Alene (Rust, 1915); specimens taken at Rose Lake September 11 and 20, 1949 (M. Jollie, in litt.); small flocks noted at Post Falls September 23, 1948, and on the open prairie at Hauser October 9, 1952, May 6, 1953, April 30, 1955, April 13, October 4, and October 17, 1956 (Burleigh).

Shoshone County. A fairly common fall migrant, in September and October, on the St. Joe National Forest, small flocks being seen then on open high ridges (Hand, 1941).

Benewah County. A fairly common fall migrant, in September and October, in the open meadows at St. Maries (Hand, 1941).

Latah County. An uncommon spring transient and a common fall transient (1948-58), small flocks occurring in the open fields and pastures from the latter part of April until the middle of May, and again from the middle of September until the latter part of October (Burleigh).

Nez Perce County. An uncommon spring transient and a common fall transient at Lewiston (1948-58); of rare occurrence there during the winter months (Burleigh).

Clearwater County. Small flocks noted at Headquarters September 15, 1951, and at Weippe September 15, 1951, and March 24, 1953 (Burleigh).

Idaho County. Several flocks seen September 20, 1941, in the Crags Mountains; a female collected at Canteen Meadow, nine miles northeast of Selway Falls (Orr, 1951).

Adams County. "Large numbers" seen at Council in mid-September of 1957 and 1958 (Newhouse, 1960).

Ada County. Noted at Blacks Creek Reservoir, twelve miles south of Boise, October 11, 1941 (Arvey, 1947).

Lemhi County. "Abundant" near Double Springs in early September, 1951 (Levy, 1962).

Bonneville County. A rare transient at Grays Lake, 1949-51; arrival dates in the spring April 16, 1950, April 8, 1951 (Steel, 1956).

South Central Idaho. "Breeds in the Salmon River Mountains"; abundant in late September and early October, 1890, "on the sage plains" (Merriam, 1891).

In the Denver Museum of Natural History there are specimens taken by Brodkorb at the following localities in the southern part of the state: Fremont County, Mount Sawtelle (10,000 feet), August; Blaine County, Quigley Creek, September; Jefferson County, Mud Lake, October; Butte County, Howe, September; Oneida County, Malad City, April.

Habits. In the southern part of its breeding range this species is limited in its distribution during the summer months to the barren rocky slopes of the higher ridges above timberline, and in Idaho it would probably never be encountered at this season of the year much below 10,000 feet. Merriam (1891) states that the Water Pipit breeds in the Salmon River Mountains, but unfortunately he does not comment on his reasons for this statement. As opportunity offered I have attempted to verify the breeding of this species in the state, but I have failed to find any suitable habitat on the higher ridges I was able to reach. However, Fichter (in litt.) reports that the Pipit was found by Lawrence B. McQueen breeding "in the vicinity of Borah Peak, Upper Pahsimeroi Drainage, Custer County" at an altitude of 9,500 feet.

In Latah County the Water Pipit was noted at rather infrequent intervals in the spring, but it was common and frequently observed in the fall. My extreme dates of occurrence at Moscow are April 19 (1949) and May 14 (1953), and September 13 (1951) and October 24 (1951). Two birds seen at Genesee March 7, 1954, were so unusually early that it is possible that they wintered at Lewiston, and ventured farther north at the first indication of spring. Otherwise my extreme dates of occurrence for Genesee are April 21 (1951) and April 24 (1952), and September 8 (1952) and October 26 (1951). I have no spring records for Potlatch, my extreme dates for the fall migration being August 31 (1955) and September 30 (1951).

At Lewiston this species was noted twice during the winter months, a single bird December 21, 1951, and a flock of approximately sixty on January 8, and again on January 13, 1954. Extreme dates of occurrence for the spring migration are April 7 (1956) and May 21 (1953), and in the fall September 4 (1953 and 1957) and November 11 (1956).

Anthus spinoletta rubescens (Tunstall)

This eastern race of the Water Pipit is found during the summer months as far west as northern Yukon, and on the basis of available specimens it

MOUNTAIN BLUEBIRD

PLATE IX

would appear to be a rare transient in northern Idaho. Males identified as *rubescens* were taken at Hauser May 6, 1953, and at Lewiston October 8, 1953, and January 8, 1954.

Anthus spinoletta pacificus Todd

This race of the Water Pipit that breeds from northern Alaska south along the coast to Oregon is a common transient in Idaho. Of sixty-five specimens taken both in the spring and in the fall in the northern part of the state, twenty-eight were found to be typical of *pacificus*, and are as follows: Kootenai County, Post Falls, female September 23, 1948, Hauser, males October 9, 1952, October 4, 1956; Latah County, Potlatch, females September 30, 1951, August 31, 1955, Moscow, males October 6, 1948, September 29, October 13 and 24, 1951, October 15, 1952, females October 10, 1949, September 13, 1951, Genesee, males October 10 and 14, 1951, March 7, 1954, females October 4, 1949, September 13, October 6 and 13, 1950; Nez Perce County, Lewiston, male September 8, 1958, females May 21, 1953, January 13, 1954, September 7 and October 24, 1955; Clearwater County, Weippe, male September 15, 1951.

Anthus spinoletta alticola Todd

On the basis of specimens taken this Rocky Mountain race of the Water Pipit occurs as a rare spring transient in the northern part of the state. Males were collected at Genesee April 21, 1951, Moscow April 23, 1951, and Hauser May 6, 1953. It is possible that further field work will reveal the presence of *alticola* as a fall transient in Idaho.

Anthus spinoletta geophilus Oberholser

This Alaskan race would appear to be the most common of the four races of the Water Pipit recorded in Idaho, for thirty specimens were taken, both in the spring and in the fall, in the northern part of the state; for this species, this is practically 50 percent of the total number collected from 1948 to 1958. These specimens are as follows: Kootenai County, Post Falls, female September 23, 1948, Coeur d'Alene, male September 23, 1950, Hauser, males April 13 and October 17, 1956; Latah County, Potlatch, female September 30, 1951, Moscow, males April 19 and October 11, 1949, September 17, 1950, October 21 and 24, 1951, April 28, 1952, April 19 and May 13, 1953, April 25, 1955, females October 4, 1950, April 27 and October 12, 1952, Genesee, males October 10 and 16, 1951, April 24, 1952, females October 16, 1950, April 21, 1951, September 8 and October 19, 1952; Nez Perce County, Lewiston, males April 13 and 28, and October 21, 1953, September 16, 1954, female May 16, 1954; Clearwater County, Headquarters, male September 15, 1951.

Waxwings: *Family Bombycillidae*

Bombycilla garrula pallidiceps Reichenow: BOHEMIAN WAXWING

General Distribution. Breeds from Alaska, central Yukon, central Mackenzie and northern Manitoba south to central Washington and northwestern Montana. Winters from southeastern Alaska, southern Mackenzie, southern Ontario and southern Quebec south irregularly to southern California, central New Mexico, northern Arkansas, central Ohio, and Pennsylvania.

Status in Idaho. A common winter resident throughout the state. Apparently nests rarely in extreme northern Idaho.

Bonner County. Taylor (1918) states that according to an article in the *Pacific Sportsman* (Vol. 2, June, 1905, page 270) a nest of the Bohemian Waxwing was found by Dr. C. S. Moody at Sandpoint that held five eggs. This is the only breeding record for the state.

Kootenai County. An irregular "winter visitor" at Fort Sherman (Coeur d'Alene); specimens taken in January and March (Merrill, 1898); common at Coeur d'Alene in the fall and winter (1910-14), being noted from November 18 until March 4 (Rust, 1915); a flock of sixteen birds seen in an apple orchard at Hauser March 12, 1957 (Burleigh).

Benewah County. An irregular, often abundant, winter "visitor" at St. Maries (1921-41); observed from November to March (Hand, 1941).

Latah County. Large flocks totalling 1,500 to 3,000 individuals noted at Moscow during the latter half of January, 1937, feeding on the berries of the Russian olive (*Eleagnus argentea*) and the mountain ash (Alcorn and Mann, 1937); a common but erratic winter resident at Moscow (1947-58); the first flocks usually appeared in early November, but there were years when this species was not recorded until late December or early January; in the spring it was only infrequently seen after early March, although in 1950 and again in 1955 small flocks were present until early April; noted at Genesee (January 1, 1951, January 19, 1952, March 4, 1956), and Viola (January 15, 1956) (Burleigh).

Nez Perce County. Noted at Lewiston only on February 1 and 5, 1950; apparently a rare winter visitant at this low altitude (Burleigh).

Clearwater County. A flock of twelve birds seen at Orofino November 25, 1954 (Burleigh).

Blaine County. First noted near Ketchum (on Rook's Creek, at 7,000 feet) on November 9, 1910; a flock of eighteen seen at Hailey on November 22, feeding on frozen apples (Jewett, 1912).

South Central Idaho. Said to be common in the winter in Lemhi Valley (Merriam, 1891).

In the Denver Museum of Natural History there are 104 specimens of the Bohemian Waxwing collected by Brodkorb at the following localities in the southern part of the state: Fremont County, Stewart Ranch, November; Jefferson County, Mud Lake, November; Madison County, Muddy

Creek, December; Bannock County, Portneuf River, January; Bingham County, Snake River, December; Bear Lake County, Montpelier, St. Charles, January, February; Cassia County, Burley, January; Twin Falls County, Twin Falls, February; Elmore County, Glenns Ferry, March.

In order both to verify the occurrence of this species in the state, and to determine whether more than one race was represented, forty-two specimens were taken at Moscow (1947-58) between the extreme dates of October 28 (1956) and April 3 (1950). All were found to be typical of *pallidiceps*.

Habits. Waxwings, regardless of species, are noted for their unpredictable movements, and this trait was characteristic of the Bohemian Waxwing as a winter resident at Moscow. Some years only small flocks appeared, other years, as in 1951, flocks comprising fully one thousand individuals were seen. Only once was this species recorded as early as the latter part of October (October 25, 1956); it was usually early November before it was seen for the first time, but in 1949 the first flock did not appear until December 23, and a year later not until January 1, 1951. There is little question but that an available food supply is the major factor in their occurrence in northern Idaho during the winter months. As long as there is an abundance of such berries as the mountain ash and Spanish olive they seem unaffected by frequent blizzards and subzero temperatures. In late winter frozen apples are accepted when there are no longer any berries left, and with the first mild weather in early spring these waxwings are commonly seen "fly catching" from the upper branches of the larger trees. Although only infrequently observed after the middle of March, a few individuals occasionally linger until early April, my latest dates of occurrence being April 5, 1950 (two birds), and April 3, 1955 (a flock of twelve).

Bombycilla cedrorum Vieillot: CEDAR WAXWING

General Distribution. Breeds from southeastern Alaska, northern Alberta, northern Ontario, central Quebec and Newfoundland south to northern California, Colorado, Oklahoma, eastern Tennessee, and northern Georgia. Winters from southern British Columbia, northern Idaho, northern Colorado, Missouri, Michigan and southern Ontario south to Panama, the Gulf coast of the United States, and central Florida.

Status in Idaho. A fairly common summer resident, and an irregular and uncommon winter resident in the northern part of the state. A scarce and local summer resident in southern Idaho.

Bonner County. A plentiful summer resident in 1917 at Clark Fork (Burleigh, 1923).

Kootenai County. Common in summer at Fort Sherman (Coeur d'Alene) from April until about August 20 (Merrill, 1898); small flocks noted at Blue Lake in 1894 (Snyder, 1900); an uncommon summer resident at Coeur d'Alene, 1910-14; a nest with three fresh eggs found June 28 on Fernan Creek (Rust, 1915); several noted at the upper end of Lake Coeur d'Alene July 1-10, 1943 (Yocom, 1946).

Benewah County. A common summer resident at St. Maries, 1921-41, from May to September (Hand, 1941).

Latah County. Noted in pairs during the summer of 1947, at Harvard, Moscow, and Deary (Johnston, 1949); a common summer resident at Harvard (1951 and 1952); a pair seen gathering nesting material July 18, 1952 (Verner, 1953); a fairly common but local summer resident (1948-58); breeding pairs noted at Princeton, Potlatch, Moscow, and Bovill; observed during the winter months at Moscow and at Genesee (Burleigh).

Nez Perce County. Reported by Bendire to breed commonly at Lapwai; nests taken June 19 and 26, 1871 (Merriam, 1891); a rare transient at Lewiston; one winter record, a small flock February 5, 1950 (Burleigh).

Clearwater County. One breeding pair noted at Headquarters August 21, 1951, and young of the year, in streaked plumage, at Weippe October 21, 1952 (Burleigh).

Adams County. One bird seen July 17, and several October 9, 1958, at Council (Hornet Creek) (Newhouse, 1960); several breeding pairs noted at New Meadows July 18, 1960 (Burleigh).

Elmore County. Noted on Rattlesnake Creek, thirty miles east of Boise, July 23, 1945 (Jollie, in litt.).

Fremont County. Several seen on Little Dry Creek in late June, 1916 (Rust, 1917).

Bonneville County. Noted in Snake Canyon, nine miles southeast of Irwin, July 13, 1949 (Jollie, in litt.); a rare transient at Grays Lake, 1949-51; arrival date June 1, 1950 (Steel, 1956); a single bird seen at Big Elk Creek August 6, 1961 (Oring, 1962).

South Central Idaho. A common summer resident in 1950 and 1951 "in suitable habitats throughout the area" (Levy, 1962).

Minidoka County. Noted at Rupert March 21, 1920 (Davis, 1935).

In the Denver Museum of Natural History there are specimens representing the breeding population of the Cedar Waxwing taken by Brodkorb at the following localities: Clark County, Medicine Lodge Creek, June, Targhee National Forest, July; Fremont County, eight miles north of Big Falls, August.

Habits. Although the Cedar Waxwing could be considered a resident species in northern Idaho, being present both during the summer months and in the winter, it actually does not fall into that category. There is an interval in the late fall, and again in the late spring, when I have failed to record it, and for a time this puzzled me. The explanation proved to be a simple one, however. The breeding race, *larifuga*, on the basis of specimens taken, occurs only during the summer months, being replaced during the winter by the northern race, *aquilonia*, that does not appear until November, and has disappeared in the spring fully a month before the breeding population arrives.

This waxwing nests later than any other species in the state, for it is usually early July before the females are incubating full sets of fresh eggs.

At Clark Fork, in 1917, I found my first nests on July 5, one with two fresh eggs, the other with five but slightly incubated. The first nest was six feet up in a small Douglas fir at the edge of a field, and was built of weed stems and wool, and lined with wool and dry pine needles. The second was fifteen feet from the ground in the top of a larch sapling, and was compactly built of larch twigs, grasses, and moss, lined with dry white pine needles. Rust (1915) states that a nest found on Fernan Creek, at Coeur d'Alene, held three fresh eggs on June 28, and was seven feet up "in a haw bush." According to Merrill (1898) the nests he examined at Coeur d'Alene were in "thorn bushes" at the edge of the river, and were loose and bulky, composed of strips of bark and "flood debris," and lined with long black fibrous moss, dry grass, rootlets, and pine needles. Verner (1953) watched a pair at Harvard on July 18, 1952, that were busily engaged in gathering nesting material.

Bombycilla cedrorum larifuga Burleigh

This western race can be distinguished from *cedrorum* by its paler coloration both above and below. It is a fairly common summer resident over much of the state; but it is not known to winter, appearing in the spring in late May, and disappearing in October. Specimens typical of *larifuga* have been taken in Idaho as follows: Latah County, Harvard, two males June 15, 1952, Potlatch, male July 13, 1952, female immature October 16, 1949, August 4, 1951, October 8, 1952, Moscow, male June 27, 1955, female July 2, 1949, male immature September 29, 1948, Boville, female July 19, 1948; Clearwater County, Headquarters, male August 21, 1951, Weippe, male immature October 21, 1952; Adams County, New Meadows, male July 18, 1960.

Bombycilla cedrorum aquilonia Burleigh

This extreme northern race of the Cedar Waxwing is found during the summer months from Alaska east through the northern part of the Canadian Provinces to Newfoundland. It can be distinguished by the uniformly dark gray of the upper parts, and by the vinaceous coloration of the under parts. It occurs as an uncommon and irregular winter resident in the northern part of the state, appearing in November and lingering in the spring as late as the latter part of April. Specimens typical of *aquilonia* have been taken as follows: Latah County, Moscow, males November 22, 1948, November 8 and December 24, 1949, April 23 and December 16, 1953, December 28, 1954, November 3, 1956, females December 3 and 15, 1949, January 4, 1950, January 27, 1951, November 15, 1952, December 25, 1953, January 30, 1954, Genesee, male February 16, 1950; Nez Perce County, Lewiston, two females February 5, 1950.

Shrikes: *Family Laniidae*

Lanius excubitor invictus Grinnell: Northern Shrike

General Distribution. Breeds from northern Alaska, central Yukon, northern Mackenzie and northern Manitoba south to northern British Columbia and northeastern Alberta. Winters from central Alaska, central Alberta, southern Manitoba, Minnesota and northern Wisconsin south to northern California, central Arizona, southern New Mexico, western Kansas, and central Missouri.

Status in Idaho. A fairly common winter resident in open country throughout the state.

Boundary County. One bird seen at Bonners Ferry November 24, 1948 (Burleigh).

Kootenai County. Common in fall at Fort Sherman (Coeur d'Alene), arriving in early November; a few in winter (Merrill, 1898); a rare winter resident at Coeur d'Alene, 1910-14; noted in January, 1913, and on December 21, 1914 (Rust, 1915); single birds seen at Coeur d'Alene November 26, 1948, and January 1, 1954, at Post Falls February 14, 1950, and at Hauser December 16, 1950, October 16 and 17, 1956, and September 26, 1957 (Burleigh).

Benewah County. An irregular and usually not uncommon winter "visitor" at St. Maries (1921-41); noted in the open valleys from October until March (Hand, 1941).

Latah County. A fairly common winter resident (1947-58), being seen almost daily in the open Palouse country from the latter part of October until early April; observed at Harvard, Princeton, Potlatch, Viola, Moscow, Genesee, Juliaetta, and Deary (Burleigh).

Nez Perce County. An uncommon winter resident; noted in the Coyote Canyon October 27, 1949, and February 1, 1952, at Lewiston at infrequent intervals between the dates of October 31 (1951) and April 1 (1957), at Ferdinand December 18, 1951, and at Winchester December 18, 1951 (Burleigh).

Clearwater County. Noted in the open prairie at Weippe November 6, 1952, and February 8, 1954 (Burleigh).

Ada County. A specimen taken at Boise February 3, 1943 (Arvey, 1947).

Blaine County. One seen near Ketchum, on Rook's Creek, November 13, 1910 (Jewett, 1912).

Bonneville County. One bird seen at Gray November 11, 1957 (Burleigh).

South Central Idaho. A specimen taken at Fort Hall October 12, 1872 (Merriam, 1891).

Jerome County. One bird noted at Eden December 10, 1957 (Burleigh).

There are also five specimens from southern Idaho in the Denver Museum of Natural History taken by Brodkorb as follows: Elmore County, Glenns Ferry, March; Jefferson County, Mud Lake, October and November; Bear Lake County, Montpelier, January.

To verify the occurrence of the Northern Shrike in the state, and to determine what race, or races, occur during the winter months, I collected a series of specimens largely in the northern part of the state. These are all typical of *invictus,* characterized by its larger size and paler upper parts, and are as follows: Kootenai County, Post Falls, male February 14, 1950, Coeur d'Alene, male January 1, 1954, Hauser, female October 17, 1956, male September 26, 1957; Latah County, Viola, female February 7, 1949, Moscow, six males between the dates of November 18, 1947, and March 28, 1956, nineteen females between the dates of November 5, 1947, and February 23, 1958, Genesee, males February 5, 1950, April 4, 1953, and April 4, 1955, female March 13, 1954, Potlatch, male February 19, 1957; Nez Perce County, Lewiston, males October 31, 1951, February 17, 1953, March 24, 1957, females November 4 and 27, 1952, January 13, 1954, January 30 and April 1, 1957; Idaho County, Ferdinand, female December 18, 1951; Jerome County, Eden, male December 10, 1957.

Habits. The Northern Shrike is possibly the least sociable of all the birds that will be encountered in Idaho, for at no time did I see even two birds together. Its preference is for the more open country, and here solitary individuals will be found perched in the top of a tree or bush, or even more commonly on a telephone pole or fence post at the side of a road. Under such circumstances it is in most cases difficult to approach, for it is at all times wary and suspicious of any interest in its activities. It is normally silent during the winter months, and only once did I hear its song. At Moscow, on March 19, 1952, one was heard uttering its repertoire of trills and short whistles, interspersed with an occasional harsh note, from the top of a telephone pole, and on collecting it I was interested to find that it was a female.

In the fall this shrike usually appears in northern Idaho in late October, and in the spring it is rarely seen after the latter part of March. At Moscow my extreme dates of occurrence are October 18 (1952) and April 14 (1955), at Genesee October 21 (1951) and April 6 (1952). At Viola it was seen as late in the spring as April 3 (1949); my earliest date of arrival at Potlatch is October 23 (1949). An unusually early record in the fall is that of the one bird noted in the open prairie at Hauser, in Kootenai County, September 26, 1957.

Lanius ludovicianus Linnaeus: Loggerhead Shrike

General Distribution. Breeds from southern British Columbia, central Alberta, central Saskatchewan, southern Ontario and southern Quebec south to Baja California, southern Mexico (Oaxaca), the Gulf coast, and southern Florida. Winters as far north as the southern half of its breeding range.

Status in Idaho. A fairly common summer resident in the southern part of the state, and a scarce and irregular spring transient in northern Idaho.

Although it was heretofore unrecorded in the northern part of the state, I noted this species at infrequent intervals in the spring, but never succeeded in recording it in the fall. In Latah County it was seen at Moscow May 15, 1951, May 11, 1952, and April 6, 1956, at Potlatch May 13, 1952, and at Genesee March 24, 1956; in Nez Perce County, at Lewiston March 21, 1953; and in Clearwater County, at Weippe March 24, 1953.

In southern Idaho it was of general distribution in the open arid country where the sagebrush predominated, but occurred during the summer months only.

Adams County. One bird seen July 12, 1958, "in arid country" south of Council (Newhouse, 1960).

Ada County. One bird seen at Boise November 7, 1957 (Burleigh).

Owyhee County. A single bird noted at Riddle May 28 to June 3, 1934 (Davis, 1935); an occasional bird noted in 1949 at Oreana June 25; in 1950 at Homedale and Marsing February 19, and at Riddle February 25; in 1951 at Murphy June 3, and at Grandview June 30 (Burleigh).

Clark County. A single bird seen August 16, 1916, between Kilgore and Rea (Rust, 1917).

Jefferson County. A common summer resident in 1961 on the Camas National Wildlife Refuge (Oring, 1962).

Bonneville County. A rare transient at Gray's Lake, 1949-1951 (Steel, 1956); one bird seen at Gray May 28, 1951 (Burleigh).

South Central Idaho. Common on the Snake River, near Blackfoot, in July, 1890; also noted then at Big Butte, along the Big Lost River and on Birch Creek; later seen at Eagle Rock August 21, in Little Lost River Valley September 11, and in the Pahsimeroi Valley September 17 (a specimen taken at Fort Hall October 3, 1872) (Merriam, 1891); a fairly common breeding bird in 1949 "in the sagebrush plains" (Levy, 1950); four birds seen May 25, 1952, in arid sagebrush country between Arco and Blackfoot (Burleigh).

Minidoka County. Noted at Rupert (1919-21) between the dates of February 18 and November 6 (Davis, 1935); a specimen taken at Acequia June 8, 1934 (Davis, 1934).

Jerome County. A specimen taken at Jerome June 30, 1949 (Levy, 1950).

Twin Falls County. Specimens taken at Hollister June 28 and July 19, 1949 (Levy, 1950).

Cassia County. An occasional bird noted at Oakley June 5, 1957 (Burleigh).

In the Denver Museum of Natural History there are thirty-nine specimens of the Loggerhead Shrike taken in southern Idaho by Brodkorb as follows: Fremont County, Big Springs, August; Blaine County, Carey, August; Bannock County, Pocatello, April; Oneida County, Malad City, April; Cassia County, Goose Creek, August; Jerome County, Jerome, August; Twin Falls County, Rogerson, July; Elmore County, Mountain Home, March; Canyon County, Deer Flat Reservoir, April.

Habits. To one familiar with the Loggerhead Shrike in the southern states its actions in its breeding range in southern Idaho come as somewhat of a surprise. In Georgia or in Louisiana, it is commonly found in the proximity of farms, and shows as little concern over the presence of man as does the robin in the towns and cities. In Idaho, however, it is a wary, suspicious bird, my observations agreeing with those of Levy (1950) who states that it "is extremely shy and hard to observe, so that a person not familiar with its habits would classify it as rare." In my experience, if approached as it perched in the top of a sage bush it at once flew for some distance, disappeared in the sagebrush, and could not be found again.

Davis (1935) cites May 20 as the earliest date for eggs at Rupert, in Minidoka County. I encountered a brood of three fully grown young, out of the nest for some time, at Grandview, in Owyhee County, June 30, 1951.

Lanius ludovicianus gambeli (Ridgway)

This race, the breeding form in Idaho, is found during the summer months as far north as southern British Columbia and as far south as northern Arizona. I have taken specimens verifying its occurrence in the state as follows: Latah County, Genesee, male March 24, 1956, Moscow, male April 6, 1956; Nez Perce County, Lewiston, male March 21, 1953; Clearwater County, Weippe, male March 24, 1953; Owyhee County, Murphy, male June 3, 1951, Grandview, female and male immature June 30, 1951; Jerome County, Jerome, male June 20, 1949; Cassia County, Oakley, male June 5, 1957; Minidoka County, Minidoka, female June 15, 1960.

Lanius ludovicianus excubitorides Swainson

This race, distinguished from *gambeli* by its larger size and paler upperparts, occurs during the summer months north to central Alberta, and on the basis of specimens taken it is a rare spring transient in northern Idaho. Males typical of *excubitorides* were collected at Moscow May 15, 1951, and at Potlatch May 13, 1952.

Starlings: *Family Sturnidae*

Sturnus vulgaris vulgaris Linnaeus: STARLING

General Distribution. Indigenous to Europe; introduced in the United States in 1890, and now largely resident from British Columbia, southern Saskatchewan, northern Ontario, eastern Quebec and Newfoundland south to California, central Arizona, southern Kansas, the Gulf coast, and central Florida.

Status in Idaho. Now a fairly common but local summer resident throughout much of the state; winters regularly but in small numbers at Moscow and Genesee, in Latah County, and commonly at Lewiston in Nez Perce County.

What is apparently the first record for Idaho is that of a single bird seen at Moscow by Bill Musgrove December 13, 1941 (Olson, 1943).

On coming to Moscow in October, 1947, I failed to note this species until December 23 when I saw a flock of approximately sixty birds at Genesee. For the following two years similar-sized flocks were observed during the winter months at Genesee and Moscow, and at Lewiston, and in 1949 Starlings were present for the first time during the spring and summer. In succeeding years this species has gradually increased in numbers and is now fairly common here throughout the year.

Levy (1959) stated that a specimen was taken at Bonners Ferry October 10, 1951, and that the Starling is "now well established" at Porthill and Bonners Ferry, Boundary County; Hauser, Kootenai County; St. Maries, Benewah County; and Moscow and Genesee, Latah County.

The first definite breeding record was reported by Jollie (1951) who found two nests at Grangeville, Idaho County, on May 12, 1951, one with six eggs, the other with five young about two-thirds grown. It would appear, however, that this species nested in Nez Perce County in 1950, for he collected a juvenile, in partial moult, at the bottom of the Central Grade, four miles east of Lewiston, on October 7.

In Clearwater County, in 1953, I noted a flock of twelve birds at Weippe March 24, and what was apparently a mated pair at Headquarters March 25.

In the southern part of Idaho the Starling was reported by Webster (1946) as "seen in numbers" in February, 1946, at American Falls, Aberdeen, and Pocatello. Two collected at Pocatello February 17 apparently represent the first specimens for the state. Levy (1952) noted one breeding pair at Idaho Falls May 28, 1951. In Adams County it was found to be common in 1957 and 1958; fully grown young were seen May 24 (Newhouse, 1960). On June 26, 1960, I noted several breeding pairs in aspen groves at the top of Targhee Pass, Fremont County (altitude 7,000 feet) one pair feeding young in the nest on that date.

Habits. Although a difference of opinion exists as to the actual number involved, it would appear that in 1890 and 1891 one hundred Starlings were liberated in Central Park, in New York City. This was the first successful introduction, others attempted as early as 1872 resulting in failure. Once satisfactorily established the increase in the breeding population saw the Starling gradually extend its range in every direction, and in just fifty years the first venturesome individual had reached Idaho. In the years to come it will probably become increasingly common in the state; being of doubtful value from an economic standpoint, this increase in numbers has been viewed with some apprehension.

In nesting a cavity is selected, and individual pairs are seldom very particular in this respect, the main requirement being that there is sufficient space to accommodate the growing nestlings. One nest found by Jollie at Grangeville was in an apple tree in an old orchard, the other "in a box elder in a small grove." The birds I found in 1960 nesting in aspen groves at the top of Targhee Pass had accepted old holes originally used by the Red-naped Sapsucker, in this instance driving away the Tree Swallows that in 1957 were nesting there.

Vireos: *Family Vireonidae*

Vireo solitarius (Wilson): SOLITARY VIREO

General Distribution. Breeds from northern British Columbia, southern Mackenzie, northern Ontario, southern Quebec and Nova Scotia south to Baja California, southern Nevada, western Mexico (Sonora and Chihuahua), western Texas, central Minnesota, northern Wisconsin, eastern Tennessee and northwestern South Carolina. Winters from southern Arizona, northern Mexico (Nuevo Leon), the Gulf coast and South Carolina south to northern Nicaragua and Cuba.

Status in Idaho. A fairly common but rather local summer resident in the more heavily wooded areas of the state.

Bonner County. Fairly plentiful during the summer of 1917 on Trestle Creek, north of Clark Fork, but not noted elsewhere (Burleigh, 1923).

Kootenai County. Arrives at Fort Sherman (Coeur d'Alene) about the tenth of May; breeds "moderately" in pine woods (Merrill, 1898); an uncommon summer resident at Coeur d'Alene, 1910-14 (Rust, 1915).

Shoshone County. A common summer resident, 1921-41, on the St. Joe National Forest, occurring from early May until September in both the Canadian and Transition Zones (Hand, 1941).

Latah County. A fairly common and generally distributed summer resident in 1947 (June 1-August 16); nests with young found in late June at Harvard (Johnston, 1949); a fairly common summer resident on the wooded ridges north and east of Moscow (1948-58), usually arriving in the spring in early May and lingering in the fall until early October (Burleigh).

Nez Perce County. Reported by Bendire as nesting at Fort Lapwai in June, 1871 (Merriam, 1891); an extremely scarce transient at Lewiston, being unrecorded in the spring and noted but twice during the fall migration over an interval of ten years, on August 13, 1950, and again on September 15, 1952 (Burleigh).

Clearwater County. A single bird noted at Weippe September 15, 1951 (Burleigh).

Adams County. Specimen now in the Museum of Vertebrate Zoology, Berkeley, taken 3 miles west of Payette Lake (Arvey, 1947).

Lemhi County. One breeding pair noted June 6, 1949, in open pine woods on Color Creek, north of Shoup (Burleigh).

Fremont County. A common summer resident; a nest with four fresh eggs found July 6, 1916, on Little Dry Creek (Rust, 1917).

Jefferson County. Fall transients noted daily, August 21-29, 1961, on the Camas National Wildlife Refuge; a female in immature plumage collected August 22 (Oring, 1962).

Cassia County. A rather scarce summer resident on the juniper-covered ridges south of Oakley, where singing males were collected June 28, 1949 (M. Jollie), and June 23, 1950 (Burleigh); another singing male also noted at the Silent City of Rocks June 6, 1951 (Levy, 1962).

Habits. The distribution of Cassin's Vireo in Idaho is apparently influenced by altitude, for while a fairly common summer resident between 2,500 and 3,000 feet, it is extremely scarce or wanting, despite suitable habitat, above 3,000 feet. This would account for its scarcity in the southern part of the state where it has been rarely recorded during the summer months. I failed to note it then even as far south as Clearwater County, and it has yet to be reported from Idaho County. The one record from Adams County would indicate that it does occur sparingly to an altitude of 5,000 feet, but being a species not easily overlooked, there can be little question as to its absence over much of the state.

In Latah County it normally appeared in the spring in early May and was only infrequently seen after early October. My extreme dates of occurrence at Moscow are April 30 (1948), average May 5, and October 11 (1951), average October 1. At Potlatch my latest date in the fall is October 2, 1950.

The southward movement in the fall would appear to be well underway in August. The single bird seen at Lewiston August 13, 1950, was feeding in willows fringing the Snake River, and on being collected was found to be an adult female in partial moult. Oring (1962) reported that as many as four individuals were noted daily the last week in August on the Camas National Wildlife Refuge, in the southeastern corner of the state.

Vireo solitarius cassinii Xantus

To verify the occurrence of this species in Idaho a small series of specimens was taken in the northern part of the state; all were found to be typical of the northern Rocky Mountain race, *cassinii*, that breeds from southern British Columbia south to California and Nevada. They are as follows: Latah County, Moscow, males April 30, May 8, and September 3, 1948, May 6, 1949, May 1 and 2, 1950, May 8 and October 11, 1951, May 8, 1952, October 2, 1953, May 5, 1955, May 3, 1957, females September 11, 1950, October 5, 1951, Potlatch, male October 2, 1950; Nez Perce County, Lewiston, female August 13, 1950; Clearwater County, Weippe, male September 15, 1951.

Vireo solitarius plumbeus Coues

The two specimens taken on the juniper-covered ridges south of Oakley, in Cassia County, males June 28, 1949, and June 23, 1950, were found to represent this southern Rocky Mountain race, heretofore unrecorded as far north as southern Idaho. Although known to date only from Cassia County, it probably occurs during the summer months along the extreme southern edge of the state where there is suitable habitat.

Vireo olivaceus caniviridis Burleigh: RED-EYED VIREO

General Distribution. Breeds rather locally throughout Washington, Idaho, and northern Oregon. Accidental in Alaska. Winter range undetermined.

Status in Idaho. A local but common and widely distributed summer resident in the northern part of the state; less numerous and reported to date in but a few widely separated areas in southern Idaho during the summer months.

Boundary County. An occasional singing male seen at Porthill June 26, 1957, in woods bordering the Kootenai River (Burleigh).

Bonner County. A plentiful summer resident in 1917 at Clark Fork occurring in deciduous woods along the Clark Fork River and the smaller streams (Burleigh, 1923); an occasional singing male seen at Sandpoint June 21, 1957, in cottonwoods at the edge of Lake Pend Oreille (Burleigh).

Kootenai County. Abundant in summer at Fort Sherman (Coeur d'Alene), arriving about May 20; occurs in cottonwoods and aspens; several nests found (Merrill, 1898); a common summer resident at Coeur d'Alene (1910-14); a nest with four slightly incubated eggs found at Fernan Lake June 27 (Rust, 1915); an occasional bird noted at Coeur d'Alene July 4, 1949, and again on July 28, 1960, in cottonwoods at the edge of Lake Pend Oreille; a fledgling barely out of the nest collected on this latter date (Burleigh).

Shoshone County. Specimen taken by C. Engler on Nine Mile Creek, four miles northeast of Wallace, July 15, 1938 (Jollie, in litt.).

Benewah County. A common summer resident at St. Maries (1921-41); present from May until August (Hand, 1941); frequently seen along the St. Joe River at St. Maries July 30-31, 1960, and fully grown young of the year taken then (Burleigh).

Latah County. A singing male noted at Juliaetta August 12, 1947 (Johnston, 1949); an uncommon summer resident at Harvard, 1951-52; seen as late as August 8, 1951 (Verner, 1953); a fairly common but local summer resident (1948-58), being limited in its distribution to the larger cottonwoods along the streams; noted at Princeton, Potlatch, and Moscow (Burleigh).

Nez Perce County. An uncommon and local summer resident; noted at Culdesac June 30, 1949, at Lapwai July 12, 1951, and at Lewiston between the dates of June 6 (1951) and August 21 (1956) (Burleigh).

Clearwater County. This vireo found to be fairly plentiful at Orofino June 12, 1951, singing males being frequently noted in woods bordering the Clearwater River; an occasional singing male seen at Elk River June 25, 1951 (Burleigh).

Idaho County. Specimen taken four miles west of Meadow Creek (Arvey, 1947); several singing males noted south of White Bird June 24, 1958, in cottonwoods on Skookumchuck Creek (Burleigh).

Washington County. Two singing males seen at Cambridge June 4, 1951, in woods bordering the Weiser River; fairly plentiful June 7, 1952, in cottonwoods at the edge of East Brownlee Creek, thirty miles northwest of Cambridge (Burleigh).

Boise County. Two breeding pairs noted at Horseshoe Bend June 21, 1950, in cottonwoods at the edge of the Payette River (Burleigh).

Elmore County. Noted on Rattlesnake Creek, thirty miles east of Boise, July 23, 1949 (Jollie, in litt.).

Lemhi County. Two singing males seen at Shoup June 5 and 6, 1949, in woods fringing Colson Creek (Burleigh).

Jefferson County. Fall migrants seen in 1961 on the Camas National Wildlife Refuge, a single bird August 21, and two August 22 (Oring, 1962).

Bonneville County. Noted in the Snake River Canyon, nine miles southeast of Irwin, July 13, 1949 (Jollie, in litt.).

Minidoka County. Migrants noted at Rupert May 17 and September 1, 1919, May 20, 1920, and May 6, 1921 (Davis, 1935).

Vireo olivaceus canivividis can be distinguished from the nominate race by the grayish wash of the upperparts and the light olive gray pileum (Burleigh, 1960). In describing this western race of the Red-eyed Vireo thirty-eight specimens were available from Idaho for comparison with similar material from the eastern United States, and are as follows: Bonner County, Hope, female June 13, 1903, Sandpoint, males June 21, 1957, July 27, 1960, Clark Fork, male July 25, 1960, females July 25 and 26, 1960; Kootenai County, Coeur d'Alene, two males July 4, 1949, fledgling male July 28, 1960; Benewah County, St. Maries, male June 22, 1948, July 30, 1960, immature male July 31, 1960, female July 31, 1960; Latah County, Princeton, male May 30, 1949, Potlatch, male May 21, 1948, females September 4, 1948, September 12, 1951, immature female July 19, 1950, Moscow, males August 27, 1949, July 11, 1951, June 30, 1952, immature male September 16, 1957, females August 11, 1948, September 7, 1949, July 29, 1960; Nez Perce County, Lewiston, males July 24, 1950, June 6, 1951, female August 21, 1956, Culdesac, male June 30, 1949, Lapwai, male July 12, 1950; Clearwater County, Crofino, male June 12, 1951, Elk River, male June 25, 1951; Washington County, Cambridge, males June 4, 1951, June 7, 1952; Boise County, Horseshoe Bend, male June 21, 1950; Idaho County, Graves Creek, male June 17, 1951, White Bird, male June 24, 1958; Lemhi County, Shoup, male June 5, 1949.

Habits. Few birds have as exacting habitat requirements as does the Rey-eyed Vireo in Idaho. In my experience it is found only where cottonwoods border either rivers or the smaller streams. This requirement applies not only to the summer months, but to the period of migration as well; thus there are wide areas within its breeding range where it does not occur at any time of the year. Altitude is apparently also a limiting factor, for despite optimum conditions at higher elevations it has rarely been noted above 2,500 feet.

It is one of the last of the summer residents to appear in the spring, seldom being observed before the end of May. In Latah County my earliest record for the spring migration is that of a single bird seen at Potlatch May 21 (1948). In the fall only an occasional individual is noted after early September, my latest dates of occurrence being September 12 (1951) at Potlatch, and September 21 (1948) at Moscow.

Bent (1950) cites September 16 as a late date of departure at Bayview, in Kootenai County.

Elsewhere within the breeding range of this vireo the nest is said to average from five to ten feet from the ground, and this average would appear to be true in Idaho. Those found by Merrill (1898) at Coeur d'Alene were all within six feet of the ground, while the one reported by Rust (1915) as holding four slightly incubated eggs on June 27 was five feet up in an alder at the edge of Fernan Lake.

Vireo gilvus leucopolius (Oberholser): WARBLING VIREO

General Distribution. Breeds in eastern Washington and northern Idaho south to central-eastern California, southern Nevada, and southwestern Utah. Winter range undetermined, but probably in Mexico.

Status in Idaho. A common summer resident in suitable habitat throughout the state.

Bonner County. An occasional singing male seen at Sandpoint June 24, 1957 (Burleigh).

Kootenai County. Arrives at Fort Sherman (Coeur d'Alene) in May; breeds sparingly (Merrill, 1898); a common summer resident at Coeur d'Alene, 1910-14 (Rust, 1915).

Shoshone County. A common summer resident, 1921-41, on the St. Joe National Forest, frequenting the "deciduous growth" in the valleys; present from May until September (Hand, 1941).

Benewah County. Noted in woods bordering the St. Joe River at St. Maries July 30 and 31, 1960 (Burleigh).

Latah County. Fairly common in 1947 (June 1-August 16) (Johnston, 1949); a common summer resident at Harvard in 1951 and 1952; two nests found July 1, 1951, four eggs in each (Verner, 1953); a common and well-distributed summer resident in the county, 1948-58, rarely appearing in the spring before the middle of May, and lingering in the fall until the latter part of September (Burleigh).

Nez Perce County. An uncommon summer resident at Lewiston, 1948-58; noted on Hatwai Creek, and in willows bordering the Clearwater River; latest dates of departure in the fall September 23, 1951, and September 21, 1956 (Burleigh).

Clearwater County. Found to be a fairly common summer resident at Weippe and at Headquarters, 1952-56, occurring in the deciduous underbrush bordering the streams (Burleigh).

Idaho County. A few noted in July, 1948, in the Lolo Pass region, below 5,000 feet (Orr, 1951).

Adams County. Noted at Council August 25, 1958 (Newhouse, 1960).

Washington County. Several singing males seen June 5, 1952, on East Brownlee Creek, thirty miles northwest of Cambridge (Burleigh).

Owyhee County. An occasional singing male seen June 29, 1951, in deciduous underbrush at Silver City (altitude approximately 6,000 feet) (Burleigh).

Lemhi County. Found to be fairly plentiful at Shoup, in the Bitterroot Mountains, June 4-6, 1949 (Burleigh).

Custer County. An occasional bird noted at Stanley July 16, 1958, and at Mackay July 8, 1960 (Burleigh).

Blaine County. This little vireo found to be a plentiful summer resident in this part of the state (June 24-28, 1950), both in the valleys in the vicinity of Ketchum and Sun Valley, and in willows fringing the streams on the mountainsides to an altitude of 8,000 feet on Easley Peak, and 10,000 feet on Hyndman Peak (Burleigh).

Fremont County. Fairly common June through August, 1916, "in willows and aspens" (Rust, 1917); singing males noted in aspens at Henrys Lake (6,700 feet) June 11, 1957, and at St. Anthony June 30, 1960 (Burleigh).

Clark County. Several pairs noted on Signal Peak June 19 and July 15, 1961 (Oring, 1962).

Jefferson County. Fall migrants seen daily on the Camas National Wildlife Refuge July 28 through August 28, 1961 (Oring, 1962).

Bonneville County. An abundant summer resident at Grays Lake, 1949-51 (Steel, 1956); this species found to be a plentiful summer resident at Gray (June 8-17, 1949), being noted in the stream bottoms (6,400), and in the aspens on Caribou Mountain to an altitude of 8,500 feet (Burleigh).

South Central Idaho. Common in the Lost River Mountain in July, 1890; two specimens taken in the Salmon River Mountains in August (Merriam, 1891); fairly common during the summer of 1949 in the stream bottoms in the south-central part of the state (Levy, 1950).

Minidoka County. A fairly common summer resident at Rupert, 1919-21 (Davis, 1935).

Cassia County. Several singing males seen in aspen groves at the Silent City of Rocks June 12, 1960 (Burleigh).

In order to determine what race or races of *Vireo gilvus* occur in Idaho, both as breeding birds and as transients, a series of specimens was taken (1948 through 1958, and 1960) in various parts of the state. All were found to represent the Great Basin form *leucopolius*, distinguished from *swainsonii,* the breeding population of the Rocky Mountain region, by the paler more grayish upperparts, and whiter underparts. These specimens are as follows: Benewah County, St. Maries, immature male July 31, 1960; Latah County, Potlatch, fifteen specimens between the dates of May 16 (1948) and September 16 (1950), Moscow, seventeen specimens between the dates of May 8 (1949) and September 30 (1956); Nez Perce County, Lewiston, immature male September 23, 1951, male September 21, 1956; Clearwater County, Headquarters, male June 18, 1952; Washington County, Cambridge, female June 5, 1952; Owyhee County, Silver City, male June 29, 1951; Custer County, Stanley, male July 16, 1958, Mackay, male July 8, 1960; Blaine County, Ketchum, male June 24, 1950, Sun Valley, males June 28, 1950, July 1, 1960; Fremont County, Henrys Lake, male June 11, 1957, St. Anthony, female June 30, 1960; Bonneville County, Gray, male June 2, 1952; Cassia County, Silent City of Rocks, male June 12, 1960.

Habits. The Warbling Vireo, unlike its near relatives in Idaho, is not concerned with altitude. It is apparently satisfied wherever suitable habitat

WESTERN TANAGERS

PLATE X

of deciduous underbrush on or near water exists; thus it can be found nesting at Lewiston (738 feet) and on the higher ridges to at least 10,000 feet (Hyndman Peak, in Blaine County).

It appears in the spring in early May, its arrival, as might be expected, being influenced to some extent by the altitude, and also by weather conditions. At Moscow the average date of arrival is May 15, the earliest it has been observed being May 8 (1949). Davis (1935) cites as arrival dates for Rupert, in Minidoka County, May 17, 1919, May 20, 1920, and May 19, 1921. At Gray, at an altitude of 6,400 feet, a single bird was seen in an aspen grove May 26, 1951, this being the earliest this species has been recorded here in the spring.

In early September there is a noticeable decrease in the number of Warbling Vireos present in Latah County, but a few linger until the end of the month. My latest date of departure for Potlatch is September 16 (1950), for Moscow September 30 (1956).

In the eastern United States this vireo feeds and nests in the upper branches of the larger trees, but in Idaho its habits are radically different. Deciduous underbrush comprising such species as the willow, the alder, and the aspen seems to satisfy all its requirements, and here its nest can be found, usually within five or six feet of the ground. Rust (1920) made a careful study of a breeding pair of Warbling Vireos at Coeur d'Alene that, on May 24, 1919, had just started the construction of their nest, four and a half feet from the ground in the fork of a small willow. It was completed on May 30, and was built of dry grasses, white string, down from willow seeds, bits of lichen, cotton, and cow hair. As far as he could determine it was built entirely by the female, but once the four eggs were laid, on June 7, both birds took their turn at incubating. The male was frequently noted singing on the nest, and was very tame, not leaving until the nest was almost touched. The eggs hatched in twelve days, and at the end of fifteen days, on July 5, the young were fully fledged and ready to venture into the world.

Verner (1953) states that the two nests that he found at Harvard in July, 1951, were both five feet from the ground in alders.

Wood Warblers: *Family Parulidae*

Vermivora peregrina (Wilson): TENNESSEE WARBLER

General Distribution. Breeds from southern Yukon, central Mackenzie, northern Ontario, northern Quebec and Newfoundland south to southern British Columbia, northern Montana, southern Manitoba, northern Michigan, northern New York, southern Maine, and Nova Scotia. Winters from southern Mexico (Guerrero and Oaxaca) to Colombia and northern Venezuela.

Status in Idaho. Of accidental occurrence in the northern part of the state.

The only record for the occurrence of this species in Idaho is that of a female that I collected at Potlatch, in Latah County, September 13, 1949.

Habits. Although the Tennessee Warbler breeds commonly north of Idaho in the Canadian Provinces of British Columbia and Alberta, its migration route is such that it will always be of accidental occurrence in the state. The Continental Divide is apparently an effective barrier both in the spring and in the fall, so while of regular occurrence in eastern Montana it is the exceptional individual that will be found farther west in the northwestern United States. It may be more common, however, than the one record would indicate, for its close resemblance to the Orange-crowned Warbler could cause it to be easily overlooked.

Vermivora celata (Say): ORANGE-CROWNED WARBLER

General Distribution. Breeds from central Alaska, central Mackenzie, northern Ontario and northwestern Quebec south to Baja California, southeastern Arizona and western Texas, and to southern Saskatchewan, southern Manitoba and central Ontario. Winters from southern California, central Arizona, southern Texas, the Gulf coast and South Carolina south to Guatemala and southern Florida.

Status in Idaho. A fairly common but local summer resident throughout the state; one winter record for Latah County.

Bonner County. One pair noted during the summer of 1917 in an open meadow below the Trestle Creek Lookout Station north of Clark Fork; male heard singing throughout July (Burleigh, 1923).

Kootenai County. Several specimens taken in May at Fort Sherman (Coeur d'Alene) (Merrill, 1898).

Shoshone County. An uncommon migrant on the St. Joe National Forest, 1921-41, in May and in August (Hand, 1941).

Latah County. A fairly common summer resident, June 1-August 16, 1947; a male collected on Paradise Ridge on June 26 (Johnston, 1949); a fairly plentiful but local summer resident on the wooded ridges north and east of Moscow (1948-58), appearing in the spring in late April, and lingering in the fall until early October; one winter record, a single bird seen daily in the city limits of Moscow December 19-22, 1948 (Burleigh).

Nez Perce County. A rather scarce migrant at Lewiston, 1948-58, being noted but once in the spring, and at infrequent intervals in the fall (Burleigh).

Valley County. Two birds seen at McCall September 18, 1955, feeding in willows fringing a stream (Burleigh).

Owyhee County. One breeding pair noted on a wooded ridge at Triangle (altitude 6,500 feet) June 25, 1949 (Burleigh).

Lemhi County. One specimen taken in the Salmon River Mountains August 22, 1890 (Merriam, 1891).

Bonneville County. A "very common" summer resident at Grays Lake, 1949-51 (Steel, 1956); an occasional singing male seen in the aspens on Bear Island, near the middle of Grays Lake, May 27, 1951 (Burleigh).

Bear Lake County. Noted at Bloomington Lake July 10, 1949 (M. Jollie, in litt.).

Cassia County. A breeding male, now in the collections of the Museum of Vertebrate Zoology, Berkeley, taken by W. B. Davis on Mount Harrison, ten miles south of Albion, June 13, 1936.

In the Denver Museum of Natural History there are eighteen specimens of the Orange-crowned Warbler collected by Pierce Brodkorb as follows: Canyon County, Boise River, two miles north of Caldwell, April; Owyhee County, Silver Mountains, May; Jordan Creek, May; east slope of the Florida Mountains, May; Jefferson County, Rigby, May; Bear Lake County, Fish Haven, May; Franklin County, Emigration Canyon, June.

Habits. In Latah County this species invariably appeared in the spring in late April, and in the fall it was always present until after the first week in October. My extreme records of occurrence for Moscow are April 22 (1950) and October 15 (1951), and for Potlatch April 16 (1950) and October 1 (1956). Altitude was apparently no limiting factor in its distribution, for it was equally common during the summer months on Moscow Mountain (2,500 feet), and at Grays Lake (6,400 feet). At Lewiston it occurred only as a rather uncommon migrant, but this was probably due to the scarcity of suitable habitat at this low altitude, 840 feet. It was noted but once in the spring, on May 16, 1953, and in the fall on September 23 and October 4, 1951, September 14, 1952, October 8, 1955, and September 22, 1957.

The one bird seen at Moscow in December, 1948, appeared daily for four days in my backyard, and fed on apples still remaining on the tree.

Vermivora celata orestera Oberholser

This Rocky Mountain race, distinguished from the nominate race by being larger and more yellowish both above and below, is the breeding form in Idaho. To verify its occurrence in the state a series of specimens was taken, largely in the more northern counties, that proved typical of *orestera* both in measurements and color. These were as follows: Latah County, Moscow, between the extreme dates of April 22 (1950) and October 3 (1957), Potlatch, between the extreme dates of April 16 (1950) and September 16 (1956); Nez Perce County, Lewiston, male October 4, 1951, females September 14, 1952, September 22, 1957; immature female September 23, 1951; Valley County, McCall, female September 18, 1955; Caribou County, Wayan, male May 22, 1951.

A male collected at Moscow May 3, 1948, is intermediate in its characters, having the measurements of *orestera* and the yellowish green coloration of the coast race, *lutescens.*

Vermivora celata celata (Say)

The nominate race of the Orange-crowned Warbler occurs during the summer months north of Idaho in Alberta, and on the evidence of actual specimens, it is a rare transient in the state, both in the spring and in the fall. At Potlatch a male was taken August 31, 1952, and females May 12, 1948, September 16, 1956, and September 13, 1957, and at Lewiston a male May 16, 1953.

Vermivora ruficapilla ridgwayi van Rossem: NASHVILLE WARBLER

General Distribution. Breeds from southern British Columbia and northwestern Montana south to central California, central Nevada and northern Utah. Winters from northern Mexico (Sonora and Durango) south to Guatemala.

Status in Idaho. An uncommon and rather local summer resident over most of the state.

Bonner County. Noted on the south slopes of the mountains north of Clark Fork from early July until late August, 1917 (Burleigh, 1923); a singing male seen in underbrush on Jeru Creek, north of Sandpoint, June 24, 1957 (Burleigh); September 12 cited by Bent (1953) as a late date of departure at Bayview.

Kootenai County. "Not uncommon" at Fort Sherman (Coeur d'Alene) during May; "breeds" (Merrill, 1898); April 29 cited by Bent (1953) as an early date of arrival at Coeur d'Alene.

Shoshone County. A rather uncommon migrant, 1921-41, on the St. Joe National Forest; possibly breeds; present in late April and May, and again in July and August; has been noted occasionally in June (Hand, 1941).

Latah County. A singing male noted on Moscow Mountain June 3, 1947 (Johnston, 1949); an uncommon migrant and a rare summer resident (1948-58) in the wooded areas north and east of Moscow (Burleigh).

Nez Perce County. The only record for Lewiston is that of a single bird seen September 6, 1953, feeding with other warblers in willows fringing a stream (Burleigh).

Clearwater County. One bird seen at Headquarters August 18, 1953 (Burleigh).

Washington County. This species found to be a fairly common summer resident in 1952 on East Brownlee Creek, thirty miles northwest of Cambridge; it was first noted in the spring on May 6; a month later, on June 7, singing males were seen from time to time in underbrush in the valley (Burleigh).

Lemhi County. Two singing males noted at Shoup June 4-6, 1949, one in underbrush bordering Colson Creek (3,800 feet), the other near the top of a ridge facing the Salmon River (4,200 feet) (Burleigh).

To verify the occurrence of this species in the state a small series of specimens were taken, 1948 through 1955, largely in northern Idaho. All were found to be typical of *ridgwayi*, distinguished from the nominate race by the brighter yellow underparts and the grayish, less green, upperparts. These are as follows: Latah County, Moscow, males May 3 and 6, 1948,

April 24 and 29, and July 10, 1949, May 1 and 3, 1950, April 25, 1952, April 26, 1953, May 5 and 13, 1955, females August 9 and September 17, 1948, April 24, 1949, May 12, 1950, May 13, 1953, Potlatch, males May 7, 1950, May 2, 1954; Clearwater County, Headquarters, female August 18, 1953; Washington County, East Brownlee Creek, male May 6, 1952; Lemhi County, Shoup, male June 6, 1949.

Habits. Few birds are more local in their occurrence in Idaho than is the Nashville Warbler. Its preferred habitat would appear to be deciduous underbrush in ravines on the mountainsides, but in such a spot only infrequently would a singing male be seen during the spring and early summer months. It undoubtedly breeds throughout the state, but there are only a few published records for its occurrence, a further indication of its peculiarly spotted distribution.

At Moscow a few pairs nested on Moscow Mountain, north of the city, and here it was a regular and not uncommon migrant both in the spring and in the fall, being most numerous in early May, and again in early September. My extreme dates of occurrence are April 21 (1950) and September 17 (1948). At Potlatch migrants were noted on but three occasions, May 12 and September 4, 1948, and May 7, 1950.

Vermivora virginiae (Baird): Virginia's Warbler

General Distribution. Breeds from southern Idaho and northern Colorado south to southeastern California, southern Nevada, southeastern Arizona and northern New Mexico. Winters in southern Mexico.

Status in Idaho. A fairly common summer resident in Cassia County and doubtless elsewhere along the southern edge of the state where there is suitable habitat.

The Virginia's Warbler was first recorded in Idaho by Brodkorb (1938) who collected two adult males at Joe's Gap, six miles northeast of Montpelier, August 24, 1934.

It was next reported for the state by Arvey (1949) who collected an adult male one mile west of Bancroft, in Caribou County, August 13, 1948.

It was found to be a fairly common summer resident at the Silent City of Rocks, west of Almo, in Cassia County, June 19-21, 1949, and again on June 12, 1960. Specimens were taken on both of these dates (Burleigh).

Habits. This small warbler frequents dense underbrush, and in its daily activities it rarely ventures more than six or eight feet from the ground. In common with the other *Vermivora* it is a restless, active bird, but being shy and adept at keeping out of sight it must be searched for to be seen. In other parts of its breeding range it is found in deciduous underbrush, scrub oak being especially favored, but in Idaho its distribution, in my experience, is limited to mountainsides covered with dense thickets of mountain mahogany (*Cercocarpus ledifolius*). Such being the case, its occurrence in the state will be both limited and local, but wherever the mountain mahogany predominates on mountain slopes the Virginia's Warbler should nest in at least limited numbers.

Dendroica petechia morcomi Coale: YELLOW WARBLER

General Distribution. Breeds from southern British Columbia and western Montana south to Baja California, northern Arizona, central New Mexico, and northwestern Texas. Winters from southern Baja California and southern Mexico (Guerrero and Veracruz) south to Ecuador, Colombia, and French Guiana.

Status in Idaho. A common and generally distributed summer resident throughout the state.

The Yellow Warbler is one of the most common and widely distributed birds in Idaho. Wherever there is deciduous underbrush bordering streams this familiar warbler will be found, regardless of altitude.

Bonner County. Found to be a common summer resident in 1917 at Clark Fork, in deciduous underbrush about the town (Burleigh, 1923).

Kootenai County. Abundant at Fort Sherman (Coeur d'Alene) during the summer; arrives in early May; nests found held five eggs (Merrill, 1898); a common summer resident, 1910-14, at Coeur d'Alene; nest with five eggs found on June 11, and young able to fly on June 14 (Rust, 1915); common in the willows at the upper end of Lake Coeur d'Alene July 1-10, 1943 (Yocom, 1946); a singing male, an early spring arrival, seen May 4, 1950, in willows fringing Lake Coeur d'Alene (Burleigh).

Shoshone County. A very common summer resident on the St. Joe National Forest "in the Transition Zone in the valleys"; noted from early May until August (Hand, 1941).

Latah County. Observed during the summer of 1947 in deciduous growth along the streams; an adult male collected August 12 (Johnston, 1949); a common summer resident at Harvard, 1951-52; in 1952 an adult was seen feeding young July 3, and a nest was found July 18 that held four fully fledged young (Verner, 1953); a common and widely distributed summer resident throughout the county, 1948-58, occurring wherever there were willows bordering streams and ponds (Burleigh).

Nez Perce County. A common summer resident at Lewiston, 1948-58, frequenting willows bordering the Clearwater and the Snake rivers (Burleigh).

Adams County. A common summer resident at Council, 1957-58, extreme dates of occurrence being May 6 and August 25 (Newhouse, 1960).

Washington County. Singing males seen in woods bordering the Snake River at Weiser June 4, 1952, and on the Weiser River at Cambridge June 7, 1952 (Burleigh).

Ada County. Several singing males seen at Boise June 22, 1949, in willows fringing a stream (Burleigh).

Owyhee County. Common at Riddle May 28 through June 3, 1934; two specimens collected (Davis, 1934); an occasional singing male noted in deciduous underbrush at Three Creek May 31, 1951 (Burleigh).

Lemhi County. Frequently noted at Salmon June 7, 1949, in woods bordering the Salmon River (Burleigh).

Fremont County. Common along the streams June through August, 1916; two nests found on Little Dry Creek June 16, in each five eggs (Rust, 1917); several singing males seen in aspens in Targhee Pass (altitude 7,000 feet) June 27, 1960 (Burleigh).

Blaine County. Found to be a common summer resident at Ketchum June 24-28, 1950, occurring along the streams in the valleys, and in aspen groves on the mountainsides to an altitude of 8,000 feet on Easley Peak (Burleigh).

Jefferson County. Common on the Camas National Wildlife Refuge June 12 through August 28, 1961 (Oring, 1962).

Bonneville County. A common summer resident at Grays Lake, 1949-51; arrival dates May 17, 1950, May 17, 1951 (Steel, 1956); two birds seen on Eagle Creek, north of Gray, on the rather late date of August 26 (1955) (Burleigh); an occasional singing male noted at Alpine May 28, 1951, in woods bordering the Snake River (Burleigh).

South Central Idaho. Common in July, 1890, on the Snake River, near Blackfoot, and along the Big Lost River, and on Birch Creek and the Lemhi River in August (Merriam, 1891); a fairly common "breeder" in 1949 in the "south central counties" (Levy, 1950).

Minidoka County. A fairly common resident at Rupert, 1919-21; extreme dates of occurrence May 9 and September 3; eggs June 17 (Davis, 1935).

Cassia County. Noted at Almo June 19, 1949, and at Burley, on the Snake River, June 18, 1949, and June 2, 1955 (Burleigh).

In view of the possibility that more than one race occurred in Idaho a series of specimens was collected throughout the state (1948-58), on various dates from late April until early September. Three races, *aestiva*, *amnicola*, and *rubiginosa*, breed north of Idaho in Alaska, British Columbia, and Alberta, and it seemed logical to assume that one or more might be present, at least in the more northern counties, in the spring and again in the fall. However, without exception all, on critical examination, were found to represent the breeding form, *morcomi*, occurring over the larger part of the Rocky Mountain region. These specimens were taken as follows: Bonner County, Clark Fork, male June 12, 1950; Kootenai County, Coeur d'Alene, male May 4, 1950; Shoshone County, Smelterville, male, female May 24, 1952; Latah County, Princeton, female immature August 24, 1950, Potlatch, nineteen specimens between the extreme dates of April 30 (1949) and September 6 (1948), Viola, female May 18, 1948, Moscow, twenty-four specimens between the extreme dates of May 5 (1948) and August 17 (1949); Nez Perce County, Lewiston, thirty specimens between the extreme dates of May 16 (1950) and September 8 (1951); Clearwater County, Headquarters, male immature August 2, 1952; Washington County, Weiser, male June 4, 1952, Cambridge, male June 7, 1952; Ada County, Boise, male June 22, 1949; Owyhee County, Three Creek, male May 31, 1951; Lemhi County, Salmon, male June 7, 1949; Fremont County, Targhee Pass, male June 27, 1960; Blaine County, Easley Peak (8,000 feet), male June 25, 1950, Sun Valley, male June 28, 1950; Bonneville County, Gray, males June 9 and 12,

1949, August 26, 1955, Alpine, male May 28, 1951; Caribou County, Soda Springs, male May 20, 1951; Bear Lake County, Paris, male May 26, 1952; Cassia County, Burley, males June 18, 1949, June 2, 1955.

Habits. In Idaho the Yellow Warbler is rarely seen anywhere but in deciduous underbrush at the edges of streams and the larger bodies of water. In migration it can be found feeding in the cottonwood groves along the rivers, but it consistently shuns conifers at all times. Altitude is apparently unimportant in limiting its distribution, for I have found it equally common at Lewiston (738 feet) and on the higher ridges to at least 8,000 feet (Easley Peak, in Blaine County). In the valleys its preference is for willows, while at the higher elevations it is largely confined to the aspen groves.

In northern Idaho it usually appears in the spring in early May, and in the fall it is only infrequently seen after late August. My extreme dates of occurrence for Potlatch are April 30 (1949) and September 8 (1956), for Moscow May 5 (1948) and August 17 (1949), and for Lewiston May 4 (1953) and September 8 (1950).

Although it feeds to a large extent in the willows the nest, in most instances within five or six feet of the ground, is constructed in any bush or shrub that offers it sufficient concealment. One that I found at Potlatch May 10, 1949, already half-built, was in a birch. Rust states that a nest he found at Coeur d'Alene was in a spirea bush, and that the two he observed on Little Dry Creek, in Fremont County, were both in rose bushes.

Dendroica caerulescens caerulescens (Gmelin): BLACK-THROATED BLUE WARBLER

General Distribution. Breeds from western Ontario, southern Quebec, and Prince Edward Island south to central Minnesota, central Michigan, northern Pennsylvania, and northern New Jersey. Winters in the Bahamas, Cuba, Puerto Rico, and the Virgin Islands.

Status in Idaho. Of accidental occurrence in northern Idaho.

There is one record for this species for the state. On January 10, 1955, I collected a male on Hatwai Creek, east of Lewiston, as it fed in underbrush bordering the stream. It had been observed the previous day, but it was so shy and difficult to approach that I failed to secure it then.

Habits. In view of its range in the eastern part of the continent, it was rather surprising to encounter a Black-throated Blue Warbler in northern Idaho in January. It so happened that I carried on no field work on Hatwai Creek during the fall or early winter months in 1954, so I rather suspect that this warbler appeared there during the height of the fall migration and, beguiled by the mild weather, lingered on. It is questionable, however, if it would have survived the winter, for the day I collected it was characterized by a steady snowfall, and by evening there was over an inch of fresh snow on the ground. The appearance of this species in recent years in Manitoba and Saskatchewan suggests a gradual extension of its breeding range westward, but even so it will always be a very rare straggler in Idaho.

Dendroica coronata (Linnaeus): MYRTLE WARBLER

General Distribution. Breeds from northern Alaska, northern Yukon, Mackenzie, central Quebec and Newfoundland south to northern British Columbia, central Alberta, southern Manitoba, central Michigan and eastern Pennsylvania. Winters on the Pacific coast from Oregon to Baja California, and from Kansas, the southern Great Lakes region and southern New England south through Mexico and Central America to Panama.

Status in Idaho. An uncommon transient both in the spring and in the fall in the northern part of the state, and a rare spring transient in southern Idaho.

Possibly because of its close resemblance to the Audubon's Warbler, this species was apparently completely overlooked in past years by those interested in the avifauna of Idaho, and was not recorded for the state until I took a specimen at Moscow May 20, 1948. In succeeding years the Myrtle Warbler proved to be a regular but rather uncommon transient in Latah County, one or two individuals being noted at infrequent intervals in the spring and in the fall.

Kootenai County. One bird noted at Coeur d'Alene October 10, 1952.

Latah County. Recorded at Moscow May 20 and October 30, 1948, May 18 and October 4, 1950, May 8, 1954, October 12, 1955, at Viola October 10, 1948, at Potlatch October 2 and 8, 1949, October 7, 1956.

Nez Perce County. One bird, a male in full breeding plumage, seen at Lewiston May 10, 1954.

Adams County. One bird noted at New Meadows November 6, 1957 (Burleigh).

Levy (1959) reports specimens taken at Moscow April 22 and 26, 1950. Steel (1956) found this species a rare transient at Grays Lake, in Bonneville County, noting it in 1950 on April 22 and 26.

Habits. It is not surprising that the Myrtle Warbler has been so completely overlooked as a transient in Idaho, for unless carefully looked for its presence would never be suspected. Almost without exception the individuals I have seen were feeding with restless flocks of Audubon's Warblers, and as the one character separating the two species under such circumstances is the lack of any yellow in the throat of *coronata* it required careful scrutiny to distinguish the one bird usually found in such a flock. Once in the hand the larger size and the diagnostic tail pattern would readily confirm the identification. During the summer months this species prefers conifers, both for feeding and nesting, but in migration it feeds in such deciduous hardwoods as the willow and the cottonwood, ordinarily never far from the ground.

Dendroica coronata coronata (Linnaeus)

Although the nominate race of the Myrtle Warbler occurs during the summer months north of Idaho in central Alberta, it apparently is a rare transient in the state. I have two records for Latah County, both for the fall migration, a male taken at Viola October 11, 1948, and a female at Moscow November 1, 1951.

Dendroica coronata hooveri McGregor

This northwestern race, distinguished by its larger size and lighter upperparts, breeds in Alaska, Yukon, and Mackenzie, and on the basis of actual specimens is the form commonly occurring in Idaho. Over an interval of ten years I collected eleven specimens that were found to be typical of *hooveri;* these are as follows: Kootenai County, Coeur d'Alene, female October 10, 1952; Latah County, Potlatch, male October 7, 1956, females October 2 and 8, 1949, October 7, 1956, Moscow, females May 20 and October 30, 1948, May 18 and October 4, 1950, October 12, 1955; Adams County, New Meadows, female November 6, 1957.

Four additional specimens are intermediate in their characters, having the measurements and tail pattern of *hooveri,* but with the yellow throat of *auduboni.* Three were taken at Moscow, a male October 4, 1948, and females September 29 and October 8, 1948, and one at Potlatch, a female September 12, 1948.

Dendroica auduboni (Townsend): AUDUBON'S WARBLER

General Distribution. Breeds from central British Columbia, southern Alberta, and southwestern Saskatchewan south to northern Baja California, southern Arizona, southern New Mexico, and western Texas. Winters from southern British Columbia, northern Idaho, central Arizona and southern Texas south through Mexico to Guatemala.

Status in Idaho. A common summer resident in the wooded areas throughout the state; winters commonly at Lewiston, in Nez Perce County, and irregularly at Moscow, in Latah County.

Bonner County. Found to be a common summer resident at Clark Fork in 1917, occurring from the valleys to the tops of the ridges; small flocks noted from the middle of August to early September (Burleigh, 1923); Bent (1953) cites April 16 as an early date of arrival at Sandpoint, and October 26 as a late date of departure at Bayview.

Kootenai County. Arrives the middle of April at Fort Sherman (Coeur d'Alene); "does not breed very commonly"; fall migration noticeable in early August, continuing until the end of September (Merrill, 1898); an abundant summer resident at Coeur d'Alene, 1910-14; departs in early October (Rust, 1915); one small flock noted in willows at the edge of Lake Coeur d'Alene October 10, 1952 (Burleigh).

Shoshone County. A common and widely distributed summer resident on the St. Joe National Forest, 1921-41; present from late April until October (Hand, 1941); an occasional bird noted on Lookout Pass (altitude 5,000 feet) July 9, 1958 (Burleigh).

Latah County. Of general distribution "in coniferous forests" June 1-

August 16, 1947 (Johnston, 1949); a common summer resident at Harvard, 1951-52; fully grown young seen August 8, 1951 (Verner, 1953); a fairly common summer resident on the wooded ridges north and east of Moscow, 1948-58; of irregular occurrence during the winter months at Moscow (Burleigh).

Nez Perce County. A regular and fairly common winter resident at Lewiston, 1948-58, the first flocks appearing in the fall as early as late August, and being noted in the spring as late as the end of May (Burleigh).

Clearwater County. A fairly common summer resident at Headquarters, 1951-55 (Burleigh).

Idaho County. Specimens taken by D. Arvey ten miles southwest of Riggins May 14, 1939 (Jollie, in litt.); frequently noted at Selway Falls in September, 1941; common in July, 1948, in the Lolo Pass region; two males taken on July 9 (at 7,000 feet) and July 13 (at 6,000 feet) (Orr, 1951).

Adams County. Noted in 1958 at Indian Valley May 6, and at Hornet Creek October 9 (Newhouse, 1960).

Owyhee County. This species found to be fairly plentiful June 2, 1951, on the higher ridges above Silver City (altitude approximately 6,000 feet) (Burleigh).

Fremont County. Common in Douglas firs in the canyons (Rust, 1917); an occasional singing male noted at Targhee Pass (altitude 7,000 feet) June 12, 1957 (Burleigh).

Clark County. Common on Signal Peak June 19 and July 14, 1961 (Oring, 1962).

Jefferson County. Transients, as many as ten each day, seen on the Camas National Wildlife Refuge August 22-29, 1961 (Oring, 1962).

Bonneville County. A very common summer resident at Grays Lake, 1949-1951; arrival dates May 17, 1950, May 18, 1951 (Steel, 1956); common at Big Elk Creek, near Palisades, August 6, 1961 (Oring, 1962).

South Central Idaho. "Abundant" in 1890 in the Salmon River and Sawtooth Mountains; two noted near Shoshone Falls October 9-11 (Merriam, 1891); a fairly common "breeder" in the south-central counties "where conifers are available" (Levy, 1950).

Minidoka County. Rare in 1911; "tolerably" common in 1913 (Kenagy, 1914); noted at Rupert May 6-13, 1919, May 2-18, 1920, and May 19, 1921 (Davis, 1935).

Cassia County. An occasional singing male noted at the Silent City of Rocks, west of Almo, June 19, 1949 (Burleigh).

Habits. Although altitude is not a limiting factor in the distribution of the Audubon's Warbler in Idaho, this species apparently is most common from 3,000 feet to 7,000 feet. It shows a definite preference for conifers, so much so that singing males seen in aspen groves on Bear Island, in Grays Lake, on May 27, 1951, seemed rather out of place. It is a hardy species, for the day it was observed north of Gray in the thick fir woods near the top of Caribou Mountain, May 24, 1951, the snow at this altitude, 8,500 feet, was still two feet in depth.

In Latah County it usually appears in the spring the latter part of April, and in the fall it is only infrequently seen after the middle of October. My extreme dates of occurrence for Potlatch are April 16 (1950) and October 10 (1948), and for Moscow April 12 (1952) and November 14 (1951) (average date of departure October 18); it was noted at Genesee as late as October 21 (1951). If the winter is relatively mild an occasional small flock will remain within the city limits of Moscow until early spring, feeding on the fruit of the Spanish olive and the mountain ash, and, when this source of food is exhausted, on frozen apples still remaining on the trees. Such was the case in 1948, and again in 1952 when a flock of twelve birds appeared in our backyard November 29, and again at this same spot at irregular intervals for the following three months.

At Lewiston this species wintered regularly, but its numbers varied from year to year. Some years only a few individuals would be present, other years scattered flocks would be seen. It was possibly most numerous during the winter of 1950-51, when several flocks containing from twenty to thirty birds were seen on January 24 and again on February 8, feeding in underbrush at the edge of the Snake River. In the fall this warbler appears at Lewiston in late August or early September (earliest date of arrival August 29, 1956); in the spring it lingers until almost the last of May (May 23, 1955, May 28, 1957).

Throughout its extensive breeding range in the western United States the Audubon's Warbler usually selects a conifer, a fir or a spruce, in which to nest, but there are instances in which deciduous hardwoods, the willow and aspen, more rarely an oak, are used. Merrill (1898) states that the majority of the nests he found at Fort Sherman (Coeur d'Alene) were "in deciduous trees and bushes, generally but a few feet from the ground." Almost without exception they were lined with black horsehair and feathers.

Although an occasional pair has been found nesting in late July it is doubtful if more than one brood is reared each year. At Clark Fork, in 1917, I watched a female gathering nesting material on July 22, but in my experience rearing a brood of young at this late date is rather exceptional.

Dendroica auduboni auduboni (Townsend)

During the summer months the nominate race of the Audubon's Warbler is limited in its distribution to the coast, occurring as far north as central British Columbia. In migration, however, there would appear to be a noticeable tendency to leave the coast, for in northern Idaho *auduboni* proved, on the basis of specimens collected, to be a not uncommon transient, especially in the fall. In all nineteen specimens were taken, four in the spring and fifteen in the fall. These were as follows: spring, males Moscow April 24, 1957, Lewiston April 28, 1949, April 8, 1955, female Moscow May 11, 1950; fall, males Moscow October 17 and December 9, 1948, November 9, 1951, December 14, 1952, October 11, 1956, Lewiston January 24, 1951 (two), November 1, 1956, females Moscow September 21 (two), and November

7, 1948, November 1, 1951, September 2, 1952, October 12, 1955, Lewiston November 16, 1956.

Dendroica auduboni memorabilis Oberholser

This Rocky Mountain race, the breeding form in Idaho, is distinguished by its larger size and more extensive black on the breast. To verify its occurrence in the state specimens, all typical of *memorabilis*, were taken in various localities, and at various dates throughout the year. These are as follows: Kootenai County, Coeur d'Alene, female October 10, 1952; Shoshone County, Lookout Pass, male July 9, 1958; Latah County, Potlatch, ten specimens, between the dates of May 1, 1948, and August 10, 1958, Viola, male May 18, 1948, Moscow, twenty-five specimens between the dates of June 6, 1948, and October 28, 1957, Genesee, female September 16, 1952; Nez Perce County, Lewiston, seventeen specimens between the dates of January 22, 1948, and September 1, 1958; Clearwater County, Headquarters, male May 10, 1955, females September 15, 1951, and May 17, 1953; Owyhee County, Silver City, male June 2, 1951; Fremont County, Targhee Pass, female June 12, 1957; Bonneville County, Gray, male May 27, 1951; Cassia County, Almo, male June 19, 1949.

Dendroica nigrescens (Townsend): BLACK-THROATED GRAY WARBLER

General Distribution. Breeds from southern British Columbia, southern Idaho, southwestern Wyoming and central Colorado south to Baja California, southeastern Arizona and southern New Mexico. Winters from southern California and southern Arizona south through Mexico to Guatemala.

Status in Idaho. A fairly common summer resident in the extreme southern edge of the state.

Owyhee County. Several noted at Riddle, and a specimen taken June 3, 1934 (Davis, 1934); found to be fairly plentiful at Triangle and specimens taken June 25, 1949 (Burleigh); noted at Idavada July 24, 1949 (Levy, 1950); an occasional singing male seen in the junipers at Three Creek May 31, 1951; one male collected (Burleigh).

Cassia County. Specimens taken on Goose Creek, ten miles south of Oakley, June 26, 1949 (Jollie, in litt.); found to be fairly plentiful on the juniper-covered ridges south of Oakley June 22-23, 1950, June 5-6, 1957, July 19-20, 1958, and June 13, 1960; specimens taken June 22 and 23, 1950, and June 13, 1960 (Burleigh).

Oneida County. An occasional male seen on the ridges north of Malad City June 8, 1955 (Burleigh).

Bannock County. Several birds noted on Buckskin Creek, east of Pocatello, June 11, 1955, and a male collected (Burleigh).

Habits. Elsewhere within its breeding range the Black-throated Gray Warbler occupies quite a diversity of habitats, fir woods in western Washington, manzanita thickets in California, scrub oaks in southern Arizona. In southern Idaho, however, it is confined entirely to low ridges covered with an open growth of large, gnarled junipers. In these trees it feeds and rears its young, and is rarely seen in any other vegetation. Such a habitat occupies a rather limited area in the extreme southern edge of the state, so this warbler will never have a very extensive range in Idaho.

The nest is usually five or six feet from the ground, so one found in Cassia County June 22, 1950, five feet up in a small thick juniper, would appear to be typical of the site chosen. It held on that date half-grown young.

Dendroica townsendi (Townsend): Townsend's Warbler

General Distribution. Breeds from southern Alaska and southern Yukon south to central Oregon, northern Idaho, and northwestern Wyoming. Winters from southern California and northern Mexico (Nuevo Leon) south to northern Nicaragua.

Status in Idaho. A fairly common summer resident in the northern part of the state.

Bonner County. Found to be a fairly common summer resident in 1917 at Clark Fork, frequenting the heavier timber in the valleys; an occasional bird seen at the Trestle Creek Lookout the last of August, and as late as September 10 (Burleigh, 1923); Bent (1953) cites September 10 as a late date of departure at Priest River.

Kootenai County. Occurs in summer at Fort Sherman (Coeur d'Alene); specimens taken on June 2 and 29, 1896 (Merrill, 1898); an uncommon summer resident at Coeur d'Alene, 1910-14, "in dense timber"; a specimen taken at Fernan Lake on June 28 (Rust, 1915); Bent (1953) cites April 29 as an early date of arrival at Coeur d'Alene.

Shoshone County. A fairly common summer resident on the St. Joe National Forest, 1921-41, occurring from May to late August in "conifer forests of the Canadian Zone" (Hand, 1941).

Latah County. An "abundant" summer resident in 1947 "in the coniferous forest" (Johnston, 1949); noted at Harvard July 25, 1951, and June 29 and August 1, 1952 (Verner, 1953); a fairly common summer resident, 1948-58, in the more heavily wooded areas north and east of Moscow (Burleigh).

Nez Perce County. Apparently largely of accidental occurrence at Lewiston as a fall transient, being noted there on the unusually late date of November 24, 1956, and on September 8, 1957 (Burleigh).

Clearwater County. This species found to be fairly plentiful at Headquarters June 15, 1951, singing males being seen at intervals in the thicker woods near the tops of the ridges; in 1952 it was noted for the last time in the fall on August 27 (Burleigh).

Idaho County. Common in the Lolo Pass region in July, 1948; noted between 4,000 and 6,000 feet; singing males seen daily throughout July; two pairs feeding young out of the nest seen on Brushy Creek July 5; a male and a female collected July 6 (Orr, 1951).

Adams County. A specimen in the Museum of Vertebrate Zoology, Berkeley, taken by Robert T. Orr on July 5, 1932, three miles west of Payette Lake, marks the extreme southern limits of this species in Idaho during the summer months.

Jefferson County. Transients noted on the Camas National Wildlife Refuge August 21-29, 1961; an immature male taken August 22 (Oring, 1962).

Minidoka County. One record, September 4, 1919, at Rupert (Davis, 1935).

Habits. Were it not for its characteristic drawling song, uttered during much of the day in May and June, the Townsend's Warbler would probably go undetected over most of its breeding range. In my experience this warbler carried on its daily activities in the upper branches of the tallest trees available, and being a small bird it was extremely inconspicuous in the thick foliage of the spruce or fir in which it was feeding. Possibly for this reason very few nests have ever been found; the few that have been were all in firs and, oddly enough, within fifteen feet of the ground.

In Latah County the Townsend's Warbler appeared in the spring in early May, and in the fall it was only infrequently seen after early September. My extreme dates of occurrence for Moscow are May 1 (1952) and September 9 (1949); at Potlatch it was noted as late as September 16 (1956).

[**Dendroica striata** (Forster): BLACKPOLL WARBLER]

General Distribution. Breeds from northern Alaska, central Mackenzie, northern Quebec, and Newfoundland south to central British Columbia, central Manitoba, northern Ontario, and Massachusetts. Winters in South America from Colombia and Venezuela south to Chile and western Brazil.

Status in Idaho. Of accidental occurrence in the southern part of the state.

There is one sight record for the occurrence of the Blackpoll Warbler in Idaho.

Wilbur (1965) states as follows: "On May 5, 1963, a Blackpoll Warbler (*Dendroica striata*) was discovered at the Meader Trout Farm near Pocatello, Idaho. This bird, a male, was feeding in a willow grove with a large number of Audubon's warblers (*Dendroica auduboni*). I watched it for approximately ten minutes, then it flew to another tree and I could not relocate it."

Habits. Although breeding commonly in the Canadian Provinces north of Idaho, the Blackpoll Warbler will never be of more than casual occurrence in the state. In common with such species as the Gray-cheeked Thrush, its migration route, both in the spring and in the fall, is diagonally east and west across the continent, so only stragglers can be looked for in the Rocky Mountain region. Being easily overlooked, especially in its rather inconspicuous fall plumage, it is possibly of more frequent occurrence in Idaho than this one record would indicate.

Seiurus aurocapillus cinereus Miller: OVENBIRD

General Distribution. Breeds from southern Alberta, southeastern Montana and western South Dakota south to southeastern Colorado and central Nebraska. Winters south to Honduras and Costa Rica.

Status in Idaho. Of accidental occurrence in the northern part of the state.

There is one record for the occurrence of the Ovenbird in Idaho. On July 1, 1949, a dead bird was found lying at the side of a road at Moscow, apparently just killed by a car (Hall, 1951). It was preserved as a specimen, and is now in the Charles E. Conner Museum, at Pullman, Washington. It was identified by John W. Aldrich as typical of this western race, *cinereus.*

Habits. As the Ovenbird breeds almost directly north of Idaho, in central Alberta, it is possible that it is more common in the state in migration than this one record would indicate. It is an inhabitant of both hardwood and coniferous forests, and being quiet and inconspicuous after the nesting season is over, it could easily be overlooked. The southward movement in the fall is rarely underway before the end of July, so it is rather surprising that an individual of this species should appear in Latah County as early as the first day of the month.

Seiurus noveboracensis notabilis Ridgway: NORTHERN WATERTHRUSH

General Distribution. Breeds from northern Alaska, central southern Mackenzie, northern Ontario and northern Quebec south to northern British Columbia, northern Idaho, northern North Dakota, northern Wisconsin, northeastern Ohio and northwestern Pennsylvania. Winters from southern Baja California and southern Mexico (Veracruz) south to northern Ecuador and southern Venezuela.

Status in Idaho. A fairly common but rather local summer resident in the extreme northern part of the state, and a rare transient south of its breeding range.

Bonner County. Sloanaker (1940) states that this species was seen at Priest Lake in July, 1935, by Mrs. E. L. Dennis; I noted one breeding pair at Hope June 13, 1950, in swampy woods bordering the Pack River; the male was frequently heard singing that morning.

Kootenai County. Sloanaker (1941) states that a specimen was collected at Coeur d'Alene in 1928 by Charles F. Hedges.

Benewah County. Noted from May 17 through August 12, 1936, at St. Maries; throughout June and early July "from two to five or six" singing males were seen in cottonwood and willow swamps (Hand, 1937); a "restricted but not rare" summer resident at St. Maries (Hand, 1941); several breeding pairs noted "in the flooded timber lands" between St. Maries and Lake Chatcolet June 19, 1951 (Levy, 1959); singing male noted in swampy woods bordering the St. Maries River May 24, 1952, June 30, 1956, May 24 and June 14, 1957 (Burleigh).

Shoshone County. One bird, a fall transient, seen at Clarkia July 17, 1948 (Burleigh).

Latah County. This species found to be a very rare transient here, being recorded but once over an interval of eleven years (1948-58); on August 12, 1950, a single bird was noted at Potlatch, in willows fringing a pool near the bank of the Palouse River (Burleigh).

Lemhi County. Two birds seen June 6, 1961, feeding "along a roadside stream" north of Baker (Oring, 1962).

Jefferson County. One bird seen on the Camas National Wildlife Refuge August 22, 1961 (Oring, 1962).

Bannock County. Bent (1953) cites May 13 as an early date of arrival at Pocatello; noted at Pocatello by Baylor (Fichter, in litt.) from May 16 to May 20, and on May 21, 1959.

Seven specimens taken in the northern part of Idaho were all found to be typical of *notabilis,* and are as follows: Bonner County, Hope, male June 13, 1950; Shoshone County, Clarkia, female July 17, 1948; Benewah County, St. Maries, males June 19, 1951, June 30, 1956, June 14, 1957; Latah County, Potlatch, male immature August 12, 1950.

Habits. Within its limited range in Idaho the Northern Waterthrush could almost be considered a common breeding bird. Its preference during the summer months is for wooded swamps where it feeds at the edges of the stagnant shallow pools, and where such conditions exist one or more pairs can be found. Frequenting as it does dense underbrush it could easily be overlooked were it not for the loud ringing song uttered by the male throughout much of the day. Although not known to breed south of Benewah County it is possible that it does nest locally and in small numbers farther south in the state. The two birds seen by Oring in Lemhi County on June 6, 1961, were considered by him as being a breeding pair, but it is not improbable that they were belated transients. More conclusive evidence is necessary before this species can be accepted as breeding in east-central Idaho.

In view of its relative abundance during the summer months in the northern part of the state, its rarity as a transient south of its breeding range proved rather unexpected. Apparently its migration route is east of the Continental Divide, and such being the case only stragglers will be found at infrequent intervals west of the Rocky Mountains.

Oporornis tolmiei (Townsend): MacGillivray's Warbler

General Distribution. Breeds from southern Alaska, southern Yukon, central Alberta and southern Saskatchewan south to central California, central Arizona, and central New Mexico. Winters from southern Baja California and northern Mexico (Sonora, Nuevo Leon) south to Panama.

Status in Idaho. A common summer resident throughout the state.

Bonner County. A fairly common summer resident in 1917 at Clark Fork; noted at the Trestle Creek Lookout from early August to September 3 (Burleigh, 1923).

Kootenai County. "Breeds rather commonly" at Fort Sherman (Coeur d'Alene); arrives the middle of May (Merrill, 1898); a "not common" summer resident at Coeur d'Alene, 1910-14 (Rust, 1915); common at the upper end of Lake Coeur d'Alene July 1-10, 1943 (Yocom, 1946).

Shoshone County. A common summer resident on the St. Joe National Forest, 1921-41, occurring in the "Transition and Canadian Zones" from May to early September (Hand, 1941).

Latah County. Common and generally distributed, June 1 through August 16, 1947 (Johnston, 1949); a common summer resident at Harvard (1951-52); young out of the nest seen July 1 and 2, 1952 (Verner, 1953); a common and well-distributed summer resident, 1948-58, appearing in the spring in early May, and lingering in the fall until late September (Burleigh).

Nez Perce County. A local and rather uncommon summer resident at Lewiston, frequenting thickets and underbrush bordering the streams that flow into the Snake and the Clearwater rivers (Burleigh).

Clearwater County. Noted at Bungalow June 19, 1952, and at Headquarters August 2, 1952, and July 16, 1953.

Idaho County. Frequently seen in July, 1948, in the Lolo Pass region, "in small forest openings where there was a dense growth of brushy shrubs"; males collected four miles southwest of Lolo Pass July 4 and 6 (Orr, 1951).

Washington County. Breeding pairs noted in underbrush at the foot of Cuddy Mountain June 5 and 7, 1952 (Burleigh).

Ada County. Bent (1953) cites May 5 as an early date of arrival at Meridian.

Owyhee County. Common at Riddle in alder and willow thickets May 28 through June 3, 1934 (Davis, 1934).

Lemhi County. An occasional singing male seen at Shoup June 4 to 6, 1949, in thickets and underbrush on the open ridges (Burleigh).

Fremont County. Occurs sparingly (1916); "parent birds" with young seen on July 16 in willows on the West Fork of Camas Creek (Rust, 1917).

Clark County. Several birds noted "in upland meadows" on Signal Peak June 19 and July 14, 1961 (Oring, 1962).

Jefferson County. Transients present on the Camas National Wildlife Refuge August 14 through August 29, 1961; common after August 22 (Oring, 1962).

Blaine County. Noted in 1960 at Ketchum, on Big Wood River, July 4, and on Trail Creek, north of Sun Valley, on July 8 (Burleigh).

Bonneville County. A common summer resident at Grays Lake, 1949-1951 (Steel, 1956); found to be fairly common at Gray June 9-17, 1949, occurring both in the valleys (6,400 feet) and on the open ridges to an altitude of approximately 8,000 feet (Burleigh); noted at Big Elk Creek, near Palisades, August 5, 1961 (Oring, 1962).

South Central Idaho. Common in 1890 in the Lost River Mountains in July, and in the Birch Creek Valley the middle of August (Merriam, 1891); a common summer resident in 1949 in south-central Idaho, "in dense thickets along streams and creeks" (Levy, 1950).

Bannock County. An occasional singing male seen on Buckskin Creek, north of Pocatello June 10, 1955 (Burleigh).

Minidoka County. Davis (1935) gives April 29, 1920, as a date of arrival at Rupert.

Cassia County. Several birds noted June 21, 1949, in thickets at the Silent City of Rocks, nine miles west of Almo (Burleigh).

Habits. The MacGillivray's Warbler is another species the distribution of which in Idaho is not influenced by altitude. At Lewiston, the lowest point in the state, it is rather uncommon during the summer months, but this is due to a scarcity of suitable habitat. Thickets and underbrush in the vicinity of water are apparently the essential requirements, and where these are found this distinctive warbler occurs. I have noted it at an altitude of eight thousand feet on Caribou Mountain, in Bonneville County, and it doubtless is present in small numbers at even higher elevations.

In Latah County my extreme dates of occurrence for Moscow are May 5 (1948) and September 30 (1950 and 1957). Adverse weather conditions in May influence its arrival in the spring; in 1953 it was May 15 before the first singing male was observed. At Potlatch my earliest date of arrival is May 6 (1950), at Lewiston May 10 (1952).

Oporornis tolmiei tolmiei (Townsend)

The nominate race is the form occurring as a summer resident over the northern half of Idaho. To determine its actual distribution specimens were collected in the northern part of the state as far south as Washington County; all were found to be typical of *tolmiei*. These are as follows Kootenai County, Coeur d'Alene, female July 29, 1948; Latah County, Harvard, male June 15, 1952, Potlatch, adult males May 10, 1949, May 13 and August 23, 1952, immature males September 8, 1950, July 27 and August 16, 1952, immature female August 2, 1958, Moscow, adult males May 5 and 17 and June 30, 1948, May 16, 1949, September 19, 1951, May 11, 1952, May 15, 1953, September 27, 1956, September 20, 1957, immature males August 10 and September 17 and 21, 1948, adult females July 9, 1948, September 11, 1949, September 30, 1950, July 16, 1951, September 30, 1957, immature female August 10, 1950; Clearwater County, Orofino, adult female August 27, 1951, Bungalow, adult male June 19, 1952, Headquarters, adult male July 16, 1953, immature male August 2, 1952; Washington County, Cuddy Mountain, adult males June 5 and 7, 1952.

Oporornis tolmiei monticola Phillips

This race occurs during the summer months from southern Oregon and southern Idaho south to central Arizona and New Mexico. It differs from *tolmiei* in having a longer tail and deeper yellow underparts. Specimens identified as *monticola* have been taken as follows: Blaine County, Sun Valley, male July 4, 1960, Trail Creek Summit (7,200 feet), male July 8,

1960; Bonneville County, Gray, males May 21, 27, and 30, 1952, female June 2, 1952; Bannock County, Pocatello, male June 10, 1955.

A male collected at Shoup, in Lemhi County, June 5, 1949, is intermediate in its characters, the tail being short as in *tolmiei* but the underparts deep yellow as in *monticola*.

[Oporornis tolmiei intermedia Phillips]

This race is characterized as being like *tolmiei* but more greenish, less yellowish above. Phillips (1947) states that a specimen taken at Coeur d'Alene in May has the characters of *intermedia*, but as the validity of this race has been questioned it does not seem advisable to place it on the accredited state list at this time.

Geothlypis trichas campicola Behle and Aldrich: YELLOWTHROAT

General Distribution. Breeds from southern Yukon, northern Alberta, central Manitoba and western Ontario south to southeastern Washington, southern Idaho, southern Wyoming, southern North Dakota and northern Minnesota. Winters south to northern Mexico (Sonora, Nuevo Leon, Tamaulipas).

Status in Idaho. A fairly common but local summer resident throughout the state.

Boundary County. Singing males noted at Porthill June 26, 1957, in underbrush bordering the Kootenai River (Burleigh).

Bonner County. This species found to be a fairly common summer resident in 1917 in the vicinity of Clark Fork (Burleigh, 1923); scattered breeding pairs noted at Priest Lake July 23, 1960 (Burleigh).

Kootenai County. Arrives at Fort Sherman (Coeur d'Alene) in May; breeds sparingly; common in September (Merrill, 1898); an uncommon summer resident at Coeur d'Alene (1910-14) (Rust, 1915).

Benewah County. A common summer resident at St. Maries, 1921-41, being most numerous "on the lower St. Joe and St. Maries Rivers"; present from May to late September (Hand, 1941); four singing males noted at St. Maries May 21, 1949, in thickets and underbrush at the edge of the St. Joe River (Burleigh).

Latah County. Uncommon and only infrequently noted during the summer of 1947; an adult male collected July 3 on the Palouse River near Princeton (Johnston, 1949); found to be a fairly common but local summer resident (1948-58), occurring wherever there was suitable habitat; definitely known to breed at Princeton, Potlatch, Moscow, and Bovill (Burleigh).

Nez Perce County. Reported by Bendire as nesting at Lapwai in 1871 (Merriam, 1891); at Lewiston noted as a breeding bird only at the reservoir east of Lewiston Orchards, at least four pairs nesting there each year (1948-58) (Burleigh).

Clearwater County. One singing male seen at Pierce June 16, 1951, in willows bordering a stream; a male in immature plumage collected at Head-quarters September 20, 1952 (Burleigh).

Adams County. One male noted in open marsh at New Meadows May 18, 1955 (Burleigh); seen "in small numbers" at Council May 31 through August 23, 1958 (Newhouse, 1960).

Washington County. This species found to be fairly plentiful at Cambridge June 4, 1951, being frequently seen in underbrush at the edge of the Weiser River (Burleigh).

Canyon County. An occasional bird noted at Melba July 16, 1960, in underbrush at the edge of the Snake River (Burleigh).

Owyhee County. Several singing males seen at Homedale June 23, 1949 (Burleigh).

Lemhi County. An occasional singing male noted at Salmon June 7, 1949, in thickets and underbrush at the edge of the Salmon River (Burleigh).

Fremont County. Several breeding pairs found in alder thickets on Targhee Pass (altitude 7,000 feet) June 27, 1960 (Burleigh).

Jefferson County. An "abundant" summer resident in 1961 on the Camas National Wildlife Refuge (Oring, 1962).

Bonneville County. A fairly common summer resident at Grays Lake (1949-51); arrival dates June 1, 1950, May 22, 1951 (Steel, 1956); several singing males noted on Eagle Creek, north of Gray, May 29, 1952 (Burleigh).

Bannock County. One singing male noted at Lava Hot Springs May 20, 1951 (Burleigh).

Bear Lake County. A breeding male collected at the north end of Bear Lake July 6, 1949 (M. Jollie, in litt.).

South Central Idaho. A fairly common summer resident in 1949 "especially in the tule-covered marshes"; a specimen taken near Buhl, Twin Falls County, July 20 (Levy, 1950); singing males noted in 1960 at Burley June 9 and Declo June 11, in Cassia County, and at Hagerman, in Gooding County, June 18 and 19 (Burleigh).

In order to verify the occurrence of this species in Idaho, and to determine whether the breeding population represented more than one race, a series of specimens was taken from early May until October at various localities throughout the state. Except in the extreme southern counties these were found to be typical of *campicola*, distinguished from *occidentalis*, the breeding form of the Rocky Mountain region, by having the upperparts grayer, less olive green, and the belly and flanks grayer, less buffy. In southern Idaho specimens taken approached *occidentalis* in their characters, but were not considered sufficiently distinct to be identified as this more southern race. Specimens of *Geothlypis trichas* collected in Idaho are as follows: Boundary County, Porthill, male June 26, 1957; Bonner County, Clark Fork, male June 13, 1950, Priest Lake, male, female, July 23, 1960; Benewah County, St. Maries, male May 21, 1949; Latah County, Princeton, male May 30, 1949, Potlatch, adult males July 21, 1951, May 5, 1957, immature males August 30, 1948, September 16, 1950, September 9, 1951, September 21, 1957, adult females August 21 and September 8, 1949, September

3, 1950, immature females August 19, 1950, September 9, 1951, August 10 and September 27, 1952, Moscow, adult males May 19, 1948, May 11, 1949, May 13 and 21, 1950, May 18, 1952, immature males September 20 and 30, 1948, adult females September 13, 1948, September 10, 1949, October 4, 1950, immature females August 31, 1948, July 23, 1949, Bovill, immature male July 19, 1948; Nez Perce County, Lewiston, adult males May 4 and 16, and June 13, 1953, May 17, 1955, June 19 and July 21, 1957, immature females September 13, 1951, August 13, 1953; Clearwater County, Pierce, male June 16, 1951, Headquarters, immature male September 20, 1952; Washington County, Cambridge, male June 4, 1951; Owyhee County, Homedale, male June 23, 1949; Canyon County, Melba, male July 16, 1960; Lemhi County, Salmon, male June 7, 1949; Fremont County, Targhee Pass, male June 27, 1960; Bonneville County, Gray, two males June 11, 1949, females June 17, 1949, May 29, 1952; Bannock County, Lava Hot Springs, male May 20, 1951; Cassia County, Burley, male June 9, 1960, Declo, male June 11, 1960; Gooding County, Hagerman, males June 18 and 19, 1960.

Habits. In Idaho the Yellowthroat will almost without exception be found in the vicinity of water. Its life is spent in thickets and underbrush, and while males commonly sing from the top of a bush or sapling both sexes are otherwise rarely observed far from the ground. Altitude is apparently largely ignored, and while I have not noted this species above seven thousand feet, this is possibly due to a lack of suitable habitat at the higher elevations.

In Latah County an occasional male will appear in the spring in early May, but it is usually the middle of the month before this species is recorded for the first time. My extreme dates of occurrence for Moscow are May 11 (1949) and October 4 (1950), for Potlatch May 1 (1948) and September 21 (1957). At Lewiston it has been observed between the dates of May 4 (1953) and September 13 (1951).

The only definite breeding records are those of Bendire (Merriam, 1891) who reported finding two nests at Lapwai in 1871, one with four eggs on June 18, and one with five eggs on June 23.

Icteria virens auricollis (Deppe): Yellow-breasted Chat

General Distribution. Breeds from southern British Columbia, southern Alberta, and southern Saskatchewan south to Baja California, and through the western Great Plains to Mexico (Jalisco, Mexico City). Winters from southern Baja California and southern Texas to central Guatemala.

Status in Idaho. A fairly common but local summer resident throughout the state.

Bonner County. One breeding pair noted at Clark Fork July 4, 1917 (Burleigh, 1923).

Kootenai County. A common summer resident at Fort Sherman (Coeur d'Alene) (Merrill, 1898).

Benewah County. A rare summer resident at St. Maries; one pair noted May 26 and 27, 1937 (Hand, 1941).

Latah County. Found to be fairly common on Moscow Mountain and on Paradise Ridge during the summer of 1947; well-fledged young seen near Moscow June 27 (Johnston, 1949); a fairly common summer resident, 1948-58, frequenting thickets and underbrush in the open valleys (Burleigh).

Nez Perce County. Reported by Bendire as breeding commonly at Fort Lapwai (Merriam, 1891); an uncommon and rather local summer resident at Lewiston, 1948-58, breeding pairs being noted on Hatwai Creek, and at the reservoir east of Lewiston Orchards (Burleigh).

Clearwater County. One singing male seen at Orofino June 16, 1951, in underbrush at the edge of the Clearwater River (Burleigh).

Idaho County. Several singing males seen at Kooskia June 28, 1951, in underbrush at the edge of the Clearwater River (Burleigh).

Adams County. Several birds seen at Council in May, 1958, "in the Gray's Creek area" (Newhouse, 1960).

Washington County. Three singing males seen at Weiser June 4, 1952, in stretches of dense underbrush bordering the Weiser River; one singing male seen the following day, June 5, on East Brownlee Creek, west of Cambridge (Burleigh).

Boise County. A specimen taken on Cinch Creek, at the Arrowrock Reservoir, June 28, 1941 (Arvey, 1947).

Ada County. One breeding pair noted at Boise June 22, 1949, in underbrush bordering a stream (Burleigh); Bent (1953) cites May 13 as an early arrival date at Meridian.

Owyhee County. Frequently heard at Riddle, and two birds seen May 28 through June 3, 1934 (Davis, 1934); an occasional singing male seen in 1949 at Homedale June 23, and at Oreana June 25, and at Reynolds Creek June 3, 1951 (Burleigh).

Canyon County. Two singing males seen near Melba July 16, 1960, in underbrush at the edge of the Snake River (Burleigh).

Lemhi County. Specimens in the Denver Museum of Natural History were taken by Brodkorb at Salmon in July.

Custer County. Several birds seen at Challis July 7, 1960, in underbrush at the edge of the Salmon River (Burleigh).

Clark County. Several birds seen July 15, 1916, on Little Dry Creek, near Spencer (Rust, 1917).

Jefferson County. An uncommon summer resident in 1961 on the Camas National Wildlife Refuge; an adult female collected there July 11; also noted along the Snake River near Roberts (Oring, 1962).

South Central Idaho. A specimen taken on Devil's Creek June 28, 1872; common in July, 1890, on Cedar Creek, in the foothills of the Blackfoot Mountains (Merriam, 1891); a common summer resident in the south-central counties in 1949, occurring "along streams and creeks" (Levy, 1950).

Minidoka County. Noted at Rupert May 17 and 31, 1920 (Davis, 1935).

Cassia County. One pair seen at Burley June 18, 1949, in underbrush bordering the Snake River (Burleigh); specimens taken June 25, 1949, on Goose Neck, ten miles south of Oakley (Jollie, in litt.).

To verify the occurrence of this species in various parts of the state nineteen specimens, all typical of *auricollis*, were taken as follows: Latah County, Potlatch, male August 16, 1952, females September 3, 1950, August 22, 1951, August 17, 1958, Moscow, males June 28, 1948, May 19, July 19 and September 10, 1949; Nez Perce County, Lewiston, males June 6 and September 13, 1951, May 10, 1952, September 8, 1954; Clearwater County, Orofino, male June 16, 1951; Idaho County, Kooskia, male June 28, 1951; Washington County, Weiser, male June 4, 1952; Ada County, Boise, male June 21, 1952; Canyon County, Melba, male July 16, 1960; Custer County, Challis, male July 7, 1960; Cassia County, Burley, male June 18, 1949.

Habits. In Idaho the Chat is a bird of the dense thickets and underbrush, where it is more often heard than seen. It has no liking for thick woods, and while the vicinity of water is not an essential requirement it takes advantage of the stream bottoms that offer it the habitat it desires. Altitude is apparently an important factor in its distribution in the state. I have never noted it above 3,000 feet during the summer months, although at 2,500 feet it can be found wherever conditions are suitable.

In Latah County it rarely appears in the spring before the middle of May, and there have been years when it was the latter part of the month before the first bird was seen. In the fall it is present in small numbers until early September, an occasional individual lingering until almost the middle of the month. At Moscow my extreme dates of occurrence are May 19 (1949) and September 10 (1949); at Potlatch my latest date in the fall is September 3 (1950). At Lewiston, in Nez Perce County, my extreme dates of occurrence are May 10 (1952) and September 15 (1957).

Wilsonia pusilla (Wilson): Wilson's Warbler

General Distribution. Breeds from northern Alaska, northern Yukon, central Mackenzie, northern Ontario, southern Labrador and Newfoundland south to southern California, northern Utah, northern New Mexico, northern Minnesota, southern Ontario, and northern New Hampshire. Winters from southern Texas and northern Mexico (Nuevo Leon) south through Mexico and central America to western Panama.

Status in Idaho. A common but local summer resident in the northern part of the state.

Boundary County. An occasional singing male seen on Harrison Peak June 25, 1957, in underbrush fringing the streams both in the valley and well toward the top of the mountain (Burleigh).

Bonner County. Fairly common, July through August, 1917, in open meadows on the higher ridges north of Clark Fork, scattered pairs being seen in underbrush bordering the streams; latest record a male noted September 10 (Burleigh, 1923).

Kootenai County. An occasional bird noted in the spring and in the fall at Fort Sherman (Coeur d'Alene) (Merrill, 1898); a single bird seen at Coeur d'Alene October 6, 1951 (Burleigh).

Shoshone County. A common summer resident on the St. Joe National Forest, 1921-41, occurring from May until the middle of September in mountain meadows in the Canadian Zone (Hand, 1941).

Latah County. A specimen reported taken by S. E. Piper on the Potlatch River July 30, 1898 (Johnston, 1949); a common transient at Moscow and at Potlatch (1948-58), especially in the fall when it was usually abundant the latter part of August; a rather scarce breeding bird on Moscow Mountain, not over one or two pairs nesting there each year (Burleigh).

Nez Perce County. An uncommon transient at Lewiston (1948-58), an occasional bird being seen in the spring from the middle of May until the first week in June, and in the fall from the middle of August until the middle of October (Burleigh).

Idaho County. Fairly common in July, 1948, "in the upper part of the Lochsa Fork watershed"; noted in alders and willows along the streams; a female collected July 4 four miles southwest of Lolo Pass (Orr, 1951).

Valley County. Four birds seen at McCall (altitude 5,000 feet) during the morning of September 18, 1955, in willows fringing a stream (Burleigh).

Owyhee County. Two birds, belated transients, seen at Reynolds Creek June 3, 1951, in underbrush at the edge of a stream (Burleigh).

South Central Idaho. Abundant the latter part of August, 1890, on Birch Creek and in the Lemhi Valley (Merriam, 1891).

Jefferson County. A common transient, August 1-29, 1961, on the Camas National Wildlife Refuge (Oring, 1962).

Bonneville County. An uncommon transient at Grays Lake, 1949-51; arrival dates June 1, 1950, May 27, 1951 (Steel, 1956).

Minidoka County. Noted at Rupert May 13 and September 4 and 19, 1919, May 16 to June 4, and September 10, 1920, and May 30, 1921 (Davis, 1935).

Cassia County. A single bird seen at Burley June 2, 1955, in underbrush at the edge of the Snake River (Burleigh).

Habits. The Wilson's Warbler is one of the latest migrants to appear in Idaho in the spring. In northern Idaho an occasional bird has been noted after the first week in May, but it is usually the middle of the month, or later, before this species is recorded for the first time. It also lingers much later in the spring than other transients, being commonly observed through the first week in June in areas where it is not known to breed. The fall migration is a very leisurely process, there being an interval of almost three months, from early August until almost the end of October, when Wilson's Warblers can be found in underbrush bordering the streams in the open valleys. At Moscow my extreme dates of occurrence are May 11 (1951) and June 7 (1951) and August 3 (1958) and October 21 (1948); at Potlatch May 9 (1955) and May 24 (1950), and August 13 (1948) and October 2

(1955); at Lewiston May 16 (1953) and June 6 (1951), and August 12 (1958) and October 16 (1950).

At the present time this warbler has not been recorded during the summer months south of Idaho County, but it is not improbable that further field work will reveal its presence as a breeding bird in the southern part of the state. It is a characteristic species of the Canadian Zone, frequenting thickets and underbrush in the vicinity of water.

Wilsonia pusilla pileolata (Pallas)

Pileolata, the breeding form in Idaho, is distinguished from the nominate race by being lighter and less greenish above, and brighter yellow below. There are no size differences. To verify its occurrence in the state the following specimens were taken over a period of eleven years, 1948 through 1958, all of them typical of *pileolata*: Boundary County, Harrison Peak, male June 25, 1957; Kootenai County, Coeur d'Alene, female October 6, 1951; Latah County, Potlatch, males September 4 and 9, 1948, May 19 and 24, 1950, August 31 and September 12, 1951, September 24, 1952, May 9 and September 25, 1955, females August 13, 1948, September 13, 1952, September 10, 1957, Moscow, males September 10 and 24, and October 21, 1948, August 15, 1949, May 18 and October 9, 1950, June 7, August 14 and 23, September 18, 1951, May 20, August 11 and 25, 1952, May 24, June 3, 1953, August 7 and 30, September 12, 1956, females August 12, October 3, 1948, September 20, 1949, August 17, 1951, August 18, September 25, October 3, 1952, August 22, 1956, August 20, 22, and 26, September 9 and 14, 1957, October 3, 1958; Nez Perce County, Lewiston, males October 16, 1950, June 6, September 1 and 2, 1951, May 16, June 4, 1953, October 8, 1955, August 13, 1956, females August 24, 1949, September 21, 1952, August 12, 1958; Clearwater County, Orofino, male August 27, 1951; Valley County, McCall, male September 18, 1955; Bonneville County, Grays Lake, male May 27, 1951.

Wilsonia pusilla pusilla (Wilson)

The nominate race of *Wilsonia pusilla* is found during the summer months north of Idaho in Mackenzie, so it is more or less to be expected that it should occur in the state as a transient, at least in small numbers. Specimens identified as *pusilla* have been taken in Idaho both in the spring and in the fall, and are as follows: Latah County, Potlatch, female October 2, 1955, Moscow, male May 31, 1955, females May 29, 1950, September 10, 1951, August 23 and September 2, 1957; Owyhee County, Reynolds Creek, male June 3, 1951; Cassia County, Burley, male June 2, 1955.

Setophaga ruticilla tricolora (Müller): AMERICAN REDSTART

General Distribution. Breeds from southeastern Alaska, southern Mackenzie, central Quebec and Newfoundland south to eastern Oregon, northern Utah, northern Colorado, central Ontario, and northern Maine. Winters from southern Baja California and southern Mexico (Puebla, Yucatan) south to Ecuador and northern Brazil.

Status in Idaho. A fairly common but local summer resident in the northern part of the state.

Bonner County. An uncommon summer resident in 1917 in the vicinity of Clark Fork (Burleigh, 1923); an occasional singing male noted at Sandpoint June 21-24, 1957, in deciduous woods bordering the streams (Burleigh).

Kootenai County. Common in summer at Fort Sherman (Coeur d'Alene); arrives the last of May (Merrill, 1898); a fairly common summer resident at Coeur d'Alene, 1910-14 (Rust, 1915); noted at the upper end of Lake Coeur d'Alene July 1-10, 1943 (Yocom, 1946); Bent (1953) cites May 11 as an early date of arrival at Rathdrum.

Benewah County. A common summer resident at St. Maries, 1921-41, occurring in deciduous woods along the streams from the middle of May until late August; noted on the St. Joe River as far as Avery (in Shoshone County), 44 miles east of St. Maries (Hand, 1941).

Latah County. Only infrequently noted during the summer of 1947; a male collected June 7, twenty miles northeast of Moscow (Johnston, 1949); found to be an uncommon summer resident at Harvard, 1951-52 (Verner, 1953); a fairly common but local summer resident, 1948-58, usually appearing in late May and being rarely seen in the fall after early September; definitely known to breed at Harvard, Princeton, Potlatch, Moscow and Deary (Burleigh).

Nez Perce County. Three singing males seen at Lapwai July 12, 1950, in swampy deciduous woods bordering a stream; recorded as a rare fall transient only at Lewiston; single birds seen in willows at the edge of the Snake River August 13 and 21, 1956 (Burleigh).

Clearwater County. Redstarts found to be fairly plentiful at Orofino June 12, 1951, in deciduous woods bordering the Clearwater River; several singing males seen at Pierce June 16, 1951, in willows fringing a stream (Burleigh).

Adams County. An occasional singing male seen at New Meadows June 28-29, 1949, in the birches along the streams (Burleigh).

Custer County. Several singing males noted at Challis July 6, 1960, in woods bordering the Salmon River (Burleigh).

Fremont County. A single singing male seen at Henrys Lake June 25, 1960 (Burleigh).

South of its breeding range the records for this species as a transient are: Jerome County, one bird seen at Jerome July 7, 1949 (Levy, 1950); Bonneville County, one bird, a female, seen on Bear Island, in Grays Lake, May 27, 1951 (Steel, 1956); Jefferson County, common on the Camas National Wildlife Refuge August 21-29, 1961; "as many as fifty were seen in a morning;" but one adult male noted during this period; an immature taken August 21 (Oring, 1962).

Specimens verifying the occurrence of this species in the state, all typical of *tricolora*, are as follows: Bonner County, Sandpoint, males June 21 and 24, 1957 and August 20, 1958; Kootenai County, Coeur d'Alene, male July 4, 1949; Shoshone County, Clarkia, female July 5, 1948; Benewah County, St. Maries, male June 22, 1948; Latah County, Princeton, males May 30, 1949, August 24, 1950, Potlatch, adult males May 21, August 13 and 30, 1948, May 26, 1949, May 24, 1950, August 2, 1951, August 10, 1952, immature male August 12, 1950, adult females May 26, August 31, 1949, August 26 and 31, 1951, immature females July 30, August 7, 1949, August 19, 1950, Moscow, adult males May 26 and 30, July 9, 1948, May 16 and September 4, 1949, June 13, 1952, June 1, 1957, June 22, 1958, July 29, 1960, immature males August 11, 1952, August 2, 1956, adult females August 14, 1949, September 17, 1952, July 8, 1958, immature females August 9, 1948, August 11, 1951, Deary, male July 2, 1950; Nez Perce County, Lapwai, two males July 12, 1950, Lewiston, male August 13, 1956; Clearwater County, Orofino, male June 12, 1951, Pierce, male June 16, 1951; Adams County, New Meadows, male June 29, 1949; Custer County, Challis, male July 6, 1960; Bonneville County, Grays Lake, female May 27, 1951.

Habits. Altitude is apparently a factor in the distribution of the Redstart in Idaho, for despite suitable habitat it is rather uncommon during the summer months above 4,500 feet. It is characteristically a bird of deciduous woods bordering streams, frequenting willows and alders at the lower elevations, and birches and aspens at the upper limits of its summer range.

In view of the long journey it makes from its winter home in the tropics, this warbler spends a rather short interval in Idaho; more often than not it is the latter part of May before the first individuals appear in the spring in the northern part of the state, and by early August there is a noticeable decrease in the numbers noted. At Potlatch my extreme dates of occurrence are May 21 (1948) and September 4 (1948), at Moscow May 16 (1949) and September 17 (1952).

Although elsewhere in its breeding range this species commonly nests in the larger trees, not infrequently some distance from the ground, in Idaho preference is apparently given to shrubs and the larger saplings. Johnston (1949) reports a nest found near Harvard June 25, 1947, that held four eggs, and was four feet from the ground "in a deciduous shrub." Another nest found near Harvard by Verner (1953) held three small young on July 1, 1952, and was thirteen feet up in an alder.

Weaver Finches: *Family Ploceidae*

Passer domesticus domesticus (Linnaeus): HOUSE SPARROW

General Distribution. Widely distributed in Europe and Asia. Introduced into the United States in 1850, and now a common resident species throughout the entire country.

Status in Idaho. Common and of general distribution throughout the state, although limited to a large extent to cities and towns, regardless of size.

What is apparently the first record for the occurrence of this ubiquitous species in Idaho is the statement of Clark P. Streator that it was noted at Pocatello in early July, 1890 (Merriam, 1891).

Rust (1915) observed it for the first time at Coeur d'Alene in the spring of 1909; by 1914 it had become a common bird in and about the town.

Jewett (1912) states that a small flock was seen at Ketchum throughout the winter of 1910.

At the present time it is doubtful if there is a town of any size in the state where this species is not found throughout the year. It has been reported from Clark County, Spencer, Dubois (Rust, 1917), Benewah County, St. Maries (Hand, 1941), Kootenai County, the upper end of Lake Coeur d'Alene (Yocom, 1946), Latah County, Moscow (Johnston, 1949), Harvard (Verner, 1953), Bonneville County, Grays Lake (Steel, 1956), Adams County, Council (Newhouse, 1960).

Habits. A characteristic of the House Sparrow that sets it apart from all other birds is its insistence in remaining in the proximity of man. For many years after it was first introduced into this country it was found only in the towns and larger cities. In time there was a limited dispersal to the farms and ranches where food and nesting sites were available, but even today it is, in Idaho, common only in the towns.

It is a hardy species, apparently unaffected by the subzero temperatures and deep snows that characterize the winters in the northern part of the state.

Rust (1915) states that a favorite nesting site at Coeur d'Alene was "the top fold of awnings after these have been rolled up during the winter." He also observed a pair that confiscated a Cliff Swallow's nest, but it fell to the ground before the eggs were laid.

Meadowlarks, Blackbirds, and Orioles: *Family Icteridae*

Dolichonyx oryzivorus (Linnaeus): BOBOLINK

General Distribution. Breeds from southern British Columbia east across the continent to central Quebec, south to northern California, central Colorado, northern Missouri, southern Indiana, northern West Virginia and central New Jersey. Winters in South America from western Brazil south to northern Argentina.

Status in Idaho. A widely distributed but rather local summer resident over much of the state.

Bonner County. Found to be fairly plentiful in 1917 in marshy meadows at Clark Fork; males still singing in early July (Burleigh, 1923); a small breeding colony noted at Sandpoint June 12, 1950 (Burleigh); a specimen in the Museum of Vertebrate Zoology, Berkeley, was taken by H. Carey at Cocolalla, twelve miles south of Sandpoint, June 27, 1937.

Kootenai County. A single male noted at the edge of an open marsh at Cataldo May 21, 1949 (Burleigh).

Benewah County. Singing males seen "on the St. Joseph River" in July (Merrill, 1898); a rare summer resident, 1910-14, in the St. Joe marshes; also noted on Wolf Lodge Creek (Rust, 1915); a common summer resident, 1921-41, at St. Maries, occurring from late May until July (Hand, 1941); two small breeding colonies noted in open marshy fields at St. Maries June 19, 1951 (Burleigh).

Shoshone County. A flock of six birds seen in an open field at Clarkia August 7, 1948; apparently a family party, one bird collected being a fully grown young male of the year; two breeding pairs noted in an open marshy field at Calder June 22, 1951 (Burleigh).

Nez Perce County. One record, an adult male feeding on July 5, 1953, with Red-winged Blackbirds in a field at the edge of the reservoir east of Lewiston Orchards (Burleigh).

Clearwater County. Six birds, apparently the adults and a brood of fully grown young, seen at Weippe August 1, 1952, feeding at the edge of a field of oats (Burleigh).

Adams County. Possibly twelve pairs found nesting in two large adjoining open fields at New Meadows June 27-28, 1949 (Burleigh); a single bird seen at Indian Valley "the last week in May," 1958 (Newhouse, 1960).

Valley County. Several singing males seen in an open marshy field at Donnelly June 4, 1957 (Burleigh).

Ada County. Singing males noted in alfalfa fields at Meridian in July, 1909 (Tracy, 1910, Wyman, 1911), and a flock of twenty-five at Meridian in August, 1911 (Wyman, 1912); Bent (1958) cites May 18 as an early date of arrival at Meridian.

Lemhi County. A single bird seen in the Lemhi Valley August 31, 1890 (Merriam, 1891); one singing male noted in an open field at Salmon June 14, 1957 (Burleigh).

Bonneville County. A fairly common summer resident, 1949-51, at Grays Lake; arrival date May 19, 1951 (Steel, 1956); recorded as still present at Grays Lake July 17, 1949 (Levy, 1950).

In order to verify the occurrence of the Bobolink in Idaho I collected the following specimens in various parts of the state: Benewah County, St. Maries, male June 19, 1951; Shoshone County, Clarkia, immature male August 7, 1948, Calder, male June 22, 1951; Nez Perce County, Lewiston, male July 5, 1953; Clearwater County, Weippe, male August 1, 1952; Adams County, New Meadows, male June 28, 1949; Lemhi County, Salmon, male June 14, 1957; Bonneville County, Grays Lake, male June 8, 1949.

Habits. The Bobolink is a denizen of wet meadows, or open marsh covered with a thick growth of grass, and this famous songster is apt to be found where such conditions exist in Idaho. Altitude would appear to be no factor, extremes at which it has been found nesting in the state being approximately 2,000 feet at Clark Fork, in Bonner County, and 6,300 feet at Grays Lake, in Bonneville County.

Although fairly common and well distributed in the more northern counties, this species is rarely observed in migration farther south in the state. During eleven years of residence in Latah County I failed to record it at any time, and in Nez Perce County I observed it but once at Lewiston, a single adult male in early July. It would appear that the route followed both in the spring and in the fall is not due north and south, and while there are insufficient data to do other than merely theorize, it could be assumed that the Bobolink enters Idaho in the spring and leaves in the early fall in the eastern part of the state west of the Continental Divide.

Because of the long journey from its winter home in South America the Bobolink remains in Idaho only long enough to rear its young. It is after the middle of May before it appears in the spring, and the southward movement is well under way before the end of July, with only an occasional individual noted after early August.

Sturnella neglecta Audubon: Western Meadowlark

General Distribution. Breeds from central British Columbia, central Saskatchewan, southern Ontario and northwestern Ohio south to Baja California, central Mexico (Zacatecas, Tamaulipas) and Louisiana. Winters north to southern British Columbia, southern Alberta, southern Manitoba, and southern Wisconsin.

Status in Idaho. A common summer resident in suitable habitat throughout the state, wintering regularly both at Lewiston, in Nez Perce County, and, although in smaller number, in Latah County; rarely elsewhere.

Bonner County. Plentiful at Clark Fork during the summer of 1917, in open fields about the town; adults noted feeding young on July 4; small flocks noticeable by the middle of September (Burleigh, 1923).

Kootenai County. Arrives at Fort Sherman (Coeur d'Alene) in early March; common in summer (Merrill, 1898); a common summer resident at Coeur d'Alene, 1910-14; extreme dates of occurrence March 27 and October 31 (Rust, 1915).

Shoshone County. A "very common" summer resident on the St. Joe National Forest, 1921-41, from March to October; rare in winter; noted both in the valleys and in the mountain meadows at the higher altitudes (Hand, 1941).

Latah County. Fairly common during the summer of 1947 in the open country (Johnston, 1949); a common resident species throughout the county, 1948-58, although less numerous during the winter months; noted in late December and in January at Princeton, Potlatch, Moscow, and Genesee (Burleigh).

Nez Perce County. A common resident species at Lewiston, 1948-58; most numerous during the winter months when scattered small flocks were seen in the open fields and pastures (Burleigh).

Clearwater County. Three birds seen at Weippe January 12, 1952, feeding on cow dung at the edge of a field; four feet of snow on the ground that day; singing males frequently noted on the open prairie south of Weippe March 24, 1952 (Burleigh).

Adams County. One small flock noted at Council February 27, 1950 (Burleigh); a common summer resident at Council in 1958, extreme dates of occurrence being March 11 and October 29; fledglings seen the last week in July (Newhouse, 1960).

Washington County. Several small flocks noted at Weiser November 23, 1951, in the open fields about the town (Burleigh).

Canyon County. A specimen in the Denver Museum of Natural History was taken by Brodkorb in January at Parma.

Ada County. A common summer resident at Boise; a specimen taken there May 12, 1943 (Arvey, 1947).

Owyhee County. Common at Riddle May 28-June 3, 1934 (Davis, 1934).

Lemhi County. Singing males seen at Shoup June 4, 1949, and at Salmon May 25, 1952 (Burleigh).

Clark County. A fairly common summer resident; several breeding pairs noted at Highbridge June 26, 1916 (Rust, 1917).

Jefferson County. A common summer resident in 1961 on the Camas National Wildlife Refuge (Oring, 1962).

Bonneville County. A common summer resident at Grays Lake, 1949-51 (Steel, 1956).

South Central Idaho. Common in 1890 "in the sage plains and valleys" until after the first snowfall in October (Merriam, 1891); an abundant breeding bird in this same general area in 1949 (Levy, 1950).

Minidoka County. A summer resident at Rupert, 1919-21; earliest date for eggs May 2 (Davis, 1935); Bent (1958) cites March 3 as an early date of arrival at Rupert.

Habits. Although the Western Meadowlark winters regularly in northern Idaho there is a noticeable decrease in numbers in late October, and it is the middle of the following March before it is common again. It is a hardy species, scattered flocks varying in size from five to twelve birds being seen in late December and January in the open fields when the ground was covered with a foot or more of snow. Its relative abundance in both Washington and Gem counties in late November, 1951, and the fact that a specimen was collected in Canyon County in January, would suggest the possibility that it also winters regularly in the southwestern corner of the state.

Breeding activities are apparently delayed in the spring until early May, but by early July the young are fully grown and able to shift for themselves. Friedmann (1934) reports a nest found in June, 1912, at Dickey, in Custer County, by L. E. Wyman that held four eggs and one of the Cowbird. At New Meadows, in Adams County, I flushed the female from a nest on May 21, 1955, that held one fresh egg. It was sunken flush with the ground, and very well concealed under a bunch of thick grass at the edge of an open field.

Sturnella neglecta confluenta Rathbun

Confluenta is distinguished from the nominate race by having the upper parts darker (the black areas more extensive), and the yellow of the underparts averaging darker. It is the breeding form in all of Idaho except the eastern corner of the state. Specimens typical of this race have been taken as follows: Kootenai County, Hauser, male October 9, 1952; Latah County, Potlatch, males March 13, 1949, February 28, 1953, February 1, 1954, January 8, 1955, Moscow, males December 4, 1947, April 20 and June 16, 1948, January 6, February 27, March 15 and December 17, 1949, March 5 and October 5, 1950, April 22, 1951, March 21 and October 20, 1952, February 26, 1953, January 30, 1955, March 13, 1956, January 21, 1957, females, April 14 and October 18, 1951, Genesee, males January 15, 1948, December 8 and 21, 1951, January 1, 1952; Nez Perce County, Lewiston, males December 18, 1947, November 11, 1948, December 1, 1949, December 13, 1950, January 21 and November 12, 1951, January 21, 1952, February 21 and December 9, 1956; Clearwater County, Weippe, male January 12, 1952; Adams County, Council, male February 27, 1950; Washington County, Weiser, male November 22, 1951; Gem County, Emmett, male November 23, 1951.

Sturnella neglecta neglecta Audubon

On the basis of specimens taken, the nominate race of the Western Meadowlark would appear to be limited in its distribution in Idaho to the eastern corner of the state. However, the number of specimens examined is insufficient to give at this time, with any degree of definiteness, the range of *neglecta* in Idaho. They are as follows: Lemhi County, Salmon, male May 25, 1952; Bonneville County, Gray, female May 25, 1951, male May 26, 1951; Caribou County, Soda Springs, male May 20, 1951; Bingham County, Blackfoot, male May 20, 1951; Jerome County, Jerome, male May 31, 1951; Bear Lake County, Montpelier, male April 27, 1954.

Xanthocephalus xanthocephalus (Bonaparte): YELLOW-HEADED BLACKBIRD

General Distribution. Breeds from central British Columbia, central Saskatchewan, central Manitoba, northern Wisconsin and northwestern Ohio south to northern Baja California, southern New Mexico, northern Oklahoma, northern Arkansas and northern Indiana. Winters from central California, southern New Mexico, central Texas and southern Louisiana south to Southern Mexico (Guerrero, Veracruz).

Status in Idaho. A common but rather local summer resident in suitable habitat throughout the state.

Kootenai County. A rare summer resident, 1910-14; two collected "on the St. Joe marshes" (Rust, 1915); small breeding colonies, each consisting of possibly a dozen pairs, noted at Rose Lake and at Cataldo May 21, 1949; a single male seen at Hauser May 6, 1957 (Burleigh).

Benewah County. Locally common in the marshes at St. Maries, 1921-41; probably breeds but noted only from April through June; seen once at Avery, in Shoshone County (Hand, 1941); what was apparently a small breeding colony of four pairs noted in an open marsh at St. Maries May 21, 1949 (Burleigh).

Latah County. A single male seen at Potlatch August 11, 1947 (Johnston, 1949); found to be an extremely scarce transient in the county, being noted on but three occasions over an interval of eleven years, 1947-58; single birds were seen at Potlatch August 24, 1951, and May 1, 1957, and at Moscow August 17, 1952 (Burleigh).

Nez Perce County. A scarce transient at Lewiston from 1949 to 1956, being infrequently seen, and in small numbers, in reeds bordering the Snake River; dates of occurrence August 2 and 19, 1949, and June 8 and July 16, 1953; nested for the first time in 1956 at the reservoir east of Lewiston Orchards, the small breeding colony consisting of six females and apparently but one male; by 1958 this colony had increased to approximately thirty females, and, as far as could be determined, three males; latest date of occurrence at the reservoir August 28 (1958) (Burleigh).

Valley County. Reported by Newhouse (1960) as common at Cascade in 1958.

Canyon County. Bent (1958) cites March 5 as an early date of arrival at Deer Flat.

Owyhee County. A small breeding colony seen in an open marsh at Riddle May 28-June 3, 1934 (Davis, 1934); noted in small numbers at Homedale June 23, 1949 (Burleigh).

Clark County. Two seen at Kilgore August 26, 1916 (Rust, 1917).

Jefferson County. An occasional flock noted at Terreton April 29, 1954 (Burleigh); a common summer resident in 1961, "during June and July," on the Camas National Wildlife Refuge; only "a few individuals" were seen in August (Oring, 1962).

Bonneville County. Found to be fairly common as a breeding bird at Idaho Falls June 7, 1949 (Burleigh); an abundant summer resident at Grays Lake, 1949-51; arrival dates, males April 8, 1950, April 5, 1951, females May 10, 1950, May 3, 1951 (Steel, 1956); a flock of approximately fifty birds seen feeding in an open field at Gray August 26, 1955 (Burleigh).

Caribou County. Several large flocks seen at Soda Springs August 25, 1955 (Burleigh).

South Central Idaho. A few noted on Big Lost River in late July, 1890, and again on September 10 (Merriam, 1891); in this same general area Levy (1950) found this species restricted in 1949 to the tule marshes, but nesting there "in large numbers."

Minidoka County. A common summer resident at Rupert, 1919-21; extreme dates of occurrence March 29 and September 18; earliest date for eggs June 28 (Davis, 1934).

Gooding County. A specimen taken at Hagerman June 16, 1940 (Arvey, 1947).

Cassia County. A flock of twenty birds, all males, seen at Burley April 23, 1954, in open marsh at the edge of the Snake River (Burleigh).

Habits. The migration route followed by the Yellow-headed Blackbirds that nest in northern Idaho would appear to be much like that of the Bobolinks that spend the summer in that part of the state. Until I found this species nesting for the first time in Nez Perce County I considered it an extremely scarce transient in northern Idaho south of St. Maries, for only rarely was it observed, and then in very small numbers.

Unlike the other blackbirds it normally does not appear in the spring until early April, and its departure in the fall takes place shortly after the young are fully grown and able to shift for themselves. In areas where it breeds there is a noticeable decrease in numbers in late July, and while flocks are observed throughout August they are few and far between. The latest date for its occurrence in the state is August 28, 1958, a single bird at the reservoir east of Lewiston Orchards.

In the spring of 1956 the water at the reservoir was unusually high, resulting in flooding a stretch of shoreline covered with a thick growth of small willows. This furnished nesting habitat suitable for this blackbird, and it was immediately taken advantage of. The depth of the water made it impossible to search these willows for nests, but the presence of six females on July 1, carrying food, left no doubt as to their successfully establishing a breeding colony here. Two years later, in 1958, this colony had more than doubled in size, and nesting activities had apparently begun earlier for on June 19 the females were seen busily engaged in carrying food to their young.

Merriam (1891) states that this species was found breeding in 1872 in Marsh Valley, in southeastern Idaho, and that a nest with four "nearly fresh" eggs was collected on June 29. It was five feet up in a clump of rushes, and was built of "dry swamp grass."

Agelaius phoeniceus (Linnaeus): RED-WINGED BLACKBIRD

General Distribution. As a breeding bird common and widely distributed on the North American continent, occurring from the Atlantic coast to the Pacific coast, and from southern Yukon and central Mackenzie south to Baja California, Mexico (Sinaloa, Veracruz), the Gulf coast, and southern Florida. Winters north to southern British Columbia, southern Manitoba, and southern Ontario.

Status in Idaho. A common and well-distributed summer resident throughout the state, occurring, regardless of altitude, wherever there is suitable habitat. Winters regularly at Lewiston, but otherwise in small numbers, and only during occasional winters, farther north.

It is doubtful if there is a bird that is present in greater numbers in the state, or is more widespread in its distribution, than is the Red-winged Blackbird. It shuns the thick woods, but otherwise, wherever there is the proximity of water, and marsh vegetation or low underbrush in which to nest, one or more pairs of this ubiquitous species will be found. It is included on all local lists that have been published, and has been recorded practically everywhere that field work has been carried on. Summarized briefly, this familiar blackbird has been reported as a common summer resident in the following localities: Kootenai County, Coeur d'Alene, Hauser; Benewah County, St. Maries; Latah County, Princeton, Potlatch, Moscow, Genesee; Nez Perce County, Lewiston; Clearwater County, Weippe, Headquarters; Idaho County, White Bird, Riggins; Adams County, New Meadows, Council, Mesa; Valley County, Cascade; Washington County, Cambridge, Weiser; Canyon County, Star, Parma; Ada County, Boise; Owyhee County, Homedale, Riddle; Elmore County, Mountain Home, Glenns Ferry; Custer County, Challis, Mackay; Blaine County, Bellevue; Clark County, Small; Fremont County, St. Anthony; Jefferson County, Mud Lake, Camas National Wildlife Refuge; Bonneville County, Idaho Falls, Grays Lake; Caribou County, Henry; Bingham County, Blackfoot; Bannock County, Pocatello; Bear Lake County, Montpelier, Fish Haven; Franklin County, Preston; Oneida County, Malad City; Minidoka County, Rupert, Acequia, Minidoka; Cassia County, Burley; Gooding County, Gooding, Hagerman; Jerome County, Jerome; Twin Falls County, Twin Falls.

Habits. The Red-winged Blackbird winters regularly at Lewiston, flocks comprising from thirty to sixty individuals being noted each year in late December and in January. In Latah County it has been noted during the winter months in small numbers in the open fields bordering the Palouse River between Princeton and Potlatch, actual dates of occurrence being January 17, 1948, January 3, 1954, January 8, 1955, and January 15, 1956. Hand (1941) states that it is "occasional in winter" at St. Maries, in Benewah County.

This species is one of the earliest migrants to arrive in the spring, the first males appearing in February when the ground is still covered with snow. In Kootenai County Merrill (1898) gives February 22 as the earliest date of arrival at Fort Sherman (Coeur d'Alene), and Bent (1958), February 12 at Rathdrum. In Latah County my earliest dates of arrival are February 13 (1952) at Genesee, February 18 (1951) at Potlatch, and February 19 (1951) at Moscow. At Weippe, in Clearwater County, at an altitude of 3,000 feet, my earliest record is that of six males seen February 28 (1954). Steel (1956) cites as arrival dates for Grays Lake (6,300 feet) males February 15, 1950, females April 8, 1950, and April 7, 1951.

Davis (1935) gives May 19 as the earliest date that fresh eggs were found at Rupert, in Minidoka County. A nest at Lewiston, on June 4, 1953, held four half-incubated eggs, and was in a thick clump of weeds in underbrush bordering a stream.

Agelaius phoeniceus nevadensis Grinnell

This Great Basin race is the form occurring over all of Idaho except the extreme southeastern corner. A series of specimens, largely taken in the breeding season, were found to be representative of *nevadensis,* and are from the following localities: Kootenai County, Coeur d'Alene, Hauser; Latah County, Princeton, Potlatch, Moscow, Genesee; Nez Perce County, Lewiston; Clearwater County, Weippe; Adams County, New Meadows; Valley County, Cascade; Washington County, Weiser; Owyhee County, Homedale; Custer County, Challis, Mackay; Jerome County, Jerome; Gooding County, Gooding, Hagerman; Minidoka County, Acequia, Minidoka.

Agelaius phoeniceus utahensis Behle

This race has a very limited range in Idaho, being found as a breeding bird only in the extreme southeastern corner of the state. Specimens representing *utahensis* have been taken in June and early July at the following localities: Fremont County, St. Anthony; Bonneville County, Idaho Falls, Grays Lake; Bannock County, Pocatello; Caribou County, Henry; Oneida County, Malad City; Franklin County, Preston; Bear Lake County, Fish Haven. Behle (1940) refers specimens from the southern edge of the state (Cassia County, Minidoka County, Gooding County, Owyhee County, Payette County) to this race, but states that they are intermediate in their characters. Specimens from these counties personally examined in connection with this study were not typical of *nevadensis,* but were considered closer in their characters to this race rather than to *utahensis.*

Icterus bullockii bullockii (Swainson): BULLOCK'S ORIOLE

General Distribution. Breeds from southern British Columbia, southern Saskatchewan, and southwestern North Dakota south to southern California, southern Arizona and southern Texas. Winters from Mexico (Sinaloa, Puebla) to Costa Rica.

Status in Idaho. A local summer resident throughout the state, but common only in the more southern counties.

Kootenai County. Breeds sparingly at Fort Sherman (Coeur d'Alene) in the cottonwoods (Merrill, 1898); a rare summer resident at Coeur d'Alene, 1910-14 (Rust, 1915).

Latah County. An adult male seen on Paradise Ridge, east of Moscow, June 15, 1947; a family group noted August 12 on Potlatch Creek, above Juliaetta (Johnston, 1949); a scarce summer resident, and rather local in its distribution (1948-58), being noted in the larger cottonwoods and willows along the streams from the middle of May until the middle of August (Burleigh).

Nez Perce County. Reported by Bendire (1895) as "abundant" at Fort Lapwai in 1871; found to be a fairly common summer resident at Lewiston (1948-58), scattered pairs being seen in the cottonwood groves along both the Clearwater and Snake rivers (Burleigh).

Idaho County. A specimen taken four miles northwest of Pollock June 27, 1940 (Arvey, 1947).

Adams County. "Not uncommon" at Council in 1958, being present from May 28 through August 1 (Newhouse, 1960).

Ada County. Bent (1958) cites April 30 as an early date of arrival at Meridian.

Owyhee County. One pair noted at Riddle May 28 through June 3, 1934 (Davis, 1934).

Lemhi County. One pair seen at North Fork June 7, 1949, in willows at the edge of the Salmon River (Burleigh).

Blaine County. One pair seen at Ketchum June 26, 1950, in cottonwoods bordering the Big Wood River (Burleigh).

Clark County. One pair seen in Little Dry Creek Canyon July 29, 1916 (Rust, 1917).

Jefferson County. A common summer resident in 1961 on the Camas National Wildlife Refuge; a male collected at Hamer on June 24 (Oring, 1962).

Bonneville County. A common summer resident at Grays Lake, 1949-51 (Steel, 1956); two pairs seen May 27, 1951, in the aspens on Bear Island, well out toward the center of Grays Lake (Burleigh).

Bannock County. Bent (1958) cites September 5 as a late date of departure at Pocatello.

Southeastern Idaho. Found breeding on Devils Creek in 1872 (Merriam, 1891).

South Central Idaho. One pair noted the middle of July, 1890, on the Snake River, near Blackfoot; also found to be common on the Big Lost River at Arco in late July (Merriam, 1891); in this same general area Levy (1950) reported this species common during the summer of 1949 in "the poplar-aspen river bottoms."

Minidoka County. A summer resident at Rupert, extreme dates of occurrence being May 6 and September 4; eggs June 1 (Davis, 1935).

Cassia County. A male collected by E. Larrison on Goose Creek, ten miles south of Oakley, June 25, 1949 (Jollie, in litt.).

Habits. Because of its rather exacting requirements the Bullock's Oriole, although well distributed in Idaho, is absent over wide areas where there is no suitable habitat. Both in migration and during the summer months it frequents the larger deciduous trees, notably cottonwoods and willows, that border the rivers and smaller streams; water is apparently not essential, however, for it can be found in dry washes where there are trees large enough to afford nesting sites. It has no liking for thick woods, and consistently shuns conifers at all times.

It is another species that spends a rather short interval in the state, for it rarely appears in the spring before the middle of May, and in the late fall it is only infrequently observed after the middle of August. At Moscow my extreme dates of occurrence are May 19 (1948) and August 17 (1953), at Lewiston May 10 (1952) and August 22 (1951).

Bendire (1895) comments on the abundance of this oriole at Fort Lapwai in 1871, stating that three occupied nests were actually observed in one birch tree. A nest found there on June 6 held four eggs, another three well-incubated eggs on June 15.

Euphagus carolinus carolinus (Müller): RUSTY BLACKBIRD

General Distribution. Breeds from northern Alaska, northern Mackenzie, northern Ontario and central Labrador south to British Columbia, central Saskatchewan, southern Ontario and southern Quebec, and through the northern Appalachians to northeastern New York. Winters from the southern part of its breeding range south to central Colorado, southern Texas, the Gulf coast, and northern Florida.

Status in Idaho. Of accidental occurrence in the northern part of the state.

This species has been recorded but once in Idaho. On November 2, 1952, I found a single bird, a female, feeding alone on swampy ground at the edge of the Palouse River north of Potlatch. It was collected to verify the identification, and found to represent the nominate race, *carolinus.*

Habits. This species bears a close resemblance to the Brewer's Blackbird, so much so that unless the possibility of encountering it is borne in mind it could easily be overlooked. It is possible therefore that it is more common in the state than the one record would indicate. Its preferred habitat, both during the breeding season and in migration, is wooded swamps, this trait being quite at variance with the preference of the Brewer's Blackbird for open fields and marshes.

Euphagus cyanocephalus (Wagler): BREWER'S BLACKBIRD

General Distribution. Breeds from central British Columbia, central Alberta, southern Manitoba and western Ontario south to Baja California, central Arizona, northern Texas, Oklahoma, and northern Illinois. Winters from the southern part of its breeding range south to Mexico (Oaxaca, Veracruz) and the Gulf coast.

Status in Idaho. A common summer resident throughout the state. Of irregular occurrence during the winter months except at Lewiston, where it winters commonly.

Bonner County. A small colony of ten pairs of these blackbirds found nesting in 1917 in an open marsh in the valley east of Clark Fork; young fairly well grown by the first week of July (Burleigh, 1923); common at Sandpoint June 12, 1950 (Burleigh).

Kootenai County. "A few pairs breed" at Fort Sherman (Coeur d'Alene); an occasional small flock noted during the winter (Merrill, 1898); an uncommon summer resident at Coeur d'Alene, 1910-14; occasional in winter (Rust, 1915).

Shoshone County. A common summer resident in the open valleys on the St. Joe National Forest, 1921-41; present from April to October.

Benewah County. One winter record (February, 1934) at St. Maries (Hand, 1941); frequently observed at Tensed June 14, 1950 (Burleigh).

Latah County. An "abundant" summer resident in 1947 (Johnston, 1949); a common and well-distributed summer resident, 1948-58; of infrequent occurrence during the winter months (Burleigh).

Nez Perce County. A common resident species at Lewiston; flocks comprising as many as 120 individuals noted during the winter months (Burleigh).

Clearwater County. Small breeding colonies noted in 1952, and, in succeeding years, at Weippe and at Headquarters; first small flocks were recorded at Weippe in the spring on April 9, 1952, and April 8, 1953, and at Headquarters April 10, 1952 (Burleigh).

Lewis County. Common at Nezperce June 20, 1952 (Burleigh).

Valley County. These blackbirds found to be already common at McCall (altitude 5,000 feet) April 12, 1958, and usually noted in pairs, although the ground that day was still covered with three feet of hard snow (Burleigh).

Adams County. Frequently seen in the open marsh at New Meadows June 27, 1949; a young bird of the year, already out of the nest, collected (Burleigh); a common breeding bird at Council, 1957-58; noted every month of the year but November; fully grown young seen by the end of June (Newhouse, 1960).

Ada County. Common and frequently seen at Boise April 17, 1949 (Burleigh).

Owyhee County. Very common at Riddle May 28-June 3, 1934 (Davis, 1934); scattered flocks, totaling several thousand birds, seen about the sheep pens at Homedale February 19-26, 1950; in view of the early date it is not improbable that these flocks represented a wintering population in this part of the state (Burleigh).

Clark County. Scattered pairs found nesting on Little Dry Creek, at Spencer, June 11-20, 1916 (Rust, 1917).

Jefferson County. A common summer resident in 1961 on the Camas National Wildlife Refuge (Oring, 1962).

South Central Idaho. In 1890 this species was found to be "abundant everywhere along the streams and about ranches and mining camps"; flocks of "fully 1000 birds" seen in the Lemhi Valley in early September (Merriam, 1891); abundant in south-central Idaho during the summer of 1949 (Levy, 1950).

Bonneville County. A common summer resident at Grays Lake, 1949-51; arrival dates, males April 13, 1951, females April 24, 1951 (Steel, 1956).

Bear Lake County. Common and frequently seen at Paris May 26, 1952 (Burleigh).

Minidoka County. A common summer resident at Rupert, 1919-21; earliest date for eggs May 13; latest date for young in the nest August 1 (Davis, 1935); Bent (1958) gives March 29 as an early date of arrival at Rupert, and November 24 as a late date of departure.

Cassia County. Common and frequently seen at Burley June 18, 1949, and at Malta June 22, 1952 (Burleigh).

Habits. The Brewer's Blackbird has no liking for the thick woods, but wherever there is open country in Idaho it will be found. Altitude is disregarded, for I found it equally common at Lewiston, at 840 feet, and at Grays Lake, at an altitude of 6,400 feet. It appears to like the vicinity of water, and in the open arid country in the southern part of the state breeding pairs can always be found where any water exists. However, where conditions are suitable it does hesitate to take advantage of nesting sites far removed from the nearest stream or open marsh.

In Latah County it usually appears in the spring in late March or early April, and in the fall it is rarely observed after the middle of October. At Moscow my extreme dates of occurrence are March 20 (1957) and October 11 (1948), at Genesee March 27 (1953) and October 21 (1950). I have three records for the winter months; at Princeton a flock of eight birds was seen January 17, 1948, and at Potlatch flocks comprising fully sixty individuals were encountered December 12, 1951, and January 3, 1954.

In nesting this species selects a wide diversity of sites, far more so than is the case with the other blackbirds. The nest may be on the ground, in a bush, or in the upper branches of a large tree; open marshes are favored, and here the thick marsh grass is used in preference to cattails or tules. Rust (1917) states that in Clark County the nests he found were in willows and in sagebrush, and in one instance on the ground. A nest found at Lewiston May 4, 1953, held two fresh eggs, and was five feet from the ground in a crotch of a cottonwood in an open grove at the edge of the Snake River. Wyman (1911) cites an experiment with a nest found in a brush pile at Meridian in July, 1909, that held three eggs. It was moved twenty-five feet to a similar situation, and the female returned to her eggs as if nothing had happened.

Euphagus cyanocephalus aliastus Oberholser

The Brewer's Blackbirds of the Columbia Basin can be distinguished from the nominate race with certainty only where the females are concerned. The males are practically indistinguishable both in respect to size and color. Females of *aliastus* are distinct from *cyanocephalus* in being lighter (less brown) below, and darker (more brown) above; there is no appreciable size difference. As a breeding bird *aliastus* has a wide distribution in Idaho, occurring everywhere except in the extreme southeastern corner of the state. A total of twenty-four females, taken at various times of the year, were found to represent *aliastus,* and are from the following localities: Bonner County, Sandpoint, June 12, 1950; Benewah County, Tensed, June 14, 1950; Latah County, Princeton, January 17, 1948, Potlatch, April 19, 1951, Viola, April 26, 1951, Moscow, June 23, 1948, April 6, 1949, July 11, 1950, April 11 and June 23, 1951, April 3, 1955, March 30, 1958, Genesee, April 28, 1951, April 1, 1952, February 16, 1958; Nez Perce County, Lewiston, April 18 and October 16, 1951; Clearwater County, Weippe, April 9,

1952, April 8, 1953, Headquarters, June 27, 1957; Lewis County, Nezperce, June 20, 1952; Adams County, New Meadows, June 27, 1949; Owyhee County, Homedale, February 22, 1950.

Euphagus cyanocephalus cyanocephalus (Wagler)

The nominate race of the Brewer's Blackbird is the form occurring throughout the Rocky Mountain region. As a breeding bird it has a very limited range in Idaho, being found during the summer months only in the northeastern corner of the state. Females representing this race, but approaching *aliastus* in their coloration, were taken as follows: Bonneville County, Gray, May 29, 1951; Caribou County, Soda Springs, August 25, 1955; Bear Lake County, Paris, May 26, 1952; Minidoka County, Rupert, June 3, 1952; Jerome County, Jerome, May 30, 1951.

Quiscalus quiscula versicolor Vieillot: COMMON GRACKLE

General Distribution. Breeds from northern British Columbia, central Mackenzie, southern Quebec and Newfoundland south to southern Colorado, southeastern Texas, northern Mississippi, northern Tennessee, and central Pennsylvania. Winters north to northern Minnesota, southern Ontario and central Nova Scotia, south to southern Mississippi, southern Georgia, and South Carolina.

Status in Idaho. Of casual occurrence in the northern part of the state.

This distinctive blackbird was first recorded in Idaho by Jollie (1951) who saw a male at Sandpoint November 19, 1950. He attempted to collect it, but it was so wary that his efforts were unsuccessful. That same year, on October 22, he collected a female a mile west of Moscow, but in Whitman County, Washington.

It was recorded for the second time in Idaho by Verner (1956) who collected a male on the Tamany Creek road south of Lewiston December 27, 1955. This specimen is now in the Charles R. Conner Museum, on the campus of the Washington State University at Pullman.

Habits. Because of its large size and its liking for open country, the grackle is a bird that cannot be easily overlooked. It would therefore appear that it has never been of more than casual occurrence in the state, and that only an occasional straggler appears in Idaho in the fall. Since it breeds commonly in British Columbia its migration route must take it east across the continent, in this way avoiding the Rocky Mountain region with its heavily wooded ridges.

Molothrus ater artemisiae Grinnell: BROWN-HEADED COWBIRD

General Distribution. Breeds from northern British Columbia, southern Mackenzie and western Ontario south to central California, southern Nevada, western New Mexico, western Nebraska, and Iowa. Winters from southern California, southern Arizona, northern Texas and Louisiana south to southern Baja California, Guerrero, and Veracruz.

Status in Idaho. A fairly common summer resident in the northern part of the state; less numerous and of local distribution in southern Idaho.

Bonner County. An occasional bird seen during the summer of 1917 in the open valley in the vicinity of Clark Fork (Burleigh, 1923).

Kootenai County. Rare; a specimen taken at Fort Sherman (Coeur d'Alene) May 25, 1896 (Merrill, 1898); noted at Hauser July 2, 1956, three adult males and an adult female feeding at the edge of an open field, and July 16, 1957, a fully grown young bird of the year, at almost the same spot (Burleigh).

Benewah County. A not uncommon summer resident at St. Maries, 1921-41; present from May until late summer (Hand, 1941).

Latah County. Noted in small numbers during the summer of 1947; a male and a female collected at Moscow June 20 and June 30 (Johnston, 1949); a fairly common summer resident (1948-58) in the more open country south and east of Moscow, usually appearing about the middle of May and being only infrequently observed after the middle of August (Burleigh).

Nez Perce County. Reported by Bendire (1895) as breeding at Fort Lapwai in 1871; an uncommon summer resident, 1948-58, at Lewiston (Burleigh).

Clearwater County. In 1952 a young bird of the year, fully grown, was seen at Weippe August 1; in 1953 three birds, a male and two females, were seen at Headquarters May 17, feeding around cows in a pasture (Burleigh).

Idaho County. One pair noted at Cottonwood June 1, 1955 (Burleigh).

Adams County. Two birds, a male and a female, noted at New Meadows May 21, 1955 (Burleigh); observed at Council May 24, 1958 (Newhouse, 1960).

Canyon County. Two males seen feeding in an open field at Nampa June 14, 1955 (Burleigh).

Owyhee County. This species noted at two widely separated spots south of Homedale June 26, 1958, three males and a female in one open field, and later in the morning three females in another field. One of the latter was collected, and found to hold an egg almost ready to be laid (Burleigh).

Custer County. Noted at Mackay (two males) May 19, 1951, and at Challis (a male, three females, and a fully grown young bird of the year) July 15, 1958 (Burleigh).

Fremont County. Two birds seen at Highbridge June 26, 1916 (Rust, 1917); three birds, two males and a female, seen at St. Anthony June 10, 1957, and three birds, again two males and a female, at Henrys Lake three days later, on June 13 (Burleigh).

Jefferson County. An uncommon summer resident in 1961 on the Camas National Wildlife Refuge (Oring, 1962).

Bonneville County. Noted for the first time at Gray on May 30, 1952, when three males, apparently belated transients, were seen feeding about cows in a pasture (Burleigh).

Caribou County. A single bird, a female, seen at Henry June 23, 1960 (Burleigh).

Bannock County. Two males seen at Pocatello June 10, 1955 (Burleigh).

Power County. Two birds, a male and a female, seen at American Falls June 9, 1955 (Burleigh).

South Central Idaho. Noted in 1890 on Big Lost River, on Birch Creek, and at Big Butte (Merriam, 1891); in this same general area it was considered by Levy (1950) to be a very scarce summer resident in 1949, his one record being three birds seen at Jerome on June 6.

Minidoka County. Davis (1935) reported this species as occurring during the summer months (1919-21) at Rupert; Bent (1958) cites as extreme dates of occurrence at Rupert May 8 and September 17.

Cassia County. Noted in small numbers at Oakley July 20, 1958, and at Burley June 9, 1960 (Burleigh).

In order to verify the occurrence of the Cowbird in Idaho, and to determine what subspecies the breeding population represented, a series of specimens was collected (1948-60) over much of the state. These were found to be typical of *artemisiae*, characterized by being larger than the other two accepted races, *ater* and *obscurus*. Localities in which these specimens were taken are as follows: Kootenai County, Hauser; Latah County, Potlatch, Princeton, Moscow, Viola; Nez Perce County, Lewiston; Clearwater County, Headquarters; Idaho County, Cottonwood; Adams County, New Meadows; Canyon County, Nampa; Owyhee County, Homedale; Custer County, Challis; Fremont County, Henrys Lake, St. Anthony; Bonneville County, Gray; Power County, American Falls; Cassia County, Burley.

Habits. Unlike the other blackbirds the Cowbird is apparently not a hardy species, for it is one of the last migrants to appear in the spring, and one of the earliest of the breeding birds to disappear in the fall. In Latah County adults were invariably gone before the end of July, only fully grown young birds of the year being seen in August and early September. My latest records for adults at Moscow are July 12, 1949 (two birds), and July 20, 1950 (five birds). Extreme dates of occurrence for Moscow, irrespective of age or sex, are May 10 (1953) and September 6 (1957), for Potlatch May 16 (1948 and 1955) and August 26 (1951). At Lewiston my latest date in the fall is September 4 (1952).

Although altitude is apparently not an important factor in the distribution of this species in Idaho, it would appear that above 6,000 feet it is rather local in its occurrence. It is not known to breed at Grays Lake (6,300 feet), despite suitable habitat, but has been found in small numbers at Henrys Lake (6,700 feet) in late June (1957).

The little breeding data available would indicate that many species are victimized by the Cowbird in Idaho. The first actual record of parasitism is that of Bendire (1895) who states that at Fort Lapwai, on June 21, 1871, he found eggs of the Cowbird in a Yellow-breasted Chat's nest. Rust (1917) reports eggs in the nests of the Brewer's Blackbird, White-crowned Sparrow and Sage Sparrow in Fremont County. At Dickey, in Custer County, eggs were found in nests of the Western Meadowlark and the Vesper Sparrow by L. E. Wyman in June, 1912 (Friedmann, 1929). At Potlatch, on June 24,

1953, I found a song sparrow's nest that held two partially-incubated eggs and one of the Cowbird. On Goose Creek, south of Oakley, in Cassia County, I watched a male Black-throated Gray Warbler on July 20, 1958, feeding a fully grown young Cowbird out of the nest for some time.

Tanagers: *Family Thraupidae*

Piranga ludoviciana (Wilson): WESTERN TANAGER

General Distribution. Breeds from southern Alaska, southwestern Mackenzie, and central Saskatchewan south to northern Baja California, southeastern Arizona, southern New Mexico and western Texas, and east to western South Dakota and northern Nebraska. Winters from northern Mexico (Baja California, Tamaulipas) south to northern Costa Rica.

Status in Idaho. A common summer resident in the more heavily forested areas throughout the state. Essentially a bird of the conifers, being found in such deciduous hardwoods as the cottonwood and the willow only in migration.

The Western Tanager is one of the new birds "discovered" by the Lewis and Clark expedition to the Pacific coast. It was described by Lewis (*Original Journals*, V:111) under date of June 6, 1806, and by Clark (*Original Journals*, V:116) under date of June 7, 1806, from specimens taken then at what is now apparently Kamiah, in Idaho County. Kamiah is accepted as the type locality for this species with the specimen collected by Lewis as the type (Jollie, 1953).

Bonner County. Found to be a plentiful summer resident in 1917 on the lower slopes of the ridges north of Clark Fork; noted at the tops of the ridges in late August (Burleigh, 1923); Bent (1958) cites September 24 as a date of departure at Bayview.

Kootenai County. Arrived at Fort Sherman (Coeur d'Alene) the last week of May; but a few bred (Merrill, 1898); frequently seen at Blue Lake during the summer of 1894 (Snyder, 1900); an uncommon summer resident, 1910-14, at Coeur d'Alene, frequenting conifers (Rust, 1915); "rather common" at the upper end of Lake Coeur d'Alene July 1-10, 1943 (Yocom, 1946).

Shoshone County. A common summer resident, 1921-41, on the St. Joe National Forest, occurring from May until September in both the Transition and Canadian Zones (Hand, 1941).

Latah County. Common "in coniferous forest areas" during the summer of 1947 (Johnston, 1949); a common summer resident at Harvard, 1951-52; young noted July 18, 1952 (Verner, 1953); a common summer resident, 1948-1958, on the wooded ridges north and east of Moscow, usually appearing after the first week in May, and being only infrequently seen after the first of October (Burleigh).

Nez Perce County. A rather scarce fall transient at Lewiston, the few dates of occurrence being July 24, 1950, August 16, 1951, and August 31, 1956 (Burleigh).

Clearwater County. A fairly common summer resident on the wooded ridges at Headquarters; latest record in the fall that of two birds seen August 27, 1952, at the Bertha Hill Lookout (altitude 5,520 feet) (Burleigh).

Idaho County. Noted September 6 and 10, 1941, near Selway Falls, and a male collected; common in July, 1948, in the Lolo Pass region (Orr, 1951); Bent (1958) cites May 10 as an early date of arrival at Grangeville.

Adams County. Two birds, apparently early fall transients, seen at Council July 15, 1958 (Newhouse, 1960).

Ada County. Bent (1958) cites May 13 as an early date of arrival at Meridian (average date May 16).

Owyhee County. Possibly twelve birds, unquestionably transients, seen at Three Creek May 31, 1951, feeding in junipers at the foot of a ridge (Burleigh).

Lemhi County. An occasional pair of these tanagers seen June 4-6, 1949, in open pine woods on the ridges north of Shoup (Burleigh).

Custer County. Several noted at Stanley August 14, 1949 (Levy, 1950).

Fremont County. Found to occur sparingly, June through August, 1916 (Rust, 1917).

Clark County. Common during the summer of 1961 on Signal Peak; an adult male collected there July 15 (Oring, 1962).

Bonneville County. A common summer resident at Grays Lake, 1949-51 (Steel, 1956); noted June 13, 1949, on Caribou Mountain, north of Gray, to an altitude of 9,000 feet; a male collected at 8,500 feet; a single bird seen at Gray May 23, 1951, the earliest to be recorded here in the spring (Burleigh).

Bear Lake County. Noted at Bloomington Lake, ten miles west of Bloomington, July 8, 1949 (Jollie, in litt.).

South Central Idaho. A male taken on the Middle Fork of the Snake River August 4, 1872; two birds seen in the Lost River Mountains in late July, 1890; common in Teton Canyon in July (Merriam, 1891).

Power County. Noted at Heglar Pass, twenty miles south of American Falls, June 29, 1949, and a female collected that day (Jollie, in litt.).

Minidoka County. Rare in 1909; "tolerably common" in 1913 (Kenagy, 1914); seen at Rupert September 7, 1919, the only record for its occurrence (Davis, 1935).

To verify the occurrence of the Western Tanager in Idaho specimens, largely representing the breeding population, were taken in various parts of the state between the dates of August 7, 1948, and May 12, 1954. They were from the following localities: Latah County, Potlatch, Moscow; Nez Perce County, Lewiston; Clearwater County, Headquarters, Weippe; Bonneville County, Gray.

Habits. This handsome tanager is so partial to conifers that it is only in migration that it can be found in Idaho in such deciduous hardwoods as the cottonwood. This preference would explain its status as a rather scarce transient at Lewiston, for otherwise altitude is no limiting factor in its distribution in the state. I found it equally common during the summer months at Moscow, at 2,500 feet, and at Gray, where it was noted from 6,300 feet to 9,000 feet, and it doubtless occurs at higher elevations than this where conditions are suitable.

In Latah County it usually appears in the spring shortly after the first of May, and in the fall an occasional bird lingers until early October. About the middle of September, however, there is a noticeable decrease in numbers, and it is only infrequently seen then. A rather unusual occurrence was the presence in 1952 of one bird in immature plumage on the campus of the University of Idaho during the last two weeks in November. It was first observed on November 17, and at intervals thereafter until November 26. At Moscow my extreme dates of occurrence otherwise are May 3 (1949) and October 15 (1951), at Potlatch May 12 (1954) and September 24 (1952).

Merrill (1898) states that on June 29, at Fort Sherman, he found a nest on which the female was incubating that was thirty feet up in a ponderosa pine.

Grosbeaks, Finches, Sparrows, and Buntings: *Family Fringillidae*

Pheucticus melanocephalus melanocephalus (Swainson): Black-headed Grosbeak

General Distribution. Breeds from southern British Columbia, southeastern Alberta and southwestern Saskatchewan south to northeastern California, southern Arizona and western Texas, and in Mexico to Guerrero and Oaxaca. Winters in Mexico from southern Sonora, southern Chihuahua and Nuevo Leon to Guerrero and Oaxaca.

Status in Idaho. A common summer resident in suitable habitat throughout the state, being less numerous, however, in southern Idaho, and rather local in its distribution.

Bonner County. Found breeding sparingly at Clark Fork in 1917 (Burleigh, 1923).

Kootenai County. A fairly common summer resident at Fort Sherman (Coeur d'Alene) (Merrill, 1898); an uncommon summer resident at Coeur d'Alene, 1910-14 (Rust, 1915).

Shoshone County. A common summer resident in the Transition Zone of the St. Joe National Forest (1921-41), occurring from May until September (Hand, 1941).

Latah County. Noted in small numbers on Moscow Mountain during the summer of 1947 (Johnston, 1949); a fairly common summer resident at Harvard 1951-52 (Verner, 1953); a fairly common and well-distributed summer resident in the more open country north and east of Moscow (1948-

58), frequenting deciduous underbrush in ravines and stream bottoms; normally present from the middle of May until early September (Burleigh).

Nez Perce County. Reported by Bendire as breeding at Fort Lapwai in 1872 (Merriam, 1891); an uncommon summer resident at Lewiston (1948-58) (Burleigh).

Adams County. Noted at Council, on the Little Weiser River, May 17 and 18, 1958 (Newhouse, 1960).

Washington County. Specimens in the Museum of Vertebrate Zoology, Berkeley, were taken on Crane Creek, fifteen miles east of Midvale, May 30, 1930.

Owyhee County. Two singing males noted at Riddle May 28-June 3, 1934 (Davis, 1934).

Fremont County. Found to occur sparingly (June through August, 1916) in deciduous underbrush along the streams (Rust, 1917).

Jefferson County. A common summer resident in 1961 on the Camas National Wildlife Refuge; a specimen taken at Roberts on June 5 (Oring, 1962).

Bonneville County. A common summer resident at Grays Lake, 1949-1951 (Steel, 1956); one singing male, the earliest spring transient noted at Gray, seen May 23, 1951, in willows on Eagle Creek (Burleigh).

Blaine County. This species found to be a fairly common summer resident in and about Ketchum, scattered pairs being seen June 24-28, 1950, in the valleys (6,000 feet) and in the aspen groves on the mountainsides to an altitude of 8,000 feet (Easley Peak) (Burleigh).

South Central Idaho. A few pairs noted in 1890 breeding on the Snake River near Blackfoot, and on Big Lost River (Merriam, 1891); an uncommon breeding bird in 1949 in this same general area (Levy, 1950).

Minidoka County. Noted at Rupert July 7, 1919 and May 27, 1921 (Davis, 1935).

In order to verify the occurrence of this species in Idaho, and to determine the race represented by the breeding population, a small series of these grosbeaks was collected, largely in the northern part of the state, between the dates of May 15, 1948, and July 2, 1960. Two males taken at Moscow May 15, 1948, and July 14, 1951, were found to approach *maculatus* in their characters; otherwise all are typical of the nominate race *melanocephalus*. Localities in which these specimens were taken are as follows: Latah County, Moscow (eight), Potlatch (five); Nez Perce County, Lewiston (two); Blaine County, Ketchum (one).

Oberholser (1919) reports specimens identified as *papago* (a synonym of *melanocephalus*) taken at Blackfoot, Bingham County, July 8, 1890; Idaho City, Boise County, June 17, 1910; American Falls, Power County, May 27, and June 4 and 5, 1911; Pocatello, Bannock County, June 16, 1911; Shelley, Bingham County, July 29 and August 4, 1911; Weiser, Washington County, June 13, 1913; South Fork of the Salmon River, twelve miles east of Warren, Idaho County, August 2, 1913; Blue Spring Hills, Oneida County, May 31, 1916.

Photo by Patricia Bailey Witherspoon, Colorado Springs, Colorado
LAZULI BUNTING

PLATE XI

Habits. The Black-headed Grosbeak is one of the later transients to appear in Idaho in the spring, for it is usually after the middle of May before the first individuals are observed. In the late summer there is a noticeable decrease in numbers, and only rarely is this species seen after late August. At Moscow my extreme dates of occurrence are May 15 (1948) and August 30 (1951), at Potlatch May 10 (1949) and September 13 (1952). My latest record at Lewiston is September 2 (1951).

This grosbeak shows a marked preference for deciduous growth in stream bottoms and ravines and even in migration is seldom found feeding in conifers. In some instances breeding activities are well under way by early June, but it is probably late June and July when most pairs are busily engaged in rearing their young. What is apparently an early breeding record is a nest that I found on Hatwai Creek, east of Lewiston, on June 6, 1951, that held two fresh eggs. It was ten feet from the ground in the top of an elderberry bush in underbrush bordering the stream. Verner (1953) reports two nests found at Harvard, one June 21, 1951, with three eggs, the other with the female incubating July 1, 1952. Both were in alders, and were flimsily built of pine needles. A nest found at Clark Fork July 4, 1917, with the male incubating, held four well-incubated eggs, and was twenty feet up in a willow in underbrush bordering a stream. It was fairly well built of coarse weed stems, lined with finer ones (Burleigh, 1923). A rather late breeding record is that of a nest found by Merriam (1891) on First Cottonwood Creek in the Teton Basin that on July 22, 1872, held two fresh eggs.

Guiraca caerulea (Linnaeus): Blue Grosbeak

General Distribution. Breeds from southern Idaho east through southern Colorado and central South Dakota to eastern Nebraska, south to West Central Texas, Baja California and northern Mexico. Winters from northern Mexico south along the Pacific coast to northern Costa Rica.

Status in Idaho. Now known to nest in small numbers at Glenns Ferry, Elmore County.

To Leon Powers, of Medford, Oregon, goes the credit for not only recording the Blue Grosbeak in the state for the first time, but for definitely establishing the fact that at least two pairs of these grosbeaks were breeding at Glenns Ferry. He comments as follows (Powers, 1969) concerning this interesting and rather unexpected discovery: "On August 21, 1967, one and one-half miles north of Glenns Ferry, Elmore County, Idaho, I observed two male and one female Blue Grosbeaks foraging in a roadside stand of sunflowers. The area was revisited on August 22, and after some searching, a male Blue Grosbeak was seen singing in the top of a stand of willows bordering nearby Canyon Creek. I was able to move quite close and view the singing male for about eight minutes. He was joined by a second bird, either a juvenile or adult female. Not until August 12, 1968 was I able to return to this part of Idaho to look for the Blue Grosbeak. I visited the same area and again found the Blue Grosbeak inhabiting the area. During the following four days I revisited the area, each day finding adult and juvenile Blue Grosbeaks of both sexes."

Although no specimen was taken it was possible to photograph birds of both sexes, the resulting pictures identifying them unmistakably as Blue Grosbeaks.

Habits. This species is essentially a bird of the more open country, being found about thickets and stretches of underbrush at the edges of fields and pastures. Like many other species it has benefited from the proximity of man, open slashings resulting from logging operations giving it the habitat it desires. Although insects are eaten, seeds form the bulk of its diet, and patches of sunflowers in the area these grosbeaks frequented near Glenns Ferry may have been at least partially responsible for their presence there. In appearance this species suggests an overgrown Indigo Bunting, but in addition to its larger size it is characterized by two distinct brown wing bars.

Passerina amoena (Say): Lazuli Bunting

General Distribution. Breeds from southern British Columbia, southern Saskatchewan and central North Dakota south to northern Baja California, central Arizona, northern New Mexico, and western Oklahoma. Winters from southern Baja California and southern Arizona south in Mexico to Guerrero and Veracruz.

Status in Idaho. A common summer resident in suitable habitat throughout the state.

Bonner County. A common summer resident in 1917 at Clark Fork (Burleigh, 1923).

Kootenai County. An uncommon summer resident at Fort Sherman (Coeur d'Alene) (Merrill, 1898).

Shoshone County. A rather common summer resident, 1921-41, on the St. Joe National Forest; present from May until August; noted in the valleys and on the more open ridges to 6,000 feet (Hand, 1941).

Latah County. Common during the summer of 1947 "in open country" (Johnston, 1949); an uncommon summer resident at Harvard in 1952, being seen there on June 23, July 1, and August 5 (Verner, 1953); a fairly common but local summer resident, 1948-58, in open country north and east of Moscow, usually appearing the middle of May, and being rarely observed in the fall after early September (Burleigh).

Nez Perce County. Reported by Bendire as common in 1871 at Fort Lapwai (Merriam, 1891); a fairly common summer resident, 1948-58, at Lewiston; noted from early May until the middle of September (Burleigh).

Adams County. Common at Council in 1958; seen from May 8 to August 10 (Newhouse, 1960).

Boise County. Noted at the Arrowrock Reservoir on Cinch Creek in 1941; a specimen taken there on June 28 (Arvey, 1947).

Lemhi County. This species frequently seen on the open ridges north of Shoup June 4-6, 1949 (Burleigh).

Fremont County. Noted in Little Dry Creek Canyon June 18, 1916 (Rust, 1917).

Teton Basin. Common in July, 1872, along the streams (Merriam, 1891).

Jefferson County. An uncommon summer resident in 1961 on the Camas National Wildlife Refuge (Oring, 1962).

Blaine County. Birds fairly plentiful at Ketchum June 24-28, 1950, singing males being seen both in the valleys (6,000 feet), and in the aspens fringing the streams on the mountainsides to an altitude of 9,000 feet (on Hyndman Peak) (Burleigh).

Bonneville County. A common summer resident at Grays Lake, 1949-51 (Steel, 1956); noted in small numbers on Big Elk Creek, near Palisades, August 5 and 6, 1961 (Oring, 1962).

South Central Idaho. A common breeding bird in 1949 "in wooded draws and stream bottoms" (Levy, 1950).

Power County. Noted at American Falls in July, 1949, and a juvenile male collected there on July 4 (Jollie, in litt.).

Minidoka County. Reported by Davis (1935) as a spring transient at Rupert, with extreme dates of occurrence April 21 (1919) and May 23 (1920).

Cassia County. Noted on Goose Creek, ten miles south of Oakley, in June, 1949, and specimens taken there on June 26 (Jollie, in litt.).

A small series of specimens to verify the occurrence of this bunting in the state was taken as follows: Latah County, Moscow, males June 3 and July 2, 1948, May 11, 1949, May 13, 1950, May 16, 1951, females June 10, 1948, May 31, 1950, juvenile males August 27 and September 10, 1949, juvenile females August 4 and September 14 and 24, 1948, August 11, 1951; Nez Perce County, Lewiston, males May 6 and June 1, 1950, May 10, 1952, May 13, 1953, females June 18 and August 13, 1953; Bonneville County, Gray, male June 15, 1949.

Habits. The Lazuli Bunting frequents deciduous thickets and underbrush in open country, and while it favors stream bottoms, water is apparently not essential for its well-being. As with so many species altitude is disregarded; it nests commonly at Lewiston (840 feet), and it has been noted to an altitude of 9,000 feet on the south slopes of the higher ridges, characterized by open pine timber and scattered thickets.

In northern Idaho the first males rarely appear before the middle of May, and not infrequently it is even later in the month before this species is recorded for the first time. At Moscow my extreme dates of occurrence are May 11 (1949) and September 24 (1948), at Lewiston May 6 (1950) and September 14, 1952.

Hesperiphona vespertina (Cooper): EVENING GROSBEAK

General Distribution. Breeds from central British Columbia east through Alberta, Saskatchewan, Manitoba and Ontario to western Quebec, south to central California and southern Arizona, in Mexico to Oaxaca and Veracruz, and in the eastern United States to northern New York and Massachusetts. Winters irregularly south to southern California, western Texas, Arkansas, and northern Georgia.

Status in Idaho. Irregularly resident throughout the state, being found in the more heavily timbered areas during the summer months, and in the open valleys from early fall until late spring.

Bonner County. One pair of these grosbeaks seen on Jeru Creek, north of Sandpoint, July 5, 1957 (Burleigh).

Kootenai County. First noted at Fort Sherman (Coeur d'Alene) May 28, 1896; females with young seen early in July; probably an "irregular summer visitor," nesting in the pines "surrounding the lake" (Merrill, 1898); a common resident species at Coeur d'Alene, 1910-14; large flocks, noted during the fall and winter, would appear to retire "to the heavy timber in the mountains" in the spring; one pair seen at Fernan Lake on August 19, and a flock of thirty young of the year noted September 1 (Rust, 1915); specimens taken at Coeur d'Alene November 26, 1948 (Burleigh) and September 14, 1949 (M. Jollie).

Benewah County. An irregular but usually common resident species at St. Maries, 1921-41, being observed there every month of the year; noted "on the highest mountain peaks" in the St. Joe National Forest except in midwinter (Hand, 1941).

Latah County. Common "in the tall conifers north of Moscow" June 1-August 16, 1947 (Johnston, 1949); common at Harvard during the summer of 1951, but scarce in 1952, the one record being that of a flock of five birds seen July 28 (Verner, 1953); resident (1948-58) throughout the county, but erratic in its occurrence, especially during the winter months when some years it was common and other years scarce (Burleigh).

Nez Perce County. A fairly common winter resident at Lewiston, 1948-58, the first small flocks usually appearing in December, and at times lingering in the spring until late May; two pairs noted in thick woods at the top of a ridge south of Lake Waha (4,300 feet) May 27, 1949 (Burleigh).

Clearwater County. A flock of sixteen birds, fully grown young of the year, seen at Orofino August 27, 1951; noted once at Headquarters, a flock of ten birds October 27, 1951 (Burleigh).

Idaho County. Three seen September 23, 1941, four miles southwest of Selway Falls; common in July, 1948, in the Lolo Pass region; two adult males collected on July 2 (Orr, 1951); a flock of sixteen seen at White Bird, at the edge of the Salmon River, February 16, 1958 (Burleigh).

Adams County. Small flocks noted at Indian Valley in late March and early April, 1958 (Newhouse, 1960).

Valley County. Noted by Bendire in July, 1877, in mountains at the headwaters of the Payette River; adults carrying food (Merriam, 1891); specimens taken (Brodkorb, in litt.) on Payette Lake in July; one male seen on Brundage Mountain, north of McCall, June 29, 1958, in thick woods near the top of the mountain (7,000 feet) (Burleigh).

Custer County. Specimens taken (Brodkorb, in litt.) on Garden Creek in August, 1935, and on Pass Creek, northeast of Mackay, in September.

Blaine County. Specimens taken (Brodkorb, in litt.) on Trail Creek in August, 1935.

Clark County. An adult male taken on Signal Peak July 14, 1961 (Oring, 1962).

Bonneville County. Two males seen and one taken August 6, 1961, on Elk Creek, eight miles southeast of Palisades (Oring, 1962).

Bear Lake County. An immature male collected August 13, 1934, in Emigration Canyon, in the Wasatch Range; five adult males taken August 12, 1935, in Joe's Gap, at an altitude of 6,800 feet (Brodkorb, in litt.).

Minidoka County. Transients noted at Rupert February 29, 1920 (Davis, 1935).

Habits. Although the Evening Grosbeak is present in Idaho throughout the year it is rather erratic in its occurrence, especially during the winter months, a characteristic common to other of the boreal finches. There were winters, as in 1947-48 and 1949-50, when flocks comprising as many as one hundred individuals were noted almost daily. There were other years, as in 1948-49 and 1951-52, when only at infrequent intervals were small flocks encountered.

During the summer months this species retires to the more heavily wooden ridges to nest; it is inconspicuous then and must be searched for to be seen. By late July or early August, however, small flocks, consisting of both adults and young of the year, appear in the open valleys, and have been frequently observed then in deciduous woods bordering the Palouse River at Princeton and at Potlatch. There is little question that this grosbeak breeds on Moscow Mountain, for on August 18, 1949, and again on August 17, 1950, fully grown young of the year were noted in the city limits of Moscow.

The seeds of the box elder are apparently preferred as a source of food, but flocks have been watched feeding on the berries of the Russian olive and mountain ash, and on one occasion on the seeds of the black locust. Orr (1951) stated that in the Lolo Pass region these birds fed about his camp where they ate bits of charcoal from the ashes of the campfires.

Hesperiphona vespertina brooksi Grinnel

Brooksi is the western race of the Evening Grosbeak that breeds from British Columbia and western Montana south to Arizona and New Mexico. To verify its occurrence in Idaho both as a breeding bird and as a winter resident, the following specimens, all typical of *brooksi,* were taken in the northern half of the state: Kootenai County, Coeur d'Alene, male November 26, 1948; Latah County, Harvard, female December 16, 1953, Potlatch, males April 10, 1949, August 23, 1952, March 13, 1953, immature male and immature female August 7, 1949, Viola, male November 23, 1952, Moscow, fifty-nine specimens between the dates of November 3, 1947, and March 7,

1958; Nez Perce County, Lewiston, males December 13, 1948, May 20, 1950, January 21, 1951, March 13, 1955, November 21, 1957, females February 8, 1951, January 19, 1957; Clearwater County, Orofino, immature male August 27, 1951; Idaho County, White Bird, male February 16, 1958; Valley County, McCall, male June 29, 1958.

Hesperiphona vespertina vespertina (Cooper)

The nominate race of the Evening Grosbeak breeds as far west as northern Alberta, so it is not surprising that it occurs as a casual winter resident in northern Idaho. Specimens representing *vespertina* have been taken as follows: Latah County, Harvard, female December 16, 1953, Moscow, males January 1, 20, and 29, and May 8, 1950, January 21 and February 16, 1956, females January 21, 1956 and March 7, 1958; Nez Perce County, Lewiston, male March 8, 1956.

In the males *vespertina* differs from *brooksi* in being lighter brown above, with the underparts yellower, and lacking to a large extent the sooty brown wash characteristic of the western race. In the females the upperparts are darker brown, the underparts grayer and less yellow.

Carpodacus cassinii Baird: CASSIN'S FINCH

General Distribution. Breeds from southern British Columbia and southern Alberta south to northern Baja California, northern Arizona and northern New Mexico. Winters over much of its breeding range, and south in Mexico to Zacatecas and San Luis Potosi.

Status in Idaho. A common summer resident in suitable habitat throughout the state; of casual occurrence in northern Idaho in winter.

Boundary County. Noted in small numbers June 25, 1957, on Harrison Peak (altitude 6,500 feet) (Burleigh).

Bonner County. Common during the summer months (1917) in open woods on the higher ridges north of Clark Fork; singing throughout July; flocks (one of fifty birds) seen in late August (Burleigh, 1923).

Kootenai County. Arrives at Fort Sherman (Coeur d'Alene) the middle of April; one of the most abundant summer birds (Merrill, 1898); one pair seen in the city limits of Coeur d'Alene June 18, 1914 (Rust, 1915); scattered pairs noted in open pine woods at Post Falls May 4, 1950, and at Spirit Lake May 6, 1953 (Burleigh).

Benewah County. A common summer resident, 1921-41, at St. Maries, being present from late March or early April until October (Hand, 1941).

Latah County. A common summer resident, 1948-58, in open pine woods on the ridges north and east of Moscow (Burleigh).

Clearwater County. One small flock noted in an open slashing at Weippe July 15, 1953; singing males frequently seen May 10, 1955, on the wooded ridges at Headquarters (Burleigh).

Idaho County. Noted infrequently in July, 1948, at "higher elevations" in the Lolo Pass region (Orr, 1951).

Adams County. Specimens in the Museum of Vertebrate Zoology, Berkeley, were taken on Smith Mountain, at an altitude of 7,500 feet, June 27 and July 9, 13, and 14, 1930.

Valley County. Scattered pairs noted in the open pine woods at McCall May 5, 1952 (Burleigh).

Boise County. Specimens taken at the head of Crooked River, in the Sawtooth Range, August 6, 1941 (Arvey, 1947).

Owyhee County. This species found to be fairly common on the open ridges at Triangle June 25, 1949, and at Silver City (6,000 feet) June 2, 1951 (Burleigh).

Lemhi County. Noted in small numbers at Shoup, in open pine woods on Colson Creek, June 5, 1949 (Burleigh).

Fremont County. Fairly common at Henrys Lake June 13, 1957 (Burleigh).

Clark County. One pair seen at Spencer June 18, 1916; also noted July 16 near the headwaters of the West Fork of Camas Creek (Rust, 1917); common on Signal Peak, northeast of Spencer, June 19 and July 14, 1961; an adult male collected June 19 (Oring, 1962).

Blaine County. Several noted on Spring Creek Trail October 27, 1910 (Jewett, 1912).

Bonneville County. A fairly common summer resident at Grays Lake, 1949-51 (Steel, 1956); an occasional pair seen June 13, 1949, in open woods near the top of Caribou Mountain (8,500 to 9,000 feet) (Burleigh); noted on Big Elk Creek August 6, 1961 (Oring, 1962).

South Central Idaho. A specimen taken at timberline in the Salmon River Mountains August 29, 1890; "large flocks" seen September 10 near the mouth of Little Lost River (Merriam, 1891); a fairly common summer resident in 1949 "in the higher coniferous forests" of the south-central part of the state (Levy, 1950).

Cassia County. One small flock seen at Almo June 19, 1949, feeding at the edge of a mountain mahogany thicket on an open mountain slope (6,500 feet) (Burleigh).

Habits. The Cassin's Finch is one of the characteristic birds of open coniferous woods, and it will be found in Idaho, regardless of altitude, where such habitat occurs. At Lewiston, in Nez Perce County, there are no conifers; thus even in migration, and during the winter months, this species has never been encountered in the cottonwood groves that border the rivers and smaller streams.

It normally appears in Idaho in the spring in late March or early April, and is rarely observed in the fall after early October. My extreme dates of occurrence at Moscow, with one exception, are March 11 (1949) and October 7 (1948), at Potlatch March 21 (1949) and September 18 (1949).

During the winter of 1950-51 small flocks unexpectedly appeared in late

December, and within the next two weeks increased in numbers until they were seen literally everywhere. The largest number noted at one time was a flock comprising fully one hundred individuals that, on January 13, were feeding in an open field at Potlatch on the seeds of weeds sticking above the two inches of snow on the ground. This unusual winter invasion terminated rather abruptly in February, a flock of thirty birds seen at Potlatch on February 18 being my last record for this species until the first singing males appeared in late March.

Carpodacus cassinii vinifer Duvall

Although at present not recognized by the A. O. U. Committee on Nomenclature, a critical study of a series of Cassin's Finches taken throughout the year, and over much of the state, showed conclusively that *vinifer* is a valid race, with characters that readily distinguish it from the nominate race. In the males the crown and upperparts are darker, the underparts variable but averaging purple rather than pink as in typical *cassinii*. Duvall (1945) summarizes this by the statement that in the males "the general appearance is more purplish, less pinkish or reddish." The females are distinctly darker both above and below. The range as given in the original description limits this subspecies to southwestern and central Idaho, but with more adequate material available it was found to be the breeding race over all of the state except possibly the extreme eastern edge.

Specimens examined in connection with this study are as follows: Boundary County, Harrison Peak, male June 25, 1957; Kootenai County, Coeur d'Alene, male August 14, 1948, Post Falls, male May 14, 1950, Spirit Lake, male May 6, 1953; Latah County, Potlatch, males September 18, 1949, January 13 and February 18, 1951, March 31, 1955, July 4, 1956, July 4, 1958, Troy, female June 25, 1948, Moscow, twenty-two males between the dates of July 21, 1948, and March 27, 1957, six females between the dates of June 19, 1948, and February 20, 1951, juvenile female August 18, 1950; Clearwater County, Weippe, two males July 15, 1953, Headquarters, female May 10, 1955; Valley County, McCall, male May 5, 1952; Owyhee County, Silver City, male June 2, 1951; Fremont County, Henrys Lake, male June 13, 1957; Bonneville County, Gray, male June 16, 1949; Cassia County, Almo, male June 19, 1949.

Carpodacus cassinii cassinii Baird

On the basis of a single specimen of the nominate race taken at Shoup, in Lemhi County, on June 5, 1949, it would appear that *cassinii* is the breeding form occurring in the extreme eastern edge of the state. Further field work is necessary, however, to determine its actual range in Idaho.

Carpodacus mexicanus (Müller) HOUSE FINCH

General Distribution. Largely resident from south-central British Columbia, northern Idaho, northern Wyoming and western Nebraska south to southern Baja California, Guerrero, and central Oaxaca.

Status in Idaho. A common resident species over much of the state; local and rather uncommon in its distribution in the extreme northern counties.

In view of the present abundance of the House Finch in Idaho, and the few published records for its occurrence in the state, it would appear that this species has increased perceptibly in numbers, and only in recent years has been found north of Nez Perce County.

Neither Merrill (1898) nor Rust (1915) reported it from Coeur d'Alene, nor did Hand (1941) note it at St. Maries, in Benewah County, during the twenty years, 1921-41, that he spent there. That it is now becoming established in Kootenai County was evident on April 2, 1958, when I noted three pairs at Post Falls, feeding about thickets in open fields.

Since the first individuals appeared at Pullman, Washington, "about the year 1919" (Jewett, *et al.*, 1953), it is probable that the House Finch could have been found then at Moscow for the first time. During my years of residence there, 1947-58, it was an abundant resident species, although its numbers during the winter months were influenced to some extent by the severity of the weather.

At Lewiston, in Nez Perce County, I also found it a common and well-distributed resident species (1947-58).

There is little suitable habitat for a species such as this in Clearwater County, so it was not surprising that it was almost totally absent. My one record is that of a single bird, a female, that was collected in an open slashing at Weippe October 16, 1955.

Farther south in the state the few published records are as follows: Davis reported it (1934) from Riddle, Owyhee County, and (1935) from Rupert, Minidoka County; Levy (1950) noted it as a fairly common breeding bird in 1949 "in farming regions, towns, and even cities" in south-central Idaho; Oring (1962) listed it as a common breeding bird at Hamer, Jefferson County. In 1944 a census of the breeding population of House Finches at Mountain Home, Elmore County, was taken by Evenden (1944) from noon until 4 p.m. on April 13. He reported 660 individuals, with an estimated population of 1000 birds. Fourteen nests, completely built but still empty, were found; also one with two fresh eggs was located.

I personally noted this species at Boise, Ada County, in 1949; at Parma, Canyon County, and Marsing and Homedale, Owyhee County, in 1950; at Burley and Oakley, Cassia County, in 1955 and 1957; at Eden, Jerome County, in 1957. Of special interest was the presence of eight birds, three of them adult males, at Henry, Caribou County, on June 22, 1960. Steel (1956) failed to note the House Finch at Grays Lake, in Bonneville County, during the spring and summer months spent there in 1949, 1950, and 1951, and there are no previous records for Caribou County. The altitude of Henry, forty miles south of Grays Lake, is approximately the same, 6,000 feet, so it would appear that this species is now attempting to establish itself at this altitude where heretofore it has been completely absent.

Habits. The House Finch, unlike the preceding species which it resembles, prefers deciduous underbrush, preferably in the vicinity of water; thus while occurring throughout the state it is somewhat local in its distribution. It consistently shuns thick coniferous woods, so it is not surprising that north of the Palouse country in Latah County it has been observed only in the open prairie in Kootenai County. It has accepted readily the advantages offered by the proximity of man, and is commonly found in towns and even the larger cities in Idaho.

The nest, compactly built of weed stems, rootlets and grasses, is in a tree or bush, usually within fifteen feet of the ground, and as concealment is an important objective, a conifer is frequently selected. Breeding activities are well under way by the middle of April and by early June flocks of fully grown young are commonly observed. Davis (1935) gives April 28 as the earliest date for eggs at Rupert, in Minidoka County.

Carpodacus mexicanus sordidus Aldrich

This race, largely limited in its distribution to the Columbia plateau of eastern Washington and Idaho, is distinct from the breeding population of the Rocky Mountain region by being darker and more grayish, less brownish, both above and below. In the males there is less of the reddish wash on the back and neck, and the red of the head, rump, throat and breast is more restricted and deeper in color.

To determine the validity of *sordidus* a series of specimens was taken in the northern part of the state, both during the breeding season and during the winter months. All were found to be typical of this race. They were collected in Kootenai County, Post Falls; Latah County, Moscow, Troy; Nez Perce County, Lewiston; Clearwater County, Weippe. Although present during the winter months at Moscow and at Lewiston, this species is less numerous from early November until the middle of March, and on the basis of specimens taken it would appear to winter in at least small numbers in southern Idaho. Specimens identified as *sordidus* were collected at Parma, Canyon County, February 18, 1950, and at Eden, Jerome County, November 14, 1957.

Carpodacus mexicanus frontalis (Say)

Frontalis is limited in its range to the southern and eastern parts of the state, but it is a common bird in this arid open country. Specimens representing this race have been taken at Emmett, Gem County, November 23, 1951; Boise, Ada County, April 17, 1949; Nampa, Canyon County, June 24

1949; Homedale, Owyhee County, June 23, 1949 and February 20, 1950; Burley, Cassia County, August 27, 1955; and Henry, Caribou County, June 22, 1960.

Pinicola enucleator (Linnaeus): PINE GROSBEAK

General Distribution. Cosmopolitan; in North America breeds from northern Alaska, northern Mackenzie, northern Ontario, northern Quebec and Newfoundland south in the mountains to central California and northern New Mexico, and to northern New Hampshire and Maine. Winters south to Kentucky and Virginia.

Status in Idaho. A fairly common resident species in the more heavily timbered areas throughout the state.

Bonner County. Noted in 1917 on the higher ridges north of Clark Fork, a flock of six on September 6, and a flock of three on September 10 (Burleigh, 1923).

Shoshone County. A local but not uncommon summer resident on the St. Joe National Forest, 1921-41, limited in its distribution then to the Canadian zone; an uncommon winter visitant in the valleys (Hand, 1941).

Latah County. An erratic winter resident at Moscow, 1947-58, usually scarce and infrequently seen, but common from late January through March, 1951 (Burleigh).

Clearwater County. A flock of seven birds seen at Ahsahka January 7, 1951, and a flock of four at Weippe February 8, 1954 (Burleigh).

Idaho County. Several seen southwest of Selway Falls September 23 and 29, 1941 (Orr, 1951).

Boise County. Single birds noted on Trail Creek, in the Boise National Forest, January 31 and February 16, 1939 (Marshall, 1945).

South Central Idaho. Breeds in the Salmon River Mountains; one taken and another noted near Timber Creek the last week of August, 1890; another taken and six others seen near Eight Mile Canyon on September 5 (Merriam, 1891).

Fremont County. A mounted specimen examined that was collected at Henrys Lake (Rust, 1917).

Blaine County. A fairly common winter resident in 1910 in the vicinity of Ketchum; first noted on November 2; specimens taken in December in willows along the Wood River (Jewett, 1912).

Bonneville County. An uncommon summer resident at Grays Lake, 1949-51 (Steel, 1956); two birds, apparently a mated pair, seen May 24, 1951, in thick woods near the top of Caribou Mountain (altitude 8,000 feet) (Burleigh).

Habits. The Pine Grosbeak is one of the more erratic of the boreal finches occurring in winter in Idaho. Usually it is only infrequently seen. There are years when it is completely absent, and only once, in eleven years of active field work, did I find it common in the northern part of the state. On January 7, 1951, the first small flock of seven birds appeared at Ahsahka, in

Clearwater County, and for the following three months, through March 31, similar small flocks were seen at frequent intervals in the vicinity of Moscow. In Latah County my earliest date of arrival in the fall is November 16 (1947).

A characteristic of this species is its tameness. It is possible to approach within a few feet of a flock feeding on the berries of a red haw (*cretaegus*) or a mountain ash, without arousing much concern, and as the birds are quiet and deliberate in their movements they are never a conspicuous part of the landscape. Elsewhere in their range they are said to eat the fruit of the box elder, but although such fare is available at Moscow throughout the winter I have never known this grosbeak to be interested in anything but fleshy fruits. In late winter, when their preferred food is largely exhausted, frozen apples still hanging on the trees are commonly consumed.

Pinicola enucleator montana Ridgway

In a series of twenty-five specimens of the Pine Grosbeak taken in northern Idaho from November through March, 1947 through 1956, only two represented the breeding population, *montana*. Both were females, and were collected at Ahsahka, Clearwater County, January 7, 1951, and at Moscow February 11, 1951. This race is known to winter as far south and east as northern Texas and western Nebraska, so it is not improbable that the breeding Pine Grosbeaks of the state are largely summer residents, and that only stragglers remain during the winter months.

Pinicola enucleator alascensis Ridgway

This northern subspecies occurs during the summer months in central Alaska, Mackenzie, and northern British Columbia. It would appear to be the race most commonly found in Idaho during the winter months, for of the twenty-five specimens collected then in northern Idaho twenty-two represented *alascensis*. They were taken as follows: Latah County, Viola, two males March 31, 1951, Moscow, males January 30, February 16 and 19, and March 30, 1951, December 27 and 28, 1953, March 7 and 11, 1956, females January 30, February 1, 16, and 19, 1951, March 7 and 11, 1956; Clearwater County, Ahsahka, male January 7, 1951, Weippe, female February 8, 1954.

Pinicola enucleator flammula Homeyer

There is but one record for the occurrence of this southern Alaskan race in Idaho. On November 16, 1947, a single bird, a female, was found in open woods partway up Moscow Mountain. It is possibly more common in the state than this one specimen would indicate.

Leucosticte tephrocotis (Swainson): GRAY-CROWNED ROSY FINCH

General Distribution. Breeds from northern Alaska, central Yukon and western Mackenzie south in the mountains to central California, eastern

Oregon, and northwestern Montana. Winters south to central Nevada and northern New Mexico, and east to northwestern Nebraska.

Status in Idaho. A common but erratic winter resident throughout the state; at the present time known to occur during the summer months only on Harrison Peak, in Boundary County.

Boundary County. A male (identified as *tephrocotis*) taken at Copeland April 8, 1950 (Levy, 1959); a male in breeding condition collected on June 25, 1957, as it fed at the edge of a deep snowdrift covering a rocky slope near the top of Harrison Peak (altitude approximately 6,500 feet) (Burleigh).

Bonner County. In the Museum of Vertebrate Zoology, Berkeley, there are specimens (three males) taken by C. F. Hedges on Soldier Creek, at Priest Lake, October 29, 1929; another male was collected by A. Olson fifteen miles northeast of Priest River October 5, 1941 (Jollie, in litt.).

Kootenai County. An "irregular fall and winter visitant" at Fort Sherman (Coeur d'Alene); none seen during the winters of 1894-95 and 1895-96; a flock of fifty noted November 3, 1896 (Merrill, 1898).

Shoshone County. Uncommon during the winter months (1921-41) on the St. Joe National Forest (Hand, 1941); a "large flock" noted on the Three Sisters Peaks, near Dismal Lake, October 21, 1950; two specimens taken found to represent the race *littoralis* (Levy, 1959).

Latah County. A small flock noted at Deary May 11, 1938 (Hand, 1941); Arvey (1947) reports a specimen taken at Moscow March 18, 1939; he gives this species the status of a "casual" winter visitant; an erratic but not uncommon winter visitant (1947-58) appearing in November and being only infrequently noted after the middle of January (Burleigh).

Nez Perce County. A fairly common winter resident (1947-58) at Lewiston, being present from early November until the latter part of March (Burleigh).

Bonneville County. A rare transient (1949-51) at Grays Lake; a flock of ten seen April 6, 1950, were apparently all *tephrocotis* (Steel, 1956).

Habits. Although the Gray-crowned Rosy Finch is present each winter over much of the state, its abundance would appear to depend on the severity of the weather. Occurring as it does during the summer months above timberline on the higher ridges it has accepted snowdrifts as a part of its normal existence, and only during periods of bad weather and low temperatures does it appear in the valleys. In Latah County flocks of varying size are seen each winter, but only in years when frequent blizzards cover the ground with a foot or more of snow are the flocks numerous. Normally such flocks comprise from twenty to forty individuals; on December 6, 1952, however, a flock of five hundred birds was seen at Genesee. My earliest date of arrival at Moscow is November 16 (1947), at Genesee October 21 (1950). At Lewiston my extreme dates of occurrence are November 1 (1952) and March 24 (1955). At Clarkston, on the opposite side of the Snake River from Lewiston, and in eastern Washington, there are sheer cliffs fronting the Snake River where large colonies of Cliff Swallows nest each year. Their nests remain intact throughout the winter, and the Rosy Finches throughout this area, both in Washington and Idaho, utilize them to roost in each night.

Leucosticte tephrocotis tephrocotis (Swainson)

On the basis of actual specimens the nominate race of the Gray-crowned Rosy Finch would appear to be rather uncommon in the northern part of the state during the winter months. It must be admitted, however, that since both *tephrocotis* and *littoralis* occur in the same flock, and that except under unusual circumstances only a few individuals are taken from the large flocks frequently encountered, it is obviously largely a matter of chance what race such individuals represent. Consequently the nominate race may be much more common than would now appear to be the case. My one record for the winter months is that of a male collected at Lewiston on January 29, 1949, from a flock of fully three hundred of these boreal finches. Eleven other individuals taken that day from this flock were all found to represent *littoralis*.

Of interest is the fact that although *littoralis* is the breeding form in eastern Washington the breeding male collected on Harrison Peak June 25, 1957, was found to be typical of the nominate race, *tephrocotis*. This evidence extends the breeding range of this subspecies from Glacier Park, in northern Montana, the farthest west in the United States it has been known to occur during the summer months, to extreme northern Idaho.

In the Denver Museum of Natural History there are thirty-four specimens of *tephrocotis* taken by Pierce Brodkorb in southern Idaho as follows: Boise, Ada County, six specimens, February 1, 1930; Montpelier, Bear Lake County, three, between the dates of January 17 and 26, 1931; Pocatello, Bannock County, twenty-five, between the dates of January 7 and 11, 1932.

Leucosticte tephrocotis littoralis Baird

This is the race that occurs most abundantly during the winter months in northern Idaho, but as it is a common summer resident of the Alpine–Arctic Zone of the Cascade Mountains of Washington its presence is more or less to be expected. To verify its presence in this part of the state a total of seventeen specimens were taken, from 1947 through 1955, as follows: Latah County, Moscow, males December 15, 1948, January 7, 1951, December 19, 1952, female January 7, 1951, Genesee, male January 11, 1950, females January 11, 1950, October 21, 1950; Nez Perce County, Lewiston, males November 2, 1947, January 29, 1949, November 1, 1952, March 24, 1955, female March 24, 1955.

Brodkorb apparently found this subspecies as plentiful in southern Idaho as the nominate race, for there are twenty-nine specimens of *littoralis* in the Denver Museum of Natural History taken by him as follows: Boise, eleven specimens, February 1, 1930; Montpelier, one, January 26, 1931; Pocatello, seventeen, between the dates of January 7 and January 11, 1932.

Leucosticte atrata Ridgway: BLACK ROSY FINCH

General Distribution. Breeds in the mountains of southwestern Montana, central Idaho, western Wyoming, northern Nevada, and northern Utah. Winters from central Idaho and northern Wyoming to northern California, northern Arizona, and northern New Mexico.

Status in Idaho. Breeds and is probably to some extent resident in the mountains in the central part of the state.

Merriam (1891) first recorded this species in Idaho, stating that in 1890 he found it common above timberline in the Salmon River Mountains; small flocks were seen "at various times," and on August 29 two specimens in immature plumage were taken.

French (1959) reported it as breeding on Hyndman Peak in the Sawtooth Mountains in 1956, young of the year being noted in September, and as being seen on Snowysides Peak in the Sawtooth Mountains, and on Borah Peak (12,000 feet), both in Custer County, in July, 1955, and on He-Devil Mountain (8,000 feet) in the Seven Devils Mountains, in western Idaho, in July, 1957.

I personally found it breeding in small numbers on Easley Peak, in the Boulder Range of the Sawtooth Mountains, twenty miles north of Ketchum, on June 25, 1950. Approximately ten birds were noted that day.

Habits. In view of the fact that this species has never been recorded in southern Idaho during the winter months it would appear that it occurs in the state in rather limited numbers at this season of the year.

Because of the depth of the snow until late June on the higher ridges where this Rosy Finch nests, it is doubtful if breeding activities are well under way before early July. The birds seen on Easley Peak on June 25 were feeding and chasing each other about on the rocky slopes and on the faces of the sheer rocky pinnacles; a female collected that day had a well developed brood patch. Despite the date the snow here still covered much of the ground with deep drifts.

Acanthis flammea flammea (Linnaeus): COMMON REDPOLL

General Distribution. Cosmopolitan; in North America breeds from central Alaska, northern Mackenzie, northern Keewatin and northern Quebec south to northern British Columbia, northern Saskatchewan, northern Ontario, southern Quebec, and Newfoundland. Winters over much of its breeding range south to northern California, northern Utah, Kansas, southern Indiana, and northern Virginia.

Status in Idaho. A common winter visitant throughout the state, but irregular in its appearance, being common some years and scarce others.

Bonner County. A specimen taken six miles south of Coolin February 19, 1939 (Arvey, 1947).

Kootenai County. A "regular winter visitor" at Fort Sherman (Coeur d'Alene); noted as late as April 11 (Merrill, 1898); uncommon during the winter (1910-14) at Coeur d'Alene; a small flock seen on the unusually late date of April 15 (Rust, 1915); a flock of possibly thirty birds seen at Coeur d'Alene March 13, 1957, feeding in alders at the edge of the lake (Burleigh).

Benewah County. An irregular winter visitor (1921-41) at St. Maries; frequent flocks noted in March, 1936 (Hand, 1941).

Latah County. A common winter visitant throughout the county (1948-1958), flocks of varying size being frequently encountered from late November until late March (Burleigh).

Nez Perce County. A scarce and rather erratic winter visitant at Lewiston, being noted only on Hatwai Creek during the late winter months; actual dates of occurrence are: 1955, one flock of six birds January 16; 1956, a flock of twelve February 24; a flock of fully sixty March 8; a flock of thirty March 12; 1957, a small flock of eight February 6 (Burleigh).

Clearwater County. Noted at Weippe in 1952, a flock of forty birds December 11, and a flock of thirty December 24, and in 1954, a flock of 100 February 16, and at Headquarters in 1953, a flock of possibly forty February 8, and in 1956, a single bird March 18 (Burleigh).

Blaine County. A single bird, a male, seen at Ketchum November 16, 1910 (Jewett, 1912).

Both to verify its occurrence in Idaho, and to determine whether more than one subspecies comprised the flocks encountered during the winter months, specimens were taken (1949 through 1957) in the northern part of the state. All were found to be typical of the nominate race, *flammea*. Summarized briefly they are as follows: Kootenai County, Coeur d'Alene, six males, six females, March 13, 1957; Latah County, Potlatch, two males January 12, 1957, Viola, three males, one female, January 12, 1951, Moscow, thirty specimens between the dates of February 5, 1949, and November 28, 1957, Genesee, two males February 12, 1956; Nez Perce County, Lewiston, males January 16, 1955 (two), February 24 (two), and March 8 (one) and 12 (two), 1956, February 6, 1957 (two), females January 16, 1955 and March 8, 1956; Clearwater County, Weippe, males December 11 (five) and 24 (two), 1952, February 16, 1954 (one), females December 11, 1952 (five), February 16, 1954 (one), Headquarters, males February 8, 1953 (two), March 18, 1956 (one).

In the Denver Museum of Natural History there are specimens taken by Brodkorb in southern Idaho, all typical of *flammea*, from the following localities: Elmore County, Glenns Ferry (February 11, 1930); Bear Lake County, Montpelier (January 17, 1931); Fremont County, St. Anthony (November 30, 1931); Gooding County, Gooding (February 17 and March 1, 1932).

Habits. The Redpoll is a hardy bird. It occurs commonly in Idaho during the winter months, but it has never been observed earlier than the latter part of November, and it is often late December or early January before the first flocks appear. The ground then is normally covered with snow, often to a depth of a foot or more, and minimum temperatures are frequently below zero, but the restless flocks of Redpolls seem entirely contented as they feed

GREEN-TAILED TOWHEE

PLATE XII

in elders bordering the streams, or on the seed of weeds sticking above the snow on the ground. Flocks encountered vary in size, but usually comprise from ten to forty individuals. The largest number I have ever recorded at one spot consisted of a flock of fully one hundred of these hardy finches that was feeding at the edge of a clearing at Weippe on February 16, 1954. At Moscow my extreme dates of occurrence are November 20 (1955) and March 24 (1951).

Spinus pinus (Wilson): PINE SISKIN

General Distribution. Breeds from southern Alaska, central Yukon, southern Mackenzie, central Quebec and Newfoundland south to northern Baja California, through the mountains of Mexico to Guatemala and in the central and eastern United States to Kansas, Iowa, central Michigan, and northern Pennsylvania. Winters over much of its breeding range and south to the Gulf coast and southern Florida.

Status in Idaho. A common resident species in the wooded areas throughout the state.

Bonner County. Common at Clark Fork during the summer of 1917, and of general distribution; small flocks noted after early July (Burleigh, 1923); a flock of two hundred birds seen on Lightning Creek, north of Clark Fork, November 25, 1948 (Burleigh).

Kootenai County. Resident at Fort Sherman (Coeur d'Alene); noted to the top of Mica Peak (Merrill, 1898); an "abundant resident" at Coeur d'Alene (1910-14); young able to fly seen June 17 (Rust, 1915).

Shoshone County. A common resident species (1921-41) on the St. Joe National Forest; of local distribution during the winter; noted every month of the year at St. Maries (Benewah County) (Hand, 1941).

Latah County. Common, and observed in small flocks, June through August, 1947 (Johnston, 1949); a common summer resident at Harvard 1951-52 (Verner, 1953); a common resident species throughout the county (1947-58); unusually abundant during the winter of 1950-51, when large flocks were frequently encountered (Burleigh).

Nez Perce County. A fairly common winter resident at Lewiston (1948-1958), flocks of varying size being seen from early January until late April (Burleigh).

Clearwater County. A fairly common summer resident (1952-56) on the wooded ridges about Headquarters; extreme dates of occurrence March 8 (1953), a small flock of four birds, and November 25 (1954), a flock of fully two hundred (Burleigh).

Idaho County. Numerous in July, 1948, in the Lolo Pass region (Orr, 1951).

Adams County. In the Museum of Vertebrate Zoology, Berkeley, there are specimens taken by Gilmore on Smith Mountain July 16 and 17, 1930.

Washington County. One pair noted at Weiser June 4, 1952, in willows at the edge of the Snake River (Burleigh).

Boise County. Specimens taken by Arvey (1947) on the Crooked River, in the Sawtooth Range, August 7, 1941, and at Horse Shoe Bend December 10, 1941.

Owyhee County. Noted at De Lamar February 19, 1950, in willows at the edge of a stream (Burleigh).

Fremont County. Noted at the head of Little Dry Creek Canyon June 15, 1916 (Rust, 1915).

Clark County. Common and frequently seen on Signal Peak June 19 and July 14, 1961 (Oring, 1962).

Jefferson County. One flock of twenty birds seen on the Camas National Wildlife Refuge August 22, 1961 (Oring, 1962).

Bonneville County. A very common summer resident (1949-51) at Grays Lake (Steel, 1956); noted near the top of Caribou Mountain (8,000 feet) June 13, 1949 (Burleigh); common on Big Elk Creek, near Palisades, August 6, 1961 (Oring, 1962).

South Central Idaho. Found "in numbers" in 1872 in the Teton Basin in July, and about Henrys Lake in early August; noted in 1890 in the Salmon River Mountains, and at Sawtooth Lake (Merriam, 1891). Levy (1950) considered this species a common summer resident in 1949 in the south-central counties, occurring "in the higher altitudes where conifers offer nesting sites."

Habits. In common with the other boreal finches the Pine Siskin is rather erratic in its occurrence in Idaho during the winter months. During most years small flocks are noted at frequent intervals, but there are winters when this species is totally absent, and an occasional year when it is surprisingly abundant. Such was the case during the winter of 1950-51, when flocks totalling a hundred or more individuals were frequently observed at Moscow from November until early February. The largest number noted at one spot that winter was a flock of approximately two thousand of these finches restlessly feeding in a large field at Lewiston January 21. In this connection it is of interest that it was this same winter that witnessed an unprecedented invasion of Cassin's Finches that had heretofore never been recorded in Idaho during the winter months.

Although the Siskin is known to nest in deciduous hardwoods it is, in Idaho, essentially a bird of the conifers during the summer months. For this reason, although altitude is apparently no factor in its distribution in the state, it occurs as a winter visitant only at Lewiston.

Orr (1951) states that in the Lolo Pass region this species was observed in July, 1948, eating charcoal from the ashes of the campfires.

Spinus pinus pinus (Wilson)

The nominate race of the Pine Siskin is the resident form in Idaho, breeding commonly throughout the wooded areas of the state, and occurring in flocks of varying size during the winter months. A series of specimens collected between the dates of May 21, 1948, and April 20, 1957, largely in the northern part of the state, were found to be typical of *pinus*. They were taken as follows: Bonner County, Clark Fork, one male and one female, November 25, 1948; Latah County, forty-nine at various times during the year, and at Potlatch, Moscow, Genesee, and Deary; Nez Perce County, Lewiston, ten, between the extreme dates of January 19, 1949, and April 20, 1957; Clearwater County, Headquarters, three males November 25, 1954; Washington County, Weiser, one female June 4, 1952.

Spinus pinus vagans Aldrich

On the basis of specimens taken this western race would appear to be an uncommon winter visitant in the northern part of the state. During an interval of nine years, 1948 through 1956, fifteen specimens collected between the middle of October and the middle of April were found to represent *vagans*, and are as follows: Bonner County, Clark Fork, male, female November 25, 1954; Latah County, Potlatch, two males October 31, 1956, Moscow, males October 16, 1948, October 21, 1955, October 22, 1956, females December 6, 1948, March 29, 1949, November 1, 1950, December 19, 1952, April 14, 1956; Nez Perce County, Lewiston, female January 28, 1954; Clearwater County, Headquarters, male November 25, 1954.

Spinus tristis pallidus Mearns: AMERICAN GOLDFINCH

General Distribution. Breeds from southern British Columbia, central Saskatchewan and western Ontario south to eastern Oregon, central Utah, western Colorado, and northern Nebraska. Winters over much of its breeding range south to southern Arizona and Texas, and in Mexico to Veracruz.

Status in Idaho. A common summer resident in suitable habitat throughout the state; less numerous and erratic in its occurrence during the winter months.

Kootenai County. A fairly common summer resident at Fort Sherman (Coeur d'Alene) (Merrill, 1898); an uncommon summer resident at Coeur d'Alene, 1910-14 (Rust, 1915).

Shoshone County. A common summer resident in the St. Joe National Forest, 1921-41, occurring in the valleys from April until November; occasional in winter (Hand, 1941).

Latah County. Common in the open country, June to August, 1947 (Johnston, 1949); uncommon at Harvard, 1951-52; one bird noted July 7, 1952 (Verner, 1953); a common and well-distributed summer resident in the county (1947-58); of erratic occurrence during the winter months, being scarce some years, and common others (Burleigh).

Nez Perce County. A fairly common resident species at Lewiston (1947-58) (Burleigh).

Clearwater County. A flock of possibly sixty birds, some of the males already in almost full breeding plumage, seen at Weippe March 25, 1953 (Burleigh).

Adams County. Specimens in the Museum of Vertebrate Zoology at Berkeley taken on Smith Mountain, at an altitude of 7,500 feet, on May 24 and 28, 1930; fairly common at Council in 1958 from May 12 to September 27 (Newhouse, 1960).

Ada County. A specimen taken at Boise March 14, 1941 (Arvey, 1947).

Fremont County. Several pairs noted in July, 1916, on Little Dry Creek (Rust, 1917).

Clark County. Specimens in the Denver Museum of Natural History taken by Brodkorb on Beaver Creek in June; "abundant" on Signal Peak June 19 and July 14, 1961 (Oring, 1962).

Jefferson County. An uncommon summer resident on the Camas National Wildlife Refuge in 1961; suddenly common the latter half of August (Oring, 1962).

Bonneville County. A fairly common resident species at Grays Lake, 1949-51 (Steel, 1956); "abundant" at Big Elk Creek August 6, 1961 (Oring, 1962).

South Central Idaho. Common at Fort Hall in October, 1872; a few noted in July, 1890, in the foothills of the Blackfoot Mountains; common on Birch Creek the middle of August (Merriam, 1891); a common breeding bird in 1950 and 1951 in the south-central counties (Levy, 1962).

Minidoka County. Noted as a breeding bird at Rupert 1919 through 1921; latest young just out of the nest seen on August 12 (Davis, 1935).

Cassia County. Specimens in the Denver Museum of Natural History taken by Brodkorb at Oakley in August.

That this species winters in the southern part of the state is well verified by specimens taken by Brodkorb from late November until early February (all in the Denver Museum of Natural History) at the following localities: Gooding, Twin Falls, Goose Creek (Cassia County), Portneuf River (Bannock County), Blackfoot, Rexburg, St. Anthony, Montpelier, St. Charles.

Specimens taken at various times of the year in the northern part of the state, between the dates of November 4, 1947, and April 28, 1957, were all found to be typical of *pallidus*, the race occurring throughout the Rocky Mountain region. This subspecies is characterized by its large size, and, in winter plumage, paler coloration.

Habits. Unlike the preceding species the Goldfinch is essentially a bird of deciduous underbrush. Even in migration it is rarely seen in the conifers, its preferred habitat being the willow and alders fringing the streams, or bordering cultivated fields and pastures in the more open country.

In common with the boreal finches it is rather erratic in its occurrence in Idaho during the winter months, for while always present during the winter it may be common one year and scarce the next. At this season of the year it can be found with flocks of Redpolls and Pine Siskins, feeding on the seeds of weeds sticking above the snow.

The prenuptial moult normally begins in early March, and by the latter part of the month the males are in almost full breeding plumage. Weather is apparently a factor in this respect for in 1952, characterized in the northern part of the state by unseasonably cold weather and deep snow on the ground until late March, flocks encountered as late as the middle of the month were still in full winter plumage.

In contrast to the breeding habits of this species in the eastern United States nesting activities are well under way by early June, and by the middle of July family parties composed of adults and fully fledged young of the year are frequently seen.

Loxia curvirostra Linnaeus: RED CROSSBILL

General Distribution. Cosmopolitan; in North America irregularly resident from southern Alaska, southern Yukon, Saskatchewan, central Ontario, central Quebec and Newfoundland south to Baja California and northern Nicaragua, and in the eastern United States to northern Wisconsin, Tennessee and North Carolina.

Status in Idaho. A common resident species in the forested areas throughout the state, but extremely erratic in its appearance regardless of locality or season.

Bonner County. Fairly plentiful during the summer of 1917 on the higher ridges north of Clark Fork, small, noisy, restless flocks being seen almost daily (Burleigh, 1923).

Kootenai County. Of irregular occurrence at Fort Sherman (Coeur d'Alene); sometimes common; noted throughout the year; males singing in February and March, and females seen then collecting nesting material (Merrill, 1898); a common resident species at Coeur d'Alene, 1910-14; numerous flocks noted during the fall and winter (Rust, 1915); Jollie (in litt.) reports specimens taken at Coeur d'Alene by H. Carey April 2, 1939, and by himself at Hauser Lake, five miles northwest of Post Falls September 14, 1949; one small flock noted in open pine woods at Post Falls May 4, 1950 (Burleigh).

Shoshone County. Resident on the St. Joe National Forest, 1921-41, but varying in abundance; most common from mid-July to October; large flocks noted in midwinter (Hand, 1941).

Latah County. Commonly noted in flocks during the summer of 1947 (Johnston, 1949); common at Harvard during the summer months of 1951-52 (Verner, 1953); a common resident species throughout the county, 1947-58, but extremely erratic in its occurrence in any wooded area, regardless of season; recorded at Potlatch, Viola, Moscow, Troy, Deary, and Juliaetta (Burleigh).

Nez Perce County. Specimens taken on Cottonwood Creek, two miles south of Gifford, October 30, 1949 (M. Jollie, in litt.).

Clearwater County. Noted at Headquarters February 24, 1953, and at Headquarters and Weippe (small flocks) September 19, 1954 (Burleigh).

Idaho County. Common in July, 1948, "in the upper Lochsa Fork watershed"; a male collected July 19, and a female July 21 (Orr, 1951).

Boise County. A flock of nine birds noted at the Deer Park Guard Station on the Boise National Forest, August 12, 1939, and for several weeks thereafter (Marshall, 1945).

Ada County. One bird collected in the Boise Valley in October, 1910, as it fed with a flock of House Finches (Wyman, 1911).

Custer County. Specimens in the Denver Museum of Natural History taken by Brodkorb at Little Redfish Lake in August.

Blaine County. Common at Ketchum from October through December, 1910 (Jewett, 1912); frequently noted in June, 1950, on the Sawtooth National Forest (Levy, 1962).

Clark County. One flock of fifteen birds seen on Signal Peak July 14, 1961 (Oring, 1962); a specimen in the Denver Museum of Natural History taken by Brodkorb in Grouse Canyon in June.

The Red Crossbill is unique in many respects, not the least being its unpredictable movements throughout the year. Casual observation would give it the status of a resident species, but while restless flocks can be seen in Idaho throughout the year such flocks may or may not represent the breeding population. This fact was clearly brought out by a critical study of specimens taken in the northern part of the state from 1948 through 1957, four recognized races being found to be present at various times of the year.

Habits. The Crossbill has many characteristics that set it apart from other birds indigenous to Idaho, and one of these is its disregard of season in which to rear its young. Too little is still known of its breeding habits, for a nest has yet to be actually found in the state, but there is little question that individual pairs nest regardless of season. Rust (1915) states that birds were seen at Coeur d'Alene on February 21, 1913, carrying nesting material, and that on May 4 young fully fledged and able to fly were noted. Orr (1951) commented on the fact that males observed on the upper Lochsa Fork watershed in Idaho County in July, 1948, were singing, and apparently nesting then. On April 4, 1949, I encountered a brood of fully grown young of the year at Troy, in Latah County, that except for their juvenile striped plumage were indistinguishable from the two adults. They were unquestionably hatched and reared during the extremely cold weather of late January and February characterized by frequent blizzards and minimum temperatures as low as 23 degrees below zero!

The favorite food of the crossbill is the seed of such conifers as the pines, firs, and spruces, and where available this seed forms the bulk of its diet. It is also very fond of salt, and it has been suggested that this unusual craving is due to the highly resinous content of the food it prefers. Marshall (1945) watched a flock of crossbills on the Boise National Forest, in August, 1939, that fed daily on salt from a salt block that had been put out for livestock and deer. Orr (1951) states that in Idaho County in July, 1948, this species was frequently observed eating charcoal from the campfires.

Loxia curvirostra pusilla Gloger

This race, characterized by its dark coloration and extremely heavy bill, represents the breeding population of Newfoundland. It wanders widely during the winter months, and on the basis of specimens taken has reached Idaho on at least one occasion, the winter of 1956-57. Males were collected then from small flocks in the open ponderosa pine woods on the south slope of Moscow Mountain on December 12, 1956, and February 17, 1957.

Loxia curvirostra bendirei Ridgway

This race, the breeding form of the northern Rocky Mountain region, is large and heavy billed as is *pusilla,* but noticeably paler in coloration. It is the crossbill most commonly observed in Idaho, for in the series of specimens collected from flocks encountered in the northern part of the state half were found to be typical of *bendirei.* They are as follows: Latah County, Potlatch, males October 24, 1948, January 21, February 12 and March 1, 1949, April 16 and August 6, 1950, November 30, 1954, February 12, 1955, Moscow, males September 1, 1948, March 26, 1949, February 17 and 24, March 2 and 16, April 22 and 28, 1957, females April 26, 1949, January 1, February 17, April 7 and 27, May 8, 1957, Troy, female immature April 4, 1949, Juliaetta, male November 10, 1949; Clearwater County, Headquarters, male September 19, 1954.

Loxia curvirostra sitkensis Grinnell

Sitkensis, a small, slender-billed race, is found on the coast from Alaska to northern California. In common with the other crossbills it would appear to be characterized by unpredictable movements regardless of season, and has been recorded in small numbers in northern Idaho. I have collected males of this race at Viola February 1, 1949, Moscow March 26, 1949, and Post Falls May 4, 1950. In the Museum of Zoology, University of Michigan, Ann Arbor, there are specimens of *sitkensis* taken by D. Arvey at Pollock, Idaho County, July 1, 1940.

Loxia curvirostra benti Griscom

This race, distinguished from *bendirei* by its smaller size and less heavy, slenderer bill, is the breeding form of the southern Rocky Mountain region. In its erratic wanderings small flocks frequently appear in northern Idaho; they have been recorded there not only during the winter months but during the spring and summer as well. In all a total of seventeen specimens of *benti* have been taken, 1948 through 1957, as follows: Moscow, males March 18 and 31 and July 13, 1950, April 7 and 17, 1951, December 12, 1956, January 1 and March 27, 1957, females July 10, 1948, April 7, 1951, Potlatch, female March 1, 1949, Deary, males (two) December 13, 1951, Weippe, male September 19, 1954.

Loxia leucoptera leucoptera Gmelin: WHITE-WINGED CROSSBILL

General Distribution. Largely resident from northern Alaska, central Mackenzie, northern Quebec and Newfoundland south to northern British

Columbia, central Alberta, northern Minnesota, southern Michigan, and southern New Brunswick. Wanders south irregularly as far as Kansas, Kentucky, and North Carolina.

Status in Idaho. Of casual occurrence in the more heavily wooded areas of the state; possibly breeds sparingly in northern Idaho.

Shoshone County. Fairly common on the St. Joe National Forest, 1921-41, but erratic in occurrence; "abundant" August 18-September 14, 1930, and July 15-October 13, 1933 (Hand, 1941).

Latah County. A flock of six birds seen January 2, 1954, on "the east side of East Twin Peak on Moscow Mountain" (Verner, in litt.).

Blaine County. Specimen taken November 6, 1910, on Rook's Creek (elevation 7,000 feet) (Jewett, 1912).

Minidoka County. Specimen taken at Rupert December 18, 1919 (Davis, 1935).

Habits. Because in size and general appearance this species so closely resembles the Red Crossbill, it is possibly more abundant in the state than the few records would indicate. During much of the year the two species occur together, and as they often feed in the upper branches of the larger conifers where they are far from conspicuous, the White-winged Crossbill could be easily overlooked. Judging from their relative abundance in Shoshone County in 1930 and again in 1933 there are apparently years when this species is present in the state in large numbers. Normally, however, it is doubtful if it is very common at any time of the year. It is suspected of breeding sparingly in the Cascade Mountains of Washington, so it is not improbable that it will eventually be found nesting in the extreme northern part of Idaho.

Chlorura chlorura (Audubon): Green-tailed Towhee

General Distribution. Breeds from southeastern Washington, southern Idaho and southeastern Wyoming south to southern California, central Arizona, and southern New Mexico. Winters from southern California, southern Arizona and southern Texas south in Mexico to southern Baja California and Morelos.

Status in Idaho. A common but local summer resident in the southern part of the state.

Owyhee County. Common at Riddle May 28-June 3, 1934; nesting (Davis, 1934); breeding specimens taken at Mary's Creek, eight miles east of Riddle June 17, 1949 (Jollie, in litt.); several birds noted at Silver City June 2, 1951 (Burleigh).

Clark County. Common in 1916 on brushy hillsides; two occupied nests found in June near Spencer (Rust, 1917); noted on Signal Peak June 19, 1961 (Oring, 1962).

Bonneville County. A common summer resident at Grays Lake, 1949-51; arrival dates June 4, 1950, and May 23, 1951 (Steel, 1956); an occasional bird noted June 13, 1949, on Caribou Mountain, north of Gray, to an altitude of 9,500 feet (Burleigh); common on Big Elk Creek August 5, 1961; specimens taken (Oring, 1962).

Bannock County. This species found to be fairly common well toward the tops of the open ridges at Pocatello June 10, 1955 (Burleigh).

South Central Idaho. Found nesting in 1872 on Conant Creek, on the Henry Fork of the Snake River, and in the Teton Basin; noted in 1890 in the mountains north of Arco, and in the canyons of the Lost River Mountains (Merriam, 1891); a fairly common summer resident in 1949 "in the higher sage brush zones" in the south-central counties (Levy, 1950).

Cassia County. Birds found to be common June 19, 1949, on the open ridges north of Almo, frequenting thickets of juniper and mountain mahogany to an altitude of approximately 6,500 feet (Burleigh); specimens taken by E. Larrison on Goose Creek, ten miles south of Oakley, June 28, 1949 (M. Jollie, in litt.).

There are specimens of this towhee at the Denver Museum of Natural History taken by Brodkorb as follows: Fremont County, Mount Sawtelle (9,500 feet), August; Teton County, Horseshoe Creek, Big Hole Mountain, July; Franklin County, Emigration Canyon, Wasatch Range, June; Cassia County, Malta, September.

Habits. Over much of its range the Green-tailed Towhee shows a decided preference for sagebrush, but in Idaho it would appear to be less demanding in its requirements, thickets and underbrush on the open ridges being readily accepted during the summer months. Altitude is apparently a factor in its distribution, for I have never noted it below 4,000 feet, and only above 6,000 feet was it present in any numbers.

Breeding activities are well under way by the middle of June, for of two nests found by Rust (1917) near Spencer on June 23, 1916, one was just completed and the other held three fresh eggs. They were "placed low in sage bushes" and were built of sage twigs and bark, lined with fine dry grasses.

Pipilo erythrophthalmus (Linnaeus): RUFOUS-SIDED TOWHEE

General Distribution. Breeds from southern British Columbia, central Saskatchewan, southern Ontario, and southern Maine south to Baja California, through Mexico to Guatemala, and to southern Louisiana, the Gulf coast, and southern Florida. Winters north to southern British Columbia, Colorado, Iowa, the southern Great Lakes region, and Massachusetts.

Status in Idaho. A common summer resident in the northern part of the state, and a scarce and rather local summer resident in southern Idaho. Winters irregularly and in small numbers in Latah County; one winter record for Nez Perce County.

Bonner County. Fairly common during the summer of 1917 at Clark Fork; a fully grown young bird of the year seen July 21 at the Trestle Creek Lookout Station (Burleigh, 1923).

Kootenai County. Arrives at Fort Sherman (Coeur d'Alene) in April; generally but sparingly distributed in summer (Merrill, 1898); a common summer resident at Coeur d'Alene, 1910-14, being present from April 15 to September 3; young able to fly noted May 18 and June 30 (Rust, 1915); specimen taken at Coeur d'Alene July 20, 1938 (Arvey, 1947).

Shoshone County. A rather common summer resident on the St. Joe National Forest, 1921-41, occurring from the valleys to "moderately high altitude"; recorded from April to August (Hand, 1941).

Latah County. Fairly common, June to August, 1947, on the mountainsides (Johnston, 1949); a fairly common and well-distributed summer resident on the open south slopes of the mountain ridges north and east of Moscow; winters irregularly and in small numbers (Burleigh).

Nez Perce County. Possibly breeds sparingly at Culdesac, a male being seen there June 20, 1949; at Lewiston an uncommon transient both in the spring and in the fall, being seen there at infrequent intervals between the extreme dates of March 8 (1954) and April 16 (1953), and August 12 (1952) and October 13 (1950); two males noted at Spalding, on Catholic Creek, February 8, 1957; in view of the early date they unquestionably wintered there; six inches of frozen snow on the ground that day (Burleigh).

Clearwater County. A fairly common summer resident, occurring wherever there was suitable habitat of thickets and underbrush in open woods, or the edges of clearings and pastures; noted in 1951 at Ahsahka April 8, Orofino June 12, and Weippe September 15; in 1953 at Greer March 24, and Headquarters March 25 (Burleigh).

Idaho County. A breeding male collected by D. Arvey ten miles southwest of Riggins May 14, 1939 (M. Jollie, in litt.); fully grown young of the year seen at Kooskia June 28, 1951 (Burleigh).

Adams County. A single bird, apparently a belated transient, seen at Indian Valley April 16, 1958 (Newhouse, 1960).

Washington County. Specimen in the United States National Museum, taken at Midvale by L. E. Wyman June 25, 1913; several birds seen May 6 and 7, 1952, in underbrush on an open ridge on East Brownlee Creek (Burleigh).

Boise County. Specimen taken July 4, 1941, on "Dutch Creek and Boise River" (Arvey, 1947).

Lemhi County. This towhee frequently seen at Shoup June 4 and 6, 1949, about thickets and stretches of underbrush on Cramer Creek (5,000 feet), and on Color Creek (6,000 feet) (Burleigh).

Oneida County. Specimen in the United States National Museum (Fish and Wildlife Service collection) taken by S. G. Jewett at Malad City July 13, 1911. This species found to be fairly common at Malad City June 8, 1955, males, occasionally a pair, being seen throughout the morning on the low ridges covered with juniper and scattered serviceberry thickets (Burleigh).

Habits. Although widely distributed in the northern part of the state the Rufous-sided Towhee is rather local in its occurrence. It has no liking for the thicker stretches of woods, frequenting thickets and stretches of underbrush along the streams and on the open south slopes of the higher ridges. Altitude is apparently a limiting factor, for I have rarely noted it during the summer months below 2,500 feet, or above 6,000 feet. Despite suitable habitat it was found to be a scarce transient only at Lewiston, and at Grays Lake (6,300 feet) there are no records for its occurrence.

In Latah County it normally appeared in the spring by the middle of March, and was rarely noted in the fall after early October. At Moscow my extreme dates of occurrence, excluding wintering individuals, are March 7 (1950 and 1954) and October 21 (1948).

This towhee would appear to be a rather hardy bird, for while it was irregular in its occurrence in Latah County during the winter months there were few years, regardless of the severity of the weather, when one or more was not recorded in late December and January. The first wintering male was encountered at Potlatch in late January, 1949, when minimum temperatures registered as low as twenty-three degrees below zero, and there were three feet of snow on the ground, and this was found to be by no means an unusual occurrence in succeeding years. Actual dates of winter occurrence are as follows: Potlatch, 1949, males January 13 and 24; Moscow, 1950, female December 28, 1951, three males January 19, 1954, two males December 24-31, 1955, female January 2, two males January 1-23, 1956, male February 5, 1957, females January 17 and 21.

Pipilo erythrophthalmus curtatus Grinnell

Curtatus, characterized by its small wing and dark flanks, is the breeding race of the northern Rocky Mountain region. A series of specimens taken largely in the northern part of the state were typical of this race, and were from the following localities: Latah County, Moscow, between the dates of April 18, 1948, and July 24, 1958, Potlatch, between the dates of January 13, 1949, and April 29, 1953; Nez Perce County, Lewiston, between the dates of March 26, 1950, and April 1, 1956, Culdesac, June 30, 1949, Spalding, February 8, 1957; Clearwater County, Orofino, June 12, 1951, Weippe, September 15, 1951, Greer, March 24, 1953, Headquarters, March 25, 1953, and April 18, 1954; Idaho County, Kooskia, June 28, 1951; Washington County, East Brownlee Creek, May 7, 1952; Lemhi County, Shoup, June 4, 1949; Oneida County, Malad City, June 8, 1955.

Pipilo erythrophthalmus montanus Swarth

Montanus is the breeding race of the southern Rocky Mountain region, and is characterized by its large wing and light flanks. There is no appreciable difference in the length of the tail of this subspecies and *curtatus.* *Montanus* has a very limited range in Idaho; it possibly occurs, at least in limited numbers, along the extreme eastern edge of the state, but to date it has been recorded only at Malad City, in Oneida County, a breeding male taken by Jewett on July 13, 1911, being referable to this race. Another breeding male that I collected at Malad City on June 8, 1955, was intermediate in its characters, having wing measurements approaching *curtatus* but the light flanks typical of *montanus*.

Calamospiza melanocorys Stejneger: LARK BUNTING

General Distribution. Breeds from southern Alberta, southern Saskatchewan, southeastern Manitoba and southern Minnesota south, east of the Rocky Mountains, to southern New Mexico and northern Texas. Winters from southern California, central Arizona, southern New Mexico and Texas south in Mexico to Jalisco and Hidalgo.

Status in Idaho. An uncommon and local summer resident in the southern part of the state.

South Central Idaho. "Half a dozen" seen in the sage plains west of Blackfoot July 17, 1890, and three between Big Butte and Big Lost River July 21 (Merriam, 1891).

Minidoka County. Noted May 29, 1921 (Davis, 1935).

Bonneville County. Rare at Grays Lake; possibly breeds (Steel, 1956); a male with enlarged testes collected in the Caribou Basin, north of Gray, May 28, 1951 (Levy, 1962).

Bingham County. A single bird, a male, seen at Aberdeen June 9, 1955 (Burleigh).

Habits. The Lark Bunting reaches the extreme western limits of its range in southern Idaho, and being essentially a bird of the Great Plains region it is not surprising that it is uncommon in the state. The northern Rocky Mountain region is an effective barrier for many species, and while a few venturesome individuals cross it in migration they will never, as in the case of the Lark Bunting, be common in Idaho during the summer months.

Passerculus sandwichensis (Gmelin): SAVANNAH SPARROW

General Distribution. Breeds from northern Alaska east across the continent to Newfoundland south through Mexico to southern Baja California and Oaxaca, in Guatemala, and in the eastern United States to Missouri, Indiana, and West Virginia. Winters north to southern British Columbia, southern Utah, Oklahoma, the northern Gulf states, and Massachusetts.

Status in Idaho. A common summer resident throughout the state; one winter record (Nez Perce County).

Boundary County. Specimen taken by Levy at Copeland April 7, 1950.

Bonner County. A fairly common resident in 1917 at Clark Fork, occurring in the open fields and pastures about the town (Burleigh, 1923).

Kootenai County. Arrives at Fort Sherman (Coeur d'Alene) in early May; breeds in small numbers on the prairie; especially common in September and early October (Merrill, 1898); a common summer resident at Coeur d'Alene, 1910-14; several specimens taken on September 29 (Rust, 1915); small flocks noted on the open prairie at Hauser October 9, 1952, April 30, 1955, and October 4 and 17, 1956, and at Rathdrum August 31, 1953 (Burleigh).

Benewah County. A local but not rare summer resident at St. Maries, 1921-41, occurring from April until September (Hand, 1941).

Latah County. Noted sparingly in the open fields, June to August, 1947 (Johnston, 1949); a fairly common summer resident, 1948-58, in the open Palouse country in the western part of the county, usually appearing in the spring in late March, and being rarely observed in the fall after the middle of October; noted at Potlatch, Viola, Moscow, and Genesee (Burleigh).

Nez Perce County. An uncommon summer resident in the open fields east of Lewiston Orchards; at Lewiston a common transient both in the spring and in the fall; one winter record, a single bird seen December 28, 1951, feeding with House Finches at the edge of a field (Burleigh).

Clearwater County. Possibly breeds in small numbers on the open prairie south of Weippe, an occasional bird being noted there August 26, 1952; small flocks present there September 16, 1951, and September 8, 1953 (Burleigh).

Idaho County. Flocks noted in September, 1941, on Burned Ridge, four miles southwest of Selway Falls; four specimens taken September 16 and 23 identified as *anthinus* (Orr, 1951).

Adams County. This species found to be fairly common at New Meadows June 27 and 28, 1949, an occasional singing male being seen then in the open fields (Burleigh); several of these sparrows seen at Council April 15 to May 6, 1958 (Newhouse, 1960).

Valley County. Noted in small numbers in the open fields south of McCall May 20, 1955, and September 10, 1958 (Burleigh).

Owyhee County. Fairly common at Riddle May 28-June 3, 1934; a breeding male taken on May 30 (Davis, 1934).

Custer County. Several fully grown young of the year noted in the meadows at Stanley July 16, 1958 (Burleigh).

Clark County. Seen in small numbers on the Camas Meadows July 16, 1916, and at Spencer August 1 (Rust, 1917).

Jefferson County. An uncommon summer resident in 1961 on the Camas National Wildlife Refuge (Oring, 1962).

Bonneville County. A very common summer resident at Grays Lake, 1949-51; arrival dates April 28, 1950, May 8, 1951 (Steel, 1956).

South Central Idaho. Several seen and one collected on the Snake River October 8, 1872; in 1890 three were taken in Birch Creek Valley August 4 and 15; observed in Lemhi Valley in late August and early September (Merriam, 1891); common "in moist grassy meadows" in south-central Idaho during the summer of 1949 (Levy, 1950).

Minidoka County. A summer resident at Rupert (1919-21), occurring between the extreme dates of April 11 and September 16; eggs June 2 (Davis, 1935).

Cassia County. Noted at Burley in open marshy fields bordering the Snake River June 18, 1949 (Burleigh).

Habits. Although found throughout the state during the summer months the Savannah Sparrow is rather local in its occurrence. It frequents open fields and meadows, and while in such a site it accepts scattered thickets it consistently shuns thick underbrush. Altitude is apparently not too important, but it would appear to limit to some extent the distribution of this species in Idaho. At Lewiston it was, despite suitable habitat, rather scarce as a breeding bird, and while it was common at Grays Lake (6,300 feet) I failed to find it in mountain meadows above this altitude.

In the northern part of the state it normally appeared in the spring in late March or early April, and in the fall was only infrequently seen after the middle of October. At Moscow my extreme dates of occurrence are March 20 (1957) and October 19 (1952), at Genesee March 21 (1953) and October 21 (1952), at Lewiston March 19 (1957) and November 1 (1953).

Passerculus sandwichensis oblitus Peters and Griscom

There is one record for the occurrence of this race in Idaho, a male typical of *oblitus* that was taken at Moscow March 20, 1957. In view of the fact that north of Idaho this subspecies does not breed farther west than Manitoba it will probably always be largely of accidental occurrence in the state.

Passerculus sandwichensis anthinus Bonaparte

This far-northern race of the Savannah Sparrow breeds from northern Alaska and northern Mackenzie south to British Columbia and Manitoba. It occurs as a fairly common transient in Idaho both in the spring and in the fall, specimens identified by John W. Aldrich as *anthinus* being taken, from 1948 through 1958, as follows: Kootenai County, Coeur d'Alene, May 4, 1950, Hauser, October 4, 1956, September 26, 1957; Latah County, Potlatch, August 31, 1949, May 4, 1955, Viola, October 10, 1948, September 13, 1949, Moscow, twenty-one specimens, in the spring between the extreme dates of March 26 (1956) and May 7 (1949), and in the fall between the extreme dates of September 15 (1952) and October 21 (1951), Genesee, April 28, 1949, October 21, 1952; Nez Perce County, Lewiston, thirteen specimens, in the spring between the extreme dates of April 19 (1949) and May 16 (1950), and in the fall between the extreme dates of September 15 (1950) and October 21 (1950); Clearwater County, Weippe, September 16, 1951; Valley County, McCall, September 18, 1955, September 10, 1958.

Passerculus sandwichensis nevadensis Grinnell

Nevadensis is the breeding race of the Rocky Mountain region, occurring during the summer months from British Columbia south to northern Arizona and east to western Nebraska. It is a common breeding bird in suitable habitat throughout Idaho, numerous specimens representing the breeding population, and identified as *nevadensis* by John W. Aldrich, being taken at the following localities: Latah County, Moscow, Genesee; Nez Perce County, Lewiston; Clearwater County, Weippe; Adams County, New Meadows; Valley County, McCall; Custer County, Stanley; Bonneville County, Gray; Cassia County, Burley. The bird seen at Lewiston on December 28, 1951, was collected, and found to be typical of this breeding population.

In the Museum of Vertebrate Zoology, at Berkeley, there are specimens of *nevadensis* collected at Grangeville, Idaho County, May 12, 1951 (E. J. Larrison); Bear Valley and Elk Creek Ranger Station, Valley County, July 14, 1932 (A. H. Miller and D. H. Blanchard); Riddle, Owyhee County, May 30, 1934 (W. B. Davis); Rupert, Minidoka County, June 13, 1934 (W. B. Davis); Elba, Cassia County, June 11-15, 1934-36 (W. B. Davis).

Specimens collected by Brodkorb in southern Idaho, in the Denver Museum of Natural History represent the breeding population, *nevadensis*, and are from the following localities, Canyon County, Parma; Owyhee County, Duck Valley; Fremont County, Mount Sawtelle, Big Spring; Bear Lake County, Montpelier, Mud Lake, Fish Haven.

Ammodramus savannarum perpallidus (Coues): GRASSHOPPER SPARROW

General Distribution. Breeds from southern British Columbia, southern Saskatchewan and western Ontario south to southern California, northern Utah, central Colorado and central Texas. Winters from central California, southern Arizona and central Oklahoma south through Mexico to central America (El Salvador), and in the eastern United States to the Gulf coast and southern Georgia.

Status in Idaho. An uncommon summer resident in the northern part of the state.

Johnston (1949) first recorded this species for Idaho. On June 19, 1947, he saw a singing male in a wheat field on Paradise Ridge, south of Moscow, and a week later, on June 27, he collected another male in a field one mile east of Moscow.

I personally found this species scarce and rather local in its occurrence. There was no lack of suitable habitat, but in only a few fields were breeding pairs present during the summer months.

In Kootenai County it was noted only in the open prairie at Hauser. Here in 1956 single birds were seen July 2 and October 18, the latter date rather late for its occurrence in the state.

In Latah County it nested at Potlatch (fully grown young of the year seen there August 4, 1951, and July 31, 1953, and at Moscow (fully grown young birds of the year seen July 18, 1949, and July 28, 1952). It was also noted at Moscow, October 9, 1948, September 4, 1949, July 18 and September 24, 1951.

In Nez Perce County it possibly breeds sparingly at Lewiston, but I noted it there on only two occasions. On May 6, 1950, two birds were flushed in the middle of an alfalfa field, and on September 11, 1956, one bird was seen in a similar spot.

In order to verify the occurrence of this species in the state twelve specimens, all found to be typical of *perpallidus,* were taken as follows: Hauser, male July 2, 1956, female October 18, 1956; Potlatch, male and female immature August 4, 1951, female immature July 31, 1953; Moscow, males July 18 and September 24, 1951, immature males July 18, 1949, July 28, 1952, female October 9, 1948; Lewiston, female May 6, 1950, male immature September 11, 1956.

Habits. Few birds are more shy or secretive than the Grasshopper Sparrow. Even its song, weak and insectlike, is not apt to betray its presence during the breeding season. Despite the fact that at both Potlatch and Moscow fully grown young of the year have been seen in July and early August, I failed to record this species in May and June when it unquestionably was present and nesting. It is therefore possibly more common in Idaho than the relatively few records indicate, and it is not improbable that future field work will reveal its presence, at least in small numbers, in the southern part of the state.

Passerherbulus caudacutus (Latham): LeConte's Sparrow

General Distribution. Breeds from southern Mackenzie and northern Ontario south to northern Montana, northern North Dakota, northern Wisconsin, and northern Michigan. Winters from central Kansas, northern Arkansas, central Alabama and South Carolina south to southern Texas, the Gulf coast and northern Florida.

Status in Idaho. Apparently of casual occurrence in the northern part of the state.

There is but one definite record for LeConte's Sparrow in Idaho. Merrill (1898) states that he collected a specimen at Fort Sherman (Coeur d'Alene) September 28, 1896.

Habits. It is doubtful if there is any other bird more difficult to become acquainted with than LeConte's Sparrow. It frequents open fields where the grass is high enough to afford it the concealment it desires, and here it must be practically walked on before it flies and reveals its presence. Under such circumstances it will go a short distance, drop back into the grass, and then be extremely difficult to find again.

One morning in early October I was following the shoreline of the reservoir east of Lewiston Orchards when a small sparrow flushed from under my feet as I crossed an area covered with thick grass. Its appearance and characteristic flight left no doubt in my mind as to its being a LeConte's Sparrow, but although I realized the importance of securing it to verify this identification I was unsuccessful in my efforts to cause it again to leave the protection of the grass in which it was hiding. This further confirmed my suspicions as to its identity, but under the circumstances I would hesitate to consider this other than a dubious sight record of a species that doubtless rarely occurs in the state.

Pooecetes gramineus definitus Oberholser: VESPER SPARROW

General Distribution. Breeds in eastern Washington, eastern Oregon, northern California, and Idaho. Winters south to southern Mexico (Guerrero and Oaxaca).

Status in Idaho. An uncommon and local summer resident in the northern part of the state; common and well distributed during the summer months in southern Idaho; one winter record for Latah County.

Bonner County. Found to be a scarce summer resident in 1917 at Clark Fork (Burleigh, 1923).

Kootenai County. Breeds sparingly at Fort Sherman (Coeur d'Alene) (Merrill, 1898); specimen taken six miles east of Harrison September 20, 1949 (Jollie, in litt.); this species found to be fairly common June 24, 1955, in the open prairie at Rathdrum; frequently noted during the afternoon; three birds seen at Hauser April 13, 1956 (Burleigh).

Shoshone County. A rare summer resident on the St. Joe National Forest, 1921-41; noted as late in the fall as September 5, 1935 (Hand, 1941).

Latah County. Found to be fairly common during the summer of 1947 on Paradise Ridge, south of Moscow (Johnston, 1949); noted during the summer months only on Paradise Ridge, but not uncommon there (1948-58); a rather scarce migrant at Moscow, both in the spring and in the fall (Burleigh); a specimen taken four miles south of Moscow December 28, 1959 (Oring, in litt.).

Nez Perce County. An uncommon migrant at Lewiston (1948-58), being noted at infrequent intervals from late March until May, and again from late August until the latter part of September (Burleigh).

Clearwater County. Noted at Headquarters April 10, 1952, and at Weippe March 24, 1953 (Burleigh).

Idaho County. Specimen taken by Dale Arvey ten miles south of Riggins July 2, 1939 (Jollie, in litt.).

Adams County. Noted at Council in 1958 from April 15 to April 28, and again from August 18 to September 6 (Newhouse, 1960).

Valley County. A single bird seen at McCall September 11, 1958 (Burleigh).

Owyhee County. Common at Riddle May 28-June 3, 1934; several nests found with young (Davis, 1934); specimens taken eight miles east of Riddle, on Mary's Creek, June 15, 1949 (Jollie, in litt.).

Custer County. A nest of the Vesper Sparrow found at Dickey in June, 1912, with two eggs and two of the Cowbird (Friedmann, 1929); one pair, the male singing, seen at Willow Creek Summit (altitude 7,200 feet) May 25, 1952 (Burleigh).

Blaine County. Scattered pairs found nesting in the vicinity of Ketchum June 24-28, 1950, occurring both in the valleys and on the open ridges to an altitude of 8,000 feet (Burleigh).

Fremont County. Several birds noted in the open fields at Henrys Lake June 13, 1957 (Burleigh).

Clark County. Found to be a fairly common summer resident in 1916; a nest with four eggs found at Spencer June 7, and one with five eggs at Highbridge June 13 (Rust, 1917).

Jefferson County. A common summer resident in 1961 on the Camas National Wildlife Refuge (Oring, 1962).

Bonneville County. A common summer resident at Grays Lake, 1949-51; arrival dates April 13, 1950, and April 21, 1951 (Steel, 1956); common in 1961 in the fields at Big Elk Creek, near Palisades (Oring, 1962).

Bear Lake County. Specimens at the University of Michigan, Ann Arbor, taken by Brodkorb at Montpelier August 17-29, 1934.

South Central Idaho. Common in 1890 along the Snake River, and in the Birch Creek, Lemhi, and Pahsimeroi valleys; also noted in late September at Sawtooth Lake (Merriam, 1891); a common breeding bird in 1949 "in the sagebrush plains" of the south-central counties (Levy, 1950).

Minidoka County. A summer resident at Rupert (1919-21); extreme dates of occurrence April 6 and November 4; eggs May 20 (Davis, 1935).

Cassia County. Specimens in the Museum of Vertebrate Zoology, Berkeley, taken at Elba by W. B. Davis June 17, 1934, and June 11, 1936; an occasional bird seen on the open ridges at the Silent City of Rocks, west of Almo, June 19, 1949 (Burleigh); specimen taken on Goose Creek, ten miles south of Oakley, June 27, 1949 (Jollie, in litt.).

Definitus is the breeding race of the northern Rocky Mountain region, and can be distinguished from *confinis* of the Great Plains by its distinctly darker and grayer upperparts. From 1948 through 1958 a small series of specimens was taken in various parts of the state, and all were found to represent this Rocky Mountain race. These specimens are as follows: Kootenai County, Rathdrum, male June 24, 1955, Hauser, male April 13, 1956; Latah County, Moscow, males April 17, 1948, May 8 and 14, 1949, May 13, September 2, 12 and 27, 1950, April 2, 1951, April 30 and August 25, 1952, females April 29, 1948, May 14, 1949, May 13, 1950, September 10, 1952; Nez Perce County, Lewiston, males September 4, 1950, April 18, 1951, May 1, 1953, March 24 and September 13, 1956, females August 27, 1950, September 13, 1951, April 28, 1952, September 1, 1953, September 19, 1956; Clearwater County, Headquarters, female April 10, 1952, Weippe, male March 24, 1953; Valley County, McCall, female May 5, 1952, male September 11, 1958; Custer County, Willow Creek Summit, male May 25, 1952; Fremont County, Henrys Lake, male June 13, 1957; Bonneville County, Gray, two males May 21, 1951; Caribou County, Soda Springs, male June 8, 1949.

In the Denver Museum of Natural History there are specimens of the Vesper Sparrow, representing the breeding population, taken by Brodkorb at the following localities: Lemhi County, Salmon; Clark County, Grouse Canyon, Medicine Lodge Creek; Bingham County, Blackfoot; Bear Lake County, Montpelier; Oneida County, Malad City; Jerome County, Jerome.

Habits. Altitude is apparently a definite factor in the distribution of the Vesper Sparrow in Idaho. It is extremely scarce if it occurs at all below three thousand feet, for in Latah County I noted it during the summer months only on Paradise Ridge. The extensive open fields at Moscow would appear to offer suitable habitat for this species, but I did not record it there other than as an uncommon migrant. In the southern part of the state it was a common breeding bird from approximately 4,000 feet to at least 6,000 feet; an occasional pair was encountered at 8,000 feet (on Easley Peak, in Blaine County), and it possibly occurs higher where conditions are suitable.

In northern Idaho the Vesper Sparrow usually appears in the spring in early April, and in the fall it is only infrequently seen after the middle of September. At Moscow my extreme dates of occurrence are April 2 (1951) and September 27 (1950); at Lewiston March 24 (1956) and May 13 (1953), and August 27 (1950) and September 19 (1956).

Throughout its breeding range in southern Idaho areas where sagebrush predominates are the preferred habitat for the Vesper Sparrow, and here the nest is on the ground at the base of or in a clump of sagebrush. This was the situation for the two nests found by Rust (1917) in Clark County, and for another nest that I found on Easley Peak, in Blaine County, that held three fresh eggs on June 25, 1950.

Chondestes grammacus actitus Oberholser: LARK SPARROW

General Distribution. Breeds in eastern Washington, eastern Oregon, Idaho, and Montana west of the Continental Divide. Winters south through Mexico to Central America (El Salvador).

Status in Idaho. A rare summer resident in the extreme northern part of the state, and a fairly common but local summer resident south of Latah County.

Shoshone County. Of casual occurrence on the St. Joe National Forest, 1921-41; noted at the Roundtop Ranger Station September 10, 1922, at the Twin Creek Ranger Station June 20, 1931, and on the upper Palouse River September 5, 1935 (Hand, 1941).

Benewah County. One pair seen at Tensed, at the edge of an old slashing, June 14, 1950 (Burleigh).

Latah County. Noted during the summer of 1947 only in the southern part of the county; several seen at Juliaetta on August 12 (Johnston, 1949); recorded once at Moscow, a single bird, in immature plumage, on August 27, 1949 (Burleigh).

Nez Perce County. A fairly common summer resident at Lewiston, 1948-58; as many as four breeding pairs seen during a morning's field work in June (Burleigh).

Adams County. Common at Council, in 1958, from May 31 through September 9 (Newhouse, 1960).

Washington County. Noted at Crane Creek, fifteen miles east of Midvale (specimen taken May 31, 1930) by R. M. Gilmore.

Ada County. Specimens in the Denver Museum of Natural History taken by A. B. Fuller at Boise July 3, 1929.

Owyhee County. An occasional bird noted June 23, 1949, in the open arid country south of Homedale (Burleigh); specimens taken by Brodkorb (Denver Museum of Natural History) at Bruneau June 5, 1932, and by W. B. Davis (Museum of Vertebrate Zoology, Berkeley) at Murphy May 24, 1935.

Jefferson County. An uncommon summer resident in 1961 on the Camas National Wildlife Refuge (Oring, 1962).

Bonneville County. Specimen in the Museum of Vertebrate Zoology, Berkeley, taken by W. B. Davis at Idaho Falls July 11, 1936; a rare transient at Grays Lake, 1949-51; one bird noted May 22, 1951 (Steel, 1956).

South Central Idaho. An uncommon summer resident in 1890; a few seen near the mouth of the Little Lost River in late July, and again on September 10 (Merrill, 1891); a fairly common summer resident in 1949 "in the sagebrush areas" in the south-central counties; a female collected at Jerome on July 16 (Levy, 1950).

Power County. Specimen taken ten miles southwest of American Falls July 3, 1940 (M. Jollie, in litt.); an occasional bird noted June 21, 1960, in the open arid country south of Massacre Rocks (Burleigh).

Minidoka County. Rare in 1909; "abundant" in 1931 (Kenagy, 1914); a fairly common summer resident at Rupert, 1919-21; extreme dates of occurrence May 7 and September 29; eggs May 20 (Davis, 1935); noted at Acequia June 14, 1960 (Burleigh).

Jerome County. An occasional bird noted at Eden June 16, 1960 (Burleigh).

Twin Falls County. A specimen in the Museum of Vertebrate Zoology, Berkeley, taken by E. C. Aldrich at Rogerson May 16, 1935.

Cassia County. An occasional bird noted at Almo June 21, 1949, and at Goose Creek, ten miles south of Oakley, June 22, 1950, and again June 13, 1960 (Burleigh).

The status of *actitus* as a valid race has been questioned by taxonomists, but a critical study of nineteen specimens taken throughout the state showed that the characters given by Oberholser readily separate the breeding population of Idaho from *strigatus* of the Rocky Mountain region. These specimens are as follows: Benewah County, Tensed, male June 14, 1950; Latah County, Moscow, immature female August 27, 1949; Nez Perce County, Lewiston, adult males August 8 and September 12, 1949, May 16, June 8, and October 13, 1950, April 28, 1952, immature male September 1, 1949, adult females September 4, 1949, September 4, 1950, immature females August 13, 1949, September 21, 1950; Owyhee County, Homedale, male

June 23, 1949; Bonneville County, Gray, female May 27, 1951; Power County, Massacre Rocks, male June 21, 1960; Minidoka County, Acequia, male June 14, 1960; Cassia County, Oakley (Goose Creek), two males June 13, 1960.

Habits. In view of its relative abundance during the summer months in eastern Washington it is rather surprising that the Lark Sparrow has never been recorded as a breeding bird in the open fields and pastures about Moscow. It presents another perplexing distributional problem, for while this species breeds north of Idaho in British Columbia and Alberta it is rare even in migration north of the Snake River.

At Lewiston, in Nez Perce County, it appears in the spring in late April or early May, and in the fall it is only infrequently seen after the middle of September. My extreme dates of occurrence are April 28 (1952) and October 13 (1950).

A nest that I found on Goose Creek, south of Oakley, held four slightly incubated eggs on June 22, 1950, and was well concealed in a clump of sagebrush at the top of an open ridge.

Amphispiza bilineata deserticola Ridgway: BLACK-THROATED SPARROW

General Distribution. Breeds from northern California, southern Idaho, and southwestern Wyoming south to Baja California, northern Sonora and northern Chihuahua. Winters north to southern California, central Arizona, and southern New Mexico.

Status in Idaho. A scarce and local summer resident in the southern part of the state, and of accidental occurrence in northern Idaho.

There is one record for this species in the northern part of the state. On May 6, 1953, I collected a male at Rathdrum, in Kootenai County, that was found feeding in underbrush at the side of a road through a large open field.

In southern Idaho it was first reported by L. E. Wyman (Duvall, 1942) who saw four individuals at Ellis, in the Pahsimeroi Valley, on June 25, 1912; a male was collected that day.

During the summer of 1959 a specimen was taken by Earl Larrison in Cassia County (Lew Oring, personal correspondence), and on August 10, 1960, five were seen and an immature male collected by Delwyn G. Berrett two miles north of Menan, in Madison County (Berrett, in litt.).

There are no other records.

Habits. The Black-throated Sparrow is one of the characteristic birds of the hot arid deserts of the southwestern United States, and with this rather exacting habitat preference it has probably never been of more than casual occurrence in southern Idaho. Over much of its range its presence is closely associated with the cane cactus (*Opuntia*), and a favored nesting site is in this or other species of cactus, such as the catclaw. The absence of such vegetation in the more arid areas of southern Idaho is undoubtedly a major factor in limiting its distribution in the state.

Amphispiza belli campicola Oberholser: SAGE SPARROW

General Distribution. Breeds in eastern Washington, Oregon, Idaho, and western Montana west of the Continental Divide. Winters south to northern Sonora and western Texas.

Status in Idaho. A fairly common but local summer resident in the southern part of the state.

Clark County. Found to be fairly common in 1916 in sagebrush areas (Rust, 1917).

Jefferson County. A female in immature plumage taken five miles southwest of Hamer August 23, 1961 (Oring, 1962).

South Central Idaho. Abundant breeding bird in 1890 "in the sage plains," and in the valleys of Birch Creek, the Lemhi River, and the Big and Little Lost Rivers; also abundant along the Snake River in October (Merriam, 1891).

Minidoka County. Abundant in 1907; rare in 1912 (Kenagy, 1941); a specimen taken at Rupert May 19, 1921 (Davis, 1935).

Jerome County. Noted at Jerome in 1949, but not elsewhere in the adjoining counties; a female collected there July 7, and a male and a female in immature plumage taken on July 20 (Levy, 1950).

In the Museum of Vertebrate Zoology, Berkeley, there are specimens taken six miles west of Murphy, Owyhee County, May 24, 1935, and seventeen miles west of Idaho Falls, Bonneville County, July 11, 1936.

In the Denver Museum of Natural History there are additional specimens taken by Pierce Brodkorb at the following localities: Owyhee County, Bruneau, July 9, 1932; Custer County, Mackay Peak, August 29, 1931; Jefferson County, Hamer, May 20, 1931; Butte County, Deadman Canyon, September 10, 1931; Jerome County, Jerome, August 7, 1932; Twin Falls County, Rogerson, July 23-31, 1932 (fourteen specimens).

A critical examination of specimens taken in Idaho showed that *campicola* is distinct from other races of *belli,* and should be recognized as a valid race. It differs from *nevadensis,* which it most closely resembles, in being larger, with the upperparts darker, more grayish, and the flanks more grayish.

Habits. The Sage Sparrow is well named, for it is found only in areas where the sagebrush predominates. In my personal experience it is a surprisingly secretive bird during the breeding season. I failed to find it in spots where I was confident it occurred, and where I did see it I had to be satisfied with a brief glimpse of one of these sparrows as it flew up from the ground ahead of me, and then could not be flushed again.

Rust (1917) reports a nest found at Spencer on July 7, 1916, that held one egg of the Sage Sparrow and two of the Cowbird.

Junco hyemalis (Linnaeus): SLATE-COLORED JUNCO

General Distribution. Breeds from northwestern Alaska east across the continent to Newfoundland, south to northern British Columbia, the central prairie provinces of Canada, central Minnesota, Wisconsin, central Michigan, and New York, and through the Appalachian Mountains to northern Georgia. Winters from southern Canada to northern Mexico, the Gulf coast, and northern Florida.

Status in Idaho. An uncommon but regular winter resident in the northern part of the state, and possibly of regular occurrence in southern Idaho, although rarely recorded there at the present time.

The only published record for the occurrence of *Junco hyemalis* in Idaho is the comment by Alden H. Miller (1941) that it probably occurs in northern Idaho but that "there are no definite records north of southern Idaho." My one record for this species in this part of the state is that of a single bird, a male, that was collected on Goose Creek, ten miles south of Oakley, in Cassia County, November 8, 1957.

In northern Idaho, at Moscow and Potlatch in Latah County, and at Lewiston in Nez Perce County, I found this junco of regular occurrence each winter (1947-58). It was present in rather small numbers, but appeared each fall in October, and usually lingered in the spring until early April. I have one record for Juliaetta, a male taken February 13, 1950.

Habits. Despite the regularity with which this species appears in northern Idaho each fall it is not surprising that it has been almost completely overlooked in past years. It has never been noted in flocks, merely single birds, rarely two, being seen with flocks of other juncos. Under such circumstances it is an inconspicuous part of the winter bird life of the state, and unless looked for its presence would in most instances not be suspected.

On the basis of actual specimens taken it normally appears in the fall about the second week in October, and in the spring it rarely lingers later than early April. At Moscow my extreme dates of occurrence are October 17 (1950) and April 22 (1950), at Potlatch October 2 (1949) and March 21 (1951), at Lewiston October 24 (1956) and April 4 (1955).

Junco hyemalis hyemalis (Linnaeus)

Although the nominate race of *Junco hyemalis* breeds commonly north of Idaho in Alaska and Mackenzie it only occurs as a rather scarce migrant in the state. Over a period of eleven years eight specimens were taken as follows: Moscow, males December 3, 1947, February 2 and November 18, 1956, female December 25, 1949, Lewiston, males March 12 and 24, and October 24, 1956, February 21, 1957.

In the Museum of Vertebrate Zoology, Berkeley, there are two specimens identified by Alden H. Miller as *hyemalis* that were taken at Moscow by M. Jollie on December 10 and 15, 1951.

Junco hyemalis cismontanus Dwight

This race breeds from southern Yukon south to central British Columbia and Alberta. It occurs as a regular but uncommon winter resident in the northern part of the state, specimens representing *cismontanus* being taken (1947-58) as follows: Latah County, Moscow, males December 27, 1947, October 9, 1948, December 13, 1949, January 9, April 3 and 22, October 17 and 18, 1950, March 28, 1956, January 17, March 27 and November 28, 1957, females April 15, 1950, October 24, 1951, Potlatch, males February 16, March 1 and October 2, 1949, November 18, 1951 (two), females February 16, 1949, January 16, 1952, January 12, 1957, Juliaetta, male February 13, 1950; Nez Perce County, Lewiston, males February 13 and December 28, 1951, February 8, 1952, April 8, 1954, April 4, 1955, January 5, 1956. The specimen taken on Goose Creek, in Cassia County, November 8, 1957, was also identified as *cismontanus*.

Junco oreganus (Townsend): OREGON JUNCO

General Distribution. Breeds from southeastern Alaska, central Alberta and southwestern Saskatchewan south to northern Baja California, western Nevada, and northwestern Wyoming. Winters over much of its breeding range south to northern Mexico (Sonora and Chihuahua) and central Texas.

Status in Idaho. A common summer resident in suitable habitat throughout the state; winters commonly at lower altitudes.

Bonner County. Common at Clark Fork during the summer of 1917, occurring both in the valleys and well up the mountainsides; a flock of approximately one hundred noted July 16 at the top of a ridge; female gathering nesting material July 17 (Burleigh, 1923).

Kootenai County. Arrives at Fort Sherman (Coeur d'Alene) in late February or early March; breeds (Merrill, 1898); fully grown young noted at Blue Lake July 18, 1894 (Snyder, 1900); a common summer resident at Coeur d'Alene (1910-14); noted from February 22 to early October; common by the first week in April; in flocks by the middle of August (Rust, 1915); common at the upper end of Lake Coeur d'Alene July 1-10, 1943 (Yocom, 1946); a flock of twelve birds seen at Coeur d'Alene January 8, 1957, feeding in underbrush at the side of a road (Burleigh).

Shoshone County. A common and widely distributed summer resident, 1921-41, on the St. Joe National Forest; abundant in migration; winters commonly in the valleys (Hand, 1941).

Latah County. Common in the forested areas June to August, 1947 (Johnston, 1949); found to be a common breeding bird at Harvard, 1951-52 (Verner, 1953); a common resident species, 1947-58, on the wooded ridges north and east of Moscow, although occurring in smaller numbers during the winter months, and limited then to thickets and underbrush in the valleys (Burleigh).

Nez Perce County. A fairly common winter resident 1947-58 at Lewiston, small flocks usually appearing in the fall in September, and being only infrequently seen in the spring after early April (Burleigh).

Clearwater County. A fairly common summer resident, 1951-56, on the wooded ridges at Headquarters, usually appearing in March, and disappearing in November; extreme dates of occurrence February 28 (1954) and November 11 (1951) (Burleigh).

Idaho County. A specimen taken at Wounded Doe Licks by C. Engler June 24, 1938 (M. Jollie, in litt.); numerous flocks noted in September, 1941, in the Selway region; two specimens taken September 11 (at Selway Falls) and one on September 20 (at Canteen Meadow); "present" in the Lolo Pass region in July, 1948; males taken July 13 and 16 (Orr, 1951).

Valley County. An occasional singing male noted at McCall (altitude 5,200 feet) April 12, 1958; ground that day still covered with fully three feet of hard snow (Burleigh).

Adams County. "Very common" at Council, 1957-58, September 19 through March 19 (Newhouse, 1960).

Washington County. Small flocks noted at Weiser February 18, 1950, and November 22, 1951; several birds seen June 6, 1952, in the fir woods at the top of Cuddy Mountain (altitude 7,600 feet); snow still in drifts five and six feet deep (Burleigh).

Ada County. Small flocks seen at Boise December 10, 1957 (Burleigh); fully grown young in immature plumage seen at Bogus Basin July 17, 1960 (Burleigh).

Owyhee County. A single bird, "probably a late straggler," seen at Riddle, June 3, 1934 (Davis, 1934); juncos fairly common at De Lamar February 19, Oreana February 21, and Homedale February 24, 1950, small flocks being noted each day; this species apparently a fairly common breeding bird at Silver City, being frequently seen June 2, 1951, on the wooded ridges about the town (8,000 to 9,000 feet) (Burleigh).

Lemhi County. Noted in small numbers at Shoup (6,000 feet) June 6, 1949, and at Lost Trail Pass (6,900 feet) June 20, 1950 (Burleigh).

Custer County. An occasional pair of juncos encountered at Willow Creek Summit (7,000 feet) May 19, 1951, and on Mount Borah (8,500 feet) July 12, 1958 (Burleigh).

Blaine County. Common near Ketchum, along Spring Creek, October 27, 1910; eventually forced to a lower altitude by deep snow (Jewett, 1912); noted in small numbers at the head of Alder Creek, north of Ketchum, June 24, 1950, and on Hyndman Peak, to an altitude of eight thousand feet, on June 27 (Burleigh).

Fremont County. Juncos found to be fairly common June 12, 1957, at Targhee Pass, on the Continental Divide, occurring in the aspen groves and in open spots on the wooded ridges at an altitude of seven thousand feet (Burleigh); several pairs noted at the head of Little Dry Creek Canyon June 18, 1916; common on the North Fork of the Snake River, north of Rea, August 25 (Rust, 1917).

Clark County. Common on Signal Peak June 19 and July 14, 1961 (Oring, 1962).

Bonneville County. A "very common resident" at Grays Lake, 1949-51 (Steel, 1956); scattered pairs noted at the top of Caribou Mountain June 13, 1949, in open fir woods between seven thousand and nine thousand feet

(Burleigh); common at Big Elk Creek, near Palisades, August 6, 1961 (Oring, 1962).

Bannock County. An occasional pair seen at Pocatello June 10, 1955, in aspen groves on Buckskin Creek (Burleigh).

South Central Idaho. Fully grown young taken in 1890 in the Salmon River Mountains the middle of August; adults noted at the lower altitudes in the Salmon River and Sawtooth mountains "later in the season"; common during migration; several noted near Shoshone Falls October 9-11 (Merriam, 1891); common in the south-central counties in 1949, occurring at higher altitudes "in the coniferous zones" (Levy, 1950).

Minidoka County. Noted at Rupert (1919-21) between the dates of September 7 and May 13 (Davis, 1935).

Habits. Juncos are hardy birds, for even during the most severe winters, when temperatures register a minimum of twenty to thirty degrees below zero, and the snow reaches a depth of three feet or more, small flocks can be encountered daily in Latah County feeding on the seeds of weeds sticking above the snow. In early March there is a perceptible increase in numbers, and for the following month numerous flocks, at times totalling as many as two hundred individuals, can be seen at the edges of the open fields in the valleys. At Lewiston, where this species occurred as a fairly common winter resident, my extreme dates of occurrence are August 21 (1957) and April 29 (1957).

On the basis of available data it would appear that *montanus* normally rears two broods each year, the first in May, the second in late June and July. Rust (1915) states that he saw a female at Coeur d'Alene gathering nesting material as early as March 27. On May 8 five nests were found, in each five eggs, and on June 27 another nest that also held five fresh eggs. He noted young already able to fly on May 19. Verner (1953) found two nests at Harvard on July 15 and 16, 1952, each with four eggs. They were "fifty yards from each other in an earth bank three feet above the road." On Moscow Mountain, north of Moscow, I flushed a female from a nest on June 4, 1950, that held four fresh eggs, and was well concealed in a bank at the side of the road. Almost without exception the nest of the Oregon Junco is on the ground, so one found at Headquarters, with the female incubating, on May 17, 1953, was of unusual interest. An old Robin's nest on a rafter under the eaves of a house was being used, the original cavity being merely relined with fine grasses and a little horse hair. In 1955 the spring was unusually cold and backward, and this weather apparently tempted the juncos to nest in small numbers in the valleys. For the first time in my experience several pairs remained throughout the summer in the Arboretum on the university campus, a brood of fully fledged young being seen there on June 16.

Breeding records for *mearnsi* are limited to three localities in Idaho, and in view of the higher altitude involved it is more or less to be expected that nesting activities are apparently delayed until June. Rust (1917) reports a nest found in Little Dry Creek Canyon, in Clark County, that held large young on July 8, 1916, and was concealed under a ledge of rock. At Targhee Pass, at an altitude of seven thousand feet, I flushed a female from a nest that held five fresh eggs on June 12, 1957, and was sunken flush with the ground and well concealed at the foot of a clump of sagebrush on an open ridge. Another nest found at Willow Creek Summit (altitude 7,000 feet) on July 14, 1958, held newly hatched young, and was as usual sunken flush with the ground and well concealed at the base of a large mountain mahogany.

Ellison (1934) states that in cutover areas at Priest River juncos were noted eating the seeds of *Pinus, monticola, Pseudotsuga taxifolia,* and *Larix occidentalis.*

Junco oreganus montanus Ridgway

Montanus is the race that occurs as a breeding bird in the northern half of the state, and south along the western edge almost to the Nevada line. It winters commonly throughout its breeding range, but during the interval from November until March it leaves the higher altitudes for the more open valleys, and it is doubtful if it can be found then above three thousand feet.

Specimens representing the breeding population have been taken at Coeur d'Alene, Potlatch, Moscow, Deary (Latah County), Headquarters, McCall, Cuddy Mountain (Washington County), and Silver City (Owyhee County).

Numerous specimens taken in Latah County from late November to early February, 1947 through 1958, were found to be typical of *montanus,* as were specimens representing wintering populations taken at Coyote Canyon (Nez Perce County), Lewiston, Council, Weiser, De Lamar, Oreana, and Homedale.

A male collected at Lewiston April 8, 1958, is a hybrid between *oreganus* and *hyemalis,* but closer to *oreganus* in its characters.

Junco oreganus mearnsi Ridgway

This distinctive race is a common breeding bird in the southeastern corner of the state. Steel (1956) considered it a common resident species at Grays Lake, but its actual status here during the winter months is open to question, as no specimens identified as *mearnsi* have been collected at Grays Lake at this time of the year. On March 21, 1967, I took a female representing this race as it fed with other juncos in underbrush on Dry Creek, four miles north of Boise. As this is a rather early date for the spring migration, it is not improbable that *mearnsi* winters in small numbers in Ada County.

During the course of my field work in the state, specimens representing the breeding population and identified as *mearnsi* have been taken as follows: Lemhi County, Shoup, female June 6, 1949, Lost Trail Pass, female June 30, 1950; Custer County, Willow Creek Summit, male, female May 19, 1951, Mount Borah (8,000 feet), male July 12, 1958; Blaine County,

Ketchum, female June 24, 1950, male Sun Valley April 14, 1964; **Fremont** County, Targhee Pass, male June 12, 1957; Bonneville County, Gray, males June 13, 1949, May 30, 1952, June 8, 1957, females June 13, 1949, June 8, 1957; Caribou County, Wayan, male May 22, 1951; Bannock County, Pocatello, female June 10, 1955; Cassia County, Albion, female June 21, 1949 (with a male Gray-headed Junco [*Junco caniceps*]; apparently a mated pair).

In the Denver Museum of Natural History there are specimens of *mearnsi* taken in 1935 by Pierce Brodkorb during the summer months in Fremont County (Sawtelle Peak), Teton County (Horseshoe Creek), Bear Lake County (Preuse Creek, Snowdrift Mountain, Home Canyon), Franklin County (Emigration Canyon).

Junco oreganus shufeldti Coale

Shufeldti is the breeding junco of southwestern British Columbia and western Washington, and as it occurs commonly on the eastern slopes of the coast ranges it is not surprising that it is a common winter resident in Idaho. Over an interval of eleven years, 1947-58, I collected seventy specimens of *shufeldti*, largely in the northern part of the state. Of this number thirty-one were typical of this race; the remaining thirty-nine were intermediate in their characters having the dark brown upperparts of *shufeldti*, and the lighter gray coloration of the head and neck characteristic of *montanus*. It would appear therefore that this winter population of *shufeldti* came to a large extent from an area of intergradation between this race and *montanus*, and were from the eastern part of the range of *shufeldti*.

Specimens typical of *shufeldti* were taken as follows: Kootenai County, Coeur d'Alene, male January 8, 1957; Latah County, Potlatch, males October 8, 1949, February 19 and December 8, 1957, Viola, male December 20, 1949, female February 4, 1951, Moscow, males November 30, 1948, January 12, September 22, October 3 and 28, December 30, 1949, January 16, 1950, October 13 and December 2, 1952, December 28, 1956, females November 9 and 19, 1948, December 23, 1949, January 20, 1957; Nez Perce County, Lewiston, males September 24 and November 12, 1949, December 4 and 9, 1956, female September 21, 1952; Clearwater County, Headquarters, males November 11, 1951, October 22, 1952; Washington County, Weiser, female November 22, 1951; Ada County, Boise, male December 10, 1957.

Specimens approaching *montanus* in their characters but closer to *shufeldti* were taken at Potlatch, extreme dates November 21 (1956) and March 23 (1958), Moscow, November 7 (1949) and April 22 (1950), Lewiston September 19 (1956) and March 17 (1957), Weiser November 22, 1951, Pocatello November 10, 1957.

In the Denver Museum of Natural History there are specimens of *shufeldti*, identified by H. C. Oberholser, taken by Pierce Brodkorb in southern Idaho as follows: Glenns Ferry, Elmore County, February 9, 1930; Blackfoot, Bingham County, February 13 and 15, 1930; Malad City, Oneida County, April 5, 1930; Blaine County, September 18, 1931; Little Lost

River, Butte County, September 25, 1931; Mud Lake, Jefferson County, October 11-27, and November 5, 1931; Bingham County, December 23, 1931; Bannock County, January 3, 1932.

Hurd (1924) states that specimens taken by R. E. Snodgrass at Orofino September 9, 1902, and by W. T. Shaw at Troy March 31, 1910, were identified as *shufeldti* by H. C. Oberholser.

Junco caniceps caniceps (Woodhouse): GRAY-HEADED JUNCO

General Distribution. Breeds from Nevada, southern Idaho, and southern Wyoming south to California, northern Arizona and northern New Mexico. Winters south to northern Mexico (Sinaloa and Durango) and western Texas.

Status in Idaho. Known at the present time as a fairly common but rather local breeding bird in Cassia County.

This species was first recorded in Idaho by W. B. Davis who took specimens (now in the Museum of Vertebrate Zoology, Berkeley) on Mount Harrison, ten miles south of Albion, June 13-16, 1936.

I personally noted this junco in small numbers at Albion (Howell Canyon) June 21, 1949, and at the Silent City of Rocks, west of Almo, June 19, 1949, and June 12, 1960. Specimens were taken on both the latter dates to verify the identification.

Habits. The Gray-headed Junco apparently has rather exacting requirements, for in my experience it occurs in Idaho only on the higher ridges (between six thousand feet and seven thousand feet) characterized by stretches of stunted junipers and extensive thickets of mountain mahogany. To date it has been recorded only in Cassia County, but further field work should reveal its presence elsewhere in the extreme southern edge of the state where similar habitat exists. It possibly winters at lower altitudes in this part of the state, but until specimens are taken at this time of the year it must be considered a summer resident only.

Spizella arborea ochracea Brewster: TREE SPARROW

General Distribution. Breeds from northern Alaska, northern Yukon, and northern Mackenzie south to northern British Columbia, southern Yukon, and central Mackenzie. Winters from southern British Columbia, southern Saskatchewan, South Dakota and northern Iowa south to northern California, central Arizona, central New Mexico, and central Texas.

Status in Idaho. A fairly common winter resident throughout the state.

In view of its regular occurrence in Idaho each winter it is rather surprising to what a large extent this distinctive sparrow has been overlooked by those interested in the avifauna of the state. There is but one published record for the Tree Sparrow in northern Idaho, that of Merrill (1898) who stated that it was rare in winter at Fort Sherman (Coeur d'Alene).

Over an interval of eleven years, 1947-58, I found this species a regular and fairly common winter resident in the northern part of the state, my records of occurrence, summarized briefly, being as follows:

Latah County. Small flocks noted at Moscow between the extreme dates of October 22 (1950) and March 27 (1955), at Potlatch February 14 and 28, 1953, and at Genesee March 7, 1954.

Nez Perce County. Noted at Lewiston each winter between the extreme dates of October 16 (1950) and April 10 (1958).

Clearwater County. One record for Headquarters, March 29, 1952; at Weippe a single bird was seen March 29, 1952, and flocks comprising eight to twelve individuals were noted during the winter of 1952-53 on the following dates: November 6, December 10 and 24, February 7 and 24, March 24.

In order to verify the presence of the Tree Sparrow in northern Idaho, and to determine the subspecies represented by this winter population, a series of specimens was taken as follows: Latah County, Potlatch, males February 14 and 28, 1953, female February 14, 1953, Moscow, males October 23 and 25, November 2 and 16, 1948, November 8, 16, and 30, 1949, January 28, 1951, December 1, 1952, November 21, 1956, females October 29, November 2 and 21, December 1, 1948, March 24, December 16 and 21, 1949, October 22 and December 28, 1950, January 24, 1954, March 27 and November 14, 1955, Genesee, male March 7, 1954; Nez Perce County, Lewiston, males October 16, 1950, November 4, 1953, January 13 and October 24, 1956, March 3 and 19, and November 1, 1957, April 4, 1958, females December 13, 1948, October 16, 1950, December 21, 1952, November 4, 1953, April 1 and 8, 1954, April 4 and 6, and November 13, 1955, March 24 and April 1, 1957, April 8 and 10, 1958; Clearwater County, Headquarters, male March 29, 1952, Weippe, males November 6, December 10 and 24, 1952, March 24, 1953, females March 29, December 10 and 24, 1952, February 7 and March 24, 1953.

Without exception all the above specimens represented the pale western race *ochracea*.

In southern Idaho there is also but one published record for the Tree Sparrow, that of Davis (1935) who reported it at Rupert, in Minidoka County, as a winter visitant, his extreme dates of occurrence (1919-21) being October 13 and April 11.

In the Denver Museum of Natural History there are specimens identified by H. C. Oberholser as *ochracea* that were taken by Pierce Brodkorb as follows: Parma, Canyon County, January 26, 1930; Burley, Cassia County, March 4, 1930; Blackfoot, Bingham County, March 12 and 17, 1930; Montpelier, Bear Lake County, January 14, 18, 24 and 25, 1931; Mud Lake, Jefferson County, October 20 and 24, and November 14 and 15, 1931; Twin Falls, Twin Falls County, February 4 and 14, 1932; Gooding County, February 21, 1932.

I noted one small flock at Salmon, Lemhi County, November 2, 1949, and took two specimens, a male and female, that day.

Habits. In view of the fact that this sparrow shuns wooded areas, and is essentially a bird of the more open country one wonders why it was given such an inappropriate name. In Idaho the flocks encountered during the winter months will be found in thickets and underbrush bordering open fields, or the sides of roads, and are not infrequently associated with juncos and song sparrows. In such a situation single birds are usually seen. The flocks that are normally observed rarely exceed six or eight individuals, the largest number noted at one time being a flock of sixteen at Moscow on December 12, 1949.

Spizella passerina boreophila Oberholser: CHIPPING SPARROW

General Distribution. Breeds from central Alaska, central Yukon, and central Mackenzie south to northern Utah, northern Colorado, and central Nebraska. Winters from southern California and northern Texas south in Mexico to Michoacan and Puebla.

Status in Idaho. A common summer resident throughout the state.

Bonner County. Common at Clark Fork during the summer of 1917 (Burleigh, 1923); again found to be a common summer resident in 1957; at Sandpoint an occasional singing male was seen June 24, 1957 (Burleigh).

Kootenai County. Arrives at Fort Sherman (Coeur d'Alene) the last week in April; common in summer (Merrill, 1898); an abundant summer resident at Coeur d'Alene, 1910-14; arrives the middle of April; common by May 1; flocks noted from early August until late September; one bird seen October 8 (Rust, 1915); one breeding pair noted at the upper end of Lake Coeur d'Alene July 1-10, 1943 (Yocom, 1946).

Shoshone County. A common summer resident on the St. Joe National Forest, 1921-41, occurring from the valleys to the higher ridges; present from late April until September (Hand, 1941).

Latah County. Common and widely distributed in the county June through August, 1947 (Johnston, 1949); an uncommon summer resident at Harvard, 1951-52 (Verner, 1953); a common summer resident throughout the county, 1947-58, usually appearing the latter part of April, and being only infrequently seen after early October (Burleigh).

Nez Perce County. A rare transient at Lewiston; two records, single birds October 16, 1951, and April 16, 1956 (Burleigh).

Clearwater County. An uncommon summer resident at Headquarters, on the wooded ridges about the town; a flock of eight birds, belated migrants, seen May 10, 1955 (Burleigh).

Idaho County. Noted in early September, 1941, in the Selway region; seen frequently in July, 1948, in the Lolo Pass region; a male carrying food collected on July 8 (Orr, 1951); several fully grown young of the year seen at White Bird Summit (4,400 feet) August 14, 1957 (Burleigh).

Valley County. This species noted on Brundage Mountain, north of McCall, June 29, 1958, an occasional pair being encountered in the more open woods almost to the top of the mountain (7,660 feet); one small flock seen at McCall (5,000 feet) September 10, 1958 (Burleigh).

Adams County. Specimens in the Museum of Vertebrate Zoology, Berkeley, taken by Gilmore on Smith Mountain July 1 and 16, 1930; fully grown young of the year seen in open woods at New Meadows June 27, 1949 (Burleigh).

Washington County. Specimens in the Museum of Vertebrate Zoology taken by Gilmore on Cuddy Mountain June 7, 15, and 17, 1930.

Boise County. Specimen taken at the junction of Dutch Creek and the Boise River July 4, 1941 (Arvey, 1947).

Elmore County. Noted in small numbers in open woods at Atlanta June 1, 1951 (Burleigh).

Owyhee County. This species found to be fairly common at Silver City June 2, 1951, occurring on the wooded ridges about the town to an altitude of eight thousand feet (Burleigh).

Lemhi County. An occasional bird noted on the wooded ridges at Shoup June 4-6, 1949 (Burleigh).

Custer County. Noted July 12, 1958, in open pine woods on Mount Borah to an altitude of eight thousand feet (Burleigh).

Blaine County. An occasional bird seen at Galena Summit (7,600 feet) July 17, 1958, and at Trail Creek Summit (7,800 feet) July 10, 1960 (Burleigh).

Fremont County. Noted in 1957 at Henrys Lake June 11, and at Macks Inn June 13 (Burleigh).

Clark County. One pair seen at the head of Little Dry Creek Canyon June 11, 1916 (Rust, 1917); common on Signal Mountain June 19, 1961 (Oring, 1962).

Jefferson County. An uncommon summer resident on the Camas National Wildlife Refuge in 1961, but abundant in late August (Oring, 1962).

Bonneville County. A common summer resident at Grays Lake, 1949-52; arrival dates June 3, 1950, May 17, 1951 (Steel, 1956); common on Big Elk Creek, near Palisades, August 6, 1961 (Oring, 1962).

South Central Idaho. Noted in July, 1872, on Conant Creek and at Fort Hall; "tolerably common" in 1890 in the foothills of the Salmon River Mountains; a specimen taken at Sawtooth Lake October 2 (Merriam, 1891); a common summer resident in 1949 in the south-central counties (Levy, 1950).

Minidoka County. Reported by Davis (1935) as a summer resident at Rupert; extreme dates of occurrence (1919-21) April 11 and October 2; eggs May 20.

Cassia County. Fairly common June 19-21, 1949, and again June 12, 1960, at the Silent City of Rocks west of Almo, frequenting the mountain mahogany thickets on the juniper covered ridges; noted in small numbers on Goose Creek, south of Oakley, June 6, 1957 (Burleigh).

To verify the occurrence of this species in Idaho specimens were taken, 1948-60, representing the breeding population in various parts of the state. All were found to represent the northwestern race, *boreophila*, and are as follows: Bonner County, Clark Fork, male June 23, 1957, Sandpoint, male June 24, 1957; Kootenai County, Coeur d'Alene, males August 14, 1948,

April 19, 1950, female September 23, 1948, Hauser, male July 21, 1952; Latah County, Potlatch, male October 1, 1956, females September 4, 1948, June 30, 1957, Moscow, twenty-three specimens between the extreme dates of April 16 (1952) and October 13 (1948); Nez Perce County, Lewiston, male April 16, 1956, female October 16, 1951; Clearwater County, Headquarters, male May 10, 1955; Idaho County, White Bird Summit, male August 14, 1957; Adams County, New Meadows, female June 27, 1949; Valley County, McCall, male June 29, 1958, female September 10, 1958; Elmore County, Atlanta, female June 1, 1951; Custer County, Mount Borah, male July 12, 1958; Blaine County, Trail Creek Summit, male July 10, 1960; Fremont County, Henrys Lake, male June 11, 1957, Macks Inn, male June 13, 1957; Caribou County, Wayan, male June 7, 1957; Bonneville County, Gray, male June 23, 1960; Cassia County, Oakley (Goose Creek), male June 6, 1957, Almo (Silent City of Rocks), male June 12, 1960.

Habits. The Chipping Sparrow, in Idaho, is essentially a bird of open coniferous woods; thick woods are consistently shunned, even in migration. Altitude is no factor in its distribution, but it does have a bearing on the species of conifers accepted by this bird during the breeding season. At lower elevations (2,000 feet to approximately 4,500 feet) it commonly occurs on the south slopes of the ridges covered by open stands of ponderosa pine. On the higher ridges it is equally common where the characteristic vegetation consists of an open growth of spruce and firs.

In Latah County the Chipping Sparrow generally appears in the spring late in April, and it is the end of September before there is a noticeable decrease in the numbers seen. At Moscow my extreme dates of occurrence are April 16 (1952) and October 13 (1948 and 1951); the average date of arrival is April 26.

Rust (1915) reports two nests found at Coeur d'Alene, one with four eggs June 11 that was in a spirea bush, the other with half-grown young June 14 that was in a "hawbush." In 1917 I succeeded in finding two nests at Clark Fork. The first held four well-incubated eggs on July 4, and was six feet from the ground in a small Douglas fir at the edge of an open field in the valley. The second held four fresh eggs on July 19, and was up five and a half feet in a small alpine fir at the top of a ridge. Both were compactly built of weed stems, rootlets, and grasses, and were lined with horsehair.

Spizella pallida (Swainson): CLAY-COLORED SPARROW

General Distribution. Breeds from northern British Columbia, southern Mackenzie, and western Ontario south to southeastern Colorado, southern Nebraska, southern Wisconsin and central Michigan. Winters from northern Mexico and southern Texas south to southern Mexico (Guerrero and Oaxaca).

Status in Idaho. Of accidental occurrence in the northern part of the state.

The Clay-colored Sparrow has been recorded on but one occasion in Idaho. On June 21, 1953, a male was collected as it sang from the top of a bush on an open slope on Paradise Ridge, south of Moscow. No others were seen at this spot, or, despite a careful search in succeeding days, in similar habitat in Latah County. At the time it was thought that this species might possibly nest sparingly in the vicinity of Moscow, but apparently this one individual was merely a straggler from its normal breeding range.

Habits. This species is partial to open country, its presence in wooded areas being confined to slashings or old burns. Brush-covered hillsides are favorite spots, and here the nest is built in a bush within a few feet of the ground. Areas like Paradise Ridge offer suitable habitat for this inconspicuous little sparrow, and as it occurs during the summer months in Montana it would not be surprising if it eventually were found nesting in Idaho.

Spizella breweri Cassin: BREWER'S SPARROW

General Distribution. Breeds from southern Yukon, central Alberta, southern Saskatchewan and southern North Dakota south to southern California, central Arizona, and northern New Mexico. Winters in the southern part of its breeding range, and south in Mexico to Jalisco and Guanajuato.

Status in Idaho. A common summer resident in the southern part of the state. Uncommon and of very local occurrence in northern Idaho.

Latah County. Uncommon; noted only on Paradise Ridge, south of Moscow, during the summer of 1947 (Johnston, 1949); an extremely scarce summer resident, 1948-58, as a breeding bird being found in small numbers only on Paradise Ridge (Burleigh).

Nez Perce County. Noted for the first time at Lewiston, during the summer months, in 1953, when singing males were seen July 13 about underbrush at the edges of the open fields east of Lewiston Orchards (Burleigh).

Adams County. Seen at Council in 1958 on April 28, and again from August 23 to September 20 (Newhouse, 1960).

Owyhee County. Common at Riddle May 28 through June 3, 1934, and nesting (Davis, 1935).

Blaine County. This species found to be fairly common on the open mountainsides north of Ketchum June 25-28, 1950, reaching an altitude of eight thousand feet on Easley Peak (Burleigh).

Clark County. Most common breeding bird in 1916 in the sagebrush areas; earliest nesting date June 16; three eggs usually found (Rust, 1917).

Jefferson County. A common summer resident in 1961 on the Camas National Wildlife Refuge; specimens taken there June 5, July 7 and 26, and August 27 and 28 (Oring, 1962).

Bonneville County. A common summer resident at Grays Lake, 1949-51 (Steel, 1956).

Power County. Specimens taken five miles southwest of American Falls July 4, 1949 (Jollie, in litt.).

South Central Idaho. A nest found on Conant Creek July 21, 1872, with three "nearly fresh eggs"; common in 1890 in sagebrush "on the Snake Plains," and in the Birch and Lemhi valleys (Merriam, 1891); an abundant breeding bird in 1949 in the south-central counties (Levy, 1950).

Minidoka County. A common summer resident at Rupert, 1919-21; extreme dates of occurrence April 11 and October 2; eggs May 20 (Davis, 1935).

Cassia County. This species found to be fairly common on the open ridges at the Silent City of Rocks, west of Almo, June 19-21, 1949 (Burleigh).

Habits. The Brewer's Sparrow is so closely associated with sagebrush in southern Idaho that it was rather unexpected to find it relatively common on the open upper slopes of Paradise Ridge, south of Moscow, where the only vegetation is scattered thickets of serviceberry. In this rather limited area as many as four singing males could be encountered in the course of an hour during the spring and early summer months. There is habitat very similar to this in the valleys, but only in late August and early September did this species leave the top of the ridge. In the spring it was usually present by the middle of May, and in the fall it lingered in small numbers until early September, my extreme dates of occurrence being May 13 (1950) and September 11 (1951). The earliest date on which I recorded this species in the valley was August 30 (1950), a single bird being seen about a thicket at the side of a road.

Spizella breweri breweri Cassin

The nominate race of *Spizella breweri* is the breeding form throughout the state, twenty specimens taken from 1948 through 1957 confirming this identification. They were collected at Moscow (sixteen specimens between the extreme dates of May 13, 1950, and September 11, 1951), at Lewiston (two males July 13, 1953), in Bonneville County (a male at Gray May 26, 1951), in Caribou County (a male at Soda Springs May 25, 1951), and a male at Pebble, in Bannock County, June 8, 1949.

Spizella breweri taverneri Swarth and Brooks

This northwestern race of the Brewer's Sparrow, occurring during the summer months in southern Yukon, British Columbia and western Alberta, is known at present as a rare fall transient in Idaho. It is not improbable, however, that further collecting will reveal its presence in larger numbers than the few records now indicate. It was first taken in the state in 1957 when I collected a female in immature plumage at Lewiston on September 24. The only other record is that of Oring (1962) who collected a male in immature plumage four miles southwest of Hamer, in Jefferson County, August 28, 1961. *Taverneri* is characterized by being larger and darker than the nominate race.

Zonotrichia querula (Nuttall): HARRIS' SPARROW

General Distribution. Breeds from northern Mackenzie and southern Keewatin south to northern Saskatchewan and northern Manitoba. Winters from southern British Columbia, Idaho, northern Colorado, Nebraska, and central Iowa south to southern California, central Arizona, southern Texas, and northern Louisiana.

Status in Idaho. Of casual occurrence during the late winter and early spring months.

Harris' Sparrow was first recorded in Idaho by Wyman (1911), who saw two birds at Nampa January 1, 1911, and collected one, a female, that day.

I have three records for the northern part of the state, single birds seen (and taken) at Lewiston April 4, 1953, at Potlatch April 19, 1953, and at Moscow January 2, 1955. The first two were males, the third a female.

Habits. In the northwestern United States the Harris' Sparrow reaches the extreme western limits of its range, so it is more or less to be expected that in Idaho it would only be of casual occurrence in migration. In my experience in Idaho single birds will be found feeding with flocks of white-crowned sparrows; as under such circumstances they could easily be over-looked, it is not improbable that this species is more common than the few records would imply. Its center of abundance in migration is on the eastern edge of the Great Plains, and it is commonly observed there in flocks of varying size, feeding about thickets and stretches of underbrush bordering open fields and roadsides.

Zonotrichia leucophrys (Forster): WHITE-CROWNED SPARROW

General Distribution. Breeds from northern Alaska, northern Yukon, northern Mackenzie, Keewatin, northern Quebec and Labrador south to central California, central Arizona and northern New Mexico, and to central Manitoba, southern Quebec, and Newfoundland. Winters from southern British Columbia, Idaho, Wyoming, Kansas, Kentucky, and western North Carolina south to southern Mexico (Michoacan, Queretaro), the Gulf coast, and Cuba.

Status in Idaho. A fairly common but local summer resident throughout the state; abundant in migration; winters irregularly and in small numbers in Latah County, commonly at Lewiston, in Nez Perce County, and possibly fairly commonly in the southwestern corner of the state.

Boundary County. This species found to be fairly common July 4, 1957, in thick brush well toward the top of Continental Mountain (altitude approximately 6,500 feet); within a rather limited area three singing males were seen, and two females carrying food (Burleigh).

Bonner County. A common fall migrant at Clark Fork in 1917; first small flock seen August 27; already fairly common by September 9 (Burleigh, 1923); scattered small flocks noted at Clark Fork September 29, 1957 (Burleigh).

Kootenai County. Fairly common at Fort Sherman (Coeur d'Alene) in the spring and in the fall (Merrill, 1898); an abundant fall migrant at Coeur d'Alene, 1910-14; observed in September and October (Rust, 1915); a single bird, an early spring migrant, seen at Coeur d'Alene April 19, 1950 (Burleigh).

Shoshone County. A common summer resident on the St. Joe National Forest, 1921-41, occurring in the Canadian and Hudsonian zones; noted at lower altitudes in migration, in May and again in September and October (Hand, 1941).

Latah County. A common migrant both in the spring and in the fall, 1947-58, numerous small flocks being noted in late April and early May, and again from late August until the latter part of November; of casual occurrence during the winter months (Burleigh).

Nez Perce County. A common winter resident at Lewiston, 1947-58, appearing in late August, and lingering in the spring until the middle of May (Burleigh).

Clearwater County. Migrants noted at Weippe October 21, 1952; a singing male, apparently a breeding bird, collected June 5, 1954, in underbrush on a wooded ridge at Headquarters (Burleigh).

Idaho County. Common in July, 1948, in willow and alder thickets "in the higher parts of the northern Bitterroot and northeastern Clearwater Mountains"; numerous flocks seen in September, 1941, in the Selway region; four specimens taken September 11-16 found to represent the race *gambelii* (Orr, 1951).

Adams County. Specimens in the Museum of Vertebrate Zoology, Berkeley, taken by Gilmore and Borell on Smith Mountain (7,500 feet) July 12 and 13, 1930, and one-half mile east of Black Lake (6,800 feet) July 27, 1930; noted at Council in 1958, on April 28, and again from September 20 through October 7 (Newhouse, 1960).

Valley County. Specimens in the Denver Museum of Natural History taken by Pierce Brodkorb on the Payette Lakes July 16 and 29, 1929; small flocks noted at McCall September 18, 1955; two birds seen near the top of Brundage Mountain, north of McCall, June 29, 1958 (Burleigh).

Washington County. Specimens in the Museum of Vertebrate Zoology, Berkeley, taken by Gilmore and Borell on Crane Creek, fifteen miles east of Midvale, May 26 and 27, and June 2, 1930; small flocks noted at Weiser February 18, 1950, and at Cambridge November 21, 1951.

Owyhee County. Reported by Jollie (in litt.) as breeding eight miles east of Riddle; a breeding male taken there June 15, 1949; small flocks, apparently representing a wintering population, noted daily at Homedale February 20-26, 1950 (Burleigh); an occasional singing male seen at Silver City June 2, 1951, on the wooded ridges at an altitude of approximately nine thousand feet (Burleigh).

Blaine County. This species found to be a common summer resident at Ketchum, being seen, June 24-28, 1950, in underbrush along the streams in the valley, and on the mountainsides from an altitude of 7,000 feet to approximately 10,000 feet (Easley Peak and Hyndman Peak); noted in small number July 17, 1958, in willow thickets at the headwaters of the Salmon River (6,500 feet) (Burleigh).

Fremont County. An occasional singing male seen in underbrush bordering Henrys Lake June 11, 1957, and at Targhee Pass (7,000 feet) June 27, 1960 (Burleigh).

Clark County. Several pairs noted on Little Dry Creek in June, 1916 (Rust, 1917); common on Signal Peak June 19 and July 14, 1961 (Oring, 1962).

Jefferson County. Several birds in immature plumage seen on the Camas National Wildlife Refuge August 28-29, 1961 (Oring, 1962).

Bonneville County. A common summer resident at Grays Lake, 1949-51 (Steel, 1956); an occasional bird noted June 13, 1949, in the open fir woods near the top of Caribou Mountain (altitude 9,500 feet), and a single bird at this same spot May 24, 1951; on this latter date the snow still covered the ground in deep drifts (Burleigh); this species fairly common May 28, 1951, in alder thickets bordering a stream in Caribou Basin, north of Gray (Burleigh); common on Big Elk Creek, near Palisades, August 6, 1961 (Oring, 1962).

Caribou County. Several singing males noted June 1, 1952, in underbrush fringing a stream two miles west of Freedom, Wyoming (Burleigh).

Franklin County. Specimen in the Denver Museum of Natural History taken by Pierce Brodkorb in Emigration Canyon June 5, 1930.

South Central Idaho. A specimen taken at Fort Hall October 13, 1872 (recorded as *intermedia*); common in 1890 in the Pahsimeroi Mountains the middle of September; adults taken (recorded as *leucophrys*); "dozens were shot" at Sawtooth Lake in late September and early October; many seen at Shoshone Falls October 9-11 (Merriam, 1891); an uncommon breeding bird in 1949 "at the higher altitudes" in the south-central counties (Levy, 1950).

Minidoka County. Noted at Rupert March 20 through May 13, and September 16, 1919, March 13 through May 18, and September 20, 1920, and April 12, 1921 (Davis, 1935).

Cassia County. Fairly common June 19-21, 1949, in thickets and underbrush at the Silent City of Rocks, west of Almo (Burleigh); noted on Goose Creek, ten miles south of Oakley, June 25, 1949, and a breeding female collected that day (Jollie, in litt.); several small flocks seen at Burley November 13, 1957, in underbrush at the edge of the Snake River (Burleigh).

Habits. The White-crowned Sparrow as a breeding bird in Idaho will be found on the higher ridges, frequenting by preference alder and aspen thickets along the streams that are fed by melting snow until the late summer. In my experience it rarely nests below five thousand feet, and is most common between 6,500 feet and 7,500 feet. Breeding activities would appear to be at their height in June and early July. Rust (1917) found a nest on Little Dry Creek, in Clark County, that on June 20, 1916, held five eggs, while on Continental Mountain, in Boundary County, females seen July 4, 1957, were carrying food to young still in the nest.

It is a hardy species, for the first males arrive on their breeding grounds in May when the ground it still covered with deep snow, and freezing temperatures at night are the rule rather than the exception. This hardiness is emphasized by the presence of small flocks in Latah County during winters characterized by frequent blizzards and subzero temperatures.

In the fall the first arrivals in late August and early September are invariably young of the year. They gradually increase in numbers, and by the middle of September, when the first adults are noted, flocks consisting of birds in immature plumage are common and widely distributed.

Zonotrichia leucophrys oriantha Oberholser

Oriantha, distinguished from the nominate race by its paler coloration, and from *gambelii* by its black lores, is the breeding race in Idaho. Specimens representing breeding populations, and having the characters of *oriantha,* were taken in various parts of the state as follows: Boundary County, Continental Mountain, one male, two females, July 4, 1957; Clearwater County, Headquarters, male June 5, 1954; Valley County, Brundage Mountain, male June 29, 1958; Owyhee County, Silver City, male June 2, 1951; Blaine County, Easley Peak (7,000 feet), male June 25, 1950, Hyndman Peak (10,000 feet), male June 27, 1950, Headwaters of the Salmon River, two males July 17, 1958; Fremont County, Henrys Lake, male June 11, 1957, Targhee Pass (7,000 feet), male June 27, 1960; Bonneville County, Gray, males June 13, 1949, May 30, 1952, Caribou Basin, male May 28, 1951; Caribou County, Wayan, two males May 22, 1951, two miles west of Freedom, Wyoming, male May 31, 1952; Cassia County, Silent City of Rocks, two females June 19, 1949.

Since *oriantha* reaches the northern limits of its breeding range in Idaho it was not surprising that it proved to be a rather scarce migrant at Lewiston. Here specimen representing this race was taken August 28, 1958. In southern Idaho a specimen of *oriantha* was taken at Homedale February 20, 1950.

Zonotrichia leucophrys gambelii (Nuttall)

This race of the White-crowned Sparrow is a common migrant throughout the state, flocks being present from the latter part of April until the middle of May, and again from late August until the middle of November. Numerous specimens have been taken, 1947 through 1958, in the northern part of the state. At Moscow specimens of *gambelii* have been collected between the extreme dates of April 20 (1952) and May 13 (1950), and August 27 (1953) and November 30 (1947). At Lewiston, where it winters commonly, between the dates of August 27 (1950) and May 16 (1953). Specimens representing the winter months have been taken on the following dates: Moscow, December 8, 1948, January 8, 1951, December 13, 1952, January 24, 1954, January 12, 1955; Lewiston, December 27, 1948, January

19, 22 and 29, February 13, and December 29, 1949, January 11, 1950, January 1, and December 21, 1951, January 24, 1952.

Zonotrichia atricapilla (Gmelin): GOLDEN-CROWNED SPARROW

General Distribution. Breeds from western Alaska and central Yukon to southern British Columbia and southern Alberta, and in the Cascade Mountains to northern Washington. Winters from southern British Columbia south to northern Baja California.

Status in Idaho. Of casual occurrence in the northern part of the state during the fall migration; recorded once in southern Idaho.

The Golden-crowned Sparrow is another species that has apparently been largely overlooked by those interested in the avifauna of Idaho. Its occurrence during the fall months is somewhat erratic, but there are few years when at least one or two cannot be recorded in the northern part of the state. My records, based in each instance on specimens taken to verify the identification, are as follows: Moscow, September 7 and October 1, 1948, September 20, 1949, September 27, 1956; Potlatch, September 29, 1949, October 6, 1955, September 16 and 28, and October 1, 1956.

Habits. It is possible that the Golden-crowned Sparrow is not an uncommon migrant in Idaho, for it is far from conspicuous during its relatively brief appearance in the state. Without exception single birds have been seen feeding with flocks of White-crowned Sparrows in underbrush bordering open fields, and under such circumstances it could easily escape observation. It has been found during the spring months in eastern Washington, but I failed to record it in Idaho at that time of the year. However, Fichter (in litt.) reports a single bird seen in his backyard at Pocatello on May 6 and 20, 1965, the only record for the southern part of the state.

Zonotrichia albicollis (Gmelin): WHITE-THROATED SPARROW

General Distribution. Breeds from southern Yukon, central Mackenzie, central Quebec and northern Newfoundland south to central British Columbia, southern Saskatchewan, central Minnesota, northern Ohio, and northern West Virginia. Winters from eastern Kansas, southern Illinois, southern Ohio and Massachusetts south to southern Texas, the Gulf coast, and northern Florida.

Status in Idaho. Of casual occurrence in the state during the fall and early winter months.

The White-throated Sparrow was first recorded in Idaho by Wyman (1912) who collected a male in immature plumage and a female at Nampa, in Canyon County, November 2, 1911.

At Moscow I collected an adult female on October 7, 1948, and an adult male on November 30, 1956, and at Lewiston a female in immature plumage January 1, 1955.

Habits. This is another species that can be easily overlooked. The few individuals that I have encountered were feeding with flocks of juncos, and it was largely by chance that their presence was detected. Despite the fact that it breeds commonly in northern British Columbia and Alberta it is nowhere common in migration in the western United States, so it would appear that in its journeys to and from its summer home it follows a route that takes it east of the Rocky Mountain region.

Passerella iliaca (Merrem): Fox Sparrow

General Distribution. Breeds from northern Alaska, central Mackenzie, northern Quebec and northern Labrador south in the mountains to southern California, central Utah and central Colorado, and to central Saskatchewan, southern Manitoba, central Ontario, southern Quebec and Newfoundland. Winters on the Pacific coast from southern British Columbia to northern Baja California, and from southern Utah, Colorado, eastern Kansas, southern Iowa, southern Michigan and New Brunswick south to southern Arizona, southern Texas, the Gulf coast, and central Florida.

Status in Idaho. A fairly common summer resident throughout the state; one winter record for Latah County.

Boundary County. Noted in deciduous underbrush near the top of Harrison Peak (6,000 feet) July 5, 1957 (Burleigh).

Bonner County. Present after August 1, 1917, in open meadows at the top of the higher ridges north of Clark Fork (Burleigh, 1923).

Kootenai County. A rare migrant at Fort Sherman (Coeur d'Alene); specimens collected in May (Merrill, 1898); two birds seen April 19, 1950, in underbrush bordering Lake Coeur d'Alene (Burleigh).

Shoshone County. A common summer resident, 1921-41, on the St. Joe National Forest, occurring from late March until September "in the Transition and Canadian Zones" (Hand, 1941); noted at Avery June 19, 1951, in willows at the edge of the St. Joe River (Burleigh).

Benewah County. Several Fox Sparrows noted June 19, 1961 at Emida Summit (Oring, in litt.).

Latah County. Fairly common in the county June through August, 1947 (Johnston, 1949); uncommon at Harvard, and only infrequently seen during the summers of 1951-52 (Verner, 1953); a fairly common and well-distributed summer resident, 1948-58, usually appearing in late March or early April, and being rarely seen after the middle of September; one winter record, a single bird at Potlatch February 4, 1956, with a flock of Juncos in underbrush at the edge of the Palouse River (Burleigh).

Nez Perce County. This species found to be an extremely scarce spring transient at Lewiston, the few records being of single birds seen April 16 and 25, 1953, and March 20, 1955; it has never been noted there during the fall months (Burleigh).

Clearwater County. An uncommon summer resident in the vicinity of Headquarters; earliest record in the spring is one bird seen April 10, 1952; on that date the snow on the ground was still a foot deep, and the temperature at daylight registered twenty-two degrees (Burleigh).

Idaho County. "Exceedingly" scarce in 1948 "in the Bitterroot-Clearwater area"; one record, a pair seen July 8, six miles southwest of Lolo Pass; the male collected (Orr, 1951).

Adams County. Specimens in the Museum of Vertebrate Zoology, Berkeley, were taken by A. E. Borell on Smith Mountain (7,500 feet) July 13 and 14, 1930, and by R. M. Gilmore one-half mile east of Black Lake July 29, 1930; noted in small number at New Meadows May 21, 1955 (Burleigh).

Valley County. Noted in small numbers on Brundage Mountain (7,500 feet) June 29, 1958 (Burleigh).

Owyhee County. One specimen taken at Riddle June 3, 1934 (Davis, 1934); specimens taken on Mary's Creek, eight miles east of Riddle, June 19 and 20, 1949 (M. Jollie, in litt.); noted in small numbers at Triangle June 25, 1949, and at Silver City (6,000 feet) June 2, 1951 (Burleigh).

Blaine County. This species found to be a fairly common summer resident in the vicinity of Ketchum, June 24-28, 1950, occurring in underbrush bordering the streams in the valley (Burleigh).

Butte County. Noted in small numbers at Arco May 19, 1951 (Burleigh).

Bonneville County. A fairly common summer resident at Grays Lake, 1949-51; arrival date April 17, 1950 (Steel, 1956).

Bannock County. Noted in small numbers on Buckskin Creek, north of Pocatello, June 10, 1955 (Burleigh).

Bear Lake County. Specimens in the Denver Museum of Natural History were taken by Pierce Brodkorb on the Bear River, at Montpelier, in May, and in the Snowdrift Mountains, eighteen miles east of Montpelier, in June.

South Central Idaho. Found to be an uncommon summer resident "in higher elevations" (Levy, 1950).

Minidoka County. Noted at Rupert April 9, 1920 (Davis, 1935).

Cassia County. Fairly common, June 19-21, 1949, at the Silent City of Rocks, west of Almo (Burleigh).

Habits. To one familiar with the Fox Sparrow in the eastern part of the continent its distribution in Idaho comes somewhat as a surprise. Shunning the fir and spruce thickets on the mountainsides, where one would expect to find it, it spends the summer months in the deciduous underbrush, willows and alders, bordering the streams. Here it is shy and inconspicuous, and were it not for the clear ringing song of the male it could easily go unnoticed.

Its appearance in the spring in northern Idaho is apparently influenced to a large degree by the weather. When the winters are relatively mild it has been noted as early as the first week in March, but there are years when it is early April before it is seen for the first time. At Moscow my earliest date of arrival is March 8 (1950). The average date (1948 through 1958) is March 21. In the late summer the Fox Sparrow gradually disappear from the stream bottoms, and are only infrequently seen after early September. At Moscow my latest date in the fall is October 8 (1948).

Breeding activities would appear to begin shortly after the birds arrive in the spring, for on May 14, 1950, well-grown young already out of the nest were seen at the edge of the Palouse River at Potlatch.

Passerella iliaca schistacea Baird

This is the race having the widest distribution in Idaho, being found during the summer months in all but the extreme southern part of the state. Specimens typical of *schistacea* have been taken as follows: Boundary County, Harrison Peak, male July 5, 1957; Kootenai County, Coeur d'Alene. male May 4, 1950, female April 19, 1950; Latah County, Harvard, male July 8, 1953, Potlatch, males March 29, 1950, April 20, 1952, April 14, 1954, Moscow, males August 2, 1948, March 14 and 17, 1950, April 7, 1953, females October 8, 1948, March 11 and April 12, 1950, April 7, 1953; Nez Perce County, Lewiston, males April 16, 1953, March 20, 1955; Adams County, New Meadows, male May 21, 1955; Blaine County, Ketchum, males June 24 and 28, 1950; Butte County, Arco, female May 19, 1951.

Passerella iliaca olivacea Aldrich

This race nests in eastern Washington, and possibly to a limited extent in the Palouse Country of Idaho, but its actual status in the state has yet to be determined. Specimens typical of *olivacea* were taken during March and April when Fox Sparrows were migrating to their breeding grounds, so in each instance individuals collected could have been transients and not birds that would have remained to nest. These specimens are as follows: Latah County, Potlatch, male March 24, 1958, Moscow, males March 8 and 15, 1950; Nez Perce County, Lewiston, female April 25, 1953; Clearwater County, Headquarters, male April 10, 1952. Of interest is the fact that my one winter record, a male collected at Potlatch February 4, 1956, is typical of *olivacea*.

Eight additional specimens proved to be intermediate in their characters, and while closer to *schistacea* approached *olivacea* in the color of their upperparts. These were taken at Moscow April 29, 1948, March 24 and May 28, 1950, May 8, 1951, March 31 and April 4, 1952, and April 2, 1953, and at Potlatch March 21, 1949. Another specimen taken at Moscow September 30, 1952, is intermediate between *olivacea* an *altivagans*.

Passerella iliaca swarthi Behle and Selander

This race occurs as a breeding bird only in the extreme southern part of the state. Specimens of *swarthi* were taken at Pocatello by Jewett June 17, 1911; by Arvey April 2, 1939; and by me at Gray June 17, 1949, and May 23, 1951, at Pocatello June 10, 1955, at the Silent City of Rocks June 19, 1949, and June 8, 1951, and at Triangle June 25, 1949.

Behle and Selander (1951) report specimens of this race taken in Owyhee County (Riddle), Bannock County (Pocatello), and Bear Lake County (Paris).

Passerella iliaca sinuosa Grinnell

This Alaskan race is apparently an uncommon transient in Idaho. Specimens of *sinuosa* have been collected at Moscow both in the spring and in the fall, and as all were taken in 1950, it is not improbable that there are occasional years when there is a definite movement of this dark race away from the coast. I collected a female March 11 and a male March 20, Levy (1959) a male March 27, and a female October 1.

Melospiza lincolnii (Audubon): LINCOLN'S SPARROW

General Distribution. Breeds from northwestern Alaska, central Yukon, southern Mackenzie, northern Quebec and Newfoundland south in the mountains of the western United States to southern California, central Arizona and northern New Mexico, and to southern Manitoba, northern Minnesota, northern Wisconsin, northern Michigan, and northern New York. Winters from northern California, central Arizona, Oklahoma, central Missouri and northern Georgia south to Central America (El Salvador), the Gulf coast, and central Florida.

Status in Idaho. A fairly common but local summer resident in suitable habitat throughout the state; in the spring a scarce transient in the valleys, but common in the fall.

Bonner County. An occasional pair noted during the summer of 1917 in open meadows at the tops of the ridges north of Clark Fork; timid and difficult to approach (Burleigh, 1923).

Kootenai County. A specimen taken near Garwood September 29, 1914 (Rust, 1915).

Shoshone County. A locally common summer resident, 1921-41, in the Canadian Zone; "the typical bird about meadows at the Twin Creek Ranger Station" (Hand, 1941).

Latah County. Two specimens, a male and a female, taken by S. E. Piper on the Potlatch River July 12, 1898 (Johnston, 1949); a rather scarce spring transient and a common fall transient (1948-58) in the more open valleys throughout the county (Burleigh).

Nez Perce County. A scarce spring transient and a fairly common fall transient (1948-58) at Lewiston (Burleigh).

Adams County. Specimens in the Museum of Vertebrate Zoology, Berkeley, taken by A. E. Borell a half-mile east of Black Lake July 26, 1930, and by D. H. Blanchard three miles west of Payette Lake July 5 and 6, 1932.

Valley County. Specimens in the Museum of Vertebrate Zoology, Berkeley, taken by D. H. Blanchard five miles east of Warm Lake July 8 and 9, 1932.

Custer County. A specimen taken at Clayton August 14, 1949 (Levy, 1950); an occasional bird noted at Stanley July 16, 1958, in willow thickets at the edge of the Salmon River (Burleigh).

Blaine County. This species found to be fairly common at Ketchum July 24-28, 1950, occurring in thickets and underbrush bordering both the Big Wood River and the smaller streams (Burleigh).

Fremont County. Noted sparingly during the summer of 1916 along streams in the canyons (Rust, 1917); a specimen in the Museum of Vertebrate Zoology, Berkeley, was taken by R. W. Smith at Ashton August 15, 1939; M. Jollie (in litt.) noted this species fifteen miles east of Drummond July 17, 1949, and collected two breeding males there that day.

Bonneville County. A rare summer resident at Grays Lake, 1949-51 (Steel, 1956); in willow thickets on Eagle Creek, north of Gray, three singing males were seen June 11, 1949, and a female in immature plumage was collected at this same spot August 26, 1955 (Burleigh); in the Caribou Basin, north of Gray, two singing males were seen May 28, 1951 (Burleigh).

South Central Idaho. In 1890 specimens were taken September 16 at an altitude of 9,700 feet in the Pahsimeroi Mountains, and at Sawtooth Lake September 28 (Merriam, 1891); a fairly common breeding bird in 1949 along streams "of the higher montane areas" in south-central Idaho (Levy, 1950).

Cassia County. A specimen taken on Goose Creek, ten miles south of Oakley, September 12, 1951 (Levy, 1962).

Habits. In Idaho the Lincoln's Sparrow is, during the summer months, typically a bird of the high alpine meadows. I have never recorded it then below six thousand feet but above this altitude it is a fairly common breeding bird to at least nine thousand feet. Being at all times rather shy and secretive it has to be looked for to be seen, and were it not for the clear bubbling song of the male, suggestive of a wren, this species could be easily overlooked on its breeding grounds.

In the northern part of the state it is only infrequently seen during the spring migration, but in the fall it is common and can be seen daily from late August until early October. It never occurs in flocks, single birds, rarely two and never more than three, being found in thickets and stretches of underbrush in the more open valleys. My extreme dates of occurrence for Potlatch are September 1 (1952) and October 8 (1952), for Moscow August 30 (1950) and October 9 (1950), for Lewiston August 29 (1950) and October 16 (1950 and 1951).

Melospiza lincolnii alticola (Miller and McCabe)

Alticola is the race that breeds throughout the Rocky Mountain region. It can be distinguished from *lincolnii*, the nominate race, by its larger size and grayer upperparts. Specimens representing the breeding population were taken in Custer County (Stanley, July 16, 1958), Blaine County (Ketchum, June 26, 1950), and Bonneville County (Gray, June 11, 1949, August 26, 1955, Caribou Basin, May 28, 1951). In the northern part of the state *alticola* was found to be a rather uncommon transient in the spring, my few records, based on specimens (in each instance males), being as follows: Moscow, April 29, 1948, April 26, 1949, Potlatch, May 10, 1953, Lewiston, April 6, 1955, April 1 and 8, 1956, April 12 and May 4, 1957. In the fall, however, it was common, and noted almost daily in thickets and underbrush in stream bottoms, and at the edges of fields and pastures. Numerous specimens were taken typical of this race, extreme dates of occurrence being as follows: Moscow August 30 (1950) and October 9 (1950), Potlatch September 1 (1952) and October 2 (1955), Lewiston August 29 (1956) and October 16 (1950).

Melospiza lincolnii lincolnii (Audubon)

Although the status of the nominate race of the Lincoln's Sparrow is at present that of a scarce fall transient in the state, it is not improbable that the breeding populations in the extreme northern counties represent *M. l. lincolnii*. Specimens, however, are unfortunately not available to determine this point. My few records for the fall migration are of females taken at Lewiston October 4 and 16, 1951, and at Potlatch October 8, 1952, and September 13, 1957.

Melospiza georgiana ericrypta Oberholser: SWAMP SPARROW

General Distribution. Breeds from southern Mackenzie, central Quebec and Newfoundland south to northern British Columbia, central Alberta, northern North Dakota, northern Minnesota, and southern Quebec. Winters south to Mexico (Jalisco and Tamaulipas), eastern Texas, the Gulf coast, and northeastern Florida.

Status in Idaho. A rare fall transient and possible winter resident in the northern part of the state.

The only records for the occurrence of this species in Idaho are of two birds, both males, that I collected at Lewiston December 1 and 21, 1953. Both were found to represent the pale western race, *ericrypta*.

Habits. In view of the fact that the Swamp Sparrow breeds commonly north of Idaho, in Alberta, it is probably more numerous in migration than the above records indicate. Single birds feeding with flocks of other sparrows can be easily overlooked, and while it prefers the vicinity of water it can be found just as often about thickets and underbrush far removed from the nearest stream. Consequently it could occur almost anywhere in the more open valleys, and to see one would usually necessitate a careful scrutiny of the numerous flocks of sparrows encountered during the fall months.

Melospiza melodia (Wilson): SONG SPARROW

General Distribution. Breeds from southern Alaska, southern Yukon, southern Mackenzie, central Quebec and Newfoundland south to southern Mexico (Michoacan, Puebla), and to northern Kansas, northern Arkansas, northern Georgia, and western North Carolina. Winters north to southern British Columbia, South Dakota, southern Michigan, southern Quebec, and central New Brunswick.

Status in Idaho. A common resident species throughout the state, although less numerous during the winter months; rarely recorded from November to February above five thousand feet.

Few birds are more numerous or have a wider distribution in Idaho than the Song Sparrow. Thickets and underbrush at the edge of, or near, water are given preference, but a brushy site is not infrequently accepted some distance from the nearest stream or marsh. This species is essentially a bird of the Transition Zone, but where there is suitable habitat it breeds commonly to an altitude of approximately 6,600 feet (Henrys Lake). It is not known to breed higher than this, and it is doubtful if it does so. Localities where the Song Sparrow has been recorded in Idaho during the summer months, in most instances as occurring commonly, are too numerous to be listed in any detail, but include the following: Boundary County (Porthill, Bonners Ferry); Bonner County (Clark Fork, Priest Lake); Kootenai County (Coeur d'Alene, Blue Lake); Benewah County (St. Maries); Latah County (Harvard, Potlatch, Moscow, Genesee); Nez Perce County (Lewiston); Clearwater County (Ahsahka, Weippe, Headquarters); Lewis County (Craigmont); Idaho County (Cottonwood, Grangeville, White Bird, Riggins); Adams County (New Meadows, Council); Valley County (McCall); Washington County (Cambridge, Weiser); Canyon County (Parma, Caldwell); Boise County (Horseshoe Bend); Ada County (Boise); Elmore County (Mountain Home, Glenns Ferry); Owyhee County (Homedale, Three Creek, Triangle, Riddle); Lemhi County (Salmon); Custer County (Challis): Blaine County (Sun Valley, Ketchum); Fremont County (Ashton, Henrys Lake); Clark County (Spencer); Jefferson County (Camas National Wildlife Refuge); Madison County (Rexburg); Bonneville County (Grays Lake); Caribou County (Wayan, two miles west of Freedom, Wyoming); Bingham County (Blackfoot); Bannock County (Lava Hot Springs); Franklin County (Preston); Bear Lake County (Montpelier); Oneida County (Malad City); Minidoka County (Rupert); Gooding County (Hagerman); Cassia County (Burley, Declo).

Habits. At Coeur d'Alene Merrill (1898) states that the Song Sparrow is common in summer, and has been noted as late as December 10 and as early as the last week in February; a brood of fully fledged young was seen as early as May 25 (1896); the nests that he found were all above the ground, in bushes and small trees, and were substantially built of dead leaves and strips of cottonwood bark, deeply cupped and lined with finer material. Two broods are reared each year; early nests hold five eggs, later ones three or four.

Rust (1919) made a careful study of this species at Coeur d'Alene, and summarizes briefly the results of several years of observation as follows: He considers the Song Sparrow as partially resident in Kootenai County; birds noted from November to February were apparently all males; his earliest breeding record is a nest that held four fresh eggs on April 12, 1918, and was eighteen inches up in a spirea bush; two broods are reared each year, the first from after the first week in April until the first week in May, the second from the first to the third week in June; the first nests are always bulky, are usually in bushes partly submerged in water, and are built of "dead blades and culms" of sedge, lined with fine grasses and horsehair; the incubation period is twelve days, and the young are in the nest from fourteen to sixteen days.

In Latah County Verner (1953) found a nest at Harvard July 17, 1952, which held three fresh eggs, and was three feet up in a red haw (*cretaegus*). At Potlatch I saw fledglings out of the nest at least several days on May 21, 1948, and on June 24, 1953, I found a nest with two partially incubated eggs and one egg of a Cowbird. It was a foot from the ground in a small bush at the edge of the Palouse River, substantially built of weed stems and grasses and well lined with fine grasses.

Melospiza melodia montana Henshaw

As one might suspect from its name, *montana* is the race occurring as a breeding bird in the Rocky Mountain region. In Idaho it occupies all of the southern two-thirds of the state except for a relatively narrow strip along the Oregon state line. On the basis of breeding specimens taken from late April until August, New Meadows in Adams County, and Salmon in Lemhi County, mark the extreme northern limits of this race in the state. These specimens, typical of *montana,* include the following: Adams County, New Meadows, male April 22, 1954, female May 18, 1955; Lemhi County, Salmon, male June 7, 1949, female immature July 10, 1958; Custer County, Challis, males May 25, 1952, July 15, 1958, female May 25, 1952; Blaine County, Ketchum, male June 26, 1950, Sun Valley, male April 25, 1954; Fremont County, Ashton, male August 15, 1939, Henrys Lake, male June 11, 1957; Clark County, Spencer, male June 3, 1931; Madison County, Rexburg, male June 21, 1945; Bonneville County, Grays Lake, males June 9, 1949, May 23, 1951, May 27, 1952; Caribou County, Wayan, male May 22, 1951; two miles west of Freedom, Wyoming, male May 31, 1952; Bannock County, Lava Hot Springs, male May 20, 1951; Minidoka County, Rupert, June 5, 1934; Cassia County, Elba, male June 15, 1934, Burley, males April 23, 1954, June 2, 1955, female April 23, 1954.

Melospiza melodia inexpectata Riley

This race, distinguished by its darker coloration, breeds from Alaska south to British Columbia and Alberta, and is apparently a not uncommon winter resident in Idaho, appearing in late September and lingering in the spring until early April. Specimens verifying its occurrence in the state were taken as follows: Bonner County, Sandpoint, male September 27, 1957; Latah County, Moscow, males November 14, 1955, January 31, 1956, females April 4, 1949, January 12, 1955; Nez Perce County, Lapwai, male November 13, 1949, Lewiston, males March 8, 1952, March 21, 1956, females February 13, 1949, October 23, 1950; Idaho County, Lowell, female March 26, 1950, Riggins, male November 16, 1957; Cassia County, Burley, female November 13, 1957.

Melospiza melodia merrilli Brewster

Merrilli was described from a specimen taken by Merrill at Fort Sherman (Coeur d'Alene) March 6, 1895 (Brewster, 1896). It has a rather limited range, occurring during the summer months from southern British Columbia and Alberta south to eastern Washington, northern Idaho, and northwestern Montana. It is a common resident species in the northern third of the state, although in an occasional year there is a noticeable decrease in numbers from early December until late February. Over a period of eleven years (1947-58) specimens of *Melospiza melodia* were taken at various times of the year in northern Idaho, and *merrilli* was found to be the breeding form from Boundary County (Porthill) to Idaho County (Grangeville). Only a limited amount of field work was carried on during the winter months in the southern part of the state, but specimens of *merrilli* were taken then at Cambridge (November 21, 1951), Burley (November 14, 1957), and Riggins (November 16, 1957).

Melospiza melodia fisherella Oberholser

Fisherella also has a rather limited range, occurring as a breeding bird from eastern Washington and Idaho south to central California and western Nevada. Its distribution in Idaho extends from Nez Perce County (Lewiston) south along the western edge of the state to Owyhee County (Riddle). Over much of this distance it is largely confined to the valleys of the Salmon and Snake rivers, although at the extreme northern part of its range it is found on the Clearwater River as far east as Weippe in Clearwater County, and in southern Idaho east at least to Horseshoe Bend, in Boise County, on the Payette River. Localities in which breeding specimens of *fisherella* were taken are as follows: Clearwater County, Ahsahka, Orofino, Weippe; Nez Perce County, Lewiston; Lewis County, Craigmont; Idaho County, Cottonwood, Grangeville, White Bird, Riggins; Washington County, Cambridge, Weiser; Canyon County, Parma, Caldwell; Boise County, Horseshoe Bend, Ada County, Boise; Owyhee County, Homedale, Three Creek, Triangle, Riddle.

In Latah County, north of its breeding range in Idaho, *fisherella* occurs in small numbers during the winter months, extreme dates of occurrence, based on specimens taken, being December 12 (1951), at Princeton, and April 6 (1952), at Genesee. There is also one record for the breeding season, a male taken at Moscow June 3, 1948. In view of the fact that this race occurs during the summer months over much of eastern Washington it is logical to assume that the individuals recorded from Latah County are stragglers from west of the range of *merrilli,* and do not represent breeding populations of *fisherella* from farther south in the state.

Rhynchophanes mccownii (Lawrence): McCown's Longspur

General Distribution. Breeds from southern Alberta, Saskatchewan, and Manitoba south to northern Colorado and northern Nebraska. Winters from central Arizona, northern Colorado and central Oklahoma south to northern Mexico (Sonora, Durango) and southern Texas.

Status in Idaho. Apparently a rare summer resident in the extreme southeastern part of the state.

There is one record for the occurrence of this species in Idaho. On August 6, 1890, Vernon Bailey collected a female in immature plumage "at the sink of Birch Creek," in Butte County (Merriam, 1891). This specimen is now in the collections of the United States National Museum.

Habits. Idaho marks the extreme western limits for McCown's Longspur as a breeding bird, so it has probably never nested in any numbers in the state. It is the middle of September before the southward movement in the fall is under way, so the presence of an individual in immature plumage in Butte County in early August would suggest that at least one pair reared their young there. Longspurs are characteristic birds of open shortgrass prairie country, and it is in such a site that this species should be watched for in future years.

Calcarius lapponicus alascensis Ridgway: Lapland Longspur

General Distribution. Breeds in western and northern Alaska, northern Yukon, and northern Mackenzie. Winters from southern British Columbia, northern Montana and southwestern South Dakota south to northern California, northern Arizona, and northern Texas.

Status in Idaho. A scarce and irregular winter visitant throughout the state.

In northern Idaho the Lapland Longspur was recorded by Merrill (1898) at Fort Sherman (Coeur d'Alene), a specimen being taken there November 13, 1896; it was noted by Levy (1959) in Boundary County, a male being taken September 16, 1950, from a flock of six at Phoebe's Tip, in the Selkirk Mountains.

There are specimens of this longspur in the Denver Museum of Natural History taken by Brodkorb in the southern part of the state, as follows: Cassia County, thirteen miles south of Burley (February); Gooding County, Gooding (February 25, 1932); Elmore County, Glenns Ferry (March 3, 1932).

Habits. My rather limited experience with this species has given me the impression that it is difficult to observe, and very easily overlooked. Frequenting open fields where the grass is short and sparse, it depends for protection on its protective coloration; when approached it remains motionless and practically invisible until almost stepped on. Only then will it fly, and once in the air it may go so far as to be almost out of sight before it drops to the ground again. Under these circumstances its presence could remain undetected even though flocks were to winter regularly in suitable habitat. Consequently, although it would appear to be a scarce winter visitant in Idaho, further study might change this conception of its present status.

Plectrophenax nivalis nivalis (Linnaeus): Snow Bunting

General Distribution. Cosmopolitan; in North America breeds from northern Ellesmere Island and northern Greenland south to southern Alaska, central Mackenzie and northern Quebec. Winters from southern Alaska, central Saskatchewan, southern Ontario, southern Quebec and Newfoundland south to northern California, northern Utah, central Kansas, southern Indiana, and Georgia.

Status in Idaho. A not uncommon but erratic winter visitant throughout the state.

Boundary County. "Many large flocks" seen at Copeland November 6, 1951 (Levy, 1959).

Bonner County. A flock of twenty seen near Sandpoint October 18, 1951 (Levy, 1959).

Kootenai County. An irregular winter visitor at Fort Sherman (Coeur d'Alene); large flocks noted on the prairie (Merrill, 1898); rare and irregular at Coeur d'Alene during the winter months (1910-14); one specimen taken (Rust, 1915).

Latah County. A single bird seen at Genesee February 8, 1956, feeding with Horned Larks at the side of a road (Burleigh).

Nez Perce County. A flock of twelve birds seen November 4, 1952, feeding in an open field at the edge of the reservoir east of Lewiston Orchards (Burleigh).

There are specimens in the Denver Museum of Natural History taken in southern Idaho by Brodkorb as follows: Bear Lake County, Indian Creek, two males, three females February 8, 1931; Power County, American Falls, females January 13, 18 and 22, 1932; Cassia County, thirteen miles southwest of Burley, male February 3, 1932, females January 22 and February 2, 1932.

Habits. The Snow Bunting is one of the hardiest of the boreal finches, for it occurs during the summer months farther north than any other small land bird. Its presence in Idaho during the winter would appear to be governed to a large extent by the severity of the weather in the southern part of its breeding range; unless the depth of the snow eliminates to a large extent its food supply it can, apparently, successfully survive long intervals of subzero temperatures. As a result its movements are quite unpredictable, and it is only during an exceptional year that flocks of any size are encountered in the state. It is characteristically a bird of the more open country, avoiding wooded areas at all times.

Species	Type Locality	Present Status of Name
1. *Bonasa umbellus phaia* Aldrich and Friedmann *Condor*, 45, no. 3, May 24, 1943, p. 98.	Priest River	In Use
2. *Actitis macularia rava* Burleigh, *Auk*, 77, no. 2, April 1960, pp. 210-12.	Lewiston, Nez Perce County	In Use
3. *Megascops flammeolus idahoensis* (Merriam), *Auk*, 9, no. 2, April, 1892, pp. 169-71.	Ketchum	Synonym of Otus flammeolus flammeolus
4. *Chordeiles minor twomeyi* Hawkins, *Condor*, 50. no. 3, May-June, 1948, pp. 131-32.	Owyhee County	In Use
5. *Colaptes cafer canescens* Brodkorb, *Occa. Papers Mus. Zool. Univ. Mich.*, no. 314, May, 1935, pp. 1-3.	Bear Lake Outlet (5,900 feet) 4 miles southwest of Montpelier, Bear Lake County	Synonym of Colaptes cafer collaris
6. *Asyndesmus lewis* (Gray), *Gen. Birds*, vol. 3, 1849, App., p. 22.	2 miles north of Kamiah	In Use
7. *Dendrocopos pubescens parvirostris* Burleigh, *Murrelet*, 41, no. 3, Sept.-Dec., 1960.	Moscow	In Use
8. *Contopus sordidulus sciccicola* Burleigh, Proc. Biol. Soc. Washington, 73, Dec. 30, 1960, pp. 145-46.	Potlatch	In Use
9. *Perisoreus canadensis bicolor* Miller, *Trans. San Diego Soc. Nat. Hist.* 7, no. 25, Oct. 6, 1933, p. 294.	4 miles west Meadow Creek elevation 3,000 feet, Boundary County	In Use

10. *Nucifraga columbiana* (Wilson) *Amer. Orn.*, vol. 3, 1811, pp. XV, 29, pl. 20, fig. 2.	Clearwater County, about 2 miles north of Kamiah	In Use
11. *Parus gambeli grinnelli* (von Rossem), *Auk*, 45, no. 1, Jan. 19, 1928, p. 104.	Priest Lake, Bonner County	In Use
12. *Parus rufescens caliginosus* Burleigh, *Proc. Biol. Soc. Washington*, 72, April, 1959, pp. 15-16.	Moscow	In Use
13. *Sitta canadensis clariterga* Burleigh, *Auk*, 77, no. 2, April, 1960, pp. 212-14.	Headquarters, Clearwater County	In Use
14. *Troglodytes troglodytes salebrosus* Burleigh, *Proc. Biol. Soc. Washington*, 72, April, 1959, pp. 16-17.	Dismal Lake, Shoshone County	In Use
15. *Hylocichla guttata dwighti* Bishop, *Proc. Biol. Soc. Washington*, 46, Oct. 1933, pp. 201-5.	Priest Lake	Synonym of Hylocichla guttata oromela
16. *Hylocichla fuscescens subpallida* Burleigh and Duvall, *Proc. Biol. Soc. Washington*, 72, May, 1959, pp. 33-35.	Moscow	In Use
17. *Bombycilla cedrorum larifuga* Burleigh, *Proc. Biol. Soc. Washington*, 76, Aug. 2, 1963, pp. 178-79.	Headquarters, Clearwater County	In Use
18. *Vireo olivaceus caniviridis* Burleigh, *Auk*, 77, no. 2, April, 1960, pp. 214-15.	Moscow	In Use
19. *Piranga ludoviciana* (Wilson), *Amer. Orn.* vol. 3, 1811, p. 27.	about 2 miles north of Kamiah	In Use
20. *Chlorura chlorura* (Audubon), *Orn. Biogr.*, vol. 5, 1839, p. 336.	20 miles southwest of Blackfoot	In Use

21. *Amphispiza belli campicola* Oberholser, *Jour., Wash. Acad. Sci.*, vol. 36, no. 11, Nov. 15, 1946, pp. 388-89.	6 miles south of Hamer, Jefferson County	In Use
22. *Melospiza melodia merrilli* Brewster, *Auk*, 13, no. 1, Jan. 1896, p. 46.	Fort Sherman	In Use

BIBLIOGRAPHY

Adams, Lowell, Mitchell G. Hanaran, Neil W. Hosley and David W. Johnston. "The Effects on Fish, Birds and Mammals of DDT Used in the Control of Forest Insects in Idaho and Wyoming, *Journal of Wildlife Management*, Vol. 13, No. 3 (July, 1949), pp. 245-54.

Alcorn, Gordon D., and Louis K. Mann. "Winter Flocks of Bohemian Waxwings," *Murrelet*, Vol. 18, No. 1-2 (Jan.-May, 1937), p. 30. Moscow, Jan., 1937.

Aldrich, John W. "A New Fox Sparrow From the Northwestern United States," *Proc. Biol. Soc. Washington*, Vol. 56 (Dec. 8, 1943), pp. 163-66.
Olivacea considered as probably being the breeding form in northern Idaho.

———————. "Relationships of the Canada Jays in the Northwest," *Wilson Bulletin*, Vol. 55, No. 4 (Dec., 1943), pp. 217-22.
Bicolcr the resident form in northern Idaho: *capitalis* in southern Idaho.

———————. "A New House Finch From the Palouse Country of the Northwestern United States," *Proc. Biol. Soc. Washington*, Vol. 62 (April 27, 1949), pp. 29-30.
Carpodacus mexicanus sordidus (sn) the resident form in northwestern Idaho.

———————. "Notes on the Races of the White-breasted Nuthatch," *Auk*, Vol. 61, No. 4 (Oct., 1944), pp. 592-604.
Tenuissima the resident race in Idaho.

———————. "Speciation in the White-cheeked Geese, *Wilson Bulletin*, Vol. 58, No. 2 (June, 1946), pp. 94-103.
Branta canadensis moffitti the breeding race in Idaho.

———————. "The United States Races of the Bob-white," *Auk*, Vol. 63, No. 4 Oct., 1946), pp. 493-508.
Colinus virginianus virginianus, c. v. mexicanus, c. v. taylori recorded from Nampa.

———————. "New Subspecies of Birds from Western North America," *Proc. Biol. Soc. Washington*, Vol. 59 (Octo. 25, 1946), pp. 129-36.
Centrocercus urophasianus phaios, Telmatodytes palustris pulverius, Catherpes mexicanus griseus, Dumetella carolinensis ruficrissa, spinus pinus vagans (all occurring in Idaho).

———————. "A Review of the Races of the Traill's Flycatcher," *Wilson Bulletin*, Vol. 63, No. 3 (Sept. 1951), pp. 192-97.
Empidonax traillii adastus the breeding form in Idaho.
Empidonax traillii campestris a migrant in northern part of state.

Aldrich, John W., and Allen J. Duvall. "Distribution of American Gallinaceous Game Birds," *Fish and Wildlife Service Circular 34*, 1955.
Ranges given for species occurring in Idaho.

———————. "Distribution and Migration of Races of the Mourning Dove," *Condor*, Vol. 60, No. 2 (March-April, 1958), pp. 108-28.
Specimens of *marginella* recorded from numerous areas in Idaho.

Aldrich, John W., and Herbert Friedmann. "A Revision of the Ruffed Grouse," *Condor*, Vol. 45, No. 3 (May-June, 1943), pp. 85-103.
Bonasas umbellus phaios described from Priest River.
B. u. affinis, B. u. umbelloides, B. u. incanus recorded from the state (Idaho).

Aldrich, John W., et. al. "Migration of Some North American Waterfowl," *U.S. Fish and Wildlife Service, Spe. Sci. Report* (Wildlife), No. 1: 1-48.
Idaho returns on banded ducks.

Allen, J. A. "Geographical Variation in the Number and Size of the Eggs of Birds," *Bul. Nutt. Orn. Club*, Vol. 1, No. 3 (Sept. 1876), pp. 74-75.
Icteria virens longicauda nesting "abundantly" at Fort Lapham, Idaho Territory; four eggs "almost invariably laid."

______________. "The North American Species of the Genus *Colaptes*, considered with Special Reference to the Relationships of *C. auratus* and *C. cafer*," *Bull. Am. Mus. Nat. History*, Vol. IV, No. 1 (March, 1892), pp. 21-44.
One hybrid specimen examined from Idaho.

Allen, Robert Porter. "The Whooping Crane," *Research Report No. 3, Nat. Aud. Soc.* (June, 1952), pp. 1-246.
Cites Idaho records.

American Ornithologists' Union. *Check-list of North American Birds*, 5th ed., 1957. Prepared by an A. O. U. Committee, Alexander Wetmore, chairman.

Anthony, A. W. "A New Subspecies of the Genus *Dryobates*," *Auk*, Vol. 13, No. 1 (Jan. 1896), pp. 31-34.
Dryobates villosus montanus recorded from Idaho.

Arvey, M. Dale. "Black-billed Cuckoo in Idaho," *Condor*, Vol. 43, No. 6 (Nov.-Dec., 1941), p. 291.
Female taken July 10, 1941, in Boise County.

______________. "Eastern Blue Jay in Idaho," *Condor*, Vol. 46, No. 4 (July-Aug., 1944), p. 205.
One seen on Moscow Mountain, seven miles north of Moscow.

______________. "A Check-List of the Birds of Idaho," *Mus. Nat. Hist.*, Univ. of Kansas Publications, Vol. 1, No. 10 (Nov. 29, 1947), pp. 193-216.
Lists 292 forms for the state.

______________. "Abundance of Richardson and Franklin Grouse in Idaho in 1948," *Condor*, Vol. 51, No. 2 (March-April, 1949), p. 98.

______________. "Virginia Warbler in Idaho," *Condor*, Vol. 51, No. 3 (May-June, 1949), p. 150.
Male, Bancroft, Bannock County.

______________. "Additions and Corrections to the Check-List of Idaho Birds," *Condor*, Vol. 52, No. 6 (Nov.-Dec., 1950), p. 275.
Seven species discussed. *Vireo huttoni* removed from the list; *spizella arborea* a migrant and *not* a breeding bird.

Bailey, Florence Merriam. "Birds of New Mexico," Judd and Detweiler, Inc., Wash., D.C., 1928, pp. 1-807.
Idaho mentioned in outlining range of many New Mexico species.

Bangs, Outram. "A Review of the Three-Toed Woodpeckers of North America," *Auk*, Vol. 17, No. 2 (April, 1900), pp. 126-42.
Picoides americanus americanus recorded from the west slope of the Bitterroot Mountains in Idaho (one specimen).

Behle, William H. "A New Race of Horned Lark From the Region of Great Salt Lake," *Condor*, Vol. 40, No. 2 (Mar.-Apr., 1938), p. 89.
Otocoris alpestris utahensis (s.n.) recorded from southern Idaho.

______________. "Distribution and Characters of the Utah Red-wing," *Wilson Bulletin*, Vol. 52, No. 4 (Dec., 1940), pp. 234-40.
Agelaius phoeniceus utahensis recorded from southern Idaho.

______________. "Additional Data Concerning the Subspecific Status of the Cormorants of Great Salt Lake," *Condor*, Vol. 43, No. 6 (Nov.-Dec., 1941), pp. 286-89.
Refers to breeding cormorants of Bear Lake, in southeastern Idaho, as subspecifically the same as Utah birds.

______________. "Clines in the Yellow-throats of Western North America," *Condor*, Vol. 52, No. 5 (Sept.-Oct., 1950), pp. 193-219.
Occidentalis and *Campicola* recorded from Idaho.

______________. "A New Race of Mountain Chickadee from the Utah-Idaho Area," *Condor*, Vol. 52, No. 6 (Nov.-Dec., 1950), pp. 273-74.
Parus gambeli wasatchensis recorded from central and southern Idaho.

______________. "A New Race of the Black-capped Chickadee From the Rocky Mountain Region," *Auk*, Vol. 68, No. 1 (Jan., 1951), pp. 75-79.
Parus atricapillus garrinus recorded from Custer County and Lake County.

——————————. "A Systematic Review of the Mountain Chickadee," *Condor*, Vol. 58, No. 1 (Jan.-Feb., 1956), pp. 51-70.
Four races—*Parus gambeli grinnelli, P. g. inyoensis, P. g. wasatchensis, P. g. gambeli*, recorded from Idaho.

Behle, William H. and Robert K. Selander. "The Systematic Relationships of the Fox Sparrows (*Passerella iliaca*) of the Wasatch Mountains, Utah, and the Great Basin," *Journal Wash. Acad. Sci.*, Vol. 41, No. 11 (Nov., 1951), pp. 364-67.
Passerella iliaca swarthi recorded from southern Idaho.

Bendire, Charles E. "American Long-eared Owl," *Ornithologist and Oologist*, Vol. 6, No. 11 (Jan., 1882), pp. 81-82.
Nesting at Fort Lapwai in 1871.

——————————. "Notes on the Habits, Nests and Eggs of *Dendragapus obscurus fuliginosus*, the Sooty Grouse," *Auk*, Vol. 6, No. 1 (Jan., 1889), pp. 32-39.

——————————. "Life Histories of North American Birds," *U.S. Nat. Mus. Spec. Bull.*, No. 1, Vol. 1, 1892, 446 pp., 12 pls. and Vol. 2, 1895, 518 pp., 7 pls.
Notes from Fort Lapwai, Idaho.

Bent, Arthur Cleveland.
Life Histories of North American Diving Birds. Bull. U.S. Nat. Mus., No. 107, pp. 1-XIII; 1-245, 1919.
Life Histories of North American Gulls and Terns. Bull. U.S. Nat. Mus., No. 113, pp. 1-X; 1-345, 1921.
Life Histories of North American Petrels, Pelicans, and Their Allies. Bul. U.S. Nat. Mus., No. 121, pp. 1-XII; 1-343, 1922.
Life Histories of North American Wild Fowl (Part 1). Bull. U.S. Nat. Mus., No. 126, pp. 1-IX; 1-250, 1923.
Life Histories of North American Wild Fowl (Part 2), Bull. U.S. Nat. Mus., No. 130, pp. 1-X; 1-311, 1925.
Life Histories of North American Marsh Birds. Bull. U.S. Nat. Mus., No. 135, pp. 1-XII; 1-490, 1926.
Life Histories of North American Shore Birds (Part 1). Bull. U.S. Nat. Mus., No. 142, pp. 1-IX; 1-359, 1927.
Life Histories of North American Shore Birds (Part 2). Bull. U.S. Nat. Mus., No. 146, pp. 1-IX; 1-340, 1929.
Life Histories of North American Gallinaceous Birds. Bull. U.S. Nat. Mus., No. 162, pp. 1-XI; 1-490, 1932.
Life Histories of North American Birds of Prey (Part 1). Bull. U.S. Nat. Mus., No. 167, pp. 1-VIII; 1-409, 1937.
Life Histories of North American Birds of Prey (Part 2). Bull. U.S. Nat. Mus., No. 170, pp. 1-VIII; 1-482, 1938.
Life Histories of North American Woodpeckers. Bull. U.S. Nat. Mus., No. 174, pp. 1-VIII; 1-334, 1939.
Life Histories of North American Cuckoos, Goatsuckers, Hummingbirds and their Allies. Bull. U.S. Nat. Mus., No. 176, pp. 1-VIII; 1-506, 1940.
Life Histories of North American Flycatchers, Larks, Swallows and their Allies. Bull. U.S. Nat. Mus., No. 179, pp. 1-XI; 1-538, 1942.
Life Histories of North American Jays, Crows and Titmice. Bull. U.S. Nat. Mus., No. 191, pp. 1-X, 1-495, 1946.
Life Histories of North American Nuthatches, Wrens, Thrashers and their Allies. Bull. U.S. Nat. Mus., No. 195, pp. 1-XI; 1-475, 1948.
Life Histories of North American Thrushes, Kinglets and their Allies. Bull. U.S. Nat. Mus., No. 196, pp. 1-VIII; 1-454, 1949.
Life Histories of North American Wagtails, Shrikes, Vireos and their Allies. Bull. U.S. Nat. Museum, No. 197, pp. 1-VII; 1-411, 1950.
Life Histories of North American Wood Warblers. Bull. U.S. Nat. Museum, No. 203, pp. 1-XI; 1-734, 1953.

Life Histories of North American Blackbirds, Orioles, Tanagers, and Allies. Bull. U.S. Nat. Museum, No. 211, pp. 1-VIII; 1-531, 1958.

Bishop, Louis B. "Two Apparently Unrecognized Races of North American Birds," *Proc. Biol. Soc. Washington,* Vol. 46 (Oct., 1933), pp. 201-5.
Hylocichla guttata dwighti described from Priest Lake, Idaho (Type male, June 23, 1929, Charles F. Hedges).

——————. "An Apparently Unrecognized Race of Redwing from Utah," *Transactions,* San Diego Soc. Nat. Hist., Vol. IX, No. 1 (Nov., 1938), pp. 1-4.
Agelaius phoeniceus sonoriensis recorded from Montpelier, Bear Lake County, Idaho.

Bond, Richard M. "Variation in Western Sparrow Hawks," *Condor,* Vol. 45, No. 5 (Sept.-Oct., 1943), pp. 168-85.
Breeding specimens examined from Coeur d'Alene and Twin Falls County.

Brewster, William. "On Kennicott's Owl and Some of Its Allies, With a Description of a Proposed New Race," *Bul. Nutt. Orn. Club,* 7, No. 1 (Jan., 1882), pp. 27-33.
Otus (Scops) asio Kennicotti recorded for Idaho.

——————. "Descriptions of a New Warbler and a New Song Sparrow," *Auk,* Vol. 13, No. 1 (January, 1896), pp. 44-47.
Description of *Melospiza fasciata merrilli,* Fort Sherman, Idaho.

Brodkorb, Pierce. "Two New Subspecies of the Red-shafted Flicker," *Occa. Papers Mus. Zool.,* Univ. Michigan, No. 314, May, 1935, pp. 1-3.
Description of *Colaptes cafer canescens.*

——————. "A New Bird for Idaho," *Auk,* Vol. 52, No. 3 (July, 1935), p. 312.
Polioptila caerulea amoenissima, im. male, collected Oct. 7, 1932, in Bear Lake County.

——————. "Virginia's Warbler in Idaho," *Auk,* Vol. 55, No. 1 (Jan., 1938), p. 125.
Two males taken Aug. 24, 1934, Joe's Gap, Montpelier, Bear Lake County (six mi. northeast).

——————. "Fossil Birds From Idaho," *Wilson Bulletin,* Vol. 70, No. 3 (Oct., 1958), pp. 237-42.

Phalacrocorax macer		
Cygnus hibbardi	new species	Twin Falls County
Porzana lacustris		Hagerman,
also		

Phalacrocorax auritius
Anas platyrhynchos

Brooks, Allan. "The Present Status of the Trumpeter Swan," *Condor,* Vol. 28, No. 3 (May-June, 1926), p. 129.
Small flock recorded as wintering in southern Idaho.

Burleigh, Thomas D. "Notes on the Breeding Birds of Clark's Fork, Bonner County, Idaho," *Auk,* Vol. 40, No. 4 (Oct. 1923), pp. 653-665.

——————. "Two New Subspecies of Birds From Western North America," *Proc. Biol. Soc. Washington,* Vol. 72 (April, 1959), pp. 15-17.
Parus rufescens caliginosus
Troglodytes troglodytes salebrosus

——————. "Occurrence of the Eastern Belted Kingfisher (*Megaceryle alcyon alcyon*) in Eastern Washington and Northern Idaho," *Murrelet,* Vol. 40, No. 2 (May-August, 1959).
Male, Lewiston, January 19, 1957.

——————. "Three New Subspecies of Birds From Western North America," *Auk,* Vol. 77, No. 2 (April, 1960), pp. 210-15.
Actitis macularia rava (Type locality—Lewiston)
Sitta canadensis clariterga (Type locality—Headquarters)
Vireo olivaceus caniviridis (Type locality—Moscow)

————————. "A New Subspecies of Downy Woodpecker From the Northwest," *Murrelet*, Vol. 41, No. 3 (Sept.-Dec., 1960).
Dendrocopos pubescens parvirostris. All of Idaho except extreme eastern edge of state.

————————. "Geographic Variation in the Western Wood Pewee (*Contopus sordidulus*)," *Proc. Biol. Soc. Washington*, Vol. 73 (Dec., 1960), pp. 141-46.
Contopus sordidulus siccicola, new subspecies.

————————. "Geographic Variation in the Cedar Waxwing (*Bombycilla cedrorum*)," *Proc. Biol. Soc. Washington*, Vol. 76, (August 2, 1963), pp. 177-180.
Two new races (Idaho) described.

————————. "*Parus rufescens levyi* a nomen novum for *P. c. caliginosus* Burleigh," *Auk*, Vol. 85, No. 4 (October, 1968), p. 695.

Burleigh, Thomas D., and Allen J. Duvall. "A New Subspecies of Veery From the Northwestern United States," *Proc. Biol. Soc. Washington*, Vol. 72 (May, 1959), pp. 33-35.
Hylocichla fuscescens subpallida

Chopp, Norman R. "Waterfowl Mortality in the Coeur d'Alene River Valley, Idaho," *Jour. Wildlife Management*, Vol. 28, No. 4 (October, 1964), pp. 692-702.

Coale, Henry K. "The Present Status of the Trumpeter Swan (*Olor buccinator*)," *Auk*, Vol. 32, No. 1 (Jan. 1915), pp. 82-90.

Cooke, Wells W. "Bird Migration in the Mackenzie Valley," *Auk*, Vol. 32, No. 4 (Oct., 1915), pp. 442-59.
Migration pattern of Red-eyed Vireo and Varied Thrush in northern Idaho.

Coues, Elliott. "Original Description of Lewis's Woodpecker," *Auk*, Vol. 9, No. 4 (October, 1892), p. 394.
"Journal" of Patrick Gass (12 mo. Pittsburgh, 1807, p. 224).

Cowan, Ian McTaggart. "Distribution of the Races of the Williamson Sapsucker in British Columbia," *Condor*, Vol. 11, No. 3 (May-June, 1938), pp. 128-29.
Sphyrapicus thyroideus nataliae (Specimen from northern Idaho).

Davis, William B. "On the Avifauna of Minidoka County and Adjacent Territory," *Murrelet*, Vol. 4, No. 1 (Jan., 1923), pp. 3-4.
Discussion, but no annotated list.

————————. "Bird Notes From Owyhee County, Idaho," *Murrelet*, Vol. 15, No. 3 (Sept., 1934), pp. 69-72.
Annotated list from Riddle, May 28-June 3, 1934.

————————. "Noon-day Feeding of the Pacific Nighthawk," *Condor*, Vol. 37, No. 3 (May-June, 1935), p. 176.
Two birds feeding at noon (June 2, 1934) two mi. s.e. of Riddle, Owyhee County, Idaho.

————————. "An Analysis of the Bird Population in the Vicinity of Rupert, Idaho," *Condor*, Vol. 37, No. 5 (Sept.-Oct., 1935), pp. 233-38.
147 species listed, 1919-21.

————————. "Broad-winged Hawk in Idaho," *Condor*, Vol. 38, No. 2 (March-April, 1936), p. 86.
Specimen taken in Owyhee County.

Davis, William B., and James Stevenson. "The Type Localities of Three Birds Collected by Lewis and Clark in 1806," *Condor*, Vol. 36, No. 4 (July-Aug., 1934), pp. 161-63.

Downing, Glenn R., and Edson Fichter. "First specimen Records of the Dunlin and the Snowy Plover in Idaho," *Condor*, Vol. 70, No. 4 (October, 1968), p. 390.

Duvall, Allen J. "Records From Lower California, Arizona, Idaho and Alberta," *Auk*, Vol. 59, No. 2 (April, 1942), pp. 317-18.
Amphispiza bilineata deserticola—Male taken by L. E. Wyman at Ellis, June 25, 1912.

—————————. "Distribution and Taxonomy of the Black-capped Chickadees of North America," *Auk*, Vol. 62, No. 1 (Jan., 1945), pp. 49-69.
Records *Parus atricapillus septentrionalis, P. a. nevadensis,* and *P. a. fortuitus* for Idaho.

—————————. "Variation in *Carpodacus purpureus* and *Carpodacus Cassinii*," *Condor,* Vol. 47, No. 5 (Sept.-Oct., 1945), pp. 202-5.
New subspecies, *Carpoducus cassinii vinifer,* recorded east to southwestern and central Idaho.

Ellison, Lincoln. "Notes on Food Habits of Juncos," *Condor,* Vol. 36, No. 4 (July-Aug., 1934), pp. 176-77.
Junco oreganus (mountanus) found to eat seeds of *Pinus monticola, Pseudotsuga taxifolia, Larix occidentalis.*

Evenden, Fred G., Jr. "Nesting of the Marsh Hawk at Mountain Home, Southern Idaho," *Murrelet,* Vol. 27, No. 3 (Sept.-Dec., 1946), p. 52.
Detailed account of nest found under construction April 17, 1944.

—————————. "Nesting Studies of the Black-billed Magpie in Southern Idaho," *Auk,* Vol. 64, No. 2 (April, 1947), pp. 260-66.
Notes on twenty nests found at Mountain Home.

Evenden, Fred G., Jr., and Joan R. Evenden. "A House Finch Census at Mountain Home, Idaho," *Condor,* Vol. 46, No. 4 (July-Aug., 1944), p. 209.
660 individuals noted in four hours.

Feduccia, J. Alan. "*Ciconia Maltha* and *Grus americana* from the Upper Pliocene of Idaho," *Wilson Bull.,* Vol. 79, No. 3 (Sept., 1967), pp. 316-18.
Fragments found near Glenns Ferry, Twin Falls County.

Fichter, Edson. "Mourning Dove Production in Four Idaho Orchards and Some Possible Implications," *Jour. of Wildlife Management,* Vol. 23, No. 4 (Oct., 1959), pp. 438-47.
A Red-headed Woodpecker seen in Idaho. Tebiwa 3:41-42, 1960.
Craters of the Moon National Monument, Butte Co.

Fisher, Walter K. "Status of *Cyanocitta stelleri carbonacea* Grinnell," *Condor,* Vol. 4, No. 2 (March-April, 1902), pp. 41-44.
Cyanocitta stelleri annectens, the race occurring in Idaho.

French, Norman R. "Distribution and Migration of the Black Rosy Finch," *Condor,* Vol. 61, No. 1 (Jan.-Feb., 1959), pp. 18-29.
Recorded from central Idaho.

Friedmann, Herbert. *The Cowbirds,* Charles C Thomas, Publisher, Springfield, Ill., Baltimore, Md., 1929, pp. 1-421.
Lists species victimized in Idaho by the Cowbird.

—————————. "Further Additions to the List of Birds Victimized by the Cowbird," *Wilson Bull.,* Vol. 46, No. 2 (June, 1934), pp. 104-14.
Sturnella neglecta and *Passerina amoena* victimized in Idaho.

Gonzales, Boyer. "Overland Journey—Texas to the Pacific," *Orn. and Ool.,* Vol. 14, No. 11 (Nov., 1889), pp. 161-62.
Mentions birds seen in Idaho from the train window.

Grinnell, Joseph. "The Origin and Distribution of the Chestnut-backed Chickadee," *Auk,* Vol. 21, No. 3 (July, 1904), pp. 364-82.
Parus rufescens rufescens recorded from northern Idaho.

Hall, Warren A. "An Oven-bird Specimen From Moscow, Idaho," *Murrelet,* Vol. 32, No. 2 (May-Aug., 1951), p. 29.
Moscow, July 1, 1949.

Hand, R. L. "Notes on the Occurrence of Water and Shore Birds in the Lochsa Region of Idaho," *Condor,* Vol. 34, No. 1 (Jan.-Feb., 1932), pp. 23-25.
Annotated list.

—————————. "The Hawk Owl in Northern Idaho," *Condor,* Vol. 35, No. 1 (Jan.-Feb., 1933), p. 32.
Seen and collected in Idaho County.

—————————. "Summer Occurrence of the Goshawk in Idaho," *Condor*, Vol. 35, No. 1 (Jan.-Feb., 1933), p. 36.
Resident in Clearwater Mountains.

—————————. "A Sight Record of the Red Phalarope (*Phalaropus fulicarius*) in Northern Idaho," *Auk*, Vol. 52, No. 2 (April, 1935), pp. 180-81.
One seen Oct. 13 and 14, 1934, St. Joe River, St. Maries.

—————————. "Comparative Abundance of Waterfowl at St. Maries, Idaho," *Murrelet*, Vol. 17, No. 2-3 (May-Sept., 1936), p. 53.
Seventeen species compared, 1933-36.

—————————. "Notes From Northern Idaho," *Auk*, Vol. 54, No. 1 (Jan., 1937), pp. 97-98.
Empidonax trailli very plen., *Salpinetes obsoletus*, two seen; *Seiurus noveboracensis*, as many as six seen (St. Maries).

—————————. "Notes on Some Birds Nesting in Northern Idaho," *Condor*, Vol. 41, No. 2 (Mar.-Apr., 1939), p. 84.
Mountain Bluebird, Robin, Cinnamon Teal—St. Joe National Forest, northern Idaho.

—————————. "Birds of the St. Joe National Forest, Idaho," *Condor*, Vol. 43, No. 5 (Sept.-Oct., 1941), pp. 220-32.
Annotated list—1921-41.

Hasbrouck, Edwin M. "The Geographical Distribution of the Genus *Megascops* in North America, *Auk*, Vol. 10, No. 3 (July, 1893), pp. 250-264.
Megascops asio macfarlanei—Nez Perce Ind. Res., Idaho.
Megascops flammeolus idahoensis—Ketchum.

Hawkins, Roland W. "A New Western Race of the Nighthawk," *Condor*, Vol. 50, No. 3 (May-June, 1948), pp. 131-32.
Chordeiles minor twomeyi, new subspecies, described from Owyhee County, Idaho.

Hayward, C. Lynn. "Important Heron Rookeries in Southeastern Idaho," *Auk*, Vol. 51, No. 1 (Jan. 1934), pp. 39-41.
Ardea herodias treganzai, Egretta thula brewsteri, Nycticorax nycticorax hoactli nesting at Bear Lake.

Hedges, Charles Foote. "Ancient Murrelet in Northern Idaho," *Condor*, Vol. 43, No. 5 (Sept.-Oct., 1941), p. 248.
Collected Dec. 29, 1929, Hayden Lake, Kootenai County.

Hoskins, Leonard W. "Sight Record of Yellow-shafted Flicker in South Idaho," *Murrelet*, Vol. 34, No. 3 (Sept.-Dec., 1953), p. 48.
Owyhee County—Sept. 27, 1952.

Hudson, George E. "Black-billed Cuckoo (*Coccyzus erythropthalmus*) at Grays Lake, Bonneville County, Idaho," *Murrelet*, Vol. 33, No. 3 (Sept.-Dec., 1952), p. 44.

Hudson, George E., and Charles F. Yocom. "A Distributional List of the Birds of Southeastern Washington," *Research Studies of the State College of Wash.*, Vol. XXII, No. 1 (March, 1954), pp. 1-56.
Frequent comments on northern Idaho records.

Hungerford, Kenneth E. "Ruffed Grouse Populations and Cover Use in Northern Idaho," *Trans. Sixteenth N. Am. Wildl. Conf.*, 1951, pp. 217-24.

—————————. "Some Observations on the Life History of the Idaho Ruffed Grouse," *Murrelet*, Vol. 34, No. 3 (Sept., Dec., 1953), pp. 35-40.

Hurd, Lucile. "Distribution of the Juncos in Washington as shown by the Washington State College Collection," *Murrelet*, Vol. 5, No. 1 (Jan., 1924), pp. 5-7.
Junco o. shufeldti recorded from Troy and Orofino, Idaho; *montanus* from Troy.

Hurley, John B. "Birds Observed in Idaho, Washington and Oregon," *Murrelet*, Vol. 7, No. 2 (May, 1926), pp. 35-36.
General account; no list; March, 1926.

Jenks, Randolph. "A New Subspecies of Pine Grosbeak From Arizona With Critical Notes on Other Races," *Condor*, Vol. 40, No. 1 (Jan.-Feb., 1938), pp. 28-35.
Lists *montana* from Idaho.

Jewett, Stanley G. "Western Records of the Catbird," *Auk*, Vol. 29, No. 1 (Jan., 1912), p. 106.
Com. in Snake River Valley from Nampa east to Pocatello, and in foothills north of Boise.
——————. "Some Birds of the Saw-tooth Mountains, Idaho," *Condor*, Vol. 14, No. 5 (Sept.-Oct., 1912), pp. 191-194.
Annotated list—Oct. 24—Dec. 20, 1910, Ketchum.
——————. "The Eastern Brant in Idaho," *Condor*, Vol. 50, No. 2 (March-April, 1948), p. 93.
Specimen shot at Sandpoint Oct. 7, 1947; first record for the state.
Jewett, Stanley G., and Walter P. Taylor, William T. Shaw, John W. Aldrich. "Birds of Washington State," *Univ. of Wash. Press*, Seattle, 1953, pp. 1-767.
Ranges of numerous races include Idaho.
Johnston, David W. "Populations and Distribution of Summer Birds of Latah County, Idaho," *Condor*, Vol. 51, No. 3 (May-June, 1949), pp. 140-49.
Annotated list—June 1-Aug. 16, 1947.
Jollie, Malcolm. "A New Bird for Washington and Idaho," *Murrelet*, Vol. 32, No. 1 (Jan.-Apr., 1951), p. 13.
Quiscalus versicolor, Moscow, Oct. 22, 1950.
——————. "A Positive Breeding Record of the Starling in Idaho," *Murrelet*, Vol. 32, No. 1 (Jan.-Apr., 1951), p. 13.
Grangeville, May 12, 1951.
——————. "A New Bird For Idaho," *Condor*, Vol. 53, No. 6 (Nov.-Dec., 1951, p. 300.
Mimus polyglottos.
——————. "Comments on the Check-list of the Birds of Idaho," *Condor*, Vol. 54, No. 3 (May-June, 1952), pp. 172-73.
Criticism of errors and omissions (both numerous).
——————. "The Birds Observed in Idaho by the Lewis and Clark Expedition, 1804-1806," *Murrelet*, Vol. 34, No. 1 (Jan.-April, 1953), pp. 1-5.
First list of Idaho birds—twenty-four species.
——————. "Plumages, Molt and Racial Status of Red Crossbills in Northern Idaho," *Condor*, Vol. 55, No. 4 (July-Aug., 1953), pp. 193-97.
Four plumages in the male Crossbill; two in the female *sitkensis, bendirei,* and *benti* recorded from northern Idaho.
——————. "New Records for Idaho," *Condor*, Vol. 57, No. 3 (May-June, 1955), p. 189.
Grus canadensis canadensis and *Clangula hyemalis* recorded in Idaho for the first time.
——————. "A Hybrid Between the Spruce Grouse and the Blue Grouse," *Condor*, Vol. 57, No. 4 (July-Aug., 1955), pp. 213-15.
Collected Nov. 12, 1950, six mi. south-southwest of Emida, Benewah County.
Jones, Victor E. "White-fronted Goose in Idaho," *Condor*, Vol. 45, No. 3 (May-June, 1943), p. 120.
One male taken at Pocatello Dec. 6, 1942.
——————. "The Starling in Idaho," *Condor*, Vol. 48, No. 3 (May-June, 1946), pp. 142-43.
Noted at Aberdeen and Pocatello.
Judd, Sylvester Dwight. "The Grouse and Wild Turkeys of the United States, and their Economic Value," *U. S. Dept. Agr. Biol. Surv. Bull.* 24, 1905, pp. 55, pls. 2.
Kenagy, Fayre. "A Change in Fauna," *Condor*, Vol. 16, No. 3 (May-June, 1914), pp. 120-23.
Affect of irrigation on "desert surroundings," Minidoka County, Idaho.
LaFave, Lynn D. "Revised status of Laridae in Eastern Washington," *Murrelet*, Vol. 46, No. 1 (January-April, 1965), pp. 7-11.
Larus hyperboreus and *Larus glaucescens* recorded at Couer d'Alene.

Levy, Seymour H. "Summer Birds in Southern Idaho," *Murrelet*, Vol. 31, No. 1 (Jan.-Apr., 1950), pp. 2-8.
Annotated list—1949.
__________. "Miscellaneous Northern Idaho Bird Notes," *Murrelet*, Vol. 40, No. 3 (Sept.-Dec., 1959).
__________. "Two New Birds Recorded for Arizona," *Condor*, Vol. 63, No. 1 (Jan., 1961), p. 98.
Buteo harlani reported collected at Genesee, Latah County, Idaho.
__________. "Additional Summer Southern Idaho Bird Notes," *Murrelet*, Vol. 43, No. 1 (Jan.-April, 1962), pp. 10-14.

Lies, Michael F., and William H. Behle. "Status of the White Pelican in the United States and Canada through 1964," *Condor*, Vol. 68, No. 3 (May-June, 1966), pp. 279-92.

Ligon, J. David. "First Record of the Gyrfalcon in Idaho," *Condor*, Vol. 70, No. 4 (Oct., 1918), p. 397. Captured by falconers eight miles east of American Falls, Power County.

Limbert, R. W. "List of the Birds of Idaho," *Arbor Day and Bird Day Manual, Idaho Bull. of Ed.*, Vol. VI, No. 3 (Feb., 1920), pp. 34-38.
A quite complete annotated list.

Linsdale, Jean M. "Geographic Variation in Some Birds in Nevada," *Condor*, Vol. 40, No. 1 (Jan.-Feb., 1938), pp. 36-38.
Parus atricapillus nevadensis (s.n.) recorded from southern Idaho.

Low, Jessop B. "Clay Bank Has Multiple Use for Wildlife," *Condor*, Vol. 47, No. 3 (May-June, 1945), pp. 132-33.
Bank, Rough-winged and Cliff Swallows, Kingfisher and Great Horned Owls noted nesting in clay bank twelve mi. from Soda Springs, Idaho.

Low, Jessop B., and Marcus Nelson. "Recent Records of Breeding Waterfowl in Utah and Southern Idaho," *Condor*, Vol. 47, No. 3 (May-June, 1945), pp. 131-132.
Canvasback nesting at Grays Lake.

Marshall, William H. "An 'Eagle Guard' Developed in Idaho," *Condor*, Vol. 42, No. 3 (May-June, 1940), p. 166.
Power lines from Hagerman to Boise protected from eagles and hawks by wooden guards (3,000 installed—20¢ each).
__________. "More Notes on Salt-feeding of Red Crossbill," *Condor*, Vol. 42, No. 4 (July-Aug., 1940), pp. 218-19.
Flock of nine Crossbills noted feeding on salt on the Boise National Forest.
__________. "Winter Bird Observations in the Boise National Forest, Idaho," *Condor*, Vol. 47, No. 4 (July-Aug., 1945), pp. 170-72.
Annotated List—twenty-three species. (Location: eighteen mi. east of Idaho City (Boise County and Elmore County), 4,800 to 8,000 feet.
__________. "Cover Preferences, Seasonal Movements and Food Habits of Richardson's Grouse and Ruffed Grouse in Southern Idaho," *Wilson Bulletin*, Vol. 58, No. 1 (March, 1946), pp. 42-52.
Boise National Forest, Sept., 1938-Sept., 1940.

McCabe, Thomas T., and Elinor B. McCabe. "Preliminary Studies of Western Hermit Thrushes," *Condor*, Vol. 34, No. 1 (Jan.-Feb., 1932), pp. 26-40.
Lists *nanus polionota* from Idaho.
__________. "Hermit Thrushes of the Northwestern States," *Condor*, Vol. 35, No. 3 (May-June, 1933), pp. 122-123.

Merriam, Dr. C. Hart, "Results of a Biological Reconnaissance of South Central Idaho," *No. Amer. Fauna, No. 5*, 1891, pp. 1-108.
Summer and fall of 1890.
__________. "The Dwarf Screech Owl (*Megascops flammeolus idahoensis* Merriam)," *Auk*, Vol. 9, No. 2 (April, 1892), pp. 169-71.
Description of new race from Ketchum, Idaho.

Merrill, J. C. "Notes on the Birds of Fort Sherman, Idaho," *Auk*, Vol. 14, No. 4 (Oct., 1897) pp. 347-57. (*Auk*, Vol. 15, No. 1 (Jan., 1898), pp. 14-22.)
Annotated List of 167 species from Nov., 1894, until Dec., 1896. (Fort Sherman on Lake Coeur d'Alene, app. where Coeur d'Alene now is.)

Miller, Alden H. "Systematic Revision and Natural History of the American Shrikes (Lanius)," *Univ. California Publ. Zool*, Vol. 38, No. 2 (Oct., 1931), pp. 11-242.
Lanius ludovicianus gambeli given as the breeding form for Idaho.

————————. "The Canada Jays of Northern Idaho," *Trans. San Diego Soc. Nat. Hist.*, Vol. 7, No. 25 (Oct., 1933), pp. 289-97.
Description of *Perisoreus canadensis bicolor.*

————————. "Speciation in the avian genus Junco," *Univ. California Publ. Zool.,* Vol. 44, No. 3 (May, 1941), pp. 173-434.
Junco oreganus mearnsi. Recorded for eastern Idaho.
Junco oreganus montanus. Recorded for northern Idaho south through Idaho, Adams, and Washington Counties, altitudinal limits from 1800 ft. in the Clearwater River Valley.
Junco hyemalis hyemalis. Wintering in southern Idaho.

————————. "The Whistling Swan in the Upper Pliocene of Idaho," *Condor,* Vol. 50, No. 3 (May-June, 1948), p. 132.

Miller, Alden H., and T. T. McCabe, "Racial Differentiation in *Passerella* (Melospiza) *lincolnii*," *Condor*, Vol. 37 (May-June, 1935), pp. 144-60.
Passerella lincolnii alticola (s.n.) recorded from "the arid mountain section of the central part" of Idaho.

Miller, Loye. "Some Pliocene Birds From Oregon and Idaho," *Condor*, Vol. 46, No. 1 (Jan.-Feb., 1944), pp. 25-32.
Grus canadensis—13 mi. nw. of Grandview, on Snake River.
Ciconia maltha
Cygnus, sp.　　　} Snake River—3.3 mi. east of Bruneau-Mountain Home
Goose, indeterminate 　} Bridge.

Moody, Charles S., M.D. "A Nesting Day in Idaho," *Oologist*, XX, No. 1 (November, 1903), pp. 9-11.
Nesting on Lake Pend Oreille, of the Western Grebe (three eggs), Avocet (four eggs), Mallard (nine eggs), Wood Duck (eight eggs), Red-winged Blackbird.

————————. "An Ornithological Iron-clad," *Oologist*, XXI, No. 7 (July, 1904), pp. 101-03.
Western Grebe nesting at Sandpoint; nest with three eggs.

Moore, Robert T. "A Review of the House Finches of the Subgenus Burrica," *Condor*, Vol. 41, No. 5 (Sept.-Oct., 1939), pp. 177-205.
Carpodacus mexicanus solitudinis (s.n.) recorded from southern Idaho.

Newhouse, Verne F. "Birds of Selected Irrigated River Valleys of West Central Idaho," *Murrelet*, Vol. 41, No. 1 (Jan.-April, 1960), pp. 1-6.
Annotated list.

Norris, Robert A. "Comparative Biosystematics and Life History of the Nuthatches *Sitta pygmaea* and *Sitta pusilla*," *Univ. of California Publ. Zool.*, Vol. 36, No. 2 (1958), pp. 119-300.
Sitta pygmaea melanotis, northern Idaho south throughout the state.

Oberholser, Harry C. "Notes on the Subspecies of *Numenius americanus* Bechstein," *Auk*, Vol. 35, No. 2 (April, 1918), pp. 188-95.
N. a. americana, the breeding form in southern Idaho.

————————. "The Geographic Races of *Hedymeles melanocephalus* Swainson, *Auk*, Vol. 36, No. 3 (July, 1919), pp. 408-416.
H. m. melanocephalus and *H. m. papago* recorded from Idaho.

————————. "The Range of the Short-tailed Mountain Chickadee (*Penthestes gambeli abbreviatus* Grinnell)," *Auk*, Vol. 36, No. 3 (July, 1919), p. 424.
Specimens from Lardo and Dickey in central Idaho.

__________. "Three New North American Birds," *Journ. Wash. Acad. Sci.,* Vol. 36, No. 11 (Nov. 15, 1946), pp. 388-89.
Amphispiza nevadensis campicola described from six mi. s. of Hamer, Jefferson County, Idaho (Type ad. male, May 16, 1931, Pierce Brodkorb).

Olson, Andrew C., Jr. "Starling in Northern Idaho," *Condor,* Vol. 45, No. 5 (Sept.-Oct., 1943), p. 197.
One noted at Moscow Dec., 13, 1941.

Oring, Lewis W. "Birds of the University of Idaho Campus," *Jour. Idaho Academy of Science,* Vol. 1, No. 2 (Oct., 1960), pp. 93-112.
Field List.

__________. "Observations on the Birds of Southeastern Idaho," *Murrelet,* Vol. 43, No. 3 (September-December, 1962), pp. 1-12.
Camas National Wildlife Refuge, Jefferson Co., Idaho.

__________. "Behavior and Ecology of Certain Ducks During the Postbreeding Period," *Jour. Wildlife Management,* Vol. 28, No. 2 (April, 1964), pp. 223-33.
Camas National Wildlife Refuge.

Orr, Robert T. "Observations on the Birds of Northeastern Idaho," *Proc. Cal. Acad. of Sciences,* Vol. XXVII, No. 1 (Mar. 7, 1951), pp. 1-14.
Sixty-seven species of birds recorded, Sept., 1941, and July, 1948.

Palmer, R. H. "Relative Abundance of Bird Species in Southeastern Idaho; Fresno County, California; Santa Clara County, California; and King County, Washington," *Murrelet,* Vol. 9, No. 2 (May, 1928), pp. 28-38.
Analysis of bird life of Bannock County, Idaho (permanent residents thirty-five, summer visitants ninety-one, winter visitants eleven, spring migrants twenty-four—total 161).

Phillips, John C. "Notes on American and Old World English Sparrows," *Auk,* Vol. 32, No. 1 (Jan., 1915), pp. 51-59.
Nampa—eight specimens taken May and June, 1911.

Phillips, Allan R. "The Races of MacGillivray's Warbler," *Auk,* Vol. 64, No. 2 (April, 1947), pp. 296-300.

Pitelka, Frank A. "Differentiation of the Scrub Jay, *Aphelocoma coerulescens,* in the Great Basin and Arizona," *Condor,* Vol. 47, No. 1 (Jan.-Feb., 1945), pp. 23-26.
Aphelocoma coerulescens nevadae, new subspecies, reported from southern Idaho.

Porter, Richard D. "The Status of Rough-legged Hawks in Idaho," *Condor,* Vol. 53, No. 5 (Sept.-Oct., 1951), pp. 257-58.

Powers, Leon. "Sight Record of the Blue Grosbeak in Idaho," *Murrelet,* Vol. 50, No. 2 (May-August, 1969), pp. 20-21.
At least two breeding pairs noted at Glenns Ferry, Elmore County.

Rand, A. L., and M. A. Traylor, "Variation in *Dumetella carolinensis,*" *Auk,* Vol. 66, No. 1 (Jan., 1945), pp. 25-28.
Specimens from Idaho noted as paler than eastern birds.

Ridgway, Robert. "The Birds of North and Middle America," *Bull. 50, U. S. Nat. Mus.,* Parts 1-8, 1901-1919.

__________. "New Species, Etc., of American Birds-II Fringillidae, *Auk,* Vol. 15, No. 4 (Oct., 1898), pp. 319-24.
Thompson's Pass, Idaho, given as southern edge of range of *Junco montanus,* new species.
Also lists *Pinicola enucleator montana* as breeding in Idaho.

Robertson, John McB. "Returns of Banded Gulls," *Condor,* Vol. 30, No. 6 (Nov.-Dec., 1928), pp. 354-55.
Banded Alberta gulls reported from Caldwell and Idaho Falls.

Royall, Willis C., Jr., and Richard E. Pillmore. "House Wren feeds Red-shafted Flicker Nestlings," *Murrelet,* Vol. 49, No. 1 (Jan.-April, 1968), pp. 4-6.
Observations made in Camas County, Idaho.

Rush, William M. *Wildlife of Idaho,* The Caxton Printers, Ltd., Caldwell, Idaho, 1942. pp. 1-299.
General account of the more common birds of the state.

Rust, Henry J. "Birds New to the Vicinity of Lake Coeur d'Alene, Kootenai County, Idaho," *Condor,* Vol. 15, No. 1 (Jan.-Feb., 1913), p. 41.
Five species recorded.

__________. "Some Notes on the Nesting of the Sharp-shinned Hawk," *Condor,* Vol. 16, No. 1 (Jan.,-Feb., 1914), pp. 14-24.
Nest with five eggs June 15, 1913, Coeur d'Alene.

__________. "An Annotated List of the Birds of Kootenai County, Idaho," *Condor,* Vol. 17, No. 3 (May-June, 1915), pp. 118-129.

__________. "Additional Notes on the Birds of Kootenai County, Idaho," *Condor,* Vol. 18, No. 2 (Mar.-April, 1916), pp. 81-82.
List of five species.

Rust, Henry J. "An Annotated List of the Birds of Fremont County, Idaho, as Observed During the Summer of 1916," *Condor,* Vol. 19, No. 2 (March-April, 1917), pp. 29-43.
June 7-Aug. 29, 1916, 103 species listed.

__________. "A Favorite Nesting Haunt of the Merrill Song Sparrow," *Condor,* Vol. 21, No. 4 (July-Aug., 1919), pp. 145-53.

__________. "The Home Life of the Western Warbling Vireo," *Condor,* Vol. 22, No. 3 (May-June, 1920), pp. 85-94.
Coeur d'Alene.

__________. "Migration and Nesting of Nighthawks in Northern Idaho," *Condor,* Vol. 49, No. 5 (Sept.-Oct., 1947), pp. 177-88.
Detailed life history study of *Chordeiles minor hesperis* at Coeur d'Alene (Made over an interval of thirty-six years).

Salinger, Herbert E. "A Pheasant Breeding Population Study on Irrigated Lands in Southwest Idaho," *Jour. Wildlife Management,* Vol. 16, No. 4 (October, 1952), pp. 409-18.

Selander, Robert K. "A Systematic Review of the Booming Nighthawks of Western North America," *Condor,* Vol. 56, No. 2 (March-April, 1954), pp. 57-82.
Chordeiles minor minor recorded once in Idaho.
     "   "   *hesperis,* the breeding race.
     "   "   *twomeyi,* not considered valid.

Selander, Robert K., and Sherman J. Preece, Jr. "Cock Roosts of Nighthawks," *Condor,* Vol. 53, No. 6 (Nov.-Dec., 1951), pp. 302-303.
Melba, Canyon County, one hundred birds (males), Buhl, Twin Falls County, fifty birds (males).

Short, Lester L., and Thomas D. Burleigh. "An Integeneric Hybrid Flycatcher (*contopus* and *Empidonax*) from Idaho," *Proc. Biol. Soc. Washington,* Vol. 72 (July 21, 1965), pp. 33-37.
Specimen taken at Moscow June 20, 1948.

Slipp, John W. "Franklin Gull in Idaho," *Condor,* Vol. 44, No. 5 (Sept.-Oct., 1942), pp. 226-27.
Occasionally in southern Idaho (four definite records).

Sloanaker, J. L. "Notes From Spokane," *Condor,* Vol. 27, No. 2 (March-April, 1925), pp. 73-74.
The White-faced Glossy Ibis and Golden Plover recorded from northern Idaho.

__________. "Spokane Bird Club Observations," *Murrelet,* Vol. 21, No. 2 (May-Aug., 1940), p. 48.
Seiurus noveboracensis recorded from Priest Lake, Idaho.

__________. "Spokane Bird Club Notes," *Murrelet,* Vol. 22, No. 2 (May-Aug., 1941), pp. 39-40.
Seiurus noveboracensis recorded from Coeur d'Alene.

BIBLIOGRAPHY 457

Snyder, John O. "Notes on a Few Species of Idaho and Washington Birds," *Auk*, Vol. 17, No. 3 (July, 1900), pp. 242-45.
Annotated list of forty-five species.

Steel, Paul E., and Elwood G. Bizeau. "Annotated List of the Avifauna in and Around Gray's Lake, Idaho," *Murrelet*, Vol. 37, No. 1 (Jan.-April, 1956), pp. 4-10.
145 species listed, 1949-51. Grays Lake, southeastern Idaho (Bonneville and Caribou counties), nine mi. long, four mi. wide; altitude 6,386 ft.
——————. "Duck Production at Gray's Lake, Idaho 1949-51," *Jour. of Wildlife Management*, Vol. 20, No. 3 (July, 1956), pp. 279-85.
——————. "Canada Goose Production at Gray's Lake, Idaho, 1949-1951," *Jour. of Wildlife Management*, Vol. 21, No. 1 (Jan., 1957), pp. 38-41.

Stewart, Robert E. "Food Habits of Blue Grouse," *Condor*, Vol. 46, No. 3 (May-June, 1944), pp. 112-20.
Seasonal food habits in Idaho (contents of sixty-eight stomachs).

Stone, Witmer. "Type Locality of Lewis's Woodpecker and Clarke's Nutcracker," *Auk*, Vol. 32, No. 3 (July, 1915), pp. 371-72.
"West of the Bitter Root Mountains in Idaho."

Sugden, John W. "The Status of the Sandhill Crane in Utah and Southern Idaho," *Condor*, Vol. 40, No. 1 (Jan.-Feb., 1938), pp. 18-22.

Swenk, Myron H., and O. A. Stevens. "Harris's Sparrow and the Study of It by Trapping," *Wilson Bull.*, Vol. 41, No. 3 (Sept., 1929), pp. 129-77.
Specimen recorded from Nampa, Jan. 1, 1911.

Taverner, P. A. "A New Subspecies of *Dendragapus* (*Dendragapus obscurus flemingi*) from Southern Yukon Territory," *Auk*, Vol. 31, No. 3 (July, 1914), pp. 385-88.
Specimens of this race examined from Preuss Mountains (Fiddle Creek).

Taylor, Walter P. "Bohemian Waxwing (*Bombycilla garrula*) Breeding Within the United States," *Auk*, Vol. 35, No. 2 (April, 1918), pp. 226-27.
Nest with five eggs Bonner County, Idaho.

Thornburg, Florence. "Scissor-tailed Flycatcher in Idaho," *Condor*, Vol. 58, No. 1 (Jan.-Feb., 1956), pp. 72-73.
One noted fifteen mi. from Sun Valley Aug. 6, 7 and 16, 1955.

Throckmorton, Michael. "Sight Record of Yellow-shafted Flicker in Southern Idaho," *Murrelet*, Vol. 34, No. 3 (Sept.-Dec., 1953), p. 48.
Hagerman, December 13, 1952.

Tracy, H. C. "The Bobolink in Idaho," *Condor*, Vol. 12, No. 2 (March-April, 1910), p. 80.
Several males seen at Meridian.

Tucker, Harold M. "Calliope Hummingbird Entangled in Grass Barbs," *Condor*, Vol. 57, No. 2 (March-April, 1955), p. 119.
Bird found dead at Caldwell in July, 1954, "entangled in barbs of a spike of grass."

Tyro, ——————. "Some Queer Habits of *Urinator imber*," *Oologist*, XI, No. 12 (December, 1894), pp. 364-366.
Habits of the Loon on Blue Lake (near Lake Pend Oreille).

Van Rossem, A. J. "A Northern Race of the Mountain Chickadee," *Auk*, Vol. 45, No. 1 (Jan., 1928), pp. 104-5.
Penthestes (*Parus*) *gambeli grinnelli* described, with type locality Priest Lake, Bonner County Idaho.

Verner, Jared. "Birds of Laird Park, Latah County, Idaho," *Murrelet*, Vol. 34, No. 1 (Jan.-April, 1953), pp. 6-8.
Annotated list—sixty-two species.
——————. "Another Idaho Record of the Bronzed Grackle," *Murrelet*, Vol. 37, No. 3 (Sept.-Dec., 1956), p. 36.
Male taken Dec. 27, 1955, Nez Perce County.

Walkinshaw, Lawrence H. "The Sandhill Cranes," *Cranbrook Ins. of Sci.*, Bull. 29, 1949, pp. 1-202.
Distribution of *tabida* in Idaho.

Ward, Henry B. "Banding White Pelicans," *Condor*, XXVI, No. 4 (July-August, 1924), p. 136-40.
Banding returns (Birds banded on Yellowstone Lake, July, 1922; one recovered on Mud Lake, forty mi. northwest of Idaho Falls, Oct. 1; another on Swan Lake, October 23.)

Webster, Harold M. "Notes from Idaho," *Auk*, Vol. 63, No. 3 (July, 1946), p. 452.
Starling and Duck Hawk reported.

Wetmore, A. "Pliocene Bird Remains From Idaho," Smithsonian Misc. Coll. 87 (20): 1-12, figs. 1-8.

Wilbur, Sanford R. "Three New Birds from Idaho." *Murrelet*, Vol. 46, No. 3 (Sept.-Dec., 1965), pp. 45-46.
Brown Thrasher, Wood Thrush and Blackpoll Warbler reported from the southern part of the state.

Wilcox, Timothy E. "Introduced Game Birds in Oregon and Idaho," *Auk*, Vol. 2, No. 3 (July, 1885), p. 315.
The Bobwhite successfully introduced in the Boise Valley.

Worcester, H. M. "Report on Marsh Owls of St. Joe Valley, Idaho," *Murrelet*, Vol. 9, No. 2 (May, 1928), p. 46.
Short-eared Owls concentrated in flooded area where rodents were unusually abundant.

__________. "Observations of Damage to Game Birds by Goshawks and Long-eared Owls," *Murrelet*, Vol. 9, No. 2 (May, 1928), p. 47.
Said to be very destructive to game birds (and meadowlawks) at St. Maries ("Long-eared Owl" probably the Great Horned Owl!)

W. S. __________. "Occurrence of the Meadowlark at Lewiston during the winter," *Young Oologist*, Vol. 2, No. 1 (May, 1885), p. 18.

Wyman, L. E. "Bobolink Again Noted In Idaho," *Condor*, Vol. 13, No. 2 (March-April, 1911), p. 75.
Singing male at Meridian, July 1909.

__________. "Harris's Sparrow (*Zonotrichia querula*) in southern Idaho," *Auk*, Vol. 28, No. 2 (April, 1911), pp. 276-68.
Female taken at Nampa.

__________. "The Catbird in Southern Idaho," *Condor*, Vol. 13, No. 3 (May-June, 1911), p. 108.
On Boise river bottoms, Aug. 1, 1909.

__________. "A Nesting Incident of the Brewer Blackbird," *Condor*, Vol. 13, No. 3 (May-June, 1911), p. 108.
Bird returns to nest after being moved twenty-five feet.

__________. "Occurrence of the Red Crossbill (*Loxia curvirostra minor*) in Southern Idaho," *Condor*, Vol. 13, No. 3 (May-June, 1911), p. 108.
One bird taken in Boise Valley, October, 1910.

__________. "Bobolink Again in Idaho," *Condor*, Vol. 14, No. 1 (Jan.-Feb., 1912).
Boise Valley—flock of twenty-five, Aug., 1911.

__________. "White-throated Sparrow in Idaho," *Auk*, Vol. 29, No. 2 (April, 1912), pp. 247.
Nampa—male and female taken.

__________. "*Oreortyx* in Idaho," *Auk*, Vol. 29, No. 4 (Oct., 1912), pp. 538-39.
Occurs in s.w. Idaho, east to Shoshone and Twin Falls.

Wythe, Margaret W. "The White-throated Sparrow in Western North America," *Condor*, Vol. 40, No. 3 (May-June, 1938), pp. 110-17.
Recorded from Nampa, Idaho, on Nov. 2.

Yocom, Charles F. "Sight Record of Old-Squaw in Idaho," *Murrelet*, Vol. 31, **No. 3** (Sept.-Dec., 1950), p. 47.
   Male New Meadows, April 1, 1950.
      "Estimated Populations of Great Basin Canada Geese over Their Breeding Range in Western Canada and Western United States," *Murrelet*, Vol. 46, No. 2 (May-August, 1965), pp. 19-26.
         Approximately 1010 pairs estimated to nest in Idaho.
Yocom, Charles F., and Iris G. Yocom. "Summer Birds Observed at Conkling Park, Kootenai County, Idaho, 1943," *Murrelet*, Vol. 27, No. 1 (Jan.-April, 1946), pp. 10-12.
   Annotated list, July 1-10, 1943, upper end of Lake Coeur d'Alene.
Yocom, Charles F., and Stanley W. Harris. "Growth Rates of Great Basin Canada Geese," *Murrelet*, Vol. 47, No. 2 (May-August, 1966), pp. 33-37.
      Included three individuals, two males and a female, from the Snake River in southwestern Idaho.

INDEX